COUNTERFEITING
AND
TECHNOLOGY

A HISTORY OF THE LONG STRUGGLE BETWEEN PAPER-MONEY COUNTERFEITERS AND SECURITY PRINTING

BOB McCABE

Whitman Publishing, LLC
PUBLISHING SINCE 1934
Whitman.com

Counterfeiting and Technology

A HISTORY OF THE LONG STRUGGLE BETWEEN PAPER-MONEY COUNTERFEITERS AND SECURITY PRINTING

© 2016 Whitman Publishing, LLC
3101 Clairmont Road · Suite G · Atlanta, GA 30329

ISBN: 0794843956
Printed in China

Correspondence concerning this book may be directed to Whitman Publishing, Attn: Counterfeiting and Technology, at the address above.

Disclaimer: No warranty or representation of any kind is made concerning the accuracy or completeness of the information presented, or its usefulness in purchases or sales. The opinions of others may vary. The author and consultants may buy, sell, and sometimes hold certain of the items discussed in this book.

If you enjoy *Counterfeiting and Technology*, you will also enjoy *100 Greatest American Currency Notes*, *A Guide Book of Southern States Currency*, *Modern Federal Reserve Notes*, the *Check List and Record Book of United States Paper Money*, the *Whitman Encyclopedia of U.S. Paper Money*, the *Whitman Encyclopedia of Obsolete Paper Money*, *United States Currency*, *A Guide Book of Counterfeit Confederate Currency*, and other books by Whitman Publishing. Whitman is a leading publisher in the antiques and collectibles and American history fields. For a catalog of related books, hobby supplies, and storage and display products, please visit Whitman Publishing online at **Whitman.com**.

Contents

Foreword

Having known author Bob McCabe for about 20 years, I am not surprised that his book is both scholarly and fascinating at the same time, despite tackling a very difficult and complex subject. Although it is titled *Counterfeiting and Technology*, the book's broader perspective goes far deeper, exploring the evolution of a few simple technologies like engraving and printing into a complex industry. Bank notes have affected nearly every aspect of our lives and history, yet few people know anything about the art and science of this work, which, due to its nature, is shrouded in mystery. McCabe has traveled to many of the largest cities in the eastern United States to ferret out original materials in libraries, museums, historical societies, and the National Archives to document this story, and from that material he has woven the fabric of a tale full of heroes and villains acting out their roles on the stage of American history.

Using his scientific background and appreciation of the need to explain mechanics, McCabe is one of the first to explain the very technical field of mechanical engraving so that the layman can understand such things as rose engines, geometric lathes, ruling machines, medallion engravers, and transfer presses. He has collected and annotated diagrams and pictures that show the operations of both ancient and 19th-century paper-making machines. He explains paper and ink chemistries in a fashion that requires no previous chemical background to understand. Nor does he forget the human side of the industry—the engravers, artists, and businessmen who gave America the most beautifully engraved and printed securities the world has ever seen; the ordinary men and women who worked in the largest money factory in the world (the Bureau of Engraving and Printing); and the motley crew of counterfeiters and "shovers" who drove the industry to find newer and better techniques for making money.

Most books about counterfeiting do not explain how the counterfeiters made imitation notes. This book does. Emanuel Ninger, a successful counterfeiter who went undetected for years, has his story and methods explained in enough detail that readers can understand his "secrets." He is simply one among many whose methods, triumphs, and downfalls are illustrated within the pages of this text. Another fascinating story is told about two young men who specialized in the new art of photomechanical printing near the turn of the century and decided to use their skills to make counterfeit $100 bills. They did this so skillfully that the U.S. government had to recall the entire series of notes. Even after they went to prison, they found a way to continue making counterfeit notes under the very noses of their guards!

With an extensive and annotated bibliography for those interested in pursuing a particular subject, as well as appendices that provide the text of original documents, descriptions of patents, lists of government officials, and even the aliases used by famous counterfeiters, this work will become a standard reference in the history of American security printing. And since McCabe never stops researching the past, future editions should be just as good as this ground-breaking first effort.

Larry Adams

Curator, The Higgins Museum

Okoboji, Iowa

Preface

There are both villains and heroes in this story, and each played a role in advancing the technology of paper money. Counterfeiting was inevitable for the same reasons that greed and larceny are natural parts of the human psyche. They have a logic all their own. Some would dismiss counterfeiting as criminal behavior, which it is, yet it is deliciously ironic that counterfeiting sometimes lead to great art, for each counterfeited note was yet another reason for a bank-note engraver to take up his burin in this battle and turn a flat piece of copper or steel into a standing Minerva, or a Neptune rising from the sea, or some other heroic figure of idealized beauty that criminal hands supposedly could not match. We marvel at the intricate beauty of the vignettes on old bank notes, at how tastefully they were designed and how skillfully they were engraved, yet we sometimes forget why vignettes were necessary. A good student of 19th-century bank-note art understands how the evil of counterfeiting and the beauty of a good engraving were intricately linked on notes, each trying to defeat the other. Today, most of the art is gone, replaced by geometric fantasies of swirling lines and strips of aluminized Mylar bearing a micro-printed text that we cannot read. Minerva and Neptune are gone, replaced by different, perhaps smaller ideas.

In writing this history, I have tried to chronicle the important developments in a somewhat secretive industry—never an easy task—and at the same time celebrate the lives of both great and lesser artists who chose a burin over a paintbrush or to be a plate printer instead of a green grocer. Time has swallowed up most of the small details of their lives. The records that survive—vital statistics, census records, obituaries, newspaper and magazine articles, letters, diaries, patents, account books, court records, and even the occasional autobiography—are only the bones of once real people and tell us little about the triumphs, the defeats, and the vagaries of their lives. The vast majority of the men and women who worked in this industry over the course of a century will never be known to us in any substantive way. Their lives are closed books, in part because they lived in a simpler and more private age, and in part because we do not celebrate the ordinary.

Counterfeiters knew that their safety depended on secrecy, so they intentionally kept their lives hidden from public view. The counterfeiters described in this book all lived in a period before any kind of state- or national-identification systems existed. There were no drivers' licenses or social security numbers, and no one had to prove their identity to sheriffs or police officers, nor to banks, hotels, landlords, or railroads. Counterfeiters used a variety of different names to hide their identity and kept their travels known to only their relatives, trusted friends, and associates. We are just now beginning to uncover their lives by the use of genealogical research, historic-newspaper databases, the records of the U.S. Secret Service at the National Archives, and the increasing availability of federal court records online.

There have been a number of books about counterfeiting in America, covering both our colonial experience with the problem and the period since the Civil War. The earliest example of this genre was William Stuart's *Sketches of the Life of William Stuart, the First and Most Celebrated Counterfeiter of Connecticut*, published by the author in 1854. It was a popular book because of its sensational material about a mean-spirited scofflaw who later repented of his crimes—a popular theme in the literature of the day. *The Government Blue Book: A Complete History*, privately printed by John S. Dye in 1880, remains the most authoritative and comprehensive work on the principle counterfeiters of the 20-year period prior to its publication. Dye had use of the archives of the Treasury Department and interviewed many of the Secret Service agents that are featured in his book. There is no better source of information on these notorious criminals, but the book says very little or nothing about their counterfeiting techniques. A similar work, but one that contains much less information about counterfeiters, is George P. Burnham's *Memoirs of the United States Secret Service*, published in 1872. It provides a number of biographical sketches of the more-successful agents in the Secret Service and does give some details of their more-famous captures, but the book is more a public relations brochure than an impartial history. So successful was this work that Burnham followed it up with a second and much better book entitled *American Counterfeits. How Detected and How Avoided*, published in 1875. Two former chiefs of the Secret Service also wrote books about their work: H.C. Whitley's *In It*, published in 1894, and A.L. Drummond's *True Detective Stories*, published in 1909, go into some detail on how they and their agents tracked down and caught counterfeiters.

Kenneth Scott's *Counterfeiting in Colonial America*, published in 1957, is a well-researched and comprehensive story. Lynn Glaser's *Counterfeiting in America*, from 1968, covers many of the most infamous counterfeiters of the middle to late 19th century and the efforts of the Secret Service to curtail their business. David R. Johnson's *Illegal Tender* (1965) and Stephen Mihm's *A Nation of Counterfeiters* (2007) are more-scholarly books. Mihm's book is the more-enjoyable "read," but both are excellent. For readers interested in modern counterfeiting, M.M. Landress's *I Made It Myself* (1973) and Robert Baudin's *Confessions of a Promiscuous Counterfeiter* (1979) are both how-to-do-it books. Landress was the more experienced and professional of these counterfeiters.

A number of retired officers of the Secret Service wrote about their experiences and got the stories serialized and published in newspapers across the country. Unlike the hurried efforts of ordinary reporters, these stories are usually drawn from official records and notebooks and are written with a concern for historical accuracy, especially those by "Captain" Patrick D. Tyrrell and the one-time chief of the Secret Service, Colonel H.C. Whitley. With this data, researchers can initiate a search of the federal records at the regional office of the National Archives and, if necessary, get photocopies of court records.

The newspapers of the United States reported a great many of the stories about counterfeiters and their crimes, and this material should never be dismissed simply because of the sensationalism and lack of professional standards in the print media of the day. Reporters often got their facts wrong or exaggerated them to please editors who just wanted to sell papers, but such stories usually provide the only convenient way of finding the date and place of a capture and (often) the names of the culprits. The diligent student will suffer through the stilted and overly dramatic dialogue to get to the few immutable facts that form a realistic story.

In contrast, the history of the *technical arts* in security printing has been much easier to write because many of the devices have survived or were described in detail in the literature.

Jacob Perkins wrote a detailed explanation of his methods in 1819 while he was in London trying to convince a committee of the Bank of England that they should use his methods to engrave and print their bank notes. Perkins invented the method of engraving individual dies and then transferring them under great pressure to a master plate of soft steel which was then hardened to make the final plate used for printing bank notes. Though he was not a bank-note engraver and spent more time on steam engineering than on security printing, he is still the single-most important person in the history of the bank-note industry, and for that he gets a whole chapter to himself (see chapter 4). His letter of 1819 to the Society for the Encouragement of Arts, Manufactures & Commerce, explaining his techniques for making bank notes, is presented in appendix C.

Waterman Lily Ormsby was the only bank-note engraver to describe the Perkins system (called siderography) so he could explain its faults. He did this in a book entitled *A Description of the Present System of Bank Note Engraving*, which he published privately in 1852. He argued that the "patchwork system" then being used to engrave notes actually facilitated counterfeiting. He further asserted that notes should be designed instead with one large vignette—taking up most of the face of the note—and that all the lettering should be interwoven into that picture. He thought mechanical engraving was easily copied and therefore, by itself, was not a sufficient safeguard against counterfeiting. His ideas were controversial and never really influenced the designers and engravers in the business, but his book was the first (and for nearly 10 years the only) detailed explanation of bank-note work.

The *Illustrated Monthly Magazine of Art*, published by Alexander Montgomery in New York for only two years, ran an article in volume I (1853) on the mechanical-engraving devices made by Cyrus Durand. The illustrations from that magazine have sometimes been used in recent works. John Durand, an art critic and son of the famous Asher Brown Durand, together with W.J. Stillman, founded and edited the *Crayon*, said to have been the best art journal of the period. Durand was left alone in this work after the second year. The *Crayon* was devoted to the fine arts and sometimes presented articles about bank-note engraving. Durand was almost certainly the author of a long, two-page article entitled "History and Progress of Bank Note Engraving" that appeared in the issue of February 21, 1855. That history is traced in rather broad outlines, but the writing is authoritative and elegant. The *Crayon* published seven volumes and seven numbers of an eighth volume from January 1855 to July 1861. *Harper's New Monthly Magazine* (usually just called "Harper's") printed a fairly detailed description of the different processes used in making paper money in 1862. The article takes the reader on an imaginary trip through the various departments of the American Bank Note Company in New York, using several of the engraving rooms, the lathe and transferring rooms, the plate vault, the ink-making room, the long-and-narrow printing room, and the ever-noxious hardening room. This was the most detailed and comprehensive examination of the bank-note industry in American periodical literature until Charles Wesley Dickinson Jr. took us all a step further with a 17-page article he wrote for *Popular Science Magazine* in March

1895. The author's father started a business making bank-note machinery in Belleville, New Jersey, in 1864. Being involved in the daily operations of that plant, the author naturally knew how every device worked. Dickinson's article is the best-written and best-illustrated description of mechanical bank-note engraving to appear in the 19th century.

None of this material, however, went into such detail that a machinist could easily make a copy of any particular device. Mechanical-engraving devices were usually described in such simple terms that one might understand their purpose but not the mechanical operations of their parts. One could see drawings or even photographs of geometric lathes and transfer presses in trade journals or magazines, but very little was written about their gear settings or how levers multiplied force. In contrast, European and especially British periodicals often published detailed works on even the more-esoteric devices, especially cycloidal and geometric lathes. Such openness may owe to cultural differences but more likely stems from the long tradition in Europe and England of hobbyists using the ornamental turning lathe. Many of Europe's monarchs and aristocrats pursued this hobby, including Louis XVI of France, Peter the Great of Russia, Friedrich-Wilhelm I of Prussia, Alphonso I of Italy, Maximilian of the Holy Roman Empire, Queen Sophie Magdalene of Denmark, King George III of England, and even the German theologian Martin Luther. Ornamental turning lathes were developed in France and Germany during the 16th and 17th centuries and had been brought to a high level of technical refinement by the time Charles Plumier had written his seminal work on the subject in 1701. Out of that tradition came the rose engine and later the "geometric pen" of the Italian mathematician Count Giovanni Battista Suardi. His book in 1752 described how mechanical devices could generate geometric curves. George Adams the younger wrote a description of the geometric pen in his *Geometrical and Graphical Essays*, published in London in 1791. Another Englishman, John Holt Ibbetson, wrote several books and pamphlets, including "A Practical View of an Invention for the better protection [of] Bank-Notes against Forgery," published in 1820. Ibbetson made both a geometric chuck and a double-eccentric chuck by his own hands and illustrated the chucks and the types of geometric patterns executed by their use. Other works by the Holtzapffel brothers, Henry Perigal Jr., William Hartley, and William Henry Northcott, to mention only a few of the English authors, all contributed to the general understanding of how geometric and other lathes worked. The *English Mechanic*, *Design and Work*, and *Amateur Mechanics*, all British magazines, printed scores of illustrated articles on the construction and use of different geometric chucks from 1866 through 1884.

In American publications of this same period, I cannot find any detailed descriptions of mechanical-engraving devices.

Fortunately, I had the pleasure of visiting with Nicolas Edwards, who came over from England to browse through my library and discuss geometric lathes and their mechanical relatives. Nicholas is the President of the Society of Ornamental Turners

and has been a long-time student of those devices. He owns two geometric lathes and is the keeper of a rose engine that belongs to the society. He understands their mechanics and operates all of them. In a Herculean feat, he was able to explain to me how the different lathes operate, so I actually began to grasp the basic principles.

Norman Underwood and Thomas V. Sullivan's *The Chemistry and Technology of Printing Inks*, published in 1915, was still relevant to the bank-note inks used over the previous century because ink chemistry evolved so slowly. Plate printing was described in numerous references during the 19th century, but only in brief detail. H.S. Neale and Theodore Isert's *The Art of Plate Printing*, published in 1927, treated the subject more extensively, but from a commercial point of view was not very helpful to bank-note students. The best explanation I found covering the fine points of inking, wiping, and pulling impressions of bank notes is the testimony given by several experts in the field in *Senate Report No. 2604*, issued during the 50th Congress, 2nd Session, and dated February 15, 1889. This is a transcript of the testimony given before a Senate subcommittee, and most of the witnesses were called from the Bureau of Engraving and Printing and the independent bank-note companies. For paper-making there is no better book than Dard Hunter's monumental *Papermaking: The History and Technique of an Ancient Craft*, published in 1947. It is an excellent introduction to the basic processes of paper-making, and the specialist can find more-technical works on specific subjects, such as bleaching, Fourdrinier machines, security chemistry, etc.

Having started this book rather late in life, I knew from long years of experience that it could never be as comprehensive, as accurate, or as skillfully written as I would like. Life is a long series of compromises, perhaps especially in the thin air of historical research, and each of us who does this kind of work eventually settles for the limitations of the pocketbook, the loss of focus due to our changing health, or the challenge of finding order in the noise and confusion of everyday life. I have persisted in this long effort because I think there is a real need for a single-reference work that sets down the basic facts of how the bank-note industry was created and evolved in the last century to become a sophisticated technology producing notes of high artistry. I have tried to distinguish between historical facts and their analysis—two very different objectives—so that readers are encouraged to turn over ideas and dissect the social, legal, and economic sinews of the system. Naturally, I am responsible for any factual errors, however innocently they were made, and even if they sometimes reveal a lack of patience with the tedious and almost constant reorganization of the bank-note companies. In the long view, I think this work will be a starting place from which others can correct my mistakes or take issue with my conclusions and constantly build a better understanding of our bank-note history.

Bob McCabe
Loxahatchee, Florida

Acknowledgements

Hundreds of people have helped me with thousands of research questions over the last 20 years or so, and I am grateful for their assistance. **Daniel Stadtfeld**, a descendant of the counterfeiting Stadtfelds mentioned in this book, has been a constant and important helper as well as a good friend whose knowledge and constructive criticism have guided my efforts. The same can be said of **Mark Tomasko**, who has written both on the history of the industry and the art it developed. **Eric P. Newman** helped me with colonial notes. **Larry Adams** gave general support and provided me with a lot of the literature I could not find elsewhere. **Dr. Wendy Woloson** helped at the Library Company of Philadelphia in finding many of the materials on the early bank-note printers there. **Mrs. Gail Moreau-DesHarnais**, a genealogist, has helped track down numerous engravers and counterfeiters. **Frances Challenor**, a retired school teacher of Latin, graciously read the first draft of each chapter and not only corrected my grammatical errors but also asked Socratic questions and offered sage advice. **Mary Donald** and **Amy Miller** in the Inter-Library Loan Department of the Broward County Library found close to 100 books and dozens of journal articles I requested over the years. Finally, I owe especial thanks to **Q. David Bowers**, the "Dean of American Numismatics" and numismatic research, who read a preliminary manuscript, corrected many of my mistakes, and suggested ways to improve the work. His contributions are greatly appreciated.

As with almost any author, my greatest supporters were my family. My son-in-law has solved all the problems I created with my computer, and my daughter and grandkids have helped in more ways than I can count. I have led a happy life in analytical chemistry for donkey's years, but triple bypass surgery and a few other machinations dreamed up by my surgeons have changed the dance. My fingers tremble because of a neurological problem, resulting in a lot of errors in my typing, and I am grateful to both Mr. Bowers and Spell-Check for their corrections.

I got started on this long quest for knowledge in 1983 when I read **Murray Teigh Bloom's** *The Brotherhood of Money*. I noticed that the book had no index, so I compiled one. That forced me to read the book a second time with a lot more concentration than I normally bring to casual reading. When I finished, I sent the index to Mr. Bloom with a brief letter congratulating him on a job well done, and from that, a long friendship and correspondence developed. I had the pleasure of visiting him and spending a long afternoon discussing bank-note stories. Since then, Murray has given me encouragement and good advice in many short notes and letters over the years, and it gives me pleasure to dedicate this book to him.

List of Illustrations

The image of the raised Massachusetts Bay Colony note of 1690 on page 17 is used with the permission of the **Smithsonian Institution's National Numismatic Collection**. The image of the 17th-century hand-roller press on page 22 is from **William Faitborne's** *The Art of Graving and Etching, 1662*. The nature-print images on page 41 come from the **Eric P. Newman Money Museum in St. Louis, Missouri** and the **Eric P. Newman Numismatic Education Society**. The white-line–engraving specimen on page 51 is original to an advertisement by **Tanner, Kearny & Tiebout** in the *Port Folio*, September 1815, and is courtesy of **The Library Company of Philadelphia**. The diagram of the patent drawing for the Perkins's Transfer Press on page 60 is used from *Barlow's Manufactures and Machinery in Great Britain*. The photograph of Perkins's Bank-Note Plant, 1809, on page 62 is from **Bathe's** *Jacob Perkins*, **Historical Society of Pennsylvania**. The drawing of Applegath and Cowper's rotary press on page 66 is courtesy of the **Museum of the Bank of England**. The specimen note of Perkins, Fairman & Heath found on page 68 is original to the *John Johnson Collection*, **Bodleian Library, Oxford, England**. The specimen note of Perkins, Bacon & Petch found on page 68 is from the author's personal collection. The specimen note engraved by Robert Branson, 1820, on page 68 is courtesy of the **St. Bride Printing Library, London, England**. The image of the Danforth, Wright & Company bank-note plant on page 77 comes from the *Illustrated Magazine of Art, 1854*. The images of the bank notes engraved by Leney & Rollinson on page 85 are courtesy of the *American Antiquarian Society*. Asher Durand's "Musidora" engraving on page 90 comes from the **Smithsonian American Art Museum**. Durand's "Ariadne" engraving on page 90 is currently located in the **Museum of Fine Arts, Houston**. Durand's painting "Kindred Spirits" on page 91 is currently located in the **Crystal Bridges Museum of American Art**. The image of George Bourne's print shop on page 98 is from **Henry Collins Brown's** *Valentine's Manual of Old New York 1922*, **New York, 1921**. The image of the new Merchants Exchange Building on page 100 was drawn by **C.I. Warne** and is used courtesy of the **Museum of the City of New York**. The image of the transfer room at the American Bank Note Company on page 103 is from **Dr. John Ellis's** *The Sights and Secrets of the National Capital: A Work Descriptive of Washington City in Its Various Phases*, **1869**. The image of the engraving department at the American Bank Note Company on page 104 is courtesy of the **New York Public Library Print Collection**. The specimen note of Rawdon, Wright, Hatch & Edson on page 106 is used from the **New York Public Library Print Collection**. The image of the Fenian Society Bond on page 126 comes from the *Essay-Proof Journal*, **Whole Number 80, 1963**. The image of the sugar mill on page 143 is available from the **McCord Museum**. The image of the Methodist Book Concern on page 172 is from the **Mechanical Curator collection**. The photograph of the United States Hotel on page 177 is from the **Lutzenberger Picture Collection**. The $3 note of Providence, Rhode Island, on page 190 is from **Stack's Bowers Galleries**. The illustration of "The Goose That Laid the Golden Eggs" on page 198 comes originally from "The Aesop for Children" illustrated by Milo Winter, sourced by **Project Gutenberg**. The image of the map on page 199 is from **Geographicus Rare Antique Maps**. The $100 Ninger counterfeit on page 209 is courtesy of the **National Numismatic Collection, National Museum of American History**. The drawing of the India Ink on page 211 is from the catalogue of the **Mackey Print Paper Company, 1897**. The "Jim the Penman" flyer on page 211 was printed by **Clement-Smith & Co.** and resides in the **National Library of Scotland**. The image of the 50-cent Fractional Currency note on page 239 is courtesy of the **American Numismatic Association**. The photograph of Benjamin Bristow on page 250 is used with permission of **Matthew Brady**. The dragon's blood on page 259 is used with permission of **Maša Sinreih in Valentina Vivod**. The diagrams on page 260 of how burins are held are found in **William Faithborne's** *The Art of Graving and Etching, 1662*. The image on page 261 of how burins cut is originally from **J.H. Baxter's** *Printing Postage Stamps by Line Engraving*, **American Philatelic Society**. The image on page 261 of intaglio lines comes from **John Easton's** *Postage Stamps in the Making*, **Faber and Faber, London, 1949**. The image on page 265 of the pole lathe is from the *Illustrated Magazine of Art, 1853*. The image of the great wheel lathe on page 266 is original to **Diderot's** *Encyclopédie*, **Volume 10 of Plates, 1772**. The photograph of the rose-engine lathe on page 266 is courtesy of **Martin Matthews**. The diagram of the rose-engine–lathe rosettes on page 267 is from **Martin Matthews's** *Engine Turning, 1680–1980*. The photograph of the barrel of rosettes on page 267 is courtesy of **Martin Matthews's** *Engine Turning, 1680–1980*. The diagram of the cycloids on page 268 can be found in **C.W. Dickinson's article in** *Popular Science Monthly*, **March, 1895**. The image of the cycloidal pattern on page 268 is from **C.W. Dickinson's article in** *Popular Science Monthly*, **March, 1895**. The diagram of the "Geometric Pen" on page 269 is from **Gardner Hiscox's** *Mechanical Movements, Powers and Devices*, **1907**. The image of the first Geometric Lathe on page 270 is used with permission of the *Illustrated Magazine of Art*, **1854**. The figure of the geometric lathe on page 270 draws from patent drawings and **Barlow's** *Manufactures and Machinery in Great Britain*. The image of Durand's geometric lathe on page 270 is used with permission from the *Illustrated Magazine of Art*, **1854**. The images of the geometric chuck on page 271 come from the **New York Historical Society**. The image of Ibbetson's geometric chuck on page 272 is courtesy of **Martin Matthews's** *Engine Turning, 1680–1980*. The Hartley geometric chuck imaged on page 272 is courtesy of **Martin Matthews**. The diagram of the gear movements on page 273 are reproduced with the permission of **Martin Matthews**. The design cut on page 273 is courtesy of **Martin Matthews's** *Engine Turning, 1680–1980*. The photograph of the Chapman cycloidal ruling machine on page 275 can be found in the **Essay-Proof Journal, October 1945**. The photographs of the Chapman geometric lathe on page 275 and 276 are courtesy of the **Bureau of Engraving and Printing**. The geometric border imaged on page 276 is from *Printing Postage Stamps by Line Engraving* courtesy of the **American Philatelic Society**. The Guillochermaschine on page 276 comes from the **Michael Kampf Catalogue**. The harmonographic pattern shown on page 276 is original to *The Daily Telegraph*. The fantasy-lathe work on page 277 is from the author's personal collection. The photograph of the campylograph on page 277 comes from **Gardner Hiscox's** *Mechanical Movements, Powers and Devices*, **1907**. The simplified pantograph on page 278 is from an ad placed in magazines by **J.G. Thompson**, 1731 North 24th Street, Philadelphia. Donkin's pantograph shown on page 279 is used in

Transactions of the Newcomen Society and is obtained by permission of the **Newcomen Society, London**. The ruling machine on page 279 is courtesy of the **Bureau of Engraving and Printing**. The two pantographs shown on page 280 are used with permission of the **Michael Kampf Catalogue**. The engraving machine shown on page 283 is from **Arthur H. Frazier's** *Joseph Saxton*, **Smithsonian Institution**. The image of Gobrecht's medal-ruling machine shown on page 285 can be found in **Arthur H. Frazier's** *Joseph Saxton*, **Smithsonian Institution**. Saxton's tracer imaged on page 285 is used with permission from **Arthur H. Frazier's** *Joseph Saxton*, **Smithsonian Institution**. The Bate medal-engraving machine shown on page 286 was drawn by **Arthur Frazier** and is used with the permission of the **Smithsonian Institution**. The Saxton medal-engraving machine shown on page 286 comes from the **Historical and Interpretive Collections of the Franklin Institute, Philadelphia**. The transfer press shown on page 287 is from the British patent drawings. The photograph of the bank-note plate on page 288 is original to the author's personal collection. The photograph of the transfer roller on page 288 is from **Mortimer Neinken's** *The United States One Cent Stamp of 1851 to 1861* courtesy of the **U.S. Philatelic Society**. Durand's transfer press is imaged on page 289 from the *Illustrated Magazine of Art*, **1854**. The Casilear-Tichenor transfer press on page 289 is found in the *Knight's American Mechanical Dictionary*, **1881 edition**. The transfer press imaged on page 289 is from **Mortimer Neinken's** *The United States One Cent Stamp of 1851 to 1861* and is used with permission of the **U.S. Philatelic Classics Society**. The photographs (RG 318-D-II-6666 / RG 318D-891) of the Chapman transfer press on page 290 and 291 come from the **Bureau of Engraving and Printing** in the **National Archives**. The parts of a transfer press imaged on page 291 come from **C.W. Dickinson's** article in *Popular Science Monthly*. The black-line/white-line conversion image on page 292 is adapted from **James H. Baxter's** *Printing Postage Stamps by Line Engraving* courtesy of the **American Philatelic Society**. The image of the modern transfer press on page 293 is used with permission of the **Michael Kampf Catalogue**. The image on page 296 of the vatman capturing pulp is taken from *Chinese Technology in the 17th Century*. The image of the triphammer on page 299 is used from *Joseph Needham's Science and Civilisation in China*. The 17th-century European paper mill on page 302 comes from an unidentified print in the **Dard Hunter Collection** at the **Robert C. Williams Paper Museum** at **Georgia Tech, Atlanta, Georgia**. The mill for hand-making paper imaged on page 303 is used from **Louis Figuier's** *Les Merveilles de L'Industrie*. The picture of the drying loft on page 303 is from **Louis Figuier's** *Les Merveilles de L'Industrie*. The Fourdrinier paper machine on page 307 can be found in the *Cyclopedia of Useful Arts and Manufactures* edited by **Charles Tomlinson**. The image of the Dickinson cylinder paper machine on page 309 is used from **Repertory of Arts, Manufacturers and Agriculture**. The image of the Gilpin paper machine on page 309 is from **Eleutherian Mills—Hagley Foundation**. The machine room on page 313 is courtesy of the **Crane & Company Museum**. The shipping room on page 314 is found in *The First 175 Years of Crane Papermaking* courtesy of the **Crane & Company Museum**. The 1890s photograph of the paper-drying building on page 322 is courtesy of the **Crane & Company Museum**. The image of boiling rags on page 324 comes from the **Crane & Company Museum**. The image of the rag-beating vats on page 325 are used with permission of the **Crane & Company Museum**. The photograph of the sizing tanks on page 325 is courtesy of the **Bureau of Engraving and Printing**. The photograph of the patent numbers on page 334 is used with permission of Fred Reed. The image of the Dodge ink mill on page 337 is courtesy of *The American Ink Maker*. The photograph of the Plymouth three-roller ink mill on page 337 comes from the author's collection. The image of the ink-grinding room on page 338 is from the author's collection. The photograph of the soy beans on page 338 is used with permission of **Midori**. The image of the 19th-century copper-plate press on page 341 is from the *Illustrated Magazine of Art*. The view of the hand-roller press on page 341 comes from the **Science Museum's Science and Society Picture Library**, London. The images of the Perkins copper-plate press on page 342 are original to the **British Library** and from the **Science Museum's Science and Society Picture Library**, London. The photograph of the steam-driven copper-plate press on page 343 is used with permission from **Barlows's *Manufactures and Machinery In Great Britain***. The image of the R. Hoe & Company Wetting Press on page 344 comes from the **R. Hoe & Company's Catalogue of 1867**. The picture of the charcoal brazier on page 345 is used with permission of the *Illustrated Magazine of Art*. The images of the copper-plate presses on pages 345 and 348 are from the **R. Hoe & Company's Catalogue of 1867**. The hand-roller press on page 346 is courtesy of **Larry Adams, curator, Higgins Museum** in Okojobi, Iowa. The Milligan press seen on page 348 is original to the **Smithsonian Institution's Graphic Arts Collection**. The Homer-Lee steam press seen on page 349 is original to the **Smithsonian Institution's Graphic Arts Collection**.

The following images are courtesy of the **U.S. Secret Service Archives**: the image on page 140 of the $2 Saint Nicholas National Bank note; the image on page 142 of the counterfeit $1 U.S. note, series 1862; the image on page 142 of the $50 United States note; the image on page 142 of the $100 Central National Bank note; the counterfeit $20 note on page 174; the counterfeit $5 note on page 180; the counterfeit $5 note on page 194; the counterfeit $50 note on page 204; the counterfeit $50 note on page 212.

The following images are used with permission from the **National Archives**: the photograph (RG 87-PC-1) of Peter McCartney on page 156; the photograph (RG 87-CA-465) of John B. Trout on page 157; the photograph (RG 87-CA-178) of James Lyons on page 160; the photograph (RG 87-PCM-880) of George Albert Mason on page 162; the photograph (RG 87-CA-125) of Lyle Levi on page 164; the photograph (RG 87-CA-128) of Wanck Hammond on page 165; the photograph (RG 87-CA-225) of Henry Cole on page 167; the photograph (RG 87-CA-744) of Nelson B. Driggs on page 175; the photograph (RG 87-PC-745) of Charles Stadtfeld on page 176; the photograph (RG 87-PC-127) of Charles Johnson on page 179; the photograph (RG 87-CA-109) of Miles Ogle on page 183; the photograph (RG 87-CA-538) of John Ogle on page 186; the photograph (RG 87-CA-180) of Billy Brown on page 188; the photograph (RG 87-PCM-925) of James B. Doyle on page 200; the photograph (RG 87-CA-142) of Charles Ulrich on page 203; the photograph (RG 87-CA-739) of Charles Hill on page 213; the photograph (RG 87-CAD-1-3) of William P. Wood on page 217; the photograph (RG 87-CAD-5-1) of John Bell on page 226; the photograph (RG 87-CAD-6-1) of A.L. Drummond on page 226; the photograph (RG 87-CAD-7-2) of William P. Hazen on page 227; the image (RG 56-AE-28) of the hand-roller presses at the bureau on page 244; the image (RG 56-AE-21) of the dies and plates in cyanide on page 246; the image (RG 318-D-6666) of the horse-drawn money wagon on page 247; the image (RG 56-AE-41B) of the sizing machines at the bureau on page 251; the image of laundering soiled currency on page 255; the image (RG 59-AE-29) of the printing room at the bureau on page 255; the image (RG 56-AE-15) on page 257 of the engraving room; the image of the lathe at the bureau on page 275; the photograph (RG 318-D-B275) of the lathe on page 276; the photograph (RG 56-AE-17) of the Hope ruling machine on page 279; the photograph (RG 56-AE-35B) on page 325 of the sizing tanks; the photograph (RG 318-D-25147) of the four-plank power-printing press on page 350.

Heritage Auctions (HA.com) provided multiple images of coins and paper money as well as some historical images. The **Library of Congress** provided certain historical images. **C. John Ferreri, Don C. Kelly, Mack Martin,** and **Mark Tomasko** also contributed images.

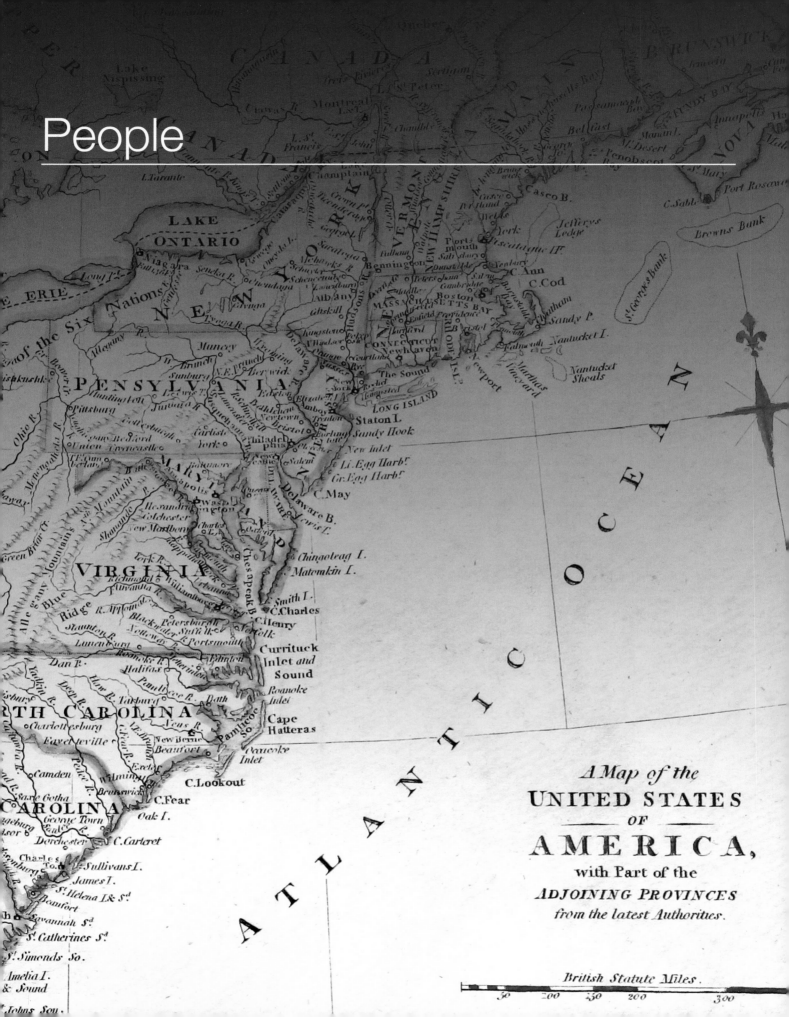

People

Chapter 1

An Experiment in Boston

Early Coins and Barter

From the very beginning of our colonial history, various commodities have been used as currency. Indian shell money, called "wampum," was used in the Massachusetts Bay Colony by the Dutch in the late 1620s. The General Court of Massachusetts set the value of the shells so that they could be used in trade. Furs, fish, cattle, and especially grain were commonly used as money in commerce. The General Court ordered that wheat and barley should be traded at the rate of four shillings per bushel, rye and peas at three shillings and four pence (3s-4d) a bushel, and Indian corn at two shillings and six pence (2s-6d). In 1635 the same court passed a law that musket balls could be used in trade at a value of a farthing apiece and that no man could be compelled to take more than 12 pence (48 musket balls) at a time in such money. Colonists were also used to the small brass and copper coins from England, the occasional English gold coins called "marks" and "nobles," and the various Dutch and Spanish coins that were brought into the colony by sailors arriving from the West Indies and the Continent. Merchants would accept certain coins and reject others depending on how well they knew a coin's value and its condition.

Gold and silver coins were often "clipped," meaning that small slivers had been cut or shaved from the edges of the coins so the shavers could eventually amass a small pile of these clippings, hammer them together, and sell them to goldsmiths and jewelers. Silver coins were sometimes "washed," meaning that they had been dunked in an acid to remove some of the metal. Coins made of gold or silver were often presented in very worn condition, and the merchants would naturally try to discount their value to compensate for the loss of the precious metal.

Transactions in "country pay," meaning wheat, barley, corn, etc., were simple enough, and two men could bargain over the fair value of these commodities. But payments in metallic coin were a more complicated matter. A legal-tender statute enacted in South Carolina in 1701 named nine varieties of silver coins and four varieties of gold. If someone presented a mixture of these coins in payment to a merchant, it required time and a good head for arithmetic to make change. These complications led many colonists to complain that a standard coinage was needed. To some extent, this was accomplished by the Spanish dollars, which were accepted everywhere without regard to their weight or condition and soon became the predominant coin throughout the colonies. In different places, these silver coins were called "pieces of eight," "eight-real pieces," "pesos," or "piastres," but the colonists always referred to them as Spanish dollars. The Spanish had established mints in Mexico as early as 1535, as well as in Peru by 1621, producing millions of such coins. By the early 17th century, there was a steady stream of these coins reaching the British colonies through their trade with the West Indies. In fact, the Spanish dollar was the world's chief coin from 1600 to about 1800 and circulated in the United States until the Act of February 21, 1857, discontinued their legal-tender status, effective two years later.

A Philip III 8-reales coin.

Although the Spanish dollars were popular, colonists persisted in their demands for coins of their own making. The legislators responded to their complaints by establishing a mint in Boston in 1652 that produced silver coins in the denominations of threepence, sixpence, and one shilling. These coins were technically illegal since the Crown had never given permission to any of the colonies to make coins. Nevertheless, the Massachusetts Bay Colony continued to make such coins until about 1660. These were nearly always struck with a 1652 date to mislead the British into thinking the total issue was much smaller than it really was.

The "Invention" of Paper Money in America

Today the concept of paper money seems simple and logical, perhaps even intuitive, but its "invention" and slow development in the Bay Colony shows it was neither. In 1681 the Reverend John Woodbridge of Newbury and certain prominent merchants in Boston began to discuss the possibility of setting up a bank of credit to be called "the Fund." That year, Woodbridge published a pamphlet entitled "Severals relating to the Fund, printed for divers reasons, as may appear." Woodbridge and his friends planned for this bank to issue notes of credit by which they could adjust debts among the members. The Fund did not issue notes for the first few years of its existence, but in 1686 Captain John Blackwell reorganized the Fund as the Bank of Credit and got approval from the General Court to purchase a rolling press on which a few "tryall notes" were later printed from an engraved copper plate.[1] Neither the plate nor any of the notes have ever been found, so it is unlikely that the Bank of Credit ever issued any notes to the public. The bank was closed in 1668.

Some European experiments with paper money had already begun, and it is reasonable to assume that a few well-read colonists in Boston had knowledge of these efforts. In July 1661 the newly organized Stockholm Bank began issuing the first European notes of credit, called *kreditivsedler*. A Dutchman named Johan Palmstruch had recommended such a plan as early as 1652, and as the Swedish government began to have serious trouble with their copper-coin currency, they were attracted to his ideas. These bank notes differed from the earlier Italian notes issued in Venice and other places. The *kreditivsedlers* were not issued against cash deposits in the Stockholm Bank but would be redeemed by the government. They were issued in even denominations (as printed on the notes) and were payable to the bearer rather than a specific person. Finally, they accrued no interest, so their value remained fixed.

A 19th-century 50-kronor note of the Stockholm Bank.

In the last half of the 17th century, a number of paper instruments appeared which represented value of one type or another. Stock certificates are an example. The earliest of these were issued by the Dutch East India Company in the early 1650s. One is presently owned by the American Stock Exchange and insured for half a million dollars. A similar certificate, issued by the English East India Company, is dated 1657. Stock certificates of this period were printed uniface on common paper and consisted of a few lines of text with spaces where the name of the owner, the date, the value, and signatures of authentication could be written.

A pamphlet published in London in 1688 explained how a bank of credit might work and mentions the successful use of bank bills in Holland and "the State of Venice."[2] The long title contains the interesting statement that the model bank proposed is "Adapted More Especially for His Majesties Plantations in America," making it all the more likely that this pamphlet made its way to Boston soon after publication. A pamphlet published in Boston in 1691 also mentions the use of bank bills in "Venice, Paris, Leghorn [the old English name for the city of Levorno, Italy] and Amsterdam," and gives an especially favorable account of how such bills circulated in Venice.[3] If the author of that pamphlet was Captain John Blackwell, as some suspect, then certainly he had read about these earliest uses of paper money by the time he was printing "tryall notes" for the Bank of Credit, and the "invention" of paper money in the Massachusetts Bay Colony may have been just an experiment based on European models.

But another monetary experiment took place much closer to Boston—one that probably had considerable influence on colonial thinking. In 1685 the French governor in Canada could not pay the army troops because the ship bringing coins was delayed by more than eight months. The governor tried various alternatives, including the offer of food on credit. In desperation, he confiscated all the playing cards in Quebec and had each card cut into four quarters. On the back of each quarter-card he wrote a value and signed his name. These cards were then "promises to pay" and circulated like coins. The experiment

worked so well that the French government later printed "card money" for use in Canada among its military forces and civil servants. It is very likely that this Canadian experiment and the London and Boston pamphlets previously mentioned were the sources for the experiment in Massachusetts that lay just around the corner.

French "card money." On the left is a seven of hearts, worth 3 sols, and on the right is a queen of diamonds, worth 15 sols.

The decision to print our first circulating paper money was made rather quickly by a small group of men in Boston in late 1690 to prevent a revolt, but it may be interesting to read first how French ambitions, English colonial affairs, and even smallpox played a role in this story, and how numerous decisions might have been made differently, putting off paper money to a much later time and for completely different reasons.

The War on the French

Beginning in 1688, the French army occasionally sent military expeditions from Canada to burn and pillage the plantations in New England, especially in the part we now call Maine. They had also armed some of the Indian tribes and put them up to the same mischief. The colonists had mounted a few expeditions against the French in retaliation, but only one of these had been even moderately successful. All had fallen far short of a decisive blow. Clearly, bigger guns were needed.

The colonists had spent the early months of 1690 planning attacks on Montreal and Quebec.

They needed ships, gunpowder, and money to pay troops, and for this they dispatched a small but speedy vessel to England in April 1690 to carry an appeal for help to their majesties William and Mary, and to the Privy Council. It was hoped that the ship would return with at least "four of five hundred barrels of powder, with shot proportional, and four or five thousand fuzees [fuses]" and perhaps the £20,000 already spent from the colony's treasury fighting the war.[4] His Royal Majesty, however, had his hands full with problems on the European continent, and he gave but little attention to the complaints from New England. What was worse, he gave them no frigates, no gunpowder, and no money! It was now up to the colonists.

The military plan the colonists devised was simple. Connecticut and New York would send a force totaling about 1,000 men marching north to Lake Champlain, joining up with about 1,500 Indians along the way. The combined forces would then get into canoes at the south end of the lake, paddle to the north end, and then march a short distance to attack Montreal. At the same time, a fleet from Massachusetts would sail around Nova Scotia, into the St. Lawrence River, and down the river to Quebec. The two forces would time their departures so that they could arrive at their assigned targets and attack them simultaneously. But if ever a plan was "star-crossed," this was it.

The forces sent by land against Montreal never got there. Count Frontenac, the French general at Montreal, heard of the English plans even before the men started marching north. The French army may have planted some of their own men in the column to sow dissension, or the colonists may simply have taken along some of the political rivalries then prevailing in New York, for we know there was bickering and dissension within the ranks all the way to Lake Champlain. The French apparently persuaded most of the Indian tribes to stay home and let the white men settle their own problems. When the colonists finally reached the lake, they found no canoes. Discouraged, and with smallpox beginning to reduce their number, the army turned around and went home. Frontenac, on hearing of this retreat, immediately sent about 3,000 foot soldiers to reinforce Quebec.

Meanwhile, the forces in Massachusetts could wait no longer, and finally, during the first week of August—much too close to the start of winter—they set sail with about 2,000 men from Nantasket, now called Hull, at the southern entrance to Boston Harbor. They had between 30 and 40 vessels, the largest of which was named *Six Friends*, armed with 44 guns and a company of some 200 men. Most of the fleet was made up of small fishing ships and coastal freighters. In addition to the usual provisions, they took along a few young drummer boys and at least two ministers. They also took along the smallpox virus, and it would do them more harm than all the French muskets. After sailing for 57 days, the fleet reached the outskirts of Quebec on October 5, and by then it was so cold that the men could walk on the ice of small lakes.

The commanding officer was a New England man, Sir William Phips, then 40 years old. Born in Pemaquid (now Bristol), Maine, in 1651, he was the son of a poor farmer

Lake Champlain, circa 1882.

and had spent his first 18 years as a sheep herder before serving as an apprentice to a shipwright, where he learned how to build ships. As a young man in Boston, he met and married a wealthy widow who taught him how to read and write. While "following the sea," he heard about a ship that had sunk off the island of Hispaniola while carrying a large cargo of silver. He also learned the approximate location of the ship and later gave such an account of it in England that the Duke of Albemarle fitted him out to make a search for the treasure. Phips sailed down to Port Royal, Jamaica, and took aboard several black divers. His first search in 1684 was a failure, but following new leads, his second attempt in 1687 was successful. With incredible luck, he found the sunken ship in such shallow water that his divers could easily reach it. Phips never learned the name of this ship and probably would not have cared much for the details of its history, but we know now that it was the *Nuestra Señora de la Pura y Limpia Concepcioñ*, a large merchant ship that had been built in the shipyard of Havana in 1620. Heavily loaded with silver from the Royal Mint in Mexico, the ship was on its way back to Spain when it hit a reef off the north coast of Hispaniola and sank in November 1641.[5] Phips recovered a treasure of about £210,000, for which he was knighted and given £16,000. He was a man of poor education and quick temper, and the historian Thomas Hutchinson said that it was only "by a series of fortunate incidents rather than by any uncommon talents, [that] he rose from the lowest condition in life to be the first man in his country."[6] What Hutchinson didn't say, however, was that Sir William, long before he had a title, was well known as a "man of the people" who enjoyed cursing with common sailors as much as he liked fist-fighting to maintain order on his ships. He had no pretensions, no hubris about his sudden wealth, and he spoke honestly and forthrightly, so the sailors and businessmen alike were impressed by what he said. That talent would play a large role in making paper money successful in British America.

Back in Quebec, Major John Walley was in charge of the troops that went ashore, and his journal gives us a detailed picture of what went wrong, day after day.[7] And things certainly did go wrong. The French were too cunning and too many, the weather too cold, the terrain too swampy, the supply of gunpowder too low, and if all that wasn't enough, too many of the men were sick with the smallpox. Out of the 2,000 men that left Boston, Major Walley was able to muster only 1,200 or so that could fight. Discipline within the ranks was terrible, the junior officers were inept, and Walley's leadership was restrained, to say the least. Several times when circumstances required an immediate tactical decision, the good major would convene a "council of war," discuss the options with his lieutenants, and then act according to their votes. Plans often went awry because of bad weather or poor execution. Finally, a week after their arrival, a storm "scattered the whole fleet, and they made the best of their way back to Boston," where Sir William Phips arrived on November 19. In his official report to King William, Phips put his losses at not more than 30 men, but Hutchinson and other historians have estimated the number was closer to 200.

While the expedition was still in Canada, some of the leading citizens of Boston began to discuss the various options for paying the troops when they returned. Naturally, there was great confidence that the colonists would defeat the French and capture their treasury, bringing home enough money to pay all the expenses of the campaign. But wiser men thought it prudent to authorize the printing of paper bills of credit in case they were needed. A draft of the hand-written authorization was drawn up on November 7, 1690, just 12 days before the colonists returned. At the same time, the committee drew up a draft of how the paper money should look.[8]

When the troops returned to Boston, those who weren't already sick with smallpox were now eager to collect the pay they had been promised, buy the food and other provisions they needed, and return to their simpler lives on farms scattered throughout the colony. The merchants of Boston were afraid that the soldiers would mutiny if they were not paid and would then compensate themselves by looting merchandise, possibly damaging or burning their shops. There was also considerable fear that the soldiers might infect the inhabitants of the city with their smallpox, and the longer they stayed in the city, the greater would be the risk of a major outbreak of the disease. Meetings were held in the top chamber of the two-story Townhouse at the head of State Street, and it was quickly decided that the colony must print the paper bills of credit they had authorized and pay the soldiers post-haste.

The First Notes

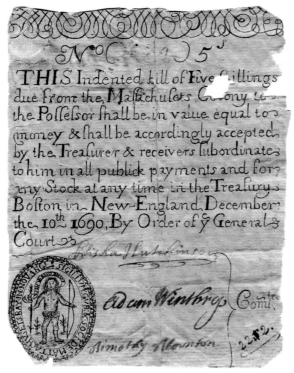

The first officially authorized paper money
in North America, December 1690.

So it was that the Massachusetts Bay Colony issued the first officially authorized paper money printed in North America, in December 1690. These first notes satisfied most of the soldiers and sailors, though not all were happy with paper money. The highly respected Sir William Phips, "merely to recommend the credit of the bills unto other persons, cheerfully laid down a considerable quantity of ready money for an equivalent parcel of them," and thus bolstered the public's confidence in the new money.[9] Soon after the notes were issued, the General Court pledged to accept them in payment of dues at a premium of five percent over and above their value in coin. This became a customary practice each time the colony issued new notes until it was stopped in 1720. The public, however, was never enthusiastic about paper money and often discounted its value. Cotton Mather said about these first notes that "those who first received them could make them yield little more than fourteen or sixteen shillings in the pound."[10] But the convenience of paper money as a common medium of exchange was one of those ideas whose time had come—as more and more people began to use these bills of credit, they became more than just a stopgap measure to avoid a mutiny and were increasingly a part of everyday life.

Cotton Mather, a moral leader of the Puritans who also held great
sway in the political and social culture of the day.

We don't know much about the denominations of the first issue of notes except that the Province Laws set the lower limit at five shillings and the higher limit at five pounds. But within two months, these limits were changed to two shillings and ten pounds, respectively, with at least eight denominations—2s, 2s-6d, 5s, 10s, 20s, 60s, 100s, and 200s. The 200s note was equal to £10 and must have been quite rare, if issued at all, since that amount was too large to use in regular transactions. No official limit was set as to the amount of money that could be printed, but Mather said the committee printed "a just number of bills." None of the official records say how many notes were engraved on each copper plate or even how many plates were engraved, but unofficial records indicate that each plate had four denominations—5s, 10s, 20s, and £5—and that £7,000 were printed initially. These notes, called "Colony bills," were printed as needed for 10 years. Only one genuine note has apparently survived from the early emissions, and it is in the collections of the Peabody-Essex Museum in Salem, Massachusetts. A note in the Smithsonian, apparently from the second emission although dated in 1690, had been raised to a higher denomination before it was seized and used as evidence at court, making it the first "raised" note in British North America of which we have any knowledge. A second raised note was in the John J. Ford, Jr. Collection and is discussed in detail in one of the Stack's auction catalogs.

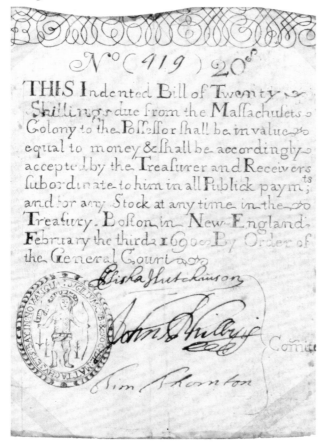

A Massachusetts Bay Colony note of 1690, the earliest paper money issued in British North America. This particular note was raised from 5 shillings to 20 shillings.

The committee in charge of printing these first notes realized they had to do something to prevent counterfeiting—which had long been a problem with coins—and after giving it some thought, they chose to print uniface indented notes from elaborately engraved copper plates. Uniface notes were those printed on one side only. Indenture was a simple procedure in which notes were printed with a special design at the top or at one end. This specially printed area of the note was called the "stub." The printed notes were bound into pads, and the stubs were cut off by scissors, usually in a slightly waved and irregular cut. Early notes were often printed with elaborate scroll work and cut so that half of the scroll remained on the issued note and the other (matching) half was on the stub. Matching serial numbers were then written on both the stub and the note proper. Naturally, the serial numbers were sequential so that no two notes were ever numbered alike. The stubs were then sewn together to form books. When notes were redeemed at the Treasury, each was compared to its corresponding stub, based on the serial numbers and denomination. If a note did not fit the cut of the parent stub, or the scroll work on the stub did not align with its counterpart on the note, or if the note bore a serial number that had already been redeemed for that denomination or of a serial number that had never been issued, it was obviously a counterfeit and could be refused. Notes printed with such stubs are said to be indented. Indenture, however, was nothing new. The procedure had been in use for several centuries in Europe in the form of indented deeds, legal records, and other important papers.

The committee also believed that the elaborate engraving printed on each note would prevent counterfeiting, since there were only a few engravers in the colony capable of such work. It was taken for granted that none of these men would be willing to risk their reputations by making counterfeit plates. The colony seal was printed on each note, bearing the image of an Indian holding a bow in one hand and a planting stick in the other. Above the Indian there is a ribbon, like a cartoon balloon, saying "Come over and help us," with the letters of the quotation so small it would be difficult for an amateur to engrave them accurately, making counterfeits more easily detected. This seal was later professionally engraved in silver in England and sent over to Governor John Endicott in 1729. That seal was copied in the engraved plate, and therefore a second printing wasn't necessary to get the seal on paper. Though paper money would take many different forms in the coming years, small, engraved printing and a seal became standard features on many colonial notes.

The seal of the Massachusetts Bay Colony, 1629.

The Engravers

No one knows who engraved the copper plates used to print the first paper money issued to the public in New England. No contemporary authors have left us a single word about the engraver. Even the usually loquacious Judge Samuel Sewall, who kept a diary for many years through this period and often commented on matters great and small, said nothing about this issue. Andrew McFarland Davis, a noted scholar of early colonial money,

read extensively in the voluminous Massachusetts archives and never found a name to match the deed. However, a few facts have come to light that offer some credible clues.

Though the engraving on these bills of credit may seem to us rough and rather crudely done, prejudiced as we are by observing 19th-century notes executed by professional bank-note engravers, we have to admit that engraving is such a difficult art that it requires a practiced hand to reach the level of craftsmanship seen on even these notes. They are certainly not the work of amateurs cutting their first plates. And who had the necessary skills to do such work? The gold and silversmiths, of course.

There were more than 20 silversmiths that practiced their trade in Boston during the last half of the 17th century, and at least 8 of these were active at the time the first paper money was engraved and printed. Two of these men have been nominated as the likely engraver—John Coney and Jeremiah Dummer. Both of them are mentioned in official records as engravers of paper money, but the challenge of proving which man was the engraver of the 1690 bills of credit has occupied scholars for many years.

John Coney (or Conny) was born in Boston on January 5, 1655, the eldest of 13 children in the family of a cooper.[11] We know that he was apprenticed to Jeremiah Dummer, one of the earliest silversmiths of Boston, and he obviously learned the craft well, for many of the finest pieces of silver made in Boston during the last quarter of the 17th century bear his mark.[12] We know that Coney engraved the plates for the currency issued by Massachusetts in 1702 because archives dated March 12, 1702–03 (*sic*), show a disbursement "to John Conny for graving 3 plates for Bills of Credit—£30.00.0."[13] The plates that Coney engraved for that issue were very similar to those of the 1690 issue, and according to David McNeely Stauffer, "approach it so closely in general design and execution, especially in the character of the decoration at the top of the note, that there is a strong possibility that both plates were made by the same man."[14] Coney also engraved the plates used to print the paper money of Massachusetts in 1708 and 1710. It has been argued that if a colony liked the job an engraver did for the first issue of its notes, then naturally they would use him again in subsequent issues, and the last three times that Coney did this work for the colony argues that he was the one who did it the first time. That's a circular argument and still bears no proof of who engraved the first issue.

Coney's private life gives little evidence that he was our mystery engraver. He married three times and fathered twelve children, of whom only five daughters grew to maturity so that he left no male descendants to carry on his name. His last child, Mehetable, lived to the age of 80 years, long enough to see the Massachusetts Bay Colony become part of an independent America. Coney seems to have been an industrious and highly skilled craftsman. He was known to be a quiet man who shunned publicity. There is no doubt that he was successful. From his record books and other accounts, he is known to have worked at his craft up to the day he died on August 20, 1722. The appraised value of his estate was given as £3,714-2s-11d, including houses and land to a value of £2,516.

John Coney taught the basic skills of silver-smithing, including engraving, to many apprentices. One of his apprentices was Nathaniel Morse. According to the *Massachusetts Archives*, volume 101, no. 525, Morse engraved and printed a plate for Massachusetts currency for which he was paid in 1735. He died in Boston in 1748. The last of the apprentices was a young Huguenot immigrant named Apollos Rivoire, who in turn taught the craft to his son, Paul Revere. Paul Revere is sometimes mistakenly called the "Father" of paper-money engraving in America, a subject we will examine in more detail later.

The only other person who might have engraved the 1690 plate was the same Jeremiah Dummer previously mentioned. He was born in Newbury, Massachusetts, in 1645, the son of Richard Dummer, an Englishman who had attained considerable wealth in the new colony and was married to the former Frances Burr, the widow of an English clergyman.[15] Of his early years we know only that he was apprenticed for

eight years to John Hull to learn the trade of the silversmith. John Hull was the first silversmith in 17th-century Massachusetts and was the first Mint Master of the colony. Dummer married John Coney's third wife's sister when he was 27 years old, and from that marriage he had 9 children, none of whom became silversmiths or engravers. 11 of his known pieces of silver bear coat-of-arms and inscriptions that show his considerable skill as an engraver.

"The Landing of the Pilgrims" at
Plymouth, Massachusetts, December 22, 1620.

Because he was so good at this type of work, he was commissioned to engrave the two copper plates used to print the paper currency of Connecticut in 1709, and those notes are so similar to the Massachusetts notes of 1690 that some writers have suggested that Dummer, not Coney, may have been the engraver of the 1690 issue. After all, both sets of notes have identical designs with an indented stub at the top and very similar scroll work through which the indented cut was made. The colonial seals are placed at the bottom and on the left side in all of these notes, and the back of the Connecticut notes bear exactly the same engraved scroll used on the backs of Massachusetts notes of the same period, meaning that they must have been printed from the same plate. Although the inscriptions on the Connecticut notes were engraved in cursive letters and those on the notes of 1689 had printed letters, there are several letters on both notes that are so similar as to appear engraved by the same hand. The inscriptions on both sets of notes are virtually identical. There is also the fact that an order of the General Court on July 2, 1692, required all colony notes to be endorsed on the back by Jeremiah Dummer and two others, which has led to the speculation that he was specifically chosen because he had engraved the plates and would be the person best qualified to detect a counterfeit. In fact, if one knew nothing about the history of these notes, one might reasonably conclude that they were engraved by just one man and that the small differences between them derive from the natural changes in skill, technique, and artistic preference acquired by the engraver during the 19 years that separated their issue. On the other hand, the Massachusetts notes of 1702 and 1708, both of which are known to be the work of John Coney, were the only paper money in the region during this period, and it would be quite natural for another engraver to copy their design when commissioned to engrave new notes for another colony. Dummer may have simply looked at the paper money he had carried in his purse for several years, thought it was a good and sufficient design, and chose to copy it when he engraved the plates for the Connecticut bills of 1709. Therefore, the similarities in work do not prove that Dummer engraved the first notes.

The similarities between Coney and Dummer's styles of engraving, and the fact that archival records attribute different notes to them, virtually eliminates all the other silversmiths from any reasonable consideration that they were the mystery engraver of the first notes. John Hull, for example, died in 1683, so he never engraved any plates for the bills of credit. It is still possible that someone may find archival or even anecdotal evidence of who engraved those first notes, but until that happens, the available evidence clearly supports John Coney in that honor.

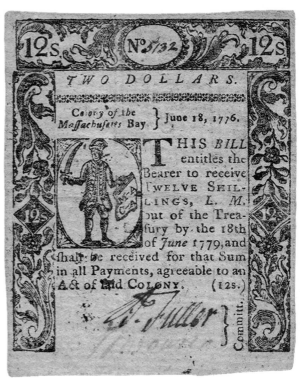

Paper currency of Massachusetts.

The Printers

Engraving is one thing and printing is another. If John Coney engraved the first plates for paper money, who printed them? The honor may belong to Bartholomew Green and his father at the press they operated in Cambridge, Massachusetts. Bartholomew was born in Cambridge on October 12, 1666, and was the son of Samuel Green, a printer. Naturally, he served his apprenticeship with his father. At the age of 21, eager to make his own fortune, he left his father's shop in Cambridge and moved across the Charles River

Compare the paper currency of Connecticut (above) with the paper currency of Massachusetts (next column right).

to Boston. His brother, Samuel Green Jr., had a successful printing shop there, and Bartholomew worked with them until his brother and sister-in-law died of smallpox in July 1690. This was the same smallpox epidemic that later in the year took so many lives in the military expedition against Quebec. Somehow, Bartholomew escaped the virus. He took over the operation of his brother's business until a fire destroyed the shop in September. Taking a few printing materials that had been salvaged from the shop (but no presses), he formed a partnership with his father. The father and son received the colony's contract to print the *Act of December 10, 1690*, that authorized the issuance of paper money, so it is reasonable to assume that they also had the contract to print the paper money mentioned in that act. Samuel Green was about 80 years old when Bartholomew joined him in Cambridge and was very likely too old to do the arduous work of printing several thousand notes. This work probably fell to his son, then 24 years old, and possibly an apprentice or two. Bartholomew went on to become the foremost printer in New England, acquiring the patronage of Harvard College and becoming the printer of the *Boston News-Letter*, the first American newspaper.

View of Harvard College at Cambridge, Massachusetts

One other possibility should be mentioned. Richard Pierce was printing in Boston as early as 1680. He probably came from the Pierce family of Essex County and served his apprenticeship under John Foster. After setting up his own shop, he became very successful, working primarily for the book trade and printing as many titles as did Samuel Green Jr. On September 25, 1690, Pierce printed for Benjamin Harris a publication called *Publick Occurencies, Both Foreign and Domestic*, which is regarded by some as the first newspaper in the British colonies, although only one edition was printed. Pierce was "well connected," having married Sarah Cotton, the granddaughter of the Reverend John Cotton of Boston, and was indirectly related to the influential Bradstreet, Dudley, and Winthrop families. These connections, as well as his business success and the fact that there were so few printers in Boston at the time, make it possible that he printed the first paper money. If so, it may have been his swan song, for he died in 1691.

Printing Technology

Although the concept of using paper bills of credit in the place of real money was new, the technology used to print the notes wasn't. Both the rolling press and engraved copper plates had been in common use for more than 100 years in most parts of Europe. Before the rolling press was invented, the common English platen press was the standard for the industry. Movable type was an alloy of lead, tin, and antimony, and the letters were usually cast in England or Holland. A printing block, or "form," of type was placed on the bed of the press and locked down by "furniture" and quoins. The type was inked with the use of leather-covered inking balls. A "puller" placed paper by hand on a wooden frame called a tympan and folded over it another frame called a frisket. These two frames were in turn folded down onto the bed of the press. The bed, with its tympan and frisket, was rolled into position directly beneath the platen. The platen was attached to a large metal screw, and when a worker turned the screw, the platen was moved downward, pressing the paper against the inked type. The chief disadvantage of this mechanism was that it could only print one sheet at a time.

A rolling press, also called a copper-plate press, was developed to print the more-complex images engraved on copper plates.

The rolling press was much simpler to operate than the platen press. A copper plate, suitably engraved, was inked in the normal way and then wiped by hand to remove the ink from the surface of the plate. Ink remained in the incised lines of the image. A dampened sheet of paper was placed over the plate, and protective felt blankets were placed on top of the paper. The plate was then run through the rollers by turning the spokes of the spider. Like the platen press, the rolling press could only print one sheet at a time, but the operation was much faster, and far less power was needed to turn the rollers.

A typical wooden-frame, copper-plate, hand-roller press of the 17th century. Notice the printer must use both hands and the pressure of his foot to turn the spider wheel.

Printing historians think the earliest roller presses were developed in the first quarter of the 16th century. When Versalius's famous work on anatomy (*De Humani Corporis Fabrica*) was printed in England in 1545, the illustrations were engraved on copper plates by Thomas Gennius and printed on a rolling press. Even the earliest patents granted in England for the printing industry mention rolling presses. Arnold Rotsipen's British Patent No. 71, issued in 1634, briefly describes his invention as a "printinge engine with wheeles & rolls," and George Tomlyn, a stationer of London, was granted a patent in 1660 and again in 1662 for printing text and flourishes on vellum and parchment by means of a "rolling printing presse and ingraven plates."[16] The fact that Tomlyn made no effort to describe the mechanism of his rolling press meant that such presses were already well known to the trade. When Captain John Blackwell reorganized the experimental banking house in Boston known as the Fund in 1686, he got permission from the General Court to purchase a rolling press to print a few "tryall notes" from engraved copper plates. Bartholomew Green and his father may have purchased the same rolling press used by Blackwell's group, moved it to Cambridge, and used it to print the notes issued in 1690. Paper money doesn't have to be printed from engraved plates, and indeed, many of the early issues were printed from typographic plates on a common press, but if you have engraved plates and want good impressions, it is essential that you use a rolling press.

We have no clear description of how the paper money was printed in 1690, but the work was probably very similar to any other type of printing except for the use of a roller press. The first concern of the printer and the committee appointed to oversee the work would have been the security of the engraved plates. They were probably kept in a locked strongbox and were only removed when the printer was ready. In 1690 there were no banks, so the plates for the bills of credit were the property of the General Court and were probably kept in the Townhouse. When needed, they would have been taken out of storage and hand-carried to the printer. Later,

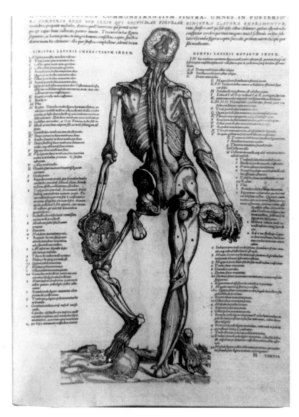

An anatomical view of a cadaver found in
De Humani Corporis Fabrica.

winter months it was sometimes necessary to heat the ink slightly so it could be worked until it had the right qualities. When all was ready, an "ink ball" or dauber was used to take up the ink and transfer it to the copper plate. By rubbing the ink ball back and forth on the copper plate, a thin film of ink was applied more or less evenly to the whole surface. And here again, heating the copper plate helped to spread the ink. Next, using a soft cotton rag, the apprentice wiped the surface of the plate until all the ink appeared to be removed except for that which remained within the incised lines of the engraving.

A sheet of paper was placed on top of the plate, and a "blanket" of felt was placed on top of the paper. These were then run under the roller under considerable pressure by turning a large wheel at one side of the press that was connected by gears to the rollers. The circular motion of the rollers caught the forward edge of the plate and carried it through the press. As the plate moved through the rollers, the pressure forced the paper into the incised line of the engraving, and the ink within those lines was absorbed onto the paper, printing exactly the same design or text engraved on the plate. These printed sheets were then hung on poles or over thin slats to dry. Finally, since several notes were usually printed on each sheet, someone had to cut apart the individual notes with scissors.

when banks began printing their own notes, the plates were typically held by the bank.

The printer previously selected the best paper to use from his available stock. This was paper that had been made in England or France from macerated linen and cotton stock and was usually coated with an animal size (an agent to stiffen the paper) to give it a hard surface so it would take ink from a quill easily. The printer may have cut large sheets of paper into the proper size he wanted to print and then dampened the paper with water to make them more pliable so they would print better. Meanwhile, an apprentice put a small amount of thick ink on a smooth flat stone and worked it back and forth with a hand roller called a "brayer" until it acquired the right consistency. Print shops were not heated overnight, so in the

Benjamin Franklin in the print shop as a "printer's devil."

Most of the work in a print shop was done by the apprentices and overseen by the printer. The apprentices were young boys, usually starting in their early teens, who contracted to work for several years without salary to learn the trade. The printer provided room and board for the apprentices, and saw to it that they went to church, kept themselves clean, and did not develop any bad habits. Isaiah Thomas was only six years old when he began his apprenticeship. Benjamin Franklin was closer to the norm when he became a "printer's devil" at age 12. The contract was called an "indenture," and it was often registered with local authorities. Working conditions were brutal. Most apprentices began work at 6:00 a.m. and worked until dark with only one hour off for breakfast and an hour for dinner. They swept floors, kept fires going, ran errands for the master and sometimes for his wife, carded wool for the stuffing of ink balls, washed type, dampened paper, composed type, delivered printing orders, and took their turn at the presses. The presses of that day, especially the platen presses, required lots of physical strength to get the work done. Usually two boys worked as a team, one inking the plates and one "pulling" the press. Pulling an impression was so hard that the "right shoulder and foot of men who constantly worked at press became enlarged, causing them to walk in a sidewise manner."[17] If the apprentice lasted the number of years required by his contract and then showed proficiency in all the skills taught him by the master printer, he became a journeyman and was free to leave and set up his own print shop. It was a common practice for master printers to give their journeymen a letter stating that they had fulfilled the obligations of their apprenticeships and had acquired the requisite skills of a printer. If a journeyman was active in his trade for a time and took in apprentices, he was entitled to call himself a master printer.

A number of printers have left diaries and letters describing the terrible working conditions of the early printing shops, and it seems that the foul odors of their work made the strongest impressions on their memories. Joseph Moxon, in his book *Mechanic Exercises*, written in 1683, describes how urine was routinely used in the making and maintenance of ink balls. These indispensable tools were leather balls that had been filled with wool or hair and attached to a wooden handle. The handles were turned on a lathe or carved in one piece, expanding at one end into a concave cup about seven inches or so in diameter that held the wool packing. The leather was usually cut from several pieces of sheepskin or dogskin. Whatever material was used had to have a fine grain and could not be porous. This leather was first soaked in a bucket of urine to make it supple and then wrung out and hung out to dry. The youngest apprentices usually got the job of preparing the leather, wringing out the urine by hand and hanging up the strips to dry. When the cup had been packed with the maximum amount of wool or hair that could be forced in by hand, the leather strips were pulled into place around the cup and nailed to it. If the leather had been properly treated, it would take up the right amount of ink and transfer it to the printing plate with great efficiency. If the inking ball became damp from excessive humidity, it would not pick up the ink very well. To get rid of the dampness, the balls were held over a flame. If they became too stiff from dried ink, the ink could be partially removed by urinating on the ball. If the balls became too greasy, one poured olive oil over them and then scraped it off when it dried. Depending on how much printing was being done, the leather strips usually wore down every couple of months and had to be replaced. In a large shop that had several ink balls, the apprentices were often making new leather and working in urine. If the printer made his own ink, he boiled linseed oil with pine resin to make the varnish and burned wood with pieces of old leather to make the black carbon soot that formed the pigment. All of this work was carried out in the back of the shop or in an adjacent room, and the aromas created were often quite offensive.

Printers at this time did not consider the engraving and printing of paper money to be a specialized branch of their trade. Except for the use of the roller press, of which there were very few in New England at the beginning of the 18th century, printing paper money was merely another job, much like any other. Since roller presses had been in use for more than 100 years, most printers understood their mechanism and could either build one or direct a skilled carpenter or mechanic to build one. When the government of the Massachusetts Bay Colony decided to issue new paper money in November 1702, it turned to John Allen for the printing, and he had John Brewer make a roller press. We don't know if Brewer worked from a mechanical drawing sent over from England, if he simply copied the parts of an existing press, or if he made the press by listening to a printer (perhaps John Allen) describe the mechanism. In fact, there were only two professional trades involved in the production of paper money in these early years—the silversmiths who engraved the printing plates and the printers who did all the rest. No one had yet built an ink mill or paper mill in the New World, so printers had to buy these supplies from the mills in England and Europe. But change was coming.

Lessons Learned

One of the lessons we can learn from this history is that the "invention" of paper money in December 1690 was not an invention at all but a pragmatic and urgent effort to avoid a riot from an unruly group of armed men. It followed a series of earlier experiments that had worked well in North America and in Europe. It would be nice if there had been a nobler idea behind the notes—something we could celebrate in poetry or in speeches given by men in white linen suits on each December the 10th—but the reality in Boston that year was far from noble. While a few learned men in the city may have known of the Chinese use of paper money or of one or two experiments in Europe, the idea that a piece of printed paper could replace a gold or silver coin must have been completely novel to the farmers and common workmen who had just returned from a brutal campaign. The same leaders who had "brilliantly" planned an attack on Quebec in the dead of winter were now offering pay in the form of paper notes.

The marvel is that these men accepted the notes at all, given that many of them came from rural backgrounds and had little or no experience in commercial transactions in coins and were completely new to the idea of paper money. These men understood that gold and silver coins had a permanent, intrinsic value, but paper had no value at all, and promises written on the paper were just that—promises, which could change at any moment and for any reason. Paper money was a daring experiment, but one that ultimately worked.

Chapter 2

Colonial Counterfeiting

Colonial Money

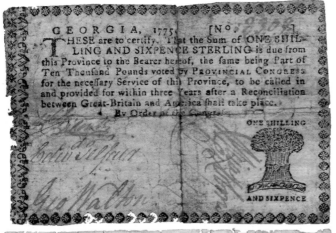

Colonial paper money from Georgia. The 1s-6d note of 1775 (top) bears the vignette of a sheaf of wheat. The "lighthouse" certificate of 1769 (bottom) bears early anti-counterfeiting codes around the border.

Although the Massachusetts Bay Colony paper money was a successful experiment in the last decade of the 17th century, it was not immediately adopted elsewhere in the colonies. South Carolina became the second colony to issue paper money but put it off until 1703, when it became necessary to support a military expedition. Connecticut, New Hampshire, New York, and New Jersey all printed money in 1709, again to fund military expeditions, and Rhode Island followed in 1710. North Carolina first issued notes in 1712, Pennsylvania in 1723, Maryland in 1733, Georgia in 1735, Virginia in 1755, and Vermont held out until 1781.[1] The Crown did not oppose the emission of paper money in the colonies and in fact often encouraged it so the colonies could pay for British military operations against their French, Indian, or Spanish enemies. To the British, it was far better to have the colonies pay for these operations out of their own pockets than to burden the Crown, and each emission of notes was eventually paid back to the colonial treasury—at least in theory—by higher taxes levied against the colonists.

There were many military conflicts in British America during the 18th century that required emergency funding or involved expenses beyond the capacity of a colony's treasury to pay. Consequently, the colonies issued a profusion of different notes to solve these and other problems. Once a colony began issuing paper money, it soon discovered other reasons to emit new issues. Many of these notes were traded or exchanged in other colonies where the ordinary citizens and merchants knew so little about them that they had trouble telling genuine notes from those that were counterfeits. On top of this, many of these notes had such simple designs and were so crudely printed that it was easy to copy them. When plates were occasionally engraved with more-elaborate designs to deter counterfeiting, would-be counterfeiters sent the real notes abroad to professional engravers, usually in England or Ireland, who then made high-quality counterfeit plates and sent them back to their American customers. Finding suitable paper was always a problem for legitimate printers until the first American paper mills were established around 1729, and even then, good-quality paper continued to be in scarce supply until long after

Independence. Printers often had to use whatever paper was available, resulting in notes having different shades of color and thicknesses that tore apart easily.

All of these problems created nearly perfect conditions for counterfeiting. A good number of men (and even a few women) took advantage of these problems with fervor and ingenuity. Although the punishments for counterfeiting in those times were usually quite harsh compared to our present laws, perhaps deterring some who were struggling with the idea, everyone knew that it would take more than just draconian laws to stop the rising tide of counterfeits. Nevertheless, the authorities continued to rely on punishment as a deterrent and offered no rewards to engravers or printers for better ideas.

Colonial paper money from Boston.

In 1691, less than a year after paper money made its debut, Robert Fenton and Benjamin Pierce were prosecuted at Cambridge, Massachusetts, for raising the denomination of at least 37 notes of the 2s and 2s-6d variety. Fenton was already notorious as a coiner, so he obviously hadn't wasted any time with the moral issues of his new venture. William Penn, the Governor of Pennsylvania, signed a warrant for Fenton's arrest in 1683 for counterfeiting "Spanish Bits and Boston Money." Since Fenton was a servant at that time and claimed that he had only followed his master's order to make a die for coins, he was given a very light punishment—one hour in the stocks. Now, eight years later and with the help of his friend Pierce, he decided he could make his fortune by simply altering the existing paper money. He and Pierce raised some notes to 10 shillings and others to 20 shillings, purchasing various goods from the wife of a Boston merchant named Nathaniel Jewell. Everyone agreed that raising the value of the notes was a criminal act since the notes were used fraudulently, and poor Jewell lost £22 of his merchandise. But since there was no specific law against raising the value of notes at this time—a fine point the freemen of the General Court had not yet considered in their rush to authorize the printing—Jewell had to prosecute Fenton and Pierce in the county courts at Cambridge and Charlestown. Fenton successfully appealed each guilty verdict, and Jewell finally had to petition the General Court on May 4, 1691. The decision of that body has not yet been found in official records.

Technically, neither Fenton nor Pierce were counterfeit engravers, just opportunists who rubbed out the denominations on bills of credit and wrote in higher denominations.

The Peregrine White Gang

The next group of counterfeiters was discovered in 1704, and they were a different breed altogether. That year, Judge Samuel Sewall wrote in his diary on July 21, "It begins to be known that the Bills of Credit are counterfeited, the Twenty-Shilling Bill."[2] Three days later, Governor Joseph Dudley issued a proclamation in the *Boston Weekly News-Letter* concerning this counterfeiting and made an unusual offer, saying:

And forasmuch as there must necessarily be a Combination of divers Persons in the said wicked

Design of Forgery and Deceit, whosoever therefore shall make discovery of them, the Person or Persons making such discovery, although themselves have been concerned therein, shall not only receive an indemnity from any punishment, but also a Reward of Fifty Pounds, to be ordered and paid them out of the Publick Treasury.[3]

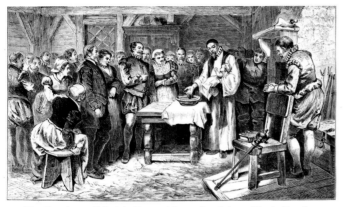

The Baptism of Virginia Dare of Roanoke Colony, North Carolina.

This gambit worked well, and within two weeks the authorities had arrested most of the counterfeiters and seized their press and counterfeit plate. One of the members of this gang was Peregrine White Jr., the son of Peregrine White, the "Mayflower Baby," so-called because he was thought to be the first child born of English parents in the New World; we now know that honor belongs to Virginia Dare of Roanoke Colony, North Carolina.[4] The elder Peregrine was 83 years old when he died at Marshfield on July 20, 1704, just a few days before his son and grandson were arrested and jailed as counterfeiters. The other members of this gang were Benoni White, the son of Peregrine White Jr., a carpenter named John Brewer (possibly the same John Brewer that made the new roller press used by John Allen to print the notes of 1702), a wine-cooper named Daniel Amos, and a "trader" named Thomas Moryan, who was then going by the name Thomas Odell. All were arrested and jailed except Odell, who fled the province.[5] Since Thomas Odell was the only one of these men who had any engraving experience and was almost certainly the engraver of these counterfeit notes, he earns the distinction of being the first true counterfeit

engraver in British America.[6] The men were tried in the Superior Court of Judicature held in Boston on November 7, 1704. Thanks to the research of Professor Kenneth Scott, the records of the trial have been retold in narrative form in his ground-breaking work, *Counterfeiting in Colonial America*.[7] Daniel Amos broke out of jail shortly after he was arrested, and no subsequent indictment against him has been found in the court records.

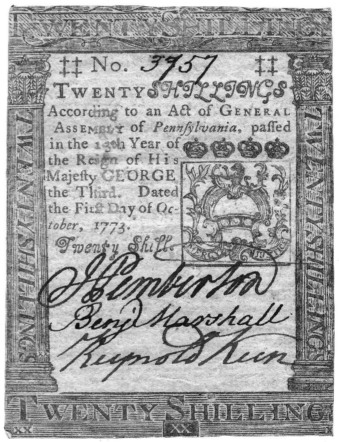

A 20-shilling note of Pennsylvania, 1773.

Thomas Odell proved to be as slippery as an eel. He was first apprehended in Stonington, Connecticut, shortly after Governor Dudley's proclamation. The Stonington jail proved to be no match for Odell's ingenuity, and he soon escaped. In May 1705 he was captured in Philadelphia, and the lieutenant governor ordered that he be extradited to Boston in irons on the sloop *Derick Adolph*. On the night of May 31, while the sloop was at anchor in Newport, Rhode Island,

Odell got out of his irons, swam ashore, and hid in a barn two miles out of town until June 6. He was recaptured and again placed in irons on the sloop and taken to Boston. He was tried there on November 6 and convicted of counterfeiting a 20-shilling note while he was in Exeter, New Hampshire. He was sentenced to be imprisoned for one year and to pay a fine of £300. By then, and perhaps long before, Odell was a career counterfeiter. He is reported in various newspapers to have escaped jail in Massachusetts in 1708 and again in 1714.[8] On both of those occasions he had been convicted of counterfeiting. Escaping from jail was not difficult in colonial times. Most jails were crudely built and were often not guarded at night because small towns could not afford to pay for overnight guards. Odell's many escapes do not signal any special Houdini-type talent for wiggling out of tight places. Curiously, he faded into oblivion about 1715, possibly in company with the Grim Reaper.

Benoni White, who was then only 18 years old, was charged with counterfeiting several 20-shilling bills during May, June, and July of 1704. He pleaded guilty and "prayed the mercy of the court," and the court swore him in to give "Queen's evidence" against the other members of the gang. There is no record that he was ever punished. John Brewer was found guilty from the testimony given by Benoni White and was sentenced to sit in the pillory for one hour on a lecture day, to have one ear cut off, to be confined in prison one year, and to pay the costs of prosecution. Governor Dudley, however, ordered that he be spared the loss of his ear. Peregrine White Jr. fared even better. He was charged with aiding and assisting in forgery and with issuing several 20-shilling bills of credit, as well as several counterfeit gold coins in Boston in July of that year. The jury found him not guilty of the forgery of paper money but guilty on the other charge. He was sentenced to pay a fine of £30, to suffer three months of imprisonment, and to pay the cost of prosecution, but it doesn't appear from newspaper accounts that any of those punishments were ever carried out. After the trial, Peregrine White Jr. claimed the £50 reward offered by Governor

Dudley in his proclamation. Since it was his testimony that led to the arrest of this gang, the court awarded him the £50 but then deducted the £30 fine.

Legal Consequences

The Peregrine White case was important because it set precedents used in many subsequent counterfeiting cases. This was the first time in New England that the court used the Crown's evidence given by two or more people to convict their associates. In cases where the evidence against the principal accused individuals was believed to be insufficient to prosecute, the Crown's attorneys could offer leniency to other (minor) defendants if they would give evidence leading to the conviction of the principal defendants. This case was also the first time the government had offered a reward for information in a criminal case and was willing to pay such money to a participant in the crime, provided his testimony led to a conviction of the others. And this case convinced the General Court that a law was clearly needed that would deter counterfeiting. Although the colony had gone 14 years without a specific law against counterfeiting, and less than £100 of bad money had been detected during that period, it was obvious that more counterfeiting would soon follow. The court immediately passed a law proclaiming:

> That whosoever shall forge, counterfeit or utter any bill in imitation of any of the bills of credit on this province, or assist in forging or counterfeiting, or engrave any plate, shall be punished in such manner as is by law provided against forgery, and be branded on the right cheek with a hot iron with the letter F [forger], and shall pay double damages to every person known to be cheated by said false bills...that whosoever shall make discovery and give information of making or putting off counterfeit bills so that the guilty person be convicted, such informer shall have as a reward £30...[9]

This law remained on the books unchanged until 1720, when the death penalty was added and it was also made illegal to counterfeit bills issued by the Province of New Hampshire and the colonies of Connecticut and Rhode Island and the Providence Plantations.

The death penalty appears on paper money to discourage counterfeiting.

Because the colonies had not yet broken away from English rule and were each given some degree of freedom to enact local laws to regulate their monetary affairs, each colony usually wrote laws that were limited to their borders. A person convicted of counterfeiting in one colony might easily escape to another colony or to another country and be safe from prosecution, free to start counterfeiting again. Ireland was a favorite refuge because it had no laws against counterfeiting English colonial money and would not extradite an alleged counterfeiter to colonial courts. The law of 1720 was therefore a daring and important step towards correcting this problem.

What? Women?

Mary Peck Butterworth was one of the first women to counterfeit paper money, making and selling more than £1,000 of notes during a seven year period before she was caught by the authorities and then released for lack of evidence. She was also one of the most resourceful and cleverest counterfeiters of the 18th century, and she was probably the most prolific single counterfeiter in New England for a long time.

We know that Mary was born in Rehoboth, Massachusetts, on July 27, 1686, the first child among the four daughters and five sons of Joseph and Elizabeth Peck. Little is known of her early life except that she was raised as a Puritan. She married John Butterworth Jr. on March 1, 1710–11 (*sic*).[10] John was a skilled carpenter when they were first married, and he later became the equivalent of a modern-day building contractor, or "housewright," and it appears that the family had a good income. They appeared to be simple, law-abiding people. But at age 30, while raising 7 children and keeping house in Rehoboth, Mary put some of her household skills to a test and found that she could make money the easy way. First she placed a piece of dampened muslin over a genuine note and applied heat by running a hot flatiron over it until the ink softened sufficiently and some of it stuck to the cloth. She then laid the cloth on a piece of blank paper and ironed it long enough to again soften the ink and transfer the design to the paper. She then burned the cloth in her fireplace to destroy the evidence of what she had done. With the crude outline of the genuine note now on paper, she sat down at her kitchen table and used a sharp quill pen to trace over the impression and fill in all the details. Looking at the true note, she was able to imitate almost exactly the thickness of various letters and design elements. We know her methods in such exacting detail because they were given by an accomplice, Nicholas Campe, at her trial in 1723.

Mary soon had three of her brothers and a sister-in-law working at this new endeavor, and then she recruited several of her husband's helpers. One of her brothers, Israel Peck, fashioned the quill pens from crow feathers and helped to fill in some of the details on the false notes. Her sister-in-law, Hannah Peck, became as good as Mary at "drawing in" the notes. Mary expanded her circle of helpers to include at least a dozen people. One of these was Daniel Smith, the town clerk of Bristol, Massachusetts, and a justice of the Bristol County Court of General Sessions. Most of the notes they copied were the Rhode Island bills of 10s, 20s, £3, and £5; the Massachusetts notes of 40s, £3, and £5; and the Connecticut bills of £5—8 different notes in all. The Rhode Island £5 notes, issued with the date July 5, 1715, were copied so accurately and so prolifically that the whole issue had to be recalled.

Eventually, one of Mary's helpers was caught passing some of the counterfeit bills at a tavern where he was entertaining three young ladies. When questioned in jail, he gave the name of an accomplice, one Nicholas Campe, who was also engaged in passing the bad notes—a "shover," as such people would later be called. Campe was arrested, and in August 1723 he confessed everything before Governor Samuel Cranston in Newport. Campe turned King's evidence and described Mary's little cottage industry in detail.[11] The Sheriff of Bristol was sent to search Mary's house, but since she had never used copper plates or a printing press, he found no material evidence of any value. And since Mr. Campe's accusations could not be proved, neither Mary nor any of her accomplices was convicted. As far as we know, Mary never returned to counterfeiting. Her only mistake was in trusting too many people with the knowledge that she played a role in these crimes. Had she been wise enough to isolate her family from any direct contact with the "passers," keeping her family's identity entirely secret, she might have become a very wealthy woman. After all, when she died of old age in Rehoboth on February 7, 1775, she was 89 years old.

The Lippincotts

Some counterfeit plates were engraved in foreign countries and then smuggled into the colonies. Probably the most notorious example of this was the case of Freelove Lippincott of Newport, Rhode Island. She is sometimes called the "first woman counterfeiter in New England." She was not a counterfeiter in the true sense of the word, for she never engraved or played any part in making counterfeit plates. Freelove was, however, the first woman ringleader of a counterfeiting gang. Her husband, Robert Lippincott, was a mariner teaching navigation in Newport in 1712, and he was probably the person who sailed to England with several genuine notes and paid an engraver to make counterfeit copper plates based on those notes.[12] The six plates brought back to Newport were used to print the £3 notes of Rhode Island, the 10s notes of Connecticut, and four notes of Massachusetts—the 3s bill, the 3s-6d bill, and the 20s and 50s bills. Apparently, Freelove and her associates printed notes from these plates using a small rolling press which was eventually thrown into the Lippincott's well to conceal the evidence. Most counterfeiting presses of this period were quite small and could be hidden in a well rather easily. This one may have been no more than a simple wooden frame to hold the copper plate. Once the plate was inked, a blank piece of paper could be placed on top of it and printed by running a heavy roller over the paper. A young man named Edward Greenman was Freelove's principal assistant. She also persuaded her brother, George Lawton, and one Henry Cooke to pass the counterfeit notes that she and Greenman were printing.

The Greenman Case

In 1713 some of Freelove's 3s-6d notes were detected as counterfeits, and the trail of inquiry lead back to her. The two Lippincotts and Edward Greenman were placed in the Newport jail to await trial. The Newport jail in those days was in very dilapidated condition, and since the prisoners had to spend several weeks there before the trial, the grand jury may have thought they had been punished enough, for the indictment was returned *ignoramus*, meaning there was no true bill and there would be no punishment. That should have ended the whole affair, but Her

Majesty's attorneys thought they had arrested the real counterfeiters, and with the consent of the general assembly, they bound the prisoners over to be tried again (double jeopardy?) at the next session of the court to be held in March 1714. Then, "The Court having Considered ye winter & ye Coldness of ye Gaol Doth Admit of Bayle . . . not less than one thousand pounds."[13] Greenman could not put up the bail, but he later escaped from jail and was fined 40 shillings *in absentia* when the court convened in March. The Lippincotts were not prosecuted in 1714, probably because Her Majesty's attorney realized the sentiments of the jury had not changed since the first hearing, and he figured he had a weak case.

The old gaol on Walnut Street, Philadelphia.
Such buildings were not very secure during this time.

While she was out on bail, Freelove printed some more notes and then either gave or sold her plates to Captain Edward Greenman of Kingston, who was an uncle of her helper, Edward. The good captain had been a member of the House of Deputies for several years and was Speaker of the House from May to October 1704. As soon as he got the counterfeit plates from Freelove, he set up a ring of operatives that included his brother, his son, Edward Greenman Jr., and another son, Silas Greenman. Silas was a man of some importance, having been a deputy

from Kingstown in 1716. He practiced forging the signatures on the various notes and became so good at it that he made it his specialty. But Silas must have been also a paragon of virtue, for when he was appointed Justice of the Peace in 1718, he decided it would be unethical to continue signing counterfeit notes.

Freelove stayed in touch with the Greenmans and eventually recruited one of her husband's students, a young man named Joseph Atwood and a nephew of Captain Greenman's, to assist them. Her health began to fail, and when her husband went to sea, she moved to Branford, Connecticut, to stay in the home of a tailor named Thomas Banks. She later got Mr. Banks to join with the Greenmans in their counterfeiting ring. At this point, the Greenmans were operating in three colonies and were the largest ring of counterfeiters in America. The notes the Greenmans were printing were eventually detected, and the evidence pointed to the captain's family.

The Greenman case became extremely important to the authorities because it involved people of such high standing, and the fear existed that if they were acquitted, it would give the appearance of a double standard of justice. Also it involved considerable damage to the currencies of three colonies —Rhode Island, Connecticut, and Massachusetts. To make certain a jury had enough credible evidence to convict, the three colonies combined their efforts and followed the same legal strategy that had been used in Massachusetts in 1704 to prosecute the Peregrine White gang. They paid rewards and granted immunity from prosecution to three members of the gang to testify against the Greenmans. Joseph Jones of Boston was paid £150. In his testimony, he revealed that he had acquired a plate from Captain Greenman in June or July 1717 and kept the plate in his house, printing notes from it for 16 or 17 months. Rhode Island paid £50 to Joseph Atwood of Newport for his testimony, in which he revealed that he had watched Captain Greenman and his two sons as they printed notes from Freelove's plates with a new roller made by the captain. Connecticut sent Thomas Banks to testify against the Greenmans, but no record has been found of the reward paid to him. The trial was held at Newport on November 26, 1718, and Captain Greenman was sentenced to have both ears cropped (cut off), to pay fines totaling £600, to give a bond of £700 to pay double damages to those who had had their bogus notes confiscated, and to stand in the pillory for one hour. Both his sons were also sentenced to stand in the pillory, lose their ears, pay fines of £300, and put up bonds of £400 for double-damage awards.[14]

The pillory was a punishment by means of locking the head and hands (and sometimes the feet) into wooden boards for a predetermined period of time.

Foreign Counterfeits

The case of Peter Woodin, a common sailor who was arrested for passing counterfeit money in Boston in January 1715, gives a more-detailed picture of the practice of having counterfeit plates engraved abroad. The *Boston News-Letter* relates the following story:

> Boston, On the 13th of January past one Peter Woodin a Sailor was Brought (before the Honorable John Clark and Samuel Checkly, Esqrs., Justices of the Peace) for putting off Counterfeit Twenty Shilling Bills of the latest impression, signed by Four Hands, who upon examination owned that whilst he was in London, (from whence he lately arrived in the Ship *Providence*) he met one Briant in George yard on Tower Hill an Engraver by Trade, who told him if he was a New-England Man, he [Briant] had a Commodity that would suit him well, shewing him a Twenty Shilling Massachusetts Bill of Credit, and [Woodin] bought of him a bundle above a Hundred for a Guiney, he also bought the Copper Plate and the Roll for a Guiney and a half, for which he was to have a Thousand Bills, Briant saying when he returned he expected a further gratification, which Woodin promised, he also owned that carried with him to London a Twenty Shilling and two Five Shilling Bills, which he sold to Captain Clark for half a Guiney, and says he saw Briant work them off but did not tell who signed them. Woodin put off about a Dozen of the said Bills, which he owned, 58 was taken with him when apprehended, and 904 taken on board the Ship with the Plate and Roll, and he lies now in Gaol to be tried. In about a Fortnights time after the Ships arrival at Cape Cod this grand Chest was Discovered as a favorable smile of Providence to this Province.[15]

None of the colonies could take any legal action against the engravers in England, Ireland, or on the Continent for making counterfeit plates or printing the paper money of New England. There were no laws in those countries against the counterfeiting of foreign bills, and indeed, there is no record of anyone in those countries having been prosecuted for such work. There were, to be sure, very harsh penalties on the books for anyone in England that counterfeited English money, and the same was true for Ireland and on the Continent. Engravers knew what was legal and what wasn't, and they often took advantage of the law whenever an opportunity permitted. Foreign counterfeiting often produced better plates and paper money because the more highly skilled engravers were still in the Old World. They could make use of better equipment, such as large printing presses, and had access to a much larger variety of inks and papers than their counterparts in New England. It is no surprise that such foreign counterfeiting plagued New England for the rest of the century. An example is this report from 1742:

> Last week Robert Neal A Mariner, belonging to Salem, who lately came hither from London in *Capt. Jones*, was apprehended and examined before two of his Majesty's Justices of the Peace for uttering false Bills of the Colony of Rhode Island in imitation of those emitted in the Year 1740, five of which Bills, were found about him *viz.* four Ten Shilling, and one of Five Shilling.
>
> Upon some further Examination he acknowledged that the said Bills were made and signed in London, and that he had brought over a Number with him, which were in a Box hid in a rocky Place at Salem, accordingly the Officers taking him along with them went to the Place he told them of, and after considerable Pains in turning over a great many large Stones, they at last found the said Box hid underneath one of them, and came to Town with it last Saturday Evening. Upon opening the Box there was found in it, four Plates engraven, one Plate containing 2 bills in imitation of the above mentioned 10/ [shilling] and 5/ [shilling] of the Colony of Rhode Island, with a Plate for the Backside of the said Bills, on another Plate, was two in imitation of the 7/ and 12/ of the Colony of Connecticut, the last Emission, and also a Plate for the Back side of the said Bills in imitation of printing Letters. In the said Box there were likewise 800 Sheets, which were struck off the Plates upon extraordinary good Paper, but none signed, *viz.* 357 Sheets of Rhode-Island at £3 and 107 £1 Old Tenor, and 440 Sheets of the Connecticut, at £1,492, 18/, Od, amounting in the whole to £2,563 18/, Old Tenor. This was a most seasonable Discovery, for the Engraving so near resembles the Original (except the Backside of the Connecticut Plate) that if he could but have obtained an accurate Signer, they might have been soon spread all over the Country to the great Damage of the Publick, which is now prevented, not one of them being out.[16]

Counterfeiting Gangs

Another trend in American counterfeiting developed early in the 18th century and continued into modern times. This was the formation of large gangs that passed paper money printed usually by a single skilled craftsman. In the early part of the century, counterfeiting was usually confined to a single family and maybe one or two close relatives or friends who passed relatively few notes in a small geographic area. The Peregrine White case in 1704 involved only five people. Freelove Lippincott and her associates also numbered only five people when they were arrested in 1713. The three Greenmans had at least five associates when they were brought before the bar. Eight people assisted Mary Butterworth in her counterfeiting, but six were relatives. In contrast, when John Potter was indicted in Rhode Island for counterfeiting in 1742, he had the company of 14 associates, and others were suspected but not formally charged. Another large gang operated in an area of Dutchess County, New York, known as the "oblong" or sometimes as the "Equivalent Tract." The Oblong gang sent their minions into the surrounding towns to purchase livestock and merchandise with counterfeit notes made at a secret location within a swamp. When the gang was finally broken up in 1745, one of the leaders made a confession in which he implicated 22 others, most of whom were never prosecuted for lack of evidence.

Owen Sullivan, a Boston goldsmith who found it was more profitable to engrave copper plates for counterfeiting than to make tankards and spoons, traveled extensively in New England and induced a large number of people to assist him. He founded the "Dover Money Club" in Dutchess County, New York, and operated there in a secret camp where he and a gang of confederates made and distributed large quantities of bogus bills. His agents passed these in Connecticut, Rhode Island, and New York. When Sullivan was finally sent to the gallows in 1756, at least 29 of his gang were known to the authorities.[17] Herman Rosencrantz was technically not a counterfeiter but was arrested in Philadelphia in 1770 for passing bogus bills. In his confession, written in jail just before he was executed, he named 17 of his confederates.[18]

Samuel Ford

Samuel Ford is yet another example of a seemingly respectable and prosperous man who let his greed get the better of his morals. Although his ancestry is difficult to reconstruct, there being so many Fords that lived in central New Jersey at the time, Samuel seems to be the son of John Ford, who was the builder of an iron forge on the Whippany River around 1710. Samuel was born in 1735, and around 1763 he built the Hibernia Iron Works, also on the Whippany River, "about four miles north of Rockaway," in the hills of northern Morris County, New Jersey. The mines and forge lay atop a rich iron-ore deposit that had become the principal iron-smelting center in America. During the Revolutionary War, it supplied cannon and shot for the Continental Army. Samuel was apparently the nephew of Colonel Jacob Ford Jr., whose Morristown mansion was used as General George Washington's headquarters during the winter of 1779 and 1780. The operation of the mine was only marginally profitable, and Ford soon decided to sell a third of the land to William Alexander, known then as Lord Sterling, and two other investors for a mere £530. Ford would later say that the financial problems with the mine had caused him to turn to counterfeiting to make up losses. His counterfeiting, however, was not very good, and he decided that a trip to Ireland to study with expert engravers there would be worth his while. He used the money from the Hibernia Iron Works sale to finance the trip. Ireland at that time was reputed to have the best counterfeiters in the world, and judging from the notes he made later, Samuel must have been a diligent student. He returned to America in June 1766 and probably brought with

him a large sum of counterfeit New Jersey notes that he and his instructor had printed. He also brought along a new bride, although he was already married.[19] When his new wife discovered his polygamy, she promptly left him. Within a month of his arrival, the Governor of New Jersey had the treasury send out public notices that large sums of bogus bills had arrived on a ship from England. England may have been the country from which the ship had originally sailed, but it was common practice in those days to stop over in Ireland at the beginning of the three-week voyage. A year later (1767), Ford was arrested in New York on a charge of passing counterfeit New Jersey bills, but no record has been found that he was brought to trial. Likely as not, he posted bail and then skipped out.

An iron forge.

Ford soon moved to Hanover (in Morris County), New Jersey, and bought land of about 130 acres in a swampy area called "the Hammock," which during much of the year was covered by water. His farmhouse was built on a drained rise surrounded by wetlands. "Ford's Hammock," as it was called, had two-feet-thick stone walls, hand-hewn beams, and a gambrel roof. Additions were made to the house in 1885 and 1937. Eventually, it was placed on the National Register of Historic Landmarks, but when taxes on the property became too much, the owner sold the land, disassembled the 280-year-old house board-by-board, and moved it to North Webster, Indiana, in 2000.[20] The inhospitable location of the original house prevented visitors from coming by and gave Ford the opportunity to set up a shop hidden in a thicket of brush where he could counterfeit notes without fear of detection. He recruited a number of people to help him pass counterfeit notes, and this group became known as the "Morristown gang."

Almost all counterfeiters make a mistake of some kind that gives them away, and Ford stupidly kept up the appearance of prosperity while living on a farm that was totally unsuitable for making an honest living. His neighbors thought something was wrong and brought the matter to the attention of the authorities. Ford was arrested at his home and taken to jail in Morristown in July 1773. He escaped jail the next day with help from Thomas Kinney, the High Sheriff, and was never found. It is now known that he went to Green Briar County, West Virginia, where he assumed his mother's maiden name (Baldwin),

became a silversmith, married, and had children. There is no evidence that he ever returned to counterfeiting.

Ford had been an accomplished counterfeiter, engraving his own plates and printing the notes himself. When he was arrested in 1773, he was probably passing counterfeits of the notes issued by New Jersey under an Act of 1764. The notes of 1764 were like those of the year before, and Eric P. Newman's book on colonial currency, *The Early Paper Money of America*, shows that the higher denominations were counterfeited. Those notes had the colonial seal on the front, but the rest of the design was scroll work, a printed text, and elaborate signatures. The back design was primarily a leaf within a frame and printed text. All of these devices could have been easily cut by a good engraver, especially one who had been trained like Ford. It would be another 70 or 80

New Jersey notes of the 1764 series—£6 (with back showing the leaf and text), £3, 30s, 15s, and 12s.

years before elaborate landscape or scenic engravings of high-artistic merit would be used to protect notes against counterfeiting. An anonymous letter published in Rivington's *New York Gazetteer* states that "his bills had stood the test of several treasurers' examination and had their sanction, which he ever made an invariable rule to secure before he passed any of his new emissions." Searches of the Ford property found his printing press, engraving tools, and counterfeit plates. Isaac Collins, the official printer for the colony, examined the press and thought that only one bill at a time could be printed on it.

Four members of the "Morristown gang" were tried and sentenced to death. They were middle-aged married men with children, and all had parents still living. All were said to be remarkably handsome, and three of them were descended from prominent families. Benjamin Cooper was one of that gang, and his father was one of the judges who heard the evidence. He ruled that his son should be hanged. A scaffold was erected on the Green in Morristown, in front of the courthouse, with the executions set for September 17, 1773. On the morning of the 17th, however, an order arrived from Governor William Franklin (Benjamin Franklin's son) to remand three of the prisoners to jail. Before a crowd estimated at 15,000, the fourth prisoner—David Reynolds—was hanged. It was said that he was the least guilty of the four, but the only one "with no friends at court."

James Smither

James Smither forms an interesting note to this survey and brings into question one of the most revered (pardon the pun) stories of American bank-note lore—that Paul Revere engraved and printed the two emissions of notes issued by the Continental Congress in 1775 and thereby became the first American engraver to make bank notes for our new country. Clarence Brigham and others have done much to establish the true facts. According to Brigham, the myth began when Benson J. Lossing published a book in 1851 entitled *Pictorial Field Book of the Revolution*, in which he gave credit for this honor to Paul Revere. Lossing changed his mind and wrote an article entitled "Continental Money" for *Harper's Monthly Magazine* that appeared in its March 1863 issue. There, he states that the colonies "employed Smithers," a gun engraver, to prepare the first plates used for printing American paper money. James Smither had come to Philadelphia from England only a few years before the Revolution and was a well-known engraver by 1775, having engraved some border cuts on notes issued by Pennsylvania dated April 3, 1772, and possibly on later notes. Thomas Paine, in a letter to the President of the Continental Congress dated April 11, 1778, said that Smither had counterfeited Continental currency for the British, and indeed, Smither seems to have show his true colors when the British left Philadelphia and he went with them to New York. On June 15, 1779, the Supreme Executive Council of Pennsylvania issued a proclamation ordering Smither to answer a charge of treason.[21]

Paul Revere.

It would be a little embarrassing if Smither is given credit for being the first engraver of notes for an independent America when he was also a counterfeiter. It comes down to the fact that Revere engraved notes for the Massachusetts Provincial Congress and not for the Continental Congress. Revere did not sign any of the notes he engraved, and he did not enter any charges for engraving notes in his Day Book, so the only evidence of his work is to be found in the journals of the Massachusetts Provincial Congress and the records of the General Court of Massachusetts. From those records and from the actual copper plates, now in the *Massachusetts Archives*, we know which notes Revere printed and when he printed them. None of that data is in question. The real question has to do with the Continental Congress sitting in Philadelphia. That body authorized the first federally issued paper money, and it appears that—Oops!—James Smither was the engraver.

The records in the *Journals of Congress* which authorized the printing of notes dated May 10

and November 29, 1775, make no mention of the engraver of the bills. Several other entries in the *Journals* make reference to the plans to print money, but they too make no mention of the engraver. Brigham and others have made an exhaustive search of the federal archives, both in the Library of Congress and at the National Archives, and in other record offices, but have found no documentary evidence of the engraver's name. But the *Journals* do tell us that a committee of five men was appointed "to get proper plates engraved, to provide paper, and to agree with printers to print the above bills." The committee, including John Adams and Benjamin Franklin, could not travel about the country to do their assigned work, so they naturally found everything within or near Philadelphia. We know, after the fact, that they got Hall and Sellers to print the notes and that the paper came

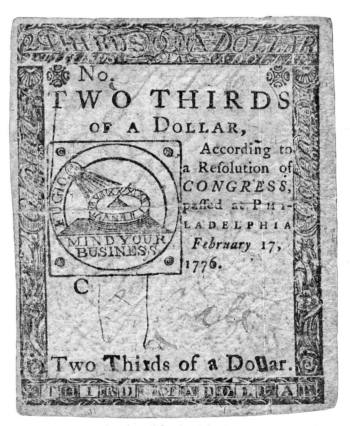

A variety of Continental notes.

from Ivy Mills, not far away—but we know nothing about the engraver.

In the article he wrote for *Harper's* in 1863, Lossing says the plates made for the first Continental notes "were rude specimens of art. The ornamental portions were engraved on type-metal, in the style of wood engraving introduced into this country by Doctor Anderson twenty years afterward; while the body of the lettering was in common movable type."

But Brigham points out that no one was paying much attention to the one man who knew personally most of the first-rate artists and engravers of the time and had unparalleled opportunity to get the facts. That was William Dunlap, born in 1766, who later put together his *History of the Arts of Design*, published in 1834, which presented for the first time the biographies of many American craftsmen. Dunlap was a careful writer who verified and corroborated his facts, so his word counts for much, and in his *History* he states flat out that "Smithers engraved the blocks for the continental money."[22]

It makes sense that Revere could not have been chosen to engrave the Continental notes because he was hunkered down in Watertown, busy engraving and printing other money. Of course, one can still argue that it doesn't matter if Revere was working for a Provincial Congress, he was still working for independence. The American Bank Note Company long touted Revere as the "father of the [bank-note] industry in the United States," so it may be difficult for their public relations department to concede that the title belongs instead to a counterfeiter and possible traitor.

Why Counterfeiting Was Easy

The preceding cases illustrate several of the reasons why it was so easy to counterfeit paper money during this period, and why it was so difficult to get convictions in court. First, the bills were so poorly designed and printed that anyone with a little artistic talent—very little in some cases—could be tempted to try their hand at imitating the notes. When Rhode Island's first paper

money was issued in 1710, for example, the notes were printed in black ink on common ledger paper from crudely engraved copper plates. The engraved designs and lettering could be easily transferred to a new copper plate by simply laying a real note on top of the plate, gluing it or tacking it in place so it would not move around, and then using a sharp needle to poke numerous small holes through the inked designs and onto the plate below to form the outline of the lettering, the scroll work, or even the provincial seal. This stage of counterfeiting requires good eyesight and some patience but hardly any other skills. When the paper is removed, the small dots left on the plate must be connected by the engraver in a continuous line of approximately the right depth and width, but this is easily accomplished after some practice.

New issues of paper money were coming out all the time to finance military operations or other emergencies, and this confused the public who had little knowledge of which notes were legal and which were worthless, especially since each colony was issuing its own set of notes in a bewildering variety of denominations. These conditions were ideal for the counterfeiter since he could take advantage of the general confusion about paper money and print rather poor-quality notes and see them passed easily in great numbers.

Most "counterfeiters" during the colonial period were not engravers but merely "passers," the people who intentionally bought counterfeit notes at a discount and then passed them to merchants or strangers at their nominal value and made a profit. Some of the passers became so proficient at this work that they made an exceptionally good living and acquired considerable property. If a person discovered that he had a counterfeit bill, he was naturally motivated to pass it to another person before it was identified as worthless and confiscated. It became such a common experience for someone to be arrested for merely possessing or passing a counterfeit bill that juries were often reluctant to bring indictments against the accused or refused to convict them unless there was other evidence that supported the accusations. Given the nature of the counterfeiter's business, there usually wasn't any other evidence. The people who worked for counterfeiters and passed false money seldom carried large amounts on their person for fear that a jury might convict them on the assumption that a large amount of bad money was evidence of a criminal connection.

Counterfeiting, of course, was not unique to any one class of people, nor to any specific time. Coins had been counterfeited for more than 1,000 years and in every corner of the world. It was certainly no surprise to anyone that paper money would follow the same course. The legal records of the colonies, and the newspapers as well, show thousands of people were either suspected or caught and prosecuted for these crimes. Many of the techniques and practices of modern counterfeiters were developed in the colonial period, with the technology of security printing being slow to respond and the legal profession doing little better.

Most counterfeiters hid their plates and small printing presses in a safe place so no physical evidence could be found and used against them in court. By 1720 it was becoming difficult for the Crown's prosecutors to win cases in all but the most flagrant violations. This situation was made even worse by the almost universal depreciation of paper money. Both colonial governments and local merchants were forced to discount its value. Bowen gives a good example of this by showing that 1 ounce of silver in Rhode Island equaled 8 shillings in paper money in 1715, then 16 shillings in 1721, 22 shillings in 1731, and 27 shillings in 1738.[23] Notes depreciated at different rates in different colonies, but the problem was very widespread, especially after 1712. Over time, the depreciation of paper money defrauds the public, for any notes they save will be worth less than when they were first acquired. This fact was a constant irritant and further eroded the public's confidence in paper money, giving them another reason to sympathize with those who were charged with possession or passing bad money.

Punishing the Counterfeiters

Compared to England, America has always been lenient towards counterfeiters. The severity of punishments varied from one judge to another, but generally, we did not hang people for financial crimes. Crowds liked to see people standing in the pillory and having their ears cut off. Thanks to the diligent research of Kenneth Scott, we know of many examples of how colonial courts punished people convicted of counterfeiting. Ann Tew, of Lancaster, Pennsylvania, was found guilty in 1765 of raising a 2-shilling Pennsylvania note to 10 shillings. She had to stand for an hour in the pillory and had both ears cut off and nailed up for the public's edification. In the Greenman case, ears flew right and left. Captain Greenman lost both ears as did his two sons, Silas and Edward Jr. Public floggings were also popular. Catherine Johnson was given 21 lashes on her bare back for passing counterfeit money in New York. She did not learn her lesson and was convicted of stealing in 1766, for which she was burned in her left thumb in the presence of the court. Branding with a hot iron on the cheek or forehead was also common. Usually a convicted person got an "F" branded on one cheek (standing for forgery) or a "C" on the forehead (standing for counterfeiter). In the most serious cases of counterfeiting, a long prison sentence and heavy fines were imposed, and on a few occasions the prisoners were hanged. The hanging of David Reynolds and Herman Rosencrantz has been mentioned. Others hanged were Sigismond Hainly Sr. in 1751 and Owen Sullivan in 1756. Joseph Bill Parker, John Wall Lovely, and Gilbert Belcher were all hanged on the same day in 1773; Bernard Repton was hanged in 1774; and David Gamble was hanged in 1780.

There were about 7-1/2 million people in England in the middle of the 18th century, but probably 7 million had never seen a Bank of England note. At the same time, 12 of our 13 colonies had issued paper money, and its use had become part of our everyday life. And yet England executed far more people for counterfeiting in the 18th century than did America. The English experiments with harsh punishments proved that under certain conditions—such as widespread poverty and/or the issuance of easily counterfeited notes—draconian legal measures do not effectively deter counterfeiting. It took the English some time to realize that a technological answer, one that made counterfeiting extremely difficult, might be the solution. Americans, on the other hand, were far more willing to try experimental methods of printing to foil the counterfeiter.

Nature Printing as a Security Device

Nature printing by I. Collins and Hall & Sellers.

Benjamin Franklin, inspired by an engraver named Joseph Breinthall, came up with a scheme to do just that—foil the counterfeiter. In 1738 he printed a 20-shilling note for Pennsylvania using a technique he called "nature printing."[24] The note made use of realistic images of three blackberry leaves and a willow leaf. Franklin noted that the "leaves not only had exceedingly complex detail, but also that their internal lines were graduated in thickness. This would make virtually impossible a fine reproduction by engraving." The technique involved the impressing of leaves or ferns on soft lead plates and then inking the plates and running them through ordinary copper plate presses to produce paper bills that reproduced the exact size, shapes, and surface textures of the original object. Franklin thought that as long as the technique was kept secret, notes made this way would be too difficult to counterfeit.[25] This technique had limited success and appeared on the colonial notes issued by Delaware, Maryland, New Jersey, Pennsylvania, and the Continental Congress. Franklin had a long experience printing notes and thinking about ways to protect notes from counterfeiting. This extended from 1731 to 1764 and included 15 issues for Pennsylvania, 1 issue for Delaware, and 3 issues for New Jersey, totaling 2,450,000 notes according to his records, which were worth £903,410. Nature printing as a security device was also used years later in the 1850s by Henry Bradbury, who used an electroplating technique that he had probably learned from Alois Auer at the Imperial Printing Office in Vienna. Both Franklin and Bradbury were correct in believing that no engraver could accurately duplicate the complexity and fine gradations of a nature print, but that same attribute also defeated the security of the technique. Once a person learned how to make a nature print, they could use any leaf of similar size and appearance to make a counterfeit nature print and no one would be the wiser. Ordinary businessmen do not examine bills under a magnifying glass and count the veins of a leaf and note their directions and bifurcations. One leaf looks like another, so the image was both too common and too complex to serve its purpose.

Continental Currency

Wars require money, and when our Revolutionary War began in 1775, we did not have enough money to do much. This problem was addressed by the Second Continental Congress, which met in secret in Philadelphia on May 10, 1775. They resolved that Congress should emit a sum of 2 million Spanish dollars for defense, and that each of the 12 confederate colonies (Georgia was not represented) would repay this money in 4 scheduled payments. The plates for this emission were engraved by Paul Revere of Boston. Originally, 403,800 notes were authorized in 9 different denominations from $1 to $20, and these notes were all issued within 3 months. Realizing that much more money was needed, Congress authorized further printings. The total had reached $6 million by the end of 1775. The cycle continued with several additional emissions until the end of 1779, when the total amount issued had reached $242 million. The currency depreciated rapidly, and by 1781 $100 in specie would buy $16,800 in paper.

$1 was a lot of money in that period, and since people were hoarding coins, it became necessary to print fractional currency. A resolution of the Continental Congress set aside $1 million on February 10, 1776, for the printing of our first fractional notes. Eric P. Newman discovered that Benjamin Franklin created the "Fugio" (I fly) legend as well as the sundial vignette seen on some notes and the "Mind your Business" legend used on others. Newman also discovered that dots in the corners of the front design reflected the denomination, with 1 dot designating 1/6 of a dollar, 2 dots for 1/3 of a dollar, 3 dots for 1/2 of a dollar, and 4 dots for 2/3 of a dollar. Newman also discovered that the devices and border designs for the fractional notes were engraved by Elisha Gallaudet. The paper for these notes was made at Ivy Mills in Chester County, Pennsylvania, by the Wilcox family.

A National Currency?

If the 13 colonies made counterfeiting easy by issuing too many notes of different designs, printing on papers of different qualities and with common black ink, and rarely using an engraved device that would be difficult to imitate, why didn't we remedy most of these problems with a single national currency once we became one nation? Like most simple questions, it has a lot of

The "Fugio" vignette on a 1787 copper and a Continental currency note.

answers. For one thing, the political mindset of the colonists did not change much when colonies became states. For a period of several years, our government operated under the Articles of Confederation (1777–1788), which were very weak and gave the federal government very little, if any, authority to overrule individual states on matters such as fiscal policy. Article IX of that document gave the federal government "the sole and exclusive right and power of regulating the alloy and value of coins struck by their own authority, or by that of the representative States." It said nothing about paper money, so politicians in the various states believed they retained the authority to issue their own (state) notes or to authorize banks within their borders to issue their own bank notes. It was a matter of "States Rights." Had the framers of the Constitution specifically made provision for the federal government to issue a national paper currency, we could have avoided some of the problems caused by the profusion of state- and local-bank notes that persisted right up to the Civil War. One can also argue that it would have pushed engravers to experiment with vignette engraving and other counterfeit deterrents much sooner. It would also have made counterfeiting a violation of federal law rather than state laws. Perhaps, though, that is too much to expect of a new nation. Perhaps it takes a kind of social Darwinism working for 50 or 60 years to select the better ideas in capitalism. Perhaps it even takes a Civil War.

Chapter 3

Philadelphia's New Inventions

1792–1820:
The Harrison Dynasty

It was not until the last decade of the 18th century that a few engravers began to specialize in bank-note work. One of the first was a transplanted Englishman named William Harrison Sr. Although he lived in America for only a few years and did nothing to advance the technical side of bank-note engraving, nor did he make any real changes in the simple, open design of our notes, he did bring over a large family and taught at least four of his sons the art of copper-plate engraving and got them started in bank-note work. The Harrisons became the first family in America to specialize in bank-note engraving and printing, and for at least three generations, these skills were passed down from father to son.[1]

An engraved view of New York.
Many bank-note engravers also did book or map engraving to start.

The senior Harrison was born in England about 1750 and is believed to have been the great-grandson of John "Longitude" Harrison, the inventor of the marine chronometer. In London he was employed for a time as a script engraver by the Bank of England, but like most others in his craft, he wasn't limited to one type of work and was often engaged to engrave maps, certificates, business cards, etc. From 1780 to about 1790, he worked as a map engraver for the British East India Company and engraved many of the Alexander Dalrymple navigation charts. In 1792 he traveled to Philadelphia to engrave bank-note plates for the newly formed Bank of the United States and the somewhat older Bank of North America.[2,3] Normally, these banks would have searched for local talent to engrave the notes and

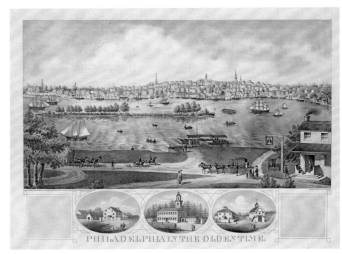

Philadelphia "In The Olden Time."

other documents they needed, and certainly there were several engravers in Philadelphia that could have done acceptable work, but the senior Harrison was chosen, probably because he had the prestige of being an English engraver and had worked at the Bank of England. While in Philadelphia, he may have heard about the rapid growth of the banking industry in America and decided to make his work for the Bank of England known to the managers of those banks, as well as his considerable engraving talents. After returning to England, he got word that he had been commissioned for the work. He left his family in London and sailed to Philadelphia, where he spent six months finishing the plates for the two banks. Apparently, he liked what he saw in this busy metropolis of some 30,000 people, and he was probably excited by the news that several more banks were planning to open their offices.

He returned to London only briefly and then packed up and returned in 1794, this time with his family. He started a successful engraving business. In the two years he was gone from Philadelphia, 11 more banks had opened their doors in North America.

Yellow fever was a deadly force in the early 19th century. This cartoon, "Yellow Jack monster," by Matthew Somerville Morgan, shows two allegorical women being attacked by the "monster" of yellow fever.

The elder Harrison brought with him a son, William Jr., who was then about 14 or 15 years old and had already worked with his father engraving maps. Another son, Charles Peter Harrison, 11 years old, had also started to engrave but was not yet ready for commercial work. The two youngest sons were Samuel, about five years old, and Richard Granville Harrison, only one year old. For the next nine years, the senior Harrison built up an engraving and plate-printing business that took on many different types of work but succeeded chiefly from the engraving of bank-note plates. One record of his success is a receipt he wrote for the Bank of the United States, dated December 15, 1798, in which he charged the bank a total of $110 for providing the copper plate and engraving a $50 post note.[4] He had obviously arrived in Philadelphia at just the right time, getting the engraving business of the two largest banks and then building on those connections to win further work. In 1803, while Harrison was at the height of his career and also a boom year for banking during which 15 new banks were established in the United States, yellow fever broke out in Philadelphia, and the old man caught the fever and died on October 18, leaving behind a secure reputation and four young sons who had all learned to use a burin.[5]

William Harrison Jr. was born in London about 1780, and by the time he was 10 years old, an obviously proud father was placing his son's name alongside his own on maps they had engraved together. His father put him to work as soon as they arrived in Philadelphia, and he engraved a map of the state of New York which was published in Mathew Carey's *American Atlas* (1795), signed *Harrison Junior sc.*[6] He probably didn't engrave any bank notes until the Bank of Trenton engaged him in that work in 1805. He started engraving for Murray, Draper, Fairman, Brewster & Company between the summer of 1810, when the company was formed, and December 1811, when Abel Brewster was bought out by his partners and his name removed from most of the plates. An example of this association is seen in a $20 Proof note that Harrison engraved for the Bank of the Potomac, which dates from 1811, when the bank was chartered and Brewster's name was still on the plate. After Brewster left the company, William Harrison (by now he had dropped the "junior" after his name) continued to engrave for Murray, Draper & Fairman for several years before moving to Georgetown, D.C., in September 1819. One reason for that move may have been the outbreak of yellow fever in Philadelphia that year, the same plague that had killed his father. In Georgetown he engraved maps for the Engineering Corps of the U.S. Army while continuing with his bank-note work.[7] It was probably while he was in Georgetown that he began to teach his son to engrave, as some of the maps are signed *Wm Harrison and David R. Harrison.* William died sometime around 1845.

Boats and ships vie for docking along the waterfront at Philadelphia.

Charles Peter Harrison, born in London in 1783, was much more a plate printer than an engraver, although he is listed as both in the Philadelphia city directories of 1820 and 1822. His father had believed that plate printing was a necessary and vital part of the business and taught his sons how to do that work. Charles was said to be the best printer in the family. David McNeely Stauffer, in his *American Engravers Upon Copper and Steel*, thought he was also a good line engraver, though not much work is attributed to him. Charles apparently formed a partnership with his brother, Richard, as their names appear together on a number of bank notes dated between 1815 and 1820. Richard probably engraved most, if not all, of these notes, and Charles did the printing. The notes are mostly from western Pennsylvania and eastern Ohio and often bear the inscription "Pitsn," indicating that the brothers had their office in Pittsburgh and probably traveled throughout the area on horseback to solicit business from the frontier banks.[8] Later, many of the notes engraved by Charles's older brother, William Jr., are also inscribed "Printed by C.P. Harrison." Charles moved to New York City with his family in 1824 and did considerable work for the banks there. The correspondence files of the Willcox paper mill contain at least three letters from C.P.

Harrison requesting bank-note paper for jobs he was then working on for the Bank of Cape Fear, North Carolina, and the Mechanics Bank. One of the letters, dated December 9, 1836, gives his address as 3 Reed Street (New York). He died in New York City in 1854 and was buried in Brooklyn's Greenwood Cemetery.

The inscription of C.P. Harrison.

Philadelphia's Dominance

Given its location, natural resources, and unique political history, Philadelphia quickly became the center of bank-note engraving in America. The town bordered the Delaware and Schuykill rivers and was also within reach of the Susquehanna and Potomac rivers, which gave the town an opening to the West. The area contained excellent farm land and forests and had become a large center for trade in lumber, iron, wheat, flour, furs, and manufactured goods such as barrels, rope, shoes, etc., in addition to goods brought in from foreign ports such as rum and sugar from the Caribbean and manufactured articles from England. A strong entrepreneurial spirit developed among the city's merchants, undoubtedly helped by the town's religious freedom, availability of capital for private loans, and virtually no interference from government. Foreigners, especially artisans and skilled craftsmen such as the Harrisons, were attracted to the city not only for its general prosperity but also for the freedom they found in the workplace. There were no craft guilds, as in Europe, to limit the number of people that could enter a profession, and everyone was free to compete for business on the basis of skill and determination.

By 1800 Philadelphia was the largest city in America, having a population of about 69,000, which was roughly 9,000 more than lived in New York City. By then the city's wharves extended nearly two miles along the Delaware River, and behind them were warehouses and the offices of ships' chandlers and the like. As one went inland, the neighborhoods changed to a mix of merchants' shops and contiguous houses. Philadelphia had grown so fast that builders could not construct housing to keep pace, and consequently rents were high. A typical shopkeeper and his family lived in a brick story-and-a-half row house that was about 17-feet wide and 25-feet deep, providing about 800 square feet of floor space on the ground floor and attic. Most of these houses had no carpets, no upholstered furniture, and only whitewashed interior walls.[9] More-successful merchants lived in larger houses, such as those built of brick by William Sansom, three-and-a-half stories in height with two rooms to a floor and leased at a yearly rental of $200. The city's streets were laid out in a grid system of rectangular blocks, but these were often cut through by small alleys where the poor lived in shacks and two-room houses. A contemporary of that day wrote that "The improved parts of the city are paved with round stones brought from the bed of the river at Trenton Falls. The footways are paved with brick and lighted by 1132 lamps, enclosed in glass lanterns, fixed on the tops of posts placed on the edges of the footway."[10] Lombardy poplars were planted at the edges of the pavement in many of the streets.

A Philadelphia brewery fronted by a busy street and surrounded by large residential facilities.

By 1810 the city had nearly 92,000 people and had become a leading center for the arts and sciences. It had more banks than any other city, had eight daily newspapers, and was the center of the American book trade. Books and magazines needed engravers to make illustrations. Publishers and magazine editors soon learned which engravers worked in a style appropriate to their publications and contracted or "commissioned" them for specific projects. By the turn of the century, Philadelphia's book trade supported a relatively large pool of such craftsmen. At least 41 engravers can be identified from the city directory and newspaper advertisements in 1810, and the number rises to 78 by 1818.[11] It is out of this pool of general engravers that some men began to do bank-note work. In the beginning (around 1810), some engravers would occasionally do the lettering for a bank-note plate to supplement their other work. Bank-note engraving was not yet a specialty, but all the necessary elements were in place, and as the American economy grew and the number of banks increased rapidly, the demand for this specialized engraving also grew.

Murray & Draper

Commodore Perry's battle on Lake Erie was drawn by Sully & Kearney; etched by C. Tiebout; and engraved by George Murray.

One of the first engravers to take advantage of this development was George Murray. He was born in Scotland but went to London as a young man and apprenticed himself to the well-known English engraver Anker Smith.[12] William Dunlap says Murray was engraving portraits in London as late as 1796, but he soon joined the Liberty Boys and eventually found it prudent to leave England, from whence he came to one of the southern states, started a business, and got married.[13] When his business failed sometime around 1800, Murray and his family moved to Philadelphia. There, he resumed his work as an engraver, primarily for the book trade, and later was hired to work on Thomas Dobson's American edition of Abraham Ree's *Cyclopedia*. Murray was especially good at engraving animals, and Dunlap said that his lions in the *Cyclopedia* "are a fair specimen and proof of his talents."[14]

Another engraver of some merit was John Draper, a native Pennsylvanian who was born in 1778 and came to Philadelphia about 1794.[15] Like Murray, he also engraved for the *Cyclopedia* from the late 1790s to 1803, and he may have met George Murray through that connection. From 1801 until 1803 he was in business for himself as a general engraver, first at 87 South Front Street (1801), then at 446 North 2nd Street (1804), and later at South 2nd Street and Carter's Alley. The first address on South Front Street was also the address of another engraver named William Carr, and the two of them may have shared the building but worked independently. During part of 1808 and most of 1809, they were partners in "Carr & Draper, Copper Plate Engravers & Printers" at 3 Norris Place. Most of their work at this time was for the book trade. John Draper's first work on bank-note plates came in 1809, as his name appears on hand-dated notes of the Bank of Washington in the District of Columbia.[16] During this period, Draper and Murray decided to go into business together. Both men had done some bank-note engraving and thought there was potential for more work of this kind. Murray's first bank-note engraving may have been as early as 1807. His name appears on notes of the Farmers & Mechanics Bank of Philadelphia in that year.[17] By 1810 Murray and Draper were partners in a firm they called "Murray & Draper, Book-Plates & Bank Note Engravers."[18]

The engraved mark of Murray, Draper, Fairman, Brewster & Co.

Abel Brewster

One of the most interesting but mercurial and querulous pioneers in the bank-note industry was an inventor named Abel Brewster.[19] He arrived in Philadelphia from Hartford, Connecticut, in October 1809. He was soon talking to engravers about his plans to produce bank notes that could not be counterfeited. Brewster said that Archibald Binny introduced him to Murray and Draper, and the four of them soon joined in a new venture.[20] Murray and Draper had also invented a plan to deter counterfeiting. The only description we have of that plan is found in a pamphlet that Abel Brewster published in 1815, and it is worthwhile to quote it here:

> This specimen represented a bill printed in colours, from a plate made of different pieces—that is, a small round piece was fitted into the plate, so as to comprehend a part of the engraved design, and then, by filling the round piece with red ink, and the rest of the plate with black ink, and pulling the piece in and printing the bill off at one operation, both colours broke in the same ornament—the round piece appeared in red, and the rest of the picture in black.
>
> They also calculated to have the plates made of steel, and to produce an exact uniformity in the margin and certain other parts of the bill with uniform and particular types. . . .[21]

Brewster's plan was quite different, and he explained it in a broad outline that he published in a Hartford newspaper in 1807 and in some detail in a pamphlet he published in Philadelphia in 1810, although he left critical parts of the process sufficiently vague so that no one else could easily duplicate his work.[22] Brewster used small punches to impress designs into copper plates, such as half-circles, small solid ovals, five-pointed stars, crosses, pentagons, hexagons, and other geometric shapes containing small designs within their borders. He liked to place pictures of familiar farm animals on his notes, as a security feature, and since he was not an engraver, he had others engrave just the outlines of cows, sheep, or horses on his dies, and he then filled in the interior parts of the figures with random, wiggly lines or small geometric shapes. When notes printed with these animals are held at a normal viewing distance, the random lines and geometric shapes blend together to give the impression of a sheep's wool or the black-and-white splotches on a Holstein cow. He called this type of work "chance or vitriolic," although he explained that "This work is like that which is produced by vitriolic acid, but not done with it. The work is effected by quite a different method, and with great pain and expense. It is impossible to make figures accurately in steel for this use, with acid—it injures the nature of the steel, and makes a rough and bungling impression."[23] He probably did this work by hand at first, but by the time he joined the company of Murray & Draper, he seems to have mounted the punches in a machine, possibly a toggle-joint press, to improve the spacing and depth of the impressions. When he worked on his press, he locked the door to the room and either worked alone or with his only assistant, David H. Mason.[24]

One of the principal features of his plan was to print a large number of notes he called "a General Standard," which would look like the actual issued notes except without the bank's name, location, or denomination. These "standards" were to be placed with merchants and handed out to the public, probably at no charge, to be used whenever it was thought prudent to check the authenticity of a proffered note. Brewster thought this would discourage and possibly eliminate counterfeiting. He may have developed this part of his plan—the use of a standard for comparison with circulating notes—from a visit he had with Jacob Perkins in 1806 and their discussion of the "check plate" that Perkins had invented.

Brewster was a difficult and contentious person, to say the least. Both the pamphlet he published in 1815 and his autobiographical memoir of 1832 reveal a paranoid personality.[25] He kept a secret journal in which he listed all the machinations and intrigues he detected among his business partners and friends. If it is ever found, it will be a fascinating work to read, not only for the aberrant psychology of its author, but also as a chronological record of the company's early progress. Eventually, Brewster's abrasive character became too much for his partners to bear, and they offered to buy his tools, secret techniques, and interest in the company. After much wrangling over money, a settlement was reached on September 5, 1811, and Brewster departed.[26]

Abel Brewster, for all his faults, played an important role in the history of the American bank-note industry. He was the catalyst that brought Murray and Draper out of their work for the book trade and into the bank-note business. When he wasn't arguing with people, he got a lot of work accomplished. Near the end of his partnership, he counted 78 plates on which he had impressed the die work. These plates formed the basic stock from which the company continued to print notes for several years. While Murray and Draper didn't accept very many of Brewster's ideas, they did take advantage of the head start he provided with his prolific work. As the number of banks in the country increased meteorically, so did the demand for new bank notes, and the company's profits soared.

Gideon Fairman

As experienced engravers, Murray and Draper knew that the key to success was to invest in talent, and they lost no time in doing just that. They kept an eye out for skilled engravers and soon recognized one of the best. Gideon Fairman was born in Newton, Connecticut, on June 26, 1774. His family was reduced to poverty when they lost their property twice to fire while he was in his teenage years. Seeing the burden of these circumstances, Gideon placed himself in an apprenticeship to Isaac Cary, a blacksmith in New Millford, just a few miles from Newton. Shortly thereafter, Richard Brunton, an English engraver of no particular merit, came to town and was shown some engravings that Gideon had made. On learning that Gideon had made his own engraving tools and had no formal instruction in the art, Brunton realized the great talent the boy possessed and advised his father to encourage him in this pursuit. At the age of 18, Gideon started on foot, with 18¢ in his pocket, and walked to Boston, where a married sister lived, and then on to Albany, New York, where he became an apprentice to Isaac and George Hutton, jewelers and engravers. Such was his talent that he soon surpassed his instructors in silver-plate engraving. At the age of 21, he went into business for himself. While in Albany, he engraved some vignettes used by banks in New York and New Orleans. He went to Newburyport, Massachusetts, in 1803 to assist William Hooker in the engraving of maps and charts for the larger towns and ports on the Atlantic coast. While there, he also did some engraving for Jacob Perkins off-and-on for several years.

The engraved imprint of Fairman, Draper, Underwood & Co.

After Gideon's wife died in 1810, Perkins asked him to go to Philadelphia to promote the introduction of steel-plate bank-note engraving—something that Perkins had been working on for a few years—and to see what the business prospects were like. Fairman, of course, visited the newly established firm of Murray, Draper & Brewster, and both sides took an immediate interest in each other. The company offered Gideon a position, and he not only decided to accept but also bought an interest in the company. He probably went back to Newburyport to sell his house and settle other affairs, but he was soon back in Philadelphia where he moved into a three-story house at 28 Sansom Street. He left for a time to fight in the War of 1812, first as a captain and later as a colonel of militia and volunteers, and thereafter he was often referred to as "Colonel Fairman."

The engraved imprint of Draper, Toppan & Co.

When the war was over, Gideon returned to Philadelphia and his old job at Murray, Draper & Fairman. This was a time when the company was one of the few "bank-note houses" in the country, and it was flooded with business. Gideon wrote his brother, David Fairman, suggesting that he come to Philadelphia to work for the company.[27] David accepted the offer and brought along a friend named Charles Toppan. According to an anonymous memoir, "The War of 1812 breaking out, Mr. Toppan applied for a commission as midshipman, through an uncle, who was a captain in the Navy, but as there were many applicants before him, his request was not granted. After remaining a short time with Jacob Perkins, the well-known inventor of Newburyport, whose inventions made a great leap forward in the progress of bank note engraving, Mr. Toppan went in 1814 to Philadelphia, in company with David Fairman, to enter the house of Draper, Murray & Fairman [sic]."[28] Charles Toppan was just 18 years old when he joined the company and was taken under the wing of Gideon Fairman to learn script engraving. Fairman was both a portrait and allegorical engraver of the first rank, and Robert Noxon Toppan, Charles Toppan's son, said that he had the "greatest talent and taste of any of the vignette engravers in the country and few equals in Europe."[29] During the next few years, two other men of phenomenal talent joined the firm as well. They were Jacob Perkins and Asa Spencer; but more about them later.

Tanner, Kearny & Tiebout

As this fledgling industry grew by leaps and bounds, other engravers were attracted to the business. One of the first was Benjamin Tanner. He was born in New York City on March 25, 1775, and moved to Philadelphia in 1799 to set up his own small general-engraving business. He was joined in 1806 by his brother, Henry Schenck Tanner, and they began to specialize in map engraving. By 1815 they had converted to a bank-note–engraving company, as the *Port Folio* magazine of that year credits Henry S. Tanner with having invented a process of bank-note engraving that would make counterfeiting much more difficult. This involved the production of white lines on a black ground in an intricate form that could not be easily duplicated by hand engraving.[30] In 1815 the Tanners were joined by Francis Kearny and Cornelius Tiebout in a new company called Tanner, Kearny & Tiebout.[31,32] In 1818 the company added the engraver John Vallance and became known as Tanner, Vallance, Kearny & Company. Vallance left within a year, and the company went out of business about 1820. Both Kearny and Tiebout lost considerable money and never returned to bank-note engraving again. Benjamin Tanner was losing his eyesight when the company dissolved, but he continued to work as a general engraver until he retired from that field in 1835 to concentrate on a check and bank-note process he called "stereographing." He died in Baltimore, Maryland, on November 4, 1848. Tanner, Kearny & Tiebout could not compete against Murray, Draper & Fairman. The catalog by James A. Haxby, *Standard Catalog of United States Obsolete Bank Notes 1782–1866*, lists 11 different banks in 7 different states for which "TK&T" engraved and printed notes, and apparently this was not enough business to make a profit.

A specimen of bank-note engraving showing white ribbons and lettering on black backgrounds.

A Few of the Lesser Lights

John Vallance was born in Scotland about 1770 and probably came to Philadelphia about 1791, where he lived and worked until he died on June 14, 1823, at the age of 53. From 1791 to 1796 he was a member of a general-engraving firm known as Thackara and Vallance, doing plates primarily for the book trade, especially Dobson's *Encyclopedia*. William

Dunlap quotes Alexander Lawson, a Scottish engraver who worked for Thackara and Vallance for two years, and who said of Vallance, "he had attempted to copy a head of Franklin, and also one of Howard, with some success. He was certainly the best engraver at this time [1794] in the United States; and had he been placed in a more favorable situation, he would have been a fine artist." Vallance was a very good script engraver, and it is said that many of the good early bank notes bear his name.

A view of the meeting house in Boston on Hollis Street, etched by John Vallance in 1788.

James W. Steel was born in Philadelphia in 1799 and was a pupil of Benjamin Tanner in 1815 before studying under George Murray for about 18 months. For a time he engraved bank-note vignettes for Tanner, Vallance, Kearny & Company. Although he was primarily a portrait and historical engraver, he is known to have engraved buildings for *Sartain's Magazine* in 1850. David Stauffer says that "at a later period in his professional life he was chiefly employed upon bank note work." He is listed in the Philadelphia city directories at 34 Sansom Street in 1835, and from 1845 to 1856 he was an independent bank-note engraver living at 80-1/2 Walnut Street. In 1858 he was at 320 Walnut Street. He died on June 30, 1879.

James Steel's brother, Alfred B. Steel, was also an engraver and worked for *Sartain's Magazine*, and then as an independent. Alfred was probably in the employ of Joseph R. Carpenter in 1869, as he was a joint patentee (with William H. Earle) of a U.S. patent for the "improvement in printing Revenue Stamps, etc., in two or more colors."

John James Barralet, although not a bank-note engraver, deserves a brief mention since he was said to have built the first ruling machine used in the United States by engravers and to have "devoted much time to the improvement of ink for copper-plate printing."[33] He was born in Ireland of French parents and studied art at the Dublin Academy, later becoming a teacher in that city. He immigrated to Philadelphia in 1795 and was thereafter chiefly employed by the book trade making illustrations. He appears to have designed some historical vignettes for other engravers. He died in Philadelphia in 1812.

The Neagles pose an interesting problem. First, there was a James Neagle, a good engraver who worked in Philadelphia from 1819 until his death on June 24, 1822, at age 53. David Stauffer says "he was possibly chiefly engaged in banknote work," but doesn't give his reason for saying that. If he was engraving bank-note vignettes, it was probably for Murray, Draper, Fairman & Company, as they were the only bank-note engraving firm in the city at that time. John B. Neagle was born in England about 1796 and came to Philadelphia as a youth. Stauffer says he was a "very good line-engraver and produced a considerable number of portraits and book illustrations." In his later life, he was engaged almost entirely on bank-note work. His relationship to James Neagle, if any, is not known.

"The First Landing of Columbus in the New World," engraved by George S. Lang.

George S. Lang, of Scottish descent but born in Chester County, Pennsylvania, in 1799, was apprenticed to George Murray and remained with him until he was about 21. He worked on some plates for Ree's *Cyclopedia*, but he was principally employed on bank-note work. His best-known work is "Washington Passing the Delaware the Evening Previous to the Battle of Trenton," after Thomas Sully. He started but never finished a large plate entitled "The First Landing of Columbus in the New World," after a design by John Barralet. His bank-note work was unsigned, and it is difficult to attribute any notes to him. He died in Philadelphia in 1866.

William Humphrys was born in Dublin, Ireland, in 1794 and came to Philadelphia early in life. He studied engraving with George Murray sometime prior to 1818 and worked for Murray, Fairman & Company, probably as a portrait and vignette engraver. After Murray died in 1825, Humphrys went to London and worked as a portrait engraver. He returned to the United States in 1843 but stayed only two years and then returned to England. His work is seen on some of the earliest English stamps, and he engraved vignettes for the London bank-note firm of Perkins, Bacon & Company. He had considerable success in England, and Clarence Brazer says that he was known as the "American engraver" when Alfred Jones visited him in 1846. He died on January 21, 1865, at Villa Novella, near Genoa, Italy, where he had gone for his health.

A New Paradigm

Christian Gobrecht, Jacob Perkins, and Asa Spencer were a new breed of fine-instrument–makers and inventors who changed the bank-note industry forever. Beginning in the early 19th century, documents of value were protected from counterfeiting by artistic engraving, and this paradigm persisted for more than 150 years. Engraving became increasingly specialized into separate departments of subject matter and technique. The old method of having one artist design and engrave a complete note gradually gave way to newer methods in which several engravers, each specialized in a particular technique, worked as a team to produce a complex note. Some engravers specialized in portrait vignettes, others depicted historic events or allegorical scenes, and still others did script engraving, square-lettering, or ornamental work, such as borders or foliage. The idea was to make it more difficult for a single counterfeiter to imitate the high level of artistic engraving on such notes. This approach, however, had only limited success.

The three Americans just mentioned—Gobrecht, Perkins, and Spencer—invented a completely new way of thinking about security printing: a second paradigm, if you will. This was mechanical engraving that went far beyond the simple use of a ruling machine to make straight lines for clouds or wavy lines depicting the ocean. They invented engraving devices that produced intricate line patterns of such mathematical precision and geometric regularity that no engraver could match them by hand, regardless of his experience. The contributions made by each of these men will be discussed in greater detail in chapter 14, but for now, a brief review of their work will suffice.

Christian Gobrecht was born just two days before Christmas in 1785 in Hanover, Pennsylvania, and was apprenticed to a clock-maker in Lancaster, Pennsylvania, before going to Baltimore, Maryland, and working there as both a clock-maker and a maker of fine instruments. In 1810 he made a metal-ruling machine for an engraver. He moved to Philadelphia in 1811 and worked for several years independently as a seal engraver and die sinker. In 1816 he joined the firm of Murray, Draper, Fairman & Company. Abel Brewster, writing in 1815, mentions that Christian Gobright (*sic*) was working for the company as a die-maker at a salary of $1,500 a year.[34] Gobrecht, working with Asa Spencer and David H. Mason, modified the design of a metal-ruling machine and in 1817 constructed a new and revolutionary instrument called the medal or medallion-engraving machine, the first of its kind. Between 1817 and 1825, he had similar machines made for a number of engravers, including Gideon Fairman and Asa Spencer, both of Murray, Draper, Fairman & Company, for Colonel Cephus Childs, for Rawdon, Clark & Company of Albany, New York, and possibly for Francis Kearny. The medallion engraver operated like a pantograph, having a tracer move over the surface of a three-dimensional medal but altering the spacing of the lines it made in a two-dimensional copy to give the visual effect of a true three-dimensional picture. This was a novel effect that had some potential for increasing the security of a bank note because ordinary hand engraving of a medallion could not produce the three-dimensional effect with the same realism.

Christian Gobrecht.

An engraving of a farmer and his family by Gobrecht.

Asa Spencer was a brilliant inventor who arguably did as much as anyone to improve the security of bank notes against counterfeiting. He was born in New England but never left a record of exactly where and when he was born. He went to New London, Connecticut, about 1800 and soon after married Elizabeth Hempster of that town. We know virtually nothing of his early years except that he worked as a clock- and watchmaker. He invented a metal-ruling machine, which he patented in 1812, for engraving clock faces and also copper and steel plates. At about that time, he began work on a machine that would imitate the intricate lines of the rose-engine turning found on watchcases. While continuing to live in New London, he apparently discussed his design for this new machine with Jacob Perkins, then widely recognized for his mechanical abilities, and Perkins suggested improvements. Perkins said he purchased the rights to this geometric lathe in August 1815, and later he introduced both the machine and Mr. Spencer to the principals of Murray, Draper, Fairman & Company. It isn't known exactly what arrangements Murray, Draper, and Fairman made with Spencer and Perkins, but the company soon had these two men as partners, and Mr. Spencer was the only person who could operate the lathe with the requisite skill and understanding of its potential. The geometric lathe revolutionized the industry and gave a distinct marketing advantage to Murray, Draper, Fairman & Company. Other bank-note companies learned to use a conventional rose engine to make similar designs, but they could not match the ease of operation and the range of geometric figures possible with the geometric lathe. Mechanical engraving did not replace the traditional line engraving, of course, but complemented it and added increased security to bank notes.

The engraved imprint of Spencer, Hufty & Danforth.

Philadelphia was not the only city in which bank-note engraving emerged as a distinct and specialized craft during this early period, but owing to Murray, Draper, Fairman & Company, the city was clearly on the leading edge of the technology and held a dominant lead in the industry. It was also in Philadelphia that bank-note–engraving companies began to change from the old-fashioned shop of two or three skilled craftsmen to more modern organizations with separate departments for designing, engraving, printing, marketing, and administration. Charles Toppan was a leader in this change, and it is primarily for his business acumen and foresight that he was so well respected in later life. The great change that would come in the late 1850s—the consolidation of several companies into one giant firm, the American Bank Note Company—would take place in New York, but a good argument can be made that the basic ideas of the division of labor within a company, coupled with knowledgeable management, originated in Philadelphia.

Chapter 4

Jacob Perkins

Jacob Perkins was undoubtedly the single–most-important figure in the American bank-note industry during the 19th century. He was a self-taught mechanical engineer of extraordinary brilliance but one whose mind was so agile and multifaceted that he never focused on any particular invention for very long. He stayed interested in bank-note security for about 30 years, but he worked on many other inventions during that time, especially high-pressure steam engines. There were other brilliant men that made important contributions to mechanical engraving—men such as Asa Spencer, Cyrus Durand, Waterman Lily Ormsby, Joseph Saxon, Herbert W. Chapman, Charles Wesley Dickinson, et al.—but each of them merely improved on existing technologies, while Perkins was a seminal thinker of the first order. He single-handedly invented a method for engraving on steel and transferring the work to other steel plates, a process he called siderography. It is easy enough to say that if Perkins had not invented this technology, someone else would have. But how long would that have taken? Perkins was aware that steel could be alternately hardened and softened, but he was the first to realize how that could be used to make bank-note plates. He was also the first to realize how that metallurgical phenomenon could be used to transfer engraved designs from one plate to another, and he was the first to invent a special press capable of making the process work. We know that Perkins also worked with Asa Spencer to improve the geometric lathe that Spencer had invented, and that he invented the D-shaped roller to replace the ordinary round rollers used on presses. He had an ability given to few men—an ability to think through a problem by reducing it to a series of simple mechanical principles.

Perkins was born into a large family on July 9, 1766. His father, Matthew Perkins, had 12 children by his first wife, Ann Greenleaf, whom he married in Newbury, Massachusetts, 3 days before Christmas 1748. Ann Perkins died in August 1762, and in January of the following year, Matthew Perkins married Mrs. Jane, the widow of Jonathan Dole. They had seven children of which Jacob was the third. Of the 19 children born to the Perkins family, 2 died before Perkins was born, so he grew up with 11 sisters and 5 brothers, most of them living in one small house in Newbury.[1]

Jacob Perkins.

We know little of Perkins's early years except that his father, a tailor, was prosperous enough to move the family to a house on the port end of town, then called Newburyport, and that Perkins had a common school education, probably being instructed by a retired nautical captain for a few pence a day. He was just nine years old when the first guns of the Revolution were fired at nearby Lexington. His parents chose his career for him when he was 12 years old, placing him in an apprenticeship with Edward Davis, a goldsmith with a shop near the town's central square. Davis is known to have done watch- and clock-making as well as gold- and silversmithing. Perkins was just three years into his apprenticeship and only fifteen years old when Davis died and left his family in a confused and financially difficult condition. Perkins took complete charge of the business and saved the Davis family from ruin.[2]

A Portuguese 6,400-reis coin, or a "half-joe."

Apparently, he continued to work in the jewelry business until he was about 20 years old. During this time, he was principally engaged in making gold and silver beads, which were then a common item of ladies' jewelry. To make these beads and other pieces of jewelry, Perkins bought whatever gold coins were available, usually old Portuguese coins called "joes" and "half-joes" that were brought in by sailors. These coins had a high gold content and were easily beaten into thin sheets that were suitable for making beads. Using dies in the shape of half-spheres, he pressed a thin sheet of gold over the die, cut it at the bottom, and then joined two of these hollow half-spheres by hammered fusion. This experience proved useful a few years later when Massachusetts had an urgent need for coins, and the United States had not yet set up a federal mint. Jacob Perkins was one of the people who had experience in making dies and applied for a job at the State Mint. The records show that he made but little money at this venture (£3-18s-10d) before the U.S. Mint opened and Massachusetts had to close down its mint operations in 1788. Perkins was considered a fairly good engraver, but he did very little work in die sinking. He was, however, a keen observer of the coin-making processes used at the mint, and this experience soon lead to his first invention.

Mints in those days made coins in several separate operations. A sheet of copper was cut into strips which were then fed by hand into a heavy fly press that punched out circular blanks. It took one man to feed the strips into the press and one or more men to pull the fly arm that operated the press. The circular blanks were then taken to another heavy press that held the dies to stamp a design into both sides of the metal blanks. If the edges of the coins were to be milled to prevent clipping, that was done in still another machine. Perkins thought that a machine could be built that would accomplish at least two of these operations in one motion, but it would take him about four years and several experiments before he perfected the design. Meanwhile, at age 24, he married Hannah Greenleaf on November 11, 1790, and they had their first child in February 1792, a daughter named after her mother. During this period, Perkins also designed and built a machine to mill the edges of coins, another machine to make nails, and began working on his first ideas for bank-note security. All this was summarized in an editorial that was published in the *Essex Journal* on July 18, 1792:

Several newspapers of the past and present week have prematurely mentioned Mr. Perkins of this town being sent for to Philadelphia, for the purpose of superintending the coinage there. Mr. Perkins' abilities in that line are fully adequate to such an appointment as the specimens he has exhibited in that line amply testify. Instead of the former method of performing the business, he invented a new machine, which cuts the metal into such circular pieces as are wanted, and give the impression at the same time—its motion is accelerated by a balance-wheel, and more than one-third of the time and labor thereby saved. He has also constructed another machine, of his own invention, for milling or lettering the edge, by which a boy can mill sixty a minute, and were it found necessary, he could apply steam to perform all the most laborious part of the business. But what is of more importance, and will be found to be of more public utility than the foregoing, is a check which he has invented, for discovering counterfeits—this is so contrived, as that one-eighth of a minute is sufficient to determine, without the possibility of a mistake, whether a piece of money is genuine or not, and any town or merchant can be supplied at a small expense with said checks, and then rest assured that an imposition will be absolutely impossible.

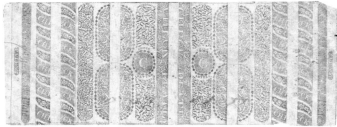

Examples of the Perkins's Patented Stereotype Steel Plate. Notice the individual replaceable dies. Perkins was the first bank-note designer to think seriously about the security of notes.

Perkins did no further work on his check-plate protector until 1798, when he began some experiments to make an actual plate. Within a few months he had a working model, as required by the Patent Office, and he patented his "Stereotype Steel Plate" on March 19, 1799.[3] Although both the model and his letters of patent were lost in the fire that destroyed the Patent Office in 1836, we have good documentation of how the plate was made.[4] As described in his 1806 pamphlet, the stereotype plate:

. . . is made up of fifty-seven case-hardened steel dies, an inch thick, and keyed together in a strong iron frame, which is screwed firm to a metal plate of an inch thickness. It is made of separate parts, in order that it should serve to print bills of any denomination, and for any banks, simply removing the dies, which contain the name of the bank, town, and denomination, and substituting others prepared for the purpose, and also that an exact uniformity might be preserved between banks in general, which could not be effected in the common way of engraving plates.

As the years passed by, the number of dies that were mounted within the frame increased to as many as 64. Once all the individual dies, including those with the name of the bank and the denomination of the bill, had been loaded into the frame, forming one complete die, it was transferred by pressure to a copper or steel plate that was in turn used to print the bank notes. In theory, the merchant who owned a printed copy of the check plate could compare that to the back of a suspect note, and if the individual dies matched exactly, the note was considered genuine. Some of the dies forming the check plate and the genuine notes were so intricately engraved and etched that it would be difficult for a counterfeiter to duplicate them. The position of these "blocks" on the back of the note was individualized for most banks and denominations and was matched to the check plate by a code letter—A, B, C, or D were used in the beginning, followed by other letters as time passed and more banks used the Perkins system. The suspect note was to be folded over along a line printed on the note and then held up against the check-plate note to make certain the engraved dies matched. If they matched and the die work on the two notes was exactly alike, the suspect note was obviously genuine.

By 1805 Perkins said that 16 banks were using his plates and that:

The standing part of these plates were elegantly engraved by Mr. James Akin, the work on the Master Steel plate or matrix occupied six or seven hundred days work, but when completed, impressions including the name of the bank and town it was consigned to, could be supplied easily by transferring to another soft steel plate which was in turn re-hardened.[5,6]

The Perkins plan sounds simple enough, but it was not completely safe from counterfeiting. The earliest notes, those of the first two decades of the 19th century, were probably seldom counterfeited, as it would be difficult to match their complex engraving. Perkins, after all, had done a good job. But soon enough, and with increasing frequency, counterfeiters learned that they could make reasonably good counterfeit plates. The counterfeits were made on copper plates since steel was still difficult to work with. Blocks were made for this work. The blocks were the same size as those on the genuine notes. White letters or denominational figures were easy to make. One simply drew the outline of the letters on the copper block or poked holes through a real note to make dots on the copper that could be connected by a burin. The area within the outline was not engraved. The area outside the outline was suitably engraved, usually by a pantograph, to make straight or wavy lines for a background. When all the finished blocks were fitted together, inked and polished, the engraved lines, filled with ink, would print, but the blank areas within the borders of letters and numbers would not print. They remained white since they were not inked. The micro-printing on the notes required the use of a pantograph, but those were easy to obtain by the late 1820s. Signature blocks posed no problems since they could be made by the technique of poking holes through a real signature with a needle.

An example of micro-printing found on a bank note.

Counterfeiters almost always made notes on banks located a good distance from the area in which they were passed. This made the notes unfamiliar to the merchants or others who accepted them. Another strategy was to engage Perkins to print notes for a "new" bank which the customer claimed to represent, presenting him with whatever fictitious documents he required. This was a scam, since the notes would be technically genuine but had no real value.

It isn't known exactly how Perkins acquired the knowledge of making hard steel soft enough that it could be engraved and then hardened so the engraved designs could be transferred to another metal or to a different soft-steel plate. It's doubtful that he learned these techniques while he worked as a jeweler because jewelers don't work in steel. It's also unlikely that he came by this knowledge while working as a die sinker for the Massachusetts mint in the late 1780s. It is possible that he read about the hardening and tempering of steel in one of several books that had appeared in the 17th and 18th centuries, but it's more likely that he learned about steel from someone who was already doing just that kind of work.[7]

As he did with most of his inventions, Perkins began with a rough knowledge of how a process should work and experimented with those ideas until he solved the technical problems and could make a practical machine or process. Sometime between 1799 and 1803 he brought the "Perkins's Process" for hardening steel to a practical level. Fortunately, we have a rather good first-hand description of the process in a fascinating series of articles written by George Escol Sellers in his later years.[8]

George Sellers was born in Philadelphia in 1808 and lived about three blocks north of the Murray, Draper & Fairman bank-note plant where Jacob Perkins did a lot of his work. As a youth, Sellers had often visited the various machine shops in his neighborhood and taken an interest in their work. His father had been one of the better mechanics of the period, and Sellers obviously acquired some of his father's mechanical talent and was already a keen observer when he first began watching Perkins working with steel, probably around the year 1818. Here is how he described the "Perkins's process:"

The steel plates were annealed in contact with oxide of iron in close retorts until soft enough to be engraved with the ease of copper plates, then they were recarbonized and hardened. I was too young at the time to fully understand the philosophy of the operation, but not too young to watch with great interest Mr. Perkins' manipulation. The care he took to have the water rapidly pass over his plates to carry off the heat forcibly impressed me.

He had small steel cylinders that he used in transferring the engravings. His mode of handling these in hardening them was very interesting to me. He heated them in what he called "mufflers," closely packed in with carbon which was made of wood charcoal and about an equal portion of a coal made of leather scrap that he burned in crucibles. I have a clear recollection of what he called his muffler furnace and also of the mufflers themselves as I have carried them to him from Miller's pottery on Filbert Street to our shop. They were tubes flattened on one side made of fire brick clay and about 1/2-inch thick. They were long enough to reach from side to side of his furnace over a charcoal fire made on a grate, charcoal being added from time to time so that the fire surrounded the mufflers.

It was a long heating process and to my boyish question of why he did not heat them in the open fire, his reply was that they would be ruined by scale if the air was not entirely excluded, and to the question as to why he was so long about it and so careful in watching the fire, he said it was necessary as a part of the hardening process.

I do not think the wood and leather coal dust were all he used in packing his cylinders in the mufflers, but I collected the leather scraps for him and when burned pounded them together with the wood coal in a great iron mortar. When Perkins was satisfied his cylinders were in condition for their cold bath, if from any cause they refused to be punched from the muffler, he never hesitated to break the muffler, seize the cylinder with heated

tongs and plunge it into a gushing stream from a hydrant.[9]

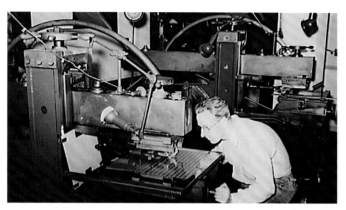

A siderographer transfers stamp images from a die to a plate at the Bureau of Engraving and Printing.

Using the basic procedures that had long been known to some steel-makers, and following the results of his own experiments, Perkins worked out the optimum furnace parameters for hardening small steel dies. The basic science is that the high-temperature burning of organic sources of carbon, such as the wood charcoal and leather scraps that Perkins used, produces carbon monoxide gas, which delivers carbon atoms to a soft-steel object, where they slowly diffuse into its surface. This is called "case hardening." Also important are the changes in the crystal structure of the iron. Pure iron, when heated to 1,670-degrees Fahrenheit, changes its internal crystalline structure from a body-centered cubic arrangement of atoms, called "alpha iron," which is soft and ductile, to a face-centered cubic structure called "gamma iron," which can dissolve much larger amounts of carbon, making the metal harder. The temperature of the steel is critical to this process, and since Perkins had no way of measuring such high temperatures, he experimented with different ways of heating the steel until he found methods that worked. Obviously, he must have used a bellows to blow air (oxygen) into the fire to reach the high temperatures necessary, but there is no mention of this in any of his writing. Later, he found that he could soften or anneal steel by heating it in a retort packed with iron filings and then cooling it slowly. The iron filings absorbed carbon from the surface of the steel and made it softer. This is the great "secret" of siderography—that steel can be softened to the point that it is like copper and can be easily engraved; then hardened so that it can be used to transfer designs to other softer steel; and finally, when a steel plate has been finished, it can be hardened again and used to print an extraordinary number of impressions.

Before Perkins, steel was simply too hard a metal to engrave and had only rarely been used by commercial engravers. Now engravers could cut designs into small squares of softened steel. These squares, called "dies," could be hardened and transferred to a small round cylinder of soft steel. The transfer was made in a special press that Perkins had invented sometime around 1810. To transfer a design, the engraved square die, sometimes called a "bed piece," was placed on the flat bed of the transfer press and held firmly in place while a small round cylinder made of soft steel was rocked back and forth over the die under several tons of pressure until an exact replica of the original engraving was "taken up" or transferred onto the circumference of the cylinder. These soft-steel cylinders were called "transfer rolls." When finished, the transfer roll had exactly the same design as the bed piece except that the design stood out in relief instead of being recessed and was a positive image, whereas the die was a reversed image. When the soft transfer roll was rocked back and forth over the hardened die, its metal was being forced down into the lines cut on the die. Thus the same design was formed on the roll but stood out from the surface of the roll. The transfer roll could then be hardened and placed back in the transfer press to be rocked back and forth under high pressure in a specific area of an actual bank-note plate.

In this way, a virgin or blank bank-note plate made of soft steel or copper could be built up one step at a time, each step being the transfer of a separate design element engraved by a specialist—whether the design was a portrait of a classical figure, an elaborate "counter," or a block of lettering. After all the different design elements had been transferred to the bank-note plate, it could

be hardened and then used to print paper money. Perkins called this process "siderography," which means "writing in steel," and the person who operated the transfer press was sometimes called a "siderographer." The unique advantage of the transfer press was that it could exert the tremendous pressure needed to force the soft steel of its cylinder into the recessed lines of the hardened bed piece. It didn't matter if the lines engraved on the hardened die were shallow cuts or deep channels, straight or curved, wide or narrow. Under such pressure the soft steel sank into and filled those lines, taking up their shape in all three dimensions. Such great pressures had never before been needed or used in printing presses, but Perkins understood from the beginning that steel could only be used for engraving if there was a way to transfer a design with great accuracy through the soft-hard-soft-hard cycle of changes, and he alone deserves the credit for building a transfer press that would accomplish that feat.

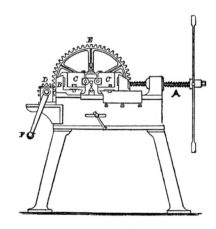

The Perkins's Transfer Press. This press transferred the image on the bed-piece to the roller die and from the roller die to the copper or steel plate.

(A) is the screw to compress the roller between frame (B). The large gear wheel (E) with a plate roller imparts the motion to the plate, and the handle and pinion gear (F)(D) provides the power.

Since steel is much harder than copper, it wears down more slowly and lasts much longer, and the engravers don't have to constantly retouch worn-out plates. By substituting steel for copper, bank-note companies could lower their cost of making bank-note plates. A typical plate printer might print 2,000 impressions from a copper plate before it was necessary to retouch the plate. Using a steel plate, the same printer might easily get 100,000 impressions.[10] Perkins said that a steel plate would print at least 150,000 impressions but copper would print only 6,000 impressions before it wore out (see appendix C). More importantly, the transfer of several independently engraved dies to the final bank-note plate was a far-better protection against counterfeiting than the old system of having all the work done by just one vignette engraver and one letter engraver. Now, several skilled engravers, each a specialist in his own particular type of engraving, could contribute small dies that would be transferred to the final plate. This multiplied the artistic challenges to the would-be counterfeiter and made it much more difficult for him to duplicate the different styles of engraving that could be placed on a bank note.

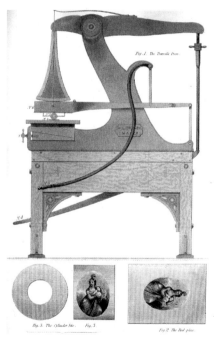

An early transfer press.

By the time Perkins had solved most of the technical problems behind siderography, he was already a successful steel-plate printer. His stereotype plates were beginning to attract the attention of several note-issuing banks, and in 1806 Perkins petitioned the General Court of Massachusetts to adopt the use of his plates in all bank notes printed within the state. He proposed giving each bank eight steel bank-note plates that

would be kept on their premises for security. The banks were to pay Perkins $4 for every eight impressions, and he would not charge them for the plates. Banks would, however, pay a yearly charge of either $30 or $100 for the right to print their notes. If their notes were counterfeited, the yearly charge would be refunded. Bills of less than $5 would be printed from copper dies and plates and the higher denominations from steel. The General Court reacted favorably to his petition but waited until 1809 to pass a banking act that required all banks in the state to use the Perkins plates exclusively. An invoice sent to the Salem Bank in 1805 charged $70 for a stereotype plate. Another invoice sent to the Essex Bank in December 1810 shows that Perkins charged 60¢ per quire of paper (24 sheets), $30 to ship the paper from Boston, a printing charge of 1¢ per note for some notes (probably those that were printed front and back), and 1/2¢ per note for others (probably the single-sided notes). From a number of such invoices sent to various banks, it would appear that the average printing order for bank notes was between 4,000 to 6,000 notes and that most notes were printed "four up," meaning four separate plates were locked together in a frame and used to print four impressions on each sheet of paper.[11]

Perkins persuaded his brother Abraham to join him in the bank-note engraving and printing business in July 1808. He even gave him a mortgage on his house at No. 14 Fruit Street in Newburyport.[12] Together, they paid for the construction of a three-story brick building to serve as a bank-note plant in the garden behind the house.[13] It was here that most of the bank-note dies and plates were engraved and then used to print the paper money of Massachusetts, Maine, and New Hampshire. The editor of the (Newburyport) *Daily Herald*, in an editorial of May 20, 1825, made an oblique reference to this fact when he reminded his readers, facetiously, that in spite of hard times, "there is more money made in Newburyport than in any other town in the Commonwealth." Unfortunately, we do not know who did the engraving or printing of the notes. After 1812 Perkins was busy with other projects and left Abraham in charge of the bank-note plant. Abraham was a good businessman who ran the plant efficiently and made a good living at this work. Still, the two brothers never became wealthy from this venture, and Abraham later found it advisable, if not necessary, to move the plant to Boston with the financing and experience of three new business partners.

The Perkins's Bank-Note Plant, 1809. Located in the back of Perkins's house at 14 Fruit Street in Newburyport, Massachusetts. A three-story building with windows.

Beginning in 1812, Murray, Draper, Fairman & Company won successive government contracts to print Interest-Bearing Treasury Notes. These were lucrative contracts and also work that enhanced the company's reputation, helping it win commercial contracts with private banks. Gene Hessler has illustrated some of these notes, showing also the archival data which indicates that the company printed 50,000 notes for the 1812 issue, another 50,000 in 1813, probably more than 100,000 notes in 1814, and probably that many again in 1815.[14] This was clearly a company that could afford Jacob Perkins.

Perkins had been loosely associated with Murray, Draper, Fairman & Company since 1812. He had met with these three men and discussed the business potential for printing bank notes. These discussions must have been positive, for Perkins and George Murray jointly patented a transfer press on June 25, 1813, and a printing press for copper and steel engravings on June 29 of the same year. In these patents, both of which were lost in the fire at the Patent Office in 1836, Murray is listed at his address in Philadelphia and Perkins at his house in Newburyport, Massachusetts. By December 1815 Perkins found that his business interests in Philadelphia far outweighed those in Massachusetts, and he moved to Philadelphia to begin working more or less full time with Murray, Draper, Fairman & Company at their bank-note plant located at 47 Sansom Street. John Draper lived on the premises, and George Murray lived just a few doors south at 48 Sansom. Gideon Fairman lived at 28 Sansom Street, and Perkins stayed there at first. Perkins was never a partner in the firm or one of its employees, but he was probably paid a consultant's fee or given some other form of compensation. In the same year, Perkins bought the rights to the geometric lathe that Asa Spencer had invented, and then he and Spencer subsequently improved it and began using it at Murray, Draper, Fairman & Company in 1816. Perkins also brought his transfer press and his singular knowledge of siderography to the company's work, providing a level of mechanical expertise that no other bank-note company could approach. Everything seemed to be going well for Perkins as the Christmas of 1818 passed. His several inventions had brought him considerable fame, perhaps some money, and probably the satisfaction of knowing that he had made important contributions to both science and mechanical engraving. His work with Murray, Draper, and Fairman was mutually advantageous, and his family life seemed stable. But beneath this tranquility, events were taking place in England that would soon have a dramatic impact on his life.

Moving To England

Counterfeiting—or forgery, as the English like to call it—had long been a problem in England just as it had in America, but it had recently begun a meteoric rise that alarmed not only the Governor and Company of the Bank of England, but also many in Parliament and even the common people. The small number of engravers who made counterfeit plates were rarely caught, but a large number of people, usually poor or from the lower-middle class, were caught passing forged notes and were given harsh punishment, including "transportation" to Australia or hanging. After a time, juries were reluctant to find such people guilty. The country banks were especially reluctant to prosecute such people given the public's sympathy for those caught and the potential damage a prosecution might bring to the bank's public relations. The directors of the country banks tried to avoid counterfeiting by using highly skilled engravers to design and make their notes, and to their credit, those efforts were increasingly successful. The Bank of England, however, did not take this approach and kept their notes simple and therefore wickedly easy to copy. The public understood this and raged against the bank's intransigence. Charles Wye Williams, in his long essay of 1818 entitled *Considerations on the Alarming Increase of Forgery on the Bank of England...*, gave the bank's statistics showing that the 12 convictions for counterfeiting in 1798 had risen to 128 convictions in just the first three months of 1817, and that the total number of counterfeited notes had risen from 17,885 in 1812 to 9,645 notes in just the first three months of 1817, or more than 100 notes a day.[15] In still another chart, one that was particularly damning, Williams showed that the records of the last session of the Old Bailey (1817) indicated that 41 persons were convicted of passing counterfeit notes, and of these 14 were sentenced to transportation and 13 were sentenced to death. Boys as young as 16 were being hanged, and some of the same age were taken from their families and homeland and transported to Australia. In the period from 1797 to 1817, slightly more than 300 people had been executed for making or passing counterfeit notes. At the height of the problem, the Bank of England alone kept 70 clerks checking all notes turned into the bank to pick out those that were counterfeit.

Even this 1950 note of the Bank of England is fairly simple in design.

The Bank of England had begun to study the problem as early as 1797, and by 1802 it had formed a Committee of Treasury that had examined 35 ideas on bank-note security. The committee, however, took no action to change the bank notes. It was reported that in 1817 there were some 10,000 engravers in England that could engrave a good likeness of a Bank of England note.[16] Sir James MacIntosh, a frequent critic of the Bank of England and a member of Parliament, said "any boy who had been six months with an engraver might imitate, so well as to make the difference imperceptible, the notes of the Bank of England."[17] Public opinion grew so antagonistic towards the bank that three separate committees were formed in 1818 to investigate the problem and make recommendations. The Bank of England's old Committee of Treasury, which had ended in 1803, was reestablished. The government formed a Royal Commission, and the Society of Arts also started an investigation. All three committees made reports after a full examination of many different proposals.

Meanwhile, Jacob Perkins had gone to Washington, D.C., in February of 1819 to attend to the company's business with the second Bank of the United States. While there, Perkins met with the

British Minister, Sir Charles Bagot. Mr. Bagot had known Perkins for two or three years and was greatly impressed with both the beauty and security of the bank notes of Murray, Draper, Fairman & Company. He had tried to persuade the Bank of England to adopt a similar system. The bank officials were duly impressed with the bank-note specimens that Mr. Bagot had sent them and decided rather quickly to offer a large cash prize to anyone who could provide a practical method by which notes could be made safe from counterfeiting. Bagot now related this information to Perkins and urged him to go immediately to London for the honor, the glory, and the cash. The year before, Perkins had also written Charles Heath, the English engraver, explaining his ideas on bank-note security, and Heath had in turn communicated those ideas and shown specimens of Perkins's work to a committee of the Society of Arts that was studying methods for improving bank-note security.[18,19] Encouragement also came from Joseph C. Dyer, a rich American who had moved to England in 1811 to establish a business promoting the interests of a number of American inventors, and he now began to act as an agent for Perkins.[20] On September 28, 1818, Dyer presented the details of Perkins's invention for printing bank notes from steel plates to a committee of the Bank of England, and meeting with favorable interest from that committee, he wrote to Perkins urging him to come to England and compete for the bank's prize money.[21]

A worker uses a transfer press to imprint the design from a cylinder die onto a bank-note plate.

After his stay in Washington, and having apparently made up his mind to try for the bank prize, Perkins went immediately to Philadelphia and met with Murray and Fairman. The partnership of this company had expired in July of 1818, and John Draper had withdrawn to an early retirement. After Draper left, the company was briefly renamed Murray, Fairman & Company. Perkins persuaded these remaining partners that the Bank of England prize was a huge opportunity, not only for the money it offered (said to be £20,000), but also for the possibility of getting the contract to print the notes for the Bank of England and the consequent enormous gain in reputation for the company. Murray and Fairman thought that Perkins would have no chance if he went to England alone and tried to talk his way into the prize. They argued that if this venture was to have any chance for success, it must be done at full tilt. A party of engravers, printers, and mechanics would have to go to England and set up a shop that could turn out specimen bank notes that were better than anything the English had seen before. The decision was made quickly with Gideon Fairman assigned to do the portrait engraving, Charles Toppan to do the letter engraving, Asa Spencer to operate the geometric lathe, Marcus Bull to do general mechanical work, and J. McCawley to do the printing. Spencer, Bull, and McCawley were given contracts that specified their wages. By the middle of May 1819, Perkins and Toppan left Philadelphia for Newburyport to say their farewells to their families there. On their return to Philadelphia, they stopped off in New London, Connecticut, to pick up Asa Spencer. They left Philadelphia on a fast-sailing ship named the *Telegraph* on May 31, 1819, with 26 cases of machinery and personal property, and arrived in Liverpool on June 28.

Perkins and his entourage lost no time in setting up shop in London at No. 29 Austin Friars Street and in making connections with both bankers and professional engravers. On December 20, Charles Heath joined the company, which now became Perkins, Fairman & Heath. George Heath, his brother, also joined the firm a little later but took no active part in the day-to-day operations. After making discreet inquires and talking with banking officials, Perkins realized that the principal obstacle to his success would be Sir William Congreve, the military governor of the Bank of England and a member of the Royal Commission that had been appointed by Parliament to find a practical solution to the problem of counterfeiting. The bad news about Congreve was that he didn't like Americans.

Congreve was then a 48-year-old military engineer. He was the eldest son of Lieutenant General Sir William Congreve. After graduating from the Royal Academy, he began working on a military rocket in the late 1790s, and after many experiments he produced a working model that he first used on a limited scale in the siege of Boulogne in 1806 and later perfected in 1808. The improved rocket was used by Lord Cochrane in an attempt to burn the French fleet in 1809. Though the rocket was not initially as successful as had been expected, its value was perceived and Congreve was made a colonel and allowed to organize two rocket companies. In 1813 he served at the battle of Leipsig, and though his rockets did not inflict much damage on the enemy, their noise and bright glare frightened the French and threw them into confusion. Consequently, the Czar of Russia showed his appreciation by making Congreve a Knight in the Order of St. Anne. On the death of his father in 1814, Colonel Congreve succeeded to the baronage and became the second Sir William Congreve. He was elected to Parliament in 1812 and became a great personal favorite of King George IV while he was the Prince Reagent. He was chosen a Fellow of the Royal Society and was highly regarded in scientific circles even though most of his inventions had to do with gun carriages, the manufacturing of gunpowder, and improvements in fireworks and military rockets. By the time Perkins arrived in England, Congreve had great influence in the Bank of England. He had his own ideas about bank-note security and had offered two plans to the bank in that connection. It would be difficult to imagine a more formidable adversary.[22]

An example of Congreve's Patent Plate on the back of a bank note.

Perkins wrote a letter to the Royal Commission on July 30, 1819, explaining the advantages of line-engraved steel plates and the basics of the siderographic system. The commission took until November to reply, probably at the insistence of Congreve who needed more time to perfect some of his own ideas. The commission's reply made no final determination and the rivalry continued. While many people offered plans to prevent forgery, three groups had clearly emerged as front runners. Most engravers and printers thought Perkins, Fairman & Heath had not only the most beautiful notes but also the most difficult to counterfeit and were therefore the company most likely to succeed. The second group, Applegath and Cowper, was little known outside the Bank of England, but they had submitted a plan to the bank's committee that seemed promising and were given £1,200 to pay for secret experiments. Finally, Sir William Congreve, who was a member of the Royal Commission but apparently thought little or nothing of the conflict of interest, also submitted a plan for making a new type of bank-note paper. When that failed, he offered a plan for printing notes in color. The Royal Commission stated in 1819 that it had considered 108 proposals, most of which had been evaluated first by the committee at the Bank of England and then passed over to the commission. The commission, however, had reached no decision.

The Society of Arts also issued a report of its investigations in the early part of 1819, but the Bank of England took no immediate action because most of its committee favored the plans put forth by Applegath and Cowper. Augustus Applegath was a prominent printer of the day and also a rather good mechanic.[23] His partner was his brother-in-law, Edward Cowper, also an ingenious machinist. They had worked together as friends and then become partners in 1817. Applegath and Cowper were the government's printers of the Bank of England's official dividend warrants and other scrip, and since they already had a "foot in the door" and had been working on a new technique for printing in color, it was natural that they would compete for the bank's prize money. Cowper had patented a process in 1816 (British Patent No. 3,974) for printing in one or more colors by using stereo plates made by the plaster process, which were afterwards bent around and fixed to a printing cylinder, inked by composition rollers, and printed from a rotary press. Cowper had also invented the composition rollers. The outstanding feature of their process, and the one that most impressed the bank committee, was their ability to print a complex design on both the front and back of a note in perfect registry. Their methods were kept secret, but we know now that they used a multi-cylinder rotary press in which the sheet of bank-note paper was carried from one cylinder to the next by means of continuous tapes. Two complete revolutions of the cylinders were necessary to print a note. The first operation of the machine was carried out with no paper. A stereotype plaster cylinder held the design of the note and was inked by several inking rollers at one side. This cylinder rotated against a second cylinder that was covered by a leather pad. The leather pad received the wet-inked design from the stereotype cylinder and in turn transferred the design to another leather pad attached to the cylinder directly above it. The two impression cylinders, each holding the inked design on their leather pads, rotated at the exact same speed and therefore printed at precisely the same time. After the leather pads were inked, paper entered the machine, passed between the two impression cylinders, and was printed. Although two revolutions of the impression cylinders were required for each note, the press operated at a good speed, and according to Cowper it could print 1,200 notes per hour.[24]

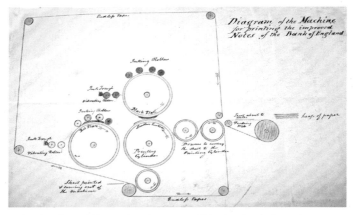

Applegath and Cowper's rotary press. This drawing is the only one known of the configuration of cylinders in the press.

Sir William Congreve's plan to stop bank-note forgery grew out of his earlier work to make coins forgery-proof. He suggested that coins be made of two parts. An irregular shape of a hard metal, such as steel, would form the first part, called the "token," and the second part, a softer metal to be called the "gauge," would be cast around the token in a circular mold forming a round coin. As a cast piece, the two parts would fit together perfectly. Without having the die from which the token was cast, counterfeiters would not be able to duplicate its irregular geometry and could not make tokens by hand that would fit so perfectly into a gauge. In a similar fashion, he suggested gold ingots could be made of a compound plate in which several pieces of gold and some harder metal would be cast into interlocking parts, and the words "Bank of England" and "Ingot" would be stamped across the different metals. Again, the precision with which the different metals were fitted together and stamped became criteria by which to judge the authenticity of the ingots. In his patent of November 1819, Congreve mentions that the processes he invented for coins and ingots would also be useful in printing, and that it would "tend to throw great difficulty in the way of forgery of banknotes and other documents which it is desirable to protect."[25] The bank committee turned down the proposals for coins and ingots, but Congreve was not deterred.

Next he proposed a new kind of bank-note paper, which he called "triple paper." This was made by first couching a thin layer of white paper, then laying an equally thin layer of a water-marked, colored paper on top of it, and finally adding another thin layer of white paper on top of the other two. After these papers were pressed and dried, they formed a homogeneous sheet that appeared white from most angles of viewing, but when held up to the light, the watermark and tint of the middle colored layer could easily be seen. The watermark was made by placing a stencil over the mould in which the pulp was drained. These stencils could be cut with elaborate fili-greed designs, making the paper extremely diffi-cult to imitate. The middle layer of paper could be formed of strips of different colors, and the stencils for the watermarks could be made differ-ent for each denomination of notes, making counterfeiting still more difficult.[26] The bank committee, however, turned down the idea of using a colored and watermarked paper, and Con-greve, always ready with an alternate plan, now went back to his work on using different metals cast in complex patterns, adapting those ideas to bank-note printing.

The "compound plate" which Congreve now proposed was actually very similar to the design of his ingot plate. This was made by cutting up a plate of a suitable metal to make a stencil, as it were, with irregularly shaped holes in various places on the plate. The plate was then laid down on a flat surface and a softer metal was poured over its back side, forming a separate, detachable plate that filled in the holes of the original plate with a perfect fit of the two metals. The two plates were then taken up together and locked in a frame. The perfectly flat front side was engraved with a graphic design and lettering that cut through both metals. The two plates could then be separated and inked in different colors, reassembled, and printed. This would give a two-colored or even a multi-colored bank note. The bank committee saw considerable merit in this plan, but they turned it down in favor of the work of Applegath and Cowper, who were still perfecting their plan.

Perkins, Fairman & Heath had submitted a number of specimen notes to the Bank of England Committee to demonstrate the effectiveness of their transfer press and the consummate skill of their vignette engraver, Gideon Fairman. Some of these specimen notes had been prepared in Philadelphia before the party left for England. The bank once again turned these notes over to their engraving department and specifically to William Bawtree, their chief engraver, to see if they could be imitated. Bawtree had a special lathe made so he could duplicate the considerable amount of machine engraving on the specimen notes. Meanwhile, Congreve had his good friend Robert Branston try his hand at copying the same notes. Branston was one of the leading wood engravers of the time, and he and his son were able to copy the machine engraving and even the micro-text on the Perkins notes by hand engrav-ing on wood and brass. The imitations were made by the Branstons in only 17 days and printed by Congreve in his pamphlet, *An Analysis of the True Principles of Security against Forgery*. Perkins had claimed that one of his notes would take an engraver three and a half years to copy, if indeed there was an engraver capable of making any copy at all. Perkins also claimed that the head of Homer on this note was engraved by one of his sons and was repeated by the transfer press to five different places.[27] A head of a woman that had been engraved by Gideon Fairman was repeated four times, there were eight ovals containing the Bank of England's charter in micro-text, pro-duced by the use of a pantograph, and there were two pieces of fancy engraving made by Asa Spen-cer's geometric lathe. It was, to be certain, a very complex design that should have deterred any engraver. The Branstons engraved the two heads on separate blocks of wood and printed them five and four times each. Branston's son copied the geometric-lathe work on brass using a fine-point run along a ruler and took only five days to com-plete the work, where Perkins had estimated it would take a professional engraver thirty months to do the same. The micro-text was engraved on copper in six days and printed intaglio. The rest of the work was printed in relief. Congreve had the Branstons copy other notes made by Perkins in similar periods of time. He argued to the bank committee that what the Branstons had done on wood could also be done on metal and then copied by the stereotyping process to print great numbers of notes, and therefore, the Perkins plan was no real security against counterfeiting. Perkins said the Branston imitation note was crude and easily detected as an imitation. Opinion was divided amongst common people, but many thought the imitation note was good enough to fool the casual observer. Bawtree's work at the bank was also nearing its finish and had produced a very good copy. The committee agreed with Congreve's argument but did not immediately issue a formal rejection of Perkins's work.

A specimen bank note engraved by Robert Branson for Sir William Congreve, circa 1820. Reduced from 4-1/2 x 8-1/2 inches.

The enlarged image shows how well Branson imitated the kind of waved-line ruling and geometric-lathe work that Perkins, Fairman & Heath claimed were impossible to duplicate.

Specimens of engraved panels, vignettes, and lathework by Perkins, Fairman & Heath, circa 1890.

A specimen note of Perkins, Bacon & Petch.

The Bank of England made a serious mistake in judging all proposals against an impossible standard. They held that if their engraving department or some independent engraver could imitate the notes produced by an inventor, then such notes did not offer a sufficient security against forgery. The bank committee failed to realize that the engraving department, with all its highly talented and specialized engravers, given enough time, would *always* be able to imitate a note design with considerable accuracy. Common counterfeiters, however, working with inferior equipment and materials, could not hope to match the high-quality work of the professionals. The problem that the English were having with bank-note forgery could have been solved, to a very appreciable degree, had the bank committee not taken such an unrealistic and absolutist position. They simply failed to realize that common things are common and rare things are rare, and it would be rare for any counterfeiter to possess the talent and knowledge necessary to imitate a professionally engraved note, especially if it were made by an esoteric method requiring machinery that common engravers did not possess and could not purchase. Garnet Terry, the Bank of England's engraver, had copied the note design submitted by Alexander Tilloch in 1797, resulting in its rejection; and now, the Branstons and Bawtree had copied the Perkins note, resulting in its rejection. The committees wanted perfection but could not find it.

The seven governors of the Bank of England's committee now favored the Applegath and Cowper notes and issued a final report to His Majesty in February 1820, recommending adoption of those notes (see appendix D). King George, however, did not immediately make a decision, perhaps waiting for the other committees to issue their reports. Meanwhile, Mr. Bawtree at the Bank of England was hard at work imitating the Applegath and Cowper notes. Finally, in September of 1821, the last group of inventors with any hope of winning—Applegath and Cowper—were informed that "in the opinion of the Committee, Mr. Bawtree's imitation is quite fatal to Messrs Applegath and Cowper's note." The bank paid compensation of more than £40,000 to Applegath and Cowper and to several workmen who had assisted then in their secret workroom at the bank. It was reported in some quarters that the bank had also paid a compensation of £5,000 to Perkins for his efforts, but Grenville and Dorothy Bathe, who examined the entries in the Perkins, Fairman & Heath company books and the official records of the Bank of England, said there was nothing to substantiate a payment was ever made to the Americans.

In the summer of 1820, Perkins, Fairman & Heath moved their bank-note plant from Austin Friars to a three-story red-brick building at No. 69 Fleet Street. Their fame had spread rapidly through the banking community, and the company soon began to print notes for the city and country banks. At that time, almost anyone with a little capital could start a country bank, and literally hundreds of these banks were in operation and wanting better-engraved notes. These provincial banks commonly issued £1 and £2 notes, so print orders were fairly large for even small banks. Perkins, Fairman & Heath is known to have made hundreds of bank-note plates for these banks during their first 10 years in business. The flood of orders that came pouring in must have offset the disappointment of losing the Bank of England prize.

In 1821 the Bank of Ireland decided their notes were simply too easy to counterfeit, and they turned to Perkins, Fairman & Heath to engrave the plates for their new bank notes. The bank had been established in 1782 with a capital of only £600,000. They hired Edward Fitzgerald of Dublin to be their first engraver, and the actual printing of notes was begun by William Wilson of Dame Street, Dublin, in the early months of 1784. These notes were printed from copper plates on paper made by Portals in England. Counterfeit notes appeared in January of 1785. By 1797 the number of counterfeit notes in circulation was so large that the bank's officials decided to offer a reward of £100 for information leading to the capture and successful prosecution of anyone who forged a note or knowingly passes a forged note. Naturally, this didn't work any better in Ireland than it had in England. The bank also issued instructions to all its clerks that they were to carefully examine all notes presented for payment, and any clerk cashing a note which was an obvious forgery would be held personally responsible. None of these measures had any appreciable effect, so the Irish Parliament passed an act that same year providing that any person found guilty of forging bank notes would be transported for life. That act, however, didn't work either, and the following year the Irish politicians, acting like those in England, substituted the death penalty for transportation. Frederick G. Hall, in his *History of the Bank of Ireland*, tells a brief but relevant story:

> *The Freeman's Journal* of 27th January, 1816, announced the death of one Robert James, at Constitution Hill, Dublin, who had forged small notes continuously since 1797 and experienced all the vicissitudes attendant on that truly adventurous

and hazardous occupation. So extensive was his practice and so numerous were his agents, that it might be truly said he had been the cause of bringing 100 poor wretches to the gallows and contributed more towards peopling Botany Bay than all the other forgers of Ireland put together.[28]

The man who did more than any other to reduce counterfeiting in Ireland was John Oldham. He was a native of Dublin, born in 1779, who had been an engraver and miniature painter for some years when he invented a consecutive numbering machine for bank notes and offered the machine to a bank in Ireland in 1809. When the bank rejected his machine, he offered it next to the Bank of Ireland. The bank officials were so impressed by the device that they interviewed Oldham and offered him the job of engineer and chief engraver. Oldham accepted the position in 1812 and began to make a number of improvements in the engraving department. One of his first innovations was to bring in an eight-horsepower steam engine to run his flat-bed press. This is probably the first use of steam to power printing presses in a bank-note plant. He also fixed one of his numbering machines to a plate-printing press so that it recorded the number of impressions made during the day. That number was compared to the number of sheets of paper issued to the printers, preventing the theft of paper. Another innovation was his use of engraved steel plates, although he was not using the Perkins process with its transfer press.[29]

A £1-10s note of the Bank of Ireland, 1814, before the Perkins process was adopted.

A £5 note of the Provincial Bank of Ireland, 1826–1837. This note is much more complex in design and was engraved by Perkins & Heath, London, using the "Patent Hardened Steel Plate."

John Oldham met Jacob Perkins and his party in Liverpool in 1819 while Perkins was showing how siderography worked. Oldham was keenly interested in the process and thought it produced beautiful notes. He took this information back to the Bank of Ireland and convinced its officials that they should adopt the Perkins process. The bank had just increased its capital by £500,000, and their order for new bank-note plates was a windfall for Perkins, Fairman & Heath. Perkins now realized that the level of business at the company was simply too large for him to manage, and he wrote to his son-in-law, Joshua B. Bacon, asking him to come from Philadelphia and take over the financial management of the company.

Not much is known about Joshua Bacon before he married into the Perkins family. He was born on April 25, 1790, in Boston, Massachusetts, and came from a respectable middle-class family. He served in the Light Infantry Company of Boston in defense of that city during the War of 1812 and married Jacob Perkins's second daughter, Sara Ann, in 1814. Perkins and Thomas P. Jones (a businessman in Philadelphia who backed Perkins in the fire-engine business) had formed a partnership in 1817 to build fire engines. Their manufacturing plant was located behind St. James's Church on North 7th Street in Philadelphia and was immediately successful, building more than 200 fire engines in the first two years.

As Perkins was getting ready to go to London in 1819, he turned over the management of the fire-engine company to Bacon, who continued to run the company efficiently. Perkins now brought his son-in-law into the company (Perkins, Fairman & Heath) to handle financial matters. He obviously trusted his son-in-law's judgment and was able to retire from the London engraving company knowing that a steady hand was at the helm.

In May 1839 Bacon took over the duties of Charles Heath as a partner in the business, and the firm became Perkins, Bacon & Company. It continued with that name until 1834, when the engraver Henry Phillipson Petch joined as a third partner (Perkins, Bacon & Petch). When Petch died in 1852, the company reverted to its old name, Perkins, Bacon & Company. Joshua Bacon died in 1863 and was buried in the Perkins family vault in Kensal Green Cemetery, in London, amongst the 500 members of British nobility buried there.

The company's largest single success did not occur until late in 1839 when the government decided to reorganize its postal system. The man responsible for that was Rowland Hill, a schoolmaster, educator, and a member of the Radical movement in England.[30] While trying to find a way to alleviate the tax burden of the people, he undertook a study of the whole British tax-revenue system and discovered that the postal system was a near perfect example of bureaucratic inefficiency and social misconduct. The postal rates were based on the distance a letter was sent, as it was in America, but since the government saw the post office as a good source of tax revenue, the postal rates were set far too high, and this discouraged the average person from using the post. Hill also documented some of the abuses of the system, and one that made him particularly irate was the fact that many people of privilege had the right to send their mail free; yet many people who did not have this franking privilege used it illegally and sent their mail without paying postage. Hill did a very thorough study of the postal system to expose its abuses and recommended practical solutions in a pamphlet he published privately, entitled *Post-Office Reform: Its Importance and Practicality*.

Hill's pamphlet caused little concern in Parliament, but his brother, Matthew, was a member of Parliament. He saw to it that Roland was invited to give evidence and explain his reforms to the Commissioners for Post Office Inquiry. The commissioners were resolutely opposed to some of his radical ideas, as were the postmaster general and other high officials in the post office. Seeing that his ideas would never win favor with the government, Hill did what any responsible radical would do—he went public with his pamphlet, and it immediately met with great success and won widespread and influential support. Numerous public meetings were held, and many petitions were sent to Parliament. Finally, the government caved in to the political pressure and appointed a Select Committee of the House of Commons to examine Hill's proposals.

Hill wanted a uniform rate of postage based only on the weight of a letter and not the distance it must travel. He proved, for example, that the cost of carrying a letter from London to Edinburgh was no more than 1/36 of a penny, rather than the current rate of 1 shilling, 1 pence. He said that if the government would lower the cost of postage, the public would use it a great deal more, and the resulting revenues from this increased use of the mail would actually be about the same or at least would cause no serious loss. Hill also argued for a prepaid fee in the form of a stamp that would be purchased and placed on the envelope by the person sending the letter. This would avoid direct payments of cash to a postal clerk, who often pocketed part of the money and sent the letter under the franking privilege or by some other subterfuge. Hill proposed a one-penny stamp for letters up to one-half ounce in weight, two pence for letters up to a full ounce, and two pence for each additional ounce or fraction thereof.

A postal-reform act embracing most of Hill's recommendations was passed in 1839 and became law on January 10, 1840. Perkins, Bacon & Petch won the bid for the printing of the stamps at 7-1/2 pence per 1,000. The design chosen was a profile portrait of Queen Victoria at the age of 15, when she was still a princess. The profile had first appeared in relief on the obverse of a medal engraved by William Wyon in 1837 to commemorate the young queen's visit to the Guildhall following her coronation. The Perkins company paid the painter Edward Henry Corbould £12 to draw the portrait. Corbould was married to one of Charles Heath's daughters. It was widely reported at the time that the portrait was engraved by Charles Heath, but later research based on company records showed that the actual work was engraved by Heath's son, Frederick Heath.[31] The stamp was printed in black ink on white paper and quickly became known as the "penny black." The same design was used on the two-pence stamps, but they were printed in blue. These were the world's first adhesive postage stamps.

The "penny black" stamp.

The Perkins company's Fleet Street plant had considerable capacity in 1840, using nearly 40 "improved rolling presses" for their work on bank notes and the book trade, but the postal contract pushed both machines and men to the limit. When Rowland Hill visited the plant in April 1840, he was shown that one plate had just been completed and work on a second plate was scheduled for completion in another week. Two presses were also ready, and a third was to be finished in one week, a fourth press in two weeks, and two more presses were in early stages of preparation. The company had committed to delivering 200,000 stamps within a week and was to continue at a rate of 240,000 stamps per day thereafter. As the additional presses came "on line," each would add 120,000 stamps per day to the production. The printing plates were kept at press both day and night for several months. Production schedules were met, and these first adhesive stamps were placed on sale on May 1, 1840.

The company continued to print the line-engraved stamps of Great Britain and its colonies until 1879. In 1855 the London firm of Thomas De La Rue & Company entered the picture with cheaper surface-printed stamps, and these gradually displaced the stamps that were printed directly from engraved plates. Over 22 billion stamps were printed from Perkins plates during those years; though not all were printed by the company. In 1844 an act of Parliament discontinued the practice of the private banks printing their own notes, and that part of the company's business declined rapidly. Henry Petch died in 1852, and Joshua Bacon died in 1863, but the company continued under its old name (Perkins, Bacon & Company), still located at No. 69 Fleet Street. It became a limited company in 1887 and moved to a modern plant in the old Southwark Bridge Buildings in Bermondsey in 1904. There, the company was under the direction of James Dunbar Heath, a grandson of the Charles Heath who had joined the company in 1818, convinced of its bright future.

Jacob Perkins lost his wife, Hannah Greenleaf Perkins, in October 1837. She had returned to Newburyport, Massachusetts, sometime in 1836. His brother, Abraham, died at his old home on Fruit Street in Newburyport on April 2, 1839. Perkins's last work with the London bank-note firm was the postal contract of 1840. After that, he retired to a more sedate life, though still occasionally involved in discussions and lectures on steam engines and related topics. Apparently he lost most of his fortune through unexplained circumstances around 1840. After 1843 he lived with his son, Angier March Perkins, an engineer of considerable reputation, at No. 18 Reagent Square. In the middle of July 1849, Jacob Perkins took to his bed with acute enteritis and died on July 30, at the age of 83 years. He was buried in the family vault at Kensal Green Cemetery. His death was little noticed in London, but he was appreciated more on the western side of the Atlantic.[32]

Chapter 5

Philadelphia Redux
1822–1858

Götterdamerung, Sort of

For a good part of the early 19th century, Philadelphia continued its lead as the bank-note capital of the country. New York City, however, with its stock exchange, large banks, and rapidly growing entrepreneurial class, was a giant financial machine whose gears were just beginning to turn. Eventually, competition between all the bank-note companies drove down profits and forced the owners to think in new ways about their survival. A few of the brightest minds argued that a consolidation of the best companies was necessary, even if it meant that some companies would be forced out of business. The industry leaders were beginning to plan ahead, becoming less dependent on good fortune and random success. Some of the great Philadelphian bank-note partnerships come to their demise in this chapter, only to be reborn in New York City under a different name.

New York was growing rapidly during the middle of the 19th century. This drawing from 1847 shows a view of Wall Street.

George Murray

Gideon Fairman left the London firm of Perkins, Fairman & Heath in July 1822 and returned to the more tranquil life of Philadelphia. As soon as he got back, he learned that his old friend and partner, George Murray, had died only a few days earlier. We know little about the end of Murray's life, except that Dunlap called him a "reckless and improvident man who died poor."

There are at least two legal documents written near the end of his life that show how desperate his financial circumstances had become. One is a note written in November 1821 to Matthew Cary, the map publisher, setting out a schedule to repay a note for $248 "due tomorrow," another note for $170 due on December 14, and still another for $300. The second document is a "warrant of attorney filed and judgment entered" binding Murray to pay Christian Gobrecht of Philadelphia the sum of $8,308 in "lawful silver money of the United States." Apparently, Murray had failed to make good on a promissory note, and this legal action was taken to protect the lender.[1] However badly Murray may have mishandled his and other people's money, we should remember that he excelled at his profession and took under his wing many young lads whom he taught the basics of line engraving—men like William Humphrys, James B. Longacre, George S. Lang, et al.

Charles Toppan

Charles Toppan and Asa Spencer also left London at about the same time as Gideon Fairman, and like him, they returned to Philadelphia. Toppan disappeared from the city directories for the next seven years, but he probably returned to his old company, now named Fairman, Draper, Underwood & Company, located at 47 Sansom Street, or he may have worked as an independent engraver.[2] Toppan did go to New York in 1825, possibly with the intention of staying there permanently, and married Laura A. Noxon of Poughkeepsie, New York.[3] After losing some money in real-estate investments, he returned to Philadelphia in 1827, and after the death of Gideon Fairman that year, he joined with his old friend, John Draper, and together with James B. Longacre they formed a new partnership called Draper, Toppan, Longacre & Company, again at 47 Sansom Street.[4] Longacre did not stay more than a few months before leaving to pursue his own engraving business. By 1828 John Draper asked Thomas Underwood to return, which he did, and the partnership was now named Draper, Underwood & Company.

Toppan left the company about the same time as Longacre and set up a shop at 28 Sansom Street as an independent engraver and printer under the name of Charles Toppan & Company. He was there from 1829 to at least 1833. Sometime around 1830, Toppan briefly joined with Peter Maverick, a famous bank-note engraver of New York. They got at least one contract—that of the Bank of Penn Township, in Philadelphia—and printed one denomination of notes with the Toppan, Maverick & Company imprint. Peter Maverick died in June 1831, and this explains the company's short life. What Maverick contributed to this note, if anything, is not known.

James Barton Longacre

An engraved portrait of Oliver Hazard Perry as it appeared in *The National Portrait Gallery of Distinguished Americans*. Perry's portrait appears on several obsolete bank notes, as does the Battle of Lake Erie during the War of 1812, of which Perry was a part.

J.B. Longacre, the son of Peter Longacre, was born in Delaware County near the Philadelphia city boundary on August 11, 1794. He showed considerable artistic talent as a youth and was taken into the family and bookstore of John Watson, who later placed him with George Murray to learn engraving. Longacre left Murray in 1819 and began to work on his own. He attracted attention in 1820 with his large plate of Andrew Jackson modeled on the painting by Thomas Sully. The head of Jackson on this painting was later engraved by the firm of Rawdon, Wright, Hatch & Edson (New York) for use in the late 1840s on a $50 note of the Canal Bank of New Orleans. For most of the 1820s, Longacre found ready employment by drawing portraits from life and then engraving them in the stipple manner. He eventually became the finest stipple engraver in America. He may have engraved bank-note vignettes for Draper, Toppan, Longacre & Company, but if so, they were not signed, and it is more likely that he was a designer for the company. Sometime around 1833, and in connection with James Herring, a portrait printer in New York, Longacre conceived the idea of publishing *The National Portrait Gallery of Distinguished Americans*, a series of 147 biographical sketches of noted statesmen and military heroes. Longacre engraved 24 of these portraits and employed many of the best engravers in the country to do the rest. However, he set such a high standard with his engravings that he had to induce some European engravers to come over to finish the series, which was published in four octavo volumes between 1834 and 1839. The art critic W.L. Andrews said in 1902, "It is a book which deserves to be well bound, for it contains the finest cabinet-sized steel engraved portraits ever executed in this country." On September 16, 1844, Longacre was appointed Engraver and Die Sinker to the U.S. Mint in Philadelphia, succeeding the late Christian Gobrecht. He designed all the U.S. coins from that date until his death. He was also employed by the government of Chile to remodel all their coins and had finished that task shortly before he died on January 1, 1869, at age 74.[5] He had married Elizabeth

Stiles of New Jersey on May 29, 1826, and she died May 1, 1850.

The $50 note of the Canal Bank of New Orleans, Louisiana.

Moving Around

The reader may be confused by the frequent changes of a bank-note company's name or the "musical chairs" that the partners played in moving from one company to another. It happened much more in America than in Europe, and there are probably many reasons for this. American engravers changed jobs often because they were in search of better opportunities. It was the American thing to do. Naturally, if they signed contracts or "articles of association," they were constrained by the terms of those documents, but the available evidence suggests that most 19th-century bank-note engravers were hired by companies and paid salaries without formal written agreements. Therefore, engravers were free to leave for whatever reason crossed their minds. That's not to say that bank-note engravers were particularly impulsive or rebellious. Like the rest of us, they had families to feed and bills to pay, but they also saw that America was full of opportunities, and that nothing ventured was nothing gained. Social, economic, and banking conditions in Europe were very different, and engravers there were less willing to take risks. So, against this background of America's meteoric growth, we see a small number of actors constantly scurrying out of one doorway and into another. While it may seem tedious to name virtually all of these partnerships and dwell on the mundane details of their histories, like a zoologist classifying seemingly identical lizards, it is precisely this kind of data that helps us to understand the dynamics of the industry during the early period of its development. Most bank-note partnerships had only a few key employees, little in the way of capital stock, and they usually existed for only a few years before changing partners. Bank-note companies also changed addresses on a frequent basis, sometimes to find larger or more secure facilities, sometimes to find a more prestigious location, and sometimes because new construction blocked the all-important light needed by their engravers.

Independent engravers often served as agents for distant bank-note companies, a symbiosis that helped both the local engraver and the parent firm. It was a common practice for engravers in a branch office to engrave dies, especially portrait vignettes or historical scenes which could stand alone and be used in almost any bank-note design, and send them to the main office, where they became part of the company's stock. Independent engravers often did business for the book trade—engraving a frontispiece, illustrating fictional stories, and engraving portraits—or doing illustrations for magazines and journals. Before photography came of age, copper-plate engraving and woodcuts were virtually the only means available for pictorial illustration. Notes issued during the colonial period often relied heavily on letter engraving. In the early 19th century, vignette engraving became increasingly important, and this was followed by the introduction of mechanical engraving. Engravers began to specialize in specific areas of art—allegorical, historical, landscape, portraits, etc.—and even in specific objects—locomotives, ships, animals, architecture, etc. Even letter engraving specialized into script and square lettering, and ornamental engravers added border elements and botanicals. Designers or "modelers" were added to company payrolls, as were siderographers, plate printers, and men to harden or anneal steel dies. After the early 1860s, women were hired at the Bureau of Engraving and Printing to count or cut notes and perform other menial tasks, and this practice spread throughout the industry.

A locomotive vignette found on a $5 bank note
of the Clinton Bank, Westernport, Maryland.

A ship vignette found on a $2 bank note
of the Lumbermen's Bank, Rockford, Illinois.

A horse vignette found on a $1 bank note
of the Bucksport Bank, Bucksport, Maine.

Bank-note customers were usually private and state banks and occasionally a railroad, steamboat, or insurance company. The bank-note salesmen sometimes stressed the artistic designs and well-executed engravings printed on good-quality paper as their selling points, but bankers were more often focused on the cost of their bank notes and cared less about their art. Business agents sometimes placed ads in newspapers and waited for inquiries from bankers, but more often they paid a personal visit to a bank, taking along a "specimen sheet" to show examples of the company's stock vignettes and the bank notes they had designed and engraved for others. Almost every company produced specimen sheets, and many of these still exist. Ordinary men, and even some ladies, had to learn the fundamentals of banking and the need to recognize counterfeit

money when they saw it. As the economy grew, so did the people's sophistication about money.

Thomas Underwood

Thomas Underwood is a good example of a highly mobile engraver. He was born February 5, 1791, in Philadelphia, the son of Robert and Jane Wagton Underwood. We know little about his social life, except that he married an intelligent woman of French descent, Aletia d'Andelot, who was 20 years his junior, and they had 8 children. Underwood was considered a good engraver. He was a partner in several firms, including the previously mentioned Fairman, Draper, Underwood & Company, which lasted from 1823 to 1827. With Fairman's death in 1827, John Draper continued with Thomas Underwood until 1833 as Draper, Underwood & Company. In 1833 two new partners were taken—Robert Bald and Asa Spencer. Bald had been an engraver with John Draper since 1823, and Spencer had worked with Draper even longer. Spencer brought along his geometric lathe, and this gave the company a considerable advantage. They were still at 47 Sansom Street in Philadelphia but soon also found business at 14 Wall Street in New York, which was negotiated by their agents, Nathaniel Jocelyn and his younger brother, Simeon Smith Jocelyn, both of whom were bank-note engravers at various times.[6]

John Draper ended his association with Bald, Spencer, and Underwood about 1835, selling his property at 47 Sansom Street and working thereafter with Charles Toppan and others. That left Bald, Spencer, and Underwood to form their own company, which they did, at the old 47 Sansom Street address, indicating they probably bought the building from Draper. The three partners styled their new company Underwood, Bald & Spencer, and for the next two years they printed for at least 18 different banks and were therefore moderately successful. In 1837 these three partners brought in the portrait engraver Samuel Hufty and set up offices at the Exchange Building in Philadelphia under the name Underwood, Bald, Spencer & Hufty. They operated a branch office in New York at 14 Wall Street under the management of the Jocelyn brothers. After 1841 they were loosely associated with Samuel Stiles, though his name does not appear in city directories. Sometime around 1840, their New York office hired Moseley I. Danforth, who had just returned from studies in London, and a die sinker named Charles C. Wright. That branch office then took the name of Danforth, Underwood & Company. Underwood remained in Philadelphia where he lived at 31 North 11th Street. The Philadelphia partnership—Underwood, Bald, Spencer & Hufty—was enormously successful, printing notes for at least 115 banks that are listed in the Haxby *Standard Catalog of United States Obsolete Bank Notes 1782–1866.* Thomas Underwood apparently made enough money in the business that he was able to retire in 1844. The next year, he moved to Lafayette, Indiana, where he died from "Asiatic Cholera" on July 13, 1849, at age 54, while his wife was two months pregnant with their last child.[7]

Danforth, Wright & Company Bank-Note Plant, 1853.
An engraver and two etchers at work.

John Draper's Partnerships

John Draper sometimes had more than one iron in the fire. While he was setting up the firm of Draper, Underwood, Bald & Spencer in 1833, he was also doing business as a partner in the firm of Draper, Toppan, Longacre & Bull, organized the same year. The Bull in this partnership was Marcus Bull, a mechanic who had gone to London with Jacob Perkins in 1819. The partnership lasted less than a year, and Bull was gone. The remaining company, styled as Draper, Toppan, Longacre & Company, was located at No. 60 Walnut Street and lasted until 1839. It also had a branch office in New York at No. 1 Wall Street. Draper then set up a larger company known as Draper, Toppan & Company which lasted until he resigned in 1844. The addresses were 103 Locust Street in 1840, then 5 Bank Place from 1840 to 1842, and finally 76-1/2 Walnut Street from 1843 to 1844. Charles Toppan was a partner from 1841 to 1844. Simeon Smith Jocelyn was an employee from 1840 to 1844, working out of various addresses in New York City. Peter H. Draper, John's son, came into the company in 1843. He probably left the next year with his father. William Cumming Smillie was a letter engraver for the firm from 1840 to 1844 and continued on after the re-organization. Charles Harrison also worked for the company from 1840 to 1841, but he remained in New York City. Draper, Toppan & Company also opened a branch office in Boston in 1843 at 60 State Street, but it changed its address several times over the next few years.

Robert Bald

Robert Bald was a bank-note engraver, but we don't know his specialty. He was born in Scotland about 1793 and came to the United States from Glasgow in 1823, when his name first appears in the Philadelphia directory. The next year the directory shows he was an engraver at No. 47 Sansom Street, the address of Draper, Underwood & Company. In 1833 he was admitted to the firm which then changed its name to Draper, Underwood, Bald & Spencer. In 1837 the firm admitted Samuel Hufty as a partner and became Draper, Underwood, Bald, Spencer & Hufty. John Draper withdrew from this company around 1837. Asa Spencer was joined by his son, Asa Spencer Jr., about 1840. Robert Bald retired in 1848 and is listed as "gentleman" thereafter in the city directories. Two of his sons, Robert L. Bald and J. Dorsey Bald, carried on the family business.

The Underwood-Bald-Spencer group of companies had plenty of competition in Philadelphia, primarily from Charles Toppan and his associates, but also from two lesser groups founded by John Draper and Charles Welsh on the one hand, and by J. Dorsey Bald on the other. Toppan had been a partner with John Draper and others for about 10 years. When Draper left the company in 1844, Toppan started a new company with Samuel H. Carpenter, at 76-1/2 Walnut Street, styled as Toppan, Carpenter & Company. Samuel H. Carpenter was an accountant who had been the assistant cashier at the large and influential banking house of Stephen Girard for several years. Toppan obviously made a wise decision hiring this young man and using his many contacts in banking circles to win bank-note contracts. Carpenter was also valued for his business and accounting skills and was one of the first men (Tracy Edson was another) to be hired by a bank-note company as a businessman.[8] Samuel's brother, Joseph R. Carpenter, had artistic talent and was soon brought into the company as a designer. In 1844 the company opened a branch office in New York, first at 16 Wall Street, then at 31 Wall Street from 1845 to 1847, and finally at 29 Wall Street during 1848 and 1849. Simeon Smith Jocelyn and his brother Nathaniel were also agents and/or engravers at that branch office, and William Cumming Smillie worked for the company out of those addresses.

The Draper, Underwood, Bald & Spencer title appears on this $5 bank note of the Phoenix Bank, Connecticut.

Some Of The Others

The Saulniers

The main office of Toppan, Carpenter & Company, which remained in Philadelphia, also hired Henry Engard Saulnier, a letter engraver who had trained under Cephas Childs and had worked off and on for Toppan since 1832. He signed the original partnership agreement (March 1844) which was to last for three years and eleven months, expiring in February 1848, but continued on with this company until it became one of the member firms of the American Bank Note Company in 1858.[9] He worked for the American Bank Note Company for a long time, possibly into the 1880s. While working for Toppan, he learned to operate the transfer press and gave up engraving to pursue that specialty. His son, Henry B. Saulnier, born in Philadelphia in 1843, also learned to engrave and became the manager of the American Bank Note Company's branch office in Philadelphia. He died November 1, 1894.

The Sartains

The Sartain family was one of the most influential and respected families in the artistic community in Philadelphia. John Sartain was born in London on October 24, 1808. He apprenticed to be an engraver and learned both line engraving and the new art of mezzotint.[10] He came to the United States in July 1830 at the age of 22, already married, and settled in Philadelphia. He was a good pictorial engraver and soon found work making prints for a number of magazines. He also began working off and on for Charles Toppan about 1832. In a letter that Sartain wrote to Joseph Willcox, of the Willcox paper mill, he mentions that he only engraved one die during his entire bank-note career and was primarily engaged in designing notes.[11] His one die was a head of Benjamin Franklin from the "French portrait," probably one of the portraits made of Franklin by Duplessis. He may have worked for other Philadelphia bank-note companies as a part-time designer. He is remembered mainly as the artist who introduced mezzotint engraving to

America. He made more than 1,500 prints for a number of magazines. Of his eight children, four of them—Samuel, Henry, William, and Emily—became artists or printers. John Sartain died in Philadelphia on October 25, 1897, shortly after finishing his autobiography, *Reminiscences of a Very Old Man.*[12]

An engraving of a portrait of Benjamin Franklin painted by J.A. Duplessis in 1783.

Charles Welsh

Charles Welsh was born in Pennsylvania about 1812. His early life has not been researched, and we know only a few details of his professional life. He became active as an independent bank-note engraver at 191 Christian Street in Philadelphia in 1841. In 1844 he appears to have been a partner with A.B. Walter, an engraver of large plates chiefly in mezzotint, and with his brother, Joseph Walter, a plate printer. That company was called Welsh & Walter, Bank Note Engravers.

Welsh joined Draper & Company in 1845. Their company consisted of John, Robert, and William Draper. In 1851 the company's name was changed to Draper, Welsh & Company at 22-1/2 Merchants' Exchange. In 1854 Nathaniel Jocelyn joined Draper & Welsh at a Philadelphia branch office at the southeast corner of 3rd and Chestnut streets. This was named the American Bank Note Company and was the first firm to use that name. Later, in 1858, Jocelyn was one of the people who helped to create the consolidation of seven bank-note companies to form a new firm also called the American Bank Note Company. Charles Welsh died sometime after 1860. Gene Hessler (*The Engraver's Line*) mentions a Charles Welsh who worked as a transfer-press

operator at the Philadelphia office of the American Bank Note Company in 1861 and 1862. This is almost certainly the same man.

John William Casilear

John William Casilear, born in New York City in 1811, is far more famous as an artist than an engraver. He began his career as an apprentice to Peter Maverick in 1826 to learn engraving. He studied painting with Asher Durand in 1831 and worked as an engraver during the 1830s. He joined the New York branch of Toppan, Carpenter & Company in 1850, and the partners changed the firm's name to Toppan, Carpenter, Casilear & Company. The main office in Philadelphia was still at 76-1/2 Walnut Street. By the middle of the 1850s Casilear was devoting all his time to landscape painting.

The talent in the New York office was fully equal to that of the Philadelphia plant, and by the middle of the 1850s included William Cumming Smillie; his brother James Smillie, a pictorial engraver; James's son, William Main Smillie, a letter engraver; and one of John W. Casilear's sons, Francis A. Casilear. The Smillies and the Casilears made important contributions to bank-note engraving, but since most of them worked in New York or other places, their biographies will come later.

The Toppan Group

Colonists pray for deliverance from an Indian attack on this engraving by Toppan, Carpenter & Co., 1856.

Toppan, Carpenter & Company also opened a branch office in Cincinnati in 1851 at 119 Walnut Street, first under the direction of Charles Jewett and later under Elijah C. Middleton, which lasted until 1858. The company also opened a branch office in Boston in 1852 at 68 State Street, which lasted until 1855, when it was then relocated to No. 20 State Street, continuing in business until the parent company joined the American Bank Note Company in 1858. They opened an office in Montreal, Canada, on Great Saint James Street, beginning in 1854, which lasted until 1858. The Haxby statistics show that the Toppan group of companies was very successful. Charles Toppan & Company printed bank notes for at least 30 different banks in 12 states. As the company's reputation grew, so did their business. Between 1844 and 1850, the period during which Samuel Carpenter was directing the company's business out of the Philadelphia plant, their imprint appears on no less than 173 different banks spread across 26 states from New England to the deep South. After 1850, when John Casilear joined the company and the New York office was busy, Toppan, Carpenter, Casilear & Company printed notes for 197 different banks. These statistics do not reveal the total number of notes printed, and obviously some of the banks were small affairs with low-volume print orders. Others failed soon after they were established. Still, the Haxby *Standard Catalog of United States Obsolete Bank Notes 1782–1866* does provide data that shows the relative sizes of the different bank-note companies, as does the *Whitman Encyclopedia of Obsolete Paper Money*. From that data, one can see that the Toppan group of companies was a major force in the industry.

Little Is Known

There were a number of bank-note engravers who worked in Philadelphia about whom we know very little. George S. Lang was born in Chester County, Pennsylvania, in 1790. W.S. Baker (*American Engravers Upon Copper and Steel*) says Lang was a pupil of George Murray in 1815. He was apparently a good line engraver, but most of his work was in unsigned bank-note vignettes. Joseph Hufty, a brother of the previously mentioned Samuel Hufty, was a copper-plate and steel engraver and was listed that way in the

Philadelphia directory in 1823. He died at an early age sometime in the mid-1820s.

"Washington Passing the Delaware," a scene engraved by George S. Lang.

Consolidation?

By the late 1840s, most of the larger Philadelphia bank-note companies had established branch offices in New York to take advantage of the larger number of skilled engravers that worked there as well as the better business opportunities. There was probably no single reason for New York's ascendancy but rather a combination of factors. Population, industry, transportation, banking, publishing, and Wall Street all had a positive effect. By the middle of the 1850s, the dominance of New York on the bank-note industry was well established, and Rawdon, Wright, Hatch & Edson was the largest bank-note company in America. But change was in the wind. As the number of bank-note companies grew, competition drove down the price the companies could charge for their services. By the middle of the 1850s, the capacity of the bank-note companies was beginning to exceed the demand for their service. As this situation grew more critical, a few far-sighted leaders in the industry began to propose that the larger companies should merge to form a giant corporation: one that could win the vast majority of new work and effectively eliminate the competition of the small, independent companies that remained. Whatever company owners thought about consolidation, they realized that if they were not invited to join, or chose not to join for some reason, their businesses might suffer greatly. It was either join or be trampled. What was it that Brutus said to his men? "There is a tide in the affairs of men, which taken at the flood, leads on to fortune. Omitted, all the voyage of their life is bound in shallows and in miseries."[13]

A two-page printed brochure for Rawdon, Wright, Hatch & Edson,
advertising their engraving and printing services.
The first page (shown) illustrates examples of their work;
the second page included a price list.

Chapter 6

New York Takes Over

Map of New York.

After the Laurentide Ice Sheet retreated from North America several thousand years ago, the area we now call New York City was left with some of the most intricate harbors in the world. By the time Verrazano arrived in 1524, the Hudson River was about 17-feet deep, enough to dock ships coming in from the Atlantic and yet shallow enough so that piers could be built at the water's edge. By 1800 New York City had a population of 80,000 people and was already a regional center of commerce. The construction of the Erie Canal in 1825 connected New York to the natural resources and commercial interests of the Midwest and allowed the city to rise to prominence as a national center of business and finance. By 1860 New York City, which was then the island of Manhattan, had a population of 600,000, and a suburb called Brooklyn added 200,000 more, making the combined metropolitan area not only the largest city in America but one of the largest cities in the world—outranked only by London, Paris, and Tokyo. The rapid growth had lead to the creation of banks and the need for bank notes. In colonial times, silversmiths and ordinary printers engraved

and printed the notes that were needed, but it didn't take long for a professional class of specialists to take over that work. Although these men were often called "bank-note engravers," they took on all kinds of engraving work, from book and magazine illustrations, name plates for doors and coffins, stationery and watch papers, to dog collars and the occasional subject plate for a print to commemorate an historic event or the portrait of a famous man. As populations increased, and there was need for greater numbers of bank notes, the secondary jobs dwindled.

William Satchwell Leney

One of the first of these early bank-note engravers in New York was William S. Leney, born in London on January 16, 1769.[1] He was apprenticed to the engraver Peltro W. Tompkins and became an accomplished portrait engraver in stipple. He was employed for Boydell's edition of Shakespeare, for which he engraved five illustrations. He was engraving under his own name in London as early as 1791. Before he came to America, he married Sarah White in Lambeth, England. Together they immigrated to America around 1805 and settled in New York City, where Leney became one of the most-successful engravers of the period, doing portraits of George Washington, John Adams, Robert Fulton, and Captain James Lawrence, among others. He also worked in line on landscape and subject plates. Stauffer says that his New York account books show that he was paid between $100 and $150 for engraving a plate, a large price for that period.[2]

Starting about 1812, Leney was associated with William Rollinson in the bank-note–engraving business. Rollinson had just invented a new ruling machine that could make wavy lines, and this created a sensation among the engravers all across

America. This was not a true partnership, however, since Leney engraved the vignettes and charged Rollinson for the copper and the engraving in each case. The Leney & Rollinson imprint is found on the notes of 33 different banks in 9 different states, according to the Haxby *Standard Catalog*.[3] They printed for 16 banks in New York alone. Leney was a prudent businessman and managed to keep his money. He left America about 1820 and bought a farm of 300 acres at Longue Pointe, Quebec, on the St. Laurence River, just below Montreal. He continued in his profession for a time and engraved the first notes of the Bank of Montreal, but he soon retired and spent the rest of his time in leisure. He and Sarah had nine children. He died at his farm on November 26, 1831, at the age 62.

Hand-colored rose prints engraved in stipple by Pierre Joseph Redouté.

A portrait engraving done in stipple of Dolly Madison after a painting by Gilbert Stuart.

William Rollinson

Born in Dudley, Worcester, England, on April 15, 1762, William Rollinson was brought up in the business of chasing fancy buttons. At the age of 20, he married Mary Johnson in Birmingham, England. At the end of November 1788, he paid 20 guineas to sail from Liverpool to New York, leaving behind his wife and first child. During the voyage, he improvised tools and began to engrave ornaments and jewelry for the officers and passengers. He arrived in New York on February 15, 1789, and within a few weeks he came to the attention of General Henry Knox, the first secretary of war. General Knox employed Rollinson to chase the Arms of the United States on a set of gilt buttons for the coat to be worn by President George Washington on his inauguration. Rollinson refused payment for his work, saying the honor was payment enough. About a year after his arrival, Rollinson went back to England and brought over his wife and child.

A portrait of James Lawrence engraved by William Rollinson in the stipple method.

For a time, Rollinson made a decent living working for silversmiths, but in 1791, without any previous knowledge of the profession or ever having seen an engraver at work, he made his first attempt at copper-plate engraving—a small bust of General George Washington in uniform. Stauffer says that Rollinson improved rapidly in the art of engraving and the scope of his work broadened accordingly. In 1795 he engraved a

"Plan of Washington." About 1800 Rollinson began engraving a portrait of Alexander Hamilton after a painting by Archibald Robertson. According to his biographers, he had no knowledge of rebiting and other processes used by those who had been brought up in the profession. Rebiting refers to the process of repeatedly etching an area of the plate, such as the background, with an acid to achieve the right tonal color, usually black. Biting roughens the surface, which then holds more ink. To make a background for the portrait, he invented a method of using a roulette inserted in a ruling machine. A roulette is a circular wheel having numerous small teeth on its periphery. This is usually mounted in a handle and rolled across an area of a plate to roughen the surface so it will hold more ink. After Hamilton was killed by Colonel Aaron Burr in a duel in 1804, his friends asked Rollinson to finish the engraving as quickly as possible. This was published by Rollinson and Robertson in 1805 and met with a good sale.

In 1811 Rollinson decided he should add banknote engraving to his skills. He gave considerable thought to the question of why counterfeiting was so easy, and based on his previous experience with ruling machines, he decided to modify his instrument so that it would make closely spaced lines in a waved fashion. He then approached William S. Leney to suggest that they had the skill and reputation to form a profitable business making bank notes. Rollinson's form letter, addressed to bankers in New York and dated March 18, 1811, reads as follows:

Sir:

The desideratum that has been long wanted to prevent the counterfeiting of Bank Notes is some kind of work that is of itself simple of appearance, and obvious at first glance, yet impossible to be imitated in the common mode of engraving. I take the liberty of laying before you a specimen of work containing all those requisites, entirely novel, and of my own invention, and which cannot be imitated by first rate artists so as to deceive common observers. It has not been until after many abortive attempts, great loss of time and expense, that I have been able to bring my invention to perfection, and to make the Note still more perfect, I have procured the assistance of Mr. William S. Leney, of this city, to engrave the vignette. In regard to both design and execution of picture work, Mr. Leney is allowed to be the first artist in America, and is a gentleman of very respectable rank in life. The other parts of the Note are engraved by myself, and if, on inspection, the novelty of the work, the mathematical accuracy of the lines, with their beautiful intersections should be deemed worthy of your encouragement, I shall be happy to execute any thing you may be pleased to order. It may also be necessary to observe, that I am not confined to the variety of figures introduced in the specimen but can vary them at pleasure, yet can always make any pattern exactly alike.

I beg leave to refer you to either of the following gentlemen in regard to my character and standing in society, Robert Lenox, Esq., or John Slidell, Esq., President of the Mechanics Bank, both of this city.[4]

A specimen of a Leney & Rollinson note shows a vertical panel at the right with the waved line ruling. Although the machine could make perfectly parallel lines that waved back and forth in concert with adjacent ones, it was also capable of making lines that were not parallel and verged toward their adjacent lines in a pattern that resembled the moiré of watered silk. Even more complex, the machine could be set to make sinusoidal lines that curved up and down like the lines traced on a modern seismograph, but with a high frequency of up and down spikes. The effect could be imitated by hand engraving, but it would require a laborious and time-consuming effort, thus giving the machine a strong advantage over the counterfeiters.

Rollinson continued to engrave to the age of 74. He wrote in his will that he was in feeble health but lived another two years and died on April 21, 1842. He was buried in New York City in St. John's graveyard, which later became Hudson Park.

Bank notes engraved by Leney & Rollinson,
showing Rollinson's waved-line metal ruling on the end panels.

Peter Maverick

Peter Maverick seems to have been destined to be a bank-note engraver.[5] His father, Peter Rushton Maverick, was one of the earliest engravers in New York as well as a die sinker and copper-plate printer.[6] His sons grew up in a household in which engraving and printing came almost as naturally as breathing. His brothers—Andrew and Samuel Maverick—both followed their father's profession. The Maverick home in those days, 3 Crown Street in Manhattan, was also a workshop and a training school for young men on their way to becoming prominent engravers. One of them was William Dunlap, a painter and theatrical producer best known to us today as an historian of the "arts of design," who had already studied in the studios of Europe and now trained with the elder Peter Maverick during 1787 and 1788, to learn the "theory and practice of etching." It is likely, though not yet proven, that Benjamin R. Tanner learned to engrave under Maverick. Francis Kearny, who later followed Tanner to Philadelphia, was apprenticed to the elder Maverick beginning in 1798. Young Peter, sitting in classes with the apprentices, learned the secret of the trade over and over again, and at the age of nine, he engraved his first work, a scene of Adam and Eve standing in the Garden of Eden next to

the Tree of the Knowledge of Good and Evil, with its forbidden fruit and a talking serpent.[7] Although this was a simple relief block, it showed that the young Peter Maverick had already learned how to transfer a drawing to the block, how to cut away the surfaces that he wanted to print as white areas, and how to fill in the outline of the picture with different kinds of strokes to show foliage, tree bark, and shadows. It was a remarkable work, considering the artist was only nine years old.

On May 15, 1802, at the ripe age of 21, the younger Peter Maverick married 19-year-old Mary Griffin. During the next seven years, the young couple moved seven times, though no one knows why. Maverick was a good engraver and constantly in demand by the New York publishers that wanted bookplates or subject plates engraved. He turned out a steady stream of diplomas, certificates, business cards, family crests, tickets, maps, and similar material. He also engraved bank notes, though it's difficult to date his earliest work in this field. His notes for the State Bank of New Jersey must have been engraved between 1812 and 1814, the only years that the bank was in operation. It's also known that Maverick did bank-note work in association with Leney & Rollinson, probably around 1812. Today the Maverick imprint, in one form or another, is found on 42 different banks in 9 different states and at least 1 foreign country (Colombia). In 1809, shortly after a sister died, Peter moved his family and shop out of Manhattan to a 20-acre farm about a mile and a half north of Newark, New Jersey. He paid $3,125 to a coach-maker in New York for the land and a house. Newark was then a town of about 8,000 people. Peter planned to set up a training school to teach engraving to apprentices. His plan was simple—at the same time they were learning basic skills, his students could help him with the workload of his busy shop, and the fees they paid for an apprenticeship would give him a steady flow of cash. Peter bought additional land adjoining his farm and began to raise merino sheep. His business ventures were successful enough that he could afford two black servants, a man named Pompey and his wife, Susan.

P. Maverick & Durand's imprint found on a bank note.

The War of 1812 was especially propitious for Peter. In the fall, a young man named Asher B. Durand was taken into an apprenticeship. Asher had been working in his father's watch-repair and clock-making shop in Maplewood, New Jersey, when he came to the notice of a painter named Enos Smith, who recognized his artistic talents. Smith convinced Asher's father that the boy should be placed with an engraver to learn those skills and recommended W.S. Leney as the best man around to teach him. Accordingly, Asher, along with his two brothers, John and Cyrus, went with Smith to see Mr. Leney in New York. They made the journey by foot from Maplewood to Newark, and then to Elizabeth Town, where they took a ferry to New York. When they finally arrived at Leney's house in the upper Bowery, they were disappointed to learn that he charged $1,000 for a five-year apprenticeship and that the family would have to pay all additional expenses. The Durand family could not afford Leney's fee, and Asher returned home. Enos Smith then suggested they apply to Peter Maverick, who already had a few apprentices and was recognized for his teaching ability. Maverick charged only $100 a year, payable at the end of a five-year term, and required the boy to pay only for his clothing and incidental expenses. Asher's father agreed to the terms.

Durand's apprenticeship ended in the fall of 1817, and almost immediately he formed a partnership with his teacher under the name Maverick & Durand. Maverick knew that Asher possessed a first-rate talent and was eager to begin business with him. Cyrus Durand joined the company in a loose partnership in 1818, and Maverick changed the name of the company to Maverick, Durand & Company. Cyrus remained in New York City with a shop at the corner of Pine Street and Broadway and used an improved version (1818) of his recently invented geometric lathe to engrave the borders of uniface notes with intricate patterns of mathematically perfect shape. The geometric shapes could not be imitated by any other engravers, and this gave a distinct advantage to the Durand shop. Asher moved to New York to join his brother, but Maverick stayed on his farm and considered the shop on Pine Street to be his branch office.

At the height of his success, Maverick became suspicious of Asher Durand's intentions. He had an understanding with Durand that he (Maverick) would have first choice of any work coming to the company, and if he declined the work, Asher could take the job. Their business relationship was strained in March 1820, when Maverick found out that Colonel John Trumbull, a former aide-de-camp to General George Washington and a painter as well, had signed a contract with Durand to engrave his 12-foot by 18-foot painting that depicted the presentation of the draft of the Declaration of Independence to Congress. The painting has since become something of a national icon, hanging in the Rotunda of the Capitol since 1826, and appearing on the back of our current $2 bill. But in 1820, Trumbull was having difficulty finding an engraver equal to the job. He wanted a foreign engraver and asked James Heath of London to do the work, but Heath required $6,000 for the job, and Trumbull refused. Trumbull then signed a contract with the Italian engraver Mauro Gandolfi at a price of $4,000. Gandolfi had come to New York in 1816 and was already famous for engravings he brought with him.[8] In the brief time he was here, however, the temperamental Gandolfi became increasingly angry with American culture. He was incensed that the Americans would not allow art students to draw from nude models, something that was never given a second thought in Europe, which he took as an indication that Americans were not serious about art and would have no appreciation for his talents. After signing the contract, Gandolfi realized he had not asked for enough money. Trumbull's painting depicted a large number of men, each portrait requiring detailed work. When Gandolfi calculated that engraving the work would take four or five years, the price agreed upon wasn't nearly enough. He expected to live in a large house at a level of luxury far beyond that given to common artists, as he had done in Bologna for most of his life. The cost of living in New York was, however, far too high to accommodate such plans. Angered by this situation, he returned to Italy. Trumbull then signed a contract with Asher Durand in 1820, whose price was only $3,000, with payments spread over four years. The engraving was finished, printed, and published in October 1823. This single work established Durand's reputation as an engraver in pure line and brought him considerable prosperity.

At the same time that the Trumbull affair was coming to light, Peter Maverick had decided he should leave Newark and return to New York City. A general depression had begun in 1817 and was at its worst in 1820. Although his business was somewhat protected from the immediate economic effects, Maverick could not help but notice that several industries had failed or moved away, that the population had decreased greatly, and that other businessmen were pessimistic about the future. Maverick took a greater-than-usual interest in his office in New York. After he learned that Durand had signed a secret contract with Trumbull on March 7, he wrote a letter asking Durand to give up his occupancy of the office on Pine Street and to stop opening the company's mail. By March 25 Maverick had discovered that Durand had taken a first choice of contracts on three occasions in the last month. Maverick also wrote that Durand had not sent him any work in the last six months, even though he knew that Maverick was having a difficult time meeting the needs of his family. Durand answered by saying that he had only broken the partnership agreement in the interest of getting the contract with Trumbull that would otherwise have gone to another engraver, and he thought the real reason for Maverick's anger was his jealousy of Durand's success. Durand was also distrustful because a number of his engravings had been published under Maverick's name without credit being given to Durand.

Subsequent letters only embittered Maverick more, and the partnership dissolved.

"The Signing of the Declaration of Independence" found on a bank note of Nebraska.

In a curious sequel to this story, Durand completed the engraving of Trumbull's "Signing of the Declaration of Independence," as it was incorrectly called, and asked Maverick to do the printing from the plate. Humiliating at that was, Maverick probably had no choice but to accede to Durand's request. He needed the money. According to the records that Stephen D. Stephens found, Maverick and his assistant, Mr. Neal, purchased a total of 506 sheets of paper from the Gilpin mill at Brandywine, Pennsylvania, at a cost of $75 a ream to do this work in January and February of 1823.[9] The records in Trumbull's account books show that the work continued for several years and that the prints sold at $20 a copy, a large price in those days.

Maverick continued to engrave bank notes, but since the field was increasingly competitive, he added lithography to his bag of tricks in 1824, only five years after the method was first used in America.[10] He also continued his apprenticeship program. One of the boys under his tutelage was John W. Casilear, who started with Maverick at the age of 15. Casilear would later study under Durand, as well, and then go on to be a banknote engraver for some years before leaving the profession to become a landscape painter. William J. Stone (1798–1865) studied engraving with Maverick, as did Maverick's two oldest daughters who worked in his shop as pupils and assistants. Emily and Maria Ann Maverick were among the first female engravers in the United States, doing portrait work in stipple and copying the original illustrations of Heath's English edition of Shakespeare for an American edition that probably dates to about 1830. Another student was John Frederick Kensett. After spending a year or so in his father and uncle's engraving shop in New Haven, Connecticut, Kensett moved to New York in 1829 to study under Peter Maverick. That same year his father died and he had to move back to New Haven where he rejoined his uncle, Alfred Daggett, in the engraving firm of Daggett, Hinman & Company. In 1835, after falling out with his uncle, he moved back to New York and joined the bank-note company of Rawdon, Wright, & Hatch, where he worked for two years. He then moved to Albany, New York, and joined the bank-note firm of Hall, Packard & Cushman, where he became highly successful as an engraver. He left Albany in 1840 to spend the next seven years studying art in Europe.

An interesting contest that took place about 1825 shows Maverick's inventive nature. Edwin and Charles Starr, with Elihu White, had invented a method of producing bank notes by letterpress (type), claiming their method was counterfeit-proof. To show confidence in their boast, they deposited a $500 forfeit with Mr. Fleming, the cashier of the Mechanics' Bank, to be awarded to anyone who could engrave a successful counterfeit. Maverick accepted the challenge and won the award. Some complained that his method should not have won since it failed to produce a raised impression on the back of the note, something that is characteristic of letterpress work. Since we don't have a detailed description of his method, or Maverick's note, it is impossible to know for certain what Maverick did, but one possibility is that he used type as punches and hammered the typefaces into soft steel or copper and then made a relief plate from the intaglio plate, printing his note from the relief plate. That would give a bank note having no impression on the back. It is also possible that he made the counterfeit lithographically.

Around the same time, Maverick designed and engraved a sheet of four bank notes (1, 2, 3, and 5 pesos) for the Republica de Colombia, but the notes were never issued. A specimen sheet of the unsigned, uniface notes remains in the United States. Simon Bolivar had just defeated the Spanish Army in South America and was establishing new, independent countries. It isn't known if Bolivar asked Maverick to design the notes or if Maverick took the project on his own initiative.

Simon Bolivar in bronze by Adamo Tadolina.

The American Academy of Fine Arts was founded in New York in 1816, and Peter Maverick was elected a member that year. But in the mid-1820s, an active and vocal group of artists within the Academy became disenchanted with the governing body, saying that the leaders lacked both business and administrative experience, were doing nothing to attract new artists, and were deaf to criticism. The opposition called themselves the "Drawing Association" and threatened to split completely with the Academy. They finally acted in 1826, founding a new institution called the National Academy of Design. Several bank-note engravers were members of this academy, including Peter Maverick, who helped to form the new academy and organized its first exhibition. The *Historic Annals of the Academy* refers to his excellent letter-engraving and bank-note work.

The last few years of Peter's life were difficult. In September of 1822 his son, Raphael, died at the age of five months. In July of the following year his daughter Caroline died at age three. In the late summer of 1825 his wife Mary, who had borne him 16 children in 23 years of marriage, became ill with "consumption," or what we now call pulmonary tuberculosis. She died on August 11, 1825. Peter soon decided to marry Matilda Brown. His children were resentful of their new mother, especially when Peter and Matilda decided to get married on May 15, the 26th anniversary of his marriage to his first wife. Peter had two children with Matilda—a daughter who lived only a short time, and a second daughter named Augusta, born on August 23, 1830. On June 7, 1831, Peter Maverick died of "decay of the heart," as it was described on his death certificate. He was then 50 years old. He was buried in St. John's cemetery, and a stone marker was inscribed "Sacred to the Memory of Peter Maverick, who departed this life June 7, 1831." Near the end of the century, the burial ground was taken by the city for a public park. Records were made of the inscriptions on the gravestones, which were then buried. The park has now become a commercial parking area, which motorists emerging from the Holland Tunnel see at their right.

After his death, an inventory was taken of Maverick's shop, showing that it was not only a large establishment but also one very well equipped. The inventory listed one copper-plate press, four presses not otherwise identified, two iron-screw presses, three lithographic presses, and one iron lithographic press. There were three ruling machines and one item listed only as a "machine," which was sold to Asher Durand. There were also 2,000 square inches of copper plate that sold at 2¢ to 3¢ an inch and unmeasured copper plate that sold for $24. His paper was of various kinds and sizes and sold for nearly $300. His lithographic stones, weighing more than two and a half tons, sold for 10¢ a pound.

Other Mavericks

There are a few other Mavericks who should be mentioned to clarify their relationships and accomplishments. Andrew Maverick, one of Peter Maverick's brothers, was born May 26, 1782. He married Catherine Dow in June 1804, moved out of his father's house, and set up his own shop for copper-plate printing. He took out a patent, dated April 17, 1810, and titled "Mode of putting on the ink in copperplate printing." That patent was lost in the fire at the Patent Office in 1836, and there is no copy or description of it. There is no evidence that Andrew ever engraved, so he is assumed to be a copper-plate printer only. He had a shop at 21 Liberty Street in New York City at the time of his death in 1826.

Peter Maverick's half-brother, Samuel, was born in New York City on June 5, 1789. On his 15th birthday, Samuel began a 6-year apprenticeship to his brother-in-law, James Woodham, to become a mariner, but that lasted only a short time. He married Mary Howell in 1808 and set up a shop for copper-plate printing. Apparently, he did a little bit of engraving for book publishers in 1824 and may have engraved one bank note, but printing was his chief occupation. He died in New York on December 4, 1845. Samuel R. Maverick was Samuel Maverick's second son. He was born on February 19, 1812. He was apparently a copper-plate printer, like his father. He moved to New Orleans in 1839 and died there on August 24 of the same year.

Asher B. Durand

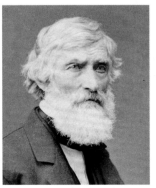

Asher B. Durand.

Asher Brown Durand was born on August 21, 1796, at Jefferson Village (now Maplewood) in the township of Springfield, Essex County, New Jersey. He was the sixth of seven brothers, two of whom, like Asher, were highly skilled. Asher's father was a descendant of Huguenots who were driven to the United States by persecution. His mother was of Dutch origin and a descendant of the early settlers of New Jersey. Asher began his education at age seven in the public school of Jefferson Village, studying reading, writing, arithmetic, grammar, geography, and the "whole of the Westminster Catechism." His education continued for five or six years and was often interrupted by the comings and goings of the itinerant teachers. These intervals of no school sometimes lasted several weeks and gave Asher time to spend in the outdoors and to work in his father's shop.

Asher's father was a watch-maker by profession, but like many others in the colonial period, he had mastered a number of trades. He was a cooper as a young man but had also learned masonry and could build an oven, chimney, or plaster a wall equal to the best. He engaged in farming to a moderate extent but excelled in repairing clocks and making watches. He was, in fact, a universal mechanic, able to fix anything that broke. Asher was a delicate child and turned more to drawing and engraving than to the mechanical arts. His older brother, Cyrus, was the opposite, becoming famous for his many inventions and versatility in all things mechanical.

After Maverick and Durand dissolved their partnership, Asher turned more and more to engraving bank-note vignettes, although he never gave up portrait work and engraved many of the famous men and women of the time. His "Musidora," a large rectangular plate engraved in 1825 and depicting a full-length, slightly draped figure of a woman standing at the edge of a stream in landscape gave proof that he was unexcelled in portrait work. Equally popular was his line engraving of John VanderLyn's 1812 painting of "Ariadne Asleep on the Island of Naxos."[11] Asher's superb portrait work can be seen in his many signed engravings for Herring and Longacre's *National Portrait Gallery of Distinguished Americans.*

The "Musidora" engraving.

The "Ariadne" engraving.

Asher was a bank-note engraver in business with Peter Maverick from 1817 to 1820 as Maverick, Durand & Company in New York City. The next two years Durand was in business for himself. From 1824 to 1827 he was a partner with his brother, Cyrus, and Charles Cushing Wright in the firm of A.B. & C. Durand, Wright & Company, and from 1828 to 1832 he was a partner with Joseph Perkins, Cyrus Durand, and Elias Wade Jr. as Durand, Perkins & Company. This latter company made the bank-note dies of Benjamin Franklin and George Washington which were later used by the firm of Rawdon, Wright, Hatch & Edson to produce the first two stamps issued by the U.S. government in 1847. After Durand, Perkins & Company dissolved in 1832, Asher continued to do vignettes for other bank-note companies, but gradually he turned to landscape and portrait painting and was identified with the Hudson River School.[12] After 1836 he gave up engraving altogether and concentrated on painting, but he still taught drawing and engraving to a number of famous students who went on to careers in the bank-note industry, including John W. Casilear, George W. Hatch, and John W. Paradise.

"Kindred Spirits."

In 1837 Durand accompanied his friend Thomas Cole on a sketching expedition to Schroon Lake in the Adirondacks of northeastern New York, and thus began a life-long fascination with landscape art. When Cole died in 1848, Durand paid tribute to him with a painting completed the next year. This work, "Kindred Spirits," shows Cole and the poet William Cullen Bryant in a Catskills landscape and became one of Durand's most famous paintings.[13] Asher spent most of his life in New York City, but he moved to his home in Maplewood, New Jersey, in 1870. He continued to work in New York for some time but died in Maplewood on September 17, 1886. He is buried in Green Wood Cemetery in Brooklyn.

Cyrus Durand

Cyrus Durand was born in Jefferson Village, Springfield Township, on February 27, 1787. Unlike his brothers, Asher and John, Cyrus did not learn to engrave, although there is some evidence that he did lettering later in life. He was always more interested in learning how things worked. His education was the same as Asher's and ended at age 14. He was always acutely aware of the limitations of his brief education. For more "advanced learning," he paid $14 for a set of the *Edinburgh Encyclopedia* and read it frequently. He then began working in his father's shop, making brass rings and sleeve buttons that he pedaled himself in Springfield. He also made silver spoons by melting silver jewelry and plate from customers and casting it in molds he made from his own designs. At age 18 he visited a clock-maker's shop and became interested in how the parts were made. Returning home, he was able to make an engine for cutting the gears and other tools for making different parts. His father probably helped design and make the tools.[14] Cyrus understood gears and clock works so well that some of his clocks were still keeping good time near the end of his life.

Cyrus married his first wife, Susan, in 1808. The years leading up to the War of 1812 were difficult for all Americans, and Cyrus was no exception. Congress passed the Non-Intercourse Act in March 1809 to prevent the shipping of goods to any British or French ports. Like its predecessor, the Embargo Act of 1807, the Non-Intercourse Act was largely unenforceable and did serious damage to the American economy. Basic provisions became extraordinarily expensive, with rye-flour for bread selling at $6 per 100-weight. About 1810, while Cyrus was working in a silversmith's shop in Newark, New Jersey, he and Asher invented a primitive turning lathe for brass and iron. As an outgrowth of that work, Cyrus soon began making machines of various kinds for the factories in the area. John Taylor, who later became a bank president in Newark, asked Cyrus to make a turning lathe for making jewelry. Taylor realized that there was only one firm in Newark that made jewelry at the time, and Newark was then a city of some 50,000 people, so the market had potential. Small jobs like these not only kept bread on the table but also gave Cyrus valuable experience in the efficient design of machinery. By 1814 Cyrus had moved his family from Maplewood to Newark, a distance of about five miles, and opened a shop there as a silversmith. That same year he volunteered to be a drummer in a company of men sent to Sandy Hook, New Jersey, to fight the British if they landed on that shore. He served three months in the army but saw no action. In 1815 he went to Rahway, New Jersey, to work in the Taurino factory making machines for spinning and carding hair for carpet manufacturers. The next year, at the request of his brother Asher, he made a ruling machine for Peter Maverick that would make both straight and waved lines. This was his first bank-note–engraving machine and was described by Asher as a "crude and simple" device, but it embarked Cyrus on a new career that would bring him fame and prosperity the rest of his life.

In 1816 Cyrus made two other machines for bank-note work. One was a ruling engine for making "water lines," and the other was a lathe for making plain ovals. The latter machine was actually a chuck that could be fitted onto a standard lathe. This chuck consisted of a sun and planet gear train that converted the circular motion of the lathe's mandrel into a cycloidal motion of the cutter to inscribe a series of ovals on a copper or soft-steel die. The chuck was technically a "cycloidal chuck" rather than a true geometric chuck, as explained in greater detail in chapter 14. About 1864, Cyrus gave the New York Historical Society his 1823 version of the so-called "geometric chuck" along with other material. He said at the time the chuck had not been used for 40 years. There is evidence that he kept improving the design and making new "geometric chucks" for bank-note companies throughout his life.[15]

The colorful lathe patterns and dies on this note were created by machines patented by Cyrus Durand.

In 1820 typhoid fever swept through Jefferson Village, killing Cyrus's wife of 12 years and 2 of his brothers. The next year he moved a short distance away to Springfield. In 1822, at age 33, he married Phoebe Wade Woodruff, the young widow of Caleb Woodruff. Cyrus and Phoebe had four children: Juliet; Jane, who married the Reverend John L. Chapman; Elias Wade, who became an engraver and artist; and Cyrus Jr., who became the first minister of Newark's Episcopal Church of St. James. Phoebe Durand lived until 1891, dying at age 100.

It was also in 1822 that Cyrus made a pantograph for reducing ovals in the borders of notes, an idea he got from the *Edinburgh Encylopedia*.[16] In 1823 he moved to New York City and entered a partnership with Charles Cushing Wright to engrave and print bank notes. There were then only five companies in the United States engaged in bank-note engraving.[17] The next year, Cyrus made a compound-lever transfer press, although he didn't apply for a patent until four years later. This transfer press was said to operate on a different principle than did the Perkins transfer press in Philadelphia, which had been kept secret. The Durand transfer press became the model for others that were built in later years but has not received the recognition it deserves, possibly because it was not an original invention and was overshadowed by Durand's "geometric chuck." It was also in 1824 that Asher Durand joined his brother and C.C. Wright in the small shop they had set up at 8 Varick Street in New York under the name A.B. & C. Durand, Wright & Company. Joseph Perkins was the fourth member of the firm. In 1827 George W. Hatch joined the company for one year. On May 1, 1828, Charles Wright left the firm after a disagreement with the Durand brothers, and Joseph Perkins was made a full partner. The firm was renamed Durand, Perkins & Company, and they relocated to 50 Wall Street. Elias Wade Jr., Cyrus's brother-in-law and a plate printer, joined the firm at that time. For several years after Durand, Perkins & Company dissolved, Elias Wade Jr. was listed in the New York City directories as a merchant, indicating that he did not pursue the printing profession.

A specimen sheet of A.B. & C. Durand, Wright & Company.

Durand, Perkins & Company produced bank notes for banks in 10 different states, but some of the contracts were small and the total volume of business was never as great as in previous Durand companies. Consequently, Cyrus had some spare time that he used to good advantage. About 1830 he made an "engine-lathe" to ornament pocket watches and pencil cases for Nelmoth, Moffits & Company in New York. In 1832, against fierce competition from new bank-note companies and a weakening market for new business, Durand, Perkins & Company was dissolved. On March 20, 1832, a New York newspaper advertised the private sale of "1 Copper Plate Printing Press, 20-inch Roller, Durand Perkins & Co. patent." The company's machinery and dies were sold to other companies. A new partnership, Rawdon, Wright, Hatch & Company, which had just added George W. Hatch, bought portrait dies of George Washington and Benjamin Franklin, which they used 15 years later to make the first two stamps issued by the U.S. government, the five-cent and ten-cent issues of 1847. Waterman Lily Ormsby, in his famous book published in 1852, mentions the sale of dies and equipment when bank-note companies dissolved, leading some authors to believe this was a common occurrence and the source of artistic dies for counterfeiters. "Going-out-of-business" sales did occur, but there is no evidence that dies were sold to the public. Bank-note engravers were conscientious men who knew full well the dangers of letting engraved dies or plates get into the wrong hands, and they exercised due caution when selling their stock. Virtually all dies and plates were sold to other bank-note companies or to individual engravers of repute.

In 1833 Cyrus settled his differences with Charles Wright and became a partner with him and Nathaniel Smith Prentice in the xylographic printing of ornamental labels. Xylography is the term used for wood engraving and prints made from such work. It became popular in the 1830s, and the fad lasted for several decades because it was fast, easier than engraving on copper or steel, and the artist could draw the lettering and images he wanted directly on the wood and then cut away the non-image areas, leaving the lettering and images in relief. These were the type of labels found on bottles of all kinds, such as for whiskey and patent medicines and on cigar boxes. It was quite a profitable business, and after two years, Cyrus retired and went to Ohio with Elias Wade Jr. with the intention of buying a farm. Less than a year later, he returned to New Jersey and joined his younger brother, Henry, and his nephew, James Madison Durand, in Camptown (now called Irvington), New Jersey, where both lived and worked in their nearby jewelry and silversmith shop in Newark. In September 1835 Cyrus paid $900 for 10-1/2 acres of land at Camptown, less than 3 miles from his boyhood home. There, he built a magnificent house designed by Alexander Jackson Davis, one of the leading architects of the 19th century. Neighbors called it "the castle on the hill," and students of architecture would later call it the most important of Davis's early works.[18] Cyrus lived there off and on, as business permitted, until the end of his life. He also paid $1,500 to purchase Enos Baldwin's grist mill and four and a half acres of the surrounding land on the Elizabeth River. He gutted the mill and used the water wheel to power machinery of his own design, manufacturing silver jewelry set with semi-precious stones. After the factory failed to make money, Durand went back into bank-note engraving as Durand & Company, a firm he established in 1839. The members of this firm cannot be determined with certainty, but it seems that Vistus Balch, an engraver, and Charles Folsom, a letter engraver, were associated with the company for a number of years.

In 1841 Durand announced the invention of the "Red Letter" as a security against the alteration of a note. The February 1843 issue of *Hunt's Merchants' Magazine and Commercial Review* announced that Durand & Company "are now prepared to execute Engraving and Printing in a style which cannot be counterfeited, or the denomination altered." The advertisement claimed that the company had discovered "a chemically unalterable red ink" to print the denominations of bank notes. Dr. James Clinton assured readers that "The results of various trials

I have made fully satisfy me [that] the red letters cannot be removed without disfiguring the face of the bill, so as to render the alteration evident."[19] Apparently, Durand & Company considered the "Red Letter" to be of such advantage to the firm that they decided against a patent. Consequently, we will have no idea of the chemicals in the red ink until a sample note is analyzed in a laboratory.[20] But the "Red Letter" did not convince the banking establishment that a counterfeiter wouldn't find a way to chemically remove the ink and then print the new denomination in some other, inferior red ink. Just because a denomination counter was red didn't mean it was genuine.

More notes using lathework created by Cyrus Durand–patented devices.

By 1843 Durand & Company was dissolved. This time, the dies, plates, and some machinery were sold at public auction, and it is possible that some of them may have found their way into the hands of counterfeiters. The July 1844 edition of *Thompson's Bank Note Reporter* warned its readers "against a number of the most dangerous frauds which have ever been passed on the public. The dies, vignettes, denominations, etc., etc., of the bank note engraving house of Durand & Company were sold at auction, and they have already fallen into the hands of counterfeiters who are manufacturing counterfeits on banks in every section of the country." The hyperbole makes this warning sound like a clever ruse to sell more copies of *Thompson's Bank Note Reporter*. Where is the evidence that engraved dies from Durand & Company were used on other notes?

Cyrus made an effort to retire from the bank-note engraving business after the fall of Durand & Company, but it was not a complete withdrawal. He continued to work as a geometric-lathe operator from time to time. In 1844 he was in Philadelphia working with Robert Draper and may have built some machinery for Draper & Company just as it was getting started. For the next six years, Cyrus lived at his "castle on the hill" and turned his mind to improving old machines and inventing new ones. These included a machine that printed designs on calico from rollers and a machine that cut figures on type-metal rollers used in printing oil-cloth.

In the late 1840s the bank-note–engraving business had improved to the extent that Cyrus began to think seriously about starting up a new company. He was finally moved to action in 1849 when he formed a new company with his son, Albert G. Durand, an engraver, and George D. Baldwin. Baldwin was listed in the New York City directory of 1848 as a "copper-plate printer," with a shop at 33 Spruce Street, but later he gave testimony before a congressional committee in which he said he was an engraver.[21] The company was formed in 1849 and named Durand, Baldwin & Company, with a shop at 40 Wall Street, but it did very little work and their notes are quite scarce. The partnership was dissolved in 1850 and Cyrus, close to age 65, decided to retire once again.

This time his retirement lasted less than a year. He went back to New York in 1851 to become the geometric-lathe operator for Danforth, Wright & Company, which then consisted of Mosely I. Danforth, Edward J. Danforth, Nicholas D. Danforth, Henry Perkins, James MacDonough, Samuel Stiles, Fitch Shepard, William D. Nichols, James Wright, Frederick Girsch, and Charles Harrison, in addition to Cyrus—a stellar crew of talented men if there ever was one. As mentioned previously, the bank-note industry in New York underwent a major reorganization in 1858, when

seven competing companies decided to join forces as one giant firm, the American Bank Note Company. As discussion of the merger became more serious, Danforth, Wright & Company found that only some of its employees were willing to join in the new venture. Therefore, the "Association" said it would accept the company under a new name, Danforth, Perkins & Company, to avoid legal problems. Cyrus Durand went with the majority of the employees into the new American Bank Note Company as their lathe operator.

The imprint of Danforth, Wright & Co. is found on a bank note of the Western Exchange in Nebraska.

As one of the few geometric-lathe operators in America, Cyrus had the respect of the new company as he and his machines were essential to their future plans. But Cyrus did not think the company was paying him an adequate salary. On June 10, 1858, a special committee was appointed to negotiate with Cyrus for his services for one year, including the use of his geometric lathe, his transfer press, the cycloidal ruling machine, and the option to buy his equipment at the end of his one year contract. Cyrus refused to sign the contract, saying it was a "one-sided" agreement to see his machinery at work for a fixed price without binding the company to buy it. Tracy Edson then recommended that "for the sake of preventing the machinery from falling into the hands of the opposition, it would be best for the company to agree to buy it at the end of the year for three thousand dollars."[22] The contract was signed, but Cyrus left the American Bank Note Company about November 1859 and joined the National Bank Note Company, where he was reunited with many old friends who had worked with him at Danforth, Wright & Company.

Cyrus stayed with the National Bank Note Company for about four years, where he produced much of the exquisite lathe work on the national currency notes printed under government contract. The government also ordered new stamps to be engraved in 1861 to replace the current stamps which were at risk of being seized and used by the Confederacy. The superb lathe work that is found on the 1-cent, 3-cent, 5-cent, 12-cent, and 24-cent stamps shows Durand's artistry at its finest. Durand left the National Bank Note Company in 1864 and went to the United States Bank Note Company when it was formed by Alfred Jones in 1865. There he engraved lathe work on currency and stock certificates for the government of Mexico. When that company failed, Cyrus went back home to live in Irvington and to tinker with improving his geometric lathe. He died there on September 18, 1868, at age 81.

The 1-cent, 3-cent, 5-cent, 12-cent, and 24-cent stamps engraved by the National Bank Note Company.

Other Durands

John Durand was a younger brother of Asher and Cyrus Durand. He died around 1820 at about the age of 28. According to the family, the elder Durand (their father) always maintained that John was the most-talented member of the family. William Dunlap, in the *History of the Rise and Progress of the Arts of Design*, says that he was "originally a jeweler, but on taking up engraving, he appeared to make progress as by inspiration." John Durand had only two years of instruction under Asher Durand before becoming an engraver. Very little of his work was published. Stauffer says that two well-engraved vignettes on the title pages of the works of William Cooper and Thomas Gray, published in New York by R & W.A. Barrow, are signed "Engraved by J. Durand."

A. Theodore Durand was a script engraver, working in New York for Casilear, Durand & Company from 1834 to 1835, and then for Casilear, Durand, Burton & Edmonds from 1835 to 1836. His relationship to the other Durands is not known.

Albert G. Durand was a son of Cyrus and Phoebe Wade Durand. He was an engraver with Rawdon, Wright, Hatch & Company from 1833 to 1834, then went to Casilear, Durand, Burton & Edmonds from 1835 to 1837, and finally showed up at Durand, Baldwin & Company from 1849 to 1850. He was married to Charlotte Durand; apparently, they had no children.[23]

Elias Wade Durand was a son of Cyrus and Phoebe Wade Durand. He was born in New York City in December 1824 and should not be confused with Elias Wade Jr., who was Phoebe Wade's brother. Elias Durand attended private schools in the city and later attended Newark Academy after his family moved to Camptown in 1836. In 1839 his father took him to New York to learn engraving. Young Elias studied with his uncle, Asher, and with other engravers until his father's company, Durand & Company, went out of business in 1843. He then spent several years in Newark at Taylor, Baldwin & Company, learning how to engrave watchcases and jewelry. Elias left Newark for New York City in 1844 to work with Thomas White, a leading jeweler of the time. He married Emma, the daughter of a local merchant, in 1846. In September of that year, he bought out his employer and continued in that occupation at 71 Nassau Street until 1850. In 1850, tired of his jewelry shop, Elias closed it down and took instructions in wood engraving from J.A. Adams.

Elias soon tired of wood engraving too and gave it up to pursue the "high art" of landscape painting. He and Asher Durand often went together to Lake George in New York to paint from nature. Elias never attained the reputation of his uncle in landscape painting. He suffered increasingly severe bouts of dyspepsia, and on advice of his physician, he closed his New York studio and retired to the cleaner air of Irvington, New Jersey, in 1857, when he was 33 years old. There, he grew strawberries and became an expert horticulturist. He also raised goldfish and sold them to supplement his income. He sadly outlived all 5 of his children and finally died on August 27, 1908, at age 84.

William Durand was a nephew of Asher Durand, possibly a son of Cyrus Durand. Stauffer says he was a man of considerable mechanical ability. He was engraving for Durand & Moore, ornamental engravers, from 1850 to 1852 and lived at home with Asher Durand. He was listed as a portrait painter in New York City in 1853 and exhibited at the Washington Art Association in 1857.

Joseph Perkins

This Perkins was born in Unity, New Hampshire, on August 19, 1788. He graduated from Williams College, a liberal arts school, in 1814. In 1818 he went to Philadelphia and learned script engraving. He set up business in that city, but in 1825 he moved to New York City to form a partnership with Asher Durand in the bank-note–engraving firm of A.B. & C. Durand, Wright & Company. He continued with them when the firm became Durand, Perkins & Company. When Asher Durand dissolved the company to turn to landscape painting, Perkins continued in business as a script engraver at his office at 4 John Street in New York until his death on April 27, 1842, after which his widow took several years to wind up the business. Joseph Perkins was not related to "the" Jacob Perkins, but by coincidence he was a partner with another Jacob Perkins, an engraver, from 1833 to 1835 as Perkins & Perkins.

George W. Hatch

George Whitfield Hatch was born in Johnstown in western New York on April 27, 1804. Almost nothing is known of his early life and education. William Dunlap, who chronicled the lives of many of our eminent engravers, once asked

Hatch for a few biographical facts, only to write later, "that I am not able to give a detailed and accurate notice of this very estimable gentleman is owing to a reserve, on his part, which is to me inexplicable." George married Mary Daniels of Albany, New York, in 1825. He was one of the first students of the National Academy of Design in 1826, and for a time he was a pupil of Asher B. Durand. Consequently, he not only designed vignettes but engraved them as well, and it can be seen from the few vignettes that he signed, or which we can attribute to him by indirect evidence, that he was obviously a good engraver in pure line. In 1827 and 1828 he was engraving with A.B. & C. Durand, Wright and Company, and in 1829 he was with Durand, Perkins & Company in their office at 50 Wall Street. The friendship between George Hatch and James Smillie began in the fall of 1830 when Smillie, then living in Quebec, decided to accept an offer made by George M. Bourne to engrave New York City scenes that Mr. Bourne had drawn. Bourne promised Smillie $10 a week to engrave his drawings, an offer that Smillie couldn't refuse. When the work became too much for any one man to engrave, George Hatch was hired by Bourne to assist. Smillie and Hatch both worked on these small, detailed, 2-3/4 by 3-1/2-inch plates. Within a few months they formed a partnership called Hatch & Smillie for the purpose of finishing the Bourne project.

In 1832 Hatch joined Ralph Rawdon, Freeman Rawdon, and Neziah Wright to establish the firm of Rawdon, Wright & Hatch. In 1834 Tracy Edson joined the company, and after one year the company's name was changed to Rawdon, Wright, Hatch & Edson. In 1841 and 1842, when Edson became a salesman and sometimes a general manager working in branch offices, James Smillie was hired, causing the company to become Rawdon, Wright, Hatch & Smillie. Smillie was apparently added to do magazine illustrations and not security engraving. When Edson returned, Smillie left, and the company's name reverted to Rawdon, Wright, Hatch & Edson. Hatch stayed with the company where he was both a designer of notes and a portrait engraver. Hessler attributes the art work on some 10 different notes and bonds to him. After Tracy Edson retired from the American Bank Note Company in 1863, George Hatch succeeded him as president and held the office until he died at Dobbs Ferry, New York, on February 13, 1866.

The book and print shop of George M. Bourne, 359 Broadway, New York, 1831.

Rawdon, Wright, Hatch & Edson

If there is any one company that displaced Philadelphia as the center of the American bank-note industry, the honor falls to Rawdon, Wright, Hatch & Edson. This company dominated the market for a quarter of a century by hiring the best talent available, having a large inventory of equipment, but above all, operating under wise and far-sighted management. The company had its origin in the career paths taken by two brothers, Ralph and Freeman Rawdon. Although Ralph Rawdon taught his younger brother, Freeman, how to engrave, the two men associated with different engravers and established different firms. Ralph Rawdon was born sometime around 1801 in Tolland, Connecticut, and was engraving in a crude manner with Thomas Kensett (the father of

the American artist John Frederick Kensett) at Cheshire, Connecticut, as early as 1813. In 1816 he moved to Albany, New York, and engraved stipple portraits over his own name. Also in that year he began working with Asaph Willard in bank-note and general engraving as Willard & Rawdon. From 1818 to 1822 he joined Vistus Balch, from Williamstown, Massachusetts, as Balch, Rawdon & Company, engaging mainly in bank-note work, and from 1823 to 1834 he was in partnership with Asabel Clark at 55 State Street in Albany as Rawdon, Clark & Company. The latter company was moderately successful for this period, and the Haxby *Standard Catalog* records their imprint on 29 different banks.

Freeman Rawdon became a partner with Neziah Wright in 1828 and formed the bank-note–engraving firm of Rawdon, Wright & Company in New York City, established at a new building called the Merchants Exchange at 55 Wall Street. The individual companies in this building had separate numbered offices, and Rawdon, Wright & Company was 35 Merchants Exchange. Their business was small and their imprint is found on the notes of only five banks listed by Haxby. On March 1, 1832, Rawdon, Wright & Company merged with Rawdon, Clark & Company to form a new firm named Rawdon, Wright, Hatch & Company. This merger brought the two Rawdon brothers together again. Tracy Edson also joined the firm on March 1, 1832, as a business administrator. Edson ran the operations for the New Orleans branch office and set up offices in Boston, Philadelphia, and Cincinnati. He was not an engraver but excelled in administrative work.

Neziah Wright was the son of Dr. Lockhart Wright and was born about 1804, probably in Lyman, New Hampshire, which was then a village of about 200 people. His early life is virtually unknown. He had a brother, Hubbard, who lived on a competency left by their father. Another brother, Ellis, went out west as a young man and was not heard from again. A sister named Abigail was born in Lyman in 1813. Neziah's daughter, Jennie, married on June 12, 1867, to Phineas C. Lounsbury, who became a governor of Vermont.

There is no question that Neziah was trained as a letter engraver. Unfortunately, he did not keep a scrapbook of his work, as some engravers did, and it is impossible to attribute any particular bank notes to his burin. At a board of directors meeting of the American Bank Note Company on May 16, 1860, he was named "Supervisor of Lettering and Transferring." He also served as the first treasurer of the American Bank Note Company, keeping that office until his retirement for reasons of bad health in May 1873.

Tracy Robinson Edson was born at Fly Creek, Otsego County, New York, about three miles from the present-day Cooperstown, on December 12, 1809.[24] He was the eldest son of William Jarvis Edson and Mary (Fairchild) Edson.[25] The family made a reasonable living farming, allowing Tracy to receive a common school education. He had two brothers, Marmont Bryan and Clement Massillon, and two sisters, Mary and Susan. When he was about 18 years old, he moved to Albany and joined the firm of Rawdon & Clark, where he "learned the business of engraving," probably as an office worker and not as an engraver.[26] He moved to New York City in the late 1820s and worked as a salesman for Rawdon, Wright & Company until 1832. He was the driving force behind the success of Rawdon, Wright, & Hatch, and his business acumen and unrelenting work ethic saved the company on more than one occasion. His natural gift for management was soon noticed by the principals of the company, and they asked him to set up and manage branch offices in other cities, including Boston, Philadelphia, Cincinnati, and New Orleans. Edson's first assignment was New Orleans. He was living there in 1835 when the company in New York suffered a major setback.

The Great Fire of 1835

The catastrophe began about nine o'clock on the very cold night of December 16, 1835. An investigation later reported that a gas pipe had burst and the escaping vapor was ignited by a coal stove in a five-story warehouse filled with merchandise and hardware. Worse conditions for a fire could hardly be imagined. An intense winter storm had frozen both the Hudson and the East rivers. Firemen had to cut holes in the ice to get to the water, and even then, the water froze in the pumps and hoses. Water had also frozen in neighborhood wells and in the 40 fire cisterns placed around the city. The reservoir at 13th Street and the Bowery was low. A fierce northerly wind whipped the fire from one building to the next, and the temperature was recorded at 17-degrees below zero. Many of the buildings were new and had iron doors and window shutters, as well as copper roofs. When they started to burn, these tightly shut buildings were like blast furnaces—so hot that the copper roofs melted and large droplets of molten copper fell, immediately solidifying on the streets below.

The Great Fire of 1835.

The entire New York Fire Department—around 1,500 strong—fought the fire with hundreds of volunteers, but it was quickly realized that they could not stop it. The time-honored option, and one used in the Great Fire of London in 1666, was to blow up buildings in the path of the fire to create a fire break. But the firemen discovered there was virtually no gunpowder in Manhattan, and a message was sent to the navy to bring a supply as fast as possible. About 2 a.m., marines arrived with gunpowder from the Brooklyn Navy Yard and began blowing up buildings. As the fire grew, it was seen as far away as Philadelphia and New Haven, Connecticut. The Philadelphia Fire Department thought all of New York was burning, and they sent 400 firemen with their equipment. A railroad connecting the two cities was still six miles short of completion, so the firemen made most of the trip in open rail-cars, but at the end of the rails they had to drag their engines and hoses through deep sand to reach the city on Saturday. Newark sent 100 men and 6 engines.

The fire destroyed nearly 700 buildings. Most of them were commercial enterprises, such as shops, warehouses, and small businesses. Thousands of New Yorkers lost their jobs. The insurance companies estimated the damages at about $25 million, a fantastic sum in those days, but the amount didn't matter much because all but 3 of the city's 26 fire-insurance companies declared bankruptcy and paid only pennies on the dollar to their customers.

There were many heroic stories that came out of this fire, as well as not a few sad ones about looting, vigilantes, and the darker side of the human mind. There were only 2 or 3 casualties, but more than 400 people were arrested for looting. The fire was not as large as the Great Fire of London which destroyed 13,000 houses, nor as large and deadly as the Chicago Fire of 1871, which killed about 300 people and left 90,000 homeless. But New York's Great Fire of 1835 gutted the financial district of the city, then the nation's financial center, and the consequences were far-reaching. Nicholas Biddle, the president of the Bank of the United States, promised to give financial aid to the city if the federal government would guarantee the loans.

The four-story Merchants' Exchange had been built in 1827 to accommodate the city's larger merchants. It housed the New York Stock Exchange Board on its second floor. It was a prestigious address, and because the city's financial leaders were constantly in the building for one reason or another, it was an ideal location for a fledgling bank-note company. On the night of the Great Fire, the interior offices of the building burned completely, and seemingly everything at Rawdon, Wright & Hatch was lost. The partners were not willing to give up their contracts to competitors, and the employees salvaged what dies and bed-pieces they could find in the ashes and started again in a temporary location while waiting for the Merchants Exchange to be rebuilt.

Construction of the new building was started in 1836 and finished in 1842. The work was given to the Boston architect Isaiah Rogers, who was then the most experienced and famous hotel architect in America. He designed the new Merchants Exchange in the Greek Revival style with massive granite Ionic columns. When the building was finished, Rawdon, Wright & Hatch were joined by James Smillie, who was made a full partner, so the company became Rawdon, Wright, Hatch & Smillie and retained that name until Edson returned from New Orleans in 1847.

The new Merchants Exchange Building after 1842. This building housed the firm of Rawdon, Wright, Hatch & Edson, the leading bank-note firm of New York.

Under Edson's careful management, the company engineered a meteoric rise to the top. A survey of the Haxby *Standard Catalog* shows that the company's imprint is found on the notes of about 344 banks as Rawdon, Wright & Hatch and on the notes of 447 banks as Rawdon, Wright, Hatch & Edson by the time the American Bank Note Company was formed in 1858. When Ralph Rawdon first entered the business in Albany, New York, he engraved for only two banks. As Rawdon & Clark in Albany, their clientele rose to 29 different banks, and from that humble beginning the company expanded to 751 banks by the late 1850s. During this time they did a very profitable business engraving and printing government and municipal bonds and stock certificates.

Edson returned to New York in September of 1847 at the request of the company, which was facing financial collapse. He stopped the immediate losses and eventually made the company profitable again. When Smillie decided to retire, the other partners made Edson a full partner, and the company was then styled Rawdon, Wright, Hatch & Edson. The next 10 years were rather pedestrian, except that the company captured much of the bank-note–printing market and made considerable money for the owners. It was generally a busy decade for the bank-note industry but one plagued by counterfeiting and a growing public distrust in paper money. The newspapers of the time published a steady stream of letters to the editors suggesting remedies for counterfeiting, including several sent to the *New York Times* by W.L. Ormsby, a bank-note engraver. Then, in the latter half of 1857, witches tending their cauldrons saw the first signs of toil and trouble.

This, of course, was the Panic of 1857. It began with the August 24 failure of the New York branch of the Ohio Life Insurance and Trust Company from a massive embezzlement scheme. The company had been a major financial force in New York, and its collapse shook the public confidence in the economy. At the same time, the Crimean War had ended, and Russia had reentered the global market, depressing the price of grain and causing hardship in America's agrarian economy. British investors began to remove funds from New York banks, further damaging the public's confidence in the economy. Many investors lost money on land speculation that depended on new railroad routes, and when the new routes failed to materialize for political reasons, thousands of these investors were ruined.

Among the several events occurring during the panic, the most dramatic was the sinking of a three-masted, wooden-hulled, 280-foot side-wheel steam ship called the SS *Central America*. The ship had already carried back East about one-third of all the gold found during the California Gold Rush and was once again on its way from Columbia to New York when it was overtaken by a hurricane in the Atlantic. There were 426 passengers on board and a crew of 102. In addition to 38,000 letters, it carried a cargo of 30,000 pounds of gold. On September 10, the crew and passengers began bailing water as fast as they could, but after 40 hours of fighting rough seas and strong winds, the captain ordered women and children into lifeboats. He and his crew, most of the male passengers, and the 30,000 pounds of gold were lost when the ship sank about 160 miles east of Cape Hatteras, North Carolina, in 8,500 feet of water. The loss of that much gold caused factories in New York to miss payrolls and some businesses to fail, but this happened after the panic had already started, so it should not be considered a "cause." The panic did not last long, and banks got back to their normal business the next year, but during the panic the banks did far less business and consequently didn't order new money from their printers. This hurt the bank-note companies and sparked a debate within the industry.

Chapter 7

The American Bank Note Company (ABNCo.)

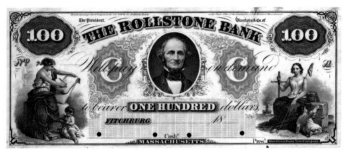

The imprint of the American Bank Note Company appears on a $100 note.

Planning a Merger

We don't know who started the discussions, or even if there was an alpha male that lead the others, but four men in particular began to argue for a change in the way the industry did business. These were Nathaniel Jocelyn, Moseley Danforth, Tracy Edson, and George Lyman. Until then, all bank-note companies were partnerships composed entirely of skilled artists, practical engravers, and agents. Most of the companies were small, and competition was fierce. Bankruptcies were common. It is generally assumed that Tracy Edson originated the idea that separate bank-note companies should merge to form one large company, but there is no hard evidence that he took the lead in that argument. The objective was economy of scale. The larger the company, it was argued, the greater its efficiency and the lower its cost in making bank notes. A larger company should have a greater appeal to potential customers since it would be more stable and could finish its work more quickly and cheaply. It would also have greater geographic reach and could compete more successfully. Even in 1858 this was not rocket science. Business mergers were not new. In the railroad industry, for example, the first merger took place in 1836, when the Maryland and Delaware Railroad merged with the Wilmington and Susquehana line, and over the years, 69 major railroads have been consolidated into today's 10 largest systems. Still, nothing like the proposed "Association" had been tried before in the bank-note industry, and it was commonly believed that the principal artists of these companies, having spent most of their lives developing an aesthetic sense of what belongs on a bank note and what doesn't, would not want to surrender their artistic freedom to businessmen.

One of the first objectives of those advocating merger was to convince Charles Toppan that their idea was fundamentally sound. This was the same Charles Toppan who had accompanied Jacob Perkins and his associates to London some 40 years earlier and who had spent much of his life raising the artistic standards of the industry. Nathaniel Jocelyn had kept a desk in Toppan's office in Philadelphia and had worked with him occasionally for several years, as had two other members of the Jocelyn family. Not surprisingly, Nathaniel is credited with selling the idea of a merger to his old friend.[1] Once Toppan was assured that art would trump commercialism in this new order, he became an active supporter, adding enormous prestige to the crusade. Nathaniel is also believed to have convinced Moseley Danforth to add his voice and reputation to the effort, and is thought to have suggested that the association be called the "American Bank Note Company," the same name that Jocelyn, Draper, Welsh & Company had used on its business cards in 1854.

George D. Lyman, who was secretary of the New York Clearing House, is credited in the official history of the American Bank Note Company as having done much to bring the several firms together. Since he knew the engravers personally and had their trust, he was able to use his office as a "neutral ground" for meetings and discussions. Recognizing his contributions to the formation of the "Association," the trustees voted to give him 20 shares of stock, then valued at $50 a share.

The transfer room at the ABNCo., circa 1860.
Note the various models of transfer presses. The man in the left foreground is hammering out an error on a plate or die.

Tracy Edson also played an important (and perhaps even the central) role in the formation of the new company, but to show their respect and admiration, the trustees voted unanimously for Charles Toppan to be the first president. Although he had been an able administrator of his own company for many years, Toppan would later write that he did not fully appreciate the many duties involved in the job. He retired on March 4, 1860, at age 63, in order "to relieve himself of the responsibilities and cares of the business." Tracy Edson then took over as president, about 13 months before the Civil War began. This was also the year in which Edson suffered an accident that dislocated his hip. He would be lame the rest of his life.

Association Period

According to the certificate of incorporation filed in the office of the New York secretary of state on April 29, 1858, the American Bank Note Company was an association of seven previously independent bank-note companies and had a nominal capital of $5,000. That money was paid to the company in one installment on June 10, 1858, and is now believed to have been a loan from Charles Toppan for the immediate purpose of filing the papers of incorporation. It did not represent the worth of the company. On September 1, 1858, the company had a capital of $1,250,000

consisting of 24,000 shares of stock at $50 a share. 20,000 of these shares were apportioned to the 25 incorporators who represented the 7 companies that formed the association. The remaining 4,900 shares were made available to the employees in a stock-purchase plan.

The seven companies that formed the American Bank Note Company were:

(1) Rawdon, Wright, Hatch & Edson, based in New York but with offices in Cincinnati, New Orleans, Montreal, and Boston. They received 23.9% of the shares of stock.

(2) Toppan, Carpenter & Company, based in Philadelphia but with offices in New York, Cincinnati, and Boston. They received 22.4% of the shares of stock.

(3) Danforth, Perkins & Company, based in Philadelphia but with offices in New York, Cincinnati, and Boston. They received 21.8% of the shares of stock. This company was actually Danforth, Wright & Company, but not all the employees wanted to join the merger, so those that did came in as Danforth, Perkins & Company.

(4) Bald, Cousland & Company, based in New York and Philadelphia. They received 13.3% of the shares of stock.

(5) Draper, Welsh & Company, based in Philadelphia but with an office in New York known as Jocelyn, Draper, Welsh & Company. They received 8.4% of the shares of stock.

(6) Wellstood, Hay & Whiting, based in New York but with an office in Chicago. They got 8.2% of the shares of stock.

(7) John E. Gavit Company, based in Albany, New York. They got 2% of the shares of stock.

Rawdon, Wright, Hatch & Edson had been a half-owner of the New England Bank Note Company since 1848, when they bought an interest from the owner, Isaac Cary. Tracy Edson convinced Isaac Cary to join the merger in return for part of the 5,591 shares given to Rawdon, Wright, Hatch & Edson. The firm of Edmonds, Jones & Smillie did not join the association until about a year later, so it was not considered an eighth incorporator but rather a new acquisition.

In the position of president of the American Bank Note Company, Tracy Edson inherited a number of problems that Toppan had chosen not to tackle. Personnel and salary problems were especially difficult. The personnel of a bank-note company were traditionally divided into two distinct camps: a few "artists," who were exceptionally good engravers and often the partners of the firm, and the "practical men," a much larger group of second-rate and apprentice engravers, siderographers, plate printers, etc. Quite often, the artists in a company knew the practical men for several years and were used to working with them. The artists naturally expected to continue working with their practical men, but the merger had given Edson too many practical men and too little work, and it fell on his shoulders to say who could stay and who must go. Another lingering problem had been the different pay scales of the original companies. Edson had to adjust these inequities, even though some people were given smaller salaries. Feelings were hurt when senior men had to accept lower positions in the new company. But Edson made the necessary changes with great skill and understanding, managing to keep the company together.

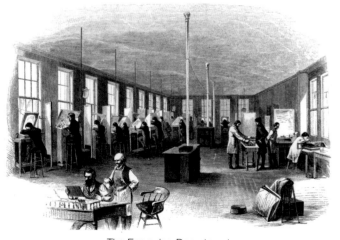

The Engraving Department
at the American Bank Note Company, circa 1860.

Printing Stock Certificates

The American Bank Note Company was immediately successful because the member companies all had existing contracts to print notes for state-chartered and private banks, and some (especially Rawdon, Wright, Hatch & Edson) had contracts to design and print bonds and other types of fiduciary paper for the government and states by combinations of engraving, lithography, and typesetting. Toppan, Carpenter & Company, for example, had won the contract to print postage stamps for the U.S. government from 1851 to 1857, which was later extended to 1861. Stock certificates and bonds were not immediately lucrative, but after the Civil War they became increasingly a larger share of the business. The American investments market got started in 1790 when the federal government decided to add up all the debts owed by the 13 states and all the federal debts due to the Revolutionary War. They issued $80 million in bonds as a result. This became the first major issue of publicly traded securities in the United States. The New York Stock Exchange traces its origin to the Buttonwood Agreement that was signed by 24 New York City stockbrokers and merchants on May 17, 1792, under a buttonwood tree outside the entrance to No. 68 Wall Street. The signers agreed to trade securities on a commission basis. The market grew rapidly after the War of 1812, expanding from government bonds to banks and insurance company stocks.

In the beginning, individuals that purchased stock in a company received a receipt that was usually about the size of a modern check. These receipts were often a printed form with no vignettes or art work. Counterfeiting was a problem and gradually drove the market to require more elaborately printed stock certificates. By the 1840s these certificates were printed in large size, on paper of good quality, and featured a vignette. Rawdon, Wright, Hatch & Edson produced the greatest number of these certificates, and as more companies went public and the annual volume of shares increased, the company made large profits "printing for Wall Street."

This was due in part to the trading of railroad stocks. The first railroad company stock to be traded was the Mohawk and Hudson in 1830, and by the 1840s, domestic-railroad stocks dominated the market for the rest of the century. The development of the telegraph around 1861 also expanded the market to other financial centers by facilitating the communication of stock prices to investors and brokers outside New York City.

After 1874, all three of the principal New York bank-note companies engraved stock certificates. They could also offer their business clients and municipal customers a complete range of services for designing certificates and bonds, engraving the kind of vignettes and borders the clients wanted, and printing these images from steel plates. The textual material could be printed lithographically in the same plant. The companies always kept their vignette and border dies and could select one or more of these from a large variety of such work. If a client wanted a vignette that was not in stock, the designing department would do the artwork. Once the art was approved by the client, it went to the engraving department, and a new die was made. These advantages satisfied clients and made that part of the business highly profitable.

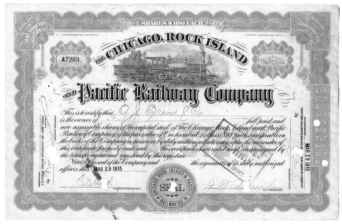

An elaborately engraved stock certificate bearing a vignette of an old locomotive—also known as "train stock."

The Patent Green Ink

William Workman, the president of the City Bank of Montreal, had been concerned about the possibility that photography would be used to make counterfeit notes. On March 2, 1857, he wrote a letter to Thomas Sterry Hunt, the chemist to the Geological Survey, to ask "your opinion as to the various tints, colors and chemical agents which have been and are now employed, as a means of protection against these frauds."[2] Taking up the challenge, Hunt surveyed the literature and conducted a number of experiments to test the resistance of ink pigments to various acids, alkalis, and solvents. His attention was drawn to a patent by George Mathews called the *Canada Banknote Printing Tint*. By July of that year, he had determined that an ink using chromium sesquioxide as a green pigment would answer all the criteria for an indestructible, non-photographic bank-note ink, and he suggested its use to Mr. Workman in a letter dated July 1, 1857.[3] Hunt had experimented with an ink made by combining stannic acid with the chromium III oxide to form what he called a mineral lake. This proved effective. When a printed bank note using this ink was photographed, a positive print would only show black ink where it should be green. Writing to a friend on August 4, 1857, Hunt mentioned:

> I have perhaps told you that I have made a fortunate discovery of a process for printing banknotes which is likely to yield me a good deal of money. It is a green ink which cannot be effaced nor copied by photography. I got a small sum for it in the United States, but a permanent right and interest in the patent in Canada. The invention is not, however, in my name, but as "Matthews Banknote Trust."[4]

George Matthews was an employee of Rawdon, Wright, Hatch & Edson in their Montreal office at the time this letter was written. When Matthews heard about the invention of this green ink, similar to the chemistry of his tint, he negotiated with Hunt and bought a right to use the ink in the United States. The Hunt formula was not completely suitable as a bank-note ink, but Matthews and his partner, George Bull Burland, improved the ink specifically for intaglio work. Matthews then wrote to his boss, Tracy Edson, in New York, and informed him of the invention. Edson was interested in buying the patent rights to the ink for use by his company and wasted no time in concluding a deal. He then announced to the public that Rawdon, Wright, Hatch & Edson had a new safeguard against counterfeiting by photography. The company printed a 20-page pamphlet about the subject in 1858 titled "A New Security for Detecting Bank Notes from Alterations and Photographic Counterfeits by the Use of the Patent Green Tint." This pamphlet was sent to many banks and given to important congressmen and state legislators. No study has been done to determine if the green tint had a quantifiable effect on attracting new customers. After all, Rawdon, Wright, Hatch & Edson wasn't the only company with an anti-photographic security feature. Jocelyn, Draper, Welsh & Company, using the name American Bank Note Company, had printed anti-photographic specimen notes in 1857, using a black ink on a red-brown background. If a counterfeiter photographed the note, the background would appear black, eliminating the contrasting colors and making it obvious that the note was not original. The red-brown background was also printed with an ink whose pigment was difficult to remove by chemical agents. In fact, the efforts made by Hunt, Eaton, and others to prevent counterfeiting by the use of special inks never did what they promised to do.[5] This was also true of the efforts to deter counterfeiting by the use of special fibers added to the paper. The Legal Tender issues of 1862 were printed by both the American Bank Note Company and the National Bank Note Company using the "Green Tint," yet they were frequently counterfeited, as were other issues. It was the efforts of the Secret Service, more than any other factor, that eventually reduced the volume of fake notes.

The Patent Green Tint caused Tracy Edson a considerable amount of trouble that he never expected. On July 14, 1864, the American Bank Note Company sued Tracy Edson. The attorneys for the American Bank Note Company (plaintiff) claimed that Tracy Edson (defendant) had wrongfully taken $38,129.58 in royalties for the use of the Green Tint, as well as another

$3,910.52 that he took under false pretenses that was owed to Matthews. There were several points of law that could be argued either for or against the plaintiff's demands, and when the defendant lost the judgment, he appealed, and a legal battle ensued that lasted until 1870.[6] During that period the Supreme Court of the City and County of New York turned the matter over to a referee, Stephen P. Nash Esquire, who eventually reported in favor of the defendant and against the plaintiff, and that the complaint should be dismissed with costs. Once again, Edson appeared to have the Midas touch.

An example of the "Patent Green Tint" used on a bank note of the Merchants Bank in the city of New York.

A specimen note of Rawdon, Wright, Hatch & Edson showing the Patent Green Tint.

Edson as an Investor

Edson was never one to let wealth pile up. He was always investing his money in new business ventures. One of the new technologies that caught his eye was the magnetic telegraph invented by Samuel Morse during the late 1830s and improved during the 1840s. In 1851, the year that Western Union was formed, there were over 50 competing telegraph companies. By 1861 the first transcontinental lines were connected. Edson saw that business information could be transmitted between distant cities in a matter of hours rather than days. He became interested in a small company called the Gold and Stock Telegraph Company, incorporated in August 1867. This company transmitted gold prices and stock quotations over private lines between a few major financial centers. Edson invested heavily in the company and took an active hand in its management. By 1869 he was made a director of the company and became its largest stockholder. Edson saw that the company could only grow if it had lines to all the major cities in the country, and the only way to achieve that goal was to set up a cooperative union with the industry's giant, the Western Union Telegraph Company. Edson once again became a salesman and convinced Western Union that a merger would be in both companies' best interest. The Gold and Stock Telegraph Company kept its name throughout Edson's lifetime and took on more and more of Western Union's business. Needless to say, Edson made a fortune from Western Union.

Samuel F.B. Morse.

The general operating department of the Western Union Telegraph Building, New York, 1875.

A young telegrapher in Boston, having invented the printing mechanism for the registration of gold and stock prices, moved to New York in 1871 to become the superintendent of the Gold and Stock Telegraph Company. This was Thomas Alva Edison. Tracy Edson became interested in Edison and helped him set up a large plant in Newark, New Jersey, to manufacture telegraphic equipment. As Edison became more interested in other scientific pursuits, he moved his laboratory to Menlo Park, New Jersey. Edison's interest in the telephone lead to Tracy Edson's interest in the investment side of the business and eventually to his purchase of stock in the American Speaking Telephone Company, the Metropolitan Telephone and Telegraph Company, and the Edison Electric Light Company. Edson also invested in Vermilye & Company (bankers), the Celluloid Manufacturing Company, the St. Nicholas Bank, the Bank of the Metropolis, the Mercantile Trust Company, the Equitable Trust Company, the Mutual Gas Light Company, and the Provident Savings Life Insurance Company. He made considerable money from the European rights to his brother's invention, the Edson Recording Steam Gauge. Behind all of this, he had a reliable cash cow in the American Bank Note Company. By the time he retired from the American Bank Note Company in 1863, Edson was already the richest man in the bank-note business. He continued as a trustee for another dozen years. By the time he died in 1881, his estate was valued at $1,681,500.

Edson lived a quiet life at home with his mother, two sisters who never married, a brother, Marmont, who also never married, and a 20-year-old Irish servant. Edson cared little for the trappings of wealth, living most of his life in two apartments in New York City, the last one being at 16 East 17th Street. His two sisters never went out into society and never stepped foot outside New York City. Unlike Tracy, they knew nothing about the investment business and relied entirely on their brother to support them.

By the time the anti-photographic inks were developed, the first dark clouds of the Civil War were beginning to stir, and businessmen, especially bankers, were growing more nervous with each passing month. For most banks, changing the design of their currency was an expensive move, and given the anxiety of the times, few banks chose to change their notes to an anti-photographic ink. But Edson's pamphlet on the subject, and perhaps the earlier anti-photographic specimen notes of Jocelyn, Draper, Welsh & Company, had convinced the newly appointed director of the National Currency Bureau, Spencer M. Clark, that such protection should be used in the first National Bank Notes that were then being planned. Clark had been gathering ideas for some time about the design of the new currency. He had obviously read W.L. Ormsby's book and agreed with that author's conclusions about bank-note security. In a letter that Clark wrote to Secretary Salmon Chase on March 28, 1863, he argued:

> The notes now in use, made up of separate dies, actually afford facilities for counterfeiting, from their patch-work composition . . . to counterfeit it by photography, which is the readiest way to deceive the masses who handle notes, particularly those who most receive and pay small notes, a non-photographic material should be introduced into, and be inseparable from, the paper, so that a photograph or phototype should present a defaced or mottled appearance, easily distinguished by all.[7]

A $5 U.S. "greenback."

Clark didn't get everything he wanted in the new notes, but the proposal to use anti-photographic ink was accepted, and the American Bank Note Company was required to use this ink on the national currency. The Patent Green Tint used on the backs of the new notes lead to the custom of calling them "greenbacks."

From the very beginning, the American Bank Note Company was involved in the preparation of government securities. Rawdon, Wright, Hatch & Company had printed these securities for a long time, so it was completely normal for Tracy Edson to go to Washington, D.C., in early July 1861 to see if he could get the contracts to print government loans.[8] He knew the government was having a serious cash-flow problem and that Secretary Chase had decided to follow the plan suggested by George D. Lyman. Chase was a lawyer, but he didn't have a firm grasp of financial matters. George Lyman, on the other hand, had worked at the Bank of North America and was then the manager of the New York Clearing House. He had a feasible plan to finance the war. On June 20, 1861, Lyman wrote to Secretary Chase and suggested that the government should "borrow from the people." "People of the loyal states," he said, are "ready to support their government; let then the government debt be distributed among them in small amounts. . . . they will show the world that a government dependent upon the people may be as strong and as rich in resources as it is free."[9]

The American Bank Note Company had already engraved and printed the $20,000,000 of treasury bonds authorized by the Act of June 14, 1858, as well as $7,000,000 of bonds issued under the Act of June 22, 1860, and $10,000,000 of Treasury Notes authorized by the Act of December 17, 1860, so the company was experienced in this type of work. All three of the largest New York bank-note companies prepared bonds, Treasury Notes, and other securities, and the American Bank Note Company and National Bank Note Company also printed the Legal Tender Notes of 1861 and 1862. Towards the end of the war, the American Bank Note Company often prepared plates which were then printed at the Treasury Department's National Currency Bureau, the forerunner of the present-day Bureau of Engraving and Printing.

This was also a time when the congressional debates over a national currency had clearly indicated a resolve to print such money, although the enabling legislation was not passed until February 1863 (National Currency Act), so Edson had several objectives to pursue on his trip to Washington, D.C. The government gave very little time to the New York companies to prepare designs for the seven intended denominations. Because some companies could not finish their designs on time, the government had to extend the bidding three weeks. Contracts were finally awarded to all three of the New York bank-note companies— the American Bank Note Company, the National Bank Note Company, and the newly formed Continental Bank Note Company. The American Bank Note Company got the contract to engrave and print the $10, $20, $50, and $100 denominations. The National Bank Note Company was to engrave and print the $500 and $1,000 denominations, and the Continental Bank Note Company got the $5 denomination. Actually, the Continental Bank Note Company got the best deal because of the volume of $5 notes needed. A later revision of the National Currency Act, passed in June 1864, gave the contract for engraving and printing the $1 denomination to the American Bank Note Company and the $2 notes to the National Bank Note Company. Most of these affairs were handled by John J. Cisco, the assistant secretary of the Treasury, whose offices were in New York. He worked directly with the officers of the various bank-note companies. There was such a demand for the National Bank Notes that the New York companies had trouble keeping up, and the National Bank Note Company was unable to meet the volume of notes under its contract. James Smillie, an engraver at the National Bank Note Company, said that, "Within a short time, all the stockholders were wealthy." And this was true also at the other bank-note companies.

Gray Is A Good Color

In April 1861 an informer notified the U.S. marshal's office in New York City that both the American Bank Note and the National Bank Note companies were printing money for the Confederate States of America. Two deputy marshals raided the offices of the American Bank Note Company and found 18 engraved-steel bank-note plates in their vaults that had been made for the C.S.A. The company's officers stated that they had stopped printing bank notes as soon as the president had issued his proclamation against dealing with the enemy on April 18, 1861. The informer, however, stated that the two companies had continued to print the notes as late as four days before the raid, and therefore they may have been in violation of that proclamation by a few days. According to a newspaper account, the deputy marshals went within one hour to the National Bank Note Company and took possession of two plates of cancelled Treasury Notes of $10, $20, $50, and $100 denominations.[10]

The imprint of the National Bank Note Company is found on a Confederate States of America $1,000 note.

Given the animosity of the Northern states toward anything to do with the South at this time, one would expect such a revelation would have caused an uproar in the newspapers and possibly public demonstrations against the two companies. But the issue was hardly noticed, if at all. Then, after the war, these dirty little problems which had been swept under the rug so carefully by lawyers were suddenly brought to light by the same profession.

Both companies were embarrassed by the revelation on May 8, 1874, that they had tried to get a contract to print the bank notes and other securities of the Confederacy both before and after the Civil War began. The discovery came about during a meeting of the Banking and Currency Committee while they were engaged in hearing the representation of the New York bank-note–printing companies against the Columbian Bank Note Company of Washington, D.C. The issue being argued was the claim of the New York companies that the printing of fractional currency, legal tenders, and bonds should be done only in New York, thereby excluding the Washington company. During the arguments, the attorney for the Columbian Bank Note Company introduced copies of two letters sent to C.G. Memminger, secretary of the Confederate Treasury, and E.C. Elmore, the Confederate treasurer. These letters had been written by Tracy Edson for the American Bank Note Company and J. MacDonough, secretary of the National Bank Note Company, and were a part of the rebel archives captured by the Union Army after the war. The war had begun on April 12, 1861, when Confederate forces fired on Fort Sumter. The letter from the American Bank Note Company was written on March 2, 1861, when it was obvious to everyone that war was just around the corner and any offer from northern bank-note companies to print Confederate currency would clearly be an illegal act of aiding the enemy. The letter of the National Bank Note Company was sent after the fall of Fort Sumter. No formal contracts were ever realized, but the Confederacy did make some small payments for the design work proposed by the northern companies. Some of these payments were affected by G.B. Lamar, their agent in the North.[11]

Although these disclosures were embarrassing to both companies, the public paid no attention. The war had been over for nine years, and neither of the New York bank-note companies was engraving and printing U.S. currency. Sometimes it is best to let sleeping dogs lie.

As the Civil War gradually wore down the Confederate defenses, the American Bank Note Company began to see that its real competition was not another bank-note company but the government's Treasury Department. By 1863 the Treasury was engraving and printing compound-interest notes, five-percent Treasury Notes, and fractional currency. In his report of 1864, Spencer M. Clark, the director of the National Currency Bureau, listed his equipment as 15 transfer presses, 72 hydraulic presses for fractional currency, 96 hand presses, 14 sealing presses, 6 ink mills, and 22 numbering machines. He also had 237 men and 288 women in his work force. The bank-note companies legitimately began to worry that the government was about to take over the engraving and printing of all currency and securities, but the government works slowly, and this didn't happen for more than a decade. Regardless, the American Bank Note Company quickly began to look to foreign bank-note and stamp contracts as an alternate source of income.

Two of the earliest contracts came from the national banks of Greece and Colombia. Each of those countries placed large orders with the company in 1862. By 1865 the American Bank Note Company was printing bank notes for several British territories as well as Brazil, Ecuador, Uruguay, Peru, and Argentina. They also printed government bonds for Peru and stamps for Argentina. Most of these contracts were negotiated by a traveling salesman named Albert Goodall, who was eventually to serve the company as its president.

A 25-drachmai note of the National Bank of Greece, engraved by the American Bank Note Company.

The ABNCo.
After the Consolidation

Congress decided in 1877 that all government currency and securities should be engraved and printed in the Bureau of Engraving and Printing, although there was no specific enabling legislation granting that authority, only appropriation acts for the bureau. The three largest bank-note companies had known for several years that this was coming. An earlier act in 1875 had restricted their participation to not more than one printing (face or back) on a national-currency note, and even before that it was obvious the government could save money by doing their currency production "in house." With the loss of currency printing, and the fact that the American Bank Note Company held a monopoly on printing foreign currency, stock certificates, and bonds, the National Bank Note and Continental Bank Note companies were faced with some hard decisions. They believed the only way to survive was to merge with the American Bank Note Company. The three companies decided to do this in December 1878, and the "consolidation," as it was called, was ratified on January 31, 1879. The new company, retaining the name American Bank Note Company, was incorporated on February 4, 1879, with a capital of $100,000 in the form of 72,000 shares of stock. The stock was apportioned so the original American Bank Note Company got 28,000 shares, or 40%; the National Bank Note Company got 24,480 shares, or 34%; and the Continental Bank Note Company got 18,720 shares, or 26% of the stock. Albert Goodall of the American Bank Note Company was named to continue as president of the consolidated company. The National Bank Note Company closed its offices at 1 Wall Street, and the Continental Bank Note Company closed its Greenwich Street offices. All operations were shoe-horned into the American Bank Note Company offices at 142 Broadway.

The new, consolidated American Bank Note Company continued to expand its overseas currency markets, especially in South and Central America, and eventually they were producing the notes of most of the countries in the Western Hemisphere. This period brought together some of the greatest designing and engraving talent of any bank-note company in history. The foreign notes, especially those printed for private banks, often featured exotic scenes of indigenous flora and fauna, pre-Columbian architecture, waterfalls and other natural wonders, native peoples and industries, and neo-classical allegories. Foreign-government issues usually stuck to the prosaic depiction of national heroes and royalty. America's paper money became gradually better designed from about 1870, reaching its pinnacle in the "Educational Series" of Silver Certificates issued in 1896. The foreign bank notes from the American Bank Note Company also reached new levels of artistic beauty during the last 30 years of the 19th century, lasting another 20 years or so into the new century.

Traveler's Checks

The American Bank Note Company was always a forward-looking and innovative company, and this lead the way in 1891 to their involvement with a new form of security document—the traveler's check. This began when the American Express Company was founded in 1850 in Buffalo, New York, by Henry Wells, William Fargo, and John Butterfield as an express company to move freight. Between 1888 and 1890, James C. Fargo, a brother of William Fargo, took a trip to Europe and carried with him the traditional letters of credit from American banks so he could get foreign cash by cashing personal checks. Although he was the president of the American Express Company and a wealthy man who had impeccable credentials, he found it difficult to get cash in many of the European cities. When he returned home, frustrated by this experience, he asked Marcellus Fleming Berry, an agent of the company, to create a better solution than the letter of credit. Mr. Berry created the American Express Traveler's Cheque in denominations of $10, $20, $50, and $100. The contract to engrave and print the traveler's checks was awarded to the American Bank Note Company, who designed the checks to look like currency. The experiment was enormously successful, and the checks soon became the most widely used form of exchange in the world.

An American Express Company traveler's check engraved and printed by the American Bank Note Company.

Stamps by the Billions

In 1893 the American Bank Note Company designed, engraved, and printed the first commemorative stamps issued by the United States. These 16 stamps were called the "Columbian Issues" in order to commemorate the 1893 World Columbian Exposition held in Chicago. The American Bank Note Company printed over 2 billion stamps whose face value exceeded $40 million. The stamps were oblong and double the usual size to give the engravers enough room to reproduce famous paintings depicting different events in the life of Christopher Columbus. The unsold stamps were destroyed in April 1894. Three different engravers worked on this series— Alfred Jones, then 74 years old, Charles Skinner, age 48, and Robert Savage, in his early 20s. Robert Savage is credited with engraving the 3-cent, 6-cent, 10-cent, $1, and $3 stamps without the collaboration of any other engravers. Alfred Jones engraved the one-cent stamp and worked with Skinner on several other values. It was normally the practice for several engravers to work on each design. Purists objected to these stamps, saying they were created merely to make money for the post office, but the public loved them nevertheless. This was the last time the American Bank Note Company printed stamps for the U.S. government for 50 years.

The counterfeiting of U.S. postage stamps got started during the last quarter of the 19th century. Virtually all counterfeit stamps were made by offset lithography. The Bureau of Engraving and Printing took over the production of all stamps on July 1, 1894, after a contentious dispute over the legality of awarding it the contract. The first known attempt to defraud the post office came on March 31, 1895, when an ad was placed in the *Chicago Tribune* offering to sell two-cent U.S. postage stamps at a discount. The counterfeiting of revenue stamps had a much longer history.

New York Stock Exchange

The New York Stock Exchange, circa 1907.

The floor of the New York Stock Exchange, circa 1907.

One of the most controversial aspects of the long history of the American Bank Note Company was its relationship with the New York Stock Exchange. Right from the beginning, the American Bank Note Company had won a fair share of Wall Street's business, engraving and printing stock certificates, bonds, etc. In November 1874 the Committee on Securities of the New York Stock Exchange issued a formal announcement:

> The numerous frauds practiced upon the community in the Counterfeiting of Stocks and Bonds, and the altering of Certificates from smaller to larger denominations, have compelled the Stock Exchange to use all precautions in their power against them, and to require in all future applications to place Securities on the List, that they shall be carefully engraved by some responsible Bank Note Engraving Company. They recommend that Certificates of Stock of One-hundred Shares should have the denomination conspicuously engraved thereon, and the Certificates of lesser denominations should be of a different style and color. Many companies have already adopted this plan, and any that are still using a printed or lithographed Certificate, are requested, for their own protection, as well as that of the public, to cease doing so, and to change to an engraved one at their earliest convenience. [This was finally adopted December 23, 1874.]

The rules issued by the stock exchange relating to the engraving and printing of certificates were seen by most people as consistent with the protection of securities. In 1885 the exchange ruled that specimen certificates must be on file with the exchange. In 1887 the exchange ruled that work must be done by an approved bank-note company, that two plates must be used—a face plate for black printing and a tint plate for color—and that signatures must be hand-written. In 1890 the exchange ruled that all text must be engraved by hand, and that odd-lot certificates must have punch panels to prevent altering the number of shares written or typed on the certificate. The exchange also required that major portions of the certificates must have steel-engraving, and that

human figures must be shown in vignettes because "human flesh tones and flowing robes allow the engraver to develop light and dark areas through the use of fine and heavy lines. . . . Photographic reproductions of genuine securities flatten out the lines, causing a muddled or mottled appearance."[12]

Drawings of the American Bank Note Company, including the plate room, the ware room, the printing room, and the counting and packing room.

Engraving and printing securities was a very lucrative part of the bank-note business, and the American Bank Note Company not only wanted to preserve their position but also took every opportunity to eliminate the competition. By the late 1870s the owners of rival bank-note companies began to suspect that the American Bank Note Company had an unethical influence on the New York Stock Exchange. An increasing number of private companies found that they had no choice in selecting a firm to engrave and print their stock certificates, and they began to complain as well. A reporter from the *New York Times* was assigned to investigate these complaints in 1884. He interviewed people who were interested in the engraving of securities, including officers of loan and trust companies, railroad officials, and brokers doing business with the stock exchange. His report upset the business community:

> . . . the Stock List Committee will agree to receive securities engraved by the American Bank Note Company before they have begun, but will not promise to receive the work of any other company until after examination. Whenever a railroad company chooses to take the risk and have its bonds engraved by some other company, the securities are rejected by the Stock List Committee, and the company is, at the end, obliged to go to the American Bank Note Company or the Franklin. Among the corporations which have had securities printed by other bank note companies and rejected, and have had to have them done by the American, are the Baltimore and Ohio Railroad, the Rome, Watertown and Ogdensburg, the Ohio and Mississippi, the Denver, Utah and Pacific, the Oswego and Syracuse, the New-York, Susquehana and Western, and the Austin and Northwestern. The State of Virginia has also been a sufferer.

> "I consider the course of the Stock List Committee unjust," said an officer of a trust company. "I am convinced that there are bank note companies in the city which can meet all the requirements of the Stock Exchange. I know that their prices are lower than those of the American, and I know their work is always rejected or else

no action is taken on their applications. It does not look like fair treatment, does it?"

"I know," said a member of the Stock Exchange, "that the American Bank Note Company has a monopoly of the business. I have been compelled to get work done by them for $2,000 which I could have had done elsewhere for $1,400, but the Stock List Committee would only guarantee to accept work by the American. I am going to bring the matter up before the Governing Committee."

"Yes," answered a railroad contractor who does a large business with the American Bank Note Company. "I know, and it is generally well known, that the American company has a monopoly in printing securities which are to be listed on the Stock Exchange. What has been already stated to you is correct, there are other companies which can do the work just as well, and can give just as good security, but they cannot get their work accepted, even in spite of the fact that their prices are lower."

"What I want to know," said another gentleman, "is this: why shouldn't a railroad company be permitted to judge for itself on this question of security? It is quite as much interested in it as the Stock Exchange can be, yet the Stock List Committee compels it to go to the American. Any railroad which proposes to list bonds, will not take the risk of having them rejected when they learn that the committee will not guarantee to accept any work except that of the American. I am acquainted with the work of other bank note companies and know they can do as well as the American. I am acquainted with the responsibility of their Directors, and think it should be satisfactory to the Stock Exchange."

It is asserted that American [Bank Note Company] Directors hold over one-half the stock of the Franklin [Bank Note Company], and that a show of competition is kept up between them which is not genuine. It is also asserted that a subcommittee was appointed by the Stock Exchange Governors to examine the condition of the minor [bank note] companies and that a report favorable to certain ones was returned, but was quietly buried without action. The business of engraving securities amounts to $3,000,000 per year, and has been practically controlled by the American company since 1858. Not more than 5 percent of the business is done by other companies. Minor companies, it is asserted, have been invariably swallowed up by the American.[13]

In spite of the bad publicity that the American Bank Note Company received in the *Times* article, nothing was done about the monopoly until George Kendall began to fight both the American Bank Note Company and the New York Stock Exchange in the press and on billboards in the early part of the 20th century.

Tilting at Windmills — George Kendall

George H. Kendall was born at Slatersville, near Boston, in 1854 and moved to New York City when he was 18 years old. He was in charge of the art department at the *Daily Graphic* for a short time. He set up business as a bank-note engraver in 1877 at 285 Broadway. In 1880 he established the Kendall Bank Note Company at 100 Church Street and filed a certificate of incorporation dated March 12, 1881, that shows the capital stock was $10,000 divided into 1,000 shares.[14] Kendall also established the New York Bank Note Company just a little over eight months after setting up the Kendall Bank Note Company at the same address—87 Liberty Street in New York City. It is curious that he chose the name "New York Bank Note Company," since an earlier firm with that name did such a terrible job of printing fractional currency that the notes were deemed unfit for use. Operating as the New York Bank Note Company, the Kendall firm was allowed to engrave corporate certificates and bonds for members of the New York Stock Exchange until 1892. Then, the order went out that the company's work would no longer be accepted by the powerful Stock Listing Committee. Kendall began a campaign against the stock exchange and the American Bank Note Company as a result. His efforts consisted mostly of charges he made to newspaper reporters, but in 1908 he began to

write to various officials in the New York State government, including the governor, Charles E. Hughes. The governor turned this matter over to Horace White, the lieutenant governor and a recognized financial expert. Lieutenant Governor White's report to Governor Hughes documented the monopoly that Kendall had alleged:

New York, June—, 1909
Honorable Charles E. Hughes,
Governor, Albany, New York

Sir: The committee appointed by you on the 14th of December, 1908, to make an inquiry into facts regarding speculation in securities and commodities have received from the New York Bank Note Company a complaint that the stock exchange prevents any company except the American Bank Note Company from engraving any securities dealt in on that exchange, thereby creating a hurtful monopoly. This complaint, originally addressed to yourself, was, at your instance, referred to us. As the subject matter does not strictly appertain to speculation, the committee have directed me to reply to you in a communication separate from our general report.

We have given the officers of the stock exchange an opportunity to reply to this complaint. They say that on several former occasions they examined the work of the New York Bank Note Company, and its predecessor, the Kendall Bank Note Co, and found that it did not meet the requirements of the exchange as to goodness of work, safeguards for plates, etc., and that the following named corporations are now eligible for such work to be used in dealings on the Stock Exchange: American Bank Note Co, International Bank Note Co, Western Bank Note & Engraving Co of Chicago, British American Bank Note Co for Canadian securities, and Bradbury, Wilkinson & Co of London, England, for securities other than American or Canadian.

It appears to have been the practice of the American Bank Note Co, or the company which owns it, the United Bank Note Corporation, to absorb any other company that acquired the right to do work in the United States for the New York Stock Exchange. In this way, the Homer-Lee Bank

Note Co and the Franklin Bank Note Co were absorbed in 1904, and the International Bank Note Co and the Western Bank Note & Engraving Co in 1905, although the corporate existence of the two last-named companies is still preserved. The officers of the exchange admit that the companies which issue securities are sufferers from this monopoly, both as to prices charged for engraving and as to promptness of delivery, and say that the exchange would be glad to be delivered of such monopoly.

From sources not connected with any of the parties to this controversy we learn that although the stock exchange will accept the work of certain foreign engraving companies, they will accept it only for foreign securities, and that attempts by American corporations to avail themselves of competitive prices by securing bids from foreign engravers have been thus defeated. From this it would seem that other considerations than the goodness of the work and carefulness in guarding the plates, are here operative, and that the Stock Exchange has not rid itself of the evils of monopoly.

Yours, very sincerely,
Horace White, Chairman[15]

In April 1910 Kendall asked for and got a hearing before the Ways and Means Committee of the State Assembly. At that meeting, Kendall made several charges against the "conspirators" as outlined in this article in the *New York Times*:

. . . He added that the American and subsidiary companies were owned by members of the Stock Exchange, and that prices charged by it were double the amount which would yield an ordinary profit. He read four letters, two of which he said he sent to the Stock Exchange and two purporting to be replies. The Stock Exchange in one of the letters, said that the New York Bank Note Company's work had been found to be unsatisfactory.

Mr. Kendall asserted that the loss to the stock-buying public through the monopoly held by the American company was about $5,000 a day, or $1,500,000 a year.

"At one time," Mr. Kendall said, "the [New York Bank Note] company received through

George J. Gould an order to furnish the certificates for the Western Union Company. The Exchange served notice that after a certain time certificates must be those supplied by the American Bank Note Company. Mr. Gould replied that if the Exchange insisted, he would withdraw all his companies and place them in the Consolidated Exchange. That brought the Stock Exchange to terms.

". . . In what little work we have done, the Exchange has made trouble for us. For instance, in the case of the Western Union, if we finished the certificates in brown, they would demand that we do the work over again in green, or vice versa. However, in spite of this, we were able to make a net profit at about 40 per cent the cost charged by the American company."[16]

When that testimony failed to get any immediate results from the state government, Kendall placed his attacks on giant painted billboards on his building at 75 Sixth Avenue so they could be seen by passengers riding past on the elevated railroad. One of these signs measured 12-feet tall and 47-feet long, with the bold title reading "Thieves of the New York Stock Exchange!"[17] Kendall's righteous ranting against the New York Stock Exchange played a small but helpful role in making the public aware of the unethical use of power by Wall Street bankers and business tycoons. The public anger lead to demands for an investigation of Wall Street, and this was noticed by Charles Lindbergh Sr., a congressman and father of the famous aviator. This demand was taken up by Louisiana-congressman Arséme Pujo, who formed a subcommittee of the House Committee on Banking and Currency and forced a number of prominent financiers, such as J.P. Morgan and George F. Baker, to appear before the committee and testify. It was claimed by those who knew him that the stress of testifying before the Pugo Committee contributed to J.P. Morgan's death. The Pujo Committee found that a cabal of financial leaders, known as "the Money Trust," was abusing their public trust to consolidate control over many industries, and this lead to public support for the ratification of the 16th Amendment in 1913 and the passage of the Federal

Reserve Act that same year. If "mighty oaks from little acorns grow," then George Kendall planted one of those acorns.

George Kendall, president of the New York Bank Note Company.

Not content with one oak tree, George Kendall wanted a whole forest, so in 1913 he went to see New York governor William Sulzer to get some legislation passed that would force the New York Stock Exchange to end the monopoly given to the American Bank Note Company. Governor Sulzer listened to Kendall's complaints and referred him to Senator Stephen J. Stilwell, the person who had introduced most of the governor's stock exchange bills in the Senate. Senator Stilwell introduced Mr. Kendall to Mr. Lewis, the Senate clerk, and told Kendall that it would cost him $250 to have the proposed bill drawn up in proper fashion. It was illegal to demand a fee for this service, but Kendall said nothing at the time. Later, Senator Stilwell demanded $3,500 to bring about a favorable report on the bill. Kendall was infuriated and decided to go public with the bribery attempt. He made his charges in a public forum so the Senate would have to act on them. Stilwell temporarily resigned his position on the Senate Judiciary Committee, and that body, controlled by Tammany Hall, decided to hear the evidence, even though it concerned one of their own members and would be a conflict of interest.

Kendall knew from previous experience that everything in this case had to be documented in writing, and, when possible, by witnesses that could attest to what had been said in verbal communications. He made sure to send carefully worded messages to the senator by telegram rather than by letter, paying the extra fee for a signed receipt of delivery. Kendall also had four telephones installed in his office that were connected to the same trunk line, so it was possible to have four of his employees listen in on conversations he had with the senator. One of Kendall's employees knew the senator well enough to recognize his voice and could swear to his identity. Another of Kendall's employees was a stenographer and could take down the conversations verbatim. Kendall had planned his conversations intelligently and repeatedly made reference to the senator's demand for $3,500. He then informed the governor of Senator Stilwell's attempted bribery and the evidence he had collected to prove it. The governor insisted that Kendall give the original evidence to the attorney general for legal review. After the attorney general decided the evidence was compelling, the governor instructed him to try the senator before the Judiciary Committee, let them decide if he was guilty or not, and present the facts to the Senate. This was done in open sessions, but the committee voted 28 to 21 that Kendall's accusations were not sustained. This created an outrage in the press, and the governor decided to turn the evidence over to a Grand Jury.

The Grand Jury heard the same evidence that was presented to the Senate Judiciary Committee but found the senator guilty of bribery. He was disbarred and sentenced to serve four to six years in Sing Sing Prison.[18] George Kendall's 30-year fight with the stock exchange and the American Bank Note Company ended when he died on April 24, 1924, at his apartment in the Sherman Square Hotel at Broadway and 71st Street.[19]

But we can't bury George Kendall without telling another story about his long fight with the American Bank Note Company. In 1882 the Commonwealth of Virginia approved an act known as Chapter 81 to fund the public debt by issuing $21 million in bonds in a sinking fund. Bids were solicited from reputable bank-note companies and three responded: the American Bank Note Company, the Western Bank Note Company in Chicago, and the Kendall Bank Note Company of New York. The bid of the Chicago company was rejected by all three commissioners of the sinking fund. The American Bank Note Company was the high bidder by about $1,500. Since the Kendall company met all the requirements—including a $100,000 surety bond to guarantee the completion of the work, a presentation of specimens of their work, and a list of the officers of the company to show that they were a reputable firm—the contract for engraving and printing of the bonds was awarded to them.

George Kendall immediately left for Richmond to meet with one of the commissioners to get the specifications of the contract. In an affidavit that Kendall submitted later, he stated that he met with S. Brown Allen, the first auditor, at his office in the capitol, and later that day Mr. Allen asked if he could meet with Mr. Kendall privately in the afternoon at his hotel room.[20] At that meeting, "the said S. Brown Allen there expressed unwillingness to award the contract to the Kendall Bank Note Company, saying his [political] party were under obligations to the American Bank Note Company for the sum of $5,000 advanced to help the campaign of United States Senator Mahone. Kendall further alleged that Mr. Allen had said that he might influence his party to accept the Kendall Bank Note Company's offer if Mr. Kendall would make a 'rebate' of $1,000, and that a present for his [Allen's] trouble would not be objectionable."

Kendall would not go along with this bribe, and Mr. Allen got an injunction to prevent the Kendall company from continuing to print the bonds. After an investigation was held and testimony was given by both sides, the court lifted the injunction, exonerated George H. Kendall of all charges, and let the Kendall company continue with its work on the printing of the bonds. Albert Goodall, speaking for the American Bank Note Company, denied that his company had

ever given even one cent for Senator Mahone's campaign.

A $2 note of the John McK. Gunn Banking House, engraved by the New York Bank Note Company.

Porter & Robertson vs. the ABNCo.

The internal affairs of the American Bank Note Company were often stormy, especially on matters of management. One of the more dramatic episodes occurred at the end of 1902, when charges of mismanagement were made public by two shareholders, Louis H. Porter and W.T. Robertson. Their complaints were especially important to the other shareholders because the plaintiffs were so well known. Louis H. Porter, a prominent lawyer, was the son of Timothy H. Porter, a trustee of the American Bank Note Company from 1879 to 1894. W.T. Robertson was the son of Touro Robertson, who helped to establish the Continental Bank Note Company and who held many of the patents for machinery used by the American Bank Note Company.

The charges made by these two men were carefully documented and printed in a circular that was sent to all shareholders. According to the *New York Times*,

> The circular declares that the Directors who control the company represent only 5,811 shares of stock, and that they are not managing the affairs of the company solely in the interest of the stockholders at large. The circular intimates that several officials are being overpaid, and that the best offices are held by friends and relatives of E.C. Converse, the dominating power on the board. The circular declares that the stockholders can get no information about the business of the company,

and the statement of its condition given out in the last annual meeting is unintelligible, except that it shows the assets of the company to be only $28 a share, when the par value is $50.[21]

The American Bank Note Company at that time had a capital of $3 million divided into 72,000 shares of $50 each. The stock was being quoted at $59 asked and $57 bid. Porter and Robertson's complaints found a receptive audience in the shareholders across the country, and they sent their proxies to the men to be used at the next annual meeting to effect change in the company's by-laws. However, the directors of the company controlled more shares than the plaintiffs, and nothing immediately came of this minor rebellion.

An article written in 1910 and published in the *New York Times* gives a little more detail to the story:

In 1906, the corporation increased its capital to $10,000,000, when it was reorganized by William Nelson Cromwell, the lawyer. Edward C. Converse, the banker, was elected President. Between 1902 and 1906, several of the Directors, including Mr. Converse, Mr. Cromwell, its attorney, and F.L. Hine, gathered as much of the stock of the concern as possible. They paid, it is said, Louis H. Porter, a son of Timothy H. Porter, a founder of the company [*sic*], $60 a share for his 3,000 shares, and a similarly low price for some 5,000 shares held by estates in and around Boston. Shortly after this, it is said, American Bank Note stock was quoted at $90 a share.

After Mr. Cromwell and his associates had gathered up the bulk of the loose stock, articles of incorporation were filed in Albany, and the concern became known by its present title, the United Bank Note Corporation. Although the papers of incorporation were filed on February 20, 1906, it was not until two months later that the names of some of the company's real Directors became known. Seven certified to the payment of one-half of the company's capital stock as "$600,000 in money and $4,400,000 in property." These Directors were E.C. Converse, Warren L. Green, Francis L. Potts, Charles A. Moore, William Nelson Cromwell, F.L. Hine, and Andrew V. Stout. Under date of December 12, 1905, the plan of recapitalization of the American Bank Note Company had been put out by a committee composed of Messrs. Cromwell, Converse, Hine, Freeland and Green, with Sullivan and Cromwell as attorneys.

The new stock pays 4 per cent on the common and 6 per cent preferred. On April 2, 1909, the corporation published a statement which showed a surplus of $3,422,740. . .

Mr. Cromwell began to take an active interest in the affairs of the American Bank Note Company in 1902. He has the backing of President Converse and the latter's relatives, J. Macdonough and Warren L. Green, Mr. Hine, and Mrs. J. Pierpont Morgan, who inherited a financial interest in the company. Mr. Green, it is said, draws a salary at present as President of the old American Bank Note Company.[22]

The Canadian Affair

In 1896 the American Bank Note Company was awarded a contract to design, engrave, and print Canadian bank notes, stamps, debentures, stock certificates, bills of exchange, and other securities. The award of the contract to an American company created a public outcry in Canada and lead to Parliamentary debates. It was found that the minister of finance, W.S. Fielding, had acted improperly in virtually every aspect of the bid proposal. First, the government would not allow the work to be done in Montreal or Toronto but insisted it be done in Ottawa. Three or four Canadian firms read the government's specifications very carefully but found that the cost of setting up a plant in Ottawa was too great, and the other risks were also too great, so they declined to submit bids. The exception was the British-American Bank Note Company, which was based in Ottawa.

The bids for the contract were opened on November 21, 1896, and the British-American company sent along a check for $5,000 as a deposit as required by the specifications. If the government chose not to accept their bid, and there were no others, it was normal procedure to ask for new tenders from all the qualified companies. In this case, however, the government did not communicate at all with the British-American company until January 8, 1897, and then only to inform them that another company had been awarded the contract. G.B. Burland, the president of the British-American, learned that the award was given to the American Bank Note Company by reading a news story in the *Toronto Globe*. As it was later learned in an investigation, the Ministry of Finance had used the time between the opening of bids on November 21 and its letter to Burland on the following January 8 to correspond with the American Bank Note Company for the purpose of removing certain specifications in the contract that were not acceptable to the American Bank Note Company, as well as to include other specifications that virtually assured that only the American Bank Note Company could meet the requirements. There was no evidence found to prove collusion between the minister of finance and the American Bank Note Company, but the perception of wrongdoing was created by the minister's improper procedures.[23] The Canadian public was quick to ask that if Montreal and Toronto were unacceptable, why did the government give the contract to a company in New York? Canadian auditors later found that the granting of the contract to the American Bank Note Company would save the government about $150,000 over five years, and that did much to assuage the public's anger.

A $1 note engraved and printed
by the British-American Bank Note Company.

Expansion

Beginning about 1905, the American Bank Note Company began surveying the entire metropolitan district to see if there were any better locations for the company's business. They finally settled on the Hunt's Point section of the Bronx. In late November 1908 they finished negotiating the purchase of 123 lots for a large plant that would accommodate 2,500 to 3,000 employees when finished but which could be expanded to accept a workforce of 5,000.[24] The four buildings planned would house the mechanical plant, and the executive offices would remain at the handsome marble building at Broad and Beaver streets. The mechanical plant had been housed at its building at Trinity Place and Thomas Street. According to an article in the *New York Times*, "Some idea of the size of these [four] buildings may be gathered from the dimensions of the block they are to occupy. It measures 375 feet on Garrison Avenue, 225 feet on Tiffany Street, 525 feet on Barretto Street, and 404 feet on Lafayette Avenue, a total of 1,520 feet of street frontage, or more than a quarter of a mile."[25] One interesting feature of the design was the absence of any doors in the rear of the complex or on the sides. Everything and everyone would pass through a main entrance in the front. The article said that the company would employ the highest class of skilled workmen, and their salaries would range from $40 to $75 a week. The construction was expected to cost more than $2,000,000, but that did not concern the trustees too much. The company at that time had a capital reserve of $10,000,000. Warren L. Green was the president, and the company had printing establishments and sales offices in Boston and Philadelphia, as well as sales offices in Baltimore, Pittsburgh, Atlanta, St. Louis, and San Francisco.

Two Giants: National and Continental

The National Bank Note Company (NBNCo.)

The imprint of the National Bank Note Company appears on a $5 bill of the Bank of America.

As the American Bank Note Company was being formed in 1858, some of the employees of the old firm of Danforth, Wright & Company decided they would not join the association of the six other companies. As a consequence, Danforth, Wright & Company split into two companies. One of these, taking the name Danforth, Perkins & Company, took the dies and machinery of the parent firm into the American Bank Note Company. The other group of employees—George H. Danforth, Samuel Stiles, Fitch Shepard, William D. Nichols, and James Macdonough—decided to form a new company to be called the National Bank Note Company.[1] At the same time, a number of employees at the American Bank Note Company began to leave, possibly because of the crowded working conditions that resulted when the American Bank Note Company took the old offices of Rawdon, Wright, Hatch & Edson in the Merchants Exchange. In addition, several independent bank-note engravers and practical men, feeling that they could not compete against the giant American Bank Note Company, saw the National Bank Note Company as a way to survive. Drawing on this group of enormously talented men, the National Bank Note Company picked some of the best—the great James Smillie, Joseph Ives Pease, William E. Marshall, George

W. Thurber, Joseph P. Ourdan, and Cyrus Durand. The company was officially founded on October 31, 1859, and its first home was the former offices of Danforth, Wright & Company at No. 1 Wall Street.

The capital stock of the company was $60,000 divided into 1,200 shares at $50 each. The shares were divided between the original nine trustees and others in the following manner:

> Robert S. Oakley, President
>> 100 shares
>
> James T. Soutter, Vice-President
>> 50 shares
>
> Samuel Stiles, Treasurer
>> 100 shares
>
> James Macdonough, Secretary & Designer
>> 136 shares
>
> William D. Nichols, Engraving & Printing Dept.
>> 136 shares
>
> George H. Danforth, Transferring Dept.
>> 136 shares
>
> Fitch Shepard, Traveling salesman
>> 136 shares
>
> Lloyd Glover, Traveling salesman
>> 136 shares
>
> John H. Van Antwerp, Banker of Albany
>> 50 shares
>
> Seven principal engravers
>> 136 shares
>
> Three or four outside friends
>> 84 shares

The research of Clarence Brazer shows that Augustus D. Shepard was brought into the company as treasurer after Samuel Stiles died on April 3, 1861. Robert S. Oakley, the first president, was a cashier at the American Exchange

Bank in New York until the spring of 1860, after which he resigned from the bank and devoted his full time to the National Bank Note Company until he died on January 16, 1862. Lloyd Glover died suddenly on August 2, 1862, while he was away from his home in Brooklyn on a trip to Illinois. James T. Soutter, president of the Bank of the Republic at No. 2 Wall Street, left the United States in 1861 and transferred his stock to his son-in-law. Fitch Shepard, originally a cashier at the Chautaqua Bank in Jamestown, New York, joined Danforth, Wright & Company, and after the founding of the National Bank Note Company, he served as a traveling salesman with them until he was elected president in 1863.

Since the dies and machinery of Danforth, Perkins & Company had been taken into the American Bank Note Company, the newly formed National Bank Note Company had to rush to purchase equipment, make new dies, print bank-note Proofs and specimen sheets, and get them out to the salesmen to take to their customers for approval. To make matters even more hectic, three of the original trustees with administrative functions died within the first two years the company was open.

The National Bank Note Company was like other bank-note companies and required all employees to work ten hours a day, six days a week, with only four paid holidays a year. Many employees found that the housing in New York was too expensive and chose to live in New Jersey, making the long commute to New York each day by taking horse-drawn street cars to reach the Newark railroad station, then taking the train to Jersey City, and from there taking a ferry across the Hudson River to New York, from where they again had to take a horse-drawn street car to reach their job. Apprentice engravers also often took one or two hours of art lessons at night schools.

The National Bank Note Company immediately faced the problem that some of the technical processes required by government contract were owned by the American Bank Note Company, and initially they would not agree to turn them over to the competition. State laws had to be passed that allowed the National Bank Note Company to use similar or modified processes. Eventually, Secretary Chase solved the problem forcefully.[2] Since the demand for the National Bank Notes was so great, it was sometimes necessary for the American Bank Note Company and the National Bank Note Company to collaborate in their preparations, and for that reason, both company names appear on some notes. In just the first four months of 1863, the National Bank Note Company produced 4,774,284 sheets of paper money, or 89,785,024 notes.

Making Postage Stamps

The Civil War required that new stamps be issued. The North feared that the Southern states would seize the large number of postage stamps held in 8,535 post offices in the 11 Confederate states and sell then secretly in the North to help finance the war. The North also wanted to interrupt communications in the Confederacy to hurt the rebellion. The old contract with Toppan, Carpenter & Casilear was due to expire in June 1861, so Postmaster Montgomery Blair put out a request for

A sheet of 3-cent stamps printed by the National Bank Note Company for the U.S. Post Office Department.

bids on new stamps. The stamp designs were submitted to a panel of disinterested experts who picked the one from the National Bank Note Company. National's bid was also 30% less than the bid from Toppan, Carpenter & Casilear. At the time, northerners were using roughly 200 million stamps a year, so the contract was a lucrative plum for the National Bank Note Company.

On August 15, 1861, the National Bank Note Company signed a contract with the U.S. Post

Office Department to print all U.S. postage stamps until August 15, 1867. By the end of the war, the National Bank Note Company was producing over 387 million stamps a year and about 26 million stamped envelopes. To provide this production, the National Bank Note Company had to move its stamp printing to a new location with more space. This department, under the management of Charles F. Steel, was located at No. 53 Broadway. Steel had previously worked for five years supervising stamp production with Toppan, Carpenter & Company, so once he joined the National Bank Note Company, it didn't require much time to acquire the necessary machinery and teach employees how to make stamps. All of the 1861 stamp designs were the work of James Macdonough. Joseph Pease was the principal engraver on the 1-cent, 2-cent, 30-cent, and 90-cent stamps; Joseph Ourdan engraved the 3-cent and 15-cent stamps; and William Marshall did the 5-cent, 10-cent, 12-cent, and 24-cent values. The post office awarded a new contract to the National Bank Note Company on October 3, 1868, for the printing of a new series of U.S. postage stamps that are now known as the 1869 stamps. These were the first to be printed in two colors. The National Bank Note Company got the contract primarily due to the efforts of Charles F. Steel.

Charles Franklin Steel

Charles F. Steel was born on January 24, 1832, in Philadelphia, Pennsylvania, the son of Robert Steel, a widely known Philadelphia merchant. He learned the book-binding trade first, and before he was of age, he was in charge of a large concern in Indianapolis. Later, he worked for the firm of Toppan, Carpenter & Company in Philadelphia, starting with their stamp department in 1855. When that company's government contract was transferred to the National Bank Note Company in 1861, Steel decided to go with it and was hired at the National Bank Note Company on June 1, 1861, to supervise their new stamp department. On October 22, 1867, he was granted Patent No. 70,174 for embossing stamp paper. This patent addressed the perceived problem of "washing" or

removing stamp cancellations so the stamps could be used again. It was common practice for postal workers to cancel stamps either by pen and ink or by using a rubber hand stamp. Ink eradicators were available that made the job of removing the cancellations easy. The problem was probably more feared than actually practiced, because very few "washed" stamps have survived from that time, but real or imagined, it was a concern for the post office. Steel's patent used a process called "grilling" in which the fibers of the paper were broken by embossed grills to such an extent that cancelling ink would soak into the paper and could not be easily removed by solvents. The grills were applied to the paper by a relatively simple machine that used a roller with small raised pyramids of metal. When a sheet of stamp paper was run through, the machine made small pyramid-like invaginations on the paper. On December 9, 1867, Steel sold the patent rights to the National Bank Note Company for a royalty of 3¢ per 1,000 stamps. He remained with the company for the 12 years it had contracts to print stamps. Following his work with the National Bank Note Company, he became one of the founders of the Franklin Bank Note Company. He died suddenly on January 2, 1904, at his home at 255 Steuben Street, Brooklyn.

The National Bank Note Company continued to expand for several years after the Civil War. In 1866 it opened offices at No. 9 Nassau Street, and from 1870 to 1875 the engraving and printing departments were located on the upper (6th) floor of the Cooper Union for the Advancement of Science and Art, where Third and Fourth avenues merge into the Bowery on the edge of Manhattan's East Village. The members of the art department (engravers) got together for a group picture just before the National Bank Note Company consolidated with the American Bank Note Company in 1879. That picture shows Richard Berry, Thomas J. Gleason, James Macdonough, Christian Rost, Alfred Jones, and Marcus W. Baldwin, all prominent or soon-to-be prominent men in the industry. Other employees included "Pop" McCoy, an engraver of unknown specialty; David Farrington, a letter engraver; Rawdon Packer, a script engraver; Thomas Kenworthy, a letter engraver; Douglas S.

Ronaldson, a letter and ornamental engraver; Peter Perrine, a pictorial engraver; D. Cooper, a letter engraver; William Chorlton, a vignette engraver who started engraving for the National Bank Note Company when he was only 16; William E. Hidden, a designer and bank-note modeler; and William Ponickau, an engraver of unknown specialty.

An act of Congress for the fiscal year of 1878 required that all work in the engraving and printing of the U.S. currency and securities be done at the Bureau of Engraving and Printing. For all three of the New York bank-note companies, the National Bank Note and Continental Bank Note companies especially, this meant the loss of government work and the strong possibility that they would have to close. Discussions were held between the top officials of the three companies, and it was agreed, on December 27, 1878, to consolidate under the name of the American Bank Note Company. The agreement was ratified on January 31, 1879.

The Continental Bank Note Company (CBNCo.)

The imprint of the Continental Bank Note Company appears on a $1 note of the Brunswick & Albany Rail Road Company.

The Continental Bank Note Company was formed by Waterman Lily Ormsby and a group of financial backers in January 1863. Ormsby was a mechanically gifted bank-note engraver and printer who established the New York Bank Note Company in 1842, and for the next 20 years, he was engaged in that business and did commercial engraving as well. He was, for example, the favorite cylinder engraver of the Colt Arms Company. Until recently, it was thought that he closed the New York Bank Note Company and later went to work as a transfer-press operator for the Continental Bank Note Company.

Letters that Ormsby wrote to Secretary Chase in 1867 revealed a much different story. Ormsby actually never shut down the New York Bank Note Company but merely changed its name to the Continental Bank Note Company, bringing in a small group of investors so he could compete with the American Bank Note and National Bank Note companies. Ormsby was not invited to join the association of seven firms that formed the American Bank Note Company in 1858 because of an allegation that he facilitated counterfeiting. He sued the person making the allegation, and the court case was reported in all the New York newspapers, which further damaged his reputation.[3] When the Civil War started and the government needed experienced bank-note engraving companies to produce currency and other securities, Secretary Chase expressed a doubt about the character of Mr. Ormsby and said he should have nothing to do with the printing of government money. At that point, the trustees of the Continental Bank Note Company removed Mr. Ormsby from his position and replaced him with the vice-president, William D. Wilson. A request was sent to Secretary Chase asking for a full investigation of the charges against Ormsby, and the secretary turned the matter over to Hugh McCulloch, the Comptroller of the Currency. Mr. McCulloch's investigation cleared Ormsby of the charges and gave him a letter to that effect. Upon presenting the letter to the trustees of the Continental Bank Note Company, Ormsby was reinstated as "head of the practical part of the business."

Although the New York Bank Note Company had all the machinery needed to engrave and print bank notes and securities, including its own version of a geometric lathe, it had never been a large company and did not initially have the ability to handle large government contracts. Ormsby needed money to hire employees, and for that reason he brought wealthy investors into the company. Because Ormsby had a bad reputation as a result of the law suit, the trustees decided not to list him in the papers of incorporation. The trustees changed rather frequently, and except for one—Touro Robertson—they are not well known. The capital stock of the company was set at $60,000, divided into 120 shares at $500 a share.

The three officers of the company were Edward G. Steele, Touro Robertson, and his uncle, Alexander C. Wilson.[4,5]

The Continental Bank Note Company occupied the four upper floors of a building at 114 Greenwich Street (corner of Liberty Street) which was owned at the time by J.J. Cisco, the assistant secretary of the Treasury Department, and since it was his job to coordinate negotiations between the Treasury Department and the various bank-note companies in New York on matters of engraving and printing the government's currency and securities, this landlord/renter relationship would be an unethical conflict of interest by today's business standards. The Continental Bank Note Company also had a satellite office on Nassau Street in 1866. They rented additional space on Williams Street for printing in 1873, and the next year they rented space at 120 Broadway, which they occupied through 1876.

The Continental Bank Note Company brought together a group of superbly talented designers and engravers. These included Joseph Prosper Ourdan, a portrait engraver who had apprenticed with Ormsby and worked at the New York Bank Note Company as well as briefly at the Continental Bank Note Company; Henry S. Beckwith, a pictorial engraver; James S. King, an allegorical engraver; Charles Skinner, a portrait and pictorial engraver; Robert Hinshelwood, a pictorial engraver; Daniel F. Caughlan, a letter engraver; Peter Hall, a script-letter engraver; Atwood Porter, a letter engraver; Joseph Claxton, a designer and script engraver; J. Meignelle, a square-letter and script engraver; Edward Fenwick, a letter and general engraver; George W. Holding, a letter engraver; Edward P. Baker, a sales agent; and George H. Staynor, who was in charge of production. They also had the able assistance of two men who were not engravers but who made a material difference in the fortunes of the company—Touro Robertson and Charles F. Steel. Robertson proved to be mechanically inclined and made several improvements to printing presses. Charles F. Steel, who had specialized in stamp production at Toppan, Carpenter & Company, and then later at the National Bank Note Company, now came

over to the Continental Bank Note Company (1873–1877) and was instrumental in getting government contracts to print stamps. Though the Continental Bank Note Company was the last of the large bank-note companies to be established in New York during this period, and presumably had a smaller group of talented engravers and designers to choose from, the record proves that they chose well, as their employees did excellent work, fully the equal of the other companies.

The $5 first-charter note.

Though it brought them no money, the first success of the Continental Bank Note Company was to convince the government to get rid of the bronzing process that had been used on fractional currency and was intended for use on the national currency. This came about when the government first asked the three largest bank-note companies in New York, as well as Butler & Carpenter of Philadelphia, to submit designs for a national currency and Treasury Notes. All the companies submitted their designs in April 1863, but the government rejected all of them and requested new designs to be submitted by May 8. On May 26, the Continental Bank Note Company was told it would be awarded the contract to print the $5 and $10 notes, but this was later changed and the $10 note was given to the American Bank Note Company. Secretary Salmon Chase signed that contract on July 13, 1863.[6] These designs were printed on bank-note paper, with and without the bronzing, and were sent to the Treasury with the recommendation to stop using the bronzing process. That effort succeeded and the Continental Bank Note Company was told to proceed with the printing of 300,000 sheets without the bronze. Other companies were also soon told to abandon the bronzing process.

The Continental Bank Note Company also engraved and printed stock certificates and bonds and other types of securities. The most interesting of these are possibly the bonds engraved and printed for the "Irish Republic," a name used by the Fenian Brotherhood: a secret, revolutionary society organized in the United States in 1858 to achieve Irish independence from England by force. These were ornately engraved, printed in green and black with red numerals, and were made to look like currency with vignettes of famous Irishmen. Since the bonds promised six-percent interest, they were very popular.[7] They were also controversial notes since the Fenian movement created a lot of dissension between England and America.

A Fenian Society Bond engraved and printed by the Continental Bank Note Company.

On July 23, 1873, the Continental Bank Note Company was awarded the contract to print all U.S. postage stamps, later including the official and newspaper stamps, for a period of four years starting on May 1, 1874. The Continental Bank Note Company got the plates from the National Bank Note Company to continue printing the same stamps, but they added a secret mark to the plates of the lower values to distinguish them from previous issues. When the contract came up again for bidding in 1877, there were four bidders: the Standard Publishing Company of Syracuse, New York; Charles F. Steel for the Franklin Engraving and Printing Company of New York (later called the Franklin Bank Note Company); the Philadelphia Bank Note Company; and the Continental Bank Note Company.

The lowest bidder, at $9.95 per 1,000 stamps, was the Standard Publishing Company, a newspaper, job-printing, and lithographic company. The next-lowest bidder was the Continental Bank Note Company at $9.98 per 1,000 stamps. The Continental Bank Note Company protested to Postmaster General David M. Kay that the bid had been intended only for "steel-plate engravers and plate printers," which the Standard Publishing Company did not claim to be, and therefore, their bid should not have been allowed. The company also reminded the postmaster general that he had the right to reject any bid that was not in the best interest of the government. The postmaster general listened to arguments on both sides and decided to give the contract to the Continental Bank Note Company since the difference in price was trifling, amounting to only $200 per year, which would be less expensive than shipping the stamps from Syracuse to New York.[8] The Continental Bank Note Company held the contract until it merged with the American Bank Note and the National Bank Note companies in the great "Consolidation" of 1879.

The Continental Bank Note Company was the first bank-note company to be controlled by bankers rather than professional artists who specialized in bank-note work. Some of the investors in the Continental Bank Note Company, such as Touro Robertson, learned the business from the ground up, but most were interested only in the profits. It would seem that the more professionally managed companies placed less emphasis on the artistic value of their notes and securities. There are some exceptions to this rule, but one generally sees that art and business do not mix well.

Waterman Lily Ormsby

A $1 note showcasing the design principles of Ormsby's Unit System.

Waterman Lily Ormsby was not only the most colorful and provocative of the bank-note–company owners but also the most analytical and technically minded of that small group of men. He was born in Hampton, Connecticut, on September 9, 1809, the second of three children born to Leonard and Elizabeth Ormsby.[9] He grew up on the family farm in Hampton and received a normal education in the public schools. He wrote that he was a "young blacksmith in William Cobb's Shop" in Rochester, New York, in 1825. Around this time, he married his wife, Julia, and began taking instructions in engraving. Before long he was engraving book illustrations for Carter, Andrews & Company in Lancaster, Massachusetts. He was a student at the National Academy of Design in 1829. His son, Waterman Lily Ormsby Jr., was born in December 1834. Soon after, the family moved to Boston, and Waterman began engraving vignettes for the New England Bank Note Company while also working on book illustrations for the publishing trade.

There is no question that Ormsby had mechanical skills far beyond the ordinary mechanic. He is sometimes described as an inventive genius. Actually, he invented very little. In his pamphlet, "Cycloidal Configurations," written in 1862, he claims to have invented 24 separate devices for engraving, but a close examination of his list shows that most of the devices were simply modifications to existing machines—improvements, perhaps—but not original inventions. His metal-ruling machine, which dates from 1832, was capable of making both straight and waved lines, but that was hardly new. In 1833 he made a medallion-engraving machine in which the medal to be copied was held in an upright position. The next year he made a medallion engraver for metals held horizontally and invented an "Automaton," a clockwork device for enlarging or reducing the size of a drawing or engraving. The British term is "pentograph," and that idiom was sometimes used in 19th-century America. About 1835 Ormsby moved to New York City and opened a shop called Ormsby's Pentographic Establishment at 26 Vandam Street. He probably worked there as an illustrator, using a pantograph to enlarge or reduce

drawings onto a copper plate for later engraving with a burin. In January 1836 he met Samuel Colt in Samuel Hall's gun shop in New York and soon formed a strong business association with him. Later that year, he invented a machine for engraving the cylinders of Samuel Colt's revolvers. Colt liked the work so much that almost every percussion pistol he made was roll engraved by Ormsby.[10]

A Colt revolver bearing some engraving by Ormsby.

The Proof plate of the "Texas Rangers" scene found on the Walker- and Dragoon-model Colt revolvers.

Ormsby placing engraved scenes on the cylinders of revolvers was probably the first time this was done by the transferring process instead of engraving the scenes by hand, as was previously on larger flintlock and percussion guns such as rifles and shotguns. In 1838 he made a device for registering the movements of a bank-note printing press, something that John Oldham had invented for the Bank of Ireland in 1816. The next year he "invented" a "kaleidoscopic" combination of geometric-lathe work. He never explained this invention in detail, so we can't be sure how it worked, but geometric-lathe work was certainly not new.

By 1840 he had made improvements to the Bogardus transfer press. His "grammagraph" (1841) was obviously a pantograph, although Ormsby described it as a machine for making map letters. The grammagraph may have traced letters directly onto a copper plate, but again, pantograph-lettering machines were already in use. His "kaleidograph" of 1846 was not patented, and its function is not known. This is true also of "kaleido-Mosaic Engraving," invented in 1861. A few of his "inventions" pertain to engraving metal combs, pencil cases, and lockets, and lie outside the field of bank-note engraving. "Genius" is an overworked word and doesn't seem to fit Ormsby's record. None of his contemporaries spoke of him as a genius, and he apparently never applied for a patent to most of his inventions. None of this, however, takes anything away from his invention of the Unit System. That idea, which shows that he could think "outside the box," as we like to say now, could have done much to suppress counterfeiting until photography came of age. In bank-note designing, he was certainly a man ahead of his time.

It would appear that Ormsby's first efforts in bank-note engraving came in 1838 when notes were issued by the Manhattan Association with his imprint. These notes were hand-dated and denominated in $1.50, $3, $5, and $10 values. The Manhattan Association is not listed in the Haxby *Standard Catalog*, nor on any New York banking histories I've searched online, so these notes may be fairly scarce.[11] Ormsby established the New York Bank Note Company at 142 Nassau Street in 1842, and over the next 16 years or so he engraved and printed a number of notes that were issued by fraudulent banks, doing great harm to his reputation. Of the 10 banks in the District of Columbia for which he engraved notes, all were fraudulent, non-existent institutions. The Haxby *Standard Catalog* shows that he also engraved perfectly good notes for many banks in the eastern and mid-western states, but his record leaves the impression that he worked readily for unscrupulous men. The problem for Ormsby is that we do not know if he acted naively and was duped by counterfeiters or if he knew the criminal intentions of some of his clients and willingly engraved notes for them. But even without knowing his innocence or guilt, we can, at the very least, say that he facilitated counterfeiters in several instances with a reckless disregard for preventing counterfeiting. Complicating this enigma is the fact that counterfeiters could cleverly imitate honest bankers and often presented counterfeit letters of recommendation from officials. And just because a counterfeit note was imprinted with the name of a prestigious bank-note company did not mean the company had anything to do with the note. Even the venerable firm of Rawdon, Wright, Hatch & Edson appears on many counterfeit notes before the Civil War.

The Unit System

In August 1852 W.L. Ormsby published a detailed treatise entitled *A Description of the Present System of Bank Note Engraving, Showing Its Tendency to Facilitate Counterfeiting*. It was the first book to address this subject, and for almost 50 years, it was the most comprehensive and best-written description of how bank notes were made.[12] The book was intended for banking institutions and the public, but at a price of $12, when most illustrated books cost a dollar or less, it was not likely to become a best seller. Ormsby's objective was to show that the system being used to make bank notes in the United States had serious flaws which made counterfeiting fairly easy. Ormsby called this a "patchwork system" and proposed to replace it with a new method called the Unit System, based on six far-reaching requisites. His book was written in a clear, non-technical style and presented his arguments in a logical order with plenty of explanation as to why the old system didn't work. Since he had years of experience in making bank notes by the old patchwork method, he understood every aspect of the mechanical side of the business. But he also had the motivation and the honesty to look at the whole process and figure out why counterfeiting was so easy.

A $1 certificate of deposit engraved by Ormsby.

A $10 note of the Commercial Bank engraved by Ormsby.

The patchwork system worked like an assembly line. A finished note was simply an assembly of many different design elements, whether a portrait vignette, square lettering, script lettering, geometric or cycloidal lathe work, etching, ornamental engraving, tint engraving, etc. These design elements were done by engravers who specialized in one particular technique, and the siderographer then took their separate dies, hardened them, and impressed them on a soft-steel or copper plate. Gradually a bank-note plate was built up from these separate dies. Ormsby argued that the separate dies became stock items in a bank-note company's inventory and were often auctioned off when a company went out of business. Dishonest engravers made extra money by selling custom-made dies to crooks. Actually, there is very little evidence of these things happening in either newspaper accounts or the Secret Service files, but that was Ormsby's rationale to criticize the patchwork system.

Ormsby wanted to do away with all the machinery—the transfer press, ruling machines, geometric lathes—everything! Instead, an artist would engrave a single panoramic scene that covered the whole surface of a note, with the lettering so interwoven by the hand of the engraver that it formed an integral part of the whole picture.

If no dies were used, then none could find their way to the counterfeiter. If the name of the bank and the denomination were interwoven into the design, then neither could be changed without leaving evidence of the alteration. In Ormsby's Unit System there would be no more mechanical engraving. Everything would be done by hand and primarily by one artist. Lettering might require a second engraver, but it would be done within the space provided by the primary artist.

Secondly, Ormsby wanted each bank to copyright the unique design on the face of each different denomination so the designs couldn't be used for any other purpose. Every bank would have copyrighted designs, and no two banks could share the same design. A third requisite was to have all bank notes engraved on the back side. Almost all notes were engraved and printed on one side only at that time, although the idea of printing notes on the back wasn't exactly new. John Keats, an engraver in Philadelphia, had taken out a patent entitled "Printing on the Back of Bank-Notes" on April 28, 1815, but nothing seems to have come of it for many years. Printing both sides of a note would cost more for banks but would make counterfeiting more difficult.

Ormsby's fourth requisite was to have engravers make copies of the master plate by the electrotype process, which he said was the simplest and most accurate of all the transferring processes. The copies would be used to print the actual notes and the master plate would be kept in safe storage so it would never wear out or require repair. A fifth requisite would have every state enact a law requiring uniformity of size in every note issued in that state. Each denomination, however, would be of slightly greater size as the value of the note increased. All $1 notes would be the same size, all $2 notes of a slightly larger size, and so on. This would enable an observer to detect any alteration in the denomination of a note.

Finally, Ormsby thought the design selected for a note should follow some principle of indicating the locality of the issuing authority. For example, a view of Niagara Falls should be used for banks in that area, or a view of the Bunker Hill Monument should be used for banks in Charlestown or Boston. Taken together, the changes proposed by Ormsby were, indeed, radical. Yet, his arguments were logical, even if impractical. Mark Tomasko has argued that during the state-bank–note era, the printing runs were too small to support the higher engraving costs of the Unit System. This would be true for the initial set up, but probably worth the extra cost if it was an effective deterrent to counterfeiting. What Ormsby failed to appreciate was the potential of photography to duplicate any note, regardless of its artistry. We can be sure that Ormsby knew about photography, but given its primitive capabilities at that time, perhaps he discounted its potential.

Spencer M. Clark, who later headed the Bureau of Engraving and Printing, apparently read Ormsby's book and was influenced by its ideas. Ormsby was unequivocal about this fact:

> My principles did, in fact, achieve a triumph. Mr. S.M Clark adopted them in 1863—using my book as his "*vade mecum.*" The Hon. Secretary Chase himself adopted them, believing Mr. Clark to be the author.[13]

"Embarkation of the Pilgrims."

After the National Currency Act of February 25, 1863, required new designs for the Legal Tender Notes popularly called "greenbacks," Clark wrote a long letter to Secretary of the Treasury Salmon P. Chase, dated March 28, 1863, in which he stated:

> Sir: I respectfully suggest as a design for a National Currency the engraving of national historic pictures of the full size of the note to be issued, and submit, as "a model of illustrative drawing," a two-dollar note, made

up of a copy of Weir's painting of the "Embarkation of the Pilgrims," with a suitable reverse.[14]

Clark didn't get everything he wanted, but the national-historic pictures he liked were engraved for the back of the new notes. They didn't cover the whole surface of the note, as Ormsby would have liked, but they were large. Clark never acknowledged a debt to Ormsby's book for the design ideas he borrowed, but it seems unlikely that Clark would have thought of those ideas on his own initiative.

By 1854 Ormsby's reputation came under the lens of the court. Depending on whom you believe, Ormsby was either a victim of his own *laissez-faire* and a polite reluctance to question the intentions of his customers, or he knowingly worked with counterfeiters and was a counterfeiter himself. Two men at the Mercantile Agency, a credit-reporting company in New York City, made allegations to their clients about Ormsby's honesty, stating flatly that he either helped counterfeiters or that he was one of them. These allegations got back to Ormsby and he filed a lawsuit.[15] Ormsby sued Benjamin Douglas, the owner of the Mercantile Agency, for $10,000 in damages for public and malicious slander. The case was heard in Superior Court before Judge Pierrepont. During the trial, the attorneys defending Douglas alleged that Ormsby had fraudulently engraved or altered bank-note plates for eight different banks, some of which did not even exist, had engraved counterfeit labels for patent medicines, such as Moffatt's Vegetable Life Pills, and had divorced his wife so he could live with a known prostitute. Although the attorneys named the specific banks and the denominations of the counterfeits, they had no corroborating evidence to prove any of their allegations.

Judge Pierrepont ruled that "under the circumstances in evidence, the communication [Douglas's allegation] was not unlawful, there being no evidence of malice or bad faith."[16] In other words, since Douglas had repeated some of the counterfeiting stories about Ormsby in private conversations—not publicly and not maliciously—he had not slandered the plaintiff.

Ormsby appealed the ruling but lost again and had to pay $284 in appellate court costs.

It is difficult to remain dispassionate and impartial about Ormsby's possible involvement in counterfeiting. The evidence is slight and often based on second-hand allegations. Ormsby worked in an industry that could be ferociously competitive and quite capable of complicity to drive him out of the business. Hugh McCulloch, the Comptroller of the Currency, investigated the charges against Ormsby and exonerated him. The question remains unanswered if McCulloch's conclusion was made expedient by the circumstances of the war. The Union had a desperate need for companies that could print bank notes immediately, and Ormsby may have been given benefit of the doubt. In fact, we have no confessions from known counterfeiters saying that Ormsby worked for them. At least one Secret Service agent reported that Ormsby was a counterfeiter and named the notes for which he was said to be responsible. This, however, turned out to be hearsay evidence and without any proof, so the agency never pursued an indictment. Dunn and Bradstreet also reported that Ormsby was involved in counterfeiting but merely repeated hearsay.

Edward E. Dunbar worked with Ormsby at the Continental Bank Note Company for nearly four years before leaving the firm to pursue other business interests. After he left, Dunbar wrote a letter to Hugh McCulloch to recommend that Ormsby be given a job of heading up the Bureau of Engraving and Printing. Writing about Ormsby's character, Dunbar makes some interesting observations:

> . . . Persecuted men generally present vulnerable points of attack. The only weak point I have discovered in Mr. Ormsby, who it may be said has been most vigorously persecuted for many years past, is his unworldly nature, a nature coming out of the inspiration of genius, and which sometimes allows him to be the dupe of designing knaves, thus giving his enemies opportunities to misrepresent his actions and motives. I have observed Mr. Ormsby closely and found him a man without

guile, incapable of a dishonest act, and of the purest moral character. All he needs is kind appreciative treatment and he will lavish the wealth of his genius even to a foolish extent.

> . . . during the entire period he was associated with me, I found him a most faithful and competent aide, and my nature revolts at the malignant character of the efforts so persistently made by professional rivals and other interested parties to injure him and which exceed anything of the kind I ever witnessed.

> I remain your obedient servant,
> Edward E. Dunbar[17]

Ormsby left the Continental Bank Note Company in 1867 and effectively retired from the business. He went back to Hampton, Connecticut, to live on the farm he had bought for his mother, who was then 82 years old. In March 1870 he wrote a long letter to George S. Boutwell, the secretary of the Treasury, in which he explained the Unit System he had invented for bank-note designs, recounted his experience at the Continental Bank Note Company, explained how he had been forced out of the company by Touro Robertson, and then wrote:

> I will now state to the Hon. Secretary, succinctly, my object in making this communication.

> 1st. I propose to effect a reform in the business of engraving bank note and stamps by adopting the Unit System as laid down in my book, page 80, etc.

> 2nd. I propose to organize and establish the Republican Bank Note Company, to be composed of the most eminent artists and business men.

> 3rd. I propose to reduce the price of bank note work and at the same time render it far more secure from counterfeiting by adopting a new and bold style—on principles of defiance to all known methods of counterfeiting, whether by photographic, lithographic, anastatic, or any other process. . . .[18]

Nothing came of that letter, and Ormsby vanished into retirement and died quietly in Brooklyn on November 1, 1883.

Chapter 9

Rebels

As civil war became inevitable, planning in the South took on a hurried cadence. The Confederate secretary of Treasury, Christopher Gustavus Memminger, realized that loans and taxes would not raise sufficient money to pay for the rapidly mounting expenditures. The Confederacy would need a new currency, and since the South did not have a government Bureau of Engraving and Printing, Memminger knew he would have to turn to private bank-note companies to print the needed notes. The Confederate Congress authorized the printing of $1 million of Interest-Bearing Notes in early March 1861. Memminger asked Gazaway Bugg Lamar, an officer in the Bank of the Republic in New York, for his help and sent him a copy of the act authorizing the notes. Lamar, always a loyal friend of the South, contracted with the National Bank Note Company in New York to print the notes. Memminger apparently failed to tell Lamar how many notes to print of each denomination, so Lamar did the arithmetic and had equal numbers of each denomination printed. The National Bank Note Company's engravers probably modified some existing vignettes held in stock and added the appropriate lettering. The job was finished quickly, and 607 sheets of Treasury Notes arrived in Montgomery, Alabama, on April 2, 1861, just 10 days before rebel cannons opened fire on Fort Sumter. Each sheet contained four different notes bearing $50, $100, $500, and $1,000 denominations for a total of $1,001,550. These were engraved notes, and Memminger was pleased by their appearance, but also upset that Lamar had so many printed of the two higher denominations. He contacted Lamar again and asked that he have the National Bank Note Company print an additional 1,000 half-sheets of the $50 and $100 denominations. Since the National Bank Note Company already had the plates, they were able to print the notes immediately and get them ready for a waiting ship. Memminger, meanwhile, had decided to send a courier from Montgomery to New York to bring home the Treasury-Note plates, "if it can be done with safety." Before the courier could get to New York, someone told the authorities there that the National Bank Note Company was printing notes for the Confederacy, and U.S. marshals went there and seized the plates. The marshals were too late to stop the shipment of the second batch of notes, so Memminger got them but was denied the much bigger prize of the plates.

Memminger took responsibility for every aspect of supplying the Confederacy with currency—finding bank-note paper, ink, engravers, lithographic stones and printers, and eventually printing companies. When the burden of the job became too much for any one man, Sanders G. Jamison was appointed clerk on March 1, 1862, to help with the production of Treasury Notes. In February 1864 he was promoted to Chief of the Treasury Note Bureau, not unlike being made captain for the maiden voyage of the *Titanic*.

A very early counterfeit note, dated 1819, with (Abner) Reed's name imprinted below the center shield. The earlier notes were easier to counterfeit, since most of the design is lettering. The vignette of Neptune is compact and artistically unremarkable.

A counterfeit $2 note of the Merchants Bank, New Bedford, Massachusetts. This note was altered from the $2 note of the Delaware City Bank, Delaware, and has no imprint. The light-red overprint of a "Lazy 2" was probably done by a tint plate. A good engraving and a dangerous note.

Samuel Schmidt's Work

Memminger sought engravers and printers who could turn out enough notes to keep the government solvent. Agents were sent to the four corners of the Confederacy to investigate printing companies to see if they had the machinery and personnel to print money. Major George Clitherall of Mobile, Alabama, was asked to go to New Orleans immediately and talk with a printer there named Samuel Schmidt to see if he could print 5,000 impressions of Treasury Notes corresponding as nearly as possible to the $50 and $100 notes of the National Bank Note Company. Clitherall confirmed that Samuel Schmidt, with a shop called the Southern Bank Note Company at No. 12 Royal Street, was the only printer who could do the job, and a contract was made on May 13, 1861.[1] But before Schmidt could get started, the Confederate Congress authorized an issue of $20 million in non–Interest-Bearing Treasury Notes, and new orders were sent to Schmidt. No one had thought to ask Schmidt if he could handle the job. The truth was that Schmidt had only two helpers—his young son and one workman—and not nearly enough equipment. Memminger was clearly to blame for not having Major Clitherall send back a complete and thorough report on Schmidt's capabilities. Some blame also belongs to Schmidt, who always implied that he could meet any requirements.

Memminger believed that the engraving and printing of the $20 million would take Schmidt about two months to complete. As the weeks went by, Memminger sent a number of telegrams to other agents in New Orleans to ask about his progress. By July 15, 1861, Memminger was incensed that not a single note had been printed by Schmidt's firm, and he sent Dr. William Reyburn to find out the problem with Schmidt's operations and make appropriate recommendations. Reyburn suggested that the most expedient solution would be to give Jules Manouvrier, a lithographer in New Orleans, 10,000 sheets of bank-note paper and let him lithograph as many notes as he could while Schmidt continued to print from his engraved plates. The intention was to withdraw the lithographic notes as fast as Schmidt's engraved notes became available. Memminger readily agreed to this plan.

This is a printer's Proof of a genuine note from the 1850s. Compare to the counterfeit note below.

Counterfeit $5 note of the Chippewa Bank, Pepin, Wisconsin. This counterfeit note is "well executed to deceive the public," but on closer examination, one can see numerous differences, such as in the white horse and the steam locomotive. If presented outside its normal area of circulation, however, it would probably pass, depending on the quality of the paper and ink.

Finding Talent Elsewhere

Meanwhile, Memminger thought it prudent to expand his search for supplies to England and New York City. He sent Major Benjamin F. Ficklin to England to hire engravers, lithographers, and printers and to buy whatever supplies he could find to help with the production of notes. Thomas A. Bell, a prominent banker, was sent to New York for the same purpose. In Richmond, Memminger found that Louis Hoyer and his partner, Charles L. Ludwig, were willing to lend their skills to the task. Hoyer was a jeweler and watch repairman. It is said that Hoyer supplied the capital when the two men decided to engage in commercial lithography in 1858. Hoyer took no active part in any of the work at the plant. He withdrew from the partnership sometime in 1864 and returned to his native Germany in 1866.[2] Ludwig, an accomplished engraver, is said to have acquired his knowledge of lithography directly from one of Senefelder's pupils in Germany.

Hoyer and Ludwig signed a contract and began printing notes from lithographic stones on July 25, 1861. As soon as the notes reached the public, there was almost universal condemnation of their crude appearance. Bankers, newspaper editors, and even officials in the Treasury Department complained of their poor workmanship. The public was expecting to see line-engraved notes printed on good paper from steel plates. Instead, they got simple vignettes of far less detail and artistic merit, owing to the way that lithographs are made. Memminger was also disappointed, but there was nothing he could do except promise better notes in the future. As we have seen in chapter 2, the same security problems were now repeated in the crude lithographic notes of the Confederacy. Because Memminger had to use several different printers, each having their own engravers producing different vignettes and layouts, the public was easily confused about which notes were authentic and which were counterfeited.

Archer & Halpin

John H. Reagan, the Postmaster General of the Confederacy, also led a search for engravers and supplies for the production of stamps. In the autumn of 1861, John Archer, an engraver who had previously worked for the American Bank Note Company, moved to Richmond, Virginia, and made the acquaintance of John Daly, a wealthy politician. After several months, they formed the printing firm of Archer & Daly. It took almost two years before their company was fully equipped and ready to open shop to make postage stamps. By April 1863 John Archer had designed and engraved his first stamps for the Confederacy. The postmaster general was both pleased and relieved to see such excellent work. Daly left the firm that year and his name was removed from the company's title. Soon after, Frederick Halpin joined the firm and it was renamed Archer & Halpin. There, Halpin engraved the portrait of Jefferson Davis on the 10-cent C.S.A. stamp. The postage rate in the United States was 3¢ apiece, but people in the

C.S.A. paid 10¢ apiece, making the Halpin 10-cent Jefferson Davis stamp the most popular and well known of the Confederate issues.

A counterfeit $10 note of the Iron Bank, Ironton, Ohio. A superb and very dangerous counterfeit note that would have readily passed anywhere, even at the bank of issue, depending on the quality of paper and ink. Graphically, it is very good, except for the oval-portrait vignette just right of the center. It does not clearly define the shoulder line and lapels of the man.

Captain Wilkinson

Various businesses in Great Britain were amenable to the Confederate cause, or to their gold, so the Confederacy naturally sought their assistance. Captain Wilkinson, with Army Major Benjamin Ficklin, left Richmond on August 12, 1862, ran the Union Navy's blockade successfully, and made it to England. Major Ficklin had orders to sign up engravers and printers for bank-note work, as stated previously, but also to help with the Confederacy's stamp production. Setting up his headquarters in London, he entered into a contract with the firm of Thomas De La Rue to print several million postage stamps. The Union Navy had set up a blockade to prevent Confederate-friendly ships from transporting supplies into the C.S.A., so it was not surprising that a shipment of five million five-cent stamps was captured on April 27, 1862, aboard the steamer *Bermuda* off the port of Wilmington, North Carolina. A second and final shipment of 12 million stamps made it safely through the blockade. Ficklin also hired 26 lithographers in Glasgow and sent them to Wilmington on the *Giraffe*, a Scottish-built, iron-hulled, side-wheel, steam-propelled gunboat of 642 tons that he bought for £32,000 and converted into a "blockade runner" renamed the *Robert E. Lee*.[3]

Southern Bank Note Company

Meanwhile, Samuel Schmidt finally finished printing the 5,000 Interest-Bearing Notes in late August 1861. Soon after, Memminger authorized troops to seize the material, paper, and bank-note machinery belonging to the American Bank Note Company's branch office in New Orleans. Memminger did not realize that the Southern Bank Note Company, managed by Schmidt, was the southern branch of the American Bank Note Company. When informed of this, he allowed Schmidt to keep enough of the machinery and other supplies so he could continue business with his regular customers but sent the rest of his material to Richmond to be placed in the engraving and printing plant of Leggett, Keatinge & Ball. This was one more example of Memminger's left hand not knowing what his right hand was doing.

Thomas A. Ball

Thomas A. Ball has been variously described as an executive in a brokerage firm, a banker, and a lawyer. Whatever the case, he apparently had the experience and skills to go to New York City in order to find bank-note engravers and make contacts for buying paper and ink. He seems to have been just as successful as Major Ficklin. He recruited Edward Keatinge, a historical engraver at the American Bank Note Company, and George Leggett, an expert lettering engraver, and convinced both to quit their jobs and go with him to Richmond to set up their own engraving and printing company. The three men left with a wagon of bank-note supplies, taking a supposedly safe route through neutral Kentucky, but they were intercepted by Union loyalists who seized all their supplies. The men escaped with only their personal belongings and finally made it to Richmond.

Memminger set them up in a printing plant with equipment from England and printers borrowed from the Army. Joseph Daniel Pope, head of the Treasury Note Division at Columbia, wrote to Memminger about the endless bickering between the bank-note companies and had this to say: "Keatinge is much the most intelligent and practical workman of them all, and would make a capital director, but I fear he is too deeply interested as a contractor to give up the profits and take a salary."

Blanton Duncan

The most colorful personality of all the owners of the note-printing companies was undoubtedly Blanton Duncan. He was also the most erratic, divisive, vengeful, and egotistical of those men. According to Douglas Ball, Duncan's father made a "great deal of money, acquired a Bolivar County Mississippi plantation and substantial real estate holdings in Louisville, Kentucky."[4] Blanton, his only son, had a good education and was admitted to the bar of the commonwealth in the 1850s. When the war was about to begin, he did not join his father and escape to Paris but instead raised a battalion of volunteers in 1861, became a part of the army of the Shenandoah, and fought at the first battle of Manassas. In July of that year he sent a check for $500 to Memminger as a personal contribution to the Southern cause. Memminger invited him to stop by his office for a chat the next time he was in Richmond. When that meeting took place, Memminger casually mentioned the trouble he was having finding good paper for making Treasury Notes. Duncan promised to see if any paper could be found in Kentucky. Later, after finding nothing in Louisville, Duncan went to Nashville, Tennessee, and found a paper mill belonging to a Mr. Whiteman that sold the Treasury Department 350,000 sheets.

Memminger was impressed with Duncan's zeal and self-confidence and thought he would make a good administrator of a printing plant. In December 1861 he invited Duncan to come down to Richmond and set up a plant. Duncan acted immediately, investing $2,000 of his own money in the plant and equipment. He found the printing of notes was so lucrative that he cut his price for 1,000 notes from $20.00 to just $15.00, and later he cut the rates again to $12.00 per 1,000, which angered all the other plant owners. When

Union troops moved too close to Richmond, Memminger asked all the local note-printing companies to move to the relative safety of Columbia, South Carolina. Duncan made it a point to get there first, probably thinking that would give him first choice in finding a good building and buying up any printing supplies that were available. His ambitions were perhaps too manic. Duncan, possibly dressed in his splendid, custom-made uniform, confiscated materials without any legal authority to do so. Not finding everything he wanted in Columbia, he went to Charleston and confiscated printing equipment and supplies from Evans & Cogswell and the firm of F.W. Bornmann, the official printer to the state of North Carolina. An outraged Bornmann sent a letter of protest to Memminger, who was surprised to learn of Duncan's behavior. Memminger made Duncan return equipment and supplies to Bornmann and paid Evans & Cogswell for their losses. But Duncan was not a man who took criticism or punishment readily.

In retaliation, he invented malicious lies about Memminger and Pope, and when these efforts were not successful, he printed two pamphlets in which he accused the secretary of all manner of evil. Memminger decided he had had enough of Duncan's insubordination and saw to it that he never again received a contract to print notes. It was probably a difficult decision for Memminger since Duncan had proved to be an efficient operator of his plant. Douglas Ball said that Duncan's workforce averaged only 20 men, yet he produced 13 million Treasury Notes, 135,000 bonds, and still found time to print 250 books and numerous pamphlets and broadsides.[5] Duncan stayed in Columbia, living in a mansion he bought, until the end of the war. When General William Sherman entered the city and burned down the Treasury Bureau and the printing plants, Duncan shrewdly offered the use of his house to Sherman and his staff, thereby saving the property while many other houses were torched. He returned to Louisville after the war and became a successful lawyer and politician. He eventually moved to Redondo Beach, California, with other members of his family, where he died in 1896.

A counterfeit $10 note of the Hatters Bank, Bethel, Connecticut. This spurious note was overprinted with a red TEN and issued under the name of a real bank. Since it does not look like any of the genuine $10 notes of the bank, it would have been intended for use in remote areas of the country, where it was unknown. The faked imprint is Rawdon, Wright & Hatch.

James Paterson

Another player in the game was James T. Paterson. He was unknown to researchers until 1912, when his imprint—J.T. Paterson & Co., Augusta, Ga.—was found on a sheet of stamps. August Dietz began a search for information and eventually located Mr. Louis Altschuh in Washington, D.C., a lithographer who had worked for Paterson at his facilities in Richmond and Augusta, Georgia. Altschuh recalled that Paterson was a jeweler and watch repairman. He was also a friend of Charles Ludwig and frequently visited the Hoyer & Ludwig plant. Over the years, researchers, including Douglas Ball, have found bits and pieces of the puzzle and put them together to form a complex but reliable story of intrigue and deception.

When Memminger asked all the note printers to move their business to Columbia, only Ludwig was not willing to make the move, probably figuring that he had a large clientele of loyal customers in Richmond and would continue to have a thriving business. Paterson knew of Ludwig's decision and decided to take advantage of it. He wrote to Memminger and offered to buy Hoyer & Ludwig's equipment and move their plant to Columbia if Memminger would assure him that he would not give any further contracts to Ludwig and thus deprive him of the profits he hoped to make. This seemed an ideal solution to Memminger, and he authorized the purchase. Paterson purchased the greater part of Hoyer & Ludwig's equipment and supplies, taking with him 13 lithographers, including Louis Altschuh and his 2 brothers, 5 presses, and a great many lithographic stones. As soon as the facility was ready, Paterson's company began printing notes from Hoyer & Ludwig's engravings already transferred to stone. They also probably received new engravings which they transferred onto stone at Columbia. After a time, Paterson moved part of his plant to Augusta, Georgia, and printed stamps, $5, $10, and $100 notes, all bearing the date of 1862, and large quantities of state notes for Alabama and North Carolina, all dated 1863. The Augusta business was closed down after about six months and the equipment brought back to Columbia. These facts were corroborated by Louis Altschuh's brother, Frank Altschuh of Indianapolis. Paterson continued to print notes at his Columbia plant until the end of the war.

In August 1862 Ludwig decided he wanted another contract to print notes and sent a letter to Memminger. At the time, the other printers in Columbia were getting $538 for 3,000 sheets of notes. Ludwig said he was willing to do the work for $240. Memminger accepted the offer but asked that Ludwig agree to rush through the engraving of another $10 note and print a supply of notes as quickly as he could. Ludwig said he could print 5,000 sheets a day but would need $288 per 3,000 sheets. Memminger agreed to that also. When Paterson learned of the double-cross, he sent a letter of protest to Memminger, reminding him that he had promised he "would never give one dime's worth of work" to Hoyer & Ludwig. The secretary excused himself by citing the exigencies of war. Memminger thought he should avoid any further trouble with Paterson by writing to Ludwig and telling him he must not imprint the notes with the name of the company. Ludwig agreed to do that, but when the engraving was finished, he secretly added his name ("Ludwig") at the bottom of the center vignette in such small lettering that it required a magnifying glass to see it.

Cogswell & Evans

The lithographic-printing firm of Harvey Cogswell and his brother-in-law Major Benjamin F.

Evans, originally set up in Charleston, South Carolina, received a letter from Memminger in October 1862, asking them to build a plant in Columbia, South Carolina, and offering to provide as many experienced printers as their operations could use. They accepted the offer and opened their one-story brick building at the corner of Gervais and Huger streets on April 1, 1863, with 43 lithographers. During the war, they printed small-denomination currency and government bonds. Unlike other printing plants in the South, this one employed ladies to do much of the menial labor. Many of the ladies had been widowed by the war and needed the annual salary of $500. Most of them cut individual bonds or notes from printed sheets, ground ink, carried paper to and from the presses, swept the floors, etc. The company eventually put 102 presses to work. Evans proposed to print notes (both front and back) at $15 per 1,000.[6] That fee was accepted, and Cogswell & Evans became the largest lithographic-printing firm in the South, continuing their work until General Sherman came through on his infamous "March to the Sea" and burned both the town and the printing plant with it.[7]

A counterfeit $20 note of the State Bank of Indiana, Indianapolis.

The Great Theft

Jules Manouvrier was mentioned previously as a New Orleans lithographer who was recommended to Memminger as the only other printer in the city that could produce the $5 and $10 notes needed so badly to supplement the slow work of Schmidt's Southern Bank Note Company. Manouvrier was finished with the notes about the middle of August 1861. Treasury Bureau agents in New Orleans inspected the printing, counted the sheets, and gave their approval to send the notes to Richmond. But no one had explained to Manouvrier that he must place the notes in strong wooden boxes before sending them by train to Richmond. Manouvrier decided to wrap the notes in heavy brown paper and send them on their way. He had plenty of experience sending commercial print jobs this way and saw no difference with Treasury Notes.

The railroads of that period took a circuitous route to Richmond, going from New Orleans to Jackson, Mississippi, then to Selma, Alabama, where packages were off-loaded onto wagons and carried to Montgomery. From there, the packages were placed back on a train and hauled to Atlanta. The next stop was Augusta, Georgia, and then on to Columbia, South Carolina. After Columbia, the train could go either to Wilmington, North Carolina, or to Charlotte, North Carolina, and from these cities other trains would haul the money to Richmond. Somehow, the packages survived intact for most of the trip. But by the time they arrived at the freight office in the train station at Petersburg, Virginia, the brown paper on one of the packages had torn open and a freight handler named Henry Tatum saw the money. Tatum hid the packages in the freight office and told his wife that evening about his discovery. Mrs. Tatum in turn told her three brothers the next morning, and they went to the freight office and removed a large number of sheets of currency. The next day, when the shipment arrived in Richmond and was delivered to the Treasury Department, the receiving clerk realized that a theft had occurred and had the secretary come down to their office to see the packages. Memminger later wrote in a letter:

> The packages which came here were put up in brown paper which chafed through and broke open, exposing the sheets to any depreciation. No engraver ever sent bills to a bank in such condition, and if the packages were forwarded by Manouvrier, it seems to me that the loss of the impressions should be laid upon him.

A government detective named Thomas Allan was assigned to the case. He worked his way backward along the route the currency had followed and interviewed every freight handler and baggage man. As soon as he reached Petersburg and began questioning the men in the freight office, he noticed that Henry Tatum appeared to be nervous. Under pressure, Tatum broke down and told the whole story, implicating Mrs. Tatum, her brothers, and a man named William H. Goodwin.[8] No record has ever been found to show if the accused ever went to trial.

Memminger decided there was no evidence that any of the $5 notes had been taken, so he allowed those notes to be issued. For the $10 notes, it was a different story. So many notes of that denomination had been stolen that the whole issue had to be destroyed. Accordingly, a committee was appointed to oversee the burning of the notes, and their report shows that they burned $780,440, making this the largest single loss of notes in the war. The workmen and equipment that Memminger had placed with Manouvrier were removed from his premises and sent to Hoyer & Ludwig in Richmond. Manouvrier, of course, was never again given any further contracts to print notes. He went back to commercial printing in partnership with Denis Simon until at least 1870.

A counterfeit $20 note of the State Bank of Ohio.

Security Printing in the South

Four lithographers who worked in Confederate printing plants were located by August Dietz in Richmond and other cities and were interviewed at length in the 1920s about the working conditions and procedures in the various plants. Information of this type was also collected from newspaper accounts and diaries by Douglas Ball. Common to all of the accounts is the fact that the men had to work long hours, often at "breakneck" speed to meet their quotas or to earn extra money. Richard E. Hendrick, who worked for Hoyer & Ludwig from 1861 to the end of the war, told Dietz that he made $5 a week in Confederate money if he printed 200 sheets of stamps a day, but that he was also paid a bonus if he printed more than 200. When he first started, he was just able to print his quota, but as he became more experienced, he managed to print a ream—480 sheets—each day. Most of the lithographers were brought over from England and had signed contracts that guaranteed them $20 a week in gold. John Hodge was one of those men, and he wrote that by the end of the war, "on every pay day, they were besieged by brokers who offered them appalling premiums" for their gold coins.[9]

Theft was rampant in all the plants, owing primarily to the absence of security. Paper was often not counted and printers could easily take printed but unsigned notes out of the plant. Hodge wrote that in Blanton Duncan's plant, one of the printers was in the habit of "carrying off five or ten sheets of ten-, twenty-, or fifty-dollar notes every day." This individual had taken more than $200,000 of notes before he was found out. Although he was sentenced to be shot, the approach of General Sherman's troops delayed the sentence and it was never carried out.[10] After the incident, "detectives" were used to watch the men at work, and a strict paper count was adopted. This is another example of Memminger's failure to understand the security problems of printing bank notes and his poor management.

Drinking was another problem that interfered with production in some of the plants. The printers sometimes went out on strike, fueled by liquor, to protest their working conditions. Colonel Duncan had the reputation of being a "no nonsense" disciplinarian, and he once reacted to a "strike" by having the local provost marshal arrest the printers and throw them in jail until they agreed to go back to work. The owners of some plants went out of their way to make life a little more bearable for their workers. Women were hired to cook a good meal that was served at midday. The printers and their assistants were

given a short break and ate in shifts, although black workers had to eat at separate tables. The heat was oppressive in the summer, and at one point, the owners in Richmond had to suspend work during the day and use their employees during the evening and at night. The war stopped the usual delivery of ice by ships coming down from New England, and this made matters much worse. Critical supplies (ink and paper) sometimes ran out for a period of time, forcing the printers to stop work and cutting into their pay. But even with all those problems, the printing plants managed to turn out almost a billion dollars before the war was over, as well as to print large volumes of bonds of several types and postage stamps by the millions. According to one source, there were 69 types of notes printed, and if one counts the design, engraving, and printing varieties, the total comes to about 400 different variations printed with 12 kinds of paper and watermark varieties.[11]

A counterfeit note of the Bank of the State of Missouri, dated 1853. The alleged printers, Toppan, Carpenter & Casilear, always did much better work than this on genuine notes. High magnification shows this to be a rather crude specimen of engraving, but good enough to pass a casual examination.

Counterfeiting

The large number of different currency designs, most of which were poorly printed, soon lead to a wave of counterfeit notes from Tennessee, New Orleans, and even Richmond. Anyone familiar with the counterfeiting of colonial notes could have predicted the problem. If you have a number of states (or colonies) issuing a number of notes of different designs, and most of them are printed indifferently on common paper, you facilitate counterfeiting. Benner has noted that "Newspapers mention more than eighteen cases [of counterfeiting] in Richmond during the period from

August to November, when everyone—civilians, soldiers, juveniles, slaves, and prisoner of war—seemed to be engaged in the practice."[12] The most famous of those cases involved John Richardson, an Italian adventurer who called himself Louis Napoleon. During a night in the last week of February 1862, thieves broke into the printing plant of Hoyer & Ludwig and printed a number of $100 Treasury Notes for their own use. Why the plant was not guarded at night was never answered in the newspaper accounts. The authorities arrested a number of individuals, including Richardson, and his version of the story was printed in the Richmond *Daily Dispatch*. According to Richardson, he met a friend, George Elam, and had a few drinks with him. Afterwards, Elam casually suggested that the two of them "go and make some money." They went to the printing plant of Hoyer & Ludwig, broke into the office, stole eight sheets of unsigned $10 notes, and printed for themselves $800 of notes apiece. Richardson then followed Elam to a shop where they stole a genuine $10 note so they could copy the signature.

Although Elam and Richardson were equally guilty, they were not treated equally. The Richmond *Daily Dispatch* came down hard on Richardson, saying that he was an Italian of bad countenance, a person of dissolute habits, and a "doubly-dyed scoundrel, skulking out" of the Confederate Army by claiming Italian citizenship.[13] He was convicted and sentenced to be hanged but was reprieved twice by President Jefferson Davis. He was finally hanged on August 22, 1862, becoming the only person executed for counterfeiting during the Civil War. As far as is known, Elam received no punishment for his role in the crime.

Counterfeit $2 note of the Saint Nicholas National Bank, New York. This "Lazy Deuce" of the First Charter Period is a very good imitation. It is not attributed by the Secret Service to any particular engraver.

Lessons from Memminger

Memminger never created a centralized government printing office to make the Confederacy's paper money, bonds, and stamps. Instead, he tried to micromanage a number of independent contractors who operated for profit. Memminger was kept busy with the chaos—the constant quarrels between the contracting printers, instances of shoddy work, inflated bills, printers' strikes, theft, absenteeism, drinking, and the incessant difficulties in finding adequate supplies of paper, ink, and lithographic stones. Joseph Daniel Pope, the Chief Clerk of the Columbia Treasury Bureau, offered sage advice to Memminger in a letter he wrote August 18, 1862:

> I do not think we will mend the matter a great deal by putting three or four contractors in one house and calling them a Government establishment. They would quarrel still, and perhaps worse than ever. All want to be masters, and all want the profits . . .[14]

At the beginning of the war, the North did not have a centralized Bureau of Engraving and Printing either, but they did have competent and well-managed bank-note companies with large stocks of finished vignette dies and transfer rolls who could have reacted quickly to any emergency requirements. They also had vast supplies of paper and ink, hand-presses, and skilled labor. By the end of the war, the North was well on its way to centralizing bank-note production. The South had none of these material advantages and suffered from the inexperienced and clumsy management style of a Treasury secretary who didn't know the difference between lithography and steel engraving. Memminger made a lot of simple mistakes, such as giving a contract to a printer without knowing his production capabilities (Schmidt), or firing a badly needed printer (Manouvrier) for a mistake that could have been avoided if he had been provided with detailed and thorough instructions.

A genuine $5 note of the Stillwater Canal Bank, Orono, Maine, dated March 27, 1840, and imprinted by the New England Bank Note Co., Patent Stereotype Steel Plate. This note appears darker in some areas because it was circulated and thus picked up dirt. Compare it to the altered note shown below, which was not circulated and looks "cleaner."

A note altered from the $5 note shown above. The place name is misspelled "Provivence." The word "Blackstone" was placed too close to the word "Canal," and the "Rhode Island" was not printed in the same wavy style as "State of."

After the Stillwater Canal Bank failed in 1841, counterfeiters apparently got hold of the remaining stock of unissued notes, chemically erased some of the words, and reprinted them with a new bank title, etc. The date shown is August 1, 1836, which is consistent with the life of the real Blackstone Canal Bank, in operation from 1831 to 1865.

Too many decisions were left to the contractors. Ludwig, for example, had the bright idea of meeting the Treasury's requirement for money by printing a disproportionate number of $50 and $100 notes. This excess of large denomination notes caused merchants to charge a five-percent surcharge for making change. The shortage of small denominations made it difficult for the government to pay its drafts.[15] Banks throughout the South offered to sell their small-denomination notes to the Treasury at five-percent premium and said they would accept payment in Treasury Notes. Memminger at first refused the offer but later had to buy $10 million from the banks in $5, $10, and $20 notes.

A puzzling example of the Treasury's ineptitude was its requirement that finished notes be signed by hand with the names of the treasurer and the register of the Treasury to make them valid. This job could have been done quite easily by facsimile

signatures on the lithographic plates. Instead, about 70 clerks were hired to sign notes, most of them women, and even they fell behind, as seen in the communication from Memminger to E.C. Elmore, the treasurer, dated November 16, 1861:

> Sir: The deficiency in the quantity of Treasury notes finished is daily increasing, and it is necessary to make the arrangements more efficient for signing. It is ascertained that a good clerk can sign his name three thousand two hundred times within the usual office hours. You will please therefore make a regulation that each clerk shall sign at least that number of signatures each day. Those who are unable to effect this amount of work are thereby proved to be not competent clerks for this Department, and you will please report them accordingly.[16]

The use of facsimile signatures was suggested by Memminger, but the Confederate Congress never authorized the practice, and it continued to the end of the war.[17] Memminger appears to have dropped the ball on that matter, and a more insistent effort might have carried the day. In all due fairness, it should be pointed out that the Union government also had a corps of people signing notes at first, but S.M. Clark soon got permission from the secretary of the Treasury to use facsimile signatures.

As Richard Todd and others have pointed out, Memminger was never given authority "to act as his judgment alone would dictate in the management of the Confederate finances. . . ."[18] He was merely an executive officer, executing the will of the Congress, and that body did not always follow his plans. Like all legislative bodies, the Confederate Congress was a deliberative body of diverse opinions that did its business by compromise, and its policies often lacked the clear, precise focus and efficiency of a single mind. The Congress may have been its own worst enemy.

Why did the Confederacy fail? There were many reasons, but most historians have argued that financial mistakes made by the government contributed greatly to its defeat. Charles W. Ramsdell said the handling of finances was "the greatest single weakness of the Confederacy."[19] Robert Kean thought a "bankrupt Treasury" was the leading cause of the failure of Southern Independence, and that "this was the prolific source of other evils," a view shared by Douglas Ball.[20] Ball argued that the Treasury ran such an inefficient operation in the printing of notes and bonds that the government was chronically short of cash and often could not pay its soldiers. As a result, soldiers were often hungry and improperly clothed, and desertions were so frequent that more than one-fourth of the army was absent without leave by 1863. Many soldiers could not support their families at home, and this contributed to a growing crisis in the morale of the civilian population. Memminger's incompetence in working with the Congress resulted in numerous financial failures which eventually became military failures.

A counterfeit U.S. Legal Tender Note of the second issue, August 1, 1862. The most notable error is in the portrait vignette of Salmon P. Chase, where the normal white space around his head is filled in with fine black lines. Otherwise, the note is a very good imitation. This note was dangerous and very likely to pass. The Secret Service does not attribute this counterfeit to any particular engraver.

A counterfeit $50 U.S. Legal Tender Note of 1862. This was a very dangerous counterfeit, believed to have been cut by Benjamin Boyd. Hessler indicates that about 10,000 of these counterfeits were in circulation. (Friedberg-148.)

A counterfeit $100 note of the Central National Bank of New York. The plates for this counterfeit were engraved by Charles Ulrich and captured by the Secret Service in 1879. Jacob Ott was probably the printer. This is a superb counterfeit and passed readily. Many of them were sent to Germany, where they were sold cheaply to travelers headed for the United States.

Chapter 10

The Bad Boys

Dunham

A sugar-mill scene in Dunham, Quebec, Canada.

One of the first important centers of counterfeiting in North America was Dunham township in Quebec, Canada, about 10 to 12 miles north of the Vermont state line.[1] Dunham was the largest of a number of small and remote villages which did a considerable amount of counterfeiting in Missisiquoi County. After 1791, when the British government opened the area to permanent settlement, a flood of about 3,000 Americans moved into these "Eastern Townships." Catherine Day, an historian of this area of Quebec, wrote that "Numbers of worthy and desirable inhabitants were thus brought into the country; though at the same time, it must be admitted that others came in, who could only be regarded in the light of unavoidable evils, being of that irresponsible, ill-regulated class who neither feared God, nor regarded man."[2] Dunham and some of the surrounding townships, such as Frelighsburg, Stanbridge East, and Barnston, were ideal for counterfeiting since the government officials had a lingering resentment against the American immigrants and there were no laws against counterfeiting *American* bank notes until the Canadian Parliament passed one in 1810.[3] Even then, this *laissez-faire* persisted until the early 1830s, when American banking interests forced a change.

A few of these "ill-regulated" men turned to counterfeiting soon after 1800. Because of the high profits and low risks of detection, counterfeiting was attractive. One person taught another the elementary techniques, and soon the fraternity grew to large numbers. Most of these men lived along a dirt road, then called "Cogniac Street" but now known as "Chemin Hudon." Certain large families dominated the business, such as the Gleasons and the Wings. These Cogniac Street counterfeiters became known as "Coniackers," and their bogus notes were called "cony," "snags," or "boodle" in the parlance of the day.[4]

Stephen Burroughs

One of the earliest counterfeiters of this period was Stephen Burroughs, born in New Hampshire in 1765 and said to be the son of a respectable clergyman. During the mid-1780s, while posing as a minister and leading a congregation for six months, he was also passing spurious coins and was finally arrested at Springfield, Massachusetts, and confined to prison for three years at Castle Island in Boston harbor. After prison he spent several years in one criminal activity after another, including horse theft and seducing young ladies. He wrote a memoir in which he detailed many of these adventures and gained the reputation of being a rogue.[5] In 1799 he moved to the area around Stanstead, just north of the Vermont line, and soon after he started a counterfeiting operation using Philander Noble to engrave his copper plates.[6] By 1807 a Canadian newspaper noted that Burroughs had escaped from the Montreal prison for the fourth time.[7]

"The Trial of a Horse Thief," a colored lithograph by Clay, Cosack & Co., circa 1877.

Stephen had a witty, ironic sense of humor, as shown in this letter he wrote to Gilbert & Dean, exchange brokers in Boston:

Lower Canada, January 25, 1809
Gentlemen:

Having often seen your "Only Sure Guide to Bank Bills," and admiring your kind labours for the public weal in detecting the works of those ingenious rogues, I have enclosed and forwarded to your exchange office, a bill on the Shipton Bank (which had very recently commenced in operation), and I pray you will have the goodness to give the public the earliest notice should spurious bills of that Bank be discovered to be in circulation.

As I am a principal Stockholder in the Shipton Bank you will do me a favor, for which I will amply reward you by genuine prototype pewter plate bills good credit at your office, and whatever premium you will give for the Shipton Bank Bills, you may be assured shall be paid you in Bank Stock.

I wish, Gentlemen, you would be attentive to my requests and strickly examine all bills on the aforesaid Bank by the enclosed genuine bill: for such is the depravity of man, and such the success of counterfeiting, that I lately observed in one of your newspapers, that *patent buck wheat pancakes* had been so exactly counterfeited in New Jersey, that none except the Officers of the Pancake Exchange could distinguish them from the original!

I solicit your friendship, Gentlemen, in this important Business. . . .[8]

Burroughs was especially noted for his boldness in court as well as in prison. He once arrived in court, unexpectedly, to sue one of his majesty's justices of the peace for having committed him to the house of corrections as a vagabond. Naturally, he was arrested.[9] He was arrested in 1809 for felony, forgery, and fraud, and placed in prison in Montreal only to escape again.

In one of the stranger twists of history, Stephen converted to Catholicism and became a priest at the old town of Trois Rivieres (Three Rivers), about 100 miles from Montreal.[10] He died there in poverty in early 1840. Stephen's son, Edward Burroughs, began counterfeiting about the age of 18 or 19. He and his friend, Daniel Ross, were caught in Lebanon, Massachusetts, in 1807 with about $1,400 worth of counterfeit bills between them. The *Salem Gazette* stated that Edward had all the audacity, cunning, and quick apprehension of his father.[11] This may be the son who later became a distinguished judge in Quebec.

David Fowler and Selah Coles

Many Americans visited Dunham and the surrounding villages for the sole purpose of buying counterfeit money. They paid for the spurious notes in genuine notes, coins, various types of dry goods, or other supplies, especially stolen horses. A good example of the business is David Fowler and his associate, Selah Coles. David normally went to Dunham three times a year and returned with a cargo of counterfeit notes. He and Coles lived in the Bowery (New York City) and sold their "coney" to "loose women" and "idlers" of the male sex, who then circulated them for their own profit. Fowler also sold these notes to two families, "of which the parents, sons, and daughter-in-law, were engaged in the business." When Fowler was finally arrested in 1820 with $7,000 in spurious bills in his possession, he confessed that he had been carrying on the business with Dunham for eight years.[12] The police estimated that the two men had put into circulation about $300,000 worth of counterfeit bills.[13] Fowler was sentenced to prison in Vermont for a term of 13 years. Selah was arrested in New Jersey and sentenced to state prison for seven years.

The exploits of William Stuart, detailed in his autobiography, became even more widely known that those of Fowler and Coles. In one section, he says:

> I took my horse and went to Canada, to a place called the Slab City, to the firm of Crane & Staples, superior copperplate engravers. They engraved the notes of several different Banks that were presented to them. In a little more than a week they produced me notes on Barker's Exchange Bank, some on New Jersey banks, and some genuine ones [*sic*] on the Commercial Bank of Philadelphia, and also upon some others that I have forgotten.[14]

Although Stuart was writing in 1857, the counterfeiting business in the Eastern Townships had reached a prodigious level as early as 1812. A newspaper of New Hampshire, dated 1813, mentions the capture of six men who had "in their possession about fifty thousand dollars in spurious bills of various banks from Georgia to Canada." These bills had been made in Barnston, Lower Canada.[15] Another account in a Bennington, Vermont, paper dated 1820 reports the arrest of a man "on his way from the great manufacturing establishment in Canada," who had "in his possession $800,000 in spurious bills, principally on the banks of this city."[16] That "boodle" would have been the equivalent of a "king's ransom" in those days—an unimaginable fortune.

Some of the counterfeiters in this area of Quebec fled to the United States to avoid arrest or trouble from within the counterfeiting community. One was "Colonel" William Ashley, who started his operations in Vermont, fled to "Slab City" in Canada, and eventually left and came west to Boston, Ohio, in 1822. As one of the "Boston Bankers," a euphemism for counterfeiters, his business grew to become one of the largest in the West by 1832.[17] We'll meet the colonel later on in this story.

The Gleasons and the Moses

A chromolithograph by Bernhard Gillam
featuring a gladiatorial "triumph" over "boodle."

Ebenezer Gleason Sr. was the patriarch of a counterfeiting family. Although he was an illiterate farmer, he had a mind for business and put his sons to effective use. Ebenezer Jr. went to Philadelphia and served as an agent for many of the other coniackers in Dunham. Gleason and his friend Benjamin T. Moses, an engraver, were caught and indicted before the U.S. Circuit Court in Philadelphia in 1828. Gleason was sentenced to 17-years imprisonment and Moses to 12 years.[18] In later trials, their friends, Reuben Moses (Benjamin's brother) and John W. Craig, were also convicted of the same crime and sentenced to the same prison in Norristown, Pennsylvania. Two years later, all four made their escape by sawing a bar from one of the windows and scaling down the wall by means of an ingeniously constructed rope ladder. Since the sheriff had refused the four of them to have visitations with their friends, they left behind a slate in their cell on which was written: "You would not allow our friends to come and see us, so we are going to see them—Goodbye."[19] Of the four escapees, Benjamin Moses was by far the greatest loss. He was not only a bank-note engraver but had long worked for the firm of Murray, Draper & Fairman in Philadelphia, the best bank-note engravers in the business.[20] He carried back to Dunham an extensive knowledge and skill set unmatched by any of the local talent, and he and his brother Reuben became the principal engravers for the Gleason gang.

The senior Gleason and his five sons (Ebenezer Jr. and Willard being the most valuable) also formed an association with Seneca Paige, and they set up a distribution network that took millions of spurious dollars into the United States. The two Moses brothers were among their engravers, and "Doctor" Jonas Boardman, an expert forger, signed the notes with near-perfect facsimiles of the real signatures. The historian Heather Darch says that Cogniac Street became the leading supplier of counterfeit money to the United States.[21] This observation is supported by numerous complaints to the editors of newspapers of the day, such as this one to a Vermont paper:

> A letter to the editor of the *Montreal Herald*, dated at Caldwell's Manor, February 7th, states that "there is an infamous gang existing in the townships adjoining the province line, whose employment it is to manufacture and issue spurious paper money, of which the quantity that is put in circulation is truly prodigious. This nefarious traffic is carried on to such perfection and extent in all its branches, that the plates are made and engraved, the paper manufactured, the impressions made, and the signatures affixed, in huts and cabins in the woods, sometimes in barns and dwelling houses through these townships within the jurisdiction of the British government. From all parts of the United States, men come to purchase this spurious money, and having got what quantity they wish, they carry it off, and put it in circulation. At various times, our magistrates and other inhabitants, have done what they could to break it up; but it seems to be so deeply rooted, so well established and supported, that in spite of all, it is yet carried on, and will be carried on, till the legislature shall have paid it serious attention, and enact more severe laws against it, than those that are in force at present."[22]

The relief prayed for was not long in coming. In the fall of 1832, an association was formed among many of the banks in the area to protect their own interests. City banks paid $100 each to join, and about 100 of the country banks paid $25 each per annum to provide a common fund to bring to justice the many counterfeiters in Lower Canada. They chose as their solicitor E. Hersey Derby Jr. He carried on a voluminous correspondence with different people in the Canadas, including Colonel Joseph Butterfield and the sheriff of Tyngeborough, who began making plans to raid several towns. Intelligently, Butterfield went to Montreal and met the attorney general, who listened to his plans and then granted him the assistance of a large police force. Butterfield also got help from Mr. Redfield, the county attorney in Derby, Vermont.

In the autumn of 1833, two large raiding parties of about 80 men each were organized as a kind of *posse comitatus*.[23] One of these parties was assigned to go to Dunham and the other to Stanstead, only a few miles west. The "descents," as raids were then called, went off with no real violence or difficulty. 12 persons were arrested at Stanstead, and 13 were taken at Dunham. The Stanstead group was seemingly more interested in counterfeiting British half-crowns and American coins. The Dunham group yielded mostly paper-money men. The men captured at Dunham included Ebenezer Gleason Sr., on whom was found $20,000 in counterfeit bills, Ebenezer Gleason Jr., Horace Gleason, Samuel Gleason, Benjamin T. Moses, Reuben Moses, Willis Sherman, Dr. Jonas Boardman, Alexander Nelson, B.D. Wing, Artemas Howe, and a man who refused to give his first name but was known as "Jones." 13 plates of different banks were found in their possession, along with a large amount of spurious notes and a quantity of counterfeit coins, with dies for stamping. They also captured a number of costly machines along with a considerable quantity of zinc, copper, and other materials. The persons arrested at Stanstead were put in irons and placed in jail at Sherbrooke, Lower Canada, and those arrested in Dunham, considered more of a public threat, were ironed and marched under the guard of a troop of cavalry to Montreal.[24]

The first trial of the Dunham men began on September 12, 1833, before the Court of the King's Bench. Eight of these men faced eight bills of indictment for the offense of acquiring and having in their possession counterfeit notes of as many banks of the United States with intent to utter them, at one and the same time. The attorney general was anxious to have the whole group tried before one jury, but the chief justice refused to allow this since he thought it might confuse the jury. The attorney general was then forced to select one indictment—charging ten of the defendants with acquiring and passing a $10 bill of the Bank of the United States. These 10 were the usual suspects: Ebenezer Gleason and his sons, Ebenezer Jr., Willard, Samuel, and Horace; Reuben and Benjamin T. Moses; Jonas Boardman; Benjamin Dudley Wing; Artemis Howse; Lyman Jones; and Willis Sherman. After a very long trial, the jury brought in a verdict of guilty against Ebenezer Gleason, the father, who was sentenced to imprisonment for two and a half years.

A counterfeit $10 bill of the Bank of the United States.

In the second trial, the same individuals, with the exception of Lyman Jones, were brought into court on September 16. They were charged with having in their possession plates for forging the notes of the Harrisburgh Bank of Pennsylvania, the Sussex Bank, the Commercial Bank of New Jersey, and the Fulton Bank of New York. The jury brought in a verdict of guilty against Ebenezer Gleason and three of his sons, Ebenezer Jr., Horace, and Willard, as well as Benjamin Dudley Wing, Benjamin T. Moses, and Jonas Boardman. They each received sentences of two years in jail. The jury acquitted Artemis Howse, Samuel Gleason, Reuben Moses, and Willis Sherman.[25] William Crane, an engraver, was not captured during these raids but was arrested with his two sons on October 2, 1833, at Berkshire, Vermont. He was armed with a cane sword and tried, unsuccessfully, to stab one of his captors.[26] The conviction of the Dunham coniackers was made possible by the foresight and determination of the Canadian Legislature, which passed a bill shortly before the trial that made it a crime to counterfeit the currency of the United States.

A $2 note of the Commercial Bank of New Jersey.

Reuben Moses still had some charges against him pending in Montreal and had entered into a recognizance to appear on February 24, 1834. Meanwhile, however, his home on Carleton Street in Philadelphia had been searched by police and a large amount of spurious money was discovered. The police also discovered a person living there named James Stewart, generally known as Dr. Stewart, a counterfeiter since 1812. Stewart and Mrs. Moses were committed to prison in Philadelphia.[27] Reuben Moses was not at home during the raid, but police found him soon after in a hotel in Baltimore, Maryland, along with a confederate named Asa Pierce. Both had a lot of counterfeit money on them. They were convicted by a jury and sentenced to prison.[28]

Old man Gleason served his time and returned to farming. His tombstone in the Harvey Cemetery at Dunham shows he died on October 2, 1851, at the age of 84 years and 10 months.

Although he played a pivotal role in the growth and spread of the counterfeiting business, he is hardly known today. His son, Willard Gleason, was still counterfeiting in 1855 when he was captured and sentenced to the Provincial Penitentiary for seven years. Presses, plates, and a variety of counterfeiting implements were found on his premises—enough to require a two-horse team to transport them to Montreal. It was said at the time that he had "been in the business of selling at wholesale counterfeit bank notes for thirty to forty years [and] is estimated to be worth from eighty to one hundred thousand dollars."[29] Upon his release, Ebenezer P. Gleason moved to DeKalb County, Illinois, and continued his coniacking business there, as described later.

Seneca Paige

Seneca Paige was a man of some mystery. He was born in Hardwick, Massachusetts, on February 11, 1788, the second son of Foster and Amity and the grandson of Captain Timothy Paige, a "minute man" who marched to Cambridge on the Lexington alarm. Little is known of Seneca's criminal life because he wrote no confessions, gave no interviews, and may have corresponded with his associates only rarely. One newspaper said he was "a tall, slender young man, of light or fair complexion, and stutters or stammers in his speech." Another source says "He was a proud man and made a fine appearance—owned the best horses and carriage to be found in that vicinity. He is said to have accumulated an ample fortune while engaged in the snag business."[30]

The "Minute-Men" of the Revolution, published by Currier & Ives in 1876.

His career in crime seems to have started at least as early as September of 1809, when he and Harris Covert attempted to pass a spurious $3 bill of the Manhattan Bank on Samuel Beach, the postmaster of Jersey City, who immediately recognized the bill as bogus. Mr. Beach was also a county judge and arrested the two men. He found between $20,000 and $25,000 of forged notes on different banks in the United States in their possession, and they were committed to the "Hackensack Gaol."[31]

Since Seneca's father had started the first school in Dunham about 1796, and Seneca had spent part of his early years there and undoubtedly knew some of the coniackers, he and Covert must have obtained their spurious bills in that area. The amount of money they carried was so large, it is doubtful that they purchased it. Even at a very cheap price, say 10¢ on the dollar, they would have needed a small fortune to buy that "boodle." More likely, they were acting as agents for the coniackers in Quebec by placing the bogus bills in circulation in the United States on some type of profit-sharing basis.

Seneca and Harris either escaped jail in Hackensack or bribed their way out. In 1812 the bank presidents of Maryland offered a $1,000 reward for the capture of Paige and his plates.[32] He was soon captured by two police officers in New York City and taken to Baltimore for trial.[33] He and two others escaped the Baltimore jail on May 30, 1815. He was described in the local paper as being "about six feet 1 or 2 inches high, slender made, thin visage, very pleasant when spoken to, light hair and blue eyes; he is about 23 years of age. . . ."[34] He was again arrested for passing counterfeit money in Wilkesbarre, Pennsylvania, in August 1816, but he and fellow-counterfeiter James Seymour escaped from jail under suspicious conditions, and a $200 reward was offered for their apprehension.[35]

Unlike other counterfeiters, Seneca specialized in large transactions, and it was not uncommon for him to sell $50,000 to $100,000 of bogus bills at a time. He began to buy land as a speculator in 1816, purchasing a lot from his brother Gardiner in Bakersfield, Vermont. In 1819 he bought 140 acres of land from his brother Reed in Canada.[36] To disguise his "snag" business, Seneca bought a lumber business and hardware store in Dunham. This front appears to have worked because Seneca was never arrested in Canada. It seems from the available evidence that none of Seneca's brothers ever got involved in counterfeiting, but his father, Foster Paige, certainly did. In 1824 a minor war broke out between the Turner Wing faction of the Dunham counterfeiting community and those loyal to Gleason and Seneca. In a dawn attack, the Wing forces captured $4,000 in bogus notes, equipment, engraved copper plates, and several people, including old man Foster Paige, who had been running the printing press when the enemy arrived. Seneca retaliated and raided the opposition, overthrowing the Wings completely and getting back his money, his equipment, and his father.[37]

There were many other coniackers living on Cogniac Street and in nearby villages. Among these were Elijah Hurd, William Babcock, Joel Hill, Daniel Blasdell, Thomas Adams Lewis, William Crane, the Moses brothers, the Quinn brothers, the Gleason family, and the Wing family. Only a few of these were actually engravers. The rest, including Seneca Paige, worked in other aspects of the business, such as printing, signing notes, selling the "cony" to visitors, or transporting counterfeits into the United States and selling them wholesale to smaller dealers.

Seneca married Mary Ann Lee, became a member of the Provincial Parliament representing Missisquoi County, and was a justice of the peace for a short time. In spite of his legal work, he was not above using the law to help counterfeiters. It seems that a civil officer, assisted by a group of soldiers, was sent to arrest a group of counterfeiters in 1854. Seneca applied to a magistrate for a warrant to arrest these soldiers, and surprisingly, the magistrate issued the warrant. Not to be intimidated, the civil officer and the soldiers then captured Elijah Hurd of Dunham and took him to Montreal, where he was tried and sentenced to a term of seven-years imprisonment for having in his possession apparatus for copper-plate printing and a quantity of paper.[38]

But this is a strange story, because taken by itself, the evidence is not sufficient to prove Hurd's intent to counterfeit. At any rate, Seneca's bold interference did not save his old friend Elijah.

There is no evidence that Seneca engaged in the counterfeiting business after the late 1830s—not even hearsay—but it is not unreasonable to think he remained a coniacker until the early 1850s, when he took a more active role in public service and became more visible. He joined the Congregational Church in Bakersfield, Vermont, in 1855. He died in Montreal on October 11, 1856, and was buried in Bakersfield.[39]

A scene of counterfeiting money.
"Low Down and Illegal" by Arthur Young.

The raids in 1833 mark the beginning of the decline of counterfeiting in the Eastern Townships of Quebec, although local scamps continued to scratch up copper plates for another two decades or so, but never on the scale that had previously been seen. The last big raids came in 1847 and 1848 and again in 1854 and 1855, hitting townships like Barnston and Stanstead. They captured such counterfeiters as Samuel Davis and his son Thomas, Oliver Hanks, Harry Hollister, Herman and Sheldon Durkee, and J. Johnson.[40]

Elijah Hurd

Elijah Hurd was a real prize for law enforcement. He was reputed to have been one of the best workmen in counterfeiting and was known to the authorities for many years, but his seclusion and secret operations thwarted his captors for a long time. When he was sentenced in Montreal, Judge Alywin said:

As to you, Hurd—thanks to your grey hairs probably—the jury have recommended you to the mercy of the Court: but they knew nothing of your previous career, or they would have saved themselves the trouble. You know what we know—but what they did not know—that, years ago, in this same place, you were convicted of this same offense, which was then punished more severely than now. Upon that conviction you were sentenced to DEATH: the fatal day arrived when you must have expected to end your earthly existence: that sentence was not carried out, and, for the time, you escaped—but to what good purpose ? Did you become a better man? Let your subsequent history and present position answer the question. Had the jury known that history they would not have talked of mercy for you.[41]

A woodcut 18-pence note, printed by Isaac Collins in 1776, declaring "To counterfeit is *Death*."

American Counterfeiting: 1810–1850

The Eastern Townships in Quebec weren't the only part of Canada supplying counterfeit money to the United States during the early part of the century. Upper Canada (now Ontario), the land just north of the Great Lakes and southwest of Lower Canada, was also active in this business. Like Quebec, the region offered isolation, and the authorities were relatively indifferent to fighting counterfeiters. In 1816 the *Bedford Gazette*, a Pennsylvania newspaper, published notes compiled from the confessions of three members of a counterfeiting network that consisted of over 100 members "that principally reside in New York; New Brunswick, in the State of New Jersey; Philadelphia, Bristol, Lancaster, York, Berlin, Hanover, Harrisburg, Pittsburg, and in Bedford County, Pennsylvania; Steubenville, Ohio; and Berkley and Frederick Counties in Virginia."[42] This network principally employed the engravers Philander Noble (whom we've met before) from Connecticut and a person who went by the code name of "Tabitha." Both lived, at least part of the time, in Upper Canada. The paper-maker for this network resided in Virginia, with additional paper coming in from Upper Canada. Philander Noble engraved the plates for counterfeiting the notes of the Philadelphia Bank, the Union Bank of Maryland, and the Hagerstown Bank. His work was done partly at East Berlin and partly at an encampment near Pine Grove Furnace (12 miles from East Berlin) in the South Mountain, Adams County, Pennsylvania. The printing of these notes was done on the Allegheny Mountain, "about three miles north of Miller's Tavern in this [Bedford] County." Once the notes were printed, they were sent to Philadelphia, and from there to other large cities throughout the Eastern states. "It is supposed," the article states, "that upwards of 30 waggoners, who travel on the road from Philadelphia to Pittsburgh, are engaged as circulators of counterfeit paper which they receive on commission, from an inn-keeper in Philadelphia."[43] Some of the members of this gang were identified by name, description, and location.[44]

A vignette featuring "Of the Waggoner and Hercules," a fable promoting self-sufficiency and hard work. Perhaps not the same virtues, quite, as espoused by the counterfeit circulators.

Jim and Dan Brown

James Brown, or "Jim," as he was commonly called, was born about 1798 in the state of New York. In 1802 the family moved to a farm just below the present city of Youngstown, Ohio, and in 1808 they moved again to a farm of 640 acres on the west side of the Cuyahoga River, just below the village of Boston. Jim's older brother, Daniel, was born in 1788, and both boys were said to be remarkably handsome, of good physique, and to have pleasant manners.[45]

It is not known which of the two brothers was first to get into the counterfeiting business, but opportunity has a way of finding the right people. In the early 1800s Ohio was a sparsely populated area with few roads. Manufacturing was virtually non-existent, and farms served only local needs. That all changed when construction was started on the Ohio and Erie Canal in 1826. When completed in the early 1830s, it connected Cleveland on Lake Erie with the Cuyahoga River, then ran southward to Akron and on to the Ohio River on the border of Ohio and Kentucky. With the opening of the canal, the economic growth of the region was expected to expand rapidly, and the Brown brothers were well situated to become the head of counterfeiting in the Cuyahoga Valley, centered on the little town of Boston.

The Browns chose as their partners William G. Taylor of Cleveland; Abraham S. Holmes and Colonel William Ashley of Boston, Ohio; William Latta of Bath, Ohio; Jonathan De Courcey

and Thomas Johnson of Norton, Ohio; and Joshua King and Joel Keeler of Portage, Ohio.[46] Neither of the Browns engaged in passing counterfeit notes themselves but instead acted as "capitalists," buying spurious notes from wholesale dealers and distributing them to a hierarchy of "boodle" carriers and passers.[47]

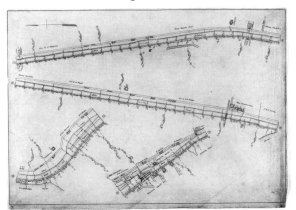

A map of the Ohio & Erie Canal plans (Lock #39 in Cuyahoga County, Ohio).

During the summer of 1826, George Darrow, Jim Brown, and William Ashley were arrested for counterfeiting in Portage County, Ohio. Their discovery was made by a Mr. George Farr, who had been given some spurious money for hogs he sold to these men. Seeking revenge, he began observing the group and undertook to join them to learn their operations and to expose them to the law. Once he gained their confidence, he was accepted as a partner and even took their oath of fidelity and agreed to murder any member who should reveal their secrets. Among the counterfeits that Farr mentioned in his evidence were $3 notes of the Manufacturers' Bank of Pawtucket and $100 notes of the Bank of Pennsylvania. He also named a person who was expected to arrive with $20,000 in notes of $3, $5, and $10 on the Western Reserve Bank.[48] As always, Jim Brown's lawyers were successful in getting delays in court or paying witnesses to fail to show.

About 1831 the counterfeiters obtained some well-engraved plates of the notes of the Bank of the United States, located in Philadelphia. These notes were current in every state of the Union and with all the countries doing business with the United States. The fact that the notes were issued by a well-established and recognized bank enhanced their reputation as a solid currency. Naturally, they became the choice of several counterfeiters. Lyman Parkes, also known as James Wilson, was a very skillful counterfeiter who produced a copperplate of the $10 note of this bank in 1835. Although the particular plate was captured, there is nothing to say that he hadn't produced similar plates earlier. Reuben Moses had also engraved these notes, but it is doubtful he got them into circulation.[49] Whoever the engraver, the Browns could have used these plates to make a fortune, but greed and bad luck got in their way.

Daniel Brown came up with the idea of using all of their spurious notes, including the notes of the Bank of the United States, to buy a ship in New Orleans and sail directly for China to buy a cargo of teas, coffees, spices, silks, and other merchandise, and then continue their purchases in India and other places. The partners of this scheme (the two Browns and William G. Taylor) figured that when they sold their merchandise in European and American ports, it would make them a fortune. To accomplish this, the partners planned to take with them $1,500,000 of spurious notes, together with the machinery and materials for turning out $2,000,000 more. They also planned to take along a number of engravers, printers, and an expert penman, all listed as "passengers." Even the captain was privy to the plan.[50]

On Christmas Eve 1830, the night before sailing, Jim Brown and Bill Taylor went on shore to "paint the town red." Although they didn't become excessively inebriated and didn't start any fights, they were noticed by the police for their "extreme liberality in the dispensation of their wealth." Police officers followed them and noticed them rowing off to their vessel anchored in mid-river. Since smuggling was then in vogue, a squad of New Orleans' finest were sent out to the ship to make a thorough search. Naturally, everything hidden on the ship was found, and the three principals were arrested and held for trial.[51]

Jim got out on bail, but his older brother, Daniel, died on August 22, 1832, while still in jail. Jim moved back to Ohio, and although his reputation

was known to his neighbors, he was elected to Justice of the Peace for Boston in 1834. In the winter of 1837, Jim moved to Akron, living in a house on Howard Street, and bought a hotel called the Summit House. He did not live in the hotel but operated it and made it the headquarters of his gang. His lawyers continued to stall the legal proceedings against him in New Orleans, and it was widely suspected that key witnesses were paid to vanish. William Taylor was acquitted in the New Orleans scheme and spent the rest of his life wandering the country.

In February 1838 Jim Brown was arrested in Akron and charged with being the mastermind of a forgery scheme in which Charles Stearns and W.J. Ames, residing in New York, and William Pitcher, formerly of Ohio, obtained genuine bank stationary from the Commercial Bank of New Orleans and forged letters and orders to obtain the original bank-note plates of the Bank of Kentucky. These plates were then taken to Messrs. Burton, Gurley & Edmonds, bank-note printers in New York, to be used to print notes. The engravers at Burton, Gurley & Edmonds became suspicious and contacted the bank to verify the order. When the scheme was discovered, the police were notified and arrested several of the principals.[52] No bank notes were actually printed, so by clever legal-defense work, Jim escaped jail once again. However, he was arrested in April 1841 for swindling the Girard Bank of Philadelphia, several banks in the west, and Jacob M. Little & Co., also of Philadelphia, by means of forged certificates of deposit on the Commercial Bank of New Orleans. The officers from Philadelphia that arrested Jim also caught a companion of his named Benjamin Stevens, a notorious counterfeiter, who had $200 in spurious notes in his possession.[53] At about the same time, Jim was getting ready to start the Farmer's and Merchant's Bank at Burlington, Wisconsin, which was then a territory. He confessed to Marshal Mills that he had acquired some $200,000 of the bills which were not yet filled out. Also, a large amount of money ready for circulation on the Exporting, Mining and Manufacturing Company at Jackson, Illinois, was found in the trunk of a confederate.[54]

A $1 note of the Exporting, Mining and Manufacturing Company at Jackson, Illinois.

Brown was given bail on posting bonds of $6,000, but on the first charge, dealing with the forgery using two banks, the witnesses from New York never appeared, and Brown was discharged. Similarly, the other charges were dismissed when it was decided there was not sufficient proof that Brown was involved. In March 1838 one of Brown's old comrades, Jonathan DeCourcey, was arrested for having in his possession $10 and $50 counterfeit bills on the Bank of Rochester, New York. To seek immunity, DeCourcey informed against Jim Brown as the source of the money. Brown was arrested and examined in early April 1838. DeCourcey claimed that Brown had offered to sell him $6,000 in spurious bills. Like many other times when Jim was arrested, he and his comrades tried just about every trick in the book to get out of trouble, including paying DeCourcey to go to Texas so he couldn't be found to give testimony. Instead, DeCourcey was captured on his way to Texas and brought back to appear at the trial. His testimony could not be shaken, and Jim was convicted and sentenced to seven-years imprisonment.[55]

Jim anticipated that he might be found guilty, so he had his attorneys make up a bill of exceptions to be carried to the State Supreme Court to ask for a writ of error. His brother-in-law made an overnight run, using fresh horses at intervals, to reach Cleveland in time to present the bill. This resulted in a new trial. At the new trial, the state's principal witness (DeCourcey) could not be found, and the proceedings against Brown were nollied (*nolle prossed*).

A similar case occurred in Portage County in June 1838. Willard W. Stevens, a resident of Akron, was arrested for dealing in counterfeit money and lodged in jail at Ravenna. He informed

the marshal that his supplier was Jim Brown and told where he could find a quantity of spurious money hidden in the cellar of his (Stevens's) house. Finding the money where indicated, the marshal got an affidavit from Stevens and then an arrest warrant. Brown was held to bail for $9,000. At the trial, a jury was impaneled and the witnesses called. All responded except Willard Stevens, who was "mysteriously" absent.[56]

A counterfeit $10 note of the Bank of Rochester, New York.

Jim's bag of magical tricks finally gave out in August 1846 while he was Justice of the Peace in Northampton, Ohio. He was charged with "making and uttering and assisting to make and utter counterfeit gold and silver coin, and counterfeit notes in the similitude of bank notes." The trial was held at the U.S. District Court in Columbus and the principal witness, John Bellows, was the son of a respected farmer in a neighboring town who alleged that Jim had sold him counterfeit money in exchange for a horse, a yoke of oxen, and other items at the rate of 20¢ per $1 for paper money and 33-1/3¢ per $1 for coin. Marshal Mills searched Brown's house in Northampton, where he found a large number of zinc and copper cups and parts of two galvanic batteries. In a trunk in the store-room, he found a large quantity of bank-note paper, one ream entire and unbroken, and in the secretary, sundry letters and other evidence of criminality.[57] The jury took two hours and returned a verdict of guilty. Judge McLean sentenced Jim to 10 years in the Ohio Penitentiary, which he began serving on August 10, 1846.

While in prison, Jim was eventually promoted to take charge of the hospital. When cholera broke out in the prison, he kept a cool head and worked constantly in caring for the sick. His devotion to the patients was appreciated by the officials of the prison to such an extent that they gladly supported the efforts then being pushed by his only daughter, Laura M. Brown, for a pardon. President Zachary Taylor granted the pardon in July 1849, and Jim was released after serving just 2 years and 11 months.

Jim's long-suffering wife, Lucy, divorced him in 1851, and his family never heard from him again. In the winter of late 1859 and early 1860, Brown and a former pupil of his named Elihu Chilson, then living in Kent County, Michigan, began a counterfeiting operation. Jim was arrested, tried, and convicted "for having in his possession, with intent to pass, a counterfeit bill," and sentenced to three-years imprisonment in the Michigan State Penitentiary. He began his sentence on March 17, 1860, and served out his full term.

Mules pulling a coal boat up a canal.

On June 17, 1865, Sheriff Burlison of Akron arrested Leonard Hill with a large amount of spurious money in his possession. Believing that Hill had acquired his money from Jim Brown, Burlison arrested him also, with another man named Thaddeus Nighman of Canton, Ohio. Between the three suspects, the haul of counterfeited postal scrip, Treasury Notes, and miscellaneous bank bills amounted to a sum between $10,000 and $12,000. Soon after, the sheriff arrested four men as part of the same gang, and his deputies arrested eight or ten others, along with a press, plates, burglars' tools, etc. They were all placed in jail in Cleveland.[58] Brown made bail and was released. While returning from Cleveland upon a coal boat on December 9, 1865, and while passing through the Peninsula lock, Jim was walking from the stern to the bow when he lost his footing and fell to the bottom of the boat,

breaking his shoulder and fracturing his skull. He was taken to Yellow Creek Basin in an unconscious condition and died on December 10, 1865, at the age of 67 years.[59]

Another Daniel Brown

Jim Brown's eldest son, born in 1820 and named Daniel after Jim's brother, also got into counterfeiting. As early as February 1838 the *Cleveland Advertiser* reported that "A young man by the name of Brown, a son of the notorious James Brown of Akron, was brought from Elyria, yesterday, to our jail."[60] That young man was Daniel M. Brown, and some $20,000 in counterfeit was found on his person. According to the account given by Samuel Lane, Dan and a companion were arrested in the saddle in Medina County and immediately taken to Elyria. Before being searched, he was permitted to go into the hotel stable and rub down his horse. On finally being searched, no counterfeit was found on his person. But when the straw bedding was searched in his horse's stall, a large amount of spurious money was found. Since there was no direct evidence that Dan had placed the money there or ever had it in his possession, he was discharged from custody. The lawmen were clearly negligent in failing to search Dan and his horse as soon as they had arrested him.

In the early 1840s Dan bought the family's 300-acre farm in Yellow Creek from his father, and on May 20, 1845, he married his cousin, Minerva A. Darrow. By 1850 they had a one-year old son, also named Daniel, living with them in Northampton. Although Dan continued to deal in spurious bank notes, he also learned how to make exceptionally good bogus coins, especially dollars, half-dollars, and quarters. They were said to be so good as to practically defy detection. In 1842 George C. Bates, the U.S. District Attorney for the state of Michigan, learned that between $40,000 and $50,000 of these finely executed bogus coins were in circulation in the southeast part of the state, and that they were the product of Dan Brown, now using the alias "Dan West." The story of Bates's search and eventual meeting with Dan are detailed in a letter that was published in the *Cleveland Leader* in November 1885.

A "Gold Rush" cartoon satirizing the desperation to head West and make a fortune, circa 1849.

Gold was discovered in California in 1849, and both Dan Brown and ex-Sheriff Samuel Lane made the trip the following year, neither knowing of the other's venture. Lane's plan was to find gold and get rich, but Dan planned on shoving counterfeit in return for gold dust. To do this with minimum risk, Dan planned on taking advantage of the current economic facts.

New York had established the first banking insurance plan with their "Safety Fund" act of 1829. This fund protected deposits in case of the bank's failure. After the financial panic of 1837, a nationwide system of Safety Fund banks was established, and they enjoyed the trust and confidence of the people. This was especially true of the State Bank of Missouri. Since California had no paper money in circulation at this time, the economy was based entirely on gold and silver coins ("hard money") or gold dust and nuggets. Dan Brown bought a large amount of counterfeit $50 and $100 bills of the Bank of Missouri, knowing that they would be eagerly accepted by the miners. It was believed that he passed between $80,000 and $100,000 of this spurious money in exchange for gold dust or real coins. By late 1850 miners and merchants realized that the paper money was counterfeit, and a vigilante party began trying to ferret out the passers of the currency. They identified "Dan West" as the principal of this scheme and learned that he was in bad

health and had already taken a steamer for Panama. They had no faster means of following him than to wait for the next steamer at the beginning of January 1851.

Here working gold miners are shown on a tobacco label, circa 1867.

Dan reached New York greatly enfeebled by scurvy, and friends then helped him get back to his home in Northampton, Ohio. There, he quickly closed his temporal affairs. The homestead was deeded to his brother, James R. Brown, in December 1850. He personally distributed his money to friends and relatives and said his good-byes. He died January 21, 1851, at the age of 31 years. According to Samuel Lane, he was buried on the home farm in Northampton, and his remains were subsequently removed to Akron Rural Cemetery and laid beside those of his wife, Minerva, who died June 27, 1874.

Lyman Parkes

Lyman Parkes was a self-taught but very talented counterfeit engraver. The "biography" of Parkes given in the *National Police Gazette* (1845) is not to be trusted on many of its facts. He was, however, clearly associated with the gang of counterfeiters on Cogniac Street in Dunham during the 1820s. On February 26, 1835, Parkes, another counterfeiter named Smith Davis, and a blacksmith named Thomas Thorpe were arrested in Philadelphia. When their rooms were searched, Willis H. Blaney, acting as an independent investigator, found a geometric lathe, a transferring press, and a printing press, as well as three copper plates for printing $10 notes of the Bank of the United States, steel dies that had been engraved by the geometric lathe, gravers, and a spectacle with an attached magnifying glass. This was a remarkable find since it indicated that Parkes had an appreciation, if not a basic knowledge, of how the geometric lathe worked and was able to make one with the help of some machinists in Philadelphia. As described earlier, this lathe had been invented by Asa Spencer and Jacob Perkins about 19 years before, when they both worked for the bank-note company of Murray, Draper & Fairman. The lathe was kept secret for a number of years afterward. These lathes and the simpler rose engines were just beginning to be used by American bank-note companies when Parkes made his. Charles Toppan, one of the leading bank-note engravers of the day, testified at the trial, saying that the Parkes lathe diverged a little bit from the one he (Toppan) was used to but obviously operated very well. One can only wonder if Benjamin Moses, who had worked at Murray, Draper & Fairman, and may have seen the geometric lathe at work, ever discussed the operation of the device with Parkes while the two engravers were in the Dunham area of Lower Canada. Parkes was found guilty and sentenced to prison.[61]

Ebenezer Philander Gleason Jr.

During 1838, Ebenezer P. Gleason Jr. of Dunham, Quebec, fame moved to Genoa, DeKalb County, Illinois. At first, he was not suspected of a criminal bent, but not long after he arrived in town, "a carpet sack well filled with counterfeit money was found in his possession."[62] The next year, one of his traveling agents was arrested in Chicago and while in jail confessed that Gleason was one of the chiefs of his gang. Gleason was arrested, but when the trial was held, the witness could not be found, and Ebenezer was set at liberty. He acquired a store, a saw-mill, and a nice farm. He married Lydia Strong on May 2, 1839, a respectable young lady of the area. According to the historian Henry Boies, the marriage lasted for a few years until a traveling doctor, named Smitch, boarded with the Gleasons and became attracted to Mrs. Gleason. When Ebenezer became ill, the doctor attended to him. After eating one day a porridge prepared by Smitch and Mrs. Gleason, he complained of the taste and soon died in convulsions and delirium. The doctor and Mrs. Gleason were arrested for murder and an order was obtained for exhumation of the body. At the autopsy, the contents of Ebenezer's stomach were examined, although in a very rudimentary way. A special term of the court was held for the trial, but the evidence from the autopsy was decided to be insufficient, and the two prisoners were released. Soon after they moved to La Salle County, where the doctor died under circumstances that lead to the suspicion that he too had been poisoned.[63]

At least two members of the Wing family from Dunham, Quebec, also moved to DeKalb County, Illinois, although I have found no evidence as yet that any of the Wings were involved in counterfeiting in Illinois.[64]

Pete McCartney

Probably the most interesting and clever counterfeiter of the 19th century was John Peter McCartney, born about 1824 of poor Irish parents. His place of birth is not yet known, but he eventually shows up on a farm near a small village called Neoga in what is now Cumberland County in central

John Peter McCartney.

Illinois.[65] Even given his humble origins, he was an educated man who could read and write quite well. He seems to have had a thirst for knowledge, learning not only engraving but papermaking and chemistry as well. As a counterfeiter he had several aliases but was known to his friends and family as simply "Pete." He grew up as a stout, active, and industrious farm boy. Like most engravers, he showed an artistic talent early in life and took to drawing naturally. His first venture into crime appears to have been on his own initiative. According to his account, this happened in the early 1840s when he was still a teenager. While he was visiting relatives in northern Illinois, he delivered produce for a farmer and was paid in dollar bills. He erased the $1 denominations on some of the bills and replaced them with "10s" that he had carefully cut off the bills of "broken banks." He glued the new denominations on the legitimate bills very skillfully and presented his finished product at the counter of a small grocery store in Indianapolis. When the clerk scrutinized the raised bill and said, "I don't know about that," Pete said he froze, wondering if he should turn and run, or say nothing. As it turned out, the clerk was merely expressing doubt that he had enough change to break the bill, and a steady silence won Pete a sizeable profit.[66]

Invigorated by his success, Pete decided to improve his meager talents by learning all he could about the counterfeiting business. He began to travel throughout the Midwest, searching for experienced hands that could teach him how to engrave, how to print, and how to "shove the queer."[67] Over time, he met some of the best men in the business and often worked with them for a short time to perfect his skills. His first teachers at a professional level were a notorious family of counterfeiters named the Johnstons.[68] At least three generations of the Johnston men made their living by counterfeiting paper money and were always ably assisted by the women of the family. William Johnston, considered the best engraver of the family, personally took young Pete under his wing and taught him the basics of engraving. After living with the Johnstons for some time, Pete worked with Ben Boyd, learning even more about engraving and plate printing. After Boyd, he went to Cincinnati, where he worked briefly with a prominent church leader and pillar of the community, Thomas Taylor, who ran a large operation making counterfeit coins. From there he went to Indianapolis and the tutelage of a German engraver named Monroe Achman.[69]

Monroe Achman had been partners with another counterfeiter named John B. Trout. When Monroe died about 1863, his widow, Abigail Achman, married Mr. Trout on September 12, 1863. She had two daughters, Almiranda and Martha Ann, from her previous marriage, and they kept the name Achman until they married. Mrs. Achman was a "shover" and taught her daughters the tricks of the trade. Mr. Trout was himself an expert engraver of counterfeit plates. Born about 1835, he was the scourge of the Mississippi Valley during the 1850s and was sentenced in 1867 to the Indiana State Prison, where he developed "consumption" (tuberculosis) and was pardoned just before his death in 1872. McCartney had studied with Monroe Achman during the late 1840s and worked with John Trout in the late 1850s.

In 1852 Pete decided to make Indianapolis his headquarters and started buying real estate. He bought a house on North Illinois Street, between First and Second streets. He also bought a house and a lot on Noble Street, another house and lot on South Street, and a whole block on West North Street. These properties were worth at least $25,000. Pete lived in the city under the alias of "Joe Wood."[70]

Pete was arrested more than 50 times during his long career in crime, but he was a good judge of men and could usually tell if an officer could be bought. He escaped from several arrests by paying policemen or sheriffs a large sum of good money to let him go. When those ploys didn't

John B. Trout.

work, Pete had no hesitancy in jumping from a train or picking a lock on a cell door and slipping away quietly in the night. He was both resourceful and daring. He was also "street smart" and trusted no one unless he knew them well. Even then, his whereabouts were sometimes revealed by "friends" in order to save themselves trouble with the law. An example of that treachery can be found in Ben Boyd, a fellow counterfeiter and Pete's brother-in-law, whom we will meet later.

The year 1864 was eventful for Pete. He settled down briefly in Springfield, Illinois, and became a "dentist" under the employ of Dr. Grenville French. On October 19 of that year, he married the same Martha Ann Achman he had met years before at Cincinnati with her sister Almiranda and her mother, Mrs. Abigail Achman, when they were printing counterfeit bills and passing them. Almiranda, or "Allie," as she was called, married Ben Boyd, making Ben and Pete brothers-in-law. Martha Ann, being from a counterfeiting family, was no newcomer to the business. She had been working with counterfeit plates since she was 13 years old and may even have had knowledge of Monroe Achman's business at an earlier age. She proved to be not only a loyal and devoted wife but an able and intelligent assistant in Pete's career.

It was also in 1864 that Captain Whitney Frank, of the Provost Marshall's office, captured a counterfeit shover in Memphis, Tennessee. The shover was an old man and may have been in prison before and knew the hardships of prison life. The gentleman offered to give the names and addresses of some counterfeiters in St. Louis if the captain would let him go free. The deal was made, and Captain Frank and his assistants went to St. Louis, made the appropriate contacts, and arranged to purchase $25,000 in counterfeit $100 greenbacks at 20¢ on the dollar. Later, a deal was made to buy the counterfeit plates for $35,000 and to buy another $100,000 of the "queer" at 20¢ on the dollar. As soon as the plates and money were exchanged, detectives appeared out of nowhere and seized the plates and $175,000 in bogus greenbacks.[71] Three of the counterfeiters (John Brown, James Vezey, and Charles Hathaway) were sent to the Old Capitol Prison in

Washington, D.C., and there they met Captain William P. Wood, superintendent of the prison and soon to be chief of the U.S. Secret Service.

The Old Capitol Prison in Washington, D.C.

Two of the suspects (Brown and Vezey) agreed to help the federal officers capture Louis Sleight in St. Louis. Captain Wood had some experience in capturing counterfeiters, so he asked the Assistant secretary of war for permission to work on the case, and the secretary agreed. The Provost Marshal of the War Department at this time was Colonel Lafayette Baker, an unscrupulous and boastful bully who took the unauthorized title of "Chief of the National Detective Police." In typical fashion, the colonel took charge of the operation. Sleight was captured along with the plates for printing nine different counterfeit notes; nine presses, including one that weighed about 3,500 pounds (probably a coin press); and dies for making $5 and $20 gold coins.[72] To save himself, Sleight agreed to borrow a counterfeit plate of the 1862- and 1863-series $20 U.S. note, the so-called "Legal Tender" Note, which had been made by the Johnston family in Indianapolis. He also promised to entrap Pete McCartney by purchasing several thousands of dollars of the counterfeit $20 bills.

Actually, there were two counterfeit plates of the $20 Legal Tender Note. The first counterfeit plate had been engraved by the Johnstons. It was a good plate but nothing spectacular. Eventually, the Johnstons decided to cut McCartney out of their gang, and when he discovered their plans, he decided to take something of value with him. He broke into their shop, stole the counterfeit plate, and made an electrotype copy from it. He replaced the original counterfeit plate and the Johnstons never suspected a thing. McCartney carefully and patiently re-engraved some parts of the plate and made it even better.

Meanwhile, Colonel Baker, Captain Wood, and their posse went straight to Indianapolis, expecting to wrap up the case and then fight for the credit. Instead, they discovered the local police had arrested Pete at the post office the day before they arrived. Captain Wood and three deputies went to the Johnston house, about two miles south of Indianapolis, early in the morning, taking everyone prisoner while they were still asleep, capturing $20 counterfeit plates, a large sum of 50-cent postal currency, and a printing press.[73] Two of the Johnston boys and Pete were put on a Pennsylvania Central train for Washington, D.C., under armed guards.[74] Pete knew he would be thrown into the Old Capitol Prison, which was infamous for its small, dank, fetid cells and torturous heat in the summer. He decided he must escape the train before it got to Washington, and since he couldn't bribe the guards, he would have to try something physically daring and unexpected.

While the train was traveling through a mountainous, rocky region near Horseshoe Bend, between Altoona and Harrisburg, Pennsylvania, at about 35 miles per hour, Pete waited until the guards were dozing, slipped the irons off his hands and feet, walked to the rear of the car, and jumped off. Surprisingly, he broke no bones but did receive bruises and abrasions. He hid for a time and eventually found friendly people who gave him food and treated his cuts.[75] Even though Louis Sleight did not figure directly in Pete's capture, Pete learned of Louis's cooperation with the lawmen and never forgave him.

Colonel Baker, Captain Wood, and the posse that had chased Pete in Indianapolis went next to Covington, Kentucky, just across the river from Cincinnati, where they arrested eight more counterfeiters and captured the plates for making

50-cent Fractional Currency and about $200,000 of finished 50-cent notes. They also captured partially finished plates for $50 Treasury Notes, a tea chest full of postal notes, and a small press used to print the notes. Altogether, they filled 14 cases with counterfeiting materials. Among the men captured were Charles Burnell, Louis Dollman, Benjamin Dean, Peter McCue, and William Minzer.[76] This was hailed in the newspapers as the largest seizure of counterfeiting materials ever made, and the success probably played an important part in Wood's decision to accept, on July 1, 1865, an appointment to be chief of the newly formed U.S. Secret Service.

During 1865 and 1866, Pete made Fort Wayne, Indiana, his base of operations. He and his gang stayed hidden in a brothel known as "Lookout Mountain," about two miles south of the city on the Piqua Road. The brothel was kept by a Mrs. Read, who was mixed up with Pete's operations for several years. Pete stayed there for a time, but after his equipment was seized by police, he moved his headquarters to another brothel in Frenchtown, Indiana, kept by a certain Mrs. Tonner and Alice Gilson, once the queen of the Fort Wayne *demi-monde*. While in Fort Wayne, Pete and Miles Ogle engraved plates for the $5 greenback Legal Tender Note, issue of March 10, 1863, and the $20 note of the same issue.

The $5 Legal Tender Note, issue of March 10, 1863. (Friedberg-63a.)

Passing counterfeit money was always risky, and Pete often stayed just one step ahead of the local sheriff or chief of police. On January 7, 1866, Pete, using the alias "Joe Wood," was arrested in East St. Louis with some $20,000 of counterfeit U.S. $50 currency on his person. He was taken before Judge Kase, who ordered him placed in jail to await the U.S. Secret Service agents. The counterfeit money was so well executed that none but the best judges could tell the difference between it and the genuine.[77] Pete's bail was made and he was released. The question was then "who made the bail?" Some citizens believed that Mayor John B. Bowman used some of McCartney's money to pay his bail in return for his agreement to let the mayor keep the rest of the genuine money. Complicating this affair is that two other men were arrested at the same time, and they were found to have $12,000 in their possession when searched at the jail. Judge Kase confiscated $11,000 of that money, and $1,000 was surrendered to Mayor Bowman. While charges were flying back and forth about the arithmetic, Pete slipped quietly out of town.

In 1866 Pete and his younger brother, Levi, were arrested at Mantoon, Illinois, by Deputy U.S. Marshal John Rittenhouse. Levi, born about 1835, was not an engraver but a dealer in the "queer," usually supplied by Pete. He was caught occasionally, the same as Pete, and usually escaped from jail. In this particular case, the information that Pete and Levi were operating in Mantoon came from an unlikely source—Pete's brother-in-law, Ben Boyd. A man named John Harmon was arrested by the Secret Service for having in his possession $1,000 in counterfeit $50 Treasury Notes. Harmon said he got the notes from Ben Boyd and John Trout, who were working together in Decatur, Illinois. Boyd and Trout were arrested shortly thereafter. Boyd wrote a letter to the Secret Service agent to bargain for his release if he gave up information about Pete's whereabouts and counterfeiting operation. The deal was made, and Pete and Levi were arrested in Mantoon and transferred to a jail in Springfield.[78] During the night of October 17, 1866, Pete and Levi escaped from jail. Doors were found unlocked. Sheriff

Grafton and his family lived on the ground floor of the jail and should have heard any noise made by escaping prisoners. It was widely believed that Mrs. McCartney had paid someone to unlock the doors and help Pete and Levi escape. She had come to Springfield to be with her husband, and, as a matter of course, the court had turned over Pete's good money to her a few days before the escape. She was also implicated by the fact that she disappeared on the same night that the two men escaped.[79]

After his escape in Springfield, Pete went to Cairo, Illinois, to lay low for a while. For some months he operated a daguerreotype studio, using the alias "Warren." While making an honest buck, he found time to study chemistry and work on improving his recipes for making good bank-note ink. After a few months of this routine, he changed his profession again and became "Professor Joseph Woods," traveling all through the west, lecturing on "Counterfeit money and how to detect it." This, of course, was a con game. The professor would give a lecture or two, and then he would circulate among the better stores in town and pass counterfeit money on unsuspecting clerks who knew his reputation and expertise and therefore never doubted he was on the "up and up." Meanwhile, his accomplices, Miles Ogle and James Lyons, were back in Fort Wayne, Indiana, printing from counterfeit plates that Pete had engraved while working in the brothels.

Pete once said that he had paid "over $70,000 in good money to escape the clutches of the law." Dishonesty cuts both ways, of course, and Pete was sometimes the victim. In the Springfield case, for example, William P. Wood, the chief of the Secret Service, and a Secret Service detective named Sam Felker, from the Chicago office, were the perpetrators of a scam. Wood visited Pete in jail and promised he would square him with the government if

James Lyons.

he would reveal the location of some plates he was alleged to own. Pete decided to trust the two men and revealed the hiding spot of the lead impressions for counterfeit plates. Wood took Ben Boyd to Champaign, Illinois, where they uncovered the plates. Wood and Felker kept the plates, possibly intending to sell them under the fictitious name of a third party to the government. Pete was outraged by the treachery.[80]

Following his escape from the Springfield jail, Pete became a fugitive for the next four years. At the end of October 1870 he and his wife, using an alias, and William Alexander, using the alias James Lyons, moved to Portland, Kentucky, and rented a house. The house needed a lot of repairs, but the trio was anxious to move in right away, so they offered the landlord an extra $50 to move the deal along. The landlord took the money, but being suspicious of the three tenants, he informed the police in Louisville that they might be burglars. The police chief assigned two detectives to watch the renters and take whatever action was appropriate. On November 4, 1870, the detectives decided they had seen enough and they raided the house. Pete was in St. Louis visiting Fred Biebusch on business, but the officers captured Mrs. McCartney and James Lyons, a printing press, a full set of engraving tools, a transfer press, a plate for making 50-cent Fractional Currency notes, inks, and plates for making various greenbacks.[81]

The Louisville police suspected that Mrs. McCartney might be of some interest to the Secret Service, so they sent a letter to the agent in St. Louis, John Eagan. Eagan left at once for Louisville, and upon arrival, he interviewed Martha McCartney in jail. Eagan had a list of all the federal securities that the Secret Service had reason to believe Pete had counterfeited. He demanded that Martha tell him where to find the plates for a $50 treasury bond, $5 and $20 Treasury Notes, and a 50-cent fractional note. Martha calmly explained that some of the material had been given to agent Sam Felker in February 1869, to get him to fix the case in Springfield, but she would get the rest of the material and give it to Eagan if he agreed to release her. Eagan said he would talk to the chief about her offer. Meanwhile, he took her and two of her children to stay at his home in St. Louis.[82]

While Eagan was trying to make arrangements for Mrs. McCartney's eventual release, Pete and Charles Johnson were arrested in Cincinnati on November 21, 1870, by the local police. Officer Haehl recognized Charles Johnson as a known counterfeiter and trailed the two men while getting "backup." When the suspects boarded the train for Indianapolis, Haehl and another officer went on board and arrested the men. The officers found two $20 counterfeit plates, a revolver, and over four hundred counterfeit bills on Johnson. They found about $3,500 in good money on Pete but no counterfeit.[83]

McCartney and Johnson were locked up in the Third Street station house. Pete requested the police to telegraph Agent Eagan in St. Louis, saying he would verify that the two men were on official business for the Secret Service and should be released. Eagan got the telegram but sent back an answer that the two men should be held until he arrived. Naturally, Pete was gone by morning. When the locks on the doors were examined, it was found that the tumblers were so loose that the bolts could have been pushed back by any sharp object, and Pete was thoroughly familiar with the way locks work. The $3,500 in good money confiscated from Pete disappeared, although it had supposedly been locked in a desk. The Chief of the Secret Service, Colonel H.C. Whitley, eventually got back $1,400 and returned it to Pete at a later date, but $2,000 was apparently stolen by the police. For some reason, Johnson did not escape with Pete. At his trial, Johnson acted as his own lawyer, putting up a spirited defense, but the jury did not buy his story that he was on his way to recover the counterfeit plates to surrender them to the government. It took the jury only a few minutes to find him guilty, and he was sentenced to prison.[84]

Pete's escape from the Third Street station house lasted only a short time before he was captured again in Decatur, Illinois. This time, Chief Whitley got considerably more cooperation from Pete and recovered over $60,000 in counterfeit money of various denominations and a complete set of new plates for printing $5 Treasury Notes. The plate was pronounced by experts to be one of the most dangerous ever cut.[85]

Pete came close to a violent death in December 1874. That year, an informant in Canada named George Albert Mason wrote to Elmer Washburn, the newly appointed Chief of the Secret Service, to report that he (Mason) was to meet an old counterfeiter named "Captain Judd" to buy some "queer" money at a certain hotel in Burlington, Iowa. The meeting was later changed to St. Louis and the Secret Service was prepared to capture this Captain Judd.[86] A meeting was arranged between Mason, "Captain Judd" (who was actually Pete McCartney), and his brother Levi McCartney. Mason planned to arrest Captain Judd to gain credit with the Secret Service so he could get a position with them. During the meeting, which took place in a hotel room, Mason pulled out a revolver and warned everyone to surrender, firing a warning shot. Pete and Levi immediately retaliated—Pete with a knife and Levi with a homemade blackjack. Pete started slashing Mason about the head and face, and Mason shot Pete in his left side, but the wound was not fatal. Pete grabbed the gun and fired at Mason but missed. Meanwhile Levi, using his rock-in-a-handkerchief blackjack, was hitting Mason over the head. The commotion scared others in the hotel, and they alerted the police station which was only a block away. Three officers quickly arrived and arrested all the parties.[87] Four days later, the Secret Service learned that Captain Judd was actually Pete McCartney.

Mason was released from custody and Pete and Levi were confined to jail. Over the next few weeks, several of Pete's associates were arrested in St. Louis and placed in the county jail with him. On the night of February 5, 1875, Pete and five of

George Albert Mason.

his friends broke out of jail and escaped. The five other escapees included such worthies as Levi McCartney, Mike Rogers (formerly of the Reno gang), John Hall (counterfeiter), James Rittenhouse (counterfeiter), and Daniel Benoni (burglar). Pete, who was still limping from the gunshot wound Mason had inflicted, dressed as an old woman and took the train to Dennison, Texas, where he had arranged to meet with the rest of his gang. Once they had settled in Texas, the various members of his gang sent for their families up north and started printing counterfeit notes from the few plates they had brought with them.[88]

Pete was captured three times within a four-month period while in Texas but always managed to bribe his way out of trouble. The other men with Pete were also arrested at different places in the state. In March 1875 Secret Service agent James L. Duckworth was sent from St. Louis to Waco, Texas, to search for Pete. He didn't have to wait long. On April Fool's Day Pete was captured in the little town of Plano, Texas. A storage receipt found on Pete was given to Duckworth and traced to Sherman, Texas, and to three large boxes containing a press, plates and dies, a large quantity of paper, and thousands of counterfeit $5 and $20 bills.[89] Pete was placed on a train for Waco under the custody of agent Duckworth and a U.S. marshal. At a lay-over in Bremond, Texas, the party of three stayed in the Higgins Hotel. While the marshal slept, Duckworth was supposed to stand guard but instead went to sleep. Pete noticed that both the guards were asleep, got up, put on Duckworth's hat, and took his leave. As a result, Bluford Wilson, the Solicitor of the Treasury, ordered that Duckworth be dismissed from the Secret Service for his negligence.[90]

Pete was recaptured and taken to Tyler, Texas, where a U.S. district judge decided to continue the case and have Pete taken by train to Austin to stand trial in July. Although Pete was shackled during the trip, he waited until the deputies were asleep and then sawed off his handcuffs and shackles. Apparently, he had gotten a multi-bladed pocket knife from one of his attorneys, broken off the file blade, and used it to make a fine saw out of another blade. Once free of his irons, he jumped up and ran to the door of the car and jumped out. His guards immediately woke and pulled the bell cord, only to find it had been cut. Once again, Pete escaped.[91]

Pete left Texas in the summer of 1875 and returned to a farm he owned in Neoga, Illinois. He owned five farms at this time, but his wife and three children lived on the farm at Neoga and several of his relatives lived within a few miles of that town. Since the Secret Service was aware of his wife's location, Pete probably hid out at a relative's farm.

On November 22, 1875, Pete and Charles Walters, his right-hand man, were arrested in Richmond, Indiana, about 60 miles east of Indianapolis, for passing counterfeit money. Marshal Louis Shafer arrested the two men and found counterfeits on both of them, and on learning that they were staying at a hotel called the Avenue House, he went there and found a satchel containing $1,800 in good money and several thousand dollars in counterfeit.[92] Naturally, they gave false names to their captors, but they were eventually identified and taken to Indianapolis for trial.[93] Pete got 15 years of hard labor in the state prison at Michigan City, Indiana. On April 25, 1877, Pete gave it one last try to escape from the prison but was discovered by a guard and prevented from leaving.

While in prison, Pete was allowed to correspond with his family, and he soon learned from one of his daughters that his wife was being unfaithful. The family physician, Dr. Lewis H. Mason, had separated from his 28-year-old wife and 6-year-old son to move in with Mrs. McCartney. Pete had left Martha with a considerable amount of both good and counterfeit money, and he expected that she would use that money to work for his release. As time went by, he realized that she was not going to help him, and he would face a bleak and painful future. He spent his time brooding over the loss of his freedom and his wife's betrayal. In 1878 he denounced Martha and Dr. Mason and stated to officials that she was in possession of counterfeit plates that he had made some years earlier and a large amount of counterfeit money. The Secret Service naturally began to watch Martha's every move.

The close surveillance was obvious to Martha and made her nervous. She was afraid that Pete would eventually tell the authorities where he had buried the plates and money out of his anger over her infidelity. She turned for advice to her husband's cousin, "Jake" McCartney, who lived about three miles away in Etna, Illinois.[94] He visited Martha on November 10, 1878, and listened to her concerns. He agreed to her request to bury the plates and the counterfeits in a safer place—one that she suggested. Jake, however, had his own concerns about helping Martha, especially after she told him that Pete might reveal the location of the counterfeit hoard and bring down the full investigative powers of the Secret Service. To protect himself and his family, Jake communicated all the information to agent E.G. Rathborne of the Secret Service. Rathborne and another agent, together with Jake, dug up the plates and money on January 21, 1879.[95] The hoard included the famous plate Pete had made of the $20 Treasury Note, as well as $21,000 of those notes, the plates for printing the $5 notes of the Traders' National Bank of Chicago, and $1,000 of those notes.

A rare, genuine Traders' National Bank of Chicago note.

Dr. Mason was arrested in late January 1879 in Hackleman, Indiana, and Mrs. McCartney on February 12 in Neoga. The trial began on March 21, 1879, in the U.S. District Court in Springfield, Illinois. The principal witness against Dr. Mason was Pete McCartney, who had been brought from prison by a writ of *habeus corpus*. Pete was allowed to meet with his wife just prior to the trial, in the presence of deputy marshals and others, and his language was noticeably vindictive, especially towards Dr. Mason. It was expected there would be quite a scene at trial and the courtroom was filled to capacity when the proceedings began.

Pete stated in court that he had known Dr. Mason since 1871 and subsequently learned that the doctor was also engaged in buying and passing counterfeit money. He said further that he and Dr. Mason had been together in Decatur, Illinois, in the early days of October 1876, and there he gave Mason several counterfeit $20 bills to pass upon different parties. Four businessmen from Decatur then testified that they recognized Dr. Mason as the person who had passed counterfeits at their businesses on or about October 6. The evidence against the doctor seemed convincing. The defense, however, called seven witnesses from Neoga, including Dr. Mason, who testified that they were absolutely positive that the doctor was in Neoga attending to his professional duties as a physician for the time stated by the prosecution witnesses, and thus could not have been outside Neoga for even one day from October 3 through October 16, 1876.[96]

Dr. Mason's trial ended when a verdict of "not guilty" was returned by the jurors and another indictment was settled by a motion for *nolle prosequi*. Pete and the lawmen said Dr. Mason was acquitted because the government witnesses were mistaken as to the time of the alleged crimes, and Dr. Mason and his friends said he was acquitted because the witnesses were mistaken about his identity. Mrs. Mason believed in her husband's innocence, except for the matter that he had left her and their son for the love of another woman, but she reconciled with him and they once again lived as a family. Martha also reconciled with Pete, and he went back to prison a wiser and less-bitter man. Martha had pleaded guilty to having in her possession counterfeit plates and money, but on motion of the district attorney, sentence was suspended and she was released on her own recognizance on bail of $500. The other indictments against her were dismissed.

Pete was released early from the Indiana State Prison on October 29, 1887, for "time served"

and good behavior. He went to New Orleans, for reasons unknown, and at age 64, with acute bronchitis, he returned to the only profession he knew. On February 18, 1888, Secret Service agent Patrick Looby arrested Pete for trying to pass a counterfeit $50 bill.[97] He was soon convicted and sent to the Ohio Penitentiary in Columbus for 10 years. He died there of bronchitis on October 21, 1890.[98] During his lifetime, Pete engraved over 50 sets of plates for printing counterfeit money. It was said that most of his plates were excellent and those that weren't were even better. He was known as the "King of the Koniackers," and the "Albrecht Durer" of the "coney" men.

The Levi and Rittenhouse Families

Another reason for Pete McCartney's success was his association with a family of horse thieves, counterfeiters, and burglars headed by Lyle Levi. The patriarch of this family was Isaac Levi, known to the Secret Service as "Old Man Levi," who was born about 1794 in Kentucky and married Rachel Ewing. The family settled near Osgood, in Ripley County, Indiana, about 1850. "Old Man Levi" and some of his sons began to deal in counterfeit money in the 1850s. Isaac and his wife had several children, including sons named Isaac ("Ike"), Eli, Thomas, and Lyle, and daughters Clarissa, Louisa, and Missouri. Ike, Lyle, and their sisters Clarissa and Missouri engaged in the distribution of counterfeit paper money and knew many of the counterfeiters of their day. The Levi house in Osgood was occasionally used by Pete McCartney as a hideout starting in 1867. He was, in fact, the principal supplier of counterfeit money to this family for several years and was an especially trusted and respected friend of Missouri Lyle (later Rittenhouse).

The house was originally a log cabin, but as the years

Lyle Levi.

passed, room after room was added on, each with its own entrance and exit, until the complex was virtually a warren secure from the knock of a sheriff. Miles Ogle visited there, as did the Driggs family and many lesser captains of the trade.

The Levi family is a good example of the way counterfeiting runs through both blood and marital relations. When Pete needed a place of refuge in the East, he usually stopped at the home of Walker "Wanck" Hammond and his wife. Wanck's wife was a daughter of Clarissa Lee, who was a niece of Lyle Levi and Missouri Rittenhouse. Mrs. Hammond's maiden name had been Florida Lee.

Wanck Hammond.

Shortly after the war, James Rittenhouse came out from the east and settled on 40 acres near Osgood. He courted Missouri Levi, who was a handsome woman, and soon married her. The Levi boys had operated a horse-stealing gang in Ohio and Kentucky for some time, but now they retreated back to Ripley County and accepted Rittenhouse into their gang. James Rittenhouse had been a skillful mechanic, and now, under the tutelage of the Levi boys, he became even better at counterfeiting gold coins, inventing his own method of imitating gold that was a marvel to the Secret Service officers. It was about this time that the Rittenhouse gang also began to circulate the very dangerous $10 counterfeit "Webster-head" notes. They contacted the Driggs gang in Dayton, Ohio, and made contact with Pete McCartney and his associates.

In 1866 Rittenhouse and some associates broke open the safe of the firm of Truett & Jacquen at Chillicothe, Illinois. They obtained a large amount of money but were never punished for that crime. In 1868 Rittenhouse, in company with the counterfeiter Miles Ogle and Mike Rogers of Council Bluffs, robbed two county treasuries in Iowa and obtained an immense amount of plunder. This created a storm, and large rewards were offered for their capture. In

consequence, the trio fled to Canada and hid there until 1871, when they finally return to the United States. Rittenhouse now had the means to buy large amounts of counterfeit money that he intended to sell at a large profit. Unfortunately, he chose to sell some of this money to a Secret Service agent in Cincinnati. He was indicted by a U.S. grand jury and admitted to a heavy bail. Naturally, he failed to appear and forfeited his bail. He was next arrested in Detroit, when he again was caught trying to sell counterfeit money. This time he escaped jail. He was free until November 2, 1874, when he was arrested on a train at Aurora, Illinois, and $300 in counterfeit bills were found on his person. In the late 1870s he was sentenced to 14-years imprisonment. Missouri had a very dramatic way about her, especially in court, and once she "fainted" trying to gain the sympathy of the jury. This time she managed to get an audience with the judge and pleaded for the release of her husband, claiming that he was dying of consumption in the hospital ward of the prison. The judge was skeptical but agreed to look into the matter. The next day the "consumptive" escaped prison and fled to Mexico.

Missouri also had her problems with the law. In October 1869 she and her brother, Lyle, were arrested and charged with having $15,000 in counterfeit money in their possession. For this transgression, Lyle was fined $100 and received a term of three years in the Southern Penitentiary of Indiana. Missouri was fined the same amount and sent to the State Reformatory for Women for three years. In 1877 Secret Service agents E.G. Rathbone and F.W. Duskirk arrested Lyle Levi, his sister, Mrs. Clarissa Lee, her daughter Alice, and Mrs. Missouri Rittenhouse for selling counterfeit money. For this, Lyle was ensconced in Indiana North Penitentiary from June 14, 1877, to December 10, 1882. Clarissa Lee was let off with a fine of $25 and sentenced to serve four months in the Jackson County jail. Her daughter, Alice, was not charged. Missouri was ordered to pay a fine of $100 and to serve three years at the State Reformatory.

Both Lyle and Missouri underwent a religious conversion at a Methodist camp meeting and signed a pledge to follow the teachings of the church. Missouri stayed with her pledge, but Lyle Levi was placed on probation and watched carefully. The church elders soon decided he was a backslider. Lyle Levi was eventually lynched by a mob, but that is another story.

Tom Ballard

Tom Ballard was born in 1840 in Poughkeepsie, New York, and was the eldest of five brothers, the others being John, William, Benjamin, and George. His father, Peter J. Ballard, was a carriage painter by trade and taught the business to each of the boys.[99] Carriages of those days were often enclosed vehicles with doors and windows to give privacy to the occupants and to protect them from the elements. The carriage bodies were painted glossy black, and the more expensive ones had scrollwork or emblems painted in gold on their doors. The Ballard family specialized in this kind of painting, but Thomas was far better at it than his brothers. In 1858 Thomas went to New York City to work for a carriage builder named Henry Hinman. Hinman was connected by marriage to Joshua ("Jock") D. Miner, a man who had served time in Ohio for counterfeiting before moving to the state of New York. At the time Tom met him, Miner was a capitalist, which meant he hired others to engrave counterfeit plates and ran a gang of shovers who passed the bad bills for good ones. Miner saw Ballard's artistic ability, thought he had potential as a counterfeit engraver, and helped him get a position with the American Bank Note Company. Miner had convinced Ballard to become a counterfeiter and wanted him to learn everything he could about bank-note manufacturing. His work at the bank-note company required him to travel to and from the note-printing bureau at the Treasury Department in Washington, D.C., although we don't know in what capacity. During these trips to the Treasury, Ballard learned the process by which bank-note paper was made. About 1863 Ballard left his legitimate job at the

bank-note company and started engraving counterfeit plates for Jock Miner and his associates. His first plate was the $1 greenback, said to be only mediocre as counterfeits go, but each succeeding plate was better than its predecessor. He set up a "factory" on the upper floor of a tenement house at No. 256 Rivington Street. His brother John worked there as a printer. Ann Adams, an aunt to the Ballards, also lived there and made the place look respectable. In 1867

"The Unicorn Norwich coach" engraved by Chas. Hunt. The side of the coach bears a gold sign that reads "Norwich to Cromer," which would have been done by a carriage painter.

Tom married Miss Julia Avery but never told her of his real occupation.[100] He lived a double life, leaving his house at 225 West 53rd Street every morning at 7 a.m. and going downtown about two miles to the factory on Rivington. There, he made bank-note paper in almost perfect imitation of the jute-fiber paper made for the Treasury Department by the Wilcox Company at Glenn Mills, Pennsylvania. Ballard also made his own ink and tinted paper when needed.

The Ballard counterfeit of the $20 bill of the National Shoe and Leather Bank of New York City came out in August 1870. Jock Miner owned the plate and sold large quantities of the notes to Henry C. Cole, who in turn sold notes to Bill Gurney and other middlemen. When Gurney was caught, he confessed to Secret Service Chief Hiram Whitley that Miner owned the plates.[101]

On the night of October 25, 1871, Ballard and Miner were caught by a Secret Service "sting" operation run by Chief Whitley and were imprisoned in the Ludlow Street Jail.[102] Ballard cooperated with the police by giving them the address of his plant. When federal agents raided the Rivington Street tenement, they found only a few items of incriminating evidence—$3,500 of counterfeit U.S. currency; a partly engraved plate for a $1,000 Treasury Note; and engraving tools. The next day, Mrs. Effie C. Cole, the wife of Miner's co-conspirator Henry C. Cole, working in the interest of her husband's release, gave detetives the address of a second counterfeiting plant. Secret Service agents went immediately to 438 West 54th Street, arrested Llewellyn Williams, a printer, and found the following: a large transfer press of the type used in bank-note companies, said to have cost $10,700; a second, smaller transfer press, said to have cost $1,200; two large roller presses for printing notes;

Henry Cole.

Hiram C. Whitley,
the second chief
of the Secret Service.

and two smaller presses for the same purpose. There were ten full sets of original bed-pieces for making transfer rolls, a full set of Treasury seals for stamping red seals on the notes, two full sets of engraver's tools, such as gravers, burnishers, calipers, etc., an unfinished plate for the $1,000 Treasury Note, finished plates for the front and back of a $20 greenback, and finished plates for the $10 National Bank of Poughkeepsie, New York, on steel. In addition, they captured a full set of steel plates for the "Lincoln head" 50-cent Fractional Currency; a second set of steel plates of the Lincoln-head scrip, but of superior quality; a set of steel plates for making seven impressions at one time of the "Stanton head" 50-cent fractional notes; another set of the Stanton-head

notes, on a steel plate to print ten impressions at a time; and a set of the Stanton-head notes on copper, for making five impressions at a time. There were numerous steel transfer rolls for making these notes; $45,000 in counterfeit money, in denominations of $2, $5, $10, $20, and $100; a large quantity of type for changing bank-title lines; 150 pounds of fiber paper; a quantity of pulp used in making fiber paper, still in the vat; and other devices for making fiber paper. And finally, there were inks and pigments for making inks, ink rollers, wiping cloths, etc.[103]

The Stanton-head 50-cent fractional note. (F-1376.)

Tom did not like sitting in jail, and on the night of November 15, 1871, he and two others escaped under mysterious circumstances.[104] Some thought Miner, being afraid of Ballard's testimony, paid for his escape.[105] For nearly three years, Tom was a fugitive from justice, and no trace could be found of him, even though a reward of $5,000 was offered. About two years after his escape, counterfeit $500 U.S. Treasury Notes began turning up. From the superior quality of the notes, the Secret Service thought it had to be the work of Tom Ballard, and they soon traced the bills to Buffalo, New York, but could not find the maker. The agents began looking for his brothers. A counterfeiter arrested in Michigan turned out to be Benjamin Ballard. Soon after, William Ballard was arrested in Lockport, New York, and George Ballard was arrested in Buffalo. By threatening George and then offering him promises of immunity, the agents were able to get him to point out Tom's house at 468 Ferry Street in Buffalo, where he lived with Aunt Adams, then 65 years of age, and a woman named Julia Ann Britton, who said she was the wife of Ben Ballard. The house was a counterfeiting plant similar to the one Tom had set up in New York City. Tom did not learn that his brother George had betrayed him until many years later. When agents raided the house, they found $9,870 in $10 National Bank Notes; 17 electrotype plates for National Bank Notes; 2 transfer rolls for making seals for National Bank Notes; 2 smooth steel plates; 1 steel plate partly engraved for a $5 bill of the Bank of British North America; 825 sheets of bond paper; 1 printing press; an electrotyping press; a large quantity of printers' ink; gold and silver solutions; bronze, acids, batteries, gelatin; and a large quantity of counterfeiting tools and materials.[106]

Tom was again placed in jail to await his trial. Pulling a nail out of a floorboard, he used it to pick the lock on his door and escape. He took a train to Cortland, where he telegraphed Henry Hinman, asking for money. The Secret Service, having suspected Hinman for some time, had ordered the telegraph office to notify them of any telegrams intended for him. They read Tom's telegram and sent him the money he had requested. When Tom went to pick up the money, agents arrested him and sent him back to jail. Then, on the night of January 16, 1875, he and four other inmates tied sheets together and slid down to the ground. Two days later, all were caught. This time, Tom was sentenced to 30 years at the Albany Penitentiary, which amounted to a life sentence given that he was 35 years old at the time. Benjamin Ballard was given a long sentence in Michigan, and his wife, the former Elizabeth Britton, got five years in the Onondaga County jail.[107] William Ballard was also sentenced to Albany Penitentiary, and George Ballard was paroled. Of the five brothers, only John remained totally free.

Tom tried several times to offer the government a method by which they could improve their bank-note paper and suppress counterfeiting in return for whatever mercy they thought appropriate. He wrote that the blue and red fibers which the government used to make a distinctive paper were too easily woven into paper by hand or else could be drawn on the paper by pen and colored ink. He proposed that various figures—such as eagles, Liberty heads, stars, etc.—be cut from a substance having a bright metallic surface (gold or silver foil) and then embedded within the paper so it could not be erased.[108] This is a technology only recently incorporated into modern bank notes. The government never expressed any interest in his offers.

On the morning of July 14, 1878, Tom tried to end his life by cutting his stomach open from his navel upward, severing an intestine. He also cut his arm and neck, and in spite of a great loss of blood, he survived. After recovering, he returned to work in the jail shoe shop. On April 16, 1879, while working in Shoe Shop No. 4, surrounded by his fellow prisoners, he attempted suicide again. Using a sharp shoe knife which had a blade a little over an inch long, he cut his throat, creating a deep slash about four inches across and just missing the main artery. At the time, Tom had a second knife in his other hand. It had a blade that was three inches long and tapered to a sharp point. Had he used the

The "Liberty head" motif has appeared in many different forms over the years.

other knife, he would surely have died. As it was, he survived once again.[109]

A reporter for the *New York Times* tried to assess the damage the Ballard family had caused the country:

> There are no estimates of the whole amount of counterfeit money that Thomas Ballard and his associates put into circulation, but John Ballard testified in court that he worked with his brother in the Rivington Street establishment for three of the eight or nine years that concern was in operation, and while he was there the output was usually about $10,000 a month. The Secret Service people estimated that the Buffalo establishment, with which Thomas had little to do, had inflated the currency $250,000. . . .[110]

If those facts are true, then the Ballard boys "inflated the currency" by about $1,210,000. The argument can be made that this relatively small amount of money did no real harm to the economy but acted instead as a stimulus, the same as any legislative act that puts an equivalent amount of money into circulation. Such an argument, of course, addresses only the economic effects and says nothing about the social effects of crime.

On June 30, 1887, President Grover Cleveland acted on the petition to pardon Tom Ballard, writing the following endorsement:

> This prisoner was sentenced for 30 years in 1875 upon a conviction of counterfeiting. He was supposed to be one of the most expert counterfeiters in the country. He has now been in prison equivalent to more than 15 years, allowing the deductions he has earned for good behavior. His conduct has been such as to cause much interest to be felt in his case by many good citizens of Albany, as I personally learned while residing in that city. The prison officials, the officers concerned in his conviction, the late District Attorney, and officers from the Department of Justice have visited the place of confinement and acquainted themselves with the circumstances of the case and many other humane and substantial citizens pray for his pardon. His wife, who has clung to him with a

true woman's devotion all these years, and who has almost worn herself out in her efforts to support and educate her daughter, just now reaching womanhood, pleaded for her erring and penitent husband's release. There is a universal belief on the part of those acquainted with the case that the prisoner's reformation is complete, and that in no circumstances could this broken down man, whose mind is fast giving way with his body, be a nuisance to society if liberated. I am of the opinion that in this case the law has been fully vindicated.[111]

Tom stayed in Albany after his release and tried to find work as an engraver in jewelry stores and printing companies, but none would employ him because of his criminal record. In a move of pure philanthropy, the state of New York awarded him a contract in 1893 to engrave the map of Fire Island. The work paid him $300.[112]

An engraved, bird's-eye-view of New York, circa 1851.

Tom's success as a counterfeiter was due, in large part, to the fact that he acquired a thorough knowledge of the technology, including paper-making and transfer work, before he actually began engraving counterfeit plates. He knew in advance that his work at the bank-note company in New York was a unique opportunity to learn the craft, and he threw himself into that study with more zeal and planning than any ordinary employee. He set up his workshop with all the usual equipment of a real bank-note company, with transfer presses, roller presses, ruling engines, transfer rolls, furnaces, and the engines for making good paper. Very few counterfeiters knew how to acquire the specialized machinery or had the experience and confidence to use them. Tom knew the technical problems that plagued most counterfeiters and skillfully worked out the solutions by observation and study. He was, indeed, the "scientific counterfeiter."

On October 4, 1891, the *Trenton Sunday Advertiser* reported that Tom Ballard had returned to Poughkeepsie, New York, was dying of consumption, and would probably not live more than a few days. He is likely buried in Poughkeepsie, but I haven't been able to find his grave.

Frederick W. Biebusch

Like Pete McCartney, Fred Biebusch stands out for his skill at evading the law and bribing his way out of trouble. But unlike McCartney, Fred was not an engraver but a capitalist. The capitalist puts up the money to run the organization. He buys the transfer press, the printing press, paper, ink, engraving tools, etc., and pays the rent on a house where money can be made with a reasonable expectation of privacy and safety. If necessary, he buys the cooperation of local lawmen or pays them to arrange escapes for those who have been arrested. He sets up a distribution system to move his counterfeit money to other parts of the country, and he sets the price for his product. Finally, he pays the salary of the engraver. Smart capitalists invest their profits in legitimate businesses to explain their wealth and to avoid the attention of the law. They are the alpha males in a sometimes ruthless, selfish, and cunning group of men whose loyalties change with the weather.

It was a tough job that many tried, and only a few survived for very long. Fred Biebusch was an exception.

Fred was born in Prussia on February 26, 1826, the son of Christian Biebusch and Henrietta Schmidt. He came to the United States in 1844 at the age of 18.[113] He married Friedericka Gerdelmann on April 5, 1849, and stayed with her until his death. He appears to have been a natural criminal, if there is such a thing, and soon became a fence for stolen goods. He kept a liquor saloon called the War Eagle on Third Street in St. Louis,

where he usually catered to a respectable clientele of river captains, steamboat officers, and business men. The police suspected his business and raided his saloon in 1850, finding a large cache of stolen property, including jewelry, watches, and silverware, all hidden behind a wall.[114] Fred managed to weasel his way out of trouble, probably by claiming he had no knowledge that the property was hidden there and that it must have belonged to the previous owner.

An 1897 Saloon.

Fred soon discovered that petty theft and fencing were not all that profitable, and he turned to counterfeiting with great zeal. He was an intelligent operator who first served his time as a simple agent for Pete McCartney. Once he had "learned the ropes," he started his own business dealings and soon ran a large network of agents who distributed counterfeit money (that he was buying and selling at a high commission) throughout Missouri, Iowa, Illinois, Kansas, and the territories. This was in the days before there was a national currency, and counterfeiting of state- and private-bank notes was rampant. Almost all the banks had their own notes, and sometimes even branch banks had different notes. A counterfeit note that was well executed could easily fool the public, and local law enforcement had limited jurisdictions and no training on tracking down the culprits. Until the Secret Service was established in 1865, the U.S. Marshal Service had the primary role of identifying and arresting counterfeiters.[115]

Fred chose his associates carefully, choosing top-flight engravers such as Pete McCartney, Ben

Boyd, and William Shelly, and men like Nelson Driggs, Louis Sleight, and John Frisby to distribute the "queer." In Missouri at that time there was a state law which provided that the testimony of any man who had served a term in the penitentiary was not admissible in the courts of the state. Fred was familiar with that provision and always followed one immutable rule—never deal directly with any man who could not prove he had been a convict. Fred dealt only with "safe" people (ex-convicts), and when negotiating a sale, he would never deliver the "queer" himself but only through a third person. No one could ever say they had received counterfeit notes from Fred.[116]

Fred was arrested in St. Louis in 1863 for passing counterfeit money. He was charged by the state of Missouri and found guilty. He challenged the sentence and won the appeal on what many considered to be a very accommodating interpretation of the statues. This case involved the charge that he "unlawfully and corruptly did, directly and indirectly, attempt, by bribing, to induce one William M. Polk to absent himself for the purpose of avoiding giving evidence in a certain cause, matter and proceeding, then pending. . . ."[117] This was typical of Fred's *modus operandi.* Whenever it was possible, he would pay a witness to take a little vacation and enjoy life. Very few people turned him down.[118]

In 1864 Colonel Lafayette Baker, Provost Marshal of the War Department, went to St. Louis to arrest a group of counterfeiters known to be working there. On August 6 Baker's group captured Fred, who was then sent to the Old Capitol Prison in Washington.[119]

Following the end of the Civil War, Colonel H.C. Whitley was made Chief of the Secret Service, and he set about reorganizing the bureau. One of his best men, Operative John Eagan, was placed in charge of the district that included St. Louis. He determined to speed up the legal processing of suspects as much as possible, to give them less chance of arranging bribes. Fred was again arrested for selling counterfeits in 1865, but this time Eagan got an early trial date and presented a wealth of corroborating evidence. One fact established at the trial was that Fred held loan

notes that could be called in on many prominent citizens of St. Louis, the total amounting to about $60,000. Unable to bribe witnesses or impeach the evidence, Fred was sentenced to 10 years in the Missouri Penitentiary.[120] But Fred had deep pockets, and after only five months, he was pardoned by Governor Thomas Fletcher. Over the next four years, he was arrested for counterfeiting four times, but each time he escaped conviction.

Finally, in February 1869 Chief Whitley sent an agent named McCabe (no relation to the author) to buy counterfeit money from Fred using marked bills. Immediately after the purchase, Fred was arrested at his house and the marked bills found on his possession. The trial was scheduled for October 1870, and during the months before the trial, Biebusch managed to bribe every witness for the government. But he forgot that he had sent an engraver named William Shelly to leave St. Louis. By sheer good luck, the Secret Service found Shelly working as an engraver at the Singer Sewing Machine Company in New York and pressured him into confessing his role as an engraver for Biebusch by offering him (Shelly) some sort of reduction in sentence if he would testify at the upcoming trial.

When the trial began, Fred was as confident of the results as he had ever been, but as soon as he saw that William Shelly was going to be a witness, he knew his conviction was certain. It was a "flight or fight" situation, and Fred decided to run from the courtroom and forfeit his $20,000 bail. Officers of the St. Louis Police then began a watch on Mrs. Biebusch, shadowing her every step. Within a week,

Colonel Lafayette Baker.

they followed her to Cabaret Island in the Mississippi River, opposite the town of Venice, Illinois. There, she was seen meeting her husband in a corn field. When Fred retired to a small hut he used for shelter, Secret Service agents and the police surrounded him and ordered his surrender. Shots were fired by both sides, and Fred tried to run away. He was eventually tackled and returned to jail.[121] At his trial, Fred faced five separate indictments. Shelly, although feeble and barely able to talk, testified fully, and Fred, then 47 years old, was convicted and sentenced to 15 years in the Missouri Penitentiary at Jefferson City, Missouri, on December 13, 1870. Fred served only five years of that sentence and then was set free by President Ulysses S. Grant. He died of "senility" in his home at 2737 Stoddard Street, St. Louis, on December 8, 1906, and is buried next to his wife at St. Peter's Evangelical Church Cemetery, along with several children and other relatives.

Nathaniel Kinsey Jr.

Nathaniel Kinsey never worked for a bank-note company, per se, but he did serve an apprenticeship with Charles A. Jewitt, a bank-note engraver and salesman for Toppan, Carpenter & Company in their branch office in Cincinnati, Ohio. Kinsey was born about 1828 in Mill Creek, Delaware, but he claimed Cincinnati as his home. With Jewitt, he specialized in landscape engraving and worked on several legitimate bank-note plates from 1850 to 1854.[122] Starting in 1854, he became an illustrator for the Methodist Book Concern for about a year, and not long after that he began engraving counterfeit notes for Edward Nevers, an old counterfeiter.[123] Nathaniel was captured in October 1864 and committed to the Old Capitol Prison in Washington, D.C. Through his attorney, he offered to turn state's evidence against parties engaged in counterfeiting in return for his freedom. The superintendent of the prison, W.P. Wood, wrote a letter to the Solicitor of the Treasury Department recommending the application, but this was turned down and Nathaniel served a long term.[124] During his counterfeiting career, he worked mostly on Fractional Currency notes: seven different plates of the 50-cent notes for seven different clients, a plate for a 10-cent note, two plates for the 25-cent notes, and a $100 greenback note. Probably his greatest claim to fame is that he taught Benjamin Boyd how to engrave. In fact he stayed friends with Boyd for a long time. He was staying in Boyd's house when it was raided in 1875, and he ran out the door to escape. He was recognized, but since there was no warrant for his arrest at the time, he was allowed to run. After that escape, he disappears from the historical records.

The Methodist Book Concern, 1893.

Benjamin E. Boyd

Benjamin Boyd was another counterfeit engraver who called Cincinnati his home. He was born there in January 1834. His father was an engraver from New York and gave his son his first instruction in the art.[125] While he was still an apprentice, not yet 21 years old, Benjamin made his first counterfeit plate on the state of Ohio. His most important teacher, however, was Nathaniel Kinsey Jr., as previously mentioned, who also lived in Ward 8, Cincinnati, not far from the Boyds. By the time he was 30 years old, Benjamin had met other famous counterfeiters and learned the secrets of their trade—men like Pete McCartney, John B. Trout, and Nelson Driggs.

Benjamin's first encounter with the law came in 1859, when he was arrested at Davenport, Iowa. He was caught engraving counterfeit plates for two shovers named Jim Vesey and Charlie

A view of Cincinnati, Ohio, circa 1848.

Hathaway, who lived in Springfield, Illinois, at the time, although Hathaway's family lived at Fort Madison, Iowa. Boyd was convicted and served two years in the Iowa Penitentiary in Fort Madison, Iowa. In the early 1860s, Benjamin became a partner of Pete McCartney, and the two engraved and printed a number of notes to be shoved by a gang of associates. One of these shovers was a young lady named Almiranda ("Allie") Achman, who we met earlier, a lady with a decidedly criminal pedigree—her father, mother, and step-father (John B. Trout) were all counterfeiters.[126] Her sister, Martha Ann Achman, had married Pete McCartney in 1864. Boyd and McCartney were arrested by the sheriff in Mattoon, Illinois, in 1865 and sent to jail at Springfield, Illinois. At about the same time, Allie Achman, along with Ed Pierce, was arrested with $26,000 of counterfeit money in her possession. Benjamin had been attracted to Allie for some time, and now he decided to buy her freedom by offering to surrender a counterfeit plate belonging to his partner, Pete McCartney. The Secret Service thought this was a good trade, so they released Allie. Benjamin wasted no time in getting her to the altar at Marine City, St. Claire County, Michigan. He was then 33 years old. He and Allie lived in a number of small towns in Illinois and Iowa, but finally they bought property in Prairie du Chien, Wisconsin, and built a home there.

Benjamin was an excellent bank-note engraver who never rushed a job. He was, in fact, considered the best letter engraver on steel anywhere in America. For the Sleight-Frisby gang, he engraved the plates for printing $50 Treasury Notes, series of 1863. He printed and sold about 6,000 pieces of this currency, representing about $300,000. Being unable to deliver the plates, he sold them

to Pete McCartney but had them in his possession when Allie was arrested. Since he engraved them, it was his craftsmanship that won the hand of his wife. In 1866 Boyd engraved the plates for printing $20 Treasury Notes, series of 1862. These plates were owned jointly by Ben Boyd, Pete McCartney, and John B. Trout. The plates were captured by the Secret Service the same year they were engraved. In 1869 Boyd engraved additional plates of the series 1862 Treasury Notes, and these were owned jointly by Joseph Kincaid, James Burdsell, and Ben Boyd. The plates were captured by the Secret Service at Greenburg, Indiana, in February 1869.[127] He also engraved the 50-cent Lincoln-head Fractional Currency note. But Benjamin's finest work, which took him 11 months to complete, was the infamous $5 plate he engraved of the Traders National Bank of Chicago, Illinois. This was considered to be one of the finest counterfeits the government had ever seen. This plate was afterwards changed to the First National Bank of Canton, Illinois, the First National Bank of Aurora, Illinois, the First National Bank of Peru, Illinois, the First National Bank of Paxton, Illinois, and two non-existent banks—The First National Bank of Cecil, Illinois, and the First National Bank of Galena, Illinois.[128] As mentioned, these plates were captured from Nelson Driggs in the raid on his premises in Centralia, Illinois, on October 21, 1875.

By the spring of 1875, Boyd's skill was evident to everyone in the Secret Service, and Elmer Washburn, the chief of the bureau, decided to place the highest priority on arresting him. He chose Patrick D. Tyrell, an agent in St. Louis, to head up the project. By June Tyrell had found Driggs by watching the wife of Dr. Milton Parker, a counterfeiter, in Nauvoo, Illinois. Mrs. Parker was an intelligent and beautiful woman, and Driggs was apparently much attracted to her and often visited. Thereafter, Tyrell watched Driggs's every movement. Before long, he came to suspect that Driggs and Boyd were meeting. In September Ben Boyd moved his wife and furniture from his house at La Clare, Iowa, to Fulton, Illinois, where he rented a large house on Prairie Street under the name of B.F. Wilson. At this point, Tyrell knew that both Driggs and Boyd had been in recent communication and that Boyd must be at work on a new plate. It was now time to call in the big guns from Washington, D.C. Accordingly, Chief Washburn, Assistant Chief James J. Brooks, and operatives E.G. Rathborne and John McDonald all came to Lyons, Iowa, to meet with Tyrell and plan simultaneous raids on Driggs and Boyd.

A counterfeit $20 Treasury Note, 1862.

The raids were carried off without a hitch and both men were caught with plenty of evidence to make convictions certain.[129] In the Boyd house, Tyrell found that cleverly mortised cavities in furniture and boxes had been used to hide engraved plates. In one box, Tyrell found $7,853 in good currency. In the woodwork of an upholstered ottoman, they found the plates for the $100 Lincoln-head Treasury Note. Later it was learned that Boyd had set a price of $6,000 for this particular plate.

$2 notes of First National banks in Illinois. Note how all have essentially the same design, save for the name of the city. This would have made counterfeiting for multiple banks with a single plate very easy.

Benjamin and his wife Allie were indicted and tried before the U.S. District Court for the Northern District of Illinois in Chicago on January 19 and 20, 1875. When the trial was over, the judge ordered that Allie was to be found "not guilty," as she was the wife of the other defendant and the judge said it was the duty of a wife to obey her husband and to protect him. This was a common practice in most courts of that time when considering the role of a counterfeiter's wife. Ben was confined to the Cook County jail while his counsel got a motion for a new trial ready. Before the motion could be presented, operative Tyrell took Ben and Allie to Springfield, Illinois, to testify as witnesses for the government in the trial of Nelson Driggs. This was later taken into consideration by the judge in Ben's motion for a new trial. The motion was denied, but Ben's sentence was reduced to 10 years. Ben served his term at the Illinois State Prison in Joliet, about 60 miles southwest of Chicago. There, he was in company with his brother-in-law, Pete McCartney. Boyd was 41 years old when he was sentenced. He served out his term and apparently stayed in Joliet, as he is listed there in the 1880 Federal Census. At the time, he reported his employment as "engraver." All the census data agrees with the known facts of his life, such as date of birth and his father and mother's places of birth. He is listed as married, but his wife's name is not shown. He was living with 37 other men in what was probably the Joliet prison. In the 1900 Federal Census, he is shown living in Ward 11, Chicago, married to a wife named "Alice," which was probably a mistake for "Allie." A newspaper of the 1880s said he was rumored to be working as a valued employee of a Chicago bank-note company.

Nelson B. Driggs

Unquestionably, Nelson Driggs ranks as either the first- or second-greatest counterfeit capitalist of the 19th century. He married into a counterfeiting family, had a beautiful wife who supported his business eagerly, and was still active as a counterfeiter in his octogenarian years. As a capitalist, he handled large amounts of money and

Nelson B. Driggs.

kept several engravers busy. He distributed his "cony" throughout the "west," meaning such states as Illinois, Iowa, Indiana, Missouri, and southern Minnesota. He knew virtually all of the famous counterfeiters of his day: men such as McCartney, Ballard, Boyd, Trout, Achman, Parker, Sleight and Frisby, Charles Hill, the Johnston family, and, to a lesser extent, the Johnsons (*sic*, different from the Johnstons). Naturally, he also had his own gang of counterfeit shovers and middlemen, some of whom were relatives. He was arrested so many times that his name became well known to the public, but he made fabulous sums of money from his ventures.

Nelson was born in 1810 in Oneida, New York. His father was Joseph Driggs, born 1780 in Bolton, Tolland County, Connecticut, and his mother was Dollie Ball, also born in Connecticut about 1782. He is said to be of Scottish lineage, but we know nothing about his ancestors there.

In 1845 Nelson was a successful businessman in Freeport, Ohio, where he owned and managed a general variety store that became one of the largest of its kind in several counties.[130] Even that early it was suspected that he was buying counterfeit money and using it in his mercantile business. So many spurious notes were traced back to his store that he was eventually forced to leave the area, and he sold his property and business to a relative. In February 1855 he was arrested in Chicago for passing counterfeit money.[131] It was found that he had $30,000 of well-executed spurious notes for the Canal Bank of New Orleans and other banks. He was tried and sentenced on March 3, 1855, receiving 10 years at the state penitentiary, which at that time was located at Alton, Illinois. Somehow, he managed to win a pardon from the governor after serving only a year and a half. It was widely suspected that money had greased the wheels of justice. In June 1857, just after he got out of prison, Nelson was caught again having counterfeits in his possession. This time he was arrested on Main Street in St. Louis carrying $5,465 in spurious notes for ten different banks, as well as four counterfeit plates. The plate for the Phoenix Bank of Chicago had omitted the letter "o" in the word "Phoenix."[132] It was about this time that Nelson became the capitalist for the Sleight and Frisby gang at Metropolis, Illinois. Sleight and Frisby, who were brothers-in-law, subsequently moved to Nauvoo, Illinois, which became a hub for many counterfeiters.[133]

Nelson and a fellow counterfeiter named John Roe were arrested at Roe's house in St. Louis on March 7, 1861, by Secret Service operative John Eagan. Eagan found $285,000 in spurious notes of various state banks and 21 full sets of counterfeit plates for those banks. While operative Eagan and his assistants were still in the house holding the men under arrest, an 18-year-old nephew of

Driggs named Henry H. Guthrie entered the house carrying a valise. Henry was promptly arrested, and the valise was found to contain 25,000 counterfeits of the $1 bill for a bank at Cadiz, Ohio, and $600 in gold. Henry was one of the six children of Samuel and Rebecca R. Guthrie that Nelson and a person named Phoebe were boarding with in the 1850 Federal Census. Another Guthrie son, John, was also in Nelson's employ as a counterfeiter.[134]

The evidence resulted in 39 separate indictments against Nelson, but he was allowed to plead guilty to just one, and for that he was sentenced to ten years in the Missouri Penitentiary. Henry Guthrie was sentenced to six years in the same prison. In 1868 Governor Fletcher pardoned Driggs.[135] Young Mr. Guthrie was also pardoned before his term was out. After his pardon, Nelson went to Louisville, Kentucky, and got back into the business of selling general merchandise. Boredom or a lack of money soon changed his plans, and he returned to St. Louis to meet with Ben Boyd and make arrangements for future counterfeiting.

Ben and Nelson went to Nauvoo, Illinois, in November 1871 and took up residence with their old friend, Louis Sleight. Nelson then began a series of botched attempts to pass counterfeit money; nevertheless, he probably carried out several successful deals that we don't know about. In 1873, operating under the alias of George Baker, he attempted to pass a counterfeit $500 U.S. Treasury Note upon the Citizen's National Bank of Des Moines, Iowa. He was caught and indicted. In October 1874 he was indicted under the name of William Jones for passing spurious money upon Henri Rochot, a jeweler of St. Paul, Minnesota. In June 1875 he was indicted under his own name for selling to Secret Service operative Charles E. Anchisi two spurious $50 U.S. Treasury Notes, series of 1869, on March 15, 1874, at Grand Junction, Mississippi. He was also indicted under his own name at the November 1875 term of the Circuit Court in Montgomery, Alabama, for conspiracy to act with George W. Simpson, Benjamin B. Bowers, Samuel R. Neill, and two others in uttering counterfeit money.[136] In each case, Nelson forfeited bail and did not return for his trial. Counterfeiters, of course, knew that a bail of a few thousand dollars was an acceptable price to pay for their freedom. By changing their name and personal appearance, they could move to another city and start all over again.

On December 23, 1873, Nelson married a lovely 23-year-old lady in La Crosse, Wisconsin. He had met her in the Hamilton County jail in Cincinnati, where both of them were serving a term for passing counterfeit money. She was Gertrude ("Gertie") Stadtfeld, a Prussian who left Europe and came over with her family when she was only six years old.[137] Her family arrived in New York harbor on the ship *Plymouth Rock*, on August 4, 1856. It was learned later that her father, Nicholas Stadtfeld, had been a counterfeiter in Prussia. In this country he ran a match factory and counterfeited "match revenue stamps" in Dayton, Ohio, probably making the old "Lucifer" matches that were in use before they were replaced by safety matches about 1865.

Charles Stadtfeld.

By now the reader may have noticed that counterfeiters often marry other counterfeiters. This was true with Pete McCartney, Ben Boyd, and now, Nelson Driggs. Gertie's sister, Mollie, married Jim (Henry) Guyon on August 19, 1874, in St. Louis, when he went under the name Henry Clinton and was a horse thief and counterfeiter in Warsaw, Illinois. Gertie's brother, Charles, was also a counterfeiter, as was a nephew, Nicolas Korn.

The Secret Service raids on the Driggs and Stadtfeld houses in Centralia, Illinois, have already been described in the sketch on Ben Boyd. The Secret Service, however, had another interest in the raids of these men beyond just ridding society of crooks. The service hoped that the testimony at the trial would give them a clue where to look for the missing plates used to print the Webster-head $10 U.S. notes, series 1869 to

1878. This plate was said to be the most perfect ever engraved by a counterfeiter, but that may be more Secret Service hyperbole than real fact. This plate was engraved for Nelson Driggs by Charles W. Hill, but the service didn't know that at the time. A general strategy was devised by Chief Bell of the Secret Service in 1888, based on the scant intelligence from the trial and from agents in the field. The chief believed that Jim Guyon, Nelson's brother-in-law, had possessed temporary ownership of the Webster-head plate, and the only way to capture the plate was through Mr. Guyon.

The Driggs family had moved to Dayton, Ohio, and built a saloon and apartment at 625 South Main Street that Nelson named "The Watch On the Rhine." Later, they moved to a splendid mansion which they renamed "The United States Hotel." This was a road house or "Oklahoma," as such places were called then, and was fitted up in elegant style and became a resting stop for counterfeiters and old soldiers on their way from the Old Soldiers Home to Dayton. It was also the headquarters for the distribution of counterfeit money to many parts of the country.

The United States Hotel near Dayton, Ohio.

Chief Bell decided that he and some agents should go to the hotel. Under disguise and using assumed names, they tried to gain the confidence of both Nelson and Gertie. Then they would buy some counterfeits, and when Guyon came to deliver the order, they would capture him and force him to reveal the location of the plates.

Unfortunately, the plan didn't work exactly as they had planned. The full details of the story are given in a number of newspapers, but suffice to say that Guyon got away, an agent was shot through his earlobe, and Bell's reputation suffered, even though he did capture $25,000 in the counterfeit notes.[138] Bell also arrested Nelson, his wife, and a "French maid" who was watching the children. The maid was actually Mary Brown, an old counterfeit distributor from those parts who was living with the Driggs family at the time.

Nelson and Gertie did not have to go to prison for this final escapade. They claimed that Chief Bell had made an agreement with them that he would not prosecute if they would help him capture Jim Guyon. The government decided that it was not worth fighting it out in court given the age of the defendants and the very small probability that they would ever engage in counterfeiting again. Nelson died on December 17, 1895, aged 86 years.[139]

The Widow Gertrude Driggs

Gertrude Driggs is simply too delightful a con artist to leave her out of this narrative. As mentioned, Nelson did not engrave but hired others to do so for him. One of his favorite engravers was Charles W. Hill, alias James W. Murphy, alias John Davis, and possibly alias Jim Guyon.[140] When Charles died at the Good Samaritan Hospital in Los Angeles in May 1901, everyone supposed he was a penniless old man. But after his death, it was discovered that he had a safe deposit box containing $142,000. The legal authorities announced that the fortune would be given to the next of kin or to anyone who had a valid claim to the money. Almost 5,000 people said they were related to Charles Hill or that he left them a will. When the wheat was separated from the chaff, only two persons had good evidence that they were valid claimants—a man from Boston named Salem Charles and Mrs. Gertrude Driggs.[141]

Gertie said that the old man known as Charles Hill had been a member of her husband's counterfeiting gang, and at the birth of her daughter, Grace Driggs, in 1888, a year before the final raid on the gang, Mr. Hill had made a will in lead pencil by which he left all his wealth to the child. Gertie had not seen him after the raid. She produced the will and traced the movements of the old man closely enough to convince many that Charles Hill was indeed a counterfeiter in the Driggs gang. She presented herself as a business-woman of 82 Wall Street, New York.

The other claimant, Salem Charles, was chairman of the street commissioners of Boston. He said that Charles Hill was really his uncle, who had run away from home as a boy and had returned with plenty of money, only to start roving again. He took Salem's niece, Miss Mary Charles, a Brimfield school teacher, with him, but finally he went on alone when she tired of travel. The case was fought by the Driggs family at their own expense, while the Charles family, having been accepted by the public administrator as the lawful heirs, had their claim defended at the expense of the state.

The most important evidence was the hand-written will. A famous handwriting expert, Professor Daniel T. Ames, testified that the lead-pencil will was a forgery, and he was followed by half a dozen lesser experts who sided with his opinion. Still, Gertie would not give up. A new point of evidence developed about the amount of hair that Charles Hill had when he died. All of Mrs. Driggs's witnesses who said they had seen Charles Hill just before he died claimed that he had a good deal of hair. Hospital nurses and others testified he was as bald as an egg. As he claimed to be 90 years old just before he died, this did not seem improbable. But Gertie, on the conviction that "in for a penny, in for a pound," went to amazing lengths to prove that Mr. Hill had hair. She hired an artist to make a "spirit photograph," showing Charles Hill had a head full of hair and claimed the photograph had been taken in 1901, just two years before the trial. The photograph, of course, was a copy of another picture of Hill that had been artificially manipulated. Gertie gave this picture to a juror named Butler while the two were alone in an elevator. It was a bald attempt to influence a juror, and when Butler reported the incident, Gertie was arrested.[142]

Ultimately, Gertie lost her case and went to jail for forgery and trying to influence a juror. The money was divided among eight members of the Salem Charles family. After she got out of jail, Gertie married a number of times and died as Gertrude Rye in 1928. She is buried today at the Greenwood Memorial Park in San Diego, California.

Who Was Jim Guyon?

After 1900 the Secret Service began to speculate that Jim Guyon may have been the counterfeit engraver Charles Hill, also known at different times as J.W. Murphy, Henry Clinton, John Davis, Jim Hank, and Jim Hamilton. There is no direct evidence of that theory, but many facts lend their support to the idea. For one thing, both Guyon and Hill were tall men, so their physical appearances do not prove they were different people. Charles Hill was believed by the Secret Service to have engraved the Webster-head plate, yet Guyon owned it. Just on the issue of who owned the plate, it makes sense to believe that Guyon and Hill were the same person. Otherwise, why would Hill have sold the plate to Guyon? Guyon had no reputation as a big-wheel counterfeit dealer. But if Guyon was Hill and related by marriage to the Driggs's family (Mollie Stadtfeld's husband), it would make sense that he would have supplied Nelson and Gertie with Webster-head notes. Guyon disappeared after the melee at the United States Hotel and was never heard from again. Charles Hill also became a drifter and was lost to the Secret Service for several years until he died.

The Johnson Family

For two generations, this large family of counterfeiters worked together, moving constantly and using numerous aliases to confuse and befuddle police and Secret Service agents everywhere. They were often confused with the *Johnston* family of counterfeiters, especially in the newspapers, and that suited them just fine. Even today, many authors attribute the exploits of one family to the other. Don Wilkie, a Secret Service agent, fell into this trap when he wrote *In It* in 1936.

The patriarch of the Johnson family was John R. Johnson, a very good engraver who made his fortune from counterfeiting during the first two or three years of the Civil War. He counterfeited Canadian money as well as American state-bank notes. He and his wife, Agnes, had eight children, including six

Charles Johnson.

sons. They were Charles, Thomas Ira, Edward, William, John, and David Henry. The girls were Jessie and Georgie, the latter being known to the newspapers as Mrs. Frank L. Bayliss. Her husband, Captain Bayliss, was a pilot on Lake Huron before his death.[143]

The two girls were trained as forgers and could duplicate the signatures on notes with great accuracy. Once they were assigned a particular signature, they would practice writing it thousands of times over the course of several months until it became as natural to them as their own signature. Jessie was considered the better at making small signatures, and she worked not only for the family but also did work for other counterfeiters. She is credited with signing $50,000 worth of $10 Treasury Notes (5,000 notes!) made by Pete McCartney for old man Brockway.

Three of the boys trained as engravers, with Edward being the best and Charles following close behind. The Secret Service believed that Charles engraved the plate for the $5 Silver Certificate, series 1891, known as the "Grant head fives" because of its off-centered vignette of Ulysses S. Grant. That was an excellent imitation, and only Charles and Edward Johnson and their accomplice, Charles Hill, were believed capable of such work. The Secret Service sent a number of its agents to find the source of the spurious notes, including Thomas B. Carter. Carter learned that Charles Johnson had sold $5,000 of the Grant-head fives to three brothers who were merchants

in Goodland, Michigan. Posing as a buyer, he persuaded the brothers to give him a letter of introduction to Johnson. Carter found Johnson in Detroit, Michigan, and tried to buy some counterfeits from him. Johnson, however, was suspicious and fled during the night. Carter found him next in Port Huron, Michigan, and arrested him. Left in charge of another agent, Johnson escaped during the night and went across the St. Claire River to Sarnia, Ontario.[144] Since Canada had no extradition treaty with the United States at that time, there was nothing more that the Secret Service could do. The Canadian police, however, caught Johnson counterfeiting Canadian money in 1888 and sent him to serve 10 years in the notorious Kingston Prison in Ontario.

The Grant-head five, a $5 Silver Certificate of 1891. (F-261.)

A counterfeit Silver Certificate.

Edward Johnson also liked to counterfeit Canadian currency. In the spring of 1880 Canada was flooded with the best counterfeits they had ever seen. Even many bank tellers could not tell the real notes from the fake ones. The Government of Canada asked John Wilson Murray, the first professional detective in the Province of Ontario, to see if he could find the source of these notes. Murray began a long search, taking with him a number of different spurious bills to show to his contacts in the underworld of counterfeit engravers and plate printers. Engravers who studied the notes carefully noticed small quirks of technique that seemed to narrow their choices to Edward Johnson and Charles Hill.

Murray continued searching for the Johnson family and finally got lucky, spotting John ("Johnnie") Johnson in a saloon in Toronto, Canada, and following him home. Murray watched the house closely for a few days until he saw Edward Johnson leave the premises. Edward was arrested on his walk into town and held in jail for questioning. Murray convinced Edward that it would be far better for him to surrender the plates he had made than to deny everything and suffer a much longer term in prison. Edward agreed with that logic and took Murray and another detective to the spot where he had buried the plates. They recovered 21 separate copper plates, all encased in solid beeswax and then wrapped in oilcloth and placed in a tin box. When Murray examined the plates later, he scored each one in a crisscross fashion so it couldn't be used again.[145]

Edward Johnson's Canadian counterfeits included the $5 and $10 notes of the Bank of Commerce, the $5 notes of the Bank of British North America, the $10 note of the Bank of Ontario, the $4 note of the Dominion Bank, and a $1 note of the Bank of Canada. It was learned later that he did not engrave the plate for the Grant-head five. That was done by Charles W. Hill, who was known to the trade as "John Hill" and sometimes as "John Murphy." Hill, whom we've met before in the sketch on Gertrude Driggs, was arrested in New York on other counterfeiting charges on August 10, 1894, and sentenced to prison. According to Edward Johnson, the plates for making the Grant-head fives were worth $40,000, if someone wanted to take the time and effort to make them again, but he doubted anyone had the talent to do as good a job

as Hill had done. He said the plates had all been made in the United States over a period of years. The Johnson family printed only one type of note each year and sold large quantities to the wholesale dealers who had them "shoved" or passed to the public.

A counterfeit $5 note of the Bank of British North America.

Different engravers sold their counterfeit notes in different ways. Charles Hill, for example, always charged $10,000 for each pair of plates (front and back) he made and would have nothing to do with the printing or the passing of the notes. He protected his identity far better than other counterfeiters, and it took the Secret Service longer to catch him than most others. Other counterfeiters usually engraved and printed their notes and then charged a fixed fee, such as 30¢ to 50¢ on the dollar, depending on the quality of the notes. The retail dealers would charge the passers still more, so they had to exchange a considerable amount of "queer" to make a decent living. Ulrich was one of the few counterfeit engravers who would make large-denomination plates, such as those for printing $500 and $1,000 notes. Most counterfeiters thought it was safer to stick with smaller denominations since they were given the least scrutiny and were of less concern to the police when they were detected. Engravers that worked for gangs usually had an agreement with the capitalist to be paid a certain percentage of the total amount printed, but Pete McCartney, who was both a capitalist and an engraver, sold some of his plates for a fixed sum and sometimes printed from his own plates and discounted the notes to other middlemen. There was no hard-and-fast rule.

Edward Johnson was placed on trial in the Fall Assizes in 1880 in Toronto, pleading guilty to each of the seven charges filed against him. The Counsel for the Crown asked the court to suspend the sentence until Edward and his daughters could be returned to the United States to answer questions. The court acceded to the request. Meanwhile, the rest of the family went into panic mode and began leaving their homes and jobs so they couldn't be found. Thomas Ira Johnson, the lame son who ran a tobacco store on King Street in Toronto, left immediately but was caught in Erie, Pennsylvania. He was jailed, but initially nothing was found. However, he carried an expensive cane, and when the top was unscrewed, a large wad of counterfeit bills was found inside. He went to prison for shoving the "queer." John Johnson was arrested in Black Rock in Buffalo, New York, and locked up for shoving. He could pay for the best legal assistance, and consequently was not convicted. Soon after, he was arrested in Toronto for shoving the $10 Bank of Commerce notes and got 10 years in Kingston Prison.

Edward Johnson did not stay out of trouble for long. About 1884 he felt the need for some excitement, so he and a friend broke into a store in Montreal one cold, winter night and stole a safe containing $6,000. They placed the safe on a cart and pulled it down the St. Lawrence River on the ice. When they got to a safe place, they blew it open by dynamite and recovered the money. Ed was caught a few days later and sent to St. Vincent de Paul Prison in Montreal for 14 years. He was out of prison for less than a year when he was captured again.[146]

The dénouement of this tangled story came about in August 1898. Virtually the entire family was arrested for questioning as a result of the diligent work of a kid detective named John R. Downey of the Detroit Police Department and his boss, Captain McDonnell. The Johnsons were scattered but lived near each other. Most were living with their mother, Agnes Johnson, at her house at 106 McGraw Avenue in Detroit, a house that David Johnson had bought for her several years before. David Henry Johnson and his wife, Emily, and two young daughters, Irene and Alma, ages 14 and 11, lived at 795 26th Street in Detroit.

Dave, or "Henry," as his wife called him, was actually captured at the house of his father-in-law, Joseph J. Weatherald, near Blenheim, in Kent County, Ontario, a short distance away. It was in the Weatherald's house that Dave engraved his counterfeits.[147] One of his daughters, Irene, died just before or during the trial, and the women of the family always appeared in full, formal mourning dress, including black gloves and veils.

The Hancock two, a $2 Silver Certificate of 1886. (F-242.)

Dave's two-story house on 26th Street was searched, and a Secret Service agent found a hidden panel behind a sideboard in a bedroom. The panel was so artfully concealed that it could only be detected by its hollow sound when tapped by the knuckles. Once opened, it revealed over $2,000 in counterfeit $2 Silver Certificates, series 1886, called the "Hancock twos" because of the vignette of General Winfield Scott Hancock, as well as the face and back plates for making more notes. A second search of the house was made and turned up some engraving tools and two double-action revolvers. Dave Johnson had always told his neighbors he worked as a traveling salesman for the Milburn wagon works of Toledo, Ohio, and they assumed his absences from home were due to that work. He appeared to be a very pious man, and he and his family were regulars at attending church.[148]

One of the reasons for tracking down the entire Johnson family was the strong suspicion that Edward or David had engraved the $2 Silver Certificates of 1891, called the "Windom twos" because they featured a vignette of the Treasury Secretary William Windom, who died in that year. The Secret Service reasoned that if they could find the Johnsons, they would find the plate. That theory turned out to be true, and the *New York Herald* gave most of the credit regarding the discovery of the plate to the Secret Service agents, while the *Detroit Journal* gave credit to the Detroit Police Department, creating some confusion about the facts. The *Journal* reporters were "on the scene" and gave vastly more details about this case than distant papers, and their reporters usually knew the police detectives personally and therefore had better access to those sources.

The Windom two, a $2 Silver Certificate of 1891. (F-245.)

The Detroit Police failed to find the Windom plates in any of their searches of the two Johnson houses. Finally, they promised the women—Mrs. Agnes Johnson and Mrs. Bayliss—that they would not be charged if they or the men gave up the plates. After thinking it over, the men decided to do the gallant thing and give up the plates, sparing the women from any prison time. This was not surprising since the Johnson men had a reputation for looking after their women. According to the *Herald*, the plates were found in the Johnson houses in Detroit. Edward went with officers to the main house. Going to a washstand in the bedroom,

> . . . [he] unscrewed an ornamental top, about six inches square. This exposed the back edge of the walnut top of the washstand, and in which there had been mortised out a place large enough to hold the back plate of the Windom note. This mortise had been closed by a piece of walnut just like the board, so that it would have been almost impossible to have discovered the hiding place, even had the top of the stand had been taken off.[149]

Edward then took the officers to David's house on 26th Street. There, "lying on his back under Mrs. Johnson's sewing machine, he unscrewed the small cabinet of drawers at one side of the machine. The top of the cabinet was a single board in which a place had been hollowed out just large enough to hold the face plate of the Windom note." Edward and David were convicted and sentenced on December 21, 1898, to serve nine years at hard labor in the Detroit House of Correction.[150] This was a light sentence. There were three indictments against them—one for having possession of the Hancock-two plates, one for having possession of the Windom-two plates, and one for making the counterfeit money.[151] Each indictment carried a maximum penalty of 15 years, so the judge could have sentenced the 2 men to 45 years each. There was no evidence against Charles Johnson, who had just gotten out of Kingston Prison. David and Edward both swore that he was not involved in making either the Hancock-two or the Windom-two plates. Charles Johnson was arrested again in Toledo, Ohio, on Thanksgiving Day, 1899, and died in the Ohio Penitentiary in mid-April 1900. Mrs. Bayliss (Georgie Johnson) and Mrs. Emily Johnson were released and moved back to their homes in Detroit.

Miles Ogle

Miles Ogle had a vicious nature and was one of the few counterfeiters who was guilty of murder. He was born in 1844 in the state of New York to German parents. His father, George Ogle, acquired a flat boat in 1862 and embarked on the Ohio River, probably at Cincinnati, with his wife and two sons, Miles

Miles Ogle.

and John. Their destination was the Mississippi River, and the main purpose of the trip seems to have been robbery. At Portland, near Louisville, Kentucky, the family was arrested but later discharged for want of evidence. At Rockport, Indiana, still further down the river, they were again suspected of robberies and an attempt was made to arrest them. As the officer came on board the boat, Miles, then about 21 years of age, shot and killed him. For this, Miles was later arrested and sentenced to five years in the Indiana State Prison, South, in Jeffersonville. During that time, Miles learned from the other inmates the finer points of robbery, theft, and counterfeiting. As his later life indicates, he must have been an attentive student.[152]

As soon as he left prison, Miles joined the infamous Reno gang, which was then terrorizing southern Indiana. In March 1868 Miles Ogle, Frank Reno, and Mike Rogers robbed the safe of the county treasurer of Mills County (Glenwood), Iowa. They were arrested by Allan Pinkerton, convicted, and sentenced to Sydney jail in that county. On the night of April 1, 1868, they dug a hole in the cell and escaped, leaving behind a note on the wall that read "April's Fool." The Reno gang soon reformed and committed the first great train robbery in the United States. Miles Ogle was one of the 12 men that robbed the Adams Express Company's railcar on the Jeffersonville, Madison, and Indianapolis train at Marshfield, Indiana, on the night of May 22, 1868. The gang

got away with about $90,000 in crisp new currency. Miles later quit the gang and then worked with Pete McCartney in 1869 and 1870 in Rolla, Missouri, and did the printing of counterfeit $5 Legal Tender Notes, the plate for which had been engraved by McCartney. Miles stole $75,000 worth of these notes from McCartney and put them in the hands of dealers and shovers in Cincinnati, proving once again that there is no honor among thieves and counterfeiters.[153]

Miles was described as a "large, stoutly built man," 6-feet tall, weighing 230 pounds, with an intelligent look, dark brown hair, and a neatly trimmed beard. His manners were those of an educated German, and his speech had a slight German accent. Unlike Pete McCartney, who sometimes seemed to enjoy risky behavior, Miles was more careful, cunning, and secretive. His business put him in contact with many counterfeiters, and after associating for a time with the infamous Johnston family, he became attracted to Ida Johnston and asked her to marry him. She accepted.

Miles was arrested in 1871 under the name George W. Wilson in Pittsburg, Pennsylvania. An indictment against him was secured in October of that year and he was allowed to post bail. Naturally, he did not show up for his trial. He apparently liked Pennsylvania, for he was arrested again on March 12, 1873, in Philadelphia for engraving plates for the $5 U.S. Treasury Notes. This time, he could not make his $12,000 bail, so he was held in jail. But on May 23, 1873, he was taken back to Pittsburg on the original indictment against George W. Wilson. Knowing he would have to serve a long prison term, Miles negotiated with U.S. district attorney Swoope to turn over four copper plates for printing $5 U.S. Treasury Notes, two steel plates for printing the "Spinner head" 50-cent Fractional Currency notes, and a large amount of counterfeit money. In addition, Miles also promised to turn over the names and addresses of other counterfeiters. Swoope may have been a legal genius, but he didn't have a clue about counterfeiters. What Miles did was a standard trick among "queersmen." They almost always had an electrotype of their plates, so losing the plates wasn't critical.

Miles was released on bail on October 18, 1873, and for a while he informed on several notorious counterfeiters who were duly arrested, but he soon stopped.

The Spinner head, a 50-cent Fractional Currency note. (F-1324.)

After he left Pittsburg, Miles went to Cincinnati and then to a small village called Cheviot. He rented a small farm and kept a country variety store. The chief of the Secret Service was close to finding him, but he sensed their presence and took flight. About August 1876 a $10 counterfeit appeared on the Richmond National Bank of Richmond, Indiana. Soon after, other counterfeits of the same denomination appeared on the Lafayette National Bank of Lafayette, Indiana. And in November still another spurious $10 bill appeared on the Muncie National Bank of Muncie, Indiana. All of these counterfeits were evidently printed from the same plate with just the title lines and signatures changed. Close examination by the experts in Washington, D.C., indicated that the plates were the work of Miles Ogle.

The Secret Service began an intensive search for Miles, and eventually they learned that he was visiting the tavern of an old friend, John McKernan, at No. 84 East Front Street, Cincinnati. McKernan was known to be a counterfeiter. Miles was followed from McKernan's tavern on different occasions to either a large livery stable kept by "J.F. Oglesby," or to a residence at No.

242 Poplar Street. The livery stable was found to belong to Miles, and the address on Poplar Street was the home of his brother-in-law, William Rhodes Johnston. This shadowing ended in the middle of November 1876 when Miles and his wife disappeared into thin air. Fortunately, they returned in early January 1877, and agents Rathbone and Tuttle kept careful watch. On a Saturday evening, January 6, Miles left the Poplar Street address and walked up the line of railroad to Brighton flats. There, he was met by William Rhodes Johnston, and the two walked together to the area called the "Commons." There, they were observed leaving the tracks and going over to a large elm tree, where they began digging in the ground. They retrieved a large valise and carried it to the Miami Railroad depot in Cincinnati where they purchased tickets for the 8:25 p.m. train for Pittsburg.

Miles was in danger if he returned to Pennsylvania. He had violated the conditions of his bail in 1873 and could be arrested any time he came back to the state. Accordingly, he paid the brakeman 50¢ to tell him when the train passed into Pennsylvania. Rathbone and Tuttle were also aware of the advantages of capturing Ogle and Johnston in Pennsylvania, so they waited patiently. As soon as the train reached a point near Collin Station, the brakeman did as directed, and agent Rathbone left his seat, walked up to Miles Ogle, stuck out his hand and said, "How do you do, Mr. Hall?" As Miles stuck out his hand to shake, Rathbone shackled one hand with handcuffs and then quickly cuffed the other hand. While this was going on, agent Frank C. Tuttle went over to Johnston, sitting about four rows behind Ogle, and stuck a revolver up to his head, shouting, "Hands up!" The two men did not offer any resistance, having been taken completely by surprise. During the arrest, however, the train passed through a long tunnel, which provided a few seconds of complete darkness. Once the train emerged into light, one of the passengers noticed a roll of money near the seat where Johnston had been sitting. The Secret Service agents were almost certain that Johnston had thrown it away, but assumptions do not hold up in court.

When searched, Miles was found to have a package of counterfeit notes in every pocket of his clothes, comprising about $2,000 in total. The notes were mostly of the Richmond, Lafayette, and Muncie $10 counterfeits that Miles was suspected of making. When the train arrived in Pittsburg on the morning of January 8, 1877, the four men checked in at the Robinson House hotel. Ogle sent word to his former attorney, Thomas M. Marshall, asking for legal assistance once again. Then, the Secret Service agents took both of their prisoners to a nearby photographer and had their photographs taken.[154] Next, the prisoners were taken to the office of the U.S. District Attorney, and the valise was searched. Knowing that Johnston could not be tied directly to any of the evidence, Miles decided to take "the rap" for everything, including the valise.

The Dexter head, a 50-cent Fractional Currency note. (F-1379.)

The valise was a heavy and stout variety, tied with cords and coated with asphaltum to keep out water. The contents consisted of a set of plates for printing counterfeit $10 notes on the national banks of Richmond, Lafayette, Muncie, and 43 electrotype plates for making changes to the original engraved plate of Richmond. There was also

a set of plates of the 50-cent notes of the "Dexter head" Fractional Currency and 52 electrotypes for printing these notes in sheets. The total amount of printed counterfeit notes came to nearly $8,000. Agents Rathbone and Tuttle returned immediately to Cincinnati and arrested John McKernan and his wife Bridget, who were the head of an extensive gang of shovers. As later found out, they had been buying large amounts of the "queer" from Miles for a long time.

Miles made a rather unusual confession to Rathbone while he was awaiting trial. Perhaps this was done to win favor or to suggest that he was genuinely ready to give up the criminal life. Whatever the reason, he told Rathbone where another "cache" or secret hiding place could be found near the elm tree in Brighton flats. Rathbone and Tuttle went there and located the spot when Miles had said the cans were located. At the time, however, the area was flooded from an overflow of Mill Creek. When this water finally receded, they went out again, but now the sod was frozen hard. Unable to dig through this soil themselves, they hired a stout Irishman to dig up the ground with a pickaxe. He eventually found a large can and a sealed tin bucket, for which they paid him $1 for his efforts. He demanded half the treasure in the cans, whatever it was. The agents told him he could leave his pickaxe in a safe place and come with them to headquarters where they would show him what was in the cans and why he couldn't have any part of it. He agreed and went to leave his tools in a bar while the agents boarded a horse car. Before the Irishman returned, the horse cars started downtown, soon followed by a burly policeman who boarded the cars and demanded to see the contents of the cans. The explanation offered by the agents did not suit the policeman, and he took them before Superintendent of Police colonel Wood. The agents showed their commissions and opened the cans for the colonel. The cans were filled with the 50-cent Dexter-head series of notes. The agents were courteously dismissed and took their prize to headquarters, where it was found that the amount of 50-cent notes came to $8,541. This raised the total amount of counterfeit money found on Ogle to $14,316.50.

The Grand Jury found true bills against Ogle and Johnston, and their trial was set for the February 1877 term of the U.S. District Court for the Western District of Pennsylvania. His Honor Judge Winthrop W. Ketchum presided. On February 23, 1877, Miles Ogle was found guilty and sentenced to imprisonment at hard labor for eight years at the Western Penitentiary at Alleghany, Pennsylvania, and to pay a fine of $8,000.[155] William Rhodes Johnston was sentenced to two-years imprisonment and to pay a fine of $2,000.

John Ogle

John Ogle.

John Ogle began his career in crime as a common burglar. He was arrested in 1864 in southern Indiana and found guilty of robbing a store. Sentenced to five years in prison at Jeffersonville, Indiana, he served out his term normally. His next exploit resulted in his capture at Cairo, Illinois, with $2,800 of counterfeit money on his person. He and the arresting officer exchanged several pistol shots, but John was overpowered.[156] He escaped from jail soon after and was eventually recaptured in Pittsburg. There, he concocted a story about a large counterfeit plant and promised to show the Secret Service its location at Oyster Point, Maryland, if they would favor his release. The service bought into this story and sent one agent to guard him while they made the trip by train. John was not shackled for some reason, and at a propitious moment he jumped from the car through the window and was free once again. He was arrested again on January 8, 1872, at a place near Bolivar, Tennessee, with $500 of counterfeit money. He was convicted in the state courts and sentenced to 10-years imprisonment. Again, he escaped from

jail on February 21, 1872, and set two burglars at liberty as well.

John was caught again in 1872 and indicted for passing $500 counterfeit bills. He was scheduled for trial in the U.S. District Court for Cincinnati but released on $5,000 bail, which he forfeited and took "French leave." On February 18, 1873, he was arrested in Cairo, Illinois, under the name Thomas Hayes, for dealing in counterfeit money. He escaped from the custody of Secret Service agent Thomas E. Lonergan on March 6, 1873, at the Relay House on the Baltimore and Ohio railroad. Lonergan knew John's background and his ties to Pittsburg, so he got on a train to search for a "needle in a haystack." Surprisingly, the first person he saw when he got off the train at Union Depot was none other than our beloved John Ogle. John was waiting for a train that was due to leave in a few minutes for the West. When Lonergan's hand touched his shoulder and he turned around to face his captor, he was so completely surprised that he offered no resistance.[157] Taken to Springfield, Illinois, he was convicted and sentenced to five years in the Joliet Illinois Penitentiary, where he served his full term. As soon as he walked out of the prison gate, he was re-arrested by a U.S. marshal to answer to a pending charge for forfeiting his bail in Cincinnati in 1872. John was tried in the district court in Cincinnati in October 1877. On December 10, 1877, he was sentenced to a term of five years at hard labor in the Ohio Penitentiary.

By now the reader will have realized that John's life is an endless cycle of arrests, jail time, and escapes, controlled by the puppet-master of his id on the stage of the American landscape. All the usual puppets are there to join him—the occasionally bungling Secret Service officer and the more-frequently bungling policeman, the jails that have mysterious holes in their walls, the store clerks that are nearly blind and accept all bank bills that are rectangular, and of course, the nattily dressed lawyers who mount ridiculous arguments against the obvious. Lewis Carroll would have loved it.

Lewis Carroll, birth-name Charles Dodgson, was a 19th-century writer known for publications in the genre of "literary nonsense." Perhaps he would have personified the Secret Service officers as dodo birds and the lawyers as flamingos.

Ogle, who was now going by the alias "Robert Rankin," was escorted to the county jail to await transportation to prison. Some painters were at work in the jail at that time but had taken a break for lunch, and the paint-streaked overalls and hickory shirt belonging to one of them lay on the floor in the corridor where Ogle had been left. He quickly realized a deception that might work to get him out of the jail. He dressed in the overalls and paint-stained shirt, picked up a bucket of paint, and walked downstairs. At the gate leading into the jail office, he raised his paint bucket to signal the turnkey that he wanted through, and the turnkey, thinking he was a painter, let him pass. Ogle walked out of jail, strolled leisurely along several streets, and went out into the countryside.[158] He went next to Brandenburg, Kentucky, working there as a stone cutter until circumstances made it prudent to leave. Afterward, he worked on a stock farm near Owensboro for two months and later traveled to Booth's Point, Dyer County, Tennessee, where he did considerable work as a carpenter. He went then to Memphis, Tennessee, but could not stay out of trouble for long. One night he went with a group of men to a house of ill repute, and as the party began drinking, they also began quarreling, and John threw a beer glass at one of the men, cutting a broad gash in his face. Ogle was arrested by a

policeman who tried to march him to the station house, but along the way, John broke loose and escaped once again. His next destination was Hughes' Point, Tennessee, where he worked as a carpenter. Returning to Brandenburg, Kentucky, he robbed a boot store of $200 worth of goods on May 28, 1878. He carried the goods to Louisville and offered them to a second-hand store for $40. A policeman happened to come into the store and was suspicious of the transaction, and he placed John under arrest. The next day the goods were identified by their owner. John tried to escape at least two more times but failed in both attempts. Afraid that he might be sent to Frankfort Penitentiary, he decided to say that he was wanted in Cincinnati. He knew the jails there and was pretty sure he could break out of them. To make the story more enticing, he said there was a reward of $200 for his return to Cincinnati. The Secret Service sent Estes Rathbone to return John to Cincinnati, and this time, he did not get away. He was sentenced to serve out his original term in the state's prison at Columbus, Ohio.

The last record of John Ogle was printed in a Baltimore newspaper that stated he had been arrested there under the aliases of Edward Davis and John Fullerhill and had been convicted in federal court for raising $1 bills to $5 and passing them. The article also mentions that Ogle was wanted in Kentucky for the murder of a neighboring farmer, who, it is alleged, he shot because the farmer's cattle got into his (Ogle's) wheat field.[159]

Joshua D. Miner

Born in Steuben County, New York, about 1824, Joshua ("Jock") Miner was a successful capitalist for many years, managing the phony money made by others. His skills were acquired naturally since his father, Joshua, and his brother, Charles M. Miner, were all counterfeiters and were imprisoned at one time or another for passing the "queer." Jock was long considered by the old-time detectives and Secret Service operatives as the "aristocrat of the coney men" because of his luxurious lifestyle. Early in his life he was arrested at Seneca Lake, New York, where he operated a sawmill on a lot adjacent to his farm. Apparently he was in the habit of paying his employees with counterfeit money mixed in with real money. On one occasion, a workman complained that he had been paid with a phony $5 note, and when confronted with the evidence, Jock grabbed the note and swallowed it. He was also accused of passing $50 spurious bills on a Buffalo, New York, bank. Public sentiment became so angry against the family that they moved to Ohio. From Coshocton, Ohio, the Miner family moved to Cleveland with "Joe" Rosencranz and started up a small counterfeiting business. Rosencranz was a writing master and could imitate anyone's signature with great accuracy. Both men were arrested and tried. Miner was convicted, but Rosencranz was acquitted.[160]

A sawmill would have been excellent cover for a counterfeiting operation.

Jock escaped from prison and eventually moved to New York City, where he set up a formidable gang of counterfeiters, including Tom Ballard as his engraver, and a number of shovers, such as Bill Gurney, "Jim" Morrison, John Simms, "Steve" Payne, "Bob" Morrisey, and Harry Cole. But a chain is only as strong as its weakest link, and the Secret Service were good at getting people to squeal. In this case, it was a well-known "coney" dealer named David Kirkbride, alias Thomas, alias Harris, alias Moore, about 26 years old and a shover for Bill Gurney. Agent Drummond of the Secret Service arrested Kirkbride at the Hudson River Depot on August 6, 1871, just as he was leaving for Chicago with $1,980 of "coney" in his pocket. Kirkbride squealed on a partner of his named David Keen, a wholesale liquor merchant when he wasn't shoving the "queer," and Keen, under the same threats, "peached" (squealed) on Harry C. Cole. Keen then agreed to cooperate with the officers in the arrest of Cole. A "sting" operation was then designed to buy counterfeit from Cole using marked money. The operation went smoothly and Harry was soon sitting behind bars.

Cole also squealed, saying that he got his "coney" from Jock Miner. The Secret Service also wanted to capture the engraver, but Cole insisted that Miner always kept the engraver's identity a secret. Even so, the agents worked out another sting operation that theoretically would nab both Miner and his engraver at the same time. Following his instructions,

William "Billy" Brown was one of the counterfeiters who escaped the Ludlow Street Jail. See note 163.

Cole told Miner that he wanted to buy the counterfeit plates of the $2 bill on the Ninth National Bank of New York City and the counterfeit $10 bill on the Farmers and Manufacturers' National Bank of Poughkeepsie. The Secret Service gave Cole $1,500 in good but marked money to pay for the plates. Miner agreed to the sale and the transfer was scheduled to take place at an assigned time on the night of October 25, 1871, at their usual meeting place in the middle of the intersection at 61st Street and the Boulevard.

This was designed to be a large operation, with several Secret Service agents disguised as laborers, carrying picks or dinner pails and appearing to be returning from work. They were to meet at the intersection at a certain time, but it was a rainy night and not all the agents arrived as scheduled. Only agents Kennoch and Drummond took part in the capture. Once Miner realized that he was about to be arrested, he threw the plates and the package of marked money into the mud, but Kennoch managed to bring him under control. Miner got several of Kennoch's fingers in his mouth and nearly bit them off, but the agent hit him with his pistol, knocking out four of his teeth and ending the scuffle. Drummond also captured his man.[161] A police carriage had to be brought to the scene so that officers with lanterns could pick up the marked money that lay scattered about in the mud. Fortunately, all the bills were recovered. At the chief's office, Drummond's captive said his name was Avery and gave his residence. When agents went to that apartment, no Avery could be found, but the name Ballard was heard. Back at the office, Mr. Avery acknowledged that he was Thomas Ballard and told all the particulars of his involvement with Miner as an engraver of counterfeit plates. He also gave the address of his "plant" on the third floor of a tenement house at 256 Rivington Street, which was promptly raided, and important counterfeiting equipment was seized.[162]

Both Miner and Ballard were confined to the Ludlow Street Jail. This prison had a kitchen, billiard room, and several "suits" that were available to prisoners with money. Ballard escaped from the jail on the night of November 15, 1871, along with two other counterfeiters.[163] His testimony was needed to convict Miner, so his escape spelled trouble for the prosecution. The Secret Service knew how important it was to keep Ballard and Miner under lock and key until their trials, so one can only wonder why the service chose Ludlow Street Jail for Ballard's incarceration, given its reputation for escapes.

Miner's trial began on December 15, 1871, and ran for 12 days.[164] Miner reportedly said that it cost him more than $25,000 for legal fees, but in truth the money went to pay for false testimony, the disappearance of witnesses, and convenient lapses of memory. Tom Ballard remained at large during the trial, but John Ballard, captured at the Rivington Street plant, gave damning testimony

that identified Miner and Hinman as the capitalists behind the whole operation.[165] Harry Cole could not give testimony because he was an ex-convict and presently under arrest. To get around this impasse, Cole was pardoned by Governor John T. Hoffman even before he was convicted. Cole's testimony was also damning, but Miner's lawyers did much to disparage his motives. And while there is no evidence of jury tampering, that remains a strong possibility. Miner was acquitted, much to the anger and embarrassment of the Secret Service.

After his trial, Miner renounced the counterfeiting business and began to devote his attention to honest pursuits. He had secured a patent for a steam-operated rock drill in the early 1870s, and this made him a lot of money. He became a contractor for the City of New York and built street sewers. He had been a widower for 15 years and, having no children, his sole companion was a niece whom he adopted as a daughter. The two resided in an elegantly furnished flat at 346 West 48th Street. He died on March 10, 1886, and was buried at Tarrytown, New York.[166]

Charles H. Smith

A $1,000 Legal Tender Note, series of 1862. (F-186c.)

Thomas Ballard wasn't the only counterfeiter who had worked for a bank-note company. Charles Henry Smith, born in Connecticut about

1820, is considered to be one of the best counterfeit engravers of the 19th century. He was once a trusted engraver at the Bureau of Engraving and Printing, later working at the American Bank Note Company and then the National Bank Note Company. According to the Secret Service, he was the tool of a counterfeiting gang headed by William E. Brockway.[167] Brockway somehow befriended Smith in the late 1850s and used him as his principal engraver for many years. Smith's work was so good that many bank tellers failed to detect his counterfeits, and even some Secret Service agents had a hard time telling his notes from the real ones. He was arrested at his house in Brooklyn, 42 Herkimer Street, on October 22, 1880. He was then 60 years old, bald on the front and top of his head, wearing glasses, but still at the top of his skills. He had engraved the $100 plates of at least six different banks, and the $1,000 plate for the six-percent bonds of the United States. Perhaps his best work was a counterfeit $50 Legal Tender Note which was judged to be so dangerous that the remaining issue had to be called in by the Treasury. Very few counterfeit engravers have ever reached that level of skill. He also engraved a superb plate for a $1,000 Legal Tender Note and a plate for a $100 compound-interest note. If we are to believe his confession to A.L. Drummond, the Secret Service agent who arrested him, Smith began to counterfeit money when he was only 18 years old, or about 1838, for a man named Hulsimer. In 1867 he finished a plate for a $1,000 Treasury Note, and the next year he engraved a plate for a $500 Treasury Note. He also admitted that he engraved a plate for a 50-cent Fractional Currency note for Jerry Cowden, a plate for a 5/20 U.S. coupon bond (captured in 1867), a plate for a 6% coupon bond (lost in 1872), and a 7/30 coupon bond.

Charles was examined before a U.S. commissioner in Brooklyn in October 1880, and after a final hearing he was released from custody on his own recognizance and agreed to appear when wanted as a witness for the government.[168] When he was interviewed by a reporter for the *Brooklyn Eagle* in September 1897, he was living in abject poverty and suffering from paresis, an impaired motion of the limbs. His son, Sidney Smith, had followed in his father's footsteps and was under indictment for counterfeiting and having in his possession false $500 Gold Certificates and $100 Canadian notes of the Bank of Montreal.[169]

U.S. Federal Census records do not tell much about this man and his family, except that he married Sarah L. in 1850 and they had nine children, of which six lived into adulthood. A son, Milton, was a lawyer and tried to help out at his father's trial, but to no effect. Francis, 38, and Grace, 36, were still living at home in 1900. In the census of 1870, Charles claimed he had real estate valued at $12,000 and personal wealth of $2,000.

Robert S. Jones

This gentleman was an engraver for the Continental Bank Note Company of New York in the 1860s. He left that firm and set up his own general-engraving shop at No. 25 St. John Street, New York. The Secret Service says he engraved a plate for the Providence Bank, Rhode Island, and a plate for the Bank of Georgia. He admitted engraving the back of a 50-cent Fractional Currency note for Jerry Cowden, similar to what Charles H. Smith did. Though he was followed by Secret Service agents and interrogated by them, there is no record of any arrest or conviction.

A $3 note of the Providence Bank, Providence, Rhode Island.

Angelo Delnoce

Another professional bank-note engraver who went bad was Angelo Delnoce, the son of a distinguished father, Luigi (Louis) Delnoce. His father was an excellent picture and portrait engraver who worked for several of the leading bank-note companies. Angelo, born in 1850, was taught to engrave by his father, and he worked for a number of years at the American Bank Note Company. He also worked for a time at a bank-note company in Buenos Ayres, Argentina. It was there, according to Secret Service records, that he conceived the idea of counterfeiting the bank notes of several South American countries. After returning to the United States, Angelo came to the attention of the Secret Service, and Chief John Brooks said there were facts in his possession about Mr. Delnoce not at all to the credit of the engraver. Angelo and his wife, Mary, had rented a two-story cottage in Hart Park, in Livingston, Staten Island, and had been there since September 1892 (or about a year) when Chief Brooks decided to raid the house. Brooks and other detectives had been watching the house for about a month. Surveillance had been difficult because the couple only went out at night and received their supplies after dark. There were parties in the house occasionally, with the parlors brilliantly lit, and dancing often went on until a late hour.

Chief Brooks raided the house at 8:30 p.m. on a Friday night, April 22, 1893, and arrested both Angelo and Mary. In searching the back rooms of the second story of the house, Brooks discovered two plate-printing presses, a proofing press, three finished steel plates for the 100-peso denomination of the Republic of Argentina, plates for the 50-, 10-, and 5-peso denominations, and a large quantity of the special paper used for printing the notes. They also found a number of the finished counterfeits which Chief Brooks said were exquisitely well done.[170]

Although the evidence made a compelling case for Angelo's conviction, his attorney offered the curious defense that the notes in evidence were not bank notes of the Argentine Republic, as charged in the indictments, but "national bank notes of a province of that country," which seems a trifling and equivocal point. Nevertheless, Delnoce walked free and never served a day in prison. On April 27 a defense motion for "arrest of judgment" was presented, and the court granted the

motion and discharged the parties from custody. Without a transcript of the testimony, the outcome of the case remains puzzling. It was rumored that Angelo and his wife returned to South America, where he worked again as a bank-note engraver.

William E. Brockway

The history of this man has been distorted so many times in the newspapers of his day that few people today know much about his early life and even less about his character. William Brockway, himself, is responsible for much of that confusion, having told a lot of lies to keep his true identity secret, a trait that is common among counterfeiters.

Reliable sources that knew him from the beginning say he was born in Essex, Connecticut, a small village on the west bank of the Connecticut River about four miles from the point where those waters run into Long Island Sound. Brockway often said that he was born on February 3, 1822, and there is no reason to doubt that. His adopted father was Captain "Joe" Brockway, the owner and commander of a small sloop that sailed periodically out of Essex Village and ran down to New York to trade a wide variety of goods. Captain "Joe" was described as a Baptist of the "hard-shelled" variety and was much respected for his honesty and integrity.

William Brockway said he was born into a family named Spencer, but his mother died while he was an infant, and his real father, an itinerant carpenter, did not want to raise him, so he gave him to a family named Brockway. That could be true, but there is no proof of that story, and his real biography begins with his life as a Brockway.

William, or "Bill," was known throughout the neighborhood for his early show of artistic talent. He especially liked caricature and sometimes practiced this in chalk on the face of his father's red barn, which fronted the old Boston and New York turnpike. These caricatures were often made of village people whom Bill apparently disliked for some reason, and he displayed these worthies in an easily recognizable but unflattering fashion.

He was roundly criticized for his disrespect, and this lead to many arguments. He was especially disliked by the pastor of his father's church because young William was quite vocal in doubting some of the pastor's beliefs. This called down the pastor's condemnation in church. The next Sunday after the disagreement, the church-goers arrived to see the meeting-house shed covered with a chalk portrait of their reverend minister's face, ornamented with huge donkey ears. This led to a fearful argument between Bill and his father, and Bill chose to pack up his few belongings and leave home, promising he would never return.[171]

The next people heard of him, the lad was working in the office of a New Haven engraver and printer.[172] The shop, located at 124 Chapel Street, was owned by Frederick P. Gorham. Bill was probably supposed to learn both engraving and printing, but he apparently preferred to devote most of his time to printing and was especially interested in a new technology called "electrotyping," which was then being used in a few advanced shops. Electrotyping provided a method by which copper could be plated onto lead by electrical current, a bar of zinc, and a chemical bath of dissolved copper sulfate. There has been some question about how Bill Brockway learned to do electrotyping. Most newspaper accounts say he attended Yale College and took a course in the subject given by Professor Silliman, but Murray T. Bloom raised legitimate questions about the accuracy of that story.[173] However he learned the basics of electrotyping, Bill soon realized this technique could be used in nefarious ways.

Gorham's shop had a contract with the New Haven Bank to print their notes, and Bill developed a scheme by which he could make an impression of the bank-note plate on lead and then plate the lead with copper. The bank-note plates and currency paper were kept by the bank and only taken out of their vault and carried over to Mr. Gorham's print shop when it became necessary to print additional bills. Two representatives of the bank were always present at the printing and kept a careful watch over their plates and special paper. Bill realized that he would

need at least one and possibly two accomplices to make his scheme work. He explained his ideas to Gorham and a part-time printer's helper. Both were impressed with Bill's careful planning and his assurances that his scheme would work with virtually no chance of detection. They agreed to help him.

Sometime later, as the bank ran low on cash, the bankers scheduled a visit to Gorham's shop. It was customary to arrange this kind of work outside normal business hours so other people would not be in the shop, possibly distracting the bank officials. In his confessions, made much later, Brockway said he kept a sheet of lead under his apron. When his assistants pretended to notice flaws in the blank currency paper and called the bankers over to the window to show the flaws, Brockway had enough time to slip the lead sheet out from his apron and place it on the press. Running the press through its normal cycle, he impressed the details of the bank-note plate directly onto the lead sheet. Then, taking the lead sheet off the press, he hid it again under his apron. When the bankers returned to the press, everything seemed normal, and when the number of sheets of bank-note paper was counted at the end of the operation, none were missing. Lead was naturally too soft to be used as a printing plate, but Bill soon plated the lead sheet with copper and made a backing of a fusible metal or plaster to support the plate.

A $1 note of the New Haven Bank, New Haven, Connecticut.

A slightly different version of this story was given in the *Journal of Commerce* (New York) for November 5, 1849, which Waterman L. Ormsby quoted in part in his book, *A Description of the Present System of Bank Note Engraving*:

About two years ago, a batch of counterfeit bills on the New Haven Bank, Conn., (Tens, Fives and Twos) made their appearance, which created much astonishment by the accuracy with which they were engraved, and the skill with which the names, etc., were filled with the pen. No trace, however could be obtained of the counterfeiters, and the affair at length passed off and was partially forgotten. Only about fifteen hundred dollars of this emission were ever discovered by the bank.

About one year ago, the five and ten dollar bills of the New Haven Country Bank, at New Haven, were counterfeited with the same mystery as to the engraving, and the same extraordinary skill in the signatures. Of this emission, some three or four thousand dollars were discovered by the bank.

The two banks, therefore, made the most vigorous and persevering efforts to detect the villains, but without success. They also warned the public to beware of the counterfeits, and immediately took measures to procure new plates and new paper, calling in their old emissions as far as possible. This was at length nearly accomplished when in August last, the officers of the New Haven Bank were astounded by the discovery that their new five dollar plate had been counterfeited, with the same exact imitation of the old, and even more perfection in the (manuscript) signatures. Of the emission, only three or four hundred dollars have been discovered by the bank.

Since the appearance of the third counterfeit, the two banks have been increasing in their efforts to solve the mystery, and bring the offenders to justice. We rejoice to say that their efforts have been at length crowned with success.

Within the last five days, Henry Knickerbocker, William E. Brockway, and a man by the name of Snyder, have been arrested at Hudson on a charge of being concerned in getting up or passing those counterfeits, or both, and having been subject to a long and rigid examination, facts were elicited which leave no reasonable doubt that some, if not all of them, were guilty. Brockway was shown to have had an active agency in getting up the counterfeits, and was probably at the bottom of the whole affair. Besides the above, three persons have been arrested at Brooklyn, one in this city and one elsewhere,

making eight, supposed to have been concerned in the villainy. The officers of justice are in pursuit of still others of the same gang. Altogether, it was one of the most dangerous combinations to defraud the public, that ever existed in this country, and we may well congratulate the community, if it is at length broken up.

The prominent part taken in the counterfeiting by Brockway was made known by Knickerbocker (who was first arrested) but not till many ineffectual efforts had been made to induce him to confess. Among other things, Knickerbocker states that he received four thousand dollars of the counterfeit from Brockway, for the purpose of getting them exchanged for other bills, but that finding some difficulty in so doing, he returned three thousand five hundred dollars of them to Brockway.

It was conclusively shown that the three counterfeits were perpetrated by the same gang. It is admitted, we understand, that the first counterfeits on those institutions must have been printed from the genuine plates. As to the recent counterfeits, on the New Haven Bank, the case is not so clear, but there would seem to be a strong presumption in favor of the supposition, from the fact that Brockway was formerly a journeyman in the office in New Haven where the genuine bills of both banks were, at that time, printed.

It further appeared that the villains had not confined their operations to the New Haven banks, but had got up and issued counterfeit twos on the North River Bank in this city [New York City], and also counterfeits on one or two other banks.

These facts we have obtained from undoubted sources , and they cannot fail to be interesting to the public.

[Ormsby's comment:] The manner in which Brockway probably succeeded in obtaining facsimiles of the bank plates, before the very eyes of the watchful director, is thus accounted for by Mr. Frederick Gorham, the proprietor of the printing establishment, whose private character is above reproach, and whose opinion is worthy of the highest respect. Mr. G remarks: "You are aware that a printer adjusts his press, the first thing, before commencing work, and in order to test whether he has the right pressure, it is usual for him to place the plate, un-inked, upon the plank, and lay a piece of waste or loose paper upon it, run it through, and then examine the effect of the pressure on the blank paper. The printer will then screw down one side or the other of his press, and perhaps repeat the performance two or three times before he commences work."

[Ormsby's comment:] Now, Mr. Brockway may have attended Prof. Silliman's lectures, and learned from them and other sources, the manner of making copies of plates by the electrotyping process, and, instead of using a worthless piece of paper, in testing his press, [he] might have used paper prepared with a metallic surface, and thus obtained a mould of the most perfect description with which to electrotype a bank plate of his own, in the course of a few hours.

Bill Brockway, at this time, was still something of an amateur criminal and didn't have the instincts of a real thief. He was smart enough to know that he should avoid capture by using shovers to exchange the counterfeit bills in respectable businesses. He gave $5,000 to one of his shovers only to discover that the man had vanished with the money. Undeterred, Bill managed to buy suitable paper and run off another 1,000 $5 bills. He learned from that lesson and never again trusted unknown people with so much money.

By the time the bank realized their notes had been counterfeited, Bill had slipped out of New Haven, leaving behind his new bride, the former Miss Mary Olmstead. He moved around Connecticut, disposing of his spurious notes, and then moved to Hudson, New York, where he joined a counterfeiting gang lead by David Keene, a Canadian. Keene had a factory for making sleighs but actually used the factory as a front for making counterfeits. When a rival gang alerted police to Keene's operation, Bill was caught in a raid and arrested. By paying a large bribe, he was permitted to escape. He set up shop in Philadelphia about 1850. There, using the guise of a "business broker," he met an eligible young lady named Margaret Welsh, married her about 1852, and settled down.[174] As his money was running low, he

decided to undertake a venture in upstate New York. There, he was seized and later sentenced to five years in Sing Sing, a large prison on the banks of the Hudson River about thirty miles north of New York City. He offered exorbitant bribes to avoid prison but was locked up anyway. His wife, who was then pregnant, pleaded with officials and perhaps paid some bribe money herself, but she got Bill released after he had served only eight months of his original sentence.

A counterfeit $5 note of the New Haven Bank.

Bill and his wife moved back to Philadelphia, bought a nice house, and led a comfortable and seemingly respectable life. Brockway was known as Colonel Spencer to his friends and neighbors. On September 3, 1852, they were blessed with their first child, a son they named William Spencer Jr., who later became a doctor. In 1854 they had a daughter, whom they named Louise Spencer. Bill had learned that he must never do anything that would connect him with counterfeiting, so he stayed in the background, using false names to conceal his real identity. He studied engravers to see if any were in precarious financial circumstances and would be willing to engrave bank-note plates for large sums of money. He also recruited plate printers and a retired transfer man to make sure that his "queer" was so good it would fool bank cashiers. No one in his organization knew their boss, and his neighbors knew only that Colonel Spencer was a business broker who had to travel out of town on a frequent basis. The Spencers then bought a large house, hired servants, and lived an increasingly luxurious life.

When the government began issuing Fractional Currency during the Civil War, Bill set up a counterfeiting shop in a house he had bought in

Mount Vernon, New York, under the supervision of a 73-year-old engraver, plate printer, and mechanic named Jonas Atkinson. He proceeded to make 50-cent notes. This shop was raided in November 1865, and Atkinson was seized with $832 in real money in his possession, and counterfeit plates for the 50-cent notes were found hidden in the shop. As it turned out, the raid was orchestrated by William P. Wood, the chief of the newly formed U.S. Secret Service. The agents did not give Atkinson back the $832 they had confiscated. However, the real significance of this raid lies in what happened next between Brockway and Chief Wood.

A few days after the raid, Bill was arrested and confessed to being a counterfeiter. He suggested to Chief Wood that they should form a loose partnership in which Bill would snitch on other counterfeiters or at least suggest who might be the engraver for certain gangs. The confession and the partnership were bizarre proposals given Bill's secretive nature. Wood accepted the proposal, and this soon became known to the public during Bill's trial, creating quite a stir in the newspapers. The public was outraged and offered dozens of theories to explain Bill's behavior. Some of these theories suggested that his wife played a pivotal role, alleging that she was afraid that her husband would be caught by Wood's trickery and sentenced to a long term in prison, and to avoid that happening, she wanted him to be safe from prosecution by appearing to be contrite and willing to help the government. An editorial in the *New York Times* is a good example of the outrage:

The dealings of the Government with counterfeiters has long been a mystery to the common mind. We believe it to be true that more of this class of offenders in proportion to the number convicted have been pardoned than any other, and for this circumstance, no satisfactory explanation has been offered. But the peculiar relations of the Government to the counterfeiters of its currency have been still further illustrated by a trial which was closed yesterday in the U.S. Circuit Court.

A man named Brockway was convicted of having been engaged in counterfeiting fifty-cent

This $5 note, dated 1865, was the subject of a counterfeit for William Brockway. The engraver of the counterfeit is not known, but judging from the excellence of the work, it may have been Charles H. Smith, whom Brockway had hired about 1860. (F-397.)

Compare the superb counterfeit to the genuine above. Such fine work made this note a very dangerous counterfeit.

stamps [Fractional Currency]. The evidence was perfectly conclusive. He had a house in Mt. Vernon, where he carried on business in concert with a man named Atkinson very extensively and the most skillful manner. In November [1865], three men under the lead of one named Savage, entered the house, seized Atkinson, upon whom they found eight hundred dollars in good money, which they divided among themselves, and also seized a variety of plates and counterfeiting tools which they handed over to the U.S. Marshal. Atkinson seems to have been let off upon the surrender of his good money, and Brockway made his escape, but soon after appeared in the Marshal's office in company with a Government employee, reclaimed a hat and coat that were seized with his "tools," talked freely of his counterfeiting operations and of the amount he would have made if he had not been broken up, and boasted that his counterfeit money was the best ever manufactured.

In a very few days, he turned up in the employ of the Government . . . . Brockway was taken into Government employ after his establishment had been broken up by William P. Wood, who is described as being at the head of the Special Detective Service under the authority of the Solicitor of the Treasury, and has known Brockway as a notorious and dangerous criminal for over two years . . . .

What does this mean? Why are counterfeiters thus made special exceptions to the ordinary process of punishing crime? Can the Government punish them in no other way than by taking them into partnership?[175]

Testimony during that trial indicated that Chief Wood was in the habit at that time of hiring counterfeiters and shovers to help him catch others in the business. In fact, a number of Secret Service operatives were former counterfeiters. Of course, this would not be ethical in today's practice and wasn't ethical under Chief Wood, but then ethics mattered little to him. We now know that he placed such criminals under the supervision of some of his agents, and Brockway was assigned to Abner B. Newcomb on January 1, 1867, at a salary of $8 a day. We know also from the testimony that the vignette on the counterfeit note was engraved by Patrick H. Reason, and that Brockway paid him $135 to do the work.[176] Atkinson would have engraved the vignette, but he had felt his hands were not as good as they should be and had hired Reason to do the job. William L. Ormsby Jr., the Superintendent of the Transfer Department of the Continental Bank Note Company, testified that the 50-cent notes turned in to the government on several occasions had, indeed,

been printed from the plates captured at Mount Vernon. Judge Shipman of the circuit court in New York heard the case and had this to say at Brockway's sentencing:

. . . Col. Wood, who says he has charge of the detective service of the Treasury Department, states that he authorized your employment, with a full knowledge of your crimes. What promises he made you, if any, does not appear; nor is it material here. Your connection with the service was long after the commission of the offenses for which you have been convicted. The United States Attorney laid your case before the Grand Jury. They indicted you, and the petit jury found you guilty. It is true, too, that Col. Wood presented himself in court, sat by your counsel, and apparently aided in your defense, while the United States Attorney was pressing your conviction. We have thus had the unseemly spectacle before this court of an officer of the Treasury Department encouraging the defense of a prisoner, while the regular prosecuting officers were presenting proofs of his guilt. . . .

There is no law which exempts employees of the Government from punishment for their offenses. Nor has Col. Wood, or any other person, except the President, the power of pardon. No one has authority to regulate, by promises to felons, the clemency of this court.[177]

Brockway was sentenced to 15 years at hard labor in the Penitentiary at Albany. Jonas Atkinson, in spite of being married to a young wife who was the mother of his children, including a babe in arms, was also sentenced to 15 years at hard labor at Albany. One reason for his harsh sentence may be the fact that he was known to have built presses and other machines for counterfeiters in the past.[178] Through the manipulations of Chief Wood, Brockway never served any time in prison.

Beginning about 1860, Brockway convinced Charles H. Smith, a talented engraver then working for the National Bank Note Company in New York, to engrave bank-note plates for him.[179] Over the years, Smith engraved a number of excellent counterfeit plates, ranging from

Fractional Currency plates to $1,000 bonds.[180] But it was another plate that got Brockway and Smith into trouble. The Union had found several ways to finance the Civil War, one of them being the printing of Interest-Bearing Treasury Notes. Several series had been printed during the war, but the series that especially interested Brockway was the "seven-thirties," authorized by an act of Congress dated March 3, 1865. They were issued in denominations of $50, $100, $500, $1,000, and $5,000. The notes had five coupons attached on the right side, each bearing the interest for six months. The notes were redeemable after three years. They were called "seven-thirties" because the annual interest rate was 7.3%, the highest rate ever paid by the U.S. Treasury. Brockway liked the $1,000 denomination best. The plates for that note were engraved by the American Bank Note Company, and the printing was done in the Bureau of Engraving and Printing. Brockway asked Charles Smith to take extra time and do his best work ever on engraving the $1,000 plate, and Smith took six full months to turn out an impeccable copy. He then set about making a plate for the $100 denomination that was almost as good. Brockway distributed these notes throughout his organization, and they began to appear in New York, Pennsylvania, and New Jersey. About $200,000 of the $100 notes were passed by Brockway's shovers before the Treasury Department detected the duplication in serial numbers and rang the alarm.[181]

There was good reason for the government to be worried by this discovery. It appeared, for a time, that someone inside the Bureau of Engraving and Printing had used original plates to print the counterfeit notes or else had the plates long enough to make lead impressions from them and then make electrotype copies. If that were true, and the story got out, the public's confidence in all government securities might plummet, and in turn, cause a drop in the price of gold. Thousands of people stood to be hurt financially if the government decided not to accept the notes. The New York investment firm of Jay Cooke &

Company had sold $80,000 of the bonds to the government in 1868. When the government decided the bonds were counterfeit, it brought suit against Jay Cooke to recover its money. Cooke's defense was to claim that the Bureau of Engraving and Printing was negligent in its handling of the original plates.[182]

A $50 seven-thirty note of 1865. (F-212d.)

At this point, the Treasury decided to call in William P. Wood and start an investigation of the Bureau of Engraving and Printing. The meeting was held in the office of the secretary of the Treasury with the assistant secretary, the treasurer of the United States, the solicitor of the Treasury, and the chief of the Bureau of Engraving and Printing all present. Wood was informed of the gravity of the situation and asked for his opinion on how best to proceed. He examined some of the notes, noting they had duplicate serial numbers, and then declared that some notes had been printed from original plates and some were counterfeit. Secretary McCulloch decided to offer a reward of $20,000 to anyone that delivered the counterfeit plates to the Treasury. Chief Wood asked if he would be eligible for the reward, and the secretary assured him that he would be paid the full reward if he could confiscate the plates.

A view of Jay Cooke & Co.
at the intersection of Nassau and Broad streets, 1873.

Chief Wood knew of Brockway's past and had suspected him from the start. When he tracked down Brockway's home in Philadelphia, he learned from the neighbors that the counterfeiter and his wife were in New York, and that Mrs. Brockway was getting ready to leave on a trip to Europe. Chief Wood went to New York and soon located the couple in the St. James Hotel. On November 19, 1867, he entered their hotel room along with a police officer at 4:00 a.m. Brockway insisted that he was named Spencer and that he knew of no one named Brockway. Chief Wood dismissed the police officer, had Brockway and his wife get dressed, and took them across the Hudson to Taylor's Hotel in Jersey City. There, he and his men began an interrogation that was "contentious and spicy" and lasted five days. By today's standards, Brockway's rights were violated since he was not allowed to have legal counsel present. On the fifth day, worn out by the almost constant interrogation, Brockway admitted who he was and offered a lavish bribe to Wood if he would let him escape. Wood wanted the plates, so he allowed Brockway to send for an attorney. Brockway chose ex-judge Sidney H. Stuart of New York, and on his advice, he agreed to surrender the plates provided Chief Wood would agree to place him on probation. The chief agreed to the deal, and the seven-thirty plates were turned over. Charles H. Smith was not arrested because Brockway was too smart to "kill the goose that

laid the golden eggs," and he kept Smith's identity secret.[183] Brockway (as Spencer) and his wife were taken to New York City to be scheduled for examination, and a bail was set for $40,000. Mrs. Brockway had secreted that amount, and more, in genuine bonds in her under-clothing. It soon came to light that the spurious notes and bonds were made from a lead impression of the genuine plates at the Bureau of Engraving and Printing, done by confederates named Eli and Edwin Langdon (father and son), and the different parts of the transfer work and printing were done by confederates in the little village of Paulsboro, in Gloucester County, New York.[184,185]

Chief Wood then tried to collect his promised reward money, but Secretary McCulloch, who had never liked Wood, gave him only $5,000 and said the remaining $15,000 would be paid to him when and if the Treasury Department won its case against Jay Cooke. Cooke's lawyers claimed their seven-thirty notes were genuine, and the government was obliged to redeem them. The gov-

"The Goose That Laid the Golden Eggs."

ernment claimed that the notes were counterfeit and therefore not a legitimate obligation on the Treasury. Wood resigned as chief of the Secret Service in 1869 and then used his time to support the government's claim in the Cooke case. When the government finally won the lawsuit, the Treasury Department used one excuse after another to delay paying the money it owed Wood, and he never collected a single penny.

In 1875 Brockway and his wife Hannah and two children moved to 264 Clermont Avenue in Brooklyn. Gone was the large house in Philadelphia and its expensive furniture and servants. Brockway, still wealthy, was now content to live a more modest life. But in 1878 counterfeit $100 notes began to appear in several states. The Secret Service suspected Brockway's involvement but didn't know where to find him. In the 1880 Federal Census, he is listed as a 58-year-old stockbroker. He had again faded into oblivion. Fortunately, an unexpected break came their way. The Brockway marriage was not going well in 1880, and after numerous spats, Brockway moved out of his house and into temporary quarters in Canarsie, an area on the south shore of Brooklyn. Mrs. Brockway went to an attorney to seek a divorce. The attorney learned from her where her husband was staying. A.L. Drummond, the chief of the New York office of the Secret Service, picked up the story at this point:

> I was in a court room one day when a lawyer whom I knew came over to me and asked why I didn't arrest old man Brockway. I told him I would be glad to do so but didn't know where he was.
>
> "Why, he is living over at Canarsie, Long Island," replied the attorney. "He goes by the name of Colonel E.W. Spencer. He has a boat, goes fishing every day and lives in fine style. I know all about him because I am the attorney for his wife."[186]

The capture of Brockway, and possibly his plates, was assigned a top priority at the Secret Service because of the excellence of the notes. Those notes were printed from plates made by Charles H. Smith and were perfect in almost every respect. Even to the trained eye they appeared to be genuine $100 notes of the Pittsburgh National Bank. Brockway even had someone steal 100 sheets of silk-threaded fiber paper from a mill in Media, Pennsylvania, that made bank-note paper.[187]

Drummond's men kept a close watch on Brockway's house in Canarsie and also on his "bachelor's apartment" at 321 West 33rd Street in Manhattan. They noticed the frequent visits made by a large, husky man. They trailed this man to a home in Brooklyn and noticed that he stayed there for about two hours and then left with a package. A quick check of the records revealed the house belonged to Charles H. Smith, who was already under suspicion for his part in previous counterfeiting cases. The surveillance of the husky man was increased. A few days later he was followed as he boarded a train for Chicago, and several agents went along as fellow passengers, unbeknownst to the suspect. When he got off the train in Chicago, he was detained and a search made of his luggage. The agents found 204 bonds of the $1,000 denomination, 1863 series.[188]

The man was identified as James Brace Doyle, a cattleman from Chicago. James B. Doyle had met Brockway sometime in 1862, and like Brockway, Doyle was a criminal entrepreneur specializing in counterfeiting. Doyle had been a farmer in Bradford, Illinois, for more than 20 years before moving to Chicago and starting a counterfeiting ring. For almost 20 years more, the two men bought legitimate businesses to launder their "queer" money. They purchased a major interest in an oil well near Pittsburg, and Brockway bought a prosperous coal business and some property in Philadelphia. Posing as legitimate businessmen, they were able to pass counterfeit $100 bills through their bank accounts with no trouble. And bank they did! Brockway and Doyle had more than 40 accounts in as many banks. They made numerous deposits of real money, occasionally spiked with hundreds of dollars of their very best counterfeits, and moved money from one account to another by bank drafts and checks. When their accounts had too much money in them, the two men would withdraw a large sum of cash and split it. Doyle

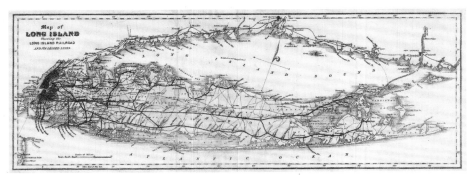

A map of Long Island, New York, dating to 1882, including Manhattan, Brooklyn, Long Island Sound, and the southern shore of Connecticut.

bought cattle and land in Illinois, Kansas, and Colorado. Brockway usually bought another business or two.

Mr. Doyle insisted that his bonds were genuine and that he had been on a legitimate business trip to New York. A Chicago banker inspected the bonds and declared them genuine. Subsequent examination by a better-qualified expert revealed the bonds were genuine, true enough, but their denominations had been raised to $1,000. The work had been done so skillfully that the banker had been fooled, but not the expert. The only questions remaining for the Secret Service were who engraved the bonds, and where was he?[189]

James B. Doyle.

Almost simultaneously (October 25, 1880), Chief Drummond and his agents raided the home of Charles H. Smith at 42 Herkimer Street in Brooklyn, finding the 60-year-old engraver at home with his wife and 18-year-old daughter. They didn't find any plates, but Drummond had a productive talk with Smith:

> Listen to me, Smith. You're an old man. For twenty-six years, you've lived in this house next door to the Superintendent of Police. You've made a lot of friends in the neighborhood and I've talked with many of them. The one thing they're emphatic about is that you won't lie. Now you tell me where the plates are that you made for Brockway.[190]

Smith thought for awhile, tears welling up in his eyes, and he finally spoke quietly, saying, "He's got them." Afterwards, he made a full written confession.[191] Brockway was arrested and hired William B. Guild Jr. to be his attorney. Mr. Guild negotiated with the Secret Service and finally reached a deal that he recommended to his client. Brockway would tell the Secret Service

where he had hidden the plates, including those for the six-percent bonds, and in return he would be given a suspended sentence from the court. Brockway agreed, and on the morning of November 25, 1880, he lead Attorney Guild, a U.S. marshal, and A.L. Drummond and two of his men to a chestnut tree in a secluded area of Richmond Hill, in the Borough of Queens, New York. One of the agents began to dig with a pick and quickly found the lead caskets holding the plates only a few inches beneath the ground. The "caskets" were six-inch lead pipes that had their ends flattened and soldered shut. When these were opened, the agents found 23 sets of steel and copper bank-note plates that had been used to print various $100, $500, and $1,000 notes, as well as plates for printing many kinds of bonds. Buried with them were glass jars that contained $350,000 in counterfeit $100 notes and a quantity of stolen fiber paper. The plates had been shellacked and wrapped in flannel to prevent rust, and the notes and bonds were in perfect condition.[192]

The next day, Brockway was taken to the U.S. District Court in Brooklyn and plead guilty to the charges filed against him by the U.S. Attorney. The government asked the judge to consider Brockway's full confession and his surrender of the plates and recommended a suspended jail sentence. Brockway walked away a free man.

"Into each life some rain must fall," said Henry Wadsworth Longfellow, and for Mr. Brockway, the rainy season was just beginning. During that winter, his wife got her divorce and most of Brockway's wealth. For many years he had placed almost everything he purchased, whether properties or businesses, in his wife's name so that the Secret Service would have no knowledge of his assets and could not seize them. Once the divorce was final, Mrs. Brockway moved to another section of Brooklyn, sold her ex-husband's properties, and lived out her life in luxury.

Meanwhile, Doyle had gone to trial in Chicago. Brockway refused to go and testify in his defense. At the trial, Doyle's lawyers tried to prove that his six-percent bonds were not counterfeit but were printed from genuine plates that might have been stolen from the Bureau of

Engraving and Printing. George W. Casilear, the chief engraver of the bureau, examined the bonds and pronounced them counterfeit.[193] After a jury pronounced Doyle guilty, his lawyers found a technical error in the way the verdict had been decided and won their motion for a new trial. At the new trial, several "experts" made a cursory examination of the bonds to see if they were printed from genuine plates or not. Secretary Folger asked Homer Lee of the Homer Lee Bank Note Company to make a thorough examination and report his findings. He gave a detailed report on the bonds and concluded that they were printed from counterfeit plates beyond any doubt.[194]

Homer Lee's testimony was the final nail driven into Doyle's "coffin." At Doyle's second trial, Brockway came to his defense, but the jury did not believe Brockway's testimony and found Doyle guilty a second time. He was sentenced on June 20, 1882, to serve 12 years at hard labor in the Chester (Illinois) penitentiary. Five years later, Doyle's lawyers appealed to President Grover Cleveland to grant a pardon to their client. The president refused, and Doyle served out his term.

President Grover Cleveland.

Brockway next formed a partnership with old friends Lewis R. Martin and Nathaniel B. Foster, Doyle's brother-in-law.[195] Doyle's wife had been a Foster when he married her. Both Martin and Foster had been counterfeiters for many years, but Brockway now proposed counterfeiting railroad bonds. Such bonds were not government securities, so the Secret Service would have no jurisdiction. The men set up their shop in a house they rented at 270 West 11th Street in Greenwich Village in New York. Brockway bought some coupon bonds of the Central Pacific and the Morris & Essex Railroad Companies, and the men started working. A.L. Drummond never

believed that Brockway would go straight, and through a tip, he learned the approximate area where Brockway was living. Drummond's agents soon spotted Brockway and tried to trail him, but they always lost him on 26th Street. Drummond recruited his 10-year-old son to follow Brockway and showed him an official picture of the counterfeiter. Brockway was not suspicious of a mere kid playing marbles on the sidewalk, and apparently he felt safe when he entered the St. James Hotel at the corner of 26th Street and Broadway. Drummond checked the hotel's register and noticed that Martin and Foster were staying in one of the rooms. Drummond turned the matter over to the police, and they raided the house in Greenwich Village and the hotel room at the St. James, finding well-executed coupon bonds of the two railroads. Brockway was arrested, and on March 5, 1884, he pleaded guilty and was sentenced to five years at hard labor in Sing Sing Prison.[196]

In Sing Sing Brockway's cellmate was Dr. Orlando E. Bradford. He was a descendant of William Bradford, a pilgrim leader and the second governor of Plymouth Colony. Orlando, needless to say, did not inherit all the good qualities of his famous relative. Instead he was an opium addict serving a 14-year term for the death of one of his girlfriends. Bradford had gotten her pregnant and then botched an abortion that he performed. His family used their political influence to try to win a release. Finally, it worked, and in June 1886 Governor David Hill pardoned Dr. Bradford.

Brockway was released from prison 18 months early for good behavior, getting out on August 4, 1887. For the next few years he lived handsomely on money he had stashed in different banks years previously. He was now 66 years old and could have lived out the rest of his life anonymously and with plenty of money. But for some reason he couldn't resist playing the game one more time. In 1893 he and Bradford agreed to counterfeit a $100 note of the Bank of Montreal, Canada, and the 1882-series $500 U.S. Gold Certificate.

An 1882-series $500 Gold Certificate. (F-1216b.)

Normally the two men would have chosen Charles H. Smith to engrave the plates, but he was now too old and dying of paresis, a kind of partial paralysis that affects muscle movement but not sensation. Charles told the men that his son, Sidney, then 39 years old, was just as good an engraver as he was, so Brockway and Bradford hired Sidney and set him up in a workroom on the second floor of a frame house at 242 Ann Street in West Hoboken, New Jersey, just across the Hudson from Manhattan. Sidney was a good engraver, but he worked much slower than his father, and he was so slow that Brockway decided to hire another engraver to help him.[197] The engraver he chose was a German immigrant who had arrived in the United States in 1853— Charles F. Ulrich.

Ulrich was then living in Cincinnati and under the close scrutiny of a Secret Service agent, William J. Burns. When Ulrich went to the telegraph office to reply to Brockway's invitation, Burns followed and covertly read the telegram. He then detained Ulrich and made him an offer he couldn't refuse—either work undercover for the Secret Service, with immunity, or serve the 15-year suspended sentence that had been imposed on him for a previous caper. Ulrich accepted Burns's offer and went to New York. He met with Brockway and was taken to the house in West Hoboken. There, he met Sidney Smith, the engraver, and Mrs. Abbie L. Smith, a cousin to Dr. Bradford but no relation to either Charles or Sidney. Abbie Smith was a 44-year-old divorcee of medium build with gray streaks in her black hair.[198] Brockway showed her how to affix red- and blue-silk fibers to the bond paper being used for the Gold Certificates.

At some point in their work, Ulrich signaled to the Secret Service that the gang was about ready to distribute their finished notes, and Chief William P. Hazen wasted no time in raiding the Ann Street workshop on a Saturday afternoon, August 3, 1895. Chief Hazen knew that none of the gang was home, but he had good information on where they lived and worked, so he went ahead with the raid and found only Abbie L. Smith and a man named William Wagner on the premises. All the others were arrested in the evening. Brockway was taken at a hotel he owned in Rockaway with a counterfeit $500 Gold Certificate and a $100 Canadian bill in his pockets. Sidney Smith was arrested at his home on 14th Street, and Dr. Bradford was captured at home. To prevent Bradford from alerting the others, he was placed under guard in his house by agents Burns and Callaghan.

During the night, Dr. Bradford managed to escape. None of the existing case files say how he escaped.[199] But newspaper reporters, after interviewing the Secret Service agents and local police, offered two main theories. The *New York Herald* took a lurid tack, suggesting that Marguerite Reynolds, a curvaceous housekeeper whose bedroom adjoined Dr. Bradford's bedroom and who was obviously on intimate terms with him, played the role of a sexual decoy, giving the good doctor the opportunity to escape:

> I learned that Miss Reynolds, the housekeeper, assisted in the escape. She made herself very agreeable to the officers and was ready to supply them with anything for their comfort for the night.

The other theory was that Miss Reynolds lured the men into her bedroom, one at a time, and chloroformed them. Both agents were temporarily suspended from duty. A month later Dr. Bradford, with his luxurious mustache and whiskers shaved off, making him look much younger than his 55 years, was located and arrested in a boarding house in New York City.[200] The officers found plates of a $100 bill in the false bottom of a bureau drawer in his room, which meant he could be charged with counterfeiting in the state of New York and would not have to be extradited to Hudson County, New Jersey, to stand trial there. Ulrich was told to stand ready to testify when the others were brought to trial.

The trial of the Brockway gang took place at the U.S. District Court in Trenton, New Jersey, beginning February 14, 1896. Dr. Bradford was tried first. He was expected to get the full penalty of 15 years. But Bradford had learned from Brockway, while they were in prison together, how valuable it could be to have a bargaining chip, such as hidden plates, if ever things went wrong. Bradford not only made a full confession of his guilt and testified about the other gang members but led the Secret Service agents to a place in Schuetzen Park, Union Hill, only two blocks away from the workshop on Ann Street, and showed them where the plates were buried. This "treasure" consisted of three plates for counterfeiting $500 Gold Certificates, two plates for counterfeiting $100 notes of the Bank of Montreal, one plate of a vignette of President Abraham Lincoln to fit into the center of the $500 plate, and counterfeit bills amounting to about $1,000,000. The trick worked, and the judge sentenced Bradford to serve only six years in the Kings County Penitentiary. Chief Hazen came from Washington, D.C., to hear Dr. Bradford's sentence. Bradford later told Hazen that three plates for counterfeiting $100 bills had been thrown into the Harlem River.[201] Although Bradford described the exact place where the plates had been tossed, no effort was made to find them, and they are probably still there, buried somewhere in the mud. Bradford asked for and was granted permission to take with him to prison $100,000 in securities. He used about $20,000 of this money to buy opium and other amenities. He died in jail in April 1899, probably from the effects of his drug habit.

William Brockway was convicted on the testimony of people living in the neighborhood of the house on Ann Street who knew that he had rented the house and who saw him visiting the place on many different occasions. But the most damning testimony came from Charles Ulrich, who told the jury the whole story of how he came to be a part of the gang and what each of the defendants did. All the defendants were sentenced by Judge Edward F. Green on March 7, 1896. Brockway was sentenced to 10 years in the State Prison at Trenton. Sidney Smith, the engraver, received six years. Mrs. Abbie L. Smith, Dr. Bradford's cousin, received four years and a $250 fine.

Brockway was 82 years old when he was paroled in February 1904. For a while he lived with some relatives in Brooklyn, then he moved to Wallingford, Connecticut, to live on a farm with his niece. After his niece died, he moved to a rooming house on Chapel Street in New Haven, then to another rooming house at 91 Olive Street.[202] It was there on the morning of December 1, 1920, that the landlord found Brockway dead in his bed. The cause of death was "illuminating gas poisoning" from a defective gas jet. He was buried in Grove Street Cemetery in New Haven.

Charles F. Ulrich

Charles Frederick Ulrich was born in Prenzlau, Prussia, about 12 miles from Berlin, on June 25, 1836. He received a normal education and was apprenticed to an engraver in 1849 when he was about 14 years old. At one point he was sent to Berlin to finish his instruction in engraving techniques. He completed four years and six months of his

Charles Ulrich.

apprenticeship and was judged to be very skillful, but his career was cut short when he had to leave suddenly for England to avoid conscription in the Prussian army. According to his confession made years later, he was in London for only six weeks, then went to Liverpool and embarked for New York City on board the *Ticonderoga* of the Black Ball Line, arriving in October 1853.[203]

Because he spoke so little English, he was unable to find work in New York as an engraver, and Ulrich said he soon fell in with a party of Englishmen who were recruiting for the British army, which was then preparing for war with Russia. Ulrich was induced to enlist in the army and was sent to Halifax, Nova Scotia, and then on to England in the HMS *Royal George*. He wound up in the unit called "the Light Brigade," and shipped out to the Crimea. He said he fought with the brigade in the battle of Balaclava, was struck over the head by a musket, and was stabbed in the side by a bayonet. He survived and was discharged in England in 1856.[204]

This $50 note was the subject of a counterfeit done by Charles Ulrich. Ulrich was one of the most talented counterfeit engravers of his time. (F-444.)

On his return to New York City, Ulrich found work as an engraver for the firm of Doty & McFarland on Williams Street. He didn't stay with them long and soon opened his own shop at the corner of Maiden Lane and Nassau Street. It was in this shop that he was first arrested for counterfeiting in 1858. Ulrich claimed he was retained to engrave a small vignette on copper for a card plate, but while he was working on this project, he was arrested by a detective of the New York City police named Robert Boyer. Boyer insisted the engraving was being done for the purpose of counterfeiting and that Ulrich was a long-time counterfeiter in England and in Germany. Ulrich was convicted and sentenced to five years in Sing Sing Prison.[205] There he told his story to the warden and suggested the warden could easily verify the facts by writing letters to

Scotland Yard and to a similar agency in Berlin. The warden took an interest in his story and wrote to Sir Richard Main, who was then in charge at Scotland Yard. Sir Richard replied that they had no records of anyone named Ulrich committing the crime of counterfeiting. Berlin also replied in the same way, so the warden asked Governor Morgan of the state of New York to conduct a full investigation. Since the story presented by the police could not be confirmed, the governor issued a full pardon in 1861.[206]

The counterfeit $50 note engraved by Charles Ulrich and captured by the Secret Service. Compare to the genuine.

Ulrich returned to New York and opened a shop opposite his old address at the corner of Maiden Lane and Nassau Street. For the next few years, Ulrich kept quiet, knowing that the New York Police detectives were constantly looking over his shoulder. In 1866 he met a capitalist named Jim Colbert through a friend, Mary Brown (the same Mary Brown we met in the story of the Driggs family). Mary Brown at that time was living with Jim Colbert. She liked Ulrich and thought he had a keen mind and great engraving talent, and so she recommended him to another friend named Charles Burnell, also a counterfeiter. She and Burnell then persuaded Ulrich to move to Cincinnati to make a plate for $100 notes of the national banks. Ulrich agreed and took with him a young lady named Kate

Gross (originally Gabenesak). Ulrich, his wife, Burnell, Mary Brown, and Ms. Gross all set up housekeeping at College Hill, some six miles from the outskirts of Cincinnati. We don't know if they were setting up a *ménage à cinq* or if they were just friends.

They decided to finish a plate that Burnell had bought from another counterfeiter, a 50-cent Fractional Currency note with a vignette of ex-Secretary Spinner. After a time, Mary Brown sent Kate Gross to Philadelphia to distribute their "queer" notes. Ulrich was apparently not up to his usually excellent workmanship and had a hard time correcting the vignette of Spinner, so his picture came out with a wild look. Meanwhile, three crooks (Tom King, John Hart, and Charles White) came down from Pittsburg posing as detectives and arrested Burnell and Ulrich. "Little Jimmy," as Burnell was called, turned over the Spinner plate, and he and Ulrich paid $1,600 to the "detectives" to let them go free. Tom King, the leader of the imposters, took the plates back to Pittsburg and started printing notes. Sometime afterwards, he was caught and sentenced to eight years in prison.[207]

Soon after this scam, Ulrich began work on a plate for making $100 notes of the Central National Bank of New York City. Skeleton plates were also made so that the name of the bank could be changed on the main plate to read Ohio National Bank of Cincinnati, Ohio, or the First National Bank of Boston, Massachusetts. 2,000 impressions were printed, equaling $200,000, and "Little Jimmy" Burnell disposed of them in only two days. He could have sold many more.

In May 1867 Kate Gross was arrested in Philadelphia for passing the "queer." She was mad at Ulrich for jilting her but became enraged when she learned that he was living with another woman. She confessed, "I knew I must break it up between them, or I should go crazy." She told the police where Ulrich was staying, and this information was passed on to Chief Wood of the Secret Service. Wood also learned that a package of good money was being sent to Ulrich from Philadelphia and would be picked up by him at the Adams Express office in Cincinnati. The chief

planted agents behind the counter dressed as clerks. When Ulrich came in to claim his package, agents captured him without resistance. Ulrich voluntarily surrendered the plates, printing press, and other machinery. He also gave Wood the plates for printing $500 National Bank Notes. These plates were pronounced by the experts at the Treasury as being equal to the genuine note in all respects. Until then, Ulrich was believed to be a mediocre engraver, but these plates changed everyone's mind. The plates were Ulrich near his best, and the Secret Service now ranked him as one of the two or three best counterfeit engravers in the country. It was decided to take Ulrich to New York and charge him there.[208]

Men playing billiards in a lithograph printed by Currier & Ives in 1869.

In June 1868 Ulrich pleaded guilty and was sentenced to 12 years at hard labor in the State Prison at Columbus, Ohio. The newspapers told a story to illustrate his intelligence. At the prison, his cell was located one floor above the billiard table in the central hall, so he had a bird's eye view of how other prisoners played the game. Ulrich had never played billiards before, the public was told, but as he watched the players, he figured out the geometry of the game and even how to hit the ball at angles that would give it spin. After a week, he began to play, and after only a few games, he was the equal of the best players.

Ulrich remained in prison for eight years and was pardoned in June 1876.[209] He stayed in Columbus for a few months in a liaison with a barkeeper's daughter and then left for Philadelphia. There he stayed at the house of Jacob Ott, a fellow German whom he had met in prison in Columbus. Ott's house was at Oak Lane, a station on the North Pennsylvania Railway about six miles north of Philadelphia. Ulrich began working on the plate of a $50 note of the Central National Bank of New York City. This work was commissioned by the capitalist Henry C. Cole. Ott was hired to be the plate printer. Ulrich stuck to the same procedures he had used before—making a superb master plate and then making skeleton plates with the bank's name left blank. He could then substitute other bank names that had approximately the same number of letters. The first counterfeit $50 bills appeared in May 1877, and the Treasury Department immediately suspected Ulrich but didn't know where to find him.

Jacob Ott, originally from Frankfort-am-Main, Germany, was a lithographer by trade and had to learn steel-plate printing in order to help Ulrich and Cole. Ott mastered the art of plate printing and made his press ready in the third floor garret of his house.[210] There, between March 1877 and April 1878, less than 13 months, he printed over half a million dollars of "queer" notes, most of which were thrown into circulation as fast as they were printed. Cole sold the notes in one large lot, and the small dealers issued them to a network of shovers on the first few days of May 1877. They were passed on the streets of Baltimore first, then New York City. Within 10 days, over $40,000 of these bills was passed.

In October 1877 Mr. Ott and company moved to a new house at Sharon Hill Station on the Philadelphia, Wilmington and Baltimore Railroad near the village of Darby, about 10 miles to the southwest of Philadelphia. Henry Cole remained in Philadelphia and continued to purchase all the supplies needed by Ulrich and Ott. Although he was considered one of the smartest operators around, Cole was sometimes curiously deficient in his attention to important details. The paper he selected for the printing of the counterfeit $50 notes of the Third National Bank of Buffalo, New York, was much too thick. Ulrich had done an excellent job of engraving, and Ott had tried diligently to print good notes, but the paper was too easily detected and lowered the price dealers were willing to pay for the notes. Ulrich protested the use of this heavy paper, but Cole insisted they work with what they had. The argument led to the temporary break-up of the trio in April 1878, with each man going his own way.[211]

A $5 note of the Third National Bank of Buffalo.

The Secret Service had been looking for Ulrich ever since he disappeared from Columbus in November 1876. Now they found him in Elizabethport, New Jersey, in April 1878, and they made sure he was followed constantly. Ulrich and Ott stayed for a time at 2041 Hope Street in Philadelphia, where Henry Cole came to visit them on several occasions and was identified by the Secret Service, who tracked him to his residence. Ulrich and Ott then moved to a furnished house at Scotch Plains, a suburb of Plainfield, New Jersey, and set up their "mill" to resume counterfeiting. The surveillance continued for a time, but on November 30, 1878, Chief James J. Brooks of the Secret Service, along with agent H.R. Curtis, made a raid on the house and found Ulrich while he was engraving a plate of the new series of $100 Treasury Notes. The workmanship of the unfinished plate suggested it would be the finest counterfeit notes ever made and certainly the best work Ulrich had ever done.

Rather than arrest Ulrich for possession of a counterfeit plate, Chief Brooks decided to use him as bait to catch others in the same business. Ulrich agreed to cooperate with the Secret Service, knowing that if he didn't, or if he tipped off his companions, he would serve a long term in prison. He continued working on the $100 plate, and the agents continued to watch and identify visitors. Finally, Cole was arrested on January 17, 1879, followed by Jacob Ott, who was arrested quietly at his place of business in New York City three days later. Ulrich was the state's witness and testified against both of his associates. Cole was sentenced to 12 years in the State Prison and to pay a fine of $2,000. Ott was sentenced to 10 years in the State Prison and also to pay a fine of $2,000.[212]

Ulrich was not immediately sentenced because of his cooperation with the prosecution. As he sat in the Trenton, New Jersey, jail, a public debate began about the proper legal course of action. Although Ulrich had not been promised immunity from prosecution, the public sentiment, and to a great extent the legal sentiment, was in his favor. A petition to President Rutherford B. Hayes asking for a full pardon of Ulrich was started by the public and signed by many influential and respectable people. The president, however, declined to act on the memorial. On April 30, 1879, the district attorney petitioned the court in Trenton to acknowledge the useful information that Ulrich had given in his testimony, and Judge Nixon was favorable to the request. Nixon permitted Ulrich to go free, on his recognizance, provided he never appear before the court again on criminal charges or he would be prosecuted to the fullest extent and rigor of the law. Ulrich made the promise and walked away a free man.

After Ulrich was released from the jail at Trenton, he was employed at one of the potteries in town as a decorator of toilet ware (ceramic and porcelain bedpans, etc.) and subsequently established himself in the same line of business. He also did some card engraving for the trade and occasionally for private individuals. He is listed in the 1880 Federal Census as living in a boarding house in Trenton with his 22-year-old wife, Mary, and a daughter also named Mary, age 2. One day while thus employed, he was visited by Charles O. Brockway, who asked him to engrave facsimiles of checks on a bank in Providence, Rhode Island.[213] Ulrich agreed to do the job but then gave the information to the Pinkerton Police Agency in New York City, and Charles Brockway's arrest was eventually made. Brockway was sentenced to a term of eight years for the offense.

In July 1882 Charles Ulrich took his wife Mary and his two young children and visited his mother in Danzig, Germany, intending to return to the United States in the fall. He left his business in the hands of two employees. Finding his mother's health failing, he wrote to say he would not return until the spring of 1883. For whatever reason, he never returned.

Charles Ulrich was probably the best counterfeit engraver in U.S. history according to the statements made by engravers at the Bureau of Engraving and Printing and officials in the Treasury Department. The precision of his work was not exceeded until the advent of photoengraving. Chief Burns of the Secret Service once told a magazine reporter that the government had adopted the Ulrich method of engraving bank-note plates and had used it ever since. Up to that time, he explained, the government had been engraving a complete plate for each bank. Ulrich engraved only one plate, leaving out the title line. He then engraved separately the title lines of the different banks and combined any one that he wished with the "skeleton" plate of the note. The government saw the efficacy of the plan and immediately utilized his ingenious method. The only problem with this story is that Pete McCartney had invented the idea several years before Ulrich.

Emanuel Ninger

Emanuel Ninger was that *rara avis*, a pen-and-ink counterfeiter. Although his technique was based on tracing the design of a real note and not freehanded drawing from a model, yet he managed to make minute alterations that improved his copies in subtle ways, elevating his work to the level of true art. Before 1909 it was legal for U.S. citizens to possess counterfeit notes as long as they did not try to pass them, and wealthy connoisseurs were eager to buy the Ninger counterfeits for their collections.[214]

Ninger was born in Austria and came to the United States with his wife, Adalia, on December 5, 1882. He was then 37 years old and a sign painter by profession. They settled in Hoboken, New Jersey, and later bought a farm just outside of Westfield, New Jersey, for $800, a purchase probably made possible by the $2,000 his wife inherited before they left Austria. In 1885 Ninger and his wife sold their farm for $1,500 and moved to a rented farm in the same vicinity, but Ninger made no serious attempt at farming. He was known to keep a few chickens, sometimes pigs, but not enough to make a living. He told people that he was drawing a pension from the Prussian government for his services in the Franco-Prussian War.

"Der Kampf un Montbeliard." A wood engraving showing a battle in January 1871 between Prussian infantry (left) and French forces (right).

The first public notice that a pen-and-ink counterfeiter was at work in the New York area was published in the *New York Times* on April 5, 1891. It read:

> In a saloon near the corner of Broadway and Wall Street a counterfeit fifty-dollar bill enclosed in a frame, hangs on the wall. It is a greenback, and nine persons out of ten would take it for the genuine article. Inspection under a magnifying glass shows that it was made with a pen and ink, and the one who made it must have been an expert with rare ability. There are others of these bills in existence, made with pen and ink, and all precisely alike. One is at the Treasury Department in Washington in the curio room of the Secret Service, and one is the property of a gentleman in Cincinnati.
>
> A great deal of hunting has been done by the Government officials for the maker of these bills, but with no success. A curious thing they have noticed is that new ones appear periodically, about once in nine months or a year. Whoever is skillful enough with his pen to execute this fine work could make

more money at legitimate business than in making fifty-dollar bills, the detectives have concluded, for this requires long and painstaking work. The conclusion has accordingly been reached that this counterfeiting is simply a fad, or perhaps a mania, with the person who does it, and is not designed as a financially profitable employment.

> Perhaps the bills are made as curiosities and not intended for circulation, but somebody's cupidity induces the possessors to pass them. From whatever motive they may be made, the process would be stopped if the Treasury officials knew the matter.[215]

The reporter didn't have all the facts, of course, and repeated Secret Service estimate that the counterfeiter made only one note every nine months to a year. Murray T. Bloom, who made a detailed study of Ninger, estimates that the real rate of production was about five or six notes a month, and since a $50 note then had a purchasing power of about $2,000 in today's money, the operation was indeed "big time."[216]

Ninger drew $10, $20, $50, and $100 notes and worked at his secret trade for 14 years before he was caught. As time passed, he began to omit some of the legal wording on the notes, but these omissions were only discovered after the fact. The *New York Times* described another note on May 19, 1891:

> ...Another turned up yesterday at the Sub-Treasury, a ten-dollar certificate. The pen-and-ink artist has omitted part of the inscriptions. For instance, the genuine bill bears the words: "This certifies that there has been deposited in the Treasury," while the counterfeit does not have these words. . . . in spite of these faults, the counterfeit is likely to escape detection in the course of ordinary business transactions. The officials believe that all of these bills are the work of one man. . . .

A year later, other omissions were described, and the reporter guessed at the method being used:

> A particularly fine counterfeit was detected at the Sub-Treasury yesterday. It is the production

of a pen-and-ink artist, who did his work so well that the bill passed through one of the city banks without any suspicion arising as to its genuineness. At the Sub-Treasury, its character was at once discovered.

The counterfeit is of a fifty-dollar greenback of the series of 1880. In the first place the operator photographed a genuine bill, getting a light picture, but sufficiently distinct to aid him on subsequent proceedings. Then, he went over the photograph with ink, in the end turning out a marvelously fine piece of work. The coloring is excellent, the design clearly reproduced, and the lettering far more accurate than is usually the case. The paper is good and has almost the right "feel."

Of course, one or two details were neglected, but they were not of a kind to attract attention. "Act of March 3, 1863," appearing over the vignette of Franklin on the genuine bill was omitted on the counterfeit. "Engraved and Printed at the Bureau of Engraving and Printing" is also missing, possibly because the artist didn't care to burden his soul with unnecessary lies.

Considering the time and care necessary to turn out the bill, it is doubtful if the counterfeiter profited greatly by his labors. It is believed he is the person who has been furnishing samples of his peculiar skill at various times for seven or eight years, but who has escaped detection so far, although Government officers have spent much time in looking for him.

Several years ago this man turned out some fifties of earlier issues than that of 1880, but most of his work has been done with twenties. The new bill is the cleverest example of his style ever seen at the Sub-Treasury.

The counterfeit was inspected by a number of bankers yesterday, and received the respectful consideration it deserved.[217]

Ninger explained his technique for tracing a genuine note, and photography had nothing to do with it.[218] His first step was to buy the best quality of bond paper, made by Crane & Company, that he could find. He then cut the paper to the same size as the genuine note he was going to trace. He placed the blank piece of paper in a jar of weak coffee to stain it slightly so it would look worn. He then placed the blank, stained paper, while it was wet, on top of the genuine note. The wet paper virtually disappeared, revealing all the details of the genuine note beneath it. He then placed the genuine note and the blank paper on top of a glass plate, and while the paper was still damp, he carried the pane of glass over to a window and propped it against the window frame at an angle of about 45 degrees. The natural sunlight again revealed all the fine lines of the genuine note. When the blank paper dried, he traced the genuine design with a sharp, hard-lead pencil and then went over the tracing with a pen and ink. Colors were added by a camel-hair brush. To duplicate the red- and blue-silk fibers that Crane & Company had added to the paper during the pulp stage of its manufacture, Ninger made small, irregular marks with pens using red and blue ink. The results were exceedingly good.

One of Emanuel Ninger's hand-drawn $100 notes, series 1880. Compare it to the genuine note shown below.

A genuine $100 note. (F-169.)

Ninger was not afraid to attempt the intricate designs of the geometric-lathe work on some of the notes. Such lathe work was supposedly the Gordian knot that counterfeiters could not untie. The lathe produced such intricate and mathematically precise designs that it was widely believed that no counterfeiter could hope to imitate them. But Ninger found a way. Rather than trying to trace every fine line of the lathe work, he "fooled the eye" (and the mind) into believing the lines were all there, a kind of *trompe l'oeil* done with the camel-hair brush. He did this so skillfully that even bank cashiers thought the notes were genuine. He also spent a great deal of time tracing the Treasury seal, which was often the weakest point of a counterfeiter's work.

In October 1892 Ninger and his wife bought a small farm for $1,500 in Flagtown, New Jersey, about 25 miles from his property in Westfield. They moved there with their three daughters, then 8, 6, and 2 years old. There, Ninger worked alone in a special room on the second floor, a room that was always locked so his children would not interfere or have any knowledge of what he was doing. He normally worked for a full month before taking some of his notes to New York City to cash. He seemed to favor saloons and liquor stores for cashing his notes. He dressed for these trips so that he looked the part of a professional businessman, wearing a great coat with a velvet collar and carrying a small black leather handbag. He avoided going into the same shop twice, walking through most of Manhattan in the search for new shops to visit on his next trip. He usually came home with most of his counterfeit bills converted into legitimate cash. According to an interview he gave to a reporter for the *New York Sun*, Ninger said his wife knew nothing about his counterfeiting and that he explained his income by telling her that he made money in speculating on stocks. It was estimated that he made about $200 to $250 a month, which placed him in the upper two percent of all wage earners. Had he stuck with sign painting, he would rarely have made more than $15 a week.

Ninger's luck ran out on March 28, 1896, during one of his weekend trips to New York City

to exchange his pen-and-ink notes for good money. On a Saturday night, near the end of his trip, he passed a $20 note at a Third Avenue grocery store. The cashier, Miss Ahrenholtze, was suspicious of Ninger from the time he entered the store. In handling the counterfeit $20 he proffered, her damp fingers smeared the serial number slightly. When she started to put the note in her cash drawer, she noticed the blurred serial number. She wet her finger on a sponge, rubbed the blurred area of the note again, and saw that the numbers became even more smeared. Ninger was just leaving the store, so Miss Ahrenholtze told a clerk to follow him. The clerk followed Ninger downtown and saw him enter a saloon at 87 Cortland Street.

The saloon was owned by W.L. Duesing, who was at the bar when Ninger came in. Ninger bought a glass of Rhine wine and a cigar and spent some time in small talk with Mr. Duesing. He paid for these items with coins. After a second glass of wine, Ninger started to leave, but on his way to the door, he appeared to remember something and returned to the bar. He asked Duesing, in his German-accented English, if he could change a $50 bill so he could pay off some workmen on Monday morning. Duesing liked to accommodate the farmers who came over from New Jersey on their weekends, so he checked his cash drawer and saw that he could change the note with $40 in cash and $10 in coin. Ninger accepted the offer, and Duesing counted out the money.

Ninger had placed his $50 note on the bar while Duesing was counting the real money. Ninger did not recount Duesing's money but shoved it in his pocket so he could hurry to meet the ferry. Duesing thought it was odd for a farmer not to count his change, so he looked again at the $50 note to make sure it was legitimate. The front of the note appeared genuine, but when he turned it over, he noticed that the back was wet from lying on the bar, and this had smeared the ink in the corner of the note. Duesing sent his barkeeper, Paul Zipper, to run after Ninger and bring him back. Zipper could not find Ninger, but acting on a hunch, he decided to run down to the ferry to see if he was there. On his way he picked up Patrolman James E. Lorrigan and quickly explained his mission. The two men raced to the ferry and saw Ninger counting his money. When arrested, Ninger claimed to have received the counterfeit note from the Union Trust Company. But Patrolman Lorrigan didn't buy the story and started walking Ninger back to the station. Ninger offered to pay back the change and to throw in five dollars for the trouble that was caused, but Lorrigan knew that the Secret Service often paid a bonus for the capture of any counterfeiter, so he refused Ninger's generous offer. Nearing the saloon, Ninger broke loose from Lorrigan and tried to run but was recaptured only a block away.

Ninger's only mistake was in using the wrong ink. Had he tested various inks to see if they were waterproof, he would have chosen India ink. In that ink, the pigment is carbon, in the form of small particles in a colloidal suspension that forms a waterproof layer when it dries. Also, shellac is added in small quantities to make the ink even more waterproof. Although Ninger

A bottle of Mackey's "Cochin" India Drawing Ink, found in an 1897 catalog.

bought his ink and pen at the art-supply shop of Alphonse Benoit on Fulton Street in New York, he probably chose an iron-gall ink that was in wide use at the time. Artists preferred to use India ink because it produces intensely black lines that give better contrast with most papers and similar materials. On the other hand, India ink has the reputation for clogging pens, due to the shellac in the ink. Iron-gall ink was always cheaper to buy but wasn't waterproof. Ninger may have been "penny wise, but pound foolish."

After his arrest, a reporter for the *New York Sun* referred to Ninger as "Jim the Penman," and this name stuck in the public's mind since it was already being used as the title of a play that was a triumph of the New York stage in 1886 and 1887. It was also playing in Boston at the time of

Ninger's arrest. The play was loosely based on the exploits of James Townsend Saward, a barrister from a good family in England who became a forger and dealt in stolen property. He went undetected for almost 30 years and specialized in forging signatures on checks. The press called him "Jim the Penman." The same sobriquet was given to Alonzo J. Whiteman, an infamous 19th-century check forger who came from a well-to-do family in New York and was a popular item in New York newspapers of the day. It was almost inevitable that the press would call Ninger "Jim the Penman."

"Jim the Penman," a play by Sir Charles Young.

Ninger was interrogated by the Secret Service. He insisted his name was "Joseph Gilber," and he claimed to be a simple farmer from Wilkes-Barre, Pennsylvania, and that he got the counterfeit $50 bill from a bank in New York. After time he grew tired of the constant questioning and confessed a number of facts about his real name and address.

Agents who went to his house confiscated two $1,000 bonds and $975 in cash, all of it legal. They also found his pens and ink bottles and brushes, which Mrs. Ninger claimed were the children's toys. Ninger later made a full confession to the Secret Service and to reporters who were allowed to interview him.

Many questions were never asked of Ninger or else he failed to answer them clearly. One involved the earliest date of his work. After Ninger was arrested, a coal dealer in Westfield named J.S. Irving remembered an incident he had with Ninger sometime in 1885, which he reported to a newspaper. Ninger had paid Mr. Irving for a delivery of a few tons of coal with a $50 bill. A few hours after Irving deposited the bill in his bank account, a cashier from the bank walked over to his shop to inform him that the bill was counterfeit. Irving remembered who had given him the note and immediately went to Ninger to demand payment. Ninger was apologetic and had a ready story about getting the note in New York. He promised to pay the coal dealer as soon as he collected the money from the New York man, and within a few days he made good on his promise, paying Mr. Irving in $5 and $10 bills that the bank accepted.

More important, however, was an incident that occurred in 1879 that had legal ramifications for Ninger's case. The first pen-and-ink note turned over to the Secret Service was found that year by a teller at the Sub-Treasury in New York. It had all the characteristics of a Ninger note, but since he did not arrive in America until 1882, how could this note have been his? One possible explanation is that Ninger made the note while still in Germany. German counterfeits of American notes were commonly sold to travelers at German ports, and it is possible that Ninger was already making counterfeits at that date and selling them to people going to

America. Lawyers were concerned because two different states, New Jersey and New York, both had cases pending against Ninger. New Jersey had the more serious case, that of *making* counterfeit notes, and New York had a lesser charge, that of *passing* counterfeit notes. Normally, the more serious case would be tried first, but lawyers worried that the 1879 pen-and-ink note would be used to suggest that such counterfeits were already circulating in the area before Ninger arrived, and therefore, he wasn't responsible for any of them. If a jury accepted this fact, giving them a reasonable doubt as to the government's claim, they might find Ninger not guilty, and that, in turn, would lessen the chance that the New York jury would find him guilty.

So Ninger was tried first in the criminal branch of the New York Supreme Court in Manhattan on May 20, 1896, before Judge Addison Brown. Ninger pleaded guilty, but his attorney, John Mayo, asked the judge for a reduced sentence, arguing that his client was nearly blind as a result of doing such intensely fine work for so many years, and that the counterfeits had hurt no

One of Emanuel Ninger's hand-drawn $50 notes.

one. If anything they were highly valued by bank-note collectors who would never think of passing them at face value. Surprisingly, the judge must have felt some sympathy for Ninger, as he gave him only six years in prison and a fine of $1 instead of the fifteen years and a fine of $5,000 that was possible. Ninger actually served only four years and two months in the Erie County Penitentiary as a result of time earned for good behavior. But immediately on release, he was informed that he would be tried in New Jersey for the indictment pending there, and he was re-arrested and taken to Trenton to be held for trial. The U.S. attorney, however, marked the two indictments *nolle prosequi*, meaning that he would not prosecute the defendant. Ninger got out of jail and virtually disappeared. Thanks to the research of Murray T. Bloom, who tracked down Ninger's grandson, Walter Dickinson, we now know that Ninger and his family moved to a small farm they bought in Oley, in Berks County, Pennsylvania. According to Dickinson, Ninger counterfeited two British-pound notes by the same pen-and-ink method he had used years before, and he passed the notes in Philadelphia. His wife, however, was fearful he would be caught again, and she insisted he stop making notes. "Jim the Penman"—Emanuel Ninger—died of nephritis on July 25, 1924, and is buried in the Oley Church cemetery.

Charles W. Hill

There is no doubt that Charles W. Hill was a gifted engraver, but he remains very much a mystery even today. What little we know of him comes near the end of his life, when he was arrested as the engraver for the Massey-Hoyt gang. Secret Service records indicate he was about 65 years of age when he was arrested in 1894.[219] His picture in those records shows a large man five-feet-ten-inches tall with wavy gray

Charles Hill.

hair, a mustache, and a short beard.[220] He was arrested in New York on August 6, 1894, following the capture a few days earlier of Samuel A. Massey and Russell B. Hoyt. Sam Massey was 60 years old and at one time the proprietor of the "Live and Let Live" Restaurant at Broadway and Fulton Street. When arrested, he had on his person 67 counterfeit $10 greenbacks. Russel B. Hoyt was once the foreman at $75 a week in Dunlap's hat manufactory on Park Avenue in Brooklyn. He lived at 315 Nostrand Avenue, Brooklyn, and was believed to have kept a counterfeiting plant at that place earlier. The tenants of that building said that the keyholes of his apartments were always stopped up and the doors kept barred. Anatonia Italia was a member of the gang, but she was arrested in May 1894 and locked up in the Erie County Penitentiary.[221]

W.P. Hazen, Chief of the Secret Service, gave newspaper reporters a lengthy but carefully guarded story about the capture of these culprits:

I regard this case as the most important that has ever been handled by any administration of the Secret Service Division of the Treasury Department. First, look at the evidence in the safe and closets. Could any set of counterfeiting paraphernalia be more complete? Of course, just now the prosecution deals with the Webster-head plate, from which we have about $13,000 in notes and with which the four prisoners are connected.

But see what luck has come to us in the seizure of the Mystic River and the Garfield twenty-dollar plates. As you see, there is no evidence on these of a single counterfeit having been struck from either set, and I believe that not one spurious note has come into circulation from them. The Garfield counterfeit is a particularly dangerous one, more so than the others. The Webster notes are marred in various ways, notably in the head vignette.

Seems to me that fate is always against the counterfeiter in one way or the other. This Webster note has a back that is magnificently executed, and the Treasury seal is splendid work, but it just happened that the vignette on the genuine bill was not well executed, and the engraver of the counterfeit plate, in trying to match it, made a botch of it. The money from the plate when "colored up" is taking. Crumple one of the "colored" bills in your pocket, go to the Astor House and take a drink, and see if the cashier doesn't give you your change unhesitatingly.

Can't tell you all about our methods and work, but I will admit that I heard of the Mystic Bank and Garfield twenty-dollar plates some months ago. Matters came to a focus over the Webster-head plates. No names, of course, to start with, last February. Murphy [Charles Hill], who is tall and big, came to this office and was very mysterious. He wanted to see me, but not in this office. I was telegraphed in Washington, and met Murphy in Jersey City.

He had a long story, a very long story, to tell about the counterfeit plates of the Mystic River Bank. He said he had made them and wanted to give them up. Of course I could do nothing but listen and advance his money. That's all in the way of business. He got about $100 from me and disappeared. As to Russell Hoyt, just look at our letter book here. Don't read the letters, but see if his name isn't mentioned as an associate of counterfeiters in 1890. He was then working for Dunlap, and rated by many as a man of exemplary conduct.

Coming down to June of this year, a gentleman inserted an advertisement in a New York newspaper as a promoter of schemes. Among answers received was one that suggested he could be of service to the Secret Service Division. He came here and Mr. Forsyth relieved him of further trouble in correspondence, and by counter-advertising tried to "connect" with the promoter's correspondent. As the slang saying is, Forsythe's advertisement. "I want the scheme: address as before," fetched him.

Of course, Forsyth and other operators went about the business in their own way, sparing no expense, exercising the greatest caution, and devoting all necessary time to the end to be obtained. They were rewarded last week when Massey's confidence had been secured, and he sold an operative thirty-four of the ten-dollar Webster notes for $100, the rate agreed upon being 30 cents on the dollar. All the notes had "had their coffee." They were stained and ready for circulation.

Massey's arrest followed, and in his pockets were found sixty-seven of the Webster head bills. Only one of them had been prepared for passing. I will not say that Massey, who is sixty years old, betrayed anyone, but when he had been lodged in Ludlow Street Jail, we were looking for Russell Hoyt, and got him the next day. This arrest, of course, made us inquisitive about the neighborhood of Danbury, Conn., as Hoyt's brother Lorenzo lived there in a prosperous looking farmhouse, and Russell had lived on a farm belonging to Joe Morgan, near Bethel.

Of course I had operatives up there, and when, last Friday, Murphy was seen in the company of Russell's landlord, Morgan, one of my men who knew of the negotiations of last February said: "Now we are getting close to the Mystic River plates."

Murphy was not molested, but Lorenzo Hoyt was put in jail on Saturday after some of the counterfeiting plant had been discovered on his farm. He had got to be very anxious because of the way the operatives were prying around, and I hear he asked when they would cease, and was informed that, if necessary, they would plow up the whole of the farm to find the press used in printing the $13,000 of counterfeits. My operatives are up there yet, and I fancy they will be as good as their word.

Now comes Murphy, a very disappointed man. For a reason that I cannot reveal, he believed that he was entitled to a reward for giving information. He came to New York this morning to get $1,000 and he got $10,000 bail. While he was in this office dickering for the reward, as he called it, Mr. Forsyth was down stairs getting papers for his arrest, and he is now in jail with Russell Hoyt and Massey.

While our case is completed to the point of having secured splendid exhibits as evidence and four prisoners, I am not ready to furnish a full pedigree of the prisoners or to tell exactly where the plates, counterfeit money, paper, ink, &c., were found on Lorenzo Hoyt's farm, except that the bundle of $12,000 was discovered under the barn. Never mind about the presses, we'll find them yet. So far as Lorenzo Hoyt is concerned, he violated the laws of the United States in Connecticut, and will be tried there.

So far, I am not prepared to say if we shall make other arrests. The operatives who are now in Connecticut may be busy up there for several days yet, and may make new discoveries and implicate other persons. For instance, we have not yet found out who made the fibre paper—may have made it themselves. Men who can make plates and turn out such money as that can make anything. When the Webster plate was finished, I suppose that the gang was in a strait for money, and they began to print on paper that had no silk fibre, but the package of $12,000 was of bills printed on fibre paper of which they had stacks.

The case is what we professionally call a "clinchem," but it will take some time fully to establish it and prepare it for the United States court. Some of the prisoners will not resist conviction. Massey said, when he was arrested:

"Well, I suppose I'm good for ten or twelve years."

As to Russell Hoyt, I've information that dates back four years to destroy any claim he may make as to respectability.[222]

Russell's brother, Lorenzo Hoyt, described by the newspapers as "a stupid-looking yokel," gave testimony that corroborated what Charles Hill had confessed. He testified that the gang boarded at Joseph Morgan's house and had two rooms there, one a bedroom, the other a small room that could only be entered through the bedroom. The door to the smaller room was always kept locked. Their press was kept in the smaller room and mounted on a bench four-feet long and two-feet high. Charles Hill operated the lever of the press, and Russell took off the printed notes. Hill and Hoyt told the Morgans that they kept the small room locked because they were working on a patent. Lorenzo Hoyt often worked in a little shop in the rear of his house. The windows were covered by paper and the door always locked. He worked there on Sundays, the only day he had off from his regular job. He sometimes took machine parts to a machinist's shop in Bethel to have them repaired, explaining he was working on an invention. He saw the press being operated by Hill and his brother and saw the notes they were making, yet he insisted he had no knowledge of their counterfeiting. The press regarded his testimony as a clumsy and tangled web of lies.[223] The counterfeit plates were found hidden in the roof of his barn, and a large cache of material was dug up in his garden. This included a $10 gold-certificate plate that had not yet been used. Agents also found a 75-pound package of bank-note paper that could have been used to print several thousand notes.[224] The set of three counterfeit plates—front, back, and seal—used for printing the Webster-head $10 U.S. Treasury Notes bore letter check 13 and the signatures of W.S. Rosecrans, register, and James W. Hyatt, treasurer.

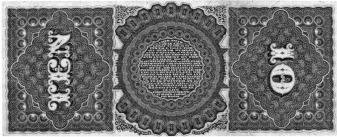

A Webster-head $10 Legal Tender Note of 1869. (F-96.)

Charles W. Hill (going by J.W. Murphy) and Russell B. Hoyt were sentenced to eight years in the Connecticut State Prison on December 7, 1894. Apparently, Hill was the only counterfeit engraver who ever voluntarily went to the Secret Service, admitting his role in a counterfeiting gang and implicating others. One naturally has to wonder about his motives. Did he act out of revenge for some perceived sleight? Did he write the letter in 1890 that implicated Russell Hoyt? There are a lot of unanswered questions remaining in this case, and it could be an interesting field of study for amateur detectives in numismatics.

Chapter 11

The Secret Service

The U.S. Secret Service was officially formed on July 5, 1865, by Secretary of the Treasury Hugh McCulloch. It was the first general-investigative agency in the U.S. government and was assigned the mission of investigating and suppressing the counterfeiting of U.S. currency and other securities.[1] The agency had a peculiar history and was not officially recognized as a distinct organization within the Treasury Department until 1883, but in the interim it derived its authority from annual appropriation acts passed by Congress.[2] Appropriation acts specify the amount of money authorized by Congress for the operating expenses of an agency and define the purposes for which the money is to be spent. This made the legal authority of the Secret Service subject to a "point of order" objection in Congress. In ordinary legislation, any appropriation act pending in Congress can be challenged by a congressman who wants to change the language of some part of the act. The congressman does this by raising a point of order. If Congress agrees to the point of order, the unwanted language is rewritten or deleted altogether. It was therefore possible, theoretically, that the agency's legal authority to investigate and arrest counterfeiters might be denied. Although there were no point-of-order objections to the appropriation acts for the Secret Service during its history, government authorities realized it would be safer to have a permanent law that defined the legal authority of the agency, and such a law was finally enacted on July 16, 1951.[3]

Secretary Hugh McCulloch.

The person most responsible for creating the Secret Service was Secretary Hugh McCulloch. He attended a cabinet meeting at the White House on April 14, 1865, a little over a month after President Abraham Lincoln began his second term of office. At that meeting, McCulloch called attention to the growing threat of counterfeiting to the public's trust in the national currency. He reviewed the efforts that had been made by his department to capture counterfeiters, but he said those efforts had not really captured the engravers and capitalists that were the backbone of the problem. Private detectives had been hired, but they had also failed to stop the flow of "queer" money. Lincoln thought for a while and then asked McCulloch if he knew of a better way to wage war against such villains. "I think so," answered McCulloch. "I think there should be a continuous organized effort, aggressive rather than defensive, and that the work should be undertaken by a permanent force managed by a directing head." The president answered, "Work it out your own way, Hugh. I believe you have the right idea." McCulloch said later that those were the last words that Lincoln said to him. About ten o'clock that night, Lincoln was assassinated.

Employees of the Secret Service hard at work.

William Patrick Wood

William P. Wood.

William P. Wood has been described as a swashbuckler and dare-devil that "shot and slashed his way through the Mexican War as the head of a column of guerilla marauders." Unfortunately, he was more than just that. He was also devious, cunning, unethical, and arrogant. Those qualities, however, were needed by the Secret Service at the beginning, when getting the job done counted for more than the Marquess of Queensberry rules. Born in Alexandria, Virginia, on March 11, 1824, Wood was the son of an immigrant engraver and die sinker. He learned mechanical skills from his father and grew up to become a very good mold-maker and general mechanic. He enlisted in the Mounted Rifles of General Samuel H. Walker in 1846 to fight in Texas. This unit later became the 3rd Regular Cavalry, and Wood became the dare-devil leader of the famous Company "C." After the war, he moved to Washington, D.C., married Miss Harriet Smith, and became the father of six children.

The Mexican army retreats at the Battle of Buena Vista, 1847.

In 1854 Wood met Edwin M. Stanton, a lawyer who had been hired to help defend an inventor named Pels Manny in a patent-infringement suit brought by Cyrus H. McCormick, the inventor of the mechanical reaper. McCormick's first reaper was patented in 1834, and Manny's first reaper, patented in 1849, was similar to the McCormick design. The crucial issue in the lawsuit was the type of blade used on the reaper to cut the grain. If Manny's blade was straight, McCormick would lose the case, and if the blade was curved, McCormick would win. In 1897 William Wood, near the end of his life, made a detailed confession in the form of an affidavit, saying that he had made a straight blade to fit the McCormick reaper at the request of Peter H. Watson, the head attorney in Manny's defense team. Manny's lawyers had located an early model of the McCormick reaper and bought it from the owner. "Colonel" Wood, as he liked to be called, took out the original, curved blade and replaced it with a straight one, using dirt and vinegar to make it look old and well-used. He said in his affidavit that he and Watson were the only two people who knew that they had rigged the evidence. The owner of the reaper swore that the machine being exhibited in court was the one he had bought from McCormick in 1840 and that he had not modified it in any way during the time he owned it. Pels Manny won the case, but it was a Pyrrhic victory because McCormick's reaper continued to dominate the market.[4]

Secretary Edwin Stanton.

Edwin Stanton became friends with Colonel Wood during the Manny trial and often helped him climb the ladder of success.[5] After Stanton became secretary of war in January 1862, he appointed Colonel Wood to be the keeper of the Old Capitol Prison in Washington, D.C. Stanton gave him the pay equivalent to a full colonel in the army, and Wood was the warden from the middle of July 1861 until he resigned on June 30, 1865. He estimated that during that time he processed more than 30,000 prisoners, including women.[6] Wood set up an intelligence system in the Old Capitol Prison in which his double-agents posed as Confederate sympathizers and told their fellow prisoners that they had frequent contact with a man that could deliver their letters to Richmond and bring back mail to Washington, with everything done secretly and without the knowledge of the prison's warden. The letters, of course, were given to Wood, who skillfully opened them and made notes of the military information they sometimes contained. He then sealed the letters and sent them to Richmond. He also opened the return mail, just as skillfully, made notes of any new developments in the South, and gave them to his double-agents to pass on to the addressees. When Stanton learned of this, he called Wood into his office and demanded to know on whose authority this practice was initiated. Wood took the "credit," but when Stanton ordered him to stop reading the prisoners' mail, Wood argued that all is fair in love and war, and the Union had a right to defend itself by every means available. Stanton was eventually won over to these arguments and permitted Wood to continue the practice, probably because the information that Wood had gleaned from opening letters had given Stanton's office lots of valuable leads on the South's war strategy, including General Robert E. Lee's plans for invading the North, which ended with the Battle of Gettysburg.

The Old Capitol Prison.

In the fall of 1864, the secretary of the Treasury, a Maine lawyer named William Pitt Fessenden, asked Stanton to lend Colonel Wood to the Treasury Department to help in the fight against counterfeiters. Stanton was agreeable to this but held Wood in his position until July 1865, when

the war was over. Wood was then assigned to his new boss, Treasury Solicitor Edward P. Jordan. Wood later reported:

> At that time it was currently reported that about half the money in circulation was counterfeit. I was permitted to use my own methods and I determined to capture the engravers and principals active in the counterfeiting business. It was also my purpose to convince such characters that it would be no longer healthy for them to ply their vocation without being handled roughly, a fact they soon discovered.
>
> In eight months I rounded up counterfeiters in nearly every state east of the Alleghenies. I made no pretense that my arrests were sanctioned by civil authority. Because my raids were made without military escort and I did not ask the assistance of State officials, I surprised the professional counterfeiter. I was threatened with every species of demolition, but took my chances at capture or being captured in those lively undertakings.

Three months after getting President Abraham Lincoln's approval to create an agency for suppressing counterfeiting, Hugh McCulloch asked William P. Wood to head such a force. Wood was the logical choice since he had already established a reputation for careful investigation and quick strikes to arrest counterfeiters. He was sworn in

William Pitt Fessenden.

as chief of the U.S. Secret Service on July 5, 1865, in the office of Edward P. Jordan, the Solicitor of the Treasury.[7] Chief Wood began his work with a force of just 15 men, most of whom were formerly private detectives; others were friends and associates. The agency's first operating budget in 1865 was $100,000.[8] Agents were paid $3 a day and had to buy their own firearms. By the end of his first year in office, Chief Wood and his operatives had captured more than 200 "counterfeiters" with the help of U.S. marshals and police officers.

Newspapers of the day noted that most of the counterfeiters were just "shovers," the people who distributed the "queer." The underworld, however, was beginning to notice the much greater risk that now plagued their profession. As President Lincoln had said, McCulloch did have the right idea—but not necessarily the best judgment in people. In some ways, Wood was the right choice to head up the new agency, but in many other respects, he was a wolf in sheep's clothing.

Daniel Stadtfeld, a good friend who specializes in researching counterfeiters, has recently discovered evidence that a noted counterfeiter, Charles Hill, was actually one of the first Secret Service agents hired by Chief Wood. Hill assumed the name James H. Walker and applied for a position with the Secret Service with a letter of recommendation from the chief of police at St. Louis, Jed Cousins. Wood himself made this entry in the *Record of Monthly Reports* in June 1865: "Perry Randolph is believed to be in Northern Indiana, having in his employ, Charles Hill, alias James H. Walker, who is engraving a plate to counterfeit some National Security." Wood had previously dismissed Walker (Hill), so he must have known exactly who he was talking about.

"The Wolf in Sheep's Clothing." A woodcut by Francis Barlow, 1687.

Chief Wood's relationship with the counterfeiter William Brockway was especially irritating to the public. Each time Brockway was arrested,

he turned over engraved counterfeit plates or revealed the locations of where they were hidden in exchange for some form of probation. Newspaper editorials were always quick to point out the ethical and moral errors in the practice of granting clemency to criminals for their cooperation, and the treatment of Brockway was held up as particularly egregious. Editorial writers asked rhetorically why police officers, the chief of the Secret Service, or anyone else, were allowed to make deals with criminals. The editors argued that the duties of law-enforcement officers were different from those of prosecuting attorneys, and Chief Wood had acted as both. Wood was especially stung by the criticism in an editorial published in the *New York Times* on June 28, 1867, entitled "Counterfeiters in the Employ of the Government." The paper criticized Wood for taking no serious action against Brockway in the Mount Vernon fractional-currency counterfeiting case, although Brockway had appeared at the marshal's office in the company of Chief Wood and "talked freely of his counterfeiting operations and of the amount he would have made if he had not been broken up, and boasted that his counterfeit currency was the best ever manufactured."[9] Brockway was not immediately prosecuted and was allowed to go freely about his business by promising to help Chief Wood to capture the actual engravers of counterfeit currency. When Brockway was eventually brought to trial against Wood's wishes, the chief acted as his voluntary counsel, "suggesting points for his defense and doing all in his power to secure his acquittal against the efforts of the regular Government officers to convict him."[10] To the public, this was clearly a conflict of interest on Chief Wood's part and suggested he was probably paid by Brockway for his help.

Chief Wood wrote a letter to the editor of the *New York Times* on the same day the editorial criticized him, ostensibly to correct certain errors of fact the he claimed were made. His "correction," however, was vague and offered no specific rebuttals of the basic facts.[11] He stayed on in his office, resigning in 1869, and was replaced by Hiram Whitley. Once he was out of the service, he became a private detective and later a newspaper reporter. In 1874 Colonel Wood contacted the Secret Service and said he had met a group of counterfeiters who offered to sell him a set of transfer rolls for making counterfeit money. Wood offered to buy the rolls if the Treasury Department would put up the money. A.L. Drummond, who was then the chief of the New York office of the Secret Service, was assigned to follow Wood discreetly and see if he could identify the counterfeiters. Drummond soon discovered that Wood wasn't negotiating with counterfeiters at all. He had confiscated the transfer rolls several years earlier and had put them aside in case he needed cash later. He was now trying to dupe the Treasury into paying him for transfer rolls that he should have turned in years before. Drummond reported his findings to Chief Elmer Washburn.

Washburn met with Wood and made him a deal. He wouldn't prosecute if Wood agreed to turn in a high-ranking counterfeiter. Wood was happy to comply with that offer and soon told the agency where they could find George Albert Mason. Chief Washburn and two other agents went to a room that Mason was renting at 548-1/2 Hudson Street and found a package of counterfeit money under his bed. Mason was an Englishman who hated Americans. Standing over six feet tall and weighing about 300 pounds, with a deep and very loud voice, he turned the proceedings of his trial into a sideshow. In the end he got 12 years at hard labor in Albany prison, Elmer Washburn got his capture, and Wood got off free.[12]

Beginning about 1869 and continuing for several years, Wood was almost delusional in his constant attacks on people he didn't like, especially those with whom he had worked in previous years. In August 1869 he issued a pamphlet attacking Secretary Boutwell and charging dishonesty on nearly all the officers of the Treasury Department.[13] As late as 1883 he was still attacking ex-Chief Hiram C. Whitley for dishonesty, saying that he originated a scheme by which he planted evidence by one team of operatives and then used a different team to arrest counterfeiters for having this planted evidence in their possession. Wood also charged chiefs J.J. Brooks and A.L. Drummond with using the same scam to boost the reputation of the Secret Service.[14] His diatribes knew no bounds, and the newspapers loved the sensational charges he made.

Colonel Wood died almost penniless on March 20, 1903, at the Soldiers' Home in Washington, D.C., and was buried in the historic Congressional Cemetery in the southeast part of that city. The Secret Service has now acted to correct an oversight, giving him a small black-granite gravestone bearing just his surname.[15] The Washington *Evening Star* in its obituary said of Wood that his "life was a continuous melodrama bordering on the tragic. . . ."[16]

H.C. Whitley

Hiram C. Whitley,
the second chief
of the Secret Service.

Hiram C. Whitley was born in Waldo County, Maine, on August 6, 1832. His father, William Whitley, a physician and surgeon, was born in Glasgow, Scotland, and was brought to America by his parents. Hiram and his parents moved to Lake County, Ohio, in 1840. He had a normal education at a Presbyterian school but left at age 15 for a more adventurous life. He got a job as a drover and took herds of cattle from the Midwest over the Alleghenies, through Pittsburgh, and on to Philadelphia. He made that trip six and a half times. On his last trip, he walked home from Philadelphia, a distance of over 500 miles, making the trip in 7 days. While still a young man, Whitley spent two years in Boston in the oyster business; he also followed the sea for a time. While in Boston, he married Miss Catherine Webster of East Cambridge in 1856. He tried mining for gold in the area around Pike's Peak in 1859 but without success. Next, he went to New Orleans, where he and his wife lived for several years. A Union sympathizer, he worked on steam boats to keep out of active service in the Confederate Army. He was working on the steamer *Starlight* at Jefferson City, Texas, when New Orleans was captured by General Butler in the spring of 1862. Returning to New Orleans, he worked for a time for Butler to rid the city of outlaws and the more obnoxious rebels. He joined the Union Army and was made a major in the 7th Louisiana Regiment. Several times he went on special missions past the federal lines and earned the respect of his superior officers. His main responsibilities were in law enforcement, and he was never hesitant to face down thugs. He was attacked by a band of outlaws seven miles south of Baton Rouge on a plantation. He shot five of his assailants, and two of them were killed outright. He also shot and killed Pedro Capdiville, a notorious desperado who had terrorized New Orleans for several years.

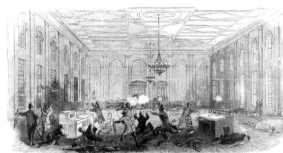

"The Riot in New Orleans," by Theodore R. Davis, 1866.

After the war, Whitley lived a short time in Boston, where he had relatives, and then moved to

Washington, D.C., bearing a letter of recommendation from General Butler. He was given a job in the Internal Revenue Bureau by Commissioner Rawlins and was directed to duty at Atchison, Kansas, where he was embroiled with investigating whiskey thieves. In 1869 he was sent to Virginia to raid moonshiners. He raided 36 stills and had many dramatic encounters with the illicit whiskey-makers in the mountains of Virginia.

Whitley was an Assistant Tax Assessor in the Internal Revenue Bureau when he was made chief of the Secret Service on May 13, 1869, following the resignation of Chief William P. Wood on May 5. His selection to become chief had come about after a casual conversation between Secretary of the Treasury George S. Boutwell and General Benjamin Butler. Secretary Boutwell had mentioned to General Butler that he was looking for a suitable person to head up the Secret Service. Butler recommended Hiram Whitley, saying he was good at scouting, good as a sniper, and one of the best cavalry leaders he had ever seen. Whitley had been promoted to lieutenant colonel but never mustered in at that rank. He had also come out of the war with a decoration for distinguished service, something that counted for much in postwar Washington, D.C.

Secretary George S. Boutwell.

As a civilian, he had remarkable success as a detective for the Internal Revenue Bureau chasing moonshiners. Whitley was still in his 40s, stood 6-feet-10-inches tall, and had a black mustache, neatly trimmed beard, and penetrating blue eyes. He was enthusiastic about changing jobs, and when he handed in his resignation, he told his boss "I'd rather be chief of the Secret Service than president of the United States."

Whitley wasted no time in reorganizing the agency, firing some of the worst employees and hiring better people to replace them. He also initiated the practice of keeping a complete record on every counterfeiter arrested, logging the information about their names, aliases, age, physical description, time and place of arrest, legitimate occupation (if any), method of operation, criminal specialty (engraver, plate-printer, shover, capitalist, etc.), and the disposition of the case in the courts. This data, sometimes with attached photographs of the arrested person, was placed on numbered pages in a multi-volume album called *Description and Information of Criminals*. William P. Wood had required each agent (then called "operatives") to send a written report to the Washington headquarters each week that listed the investigations' work in a summarized fashion. Whitley now required each operative to send a detailed weekly report that showed everything the operative did during each day of the week. These notes were filed as *Daily Reports of Agents*. Both sets of records were originally intended for confidential use by the chief and assistant chief. They read the daily reports, set priorities and made recommendations to the operatives in the field, approved of special requests for additional funding, and sometimes, based on what they had read in the reports, went personally to assist the operatives in a raid.

Another of the innovations that Whitley oversaw was the use of official badges and printed credentials. Previously, operatives had nothing by which to identify themselves to the public and to other law-enforcement officials. If an agent wanted a gun, he had to buy it with his own money. The Secret Service supplied handcuffs to its operatives but nothing else. Under Whitley, an official design for a badge was approved on August 5, 1873. It consisted of a five-pointed silver star with intricate machine engraving on each point and the engraved words "U.S. Secret Service" in the middle. Beginning March 17, 1875, Whitley saw to it that each agent received a printed credential called a "commission," prepared by the Bureau of Engraving and Printing. An operative had to pay $25 for his badge, but the cost was refunded on his retirement.

Whitley decided to move his headquarters to New York City in 1870, as that was the leading center for counterfeiters. The assistant chief and a small number of clerks remained in Washington, but the records were moved to new offices at 63 Bleecker Street in the Manhattan Borough of New York City. While he was in New York, Whitley's name was mentioned as a participant in a complex scheme to end the influence and corruption of the Board of Public Works in its *de facto* control over the city government of Washington, D.C. There was no proof that Whitley had anything to do with the political intrigues, but reporters working for sensational newspapers persistently used his name in an unfavorable context. As a result, the secretary of the Treasury thought its best that Whitley resign, which he did on September 2, 1874. Simon B. Benson, the agent in charge of the Pennsylvania District, took over as acting chief and served until October 2, when Elmer Washburn became the third chief of the Secret Service. In 1877 Hiram Whitley moved to Emporia, Kansas, and bought a farm of about 400 acres. Three years later, he moved into Emporia and became a prominent businessman. In 1880 he built the Hotel Whitley, and in the following year, the Opera House, which subsequently burned.

A Secret Service agent checking confiscated, counterfeit currency.

Whitley's legacy is that he brought much-needed change to the administration of the agency, more than doubled the number of agents to 32 men, insisted that his operatives focus more on capturing the dealers, gang leaders, capitalists, and engravers than the street-level shovers, and ordered his agents to use the threat of imprisonment to get leads from criminals rather than pay "reward" money. Congress had appropriated

$100,000 to the Treasury Department to fight counterfeiting, and Solicitor Jordan had made the money available to the first chief. Colonel Wood spent most of that money to buy leads, but much of it was wasted on false information. Every chief, including Whitley, was concerned about the agency's public image and made an effort to present their agents' work in the best possible way, sometimes stretching the truth. Consider this report that appeared in the *New York Times*:

> Col. Whitley, Chief of the Secret Service Division of the United States Treasury Department, has issued a circular explaining the system adopted by him in the detection of criminals. After showing that detectives are warranted in using minor offenders to convict other persons guilty of higher crimes, especially counterfeiting, where so much skill is required in procuring evidence. Col. Whitley recounts the obstacles in the way of convicting wealthy and apparently respectable counterfeiters. The result of Col. Whitley's mode of detection since he has been Chief of the Secret Service Officers include the capture of over ninety sets of counterfeit plates of various denominations, and upward of a million representative dollars of illegal issue, together with the apprehension of more than 1,200 offenders, many of whom are now serving out terms of imprisonment. At the present time, there are no counterfeit plates of Government money in existence in this country, and the circulation of bad money has never been known to be so scarce.[17]

In reality, Whitley's operatives affected 222 arrests for counterfeiting during his 4-year and 4-month term, as compared to the 123 arrests for counterfeiting made by William P. Wood's agents during his term of slightly over 6 years.[18] Hiram Whitley died in Emporia, Kansas, on October 16, 1919.

Elmer Washburn

Elmer Washburn.

Elmer Washburn was chief of the Secret Service for only a short time, from October 2, 1874, until October 24, 1876, a total of just 24 months. Details about his life are sketchy. He was born in Plymouth County, Massachusetts, in 1834 and may have received formal training as a mechanical engineer. Sometime after the Civil War he was made warden of Joliet Prison in Illinois, and following that, Chicago mayor Joseph Medill made him the chief of police in 1872. Washburn had a difficult time with the Chicago Police Department and was not liked by his captains. He became unpopular with the citizens of Chicago when he attempted to enforce the Sunday closing laws in 1873. Mayor Medill supported Washburn's actions, but the uproar that followed cost both men their jobs. Washburn then worked for the Illinois Central Railroad as a division chief prior to his selection to be chief of the Secret Service. The Solicitor of the Treasury appointed an investigative committee to study the Secret Service Division soon after Washburn took office. The committee made a number of recommendations that Washburn followed, including moving the headquarters of the agency back to Washington, D.C. He also rewarded the loyalty and effectiveness of his agents by increasing their salaries. He chose not to act on the recommendation that he reduce the number of employees (32) in his agency. In another innovation, his agency was apparently the first in Washington to buy and use a Sholes & Glidden Remington typewriter, the first practical-typing machine.[19] Washburn resigned his position in October 1876 and became the senior partner with his son in an engineering-consulting firm in New York.

For the most part, Washburn's short career in the Secret Service was uneventful. But in October

1875 Washburn received a report from agent Patrick D. Tyrrell that he had identified Ben Boyd and Nelson Driggs hiding in Illinois. Driggs was staying with the Stadtfeld family in Centralia, Illinois, and Ben Boyd and his wife were staying in Fulton, Illinois. Tyrrell's report rang alarms in Washington and brought out Chief Washburn, Assistant Chief Brooks, agents E.G. Rathbone and John McDonald, and an operative named Hurr, who rushed to Lyons, Iowa, to meet with Tyrrell to plan a raid on the Illinois hide-outs. Those raids are described in chapter 10 under the sketches of Ben Boyd and Nelson Driggs. The capture of those two counterfeiters was widely hailed in the newspapers and did nothing but enhance the reputation of Chief Washburn.

The Secret Service never grew to any appreciable size in the 19th century. David Johnson said that "between 1875 and 1910, the division never employed more than 47 operatives and Chief Operatives at one time. In fact, the average for that period was only 25, and for sixteen years, 1878–1898, the number of employees classified as operatives remained well below that average."[20] The pay scale ranged from $4 to $7 a day, roughly equivalent to the range of salaries in metropolitan police departments and a little less than the private bank-note companies paid their beginning engravers. Most counterfeiters were not violent people, and only a handful of Secret Service agents ever got shot. No agents were killed until 1908.

James J. Brooks

James Brooks was born in Birmingham, England, in 1824 and immigrated to the United States in 1848. In 1851 he lead a group of pioneers west to Reed's Landing in Minnesota Territory, going by rail, covered wagons, boats, and finally on foot. In 1854

James J. Brooks.

he returned East with his wife and two children, went back to England for a visit, and then returned to the United States the next year and settled in Newark, New Jersey. He did some newspaper reporting in Newark and then moved to Washington, D.C., where he became a reporter for *The Chronicle*, specializing in reporting crime cases. There, by 1859, he had earned a solid reputation for investigating and exposing corruption, fraud, and other crimes against the public. During the Civil War, he was a cavalry captain, not unlike Colonel Wood and Major Whitley. After the war, he used his political connections to get a job with the Internal Revenue Bureau, hunting the perpetrators of revenue fraud and catching tax dodgers.

While working for the Internal Revenue Bureau, Brooks was set upon by a gang of eight hoodlums and beaten severely, requiring a stay of several weeks in the hospital to recuperate. The underworld had put a price on his head, offering $500 to anyone who killed him. Two thugs from a whiskey ring in Philadelphia followed Brooks to a book store in September 1869, sneaked up behind him, and shot him four times. One of the bullets cut away a portion of one lung and lodged in his chest, where it remained for the rest of his life. The two men were caught and sent to prison, and Brooks became a hero to the public and was frequently praised in the press for his integrity and bravery. He stayed with the Internal Revenue Bureau until 1874, when he accepted a position as special assistant chief of the Secret Service under Chief Elmer Washburn.

In early 1875 Chief Washburn assigned Brooks to take over the New York District office, and in the summer of that year he sent him to Chicago to investigate the Whiskey Ring scandal. Simply put, the Whiskey Ring was a group of distillers and public officials who defrauded the government of liquor taxes. After the Civil War, liquor taxes were raised very high, in some cases as much as eight times the basic price of the liquor. Large distillers, beginning in St. Louis in 1871 but spreading quickly to Milwaukee, Cincinnati, New Orleans, and Chicago, bribed government officials in order to keep the tax proceeds. U.S. Secretary of the Treasury Benjamin H. Bristow, working without the knowledge of President Ulysses S. Grant or the attorney general and using a few highly skilled Secret Service investigators to identify the principal conspirators, struck suddenly on May 10, 1875, in a series of raids, arresting the tax dodgers and seizing their distilleries. Over the next few months, more than $3,000,000 in taxes were received, and of 238 persons indicted, 110 were convicted in federal courts. President Grant's personal secretary, General Orville Babcock, was one of the public officials indicted. He escaped conviction only because of a presidential pardon.[21] Although President Grant was not directly involved in the scandal, his pardon of Babcock, against almost everyone's advice, was viewed by Secretary Bristow and Attorney General Perrepont as a demonstration of Republican corruption. Many people saw the scandal as a plot to finance the Republican party by fraud.[22] The use of Secret Service operatives to investigate the conspiracy was one of the few times the agency had been given a special assignment outside its official mission.

The home of General Orville Babcock, Washington, D.C.

Brooks took over as chief of the Secret Service when Chief Washburn resigned in October 1876.

One of his first administrative decisions was to issue a formal manual of instructions for all operatives. Rutherford B. Hayes was elected president in 1876, and John Sherman became secretary of the Treasury on March 10, 1877. Sherman heard rumors that the Secret Service was being used for "improper purposes" and decided the only way to quell the rumors was to appoint an impartial committee to investigate the division as thoroughly as possible and report its findings. The committee left no stone unturned, looking into every aspect of the agency's work. When finished, the committee found nothing amiss and had only praise for the agency's work.

Chief Brooks stayed at the helm through some of the worst times the Secret Service endured. When he submitted his resignation to the new secretary of the Treasury in 1885, it was refused. He agreed to stay on but then found that Congress was in a pinchpenny mood and would no longer support the agency as it had previously. The agency had been spending $11,500 a year for administrative work just before Brooks took over. Now Congress gave it only $3,500 for an even greater workload. His predecessors had assistant chiefs to help them, but Brooks got no assistants. To save money, he terminated the practice of giving agents paid vacation time each year. He now advised his operatives that "Hereafter, [a] leave of absence can only be given without pay." After fighting budgetary battles for several years, Brooks once again tried to resign on February 15, 1889, but Secretary William Windom made a personal plea to Brooks to stay the course, and he finally agreed to remain with the Secret Service as a "special agent," to carry out any special investigations that might be required. Secretary Windom accepted that arrangement, and Brooks stayed on until he resigned on February 16, 1893.

Brooks served as chief for 13 years and then as special agent for another 4 years. After he left government service, he became the general manager of Gilkinson's American Detective Bureau, with headquarters in Pittsburgh. At age 72, he died of a heart condition on October 11, 1895, at his home on Bluff Street in Pittsburgh. He had carried the bullet lodged in the pericardium of his heart for over 16 years, and perhaps that contributed to his death. He left behind a widow, three sons, and four daughters.[23] His brother, John P. Brooks, was chief of the Eastern District of the U.S. Secret Service for 16 years. Like James Brooks, John was also born in England. John died at his home in Newark, New Jersey, on October 23, 1893, just two years before the death of his brother.[24]

Many of the great counterfeiters had been convicted and sent to prison by the time that Brooks left the division. Peter McCartney, who was both an engraver and a capitalist, died in prison in 1896. Frederick Biebusch, a capitalist and dealer who was arrested many times but served very little time in prison, had grown old and wealthy enough to quit the game. Ben Boyd, one of the best engravers in the underground, was now in prison. Thomas Ballard, the "scientific counterfeiter," died in prison sometime prior to 1886. Nelson Driggs died at home in 1895. Counterfeiting wasn't over, but the Secret Service had grown to such a level in efficiency and power that the public now trusted in the national currency more than ever before.

John S. Bell

John S. Bell.

John S. Bell joined the Secret Service on June 22, 1885, and rose quickly through the ranks to become chief on February 16, 1889. Bell had been formerly the chief of police in Newark, New Jersey. He was a big man with a muscular build, a mustache, and a well-trimmed beard, looking very much like the entertainer Buffalo Bill Cody. He is said to have been a polished conversationalist with a congenial personality. Bell also ran into a stingy Congress that hindered his work by not funding the Secret Service adequately. He was persistent in complaining about the lack of funding, and this may

have bothered Secretary Windom. The secretary sent him a brief note on June 2, 1890, saying, "Sir: Your services as Chief of the Secret Service will not be required from and after this date."

Chief Clerk John Cowie became the acting chief of the Secret Service on June 3, 1890, and held that position for seven months. Secretary Windom tried to get James Brooks to come back into active service and take over as chief, but Brooks declined. Windom then looked at the personnel files of several seasoned agents already working for the Secret Service. He picked Andrew L. Drummond to become the next chief, and that proved to be a wise decision.

Andrew Lewis Drummond

A.L. Drummond.

A.L. Drummond was born in Lancaster, Pennsylvania, in 1844. When the Civil War broke out, he shipped as a 16-year-old seaman on a transport carrying supplies to Union forces in the South. After he solved a minor crime during the war, he volunteered to conduct other investigations for the Union and was quite successful. After the war, he decided to open a detective agency in New York City. He entered the Secret Service in 1871 and soon solved several major cases. Chief Brooks made him the agent in charge of the New York office, and he continued in that position for 20 years until he was made chief on January 2, 1891.

During his long service in the field, Drummond experienced firsthand the many legal problems that made it difficult for U.S. attorneys to win convictions in counterfeiting cases, and he set about changing the many loopholes in the laws. Chief Drummond's usual method was to write a letter to a congressman, pointing out the legal problems with a particular law and suggesting changes that could be made to correct the deficiency. Because he was so well known to congressmen and attorneys, as well as bankers and law-enforcement officers (and perhaps because he had the look of one's grandfather, complete with glasses and a "longhorn" mustache), Drummond was well respected and had great success in getting his proposals turned into law. Before he left the Secret Service, he managed to get 14 proposed amendments on the books, giving new protection to the national currency and putting new teeth into existing laws.

Chief Drummond was particularly effective in changing the way search warrants were obtained and used. In November 1883 Drummond began a campaign to get Congress to authorize the Secret Service to obtain search warrants from a judge or magistrate. Up to that time, much of the information about counterfeiting came from paid informants. Drummond reassured Congress that if the Secret Service had its own search authority, operatives could act on an informant's information without the need to buy counterfeit money from the alleged counterfeiter to present as evidence. The operatives could raid a location and seize evidence without involving U.S. marshals or local police. If no evidence was found, at least the Secret Service would be protected from civil lawsuits.[25] Chief Drummond had testified before grand juries in Brooklyn and Manhattan, arguing that the Secret Service needed its own search authority to act quickly on information from informants and to avoid the possibility that careless or dishonest law-enforcement officers would alert the alleged crooks before a raid. In 1890 the House Committee on the Judiciary held hearings on the Drummond proposal, and a year later Congress acted on the Committee's recommendation and authorized judges or U.S. commissioners to grant search warrants to the Secret Service.[26]

While Drummond was chief, the Secret Service was asked to investigate national banks for fraud and embezzlement. Drummond had insufficient funds to carry out the mission, but he assigned eight operatives to do this work and ran the investigations as long as possible. When the money finally gave out and the investigations were stopped, the newspapers demanded their resumption. A voluntary community-service group called "A Committee of Fifty for a New Philadelphia" presented a sizable loan to the government to finance the investigations. Secret Service operatives arrested several bank directors and cashiers for a variety of financial crimes.[27] Today, these investigations would be handled by the Federal Bureau of Investigation.

Drummond proved to be the most constructive and effective chief in the agency during the 19th century. His dedication and efficient administration were well known throughout the law-enforcement community, and he could have rested on those laurels for many more years in the Secret Service. Instead, he decided the burdens of that work would best be shouldered by younger men, and he resigned as chief on January 31, 1894, to return to his family's detective agency in New York. He published a volume of reminiscences in 1909 entitled *True Detective Stories.*[28]

William P. Hazen

Chief Drummond's replacement was William P. Hazen. He had joined the Secret Service in Cincinnati, Ohio, on May 26, 1893, and less than a year later, on February 1, 1894, he was summoned to Washington, D.C., and promoted to chief. His father had been a Cincinnati police officer before setting up the Hazen Detective Agency in that city. William had worked for the company and solved several cases before joining the Secret Service.

The first major counterfeiting case to come to Chief Hazen's attention

William P. Hazen.

was a dilly. A new counterfeit $100 Silver Certificate of the 1891 series made its appearance in 1898 in Philadelphia. Hazen sent out a circular to all the banks with the following warning: "This is the most dangerous counterfeit known to the Secret Service. Its existence is considered so grave a menace as to warrant a recall of all notes of this kind from circulation." Secretary of the Treasury Lyman Gage was alarmed by the superior quality of the counterfeits. It would be one thing to call in the entire issue of 260,000 notes but quite another thing if the counterfeiter turned to other denominations and counterfeited those. Secretary Gage told Chief Hazen to devote his full time to the investigation of this case, using as many men as needed, and arranged for a senior clerk in the Treasury Department to take over the chief's administrative duties.

At the same time, Gage told Hazen that he would appoint a committee to investigate a serious matter being reported in the press. That serious matter concerned the assignment of two or three agents to safeguard President Grover Cleveland and his family while they vacationed at Gray Gables, Massachusetts. At that time, the Secret Service was not authorized to safeguard government officials. Their only mission was to suppress counterfeiting. The investigation did not reveal who authorized Chief Hazen to send the agents to protect President Cleveland and later President William McKinley as well, leaving modern historians to suspect that Hazen acted independently.[29] Retribution was quick in coming, and on February 27, 1898, Hazen was demoted to the rank of operative, but he continued to work for the Secret Service until he resigned on June 12, 1901. To replace Chief Hazen, Secretary Gage chose John E. Wilkie.

John Elbert Wilkie

U.S. Secret Service
Chief John E. Wilkie.

John Wilkie followed in his father's footsteps and became the city editor of the Chicago *Tribune*. His father had been the editorial writer for the same paper until his death in 1892. The younger Wilkie came to the attention of Secretary Gage when Chief William Hazen was demoted. Gage had asked Under-Secretary Frank Vanderlip if he knew of anyone who could handle the job. Vanderlip had also worked at the *Tribune* before going into banking, and he recommended John Wilkie, whom he knew personally. After interviewing Wilkie, Secretary Gage, who was also from Chicago, offered him the position of chief, and Wilkie accepted. He was appointed first to be an operative, and on March 1, 1898, he was promoted to the position of chief. He was then 27 years old, becoming the youngest chief in the division's history.

"Assassination of President McKinley," circa 1905.

Chief Wilkie and his men solved the Taylor-Bredell counterfeiting case and shut down the Jacobs Cigar factory that had been used as the plant for making counterfeit $100 notes. Wilkie was also in charge of counter-espionage during the Spanish American war, and in his most famous case of that time, he exposed Ramon Carranza, a former attaché of the Spanish embassy, as the ringleader of an enemy espionage network. After the war, Wilkie continued to protect the president, without an official mandate, just as William Hazen had done before him. In September 1901, President William McKinley attended the Pan American Exposition in Buffalo, New York, and stood in a receiving line to shake hands with local dignitaries. Leon Czolgosz, a Polish-born American anarchist, stepped in front of the president and shot him twice with a .32-caliber revolver. The president later died from gangrene. It took five years for Congress to finally pass legislation that authorized the use of appropriated funds "for the protection of the person of the President of the United States."[30]

Another large counterfeiting affair that occurred on Chief Wilkie's watch, though he had nothing to do with the investigation, was the Roberts case in Louisville, Kentucky, in August 1909.[31] This time, a man named John C. Roberts and his brother, Marion Roberts, were involved with a man named William Koenig, a printer, to make counterfeit Mexican currency. Marion had tried to sell some of the money to a local broker, who informed the chief of police. Marion was shadowed by local detectives who then also found his brother. John had with him a large brass-bound trunk, filled from bottom to top with crisp new 100-peso Mexican bank notes. He was just about to leave for Mexico but had decided to wait for a few days more to take delivery of a numbering machine he had ordered. Like most counterfeiters, the Roberts brothers had trusted too many people with too much information.

John E. Wilkie was a controversial chief who was famous for his ability to manipulate the press. He served for 14 years, resigning in 1912. He then went back to Chicago and took a position as vice-president with the Chicago Railway Company.

⁓ ⋆ ⁓

The Secret Service is usually considered the premier law-enforcement agency of the country, but it has endured many travails through the years, from congressional underfunding to ethical lapses by its chiefs. Agents were usually chosen who had previous police or law-enforcement experience and knew the arcane language of the underworld. Still, most of their training was "on-the-job," and they learned to live by their wits. Formal-training courses only began in the 20th century. Most agents carried guns when searching for violent criminals or making raids on suspected counterfeit plants, but very few agents were ever wounded, and none were killed in the 19th century. Most agents were basically honest, and only a handful

were ever criminally involved in counterfeiting.[32] The agency has always been small but well respected. As the world has become more complex, the Secret Service has taken on additional duties, including the protection of the president and other high officials. The agency now belongs to the Department of Homeland Security and not the Treasury Department. The camera has replaced the counterfeiter's hand engraving, and security printing is now full of optical tricks and chemical snares.

By the end of the 19th century, the Secret Service could say that only $1 in every $100,000 was counterfeit. Compared to the statistics of 40 years earlier, that was a real success. In fact, the Secret Service was more effective at suppressing counterfeiting than all the inventions of mechanical engraving combined. The geometric lathe, although marvelous, was easily duplicated by clever counterfeiters, and with the advent of the camera and photoengraving, geometric-lathe work was no more effective a protection against counterfeiting than colored inks or security papers. At its lowest, pedestrian level, this is a never-ending story of the struggle of evil against good. First one triumphs, and then the other. But on the longer and less-focused scale of history, the Secret Service has proven the wisdom of Hugh McCulloch's ideas back in 1865.

Secret Service men.

Chapter 12

The Bureau

"Beaten Out on the Anvil of History"

The financial histories of the colonies have shown that war and money are often tied together, and this was as true in 1861 as it was in 1690. As talk of rebellion became popular in the South, the financial condition of the country declined steadily and even approached bankruptcy. Secretary of the Treasury Salmon P. Chase distrusted any kind of money except specie (hard money), and he hoped he could finance the war like Albert Gallatin had in the War of 1812, by borrowing money instead of taxing products. After Confederate troops fired on Fort Sumter, and everyone realized that war was inevitable, northern politicians began to think seriously about the urgent need for money to pay for wartime expenditures and to hold together the economy.

A portrait of Secretary of the Treasury Salmon P. Chase as seen on the $1 U.S Legal Tender issue of 1862. (Friedberg-16.)

Interest-Bearing Treasury Notes

At the onset of hostilities, Congress was well aware of several ways to raise money to finance a war. Previously, the United States had borrowed money from the people. During the Revolution, the Continental Congress started borrowing from citizens on June 3, 1775, by authorizing a loan for £6,000,000. During the War of 1812, a loan of $5,000,000 was authorized on June 30, 1812, for the purpose of purchasing supplies and paying debts. The Treasury issued Interest-Bearing Notes that the public could buy with specie and which paid 5.4% interest with maturity set at 1 year from the date of issue. They were not legal tender, but they were treated as such and had a limited circulation.

"Pain's Great War Spectacle, Mexican War, Siege of Vera Cruz." This colored lithograph was printed by Sackett & Wilhelms Lithographic Company, circa 1890.

This pattern had been repeated many times during the intervening years to pay for war debts arising from domestic conflicts with Indians as well as the Mexican War, and it should not be any great surprise that the practice was continued. By the time of the Civil War, however, the process had grown to be more sophisticated, and government financial experts had learned new ways to sell fiscal paper that paid a sufficiently attractive rate of interest which would bring in millions of dollars very quickly. To do this, the Act of March 2, 1861, authorized the printing of six-percent Interest-Bearing two-year Treasury Notes. Although these new Treasury Notes were technically the first notes issued by the federal government to have backs printed in green ink, they were not called "greenbacks" because the volume printed was so low (about $35 million) and the denominations were so high ($50, $100, $500, $1,000, and $5,000) that they could not circulate as "pocket money." Except for the investment community, they were little known to the public.[1] The interest on these notes was payable semi-annually on January 1 and July 1. Because the Act of March 2, 1861, did not specify how long the notes could bear interest, President Abraham Lincoln decided to issue them in two series—one payable at 60 days and the other at 2 years. The 2-year notes were printed from "old plates," and the 60-day notes from "new plates" which were overprinted in two transparent vertical columns of a reddish-orange tint. The notes measured 7-1/2 by 3-3/4 inches and were printed on the face in black ink. All the backs were printed in green ink. Only the 60-day notes were printed in the $5,000 denomination. The National Bank Note Company, which excelled at mechanical engraving, got the contract to engrave and print the notes. To do so the company made use of a newly patented security feature on the back of each note. This was a concentric series of overlapping petals done by a combination of geometric-lathe and cycloidal-engine work with occasional rosette work and waved lines. The geometric-lathe work was done in both white line and black line. This was the first time that such elaborate mechanical engraving had been combined with lettering. Each petal bore the inscription "United States Treasury Note" and the denomination of the note. The patent for this security feature, No. 30,488, dated October 23, 1860, was assigned to James MacDonough, one of the founders of the National Bank Note Company. The purpose of the patent was to prevent counterfeiters from raising the denomination of the note. One could simply compare the denomination on the front of the note with the security device on the back to be certain they were the same. There are no reports in official records that any of these notes were ever counterfeited, but that's expected—since the notes were intended to pay interest, when presented for payment, records would indicate if a note had been counterfeited, and it would not have been honored. Therefore, counterfeiters would have had a very difficult time selling such notes.

These Interest-Bearing Notes were the first of a class of such notes, and others were authorized by acts of Congress during the Civil War. These included the Compound Interest Treasury Notes and the refunding certificates. All these notes are extremely rare, and in some cases they are unique or known only from official Proof notes. This is understandable since the notes were investment opportunities for buyers and were not handled as ordinary cash; they were kept only until the interest became payable and were then turned in for their full value.

An Interest-Bearing "one year" Treasury Note. (F-196a.)

The government also issued Interest-Bearing Treasury Notes that were called "One Year" notes because they bore interest at five percent for a period of one year. They were authorized by Congress on March 3, 1863. They were issued in seven different denominations from $10 to $5,000 and paid their interest when presented for redemption. Finally, there were also three-year notes authorized by acts of Congress on July 17, 1861; June 30, 1864; and March 3, 1865. All three issues paid 7.3% interest for a period of 3 years, the highest rate of interest ever paid by the government for its notes. They were issued in five denominations from $50 to $5,000.

Demand Notes

The Interest-Bearing Treasury Notes authorized on March 2, 1861, raised some money but not enough, and Secretary Chase went before a special session of Congress on July 4, 1861, to suggest that the North must began taxing products to raise revenues and to float loans by issuing non–Interest-Bearing Notes which would circulate as money. This was a radical idea that produced a storm of controversy in the Congress and sent a flood of letters to the editors of the larger newspapers. Chase explained that the war had worried the business community to the point that far fewer imported products were being bought, resulting in a dramatic decline in the custom duties on such imports, which had provided the largest single source of federal income up to that time. Chase was afraid that Interest-Bearing Notes would fall in value over time, especially if the war went badly for the North, and the whole financial scheme might fall apart. Congress acted quickly, and acts were passed on July 17 and August 5, 1861, authorizing $60 million in Treasury Notes. These notes were "payable on demand" but paid the holder no interest. Also, they were redeemable in coin, and the notes could be reissued. Because they had the phrase "payable on demand," the public called them "Demand Notes."

By the end of 1861, many people in the North began to doubt that the Union could win the war. Their doubts owed chiefly to the Union's losses on the battlefield. The First Battle of Bull Run, which the Confederates called "Manassas," was fought just 25 miles outside of Washington, D.C., on July 21. It resulted in a surprising defeat for the Union Army. Even more serious was the Confederate victory at the Battle of Ball's Bluff on October 21, which killed 921 Union troops and only 149 Confederate soldiers. The battle also killed a popular U.S. senator, Colonel Edward Dickinson Baker, a close friend of President Lincoln. Then, in November 1861 a Union warship, the USS *San Jacinto*, intercepted a British mail packet, the *Trent*, on the high seas just off Cuba and arrested two Confederate diplomats who were on their way to Europe to ask for recognition of the Confederacy and material support for their fight against the Union. The diplomats, James Mason and John Slidell, were taken to Boston and placed in a military prison. The *Trent* Affair angered the British greatly, and for a while it seemed that England might enter the war on the side of the Confederacy. Although President Lincoln would eventually back down and allow the captives to go on with their mission, the incident, in spite of its almost universal approval in northern newspapers, did much to worry the public. They began to quietly hoard gold coins, creating a gold shortage not only in the banks but in the U.S. Treasury as well. This complicated the government's efforts to raise loans to pay for the rapidly increasing expense of getting together an army of 600,000 volunteers.

A Civil War Confederate bond issued in Houston, Texas, dated in 1863. The total loan was for $1,000, but the individual coupons below were each denominated $35.

Secretary Chase developed a plan to pay for the war by a variety of means, but principally by using loans. Lacking any real experience in practical banking, Chase turned to his friend Jay Cooke, a Philadelphia banker, to set up a program that would sell war bonds. Cooke knew that the middle classes were not only capable of buying war bonds but were motivated by patriotism to do just that. Although he expected that wealthy citizens would buy most of the bonds, he directed an efficient advertising campaign to attract middle-class people to this market, using newspaper ads and about 2,500 salesmen. His sales force contacted almost a quarter of all northern families and sold more than $3 billion in bonds.

It was obvious to Secretary Chase and to a number of his advisors in the Treasury Department that a national currency was needed to finance the war. Now that the public had hoarded gold coins, it would be very difficult to buy all the military supplies and services using the bewildering variety of state-bank notes that were discounted at various rates. Chase hated the state-bank notes and wanted to do away with them as quickly as possible. In their place, he wanted non–Interest-Bearing Notes, but the idea that the government could print its own paper money was very much in question. Legal scholars and congressmen of both parties pointed out that the Constitution never specifically authorized the government to issue paper money, and therefore such money would not be legal. President Lincoln didn't know whom to trust on this argument and finally turned to an old friend, Colonel Richard Taylor, for advice.

The colonel suggested that the non–Interest-Bearing Notes proposed by Secretary Chase should be made "legal tender" in order to have the full backing of the government and the obligation that the public accept them in payment of all public and private debts.[2] This was a bold plan and unpopular with Congress. Most congressmen belonged to a "hard money" tradition that ran back to the Federal Convention of 1787, and the idea of issuing paper money which was not backed by gold or any other reserve, and making it a legal tender, was anathema. When the legal tenders were first proposed, Owen Lovejoy, a Republican senator from Illinois and a friend of President Lincoln, stated "There is no precipice, there is no chasm, there is no possible yawning bottomless gulf before this nation so terrible, so appalling, so ruinous as this same bill."[3]

Secretary Chase was also against the concept of making the non–Interest-Bearing Notes that he wanted into "legal tenders," and he did what he could to discourage the Congress from adopting such a plan; but as push came to shove, he finally relented in his efforts and allowed the bill to pass on January 29, 1862. Chase next had to persuade President Lincoln to issue legal-tender paper currency, and this he did, however grudgingly. This must have been a difficult decision for Lincoln, but he approved the plan. A bill was sent to Congress which resulted in vigorous and sometimes acrimonious debate. At the height of these arguments, the Republican congressman from New York, Elbridge C. Spaulding, a member of the House Ways and Means Committee, proposed a solution that was finally accepted— a national currency, payable on demand by the U.S. Treasury, but not backed by gold or silver, and legal tender for all debts, public and private, except duties on imports and interest on the public debt. This was fiat money, to be sure, and of questionable constitutionality, but Attorney General Edward Bates upheld its legality, and it took less than two weeks for Congress to adopt the Spaulding bill. Contracts were signed with two New York bank-note companies—the American Bank Note Company would engrave the printing plates for the $5 and $10 notes, and the National Bank Note Company would engrave the plates for the $20 notes. In the end the National Bank Note Company was too busy to take on the additional work of printing these notes, or had too few employees to do the job, and so the American Bank Note Company printed all the notes—initially authorized at $50 million when the contract was signed. Another $10 million was authorized on February 12, 1862. The $5 bills were finally contracted on August 5, 1861, making a total of $60 million.

The $5 notes had a "Statue of Freedom" on the left, which Gene Hessler attributes to the burin of Owen G. Hanks. The $10 note had a portrait of President Abraham Lincoln at left, which Fred Reed identifies as the work of Charles Burt. The engravers of the $20 notes are unknown. The backs of these notes all have a large field of very small denomination counters, repeated by a pantograph, as well as lettering in white-line engraving, but no geometrical lathe work. The notes were printed four to a sheet at the American Bank Note Company in New York and then sent under guard by the Adams Express Company to the Treasury Building in Washington, D.C. When received, the sheets were counted and signed by the proper officers—the treasurer and the register of the Treasury—and then trimmed and separated by ladies wielding sharp scissors. This simple trimming operation may be regarded as the first step taken by the Treasury to take over the work of the private bank-note companies and eventually to perform the majority of the operations of making money under one roof.

The "Statue of Freedom" vignette found on the face of a $20 U.S. note, March 3, 1863. The back bears green printing. (F-126b.)

Legal Tender Notes

The Demand Notes were replaced in 1862 by a new series called "United States Notes," also known as the "Legal Tender Notes" because each note was imprinted with the words "This Note is a Legal Tender." An issue of $150 million was authorized by the Legal Tender Act of February 25, 1862.[4] The notes were printed with ornately engraved backs in green ink, so they were also called "greenbacks." The total issue was eventually printed in denominations of $1, $2, $5, $10, $20, $50, $100, $500, $1,000, $5,000, and $10,000. According to Robert Friedberg's *Paper*

Money of the United States, there were five issues of these notes:

> The first-issue notes were dated March 10, 1862, and consisted of denominations from $5 to $1,000.

> The second-issue notes were dated August 1, 1862, and consisted of the denominations $1 and $2 only.

> The third-issue notes were dated March 10, 1863, and were issued in all denominations from $5 to $1,000.

> The fourth-issue notes were printed under the authority of the Congressional Act of March 3, 1863. These notes were issued in denominations from $1 to $10,000 and included the series of 1869, 1874, 1878, 1880, 1907, 1917, and 1923. Confusing the picture a bit, the notes of 1869 are titled "Treasury Notes," while all of the later issues are titled "United States Notes."

> The fifth-issue notes consisted only of the $10 denomination of the series of 1901.

One can see that the various issue periods, denominations, and signatures provide a rich variety of notes for collectors. The Treasury seal and the serial numbers were printed in red. Both the National Bank Note Company and the American Bank Note Company engraved and printed these notes until the Bureau of Engraving and Printing was established and took over the operations.

The Legal Tender Act of 1862 was controversial to say the least. Challenges to the constitutionality of the act lead to several cases heard before the Supreme Court, beginning with *Hepburn vs. Griswold* in 1870.[5] In that case, the court, headed by Chief Justice Salmon P. Chase, held that paper money violated the fifth amendment of the Constitution. (This was the same Salmon Chase that had a role in writing the Legal Tender Act when he was the secretary of the Treasury in the first place.) On the same day that *Hepburn vs. Griswold* was decided, President Ulysses S. Grant nominated two new justices to the Supreme Court. These nominees had been vetted and were known to support the idea that paper money could be a legal tender. The two new justices voted to reverse the *Hepburn* decision in *Knox vs. Lee* and *Parker vs.*

President Ulysses S. Grant.

Davis in 1871. The constitutionality of the Legal Tender Act was even more broadly upheld in *Julliard vs. Greenman* in 1884. Together, these cases are known collectively as the "Legal Tender Cases," and since they established and defined the constitutionality of our paper money, they are well-worth reading.

Compound Interest Treasury Notes

Compound Interest Treasury Notes were a special type of Legal Tender Notes. They paid interest at a rate of six percent compounded twice a year for a period of three years. They were authorized by acts of Congress on March 3, 1863, and June 30, 1864, as another attempt by the government to finance the war. They were issued in six denominations ranging from $10 to $1,000 and were legal tender at their face value. Each note was overprinted in large gold letters at the center of the face of the note, reading "Compound Interest Treasury Note." The $50 and $100 denominations were extensively counterfeited, especially by the engraver Charles H. Smith, a counterfeiter who had once worked for the National Bank Note Company (see the essay on Charles H. Smith in chapter 10).

Spencer M. Clark

The person placed in charge of the various small operations in the Currency Bureau of the Treasury was Spencer M. Clark, then 51 years old and previously the Acting Engineer in Charge of the Bureau of Construction at the Treasury and also the chief clerk of that bureau. Secretary Chase had given him the job of overseeing these new operations, but no definite plans had been made about the future of the office. It was wartime, and many treasury projects were managed on a day-to-day basis. It soon became apparent, however, that more people would be needed. One of the provisions of the Legal Tender Act required that each note should be signed by two officers: "the First or Second Comptroller, or the Register of the Treasury, and countersigned by such other officer or officers of the Treasury as the secretary of the Treasury may designate" (12 Stat. 313). Since it would be impossible for two officers to sign millions of notes and still have time for their other duties, a group of 70 clerks were hired at a salary of $1,200 a year to do nothing but sign notes with a special ink. Clark thought this solution was simply too costly and suggested to Secretary Chase that the notes could be imprinted with the facsimile signatures of the Treasury officers and thereby do away with the clerks. The secretary naturally agreed to this cost-saving measure.[6]

Spencer M. Clark on a five-cent note. (F-1239.)

Clark also proposed that "an additional evidence of lawful issue might be made with a copy of the Treasury Seal that could be printed in the Treasury Building on each note, bond or coupon issued."[7] This resulted in the secretary's approval of the scheme and an application to Congress for the necessary authority to carry it into execution. This authority was given by an act approved February 25, 1862 (12 Stat. 346). Clark said:

> He [Chase] then orally directed me to procure the necessary machinery to seal the notes, and to design a suitable copy of the seal. I complied with this order by procuring presses specially made for the purpose, on approved models, and by designing the copy of the seal now in use. This design has for its interior a facsimile of the seal adopted by the Treasury Department for its documents on a ground of geometric lathe-work, the exterior being composed of thirty-four points similarly executed. These points were designed to be typical of the thirty-four States, and to simulate the appearance of seals ordinarily affixed to public documents. It was difficult of execution and believed to be a sufficient guard against counterfeiting.[8]

Clark also reformed the trimming division and overcame the natural resistance of the ladies to change their job. Originally, the notes were separated and trimmed by a force of about 75 ladies who were paid $50 a month. Clark suggested to Secretary Chase that the work was tedious and expensive and could be done by machinery at a great savings. Chase gave him permission to build two machines and to oversee their trial operation. One machine was made for trimming the four-subject sheet of notes and the other for separating and trimming the individual notes. A small steam engine and boiler were set up in a southwest room of the south wing of the basement, and the countershafts and pulleys transferred power to the machines. The women did not want to lose their jobs and protested the use of the new devices, but Clark's calm demeanor and reputation for honest talk overcame their fears. He began his trials with four ladies and one male assistant on August 29, 1862, and this date is usually taken as the official beginning of the bureau. Clark could hardly restrain his enthusiasm in his report on these trials in January 1863:

> We commenced work on twelve thousand impressions per day, and in my original programme for the work I stated that the machines, when the operators became expert, would do thirty thousand impressions in ten hours work. So expert have the present operators become, that they now do thirty-six thousand impressions in eight hours' work. I stated in the original programme that the pay-roll for thirty thousand impressions would not exceed $1,700 per month. It has not yet in any month amounted to $1,000. The present cost of trimming and separating by machinery is forty-eight cents per thousand sheets. The cost reported from the Loan Branch, by the old method, was $2.40 per thousand. . . . The operators now work "by the piece," as it is technically termed. . . . They earn from $1.20 to $1.80 per day, depending upon their skill and industry.[9]

While Clark was busy setting up a more-efficient trimming division in the basement of the Treasury, Secretary Chase was wondering if the government could save money by having the various notes and other securities printed at the same place. It would be an enormous task to hire and organize the hundreds of people needed, but Chase had been watching Clark and liked the way he found solutions to similar problems. Clark does not mention any specific discussions about the New York bank-note companies in his reports, but he does say that Chase asked him to start thinking about other ways in which he could save the government money. When his attention turned to the cost of producing bank notes, he was shown the contracts for the first time, and after a quick study, he told the secretary that the government was paying "a rate vastly disproportionate to the services rendered."

Chase knew the recent history of the New York bank-note companies—how they had formed a coalition of all the companies of any repute and came quickly to control virtually all the talent, capital, and experience in the field.

The government's contracts had been a windfall, especially for the American Bank Note Company. It was originally formed with a cash capital of $5,000, according to the certificate of incorporation filed with the state of New York, and then created a nominal capital of $1,250,000, represented by shares which it distributed in influential quarters, but which, up to the time of the government contracts, had not reached a par value in the share market. After the company got the contract to engrave and print the government's money, it divided among its shareholders 30% per annum on its nominal capital of $1,250,000. In Chase's experience, the American and National Bank Note companies acted as one entity and took full advantage of the government's precarious condition in a time of war. He asked Clark to think seriously about the possibility of setting up a bureau that could duplicate the work of the private bank-note companies at a savings to the government and got Congress to authorize such a bureau in the second section of the act approved July 11, 1862 (Stat. 12 532).[10] Clark was probably ten steps ahead of the secretary on this Herculean project, but like the respectful employee he proved to be, he went about his planning and waited for the secretary to invent the idea.

Various names were given to the offices at the Treasury Building in which the notes coming in from New York were trimmed, separated, and sealed. None of these names were formalized by law, but since most of the employees thought the work was connected with the secretary's office, terms like "the small note department" and "small note bureau" were commonly used. Clark had stationery printed with the name "National Note Bureau" and used the letterheads in late 1862. By 1863 the term "National Currency Bureau—First Division" was well established, and in a report of 1864, Clark wrote: "In my judgment, this Division, which now only exists *ex necessitate rei*, should be organized by law as a distinct and separate Bureau, to be entitled The Engraving and Printing Bureau of the Treasury Department." The agency's present name, the "Bureau of Engraving and Printing," was apparently first used on July 31, 1868, in official correspondence with a company in New York. When a congressional committee began its investigation of the printing of government securities in November 1868, some of the witnesses identified themselves as employees of the "Bureau of Engraving and Printing." The bureau's official history concedes that there was never a specific enabling act that established the bureau or gave the agency its present name, yet there are so many references to the bureau in congressional acts and other government documents that its legitimacy has never been seriously questioned.

During this period, Secretary Chase conceived the idea of a national-banking system, and he set about defining the basic principles and working out the details. He convinced Congress of the necessity of such a system and won their support. One of his ideas was to have a uniform, permanent, national currency, and he discussed this idea with Spencer Clark. Clark was delighted with the idea and began to think about designing and printing the notes within the Treasury. Up to this point, Clark had a remarkable record of success on every project he had been assigned.

It seems highly likely that Clark was influenced by the ideas of Waterman Lily Ormsby. Following Ormsby's thinking, Clark decided that our national currency should depict "national historic pictures of the full size of the note."[11] Clark suggested specific artwork for the different denominations and gave carefully reasoned arguments for his designs in a letter he wrote to Secretary Chase on March 28, 1863. First, he suggested each note be engraved in "the highest style of the art," by a number of specialists to discourage any counterfeiter, even those who were professional engravers, from attempting to imitate the work. He also wanted anti-photographic elements, inseparable from the paper, to be used in the designs, such as inks that could not be reproduced photographically. He submitted a $2 note depicting Weir's painting of the "Embarkation of the Pilgrims" as a sample note. He explained that raising the denomination of a note was even more dangerous than counterfeits, but "if a two-dollar bill is always the picture of the 'Embarkation of the Pilgrims' and a ten-dollar bill is always the picture of 'Washington Crossing the Delaware,' the public, even those who cannot read as well as those who do not understand our language, or who cannot distinguish the numerals, will soon educate themselves to these facts in handling the money, so that they could never be deceived into taking one denomination for another."[12]

The "Washington Crossing the Delaware" vignette as seen on a $50 National Bank Note of the Kentucky National Bank of Louisville. The back bears "The Embarkation of the Pilgrims." (F-444.)

Clark also thought his national-history notes would help to teach the masses the prominent periods and central events of America's history. As an additional safeguard against photographic counterfeits, he wanted to print the denomination, date of issue, Treasury seal, and the coat of arms of the state where the bank was located in gold characters, which would be attached to the paper before the note was printed. Both Secretary Chase and Spencer Clark were eager to begin this work and seemed to have all their ducks in a line. They had the authority to design new notes and produce them at the Treasury, as granted by the second section of the Act of July 11, 1862, but there were several important people who thought the national currency should not be printed at the Treasury. Hugh McCulloch, the Comptroller of the Currency, was the principal opponent. The

contract for Legal Tender Notes (second issue) was put out on open bid and won by the American Bank Note Company. The American Bank Note Company used the portrait of Salmon P. Chase in place of the "Landing of Columbus" and used the portrait of Alexander Hamilton in place of "Embarkation of the Pilgrims." These were the first $1 and $2 notes placed into circulation.

Chase was ultimately successful, and the National Banking Act was approved on February 25, 1863 (Chapter 58, 12 Stat. 665). It established a system of national charters for banks and encouraged the development of a national currency that was based on the holdings of treasury securities by each bank. It also established the Office of the Comptroller of the Currency to organize and supervise the new banking system through regulations and examinations. The Act, however, was defective, and President Abraham Lincoln signed a revision on June 3, 1864, officially called the National Currency Act but later called the National Bank Act, subtitled "An Act to provide a National Currency, secured by a Pledge of United States Bonds, and to provide for the Circulation and Redemption thereof." Like all legislation, today this is still a work in progress and is revised from time to time as devious minds find new ways to manipulate its regulations to their advantage.

Fractional Currency

The Civil War did much to change how Americans thought about their money. Almost overnight we went from a nation using specie (gold and silver coins) as the foundation of our monetary system to a fiat money in the form of a paper currency that was based solely on the faith of the people in their government. Problems soon followed. With people hoarding so much hard money, banks were forced to suspend payment in specie, and this created a problem for merchants and businesses. Merchants resorted to the use of anything that could pass for money—base metal tokens, tickets, foreign coins, promissory notes, stamps, etc. Francis E. Spinner, then treasurer of the United States, is credited with the idea of using postage stamps as money. According to a story printed in the *Washington Star* in December 1879, General Spinner got involved when he bought some apples one day and got apples in change. He sent an aide to the post office to buy some small-denomination stamps and pasted different combinations of the stamps to small rectangular pieces of blank paper. He then passed them around his department to see what his employees thought of the idea of using them in lieu of real coins. Finding that his experimental "postal money" was universally approved, he took his idea to Congress, and they authorized the printing of currency of the same basic design in the Act of July 17, 1862.[13] The contract for this postal currency was given to the National Bank Note Company to print 5-cent, 10-cent, 25-cent, and 50-cent notes. Later, the American Bank Note Company was asked to print the backs of the notes for additional security. These notes bore facsimiles of the five-cent and ten-cent postage stamps then current. The postal currency was issued from August 21, 1862, until May 27, 1863. Similar notes issued later were authorized by an act of Congress dated March 3, 1863, and were called "Fractional Currency." It was proposed to issue $100,000 of the Fractional Currency each day, which meant the New York companies had to print 16,000 sheets of notes a day and ship them to Washington, D.C., to be counted, separated, and trimmed.

The expense of the postal currency was an enormous drain on the budget of the bureau, and Secretary Chase once again asked Clark if he would investigate the possibility of the government saving money by printing the notes in the Treasury. The Act of March 3, 1863, had already authorized the work, so only the financial analysis remained to be done. Clark reported that he would need 30 22-inch copper-plate presses, 10 18-inch presses, 4 Gordon presses for surface printing (similar to those used to print bonds), 5 new trimmers, and 10 separators. The total estimated start-up cost would be less than $20,000, a mere pittance compared to the money being paid to the New York note companies for approximately the same work.[14] Secretary Chase

approved the report, and Clark put together the equipment and plate printers and began the first note-printing operation in the bureau—the Fractional Currency—and issued the first notes on October 10, 1863.

A bronze oval on a 50-cent Fractional Currency note. Notice how the oval obscures the beautifully engraved harbor scene in the background. This was intended by Clark to be a security device, but the oval made little or no sense.

Just before the bureau began printing Fractional Currency, Clark experimented with a new process that placed a semi-transparent bronzed oval around the portrait in the center of the note. This bronzing process was technically a success, but on the five-cent note of 1863 it detracted from the wonderfully detailed harbor scene in the background that had been engraved by James Duthie. The purpose of the bronze oval was to defeat photographic counterfeits. There was no panchromatic film in those days, and the bronzed oval would appear as a solid black oval in any attempt to reproduce it photographically. Yet given the low value of these notes, photographic counterfeiting did not make economic sense. Clark liked his invention so much that he used it on some of the early bonds the bureau printed. Plate printers, however, hated the bronze oval and may have been influential in the decision to discontinue its use. It is found only on the second series of Fractional Currency. When it was decided to increase the issue of Fractional Currency, adding 10-cent, 15-cent, 25-cent and 50-cent notes, the Treasury Department decided the work could be done more cheaply by the private bank-note firms in New York, and contracts were given to the American Bank Note and National Bank

Note companies. Difficulties soon appeared as the government made increasing demands for these notes. For three years the plate printers at both companies had been paid the same scale of wages, and since these wages were among the highest of any paid to mechanical workmen, there had been no complaints. Although printers were paid by the piece, they typically made $40 or more for a standard week of 48 hours.

Strike!

The plates used to print the new Fractional Currency were two-inches wider but one-inch shorter and took more time and effort to print. Some of the plate printers at the National Bank Note Company began to complain that this change in plate size resulted in less pay. On July 26, 1869, three of the men at the National Bank Note Company signed a paper asking for an increase in pay of 10¢ additional for every 100 impressions made from the new plates. The directors of the company were incensed by this request and immediately fired the men. The management then warned all plate printers that the company would not tolerate any further complaints about wages. Two days later, 44 additional men out of 76 employed by the company walked away from their jobs, sympathizing with the men who had been fired.[15]

Word of this strike stirred up emotions among the plate printers at the American Bank Note Company, but this was immediately countered by a warning from management that no increase in wages would be granted, and anyone who was not satisfied could leave. These tactics stifled an agitation before it got started. At the National Bank Note Company, 29 of the strikers were allowed to come back to work, and for a time it seemed that this "labor action" would come to an end. The officials at the National Bank Note Company knew that they were in danger of losing their government contract if they continued to fail in meeting their daily quotas for Fractional Currency.[16] These same officials also knew that the strikers had financial support and would be able to stay the course, however long it might be. The

Plate Printers' Union at Washington, D.C., had sent the strikers a telegram on August 12 saying "Hold firm and the day is yours. We will send you $300 to-morrow and more when you want it." A communication in much the same form was received from the Plate Printers' Union in Philadelphia, pledging all the money the strikers might require, up to $1,000.[17] Many letters of support came in from Washington, Philadelphia, Chicago, Boston, and New York, and these were routinely read at the nightly meetings of the strikers, giving them moral support and a sense that their fight was more than just a local issue—that it sought a just and equitable wage for everyone in the industry. The officials at the National Bank Note Company finally gave in on August 27, 1869, but they didn't formally agree to a new contract until September 6, giving the strikers an increase of 5¢ on the backs and 10¢ on the faces of the new Fractional Currency.[18]

Fractional currency was printed in five different series, lasting to the final issue of February 15, 1876. Each series has some unique feature, and many of the notes have interesting stories behind their designs. The five-cent note of the third issue has a portrait of Spencer M. Clark at its center. This created considerable controversy in several newspapers of the day, especially the *New York Times*, and many people thought it was a good example of overweening and arrogant pride and an abuse of office. Most people, however, probably didn't even know who Spencer Clark was. When the controversy reached Congress, a law was passed (14 Stat. 25) that prohibited the use of a portrait of any living person on a security of the United States, and that law remains in effect today. At the time the law was passed, the bureau had finished engraving a new 15-cent note and was ready to print it. The note, however, showed the portraits of generals Ulysses S. Grant and William T. Sherman, both of whom were still alive, so the project was terminated and a 15-cent note was not issued until the fourth series, when a demure bust of Columbia replaced the generals. The third series of Fractional Currency did portray Francis E. Spinner, the treasurer of the United States, on the 50-cent note while he was still alive, and the 25-cent note of the same series depicted William P. Fessenden, the secretary of the Treasury, while he was still alive. The public accepted both notes without controversy.

Francis E. Spinner.

The Early Engravers

Spencer Clark had a talent for recognizing highly skilled engravers and convincing them to work at the National Currency Bureau. He kept a list of engravers who had excellent reputations and noted his preferences. He obviously wanted to hire only the best men but was hampered in this effort by the fact that the National Currency Bureau was a new (and some would say "experimental") organization, with no proven track record and considerable opposition from the established bank-note companies. He won over some of these men by going to see them at their homes in New York or elsewhere.

James Duthie must have been near the top of Clark's list. He had learned to engrave in his native England and joined the Treasury Department in 1862 at a salary of $1,600 a year to become its first portrait and pictorial engraver. Prior to the bureau, he was the junior member of Gavit and Duthie, general engravers in Albany, New York, and did many portraits and landscapes for the magazines. While working for the government, he engraved the detailed dock scene featured on all the denominations of the second series of Fractional Currency. He also engraved the essays for the "Landing of Columbus" and the "Embarkation of the Pilgrims" that were intended for the $1 and $2 bills of the second issue of the Legal Tender Notes but were never used on those notes. By late April 1864, Duthie was named Superintendent of the Artists Room in the bureau. He left the bureau about 1865 to go into business with a Mr. Idlitz, who

had conducted experiments in electrochemistry at the bureau.

Another engraver was John Francis Eugene Prud'homme. He was born on the island of St. Thomas in the West Indies on October 4, 1800, and was brought by his parents to New York City when he was eight years old.[19] About 1814 he was apprenticed to his brother-in-law, Thomas Gimbrede, to learn engraving. By the age of 21, he was engraving under his own name. He began as a portrait engraver working in stipple but soon expanded his range and became a prolific illustrator of books and magazines. He was made an Academician of the National Academy of Design in 1846 and was a curator there for several years. He became a bank-note engraver in 1852, working for one of the New York bank-note companies as a designer and engraver of decorative work. In 1869 he joined the Treasury Department in Washington, D.C., where he was a designer of ornamentation for notes and other securities. He remained with the bureau until he resigned from failing health in 1885, being then the oldest engraver in America. He died at his home in Georgetown, D.C., on June 27, 1892.[20]

Joseph Prosper Ourdan was born in New York City on February 16, 1828, the son of Joseph James Prosper Ourdan of Marseilles, France. He served an apprenticeship with Waterman L. Ormsby of New York City. Under his own name, he engraved some good portraits and made illustrations for the book trade. Later, with Rawson Packard, he produced portrait plates in mezzotint for the firm Packard and Ourdan. From 1861 to 1870 he made portraits for postage stamps at the National Bank Note Company, including the 1861 3-cent Washington, the 1862 2-cent Jackson, and the 1870 3-cent Washington, 6-cent Lincoln, 7-cent Stanton, 15-cent Webster, and 30-cent Hamilton. David M. Stauffer says he became interested in bank-note work early in his life and worked for the Continental Bank Note Company in New York as well as the American Bank Note Company's Philadelphia office before joining the bureau. At the bureau he engraved the head of Salmon P. Chase on the $1 note of the 1862 Legal Tender issue and the head of

Francis E. Spinner on the 50-cent fractional note of the third series. He is also credited with engraving a vignette modeled on a painting by Charles Schussle called "Columbus, Discovery of Land." This vignette appears in the upper-left corner of the $1 bills of the 1869 series of U.S. notes. He engraved the head of Alexander Hamilton on the $2 bill of the 1862 U.S. notes and the head of General Winfield Scott on the $500 bill of the Interest-Bearing Notes authorized by the Act of March 3, 1863. Stauffer, writing in 1907, says that Ourdan eventually became the chief of the Bureau of Engraving and Printing, but I find no evidence that he ever held such a position.

"Columbus, Discovery of Land" as seen on a $5 National Bank Note of the National Exchange Bank of Seneca Falls, New York. The back bears the vignette "Landing of Columbus." (F-397.)

Joseph Prosper Ourdan taught his father, Joseph James Prosper Ourdan, to engrave, and he too became an excellent line engraver. The father was employed by the bureau from 1865 until his death in Washington, D.C., on October 25, 1874. His son died in Washington on May 10, 1881. Vincent Le Comte Ourdan, the son of J.P. Ourdan, was born in Brooklyn, New York, in 1855. He learned to engrave with the Columbian Bank Note Company in Washington, D.C., from 1875 to 1878, and started working for the bureau in 1879. On April 7, 1880, he was elevated to "cleaner," grade 2–3, in the Engraving Division at $3 per day. He returned to the Columbian Bank

Note Company where he remained until the company went out of business.

Uzal C. Ryerson was hired by Spencer Clark in July 1863 as a transfer-press operator. He had previously been with the American Bank Note Company in New York and lived in Irvington, New Jersey. He was at the bureau only a short time, being discharged by Clark in February 1867 apparently because he "interfered with the other men's work." In testimony he gave before a congressional committee, he mentioned that when he was hired at the bureau, there was only one other man in his department, and that was Elisha Hobart.[21] Hobart was born in England and came to the United States about 1843, settling first in Albany, New York, and later moving to Boston, where he worked for Joseph Andrews. His work at the National Currency Bureau may have included the operation of the transfer press. He was killed by Confederate rifle fire while on a picnic with other Union soldiers in July 1864.

Heinrich (Henry) Gugler was another engraver hired by Clark. He was born in Germany in 1816 and came to America in 1853. He was a very good vignette and portrait engraver and found work in New York City with the bank-note companies. He joined the National Currency Bureau on January 15, 1863. He engraved the portrait of Abraham Lincoln used on the $20 bills of the Compound Interest Treasury Notes authorized by the Act of March 3, 1863, and two vignettes entitled "Victory" and "Mortar Firing" used on this same note. He also engraved the vignette entitled "The Pioneer" used on the $5 U.S. note issued in 1869 and the small-eagle vignette used on the $10 bills of that series. He left the bureau in 1866 to work privately on a life-sized portrait of Abraham Lincoln. The engraving took almost three years to complete and was the first life-sized steel-engraved portrait ever attempted.[22] It was used as the model for the four-cent stamp of 1890. Henry Gugler established a lithographic company in Milwaukee and died there in 1880.

Other engravers worked for the bureau on a commissioned basis. Most of them worked at home or out of their own offices. Charles Kennedy

Burt is a good example. In addition to a lot of work for the American Bank Note Company, mostly on South American bank notes, he also engraved a scene called "Concordia" after a piece done by the artist T.A. Liebler that was used on the face of the $1 National Bank Note of the first-charter period. He also engraved the "Landing of the Pilgrims" on the back of the same note. He engraved the Jalabert painting of Martha Washington that was used on the face of the $1 Silver Certificate of 1886. The same picture was used on the back of the $1 Silver Certificate of 1896. In 1867 he engraved the portrait of Thomas Jefferson after the painting by Gilbert Stuart which was used on the $2 U.S. note of 1869 and later the $2 Federal Reserve Note of 1918, the $2 U.S. note of 1928, and on subsequent issues. A portrait of Abraham Lincoln was engraved by Burt based on a photograph taken by Anthony Berger, a partner of Mathew Brady. It was used on a number of $5 notes. In fact, Burt did several portraits of Lincoln, including the ones used on the $10 Demand Notes of 1861, the $10 Legal Tender Notes of 1862 and 1863, the 50-cent Fractional Currency of 1869, the $100 Legal Tender Notes of 1869, the $500 Gold Certificates of 1870 to 1875, and the $500 Gold Certificates of 1882 and later issues.

The vignette called "The Pioneer" appears on the $5 U.S. note of 1869. This note is also known as the famous "Rainbow Note." (F-64.)

Burt's portrait of Salmon P. Chase appeared on the $10 Compound Interest Treasury Note of 1864. His portrait of Alexander Hamilton appeared on the $20 U.S. note of 1869. The $50 U.S. note of the 1874 series has two Burt engravings—a portrait of Benjamin Franklin after the painting by Duplessis and an allegorical "America" wearing a crown on which is printed "E Pluribus Unum." A small vignette entitled "Justice with Shield" appears on $50 Interest-Bearing Notes of 1864. Burt engraved a portrait of Silas Wright on the $50 Gold Certificate of 1862. His other subjects on U.S. currency include Thomas Benton, Brigadier General Joseph Mansfield, John Quincy Adams, Charles Sumner, General George Meade, E.D. Baker, Robert Fulton, and many small allegorical vignettes.

The Bureau Expands

The bureau began its operations in late August 1862 with one man and four women in a room in the attic of the west wing of the Treasury Building. Gradually it took over the work done by private bank-note companies. By 1877 there was no space left for expansion. The next year, Congress authorized the purchase of some land from William Corcoran, a prominent businessman in Washington, D.C., known now primarily as the founder of the Corcoran Art Gallery. The wise men at the bank-note companies in New York knew that if the Treasury was successful in getting congressional approval for the financing, the government would have an advantage over the private companies, and there would never be another chance to get the government work back. Naturally, they fought the appropriation bill in Congress. Senator Conkling was the chief opponent to the bill, and he argued against it every step of the way.[23] Eventually he lost, and the new building was completed in record time at a cost of $300,000. It was occupied by July 1, 1880. Although the building was 220-feet long and 135-feet wide and had a basement and three stories above ground, it was apparent almost from the beginning that more space would be needed. Congress set about trying to buy adjacent land, which it did in parcels, but one property owner held out for more money than the government was willing to pay. The hold-out lasted until 1891, when Congress decided to take legal action, condemned the property, went into federal court, and acquired the title by court decree, paying a little over $15,000 for the land.

The new building for the Bureau of Engraving and Printing (between 1908 and 1919).

In 1903 Congress appropriated $215,000 to buy additional land south of the new building. As the work force grew and the bureau expanded its operations, planning started for a new and larger structure. In May 1908 Congress approved $2,150,000 to buy land and erect a new building of the approximate dimensions of 300 by 500 feet. The building was to have a basement and four stories using fire-proof materials throughout. After the final plans had been drawn up, it was found that the building could not be constructed of brick with limestone trimmings, as originally planned, and still meet the established limit of cost. Also, the Committee on Public Buildings and Grounds said that such building materials would not be appropriate for a monumental building at the intended site of the secondary axis of the Mall (of Washington, D.C.). They thought granite would be a more desirable material.[24] Congress approved a new bill that allowed $250,000 for the purchase of the land and $1,900,000 for the construction of the building. The original design was for a building with 450,000 square feet of floor space, more than twice the space in the bureau's first building. The final plans, however, authorized a building in the Roman-Doric style with a steel superstructure comprising a basement, four stories, and the attic made of reinforced concrete faced with Indiana limestone and granite trim. Its length was 505

feet, and it had four wings that extended 296 feet, providing 442,000 square feet of floor space. The final cost was $2,882,000. The old building was turned over to the Treasury Department.

Working at the bureau was not always pleasant. In a letter written by Chief of the Bureau William Meredith to Secretary of the Treasury William Windom, Meredith pointed out that 210 plate printers and their assistants were crowded into a room on the third floor that allowed only 7 inches between the handles of the presses.[25] The stoves and tables used by the printers were also jammed into this space. The crowding frequently made it necessary for one printer to wait while his neighbor was pulling an impression or removing his plate to or from the stove. With 209 of these presses in daily operation, each requiring a printer and his female assistant (418 persons) besides helpers and other employees, the total occupancy was brought to about 450 people. This large number of people in close proximity to each other vitiated the air to a considerable extent, and with two gas jets burning at each of the presses, one can understand that the health conditions were not good. Since the room was immediately under the roof, which was made of iron and slate, it was extremely hot during the summer and very cold during the winter.

Hand-roller presses at the bureau in the 1890s. 169 presses were placed in this room, showing the crowding that was necessary.

The letter goes on to mention the adverse conditions in several divisions of the plant. Bank notes were dried in a sheet-iron enclosure located under the roof of the boiler house. This meant that the notes were dried too rapidly at too high a temperature, causing the paper to wrinkle at the edges. It would have been far better if the paper was dried at a low temperature for a longer period. The ink mills used to grind pigments for ink were located next to a coal pile, from which the wind blew grit into the ink while it was being ground, sometimes ruining the entire batch of ink. The dry colors used in making ink were stored in a sub-basement adjacent to the elevator, and the finely powdered colors, many of which were toxic, were carried up the elevator shaft to every floor of the building as a fine dust which was taken into the lungs of the employees. The dry colors were also injuring the fine machinery used in mechanical engraving by settling on the instruments as a form of grit.

There are memos in the archived files that show the management was concerned about the personal hygiene of the employees. This was a time when men typically wore the same shirt and trousers for a week without laundering them. The 1880 Rule Book laid out strict guidelines:

> Employees of the printing division will be requested to change working clothes once a week as far as practicable.
>
> The Superintendent of the plate branch is instructed to refuse a plate on Monday morning of each week to any printer who shall present himself in a shirt which bears evidence of having been worn at work during the previous week.

Women also wore their clothing for several days in a row before washing them. Rose water, lilac water, and other scented liquids were commonly used, but their effect soon disappeared, especially in the over-heated rooms at the bureau. Dressing rooms and lockers were provided to both men and women, and "water closets" (toilets) were located throughout the building, but the attendants in these rooms had a difficult job keeping down the unpleasant odors.

In a letter written by the chief of the bureau in 1887 and addressed to the commissioners of the District of Columbia, he complains that the streets outside the bureau were covered by clay that dropped from the wagons carrying it to the Washington Monument construction site. The clay was then ground by the wheels of the wagons and cars traveling through 14th Street and was blown into the bureau where it settled on fine machinery. Chief Graves writes that "This dust is particularly injurious to the fine transfer presses and the geometric lathe used in the engraving division."[26]

Even the new building constructed in 1914 did not solve all the problems. In spite of the fact that Director Ralph and the government architects had given a great deal of thought to the accommodations for the engraving personnel, making sure they had plenty of light and space, it was soon found that they were located too near the printing presses, and the vibration was a serious problem. In October 1925 the director was forced to move the engraving department with its 200 employees back to the old rooms it occupied in the original building, where it remained for 13 more years.[27]

How Bank Notes Were Made

Once the government had decided to issue a new note or series of notes, a model (drawing) was made by a designer who worked in the engraving division or was under contract to that department. The model was then reviewed by the superintendent of the Engraving Department, who had the authority to require changes. The model was sometimes sent out to the officials in various departments of the government to get their approval, but if that was not required for a particular note, it was sent directly to the secretary of the Treasury for his approval. As soon as everyone had signed off on the model, it was given to different engravers who specialized in various branches of the art—portrait vignettes, landscape or historical scenes, square lettering, script lettering, ornamental engraving, lathe work, etc. These engravers worked on different parts of the design, producing individual dies engraved to the right size.

The finished dies were then hardened by heating them in a solution of potassium or sodium cyanide and quenching their heat by quickly dipping them in oil or brine. Before cyanide came into general use, the practice was to place the dies in muffle furnaces with scraps of leather or pieces of bone or ivory and to heat everything at a high temperature. Cyanide has the advantage of being a richer source of carbon than organics like leather or bone. It also worked much faster than the furnace method. Unfortunately, it had the potential to kill a careless employee, and depending on how well the ventilation was working, it could have killed several people at once.

The process of hardening dies and plates by cyanide bath. Note the fume hoods—hydrogen cyanide gas is less dense than air, so it rises and goes up the fume hoods by fan-driven ventilation. The gas is extremely dangerous. The same gas was chosen later by Germans, under the name Zyklon B, to murder Jews in concentration camps.

When hardened, the die was placed on the bed of a transfer press, and a cylinder of soft steel, called a role, was rocked over the die under great pressure until the soft steel of the roll was forced into the engraved lines of the die, reproducing those lines perfectly in relief on the circumference of the roll. Several dies could be transferred to separate rolls. When the entire design of the bank note had been transferred, the soft-steel rolls were hardened by the same potassium-cyanide method that was used to harden dies. The hardened rolls with their design in relief were then transferred to a flat, soft-steel bank-note plate. It was extremely important that the operator of the transfer press, using a loupe or powerful magnifying glass, aligned the rolls precisely so the relief designs of different rolls did not overlap or appear mismatched. After the flat soft-steel plate was hardened, a relief plate was made from the original flat master plate, and then an intaglio plate was made from that. The original intaglio plate was not used for printing but stored in the vault for possible future use. The secondary intaglio plate was then cleaned, inspected, covered with a rust-preventing oil, and given to the Plate Vault Division where it was kept until needed by the Plate Printing Division. Since the bank-note plate now consisted of many individual engravings done by multiple highly trained and skilled craftsmen, it would be almost impossible for a solitary counterfeit engraver to possess all the same skills and be capable of engraving a similar plate. That was the theory that prevailed in the industry for many years, but that was before electroplating and photography became common tools.

Over the years, plate printing at the bureau has undergone a number of radical changes. From 1864 to 1869, some Fractional Currency was printed on hydrostatic presses on dry paper. From 1870 wet paper was used for virtually every job until a change to a dry-intaglio printing process was made in 1957. After 1870 paper was received from the manufacturer in sealed packages of 1,000 sheets each. A custodian looked at a job order and determined how many sheets of paper would be required. He then broke the seals on the appropriate number of packages, weighed the paper, and sent it to the wetting division. There, operatives counted the sheets and signed a tag placed within the package if the count was correct. In the early days, sheets were wetted by hand operations using wet tissues or cloths placed at regular intervals within small stacks and left for several hours. Then, the paper was sorted so that the dry sides were placed in contact with the wet cloths and again left for several hours. The damp paper was then stacked in piles of 100 sheets or in tall stacks and covered with a moist cloth to wait until the Plate Printing Division requested the paper.

The purpose of wetting the paper was to make it more pliable and easier to print. Although the hand-roller presses and the steam-driven power presses all operated by putting great pressure on the paper, moist paper was pressed down into the intaglio lines of the bank-note plate more easily than dry paper and therefore produced a better impression of the inked lines. In 1911 a machine was installed that automatically wetted paper by moving it through on a felt blanket under a spray of water. As the paper moved forward, one sheet at a time, it went through a set of heavy rubber rollers that were adjusted to press out excess water and control the amount of moisture left in the sheets. At the delivery end of the machine, the paper was removed and placed in packages of 100 sheets. The packages were taken to a stockroom, placed under moist cloths, weighted down by heavy iron plates, and allowed to stand for three or four days so the moisture got evenly distributed to every fiber in the sheets. An automatic sheet feeder was added to the machine several years later. By 1924 there were 28 automatic wetting machines in use, capable of wetting approximately 1 million sheets a day. It was found that during the winter, when the water temperature naturally fell, cold water would not permit moisture to penetrate the paper as readily as it should, so heaters were built into the systems to regulate water temperature to about 60° Fahrenheit.

As with most functions involving paper, there was an elaborate system of checks to make certain no one could take either blank or printed sheets without being detected. At the beginning of each day, the printer's assistant presented a draw slip to a clerk of the Wetting Division, giving the amount and class of paper required and the denomination of the notes to be printed. When she received the paper, she took it back to the press and counted it. If the correct number of sheets was verified, she informed the printer, who gave a receipt for it to the clerk of the Wetting Division. Clerks were the bookkeepers and had to account for every item under their charge and report any deficiencies.

A horse-drawn money wagon. The building of the Bureau of Engraving and Printing is behind the wagon.

Theft at the Bureau

From the very beginning, a few wise guys have figured out ways to steal money from the bureau, but the clerks and other watchmen have always found the evidence. One of the most famous of these episodes occurred on October 10, 1862, before the bureau was formed. At that time, the precursor agency was located in the main Treasury Building on Pennsylvania Avenue. The thief removed about $200,000 and hid the notes in a box with a hinged lid in Room 2124, near one of the building's exits. This was discovered in the late afternoon by a charwoman, Sophia Holmes. Mrs. Holmes was the widow of Melchior Holmes, a slave who had saved enough money to buy his freedom. He joined the Union Army and was killed in the first battle of Bull Run, leaving Mrs. Holmes with two children to raise. Several congressmen became interested in her plight and arranged for her to work at the Treasury Department, where she became the first African-American to be hired there. Her work as a charwoman brought her $15 a month. When she found the stolen money in the box, she knew something was amiss. She wrapped the notes in a bundle and sat down on it to await help. She knew that General Francis E. Spinner, the treasurer of the United States, ate and slept in his office. Each night he got up and made the rounds by candlelight to make sure all the vaults were locked. So at 2:00 a.m. on October 11, he approached the room where Sophia was sitting on her incredible find. She saw the light approaching and called out for him to come running. He entered the room with a drawn pistol, not knowing what to expect. When she showed him the money, he immediately called for guards. Early the next morning, an official investigation began, but the thief was never identified.

Spinner was so impressed by Sophia's honesty that he recommended she be promoted to messenger and given that position for life. President Abraham Lincoln agreed and officially commended her. Through Spinner's efforts, she was advanced in salary to $660 a year. She stayed in that job for almost 38 years, during which she became known to everyone at the bureau as "Aunt Sophie." She died October 10, 1900, exactly 38 years to the day after she discovered the stolen money. Her obituary appeared in the *New York Times*.[28]

The first true loss of Treasury Notes occurred on April 15, 1864, in the plate printers' drying room. There, a single sheet of unfinished 5% interest-bearing $20 2-year notes was taken from a parcel of 800 sheets. Suspicion was centered on a scrubbing woman, employed under surveillance to clean the room each day. One of the notes was spent at a store on Pennsylvania Avenue the day after the theft, and she was arrested and charged with the crime, though she denied the charge. The case was turned over to the solicitor of the Treasury Department and the district attorney, but they ruled that since the sheet had not been finished, the notes were not legally money. The only property taken was the bank-note paper. The case was therefore dropped, but the scrubbing woman was dismissed from government service.[29] On July 23, 1864, a theft took place in another drying room of the plate-printing division. There, 10 sheets of 50-cent Fractional Currency notes were taken, amounting to a loss of $100 (20 notes to the sheet). Mr. Neale, the superintendent of the room, had his suspicions about who stole the notes, but he had no proof. S.M. Clark, the chief of the bureau, decided to dismiss all the employees that worked in that room. This was done, and Mr. Neale was allowed

to re-hire such of them as he thought were innocent. The loss was taken out of the pay of all the employees.[30]

Another loss occurred on September 10, 1864, when one sheet of four $10 Compound Interest Treasury Notes was found missing in the sealing division. A diligent search was made, with no success, and each employee was searched as they left their shift by a committee of their number. The value of the lost notes was assessed equally upon each employee, so there was no permanent loss to the bureau.[31]

A $100 note of the First National Bank of Cincinnati, First Charter Period. (F-452.)

A more serious theft was detected in early June 1864 when a package consisting of 6,000 coupon bonds of $1,000 each was found to be short by 100 bonds, amounting to a loss of $100,000. The bonds had been printed by a New York bank-note company and forwarded in a mail car to the secretary of the Treasury, where they were received in the loan division, counted, and found to agree with the invoice. A search of the records was made and showed that the 6,000 bonds were received by Mr. Bailey, the clerk in charge of the counting room, who found them to be correct. From there, the bonds were delivered to the trimming division, where they were again counted and found to be correct. After trimming, the bonds were delivered to the sealing division, counted, found to be correct, and then sealed and delivered to the loan division of the Treasury on September 28, 1863. Nine months later, the loss was discovered. Since the loan division of the Treasury Department did not keep methodical and detailed records, there was no way to trace the handling of the bonds after they left the National Currency Bureau (BEP). Whoever stole the bonds never tried to use them, and consequently, there was no actual loss to the government except for the value of the paper.[32]

On April 29, 1867, James H.A. Schureman, who worked for the Office of the Comptroller of the Currency in the rooms connected with the vaults at the bureau, took 80 $100 bank notes intended for the First National Bank of New Jersey, not yet signed. He also took 80 $50 notes printed for the same bank for a total of $12,000. The theft was discovered on May 3 and quickly traced to Mr. Schureman. Some of the notes were found in his wife's possession. Other evidence clearly indicated that Schureman took the notes, and a jury found him guilty. Judge Fisher, however, ruled that there was a defect in the indictment serious enough that he set the verdict aside and discharged the prisoner. The language of the indictment did not match the language of the statute (Act of February 5, 1867), and the difference was fatal to the government's case.[33]

In December 1869 1 package of 50-cent Fractional Currency with a value of $750 was stolen during the turnover of two sets of employees at a time when the bureau was working day and night shifts. Within a short time, another theft took place when visitors to the bureau walked away with two sheets of $10 notes for a loss of $80. The chief of the bureau, George B. McCartee, and certain of his assistants had to pay the Treasury for those two thefts.[34] This came at a time when the bureau was still perfecting its system of checks and balances.

The numerous checks and balances of the Treasury Department had deterred theft for nearly 11 years, but that began to change during the Grant administration, especially during the winter of 1870 and 1871. In that period, Charles

E. Edwins was convicted of embezzling $5,749 from the Treasury but was pardoned by the president in March 1871 on account of his ill health. Seth Johnson, a clerk in the cash room of the Treasurer's Office, stole $37,894.[35] He was tried, convicted, and served time in prison. Frederick A. Marden, the chief clerk in the Division of Accounts in the Treasury, stole almost $12,000. Since the Bureau of Engraving and Printing did not then have a separate building but was still in the Treasury Department, the public often confused the bureau with the department, and sometimes it was thought that all the defalcations were occurring in the bureau.

Although it did not directly involve the Bureau of Engraving and Printing, there was a theft in the cash room of the Treasury Department on June 2, 1875, that created a sensation in Washington, D.C.—not so much for the money that was stolen but for the public's interest in the highly dramatic revelations that followed. The story begins with the tragic death by fire of a Universalist minister, the Reverend Benjamin B. Halleck, who was killed in a railroad accident, leaving his family in poor circumstances. General Francis E. Spinner, the treasurer of the United States, came to the relief of the family by taking the minister's son, Benjamin B. Halleck Jr., into his home for several months. Spinner saw to it that the boy was given a position in the Treasury Department. Benjamin, or "little Billy," as Spinner liked to call him, was extremely subject to influence, and this would be his downfall. Standing in the wings was the nefarious William H. Ottman, a saloonkeeper and a man who had experience in corrupting treasury clerks. He was suspected of putting up another clerk, Seth Johnson, to steal $37,894 from the Treasury some three years earlier, but Ottman was never convicted of that crime. Ottman had an accomplice, an old gambler named Theodore W. Brown, also called "Peg Leg" because of his wooden leg.

Young Halleck's duties in the cash room were to count the amount of National Bank Notes in packages being sent out by express companies and to affix a seal to each package. Ottman convinced the gullible Halleck that the theft of a single package of money would go unnoticed and, even if detected, could not be traced to him. Believing Ottman, Halleck stole a package containing $47,000 in $500 bills. Ottman had promised Halleck a full third share of the money, but in fact he paid him only small sums from time to time, putting him off by saying he would give him his saloon on Pennsylvania Avenue. Ottman gave several of the $500 bills to his friend Brown to cash into smaller notes. Brown asked a fellow gambler, John Kelly, to cash one of the $500 bills. When Kelly asked where he got so much money, Brown told him that Ottman gave him the note and asked him to cash it. Brown did not realize that Kelly harbored a secret grudge against him because he (Brown) had been the principal witness against another gambler, a friend of Kelly's, in a killing that happened some years earlier. Kelly got his revenge by writing a letter to George O. Miller, a detective on the Washington Metropolitan Police force who had been assigned to this case.

Acting on information in the letter, Miller followed Brown to the horse races in Saratoga and witnessed him cashing $500 notes. Meanwhile, Halleck had been suspected of stealing the money all along and had been followed by Secret Service agents who witnessed everything he did and everywhere he went. They knew, for example, that he frequented the saloon kept by Ottman and was friends with Peg Leg Brown. In those days, the Secret Service cooperated with the Metropolitan Police and exchanged information about their suspects. Halleck was arrested and placed in jail. General Spinner asked Halleck's wife if she would visit her husband in jail and try to get him to reveal everything he knew about the theft. Halleck confessed, and the other actors were quickly arrested. About $32,000 in new $500 notes were found deposited in Ottman's accounts in two different

Secretary of the Treasury Benjamin Bristow.

banks in Alexandria, Virginia, and that money was seized by the police.

Halleck, Ottman, and Brown were tried in federal court, and all were released on bail pending the outcome of motions made by their attorneys. Halleck gave such confusing testimony that he was acquitted at the first trial. After a mistrial was declared on the second prosecution, Halleck died. Ottman then demanded that the police give him the money they had seized from his bank deposits. In what came to be called the "Ottman Compromise," the government agreed in 1882 to keep $12,500 and return $7,500 to Ottman. The reason for this compromise was unknown, and newspaper editors asked the obvious questions—who authorized the compromise, why did they do it, and who got the rest of the money? If Ottman *was not* involved in the robbery, all of the money that had been seized belonged to him. If he *was* involved, it all belonged to the government. The *New York Times* said this compromise was one of the most disgraceful failures in the annals of criminal jurisprudence, and the *Argus* of New Philadelphia, Ohio, called the compromise the "most barefaced fraud that was ever perpetuated," and suggested the missing money had gone to the defense lawyers.[36]

Everyone had an opinion about the Halleck case. General Spinner was at first dismayed by the duplicity of his young charge, saying "How damned sorry I am to think that little Billy Halleck would have robbed me," but eventually he took a more philosophical repose, saying "I'll be damned if the ways of God are not mysterious in unraveling sorrow." Secretary of the Treasury Benjamin H. Bristow decided that the public should no longer be allowed to visit the Bureau of Engraving and Printing nor the vault at the Treasury Department. Such visits had been a popular attraction for several years.

Employee Relations

The procedures followed in the bureau were well organized and efficient. The backs of notes were printed first. After the ink dried, the printed sheets were then carried to the Examining Division where young ladies made sure each note was perfectly printed and "spoiled" notes were discarded. If perfectly printed, the sheets were sent back to the Wetting Division to go through the same process of wetting and storing as before. On their second trip through the Plate Printing Division, the sheets were printed on the faces of the notes.

The bureau was not always in charge of itself, and from time to time it had to comply with legislative acts or union demands that didn't make sense. A good example is the Sundry Civil Appropriations Act of 1889. Prior to this act, the bureau paid $1 per 1,000 impressions to the owners of the Milligan Power Press for any intaglio work done on those presses. The act limited the royalties to just 1¢ per 1,000 impressions and required the owners to keep the presses in repair. Naturally, the owners couldn't make any money with such arrangements and shut down their operations at the bureau. That move undoubtedly satisfied the Plate Printers' Union which saw the power presses as a threat to their job security and wanted the bureau to continue printing money and stamps with hand-roller presses. By 1891 the bureau couldn't keep up with the work and had

Sizing machines at the Bureau of Engraving and Printing, circa 1900. The application of size was the old method of stiffening bank notes. This was considered a "woman's job."

to start using surface presses to print certain classes of revenue stamps. The surface plates were engraved in relief.

The Act of July 1, 1898 (30 Stat. 605), showed just how powerful the Plate Printers' Union was. That act required that "all bonds, notes and checks shall be printed from hand-roller presses." Most of the hand-roller press operators were middle-aged men, and they knew that if the bureau were to go over to power presses, they would be thrown out of work at a time in their lives when it would be difficult to find employment in their field. The opposition of the American Federation of Labor against the power presses was successful. The bureau once again started buying additional hand-roller presses from R. Hoe & Company and searching for space in which to put them. The main pressroom at that time had just over 9,000 square feet of floor space jammed tight with 224 hand presses, each with a gas stove and a work table for the assistant. Additional pressrooms were set up on different floors of the building, but there was no easy solution, and the working conditions grew worse. Finally, in 1907 the provisions of the Act of 1899 were repealed, and some power presses were returned. This situation continued until 1912, when it was proposed to give the secretary of the Treasury full discretion in choosing which press to use for each class of work. This was vigorously opposed by labor and especially by the National Steel and Copper Plate Printers' Union.[37] A compromise was worked out with the limitation that not more than 1/5 of the hand-roller presses would be eliminated each year.[38] The discretionary power of the secretary of the Treasury was made permanent in 1923, and power presses soon displaced all the hand-roller presses.

The American Federation of Labor was also active in promoting increased salaries for the female employees of the bureau. These efforts began in earnest about 1909, when the female workers numbered about 900, most of them employed as assistants to the plate printers. The plate printers paid their assistants $1.25 a day, and the government paid them an extra 25¢ a day, making their average salary about $30 a month.

The female assistants working on the steam-powered presses made $1.50 a day, all of it paid by the government.

Things came to a head in March 1911, when local-labor leaders persuaded the women to form a union and affiliate with the American Federation of Labor. Joseph E. Ralph, the Director of the Bureau at the time, said that neither he nor the secretary of the Treasury had any power to increase the women's salaries since the appropriations of the bureau were based upon the estimated quantity of work required by the various departments served by the bureau. Ralph said he was sympathetic to the women's cause but was unable to help them. He also liked to point out that many of these women were the daughters of men working at the bureau and that most had been previously employed by the department stores in the city at lower wages, longer hours, and without leave of absence. The president of the women's union countered by saying that many of the older women had families to support and found it extremely difficult to manage their households with such low wages. The women eventually won increased salaries, but the same arguments persisted for many years, fueled as much by male chauvinism as any other factor.[39]

A delegation of women from the American Federation of Labor visits the White House in Washington, D.C.

An argument can be made that women actually faired pretty well at the bureau if you consider how they were treated elsewhere in the business world. And while some women may have endured difficult times, yet longevity in service seems to have been a female trait. Many women worked most of their lives at the bureau, and many handled millions of dollars in currency, some of which is now so rare that even wealthy collectors can only dream of finding the notes. Many women worked 40 or even 50 years, but the story of Emma S. Brown is unique. She came to work at the bureau in 1865 when she was just 10 years old, and she left after 59 years of service. Her family moved to Washington, D.C., from Philadelphia when her father got a job with the Treasury Department to work on the construction of one of its security vaults. While working there, he contracted pneumonia and died. The support of the family fell to his son, Alonzo Y. Brown, who joined the 188th Pennsylvania Volunteers and was killed in action during the siege of Petersburg in July 1864. Mrs. Brown was a cripple and could not work, leaving herself and Emma in abject poverty. Mrs. Brown's congressman heard of the family's plight and used his political leverage to get Emma a job with the bureau. When she retired on April 24, 1924, she was then forewoman of the trimming section of the Bureau's Examining Division.

Salary disputes were a constant problem for the directors of the bureau, especially after the plate printers and others formed unions to represent their labor demands. A good example is found in the problems facing Director Meredith in 1904. The "back printers" were being paid $4.50 a day while the "face printers" received $5 a day. The bureau had taken the position many years earlier that printing the faces of bank notes was more delicate work and required greater skill than printing the backs, and therefore only the better workmen were employed in that job and deserved slightly higher pay. The Plate Printers' Union took the opposite position and said that both types of printing required the same level of skill, and therefore the pay should be equal. The Treasury Department then pointed out that the law required that various employees of the bureau could not be paid at a higher rate than other men engaged in the same or similar work elsewhere. The only comparison available was to the wages paid by the American Bank Note Company, which were about the same as those at the bureau.

Director Meredith refused to increase the wages, and after both sides got their complaints spelled out in the press, nothing was done.[40]

George W. Casilear

George Washington Casilear, the son of Francis and Ellen Bainbridge Casilear, was born in New York City in 1825. His father, also an engraver, was the brother of the famous artist John William Casilear, which made George his nephew. He learned engraving primarily from his father, who was with the bank-note–engraving firm of Draper, Toppan & Company in New York during the early and mid-1840s. George went to California in 1849 by way of Cape Horn to make his fortune in the gold fields. He found no gold, but after he returned to New York he engraved several large plates of San Francisco and Sacramento from sketches he had made, either singly or together with his uncle, Henry Bainbridge. At that time, about 1851, he was styled as an "artist and publisher," but his engravings were published by Sarony & Major. From 1852 to 1857 George worked at various firms as an editor, a secretary, and a solicitor of patents. He probably began engraving with Toppan, Carpenter, Casilear & Company in Philadelphia, where his uncle, John W. Casilear, was a member from January 1, 1850, to October 1854. He joined the new currency bureau in the Treasury Department on December 1, 1862, as Assistant of Model Designing, and he stayed at the bureau for the rest of his professional life, some 31 years. He lived at 3019 "N" Street in Georgetown for 30 years, and while he was there it is said, "he attracted other printers

A study for a bank-note vignette of Minerva with classical figures, by John W. Casilear.

and map-makers, some from England and France and even the French colonies of the West Indies, to live nearby in rental housing at the corners of Dumbarton and 30th."[41]

In December 1864 George was custodian and served sometime as acting superintendent of engraving between 1869 and 1877. At the Paris Exposition of 1878, he was awarded a silver medal for Superior Excellence in Engraving. On April 28, 1885, during the Cleveland administration, he was replaced as superintendent of engraving by John A. O'Neil, a portrait and historical engraver who had once been the mayor of Hoboken, New Jersey. This was a political appointment and not unusual for that time. O'Neil served in that position until December 16, 1889, when Casilear once again took over the reins. Mr. Casilear was never the Chief of the Bureau, as some biographies state. He retired on October 30, 1893, and then spent a long vacation in southern France. During his service at the bureau, Casilear was often called on to testify in court on the authenticity of alleged counterfeit notes, or to explain technical issues, most notably in the trial of William E. Brockway, a famous counterfeiter, held in December 1870 (see more in the essay on William E. Brockway in chapter 10). There, as a witness for the government, he explained the *modus operandi* of engraving bond plates and pronounced the Brockway plate of the "seven-thirty" bond issue to be a counterfeit. He was one person who "knew it all." Together with George W. Tichenor, he developed a bench transfer press that is illustrated in chapter 14. He received several patents in the field of security engraving and printing (see appendix J). He died in Charlottesville, Virginia, on August 7, 1912.[42] He was survived by his wife, Jane, and several children. His relationship to Paul S. Casilear, if any, is not known.[43]

Laundering Notes

To save money at the bureau during hard times, Director Joseph Ralph is credited with the idea of washing soiled notes and returning them to circulation.[44] At the time, about 1910, it cost the government $13.50 per 1,000 notes printed, regardless of the denomination. The life span of small-denomination notes was much shorter than those of greater value simply because the small notes were handled much more often. At the time, Director Ralph noted that the $1, $2, and $5 notes—excluding National Bank Notes—comprised 43.75% of the currency printed. Most of them were returned to the bureau not because they were worn out, but simply for the reason that they were soiled. Ralph decided the notes could probably be cleaned, re-sized, and sent back into circulation. To verify this assumption, he formed a committee of experts to study the problems.[45] The committee conducted tests on single bills and found that Silver Certificates and Treasury Notes could be cleaned and re-sized economically. The soap designed specifically to do this job consisted of potash and some "high-grade" oils, which both cleaned the notes and bleached them at the same time, but it could not be used on Gold Certificates because the potash caused the yellow ink to dissolve. The National Bank Notes could not be washed because they were signed in different inks at their bank of origin, and most of those inks were water-soluble. Still, this was not a problem because the remaining Silver Certificates and Treasury Notes comprised the vast majority of the soiled notes.

A $5 Silver Certificate. (F-277.)

The committee designed a special washing machine that was essentially a vertical cylinder in which wire trays were placed that held the notes in a single layer. This arrangement prevented the notes from rubbing against each other and causing additional wear by friction. It also kept the notes separated so that both sides of a note were washed. It was found that a water temperature greater than 140-degrees Fahrenheit would injure the notes. When fully loaded, the "tub" would started revolving, continuing its washing cycle for 10 to 15 minutes. Next, the hot water was removed, and a rinse cycle was started with cold water, continuing for five minutes. Then the notes were subjected to a weak formaldehyde solution to kill any germs that were on them. Next, the notes were subjected to a bleach solution and then partly dried. They were sent through a sizing vat that contained a 10% solution of animal size with a little alum in it. The sizing vat carried the notes between a number of small, endless belts that moved over rollers. The money was fed in between these belts at one end of the vat and carried down through the solution and dropped off the other end. The notes were then placed in stacks of about four notes each, and Fuller boards (pressboards) were placed between the notes to keep them from touching each other. The stacks were taken one at a time and fed between two heavy steel rollers which exerted a pressure of 30 tons. Each stack was passed through the rollers twice, which "ironed" the notes and gave them a glossy appearance.

From their calculations, the committee reported that it cost about 1/10 of a cent to wash an individual note, far less than the cost of destroying the note and printing a new one. It was also claimed that laundering the notes would add another eight months, or roughly 56%, to their life. Further progress was made when the three separate operations were combined into one large machine, and the washing time was reduced to only three minutes. It was then possible to use only three operators for each machine and to clean between 30,000 and 40,000 notes per day per machine, depending on the skill of the operators. Eventually, 12 of the improved washing machines were made at a cost of $1,250 each and installed at various locations throughout the country.

Though it was economical, the practice of laundering soiled notes came to an end in 1918. With the outbreak of World War I, it became impossible to get adequate supplies of linen, and the Crane Paper Company had to limit the amount of linen used in each note. Eventually they had to go to an all-cotton paper. Cotton paper did not wash like linen paper did, and the

feel and appearance of the washed notes were quite different from previous years. It was decided to discontinue the washing of notes until the war ended and paper could return to a linen-cotton mixture. In 1921 the bureau was getting ready to change the linen ratio, but the Secret Service objected to washing soiled notes, saying that the practice made it difficult for the public to decide if a washed note was genuine or not. After eight years, the unwashed masses were once again given unwashed money.

Laundering soiled currency at the bureau, circa early 1900s.

A printing room at the bureau, circa 1900. During the Civil War, the Bureau of Engraving and Printing broke tradition by offering women manual-labor jobs alongside male workers. Women excelled at certain jobs, and their earnings were not only beneficial but also helped free them from purely domestic roles.

Processes

GILPIN PAPER MACHINE

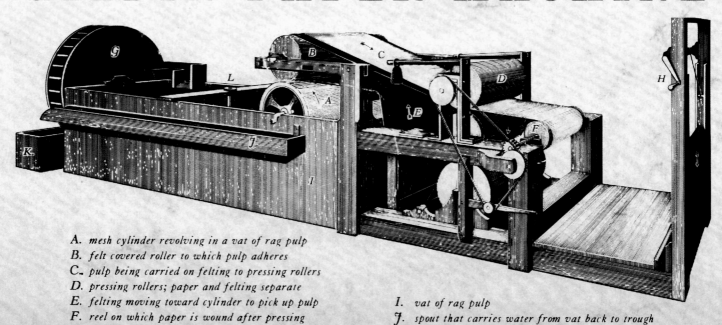

A. mesh cylinder revolving in a vat of rag pulp
B. felt covered roller to which pulp adheres
C. pulp being carried on felting to pressing rollers
D. pressing rollers; paper and felting separate
E. felting moving toward cylinder to pick up pulp
F. reel on which paper is wound after pressing
G. bucket wheel that raises water from trough into pulp vat
H. crank to tighten up felting

I. vat of rag pulp
J. spout that carries water from vat back to trough
K. trough containing water
L. agitator, or paddle that stirs pulp

Chapter 13

Line Engraving

The Workplace

A detailed vignette would have required delicate engraving tools.

As with any craftsman, an orderly workplace was essential to the bank-note engraver. The engraver worked at a table facing a window having a white, translucent screen set at an angle of about 45 to 75 degrees from the horizontal. This screen was sometimes made by tacking tracing paper to a frame. The purpose of the screen was to diffuse sunlight. If work was done in front of an open window, the light would reflect off the plate and directly into the eyes of the engraver, making it more difficult for him to see his work. By using a screen to spread diffused light over the engraving table, the lines cut by the engraver will appear, by the difference in contrast, as darker lines, as in a drawing on paper. Sidewall screens were sometimes attached to each end of the work table, extending about four feet into the room, forming a kind of booth. When doing large plates, a drawing or photograph was tacked up on the right hand screen, and on the left screen a mirror was placed to reflect and reverse the drawing. The engraver would look at the reversed or mirror image of his drawing as a guide for his engraving. In doing detailed work of small scale, such as a vignette for bank notes, a different technique was used.

Somewhere on the engraving table, or very near it, were placed the various small hand tools that the engraver expected to use every day. These included burins of different shapes and sizes, scrapers, burnishers, oval points, tracing points, chisels, hammers, calipers, etc. Several magnifying glasses were usually scattered around. A cushion, usually a leather bag filled with fine sand, was used to hold the plate while it was being cut. The cushion allowed the plate to be rotated at will. In some of the larger establishments, the engraving tables were placed next to each other in a long line that took up the whole wall, each table having its own window. In smaller companies, these tables were fewer in number and could be set apart.

The engraving room at the Bureau of Engraving and Printing in the late 1890s.

Transferring Artwork to a Die

The engraver worked on a piece of soft metal called a die, usually of soft steel but sometimes of copper. This metal die was usually in the shape of a square plate, about 2 inches by 3 inches, with a thickness of about 1/8 of an inch. The area of the die was not much larger than the actual size of the drawing. The engraver had several ways to outline the artwork on the die. In earlier times, before photography, an engraver could simply make a drawing with a fine lead pencil on the surface of the die. He would then trace the outline of the drawing with a sharp, pointed tool to make a preliminary sketch of the subject on the metal. Sometimes, an etching ground (a wax film used to protect the underlying metal from acid) was applied to the surface of the die, and a paper drawing was placed on top of the ground. A sharp needle was used to punch through the outline of the drawing. By making many punches with the needle, each spaced a short distance from the previous one and penetrating through the ground, a precise outline of the drawing was made on the die. Then, the paper was removed and nitric acid was dropped on the needle marks, eating away at the exposed metal and deepening the lines. Later, the engraver would take up his burin and retrace the bitten lines to give them the proper depth and width.

Charles Frederick Partington in his work, *The Engraver's Complete Guide* (1825), advises students to take a polished piece of copper and heat it in an oven until it is hot enough to melt a piece of white wax. Then rub a stick of white wax over the heated plate until the whole surface of the plate is covered by a thin, uniform film of the wax. Place the plate on a table, waxed side up, and let it cool. Meanwhile, take a piece of transparent tracing paper and place it over the drawing of the subject you wish to engrave. Trace the outlines of the subject as accurately as possible, using a black-lead pencil. Place the completed tracing face down on the white wax surface of the plate and place this in a press or put heavy weights on the paper for an hour or two. This transfers the pencil-lead drawing to the white wax in reversed position. The pencil marks on the white wax can now be traced with a fine point that just touches the copper plate. Melt the wax off the copper and you will find a perfect outline of the subject which you can "flesh out" with a burin.

Many engravers experimented with different recipes for making etching grounds. A number of these were described in a notebook kept by G.F.C. Smillie.[1] F.F. Girsch's etching ground for vignette engraving consisted of 10 oz. asphaltum, 5 oz. white wax, 8 oz. Burgundy wax, and 1 oz. mastic. A similar ground was used by James Bannister—3 oz. asphaltum, 1/2 oz. white wax, and 3 oz. Burgundy pitch.

A "transfer wax" was a material used for a slightly different purpose. It transferred a drawing made on a gelatin sheet to the surface of a die. A precise drawing was made of a subject, say a locomotive. That drawing was reduced by photography to the appropriate size and covered by a sheet of stiff gelatin. The drawing was easily seen through the gelatin. The engraver traced the outline of the drawing on the gelatin with a sharp point. Powdered vermillion or red chalk was rubbed on the scratched lines of the gelatin drawing, and then the excess was scraped off. Next, the gelatin sheet was turned over and placed on a steel die that had been covered by a layer of a "transfer ground." The gelatin sheet was then lightly burnished to make a vermillion impression on the ground. This is called a "red wax transfer." An etching point was used to trace the red lines on the ground. Sometimes a "rat tail" file was used, which had a sharpened point just a little blunter than a needle. Getting the right transfer ground was very important since it must hold the vermillion rigidly on the surface and be impervious to acid. All engravers learned the different characteristics of transfer ground as they progressed in their training. When the drawing had been traced through the ground and onto the die, the ground was covered with an etching acid. This bit into the steel die and "transferred" the original drawing to the die.[2] Smillie's transfer ground was made from 1/2 oz. of Burgundy pitch, 3/4 oz. yellow beeswax, and "scruples of tallow." These ingredients were boiled together, thoroughly mixed, and cooled in cold water. Then it was mixed with charcoal (or lampblack), dragon's blood, and oil.

Dragon's blood, sanguis draconis.

The size of the original drawing can be enlarged or reduced on the die or plate by using a pantograph. Pantographs are machines that use a mechanical linkage to move two different points at the same time and in the same spatial relationship to each other, except that one of the points traces the pattern or outline of a drawing, and the other point cuts a metal die or plate with the same pattern, but larger or smaller as the operator wishes. Pantographs can be set so they reproduce a pattern, such as letters, to a very small, hardly visible size. Pantographs are described in greater detail in chapter 14.

In the directions given in *The American Bond Detector*, which dates from 1869, it was suggested that the original drawing be reduced by the daguerreotype camera to the size the engraver wanted on the finished bank-note plate. The New York photographer Abraham Bogardus made daguerreotypes for the American Bank Note Company, and one of his employees, Stephen H. Horgan, who started with him in 1873, later wrote that "The pen or pencil drawings of designs for engraving on steel were reduced to proper size by the daguerreo-type method."[3] The engraver could then trace an outline of the artwork with a fine needle called a tracing point to make a series of small round dots. After the tracing was complete, he filled in the dots with red wax, cut out the section of the daguerreotype, and pressed it down on the polished metal surface of his plate. The red wax was transferred to the plate in the correct left-to-right orientation

and made a suitable outline that the engraver could follow to reproduce the drawing. This technique is also called a "red wax transfer." It is possible to skip the transfer and cut an engraving directly onto the plate, but because line engraving is so precise and unforgiving of errors, it makes better sense to transfer a drawing onto the plate and work from that.

Another method was to draw the artwork directly on the plate with a soft-lead pencil or lithographic crayon and then cut through those lines. By the 1890s a ferrotype ("tin-type") was being used by the American Bank Note Company. The photo of the drawing, or perhaps a photo of a real subject, such as a locomotive, was reduced by a camera lens to the engraving size, and the subject was automatically reversed, which was ideal for picture engraving since the engraver had to engrave in reverse. Its outline was engraved through the photographic image and onto the metallic substrate and then filled with red wax and transferred to the polished die. The tin-type survived beyond the turn of the century, perhaps as late as the 1940s, but newer photographic transfers soon replaced it. No matter what technique was used, the basic procedure was to transfer a drawing or photograph onto the surface of the plate or die and engrave that image into the metal.

A daguerreotype portrait of five women.

Burins

In line engraving, the burin, or graver, was the basic tool for cutting a line in metal. One of the first duties of an engraver when he arrived at work in the morning was to sharpen his burins. This was usually done with a sharpening stone of some kind. Sometimes these were called "oil-stones" or "whetstones." Whetstone is a compound word that uses *whet* to mean sharpening. The process of sharpening a burin or any other blade was called "stonning." Different stones were used, but the best was an "Arkansas stone," often used during the latter half of the 19th century when its superior sharpening qualities became known. Since the 1960s it has been called novaculite and is known to be a very dense, ultra-pure siliceous sediment called "bedded chert," found in the Quachita Mountains of Arkansas. A slightly inferior grade of this stone was quarried in Turkey and called "Turkey stone." The relative hardness of novaculite is 6.5 on the Mohs scale, making it just a little harder than file steel. Greek waterstone was used in Europe to sharpen knives and may have been used for burins. In fact, several stones in Europe and America were found to do a good job in sharpening carbon-steel blades and became part of the tool kits of engravers. Burins and other engraving tools were sharpened until they cut through soft steel with very little pressure from the hand. It was easy to cut a straight line with a sharp burin, and even beginning students could do this. But once a burin became dull, the line wavered, and experienced engravers could tell by the feel of the cut that the burin was losing its sharpness.

Burins come in different shapes and sizes, but generally the handles are made of wood and have a broad surface to fit into the palm of the hand. The handle holds a shaft of tempered steel that ends in a sharp point. Tempered steel is much harder than the soft steel on which the burin cuts lines. This steel shaft is sometimes referred to as "lozenge-shaped" or "diamond-shaped." The thumb and third finger of the hand are placed on opposite sides of the shaft with the forefinger resting near the point. The forefinger is a guide

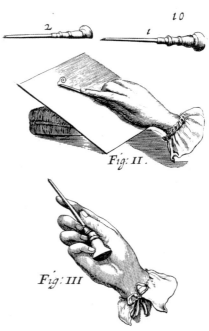

How burins are held.

only, and it does not exert pressure downward on the point.

The position of the engraver's body is important, and trained engravers were taught to position their knees in the direction they would be cutting. The elbow of the cutting hand should rest on the table, and the hand that is not cutting should rest behind the cutting hand. Long hours of practice are needed to learn these and the many other lessons that teach one how to engrave. Apprentices were first taught how to make straight-line cuts in scraps of copper, and then to broaden the cuts, to narrow the cuts, and how to end the cut gradually. Only after mastering these simple steps did they move on to more advanced techniques.

The purpose of a burin is to cut a line into metal. The line can be cut to various depths and to various widths. The range of depths can vary from 5/10,000 of an inch for the finest lines down to 1/100 of an inch for the deepest lines, which is a 20-fold increase. Experience teaches the engraver how different lines will look when they have been filled with ink and printed on paper. To become an engraver, even a letter engraver, one must first learn to draw. When the basics have been mastered, such as scale, balance, light and shadow, perspective, etc., one begins to appreciate how lines become forms. Forms are a kind of visual language recognized by the brain. Lines, then, are the language of the engraver. The burin cuts a V-shaped channel in metal. The metal that is displaced by the burin is pushed up in front and to each side, like earth is pushed up on each side of a plow as it cuts through the ground. If this burr is left on the plate, it will blur and broaden the line, so the engraver must scrape it off. If the engraver increases the pressure on the burin, he will cut a deeper and broader line. If he presses only lightly, he will cut a shallow and thin line.

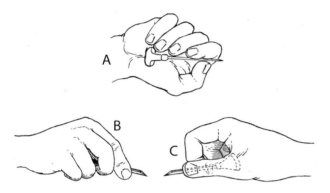

How burins cut. Both shallow and deep lines are inscribed by the same graver. Drawing "A" shows a side view of the right hand holding the graver. Drawing "B" shows the view from the other side of the hand. Drawing "C" shows the graver from below.

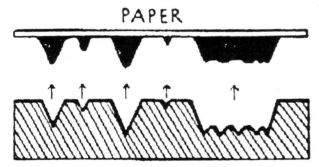

The Intaglio Process, showing how the different depths of engraved lines produce different elevations of ink on the surfaces of paper.

Partington and other instructors had long passages in their books to tell students how to engrave certain objects and textures. When sculpture is represented, for example, the stone is assumed to be white marble, so the engraving should be light and smooth, the eyes should have no pupils, and the hair should be coarse. Linen should be represented by small and closer lines than other sorts of cloth, and where there are folds in the cloth, a single light stroke is required. Woolen cloth should have two strokes instead of one, and where the strokes cross, the second stroke should be finer than the first. Shining metals, glass, and smooth water all require clean, single stokes interlined by finer strokes. For smooth water, as in a lake or pond, the strokes must be horizontal, but in rougher water, the lines should be waved. In rough seas, the waves must be drawn in bolder strokes with white caps on their tops. Rain is depicted by fine oblique lines. In representing mountains, one should frequently interrupt the lines to show the irregularities of the mountain's surface. The greater the distance to the mountains, the fewer interrupted lines are required. To get dark shadows, or to depict foliage, trees, furs, etc., one usually turns to etching.[4]

Etching

Etching refers to a technique for making intaglio plates using special tools and materials that add "tone" or "color" to the print that couldn't easily be made by simple line engraving. First, the plate or die is covered with a waxy ground that is resistant to acid. The engraver then cuts through the ground with a sharp etching point to make a line in the metal. When all the lines have been made for the drawing, the engraver places the metal plate in an acid bath, such as *aqua fortis* or pyroliginous acid, for about two hours. This acid is called the etchant, or "mordant" (French for "biting"), and it will eat away at the metal that has been exposed by the etching point. The plate is removed from the acid bath, and the remaining ground is cleaned off, leaving a shiny plate with a design etched in it. The process dates back about 500 years and has undergone much development over time. In America it was usually the practice to cut steel to show human flesh and drapery and to use etching for just about everything else.

A variety of etching acids have been used in bank-note engraving. Spencer acid is three-parts silver nitrate and one-part mercury. Spencer acids were usually used for letter engraving. Smillie's etching acid for vignettes was 1 oz. nitric acid diluted with 3 oz. acetic acid

A vignette made by etching. The etched work was done by Jas. Smillie.

Another of his formulas required 1 oz. nitric added to 50 oz. water. He sometimes etched his plates as many as seven times, letting each "wash" go for one to two minutes.

Bank-note engravers liked to use etching to achieve tonal variations or "color" in their engravings. The technique is especially good for adding shadow to a drawing or to show the play of light on a surface, such as tree bark. Such engravers often used the same techniques as the old masters to enhance their vignettes. For example, resin dust could be added to certain areas of a line engraving to show shadow or give the effect of great distance in a landscape scene. The resin dust was placed on those areas of the plate and then heated to make it stick to the copper. The engraver then added a ground to the areas of the plate he didn't want to be textured. Again, placing the plate in an acid bath ate away the resin dust and bit into the metal to give it a texture that held ink.

Etching is also used with stipple engraving to suggest the sensuous and supple character of human flesh. Here, the engraver repeatedly stabs an area with an etching point to penetrate the ground and leave numerous little round dots. Placed in an acid bath, the small dots are duplicated in the metal below and give tone to the area. Tone can also be achieved by fine-line cross-hatching or by engraving parallel fine lines.

Cross-hatching and parallel lines would give texture to an image.

Slow and Easy

Different engravers had different ways of doing their work. Some of the self-taught engravers did almost everything wrong—according to their colleagues—but managed to make good pictures. Most engravers did not start working until they had studied the preliminary drawing made on the plate and decided the order in which they would engrave the lines. The main lines were usually cut first to give an idea of how the image would look. The work, of course, was always done with the aid of a magnifying glass or loupe, and each cut was carefully planned and then made slowly. The whole process of line engraving is slow. Alan Dow, an engraver for Bradbury, Wilkinson & Company, took 18 months to engrave the portrait of Queen Elizabeth II on the £5 coin of 1990, and even then he was not satisfied with his work. Neither was the queen, who said the engraving made her look old, but added, "But then I am old." Alfred Jones, an American engraver, on the other hand, was known for his speed in finishing work.

Queen Elizabeth II as seen on the £5 gold coin of 1990.

Correcting Mistakes

To correct a mistake, one had to turn a plate or die over and hammer out the area in which the mistake was made. To find the exact area on the blank side of a plate or die, one placed calipers over the area of the mistake and squeezed softly to make an indentation on both sides of the plate. Usually this had to be repeated several times in slightly different places to cover the whole area of the mistake. Then, the blank side was hammered to elevate the corresponding area (and the mistake) on the engraved side of the plate or die. The elevated area was scraped down and polished, leaving a blank area in which new lines could be cut. Engraving mistakes didn't have to be horrendous to require correction. If a steel die was not polished to a perfect flatness, then there would be a slight tilt to the surface. An engraving on that die, no matter how excellent, would be slightly higher on one side and lower on the other. This disparity would be reproduced in the transfer press and would result in an uneven impression on the printing press. A die or plate had to be carefully prepared even before it was engraved. It must lie flat and measure the same thickness at every point.

Specialization

Engravers usually specialized in a particular area of the art, some becoming square-letter engravers, others becoming script engravers, landscape engravers, portrait engravers, historical engravers, etc. The highest form of the art was portrait engraving, and close behind that came historical engraving. The first bank notes featured only lettering, and that custom persisted for more than 100 years, although some Colonial notes had small vignettes, such as the "Sword-in-Hand" notes of Massachusetts or the elaborately engraved backs of South Carolina's notes (my favorite is the eagle eating out the liver of a chained Prometheus on the $70 note of 1779). Still, vignettes were not a regular feature on the majority of Colonial notes, and their continuous use began later. The earliest vignette may have been executed by George Murray in 1808 for the Farmers and Mechanics Bank of Philadelphia.[5] Letter engraving became highly specialized by the middle of the 19th century. Square lettering often used white-line engraving and greater use of the pantograph. Script engraving developed several styles from the very ornate flourishes seen on British notes to the simple round hand on American notes. Ornamental engraving, such as acanthus leaves and vines, required a study of basic botany. Mechanical engraving, used on the borders of notes and as a background for the denomination counters, was a combination of lathe engraving and transfer-press work. Metal ruling was a specialty within mechanical engraving, although it was sometimes done by lathe operators. Medallion engraving required training on a special ruling machine. Finally, designers and modelers had to understand the strengths and weaknesses of their engraving departments and customize their designs appropriately. Engraving supervisors had to examine work-in-progress plates to make sure the designs were well balanced, that the different parts were well engraved, that the plates would make good impressions in the printing presses, and that production was on-schedule.

The eagle eating the liver of Prometheus.

Attributions

One would think that engravers were rightfully proud of their work and therefore signed their portrait or historical vignettes, but that was not the case as very few signed vignettes have been found. Julian Blanchard examined the vignettes on approximately 1,350 bank notes in a study he conducted in 1945 but found only 52 notes that were signed by the engraver.[6] Even when engravers did sign their vignettes, it was a tradition to print the name in very small type and hide it somewhere along the border of the vignette. Students of the art have been able to attribute some unsigned vignettes to particular engravers,

but this is done primarily from historical records and not by the recognition of artistic styles. Gene Hessler, Mark Tomasko, and Roger Durand have all written extensively on identifying vignettes and their engravers. Tomasko mentions having seen notations indicating that Robert Savage had such a vast knowledge of the artistic styles of vignette engravers that he sometimes attributed vignettes for the Records Department of the American Bank Note Company for some of their acquired and predecessor-company vignettes. However attributing vignettes to a particular engraver requires thorough research and a pound of caution.

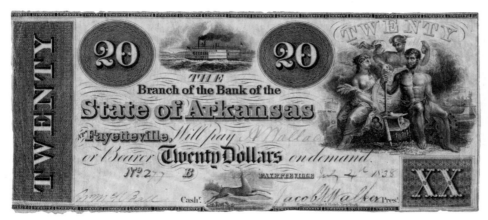

A vignette of Mercury, Ceres, and Vulcan signed by Freeman Rawdon.

A vignette of an Indian signed by George W. Hatch.

Chapter 14

Mechanical Engraving

Lathes

A lathe is a device that turns a work piece in a circular motion so that a cutting tool can be pressed against the side of the piece and shape it as it spins around. The potter's wheel was an early form of a vertical lathe, except that the artisan's hands were the cutting tool. A primitive bow drill is also an example of a vertical lathe. Surprisingly, the earliest depiction of a lathe is found in a carved relief on a wall of the tomb of Petosiris, a high priest of the Egyptian god Toth, and dates to around 300 BC. The early Romans, Greeks, and Assyrians all had primitive forms of lathes to turn wood to make spear shafts, arrow shafts, weapon handles, and more mundane things like chair legs, bedposts, bowls, and cups. Archeological excavations have shown that the Vikings made many items in wood by using pole lathes. This was an improvement over bow lathes, but the earliest depiction of a pole lathe does not occur until the 13th century, when one is clearly seen in a stained glass window of the Chartres Cathedral. A young green pole of larch or yew, mounted on the ceiling of a workshop or possibly still growing in the ground, provided the recoil of a natural "spring" as a source of power. A cord was tied at the working end of the pole and came down to wrap around the work piece and then passed below to a foot treadle. The operator, usually standing, worked the foot treadle with one leg and stood on the other leg. As the foot treadle was depressed, the cord that was wrapped around the periphery of the work piece made it spin around. At the same time, it pulled down on the working end of the spring pole. The bending of the spring pole created tension, pulling the cord up and spinning the work-piece in the opposite direction. This was reciprocating motion. First, the work piece revolved in one direction and then in the opposite direction. For safety, an operator could only cut into the work piece when it was spinning towards him, so the reciprocating motion of the pole lathe meant that half the time was wasted.

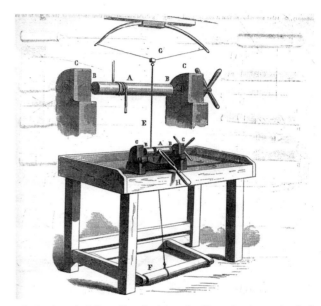

A simple pole lathe with a foot-treadle. These basic mechanical concepts were carried over into the early rose engines.

The next improvement in the lathe was the use of a "great wheel" to provide the motion to the work piece. A great wheel was usually heavily built and several feet in diameter, although size was not critical. The larger the wheel, the greater its speed and the greater its moment of inertia. The periphery of the wheel contained a groove to hold the drive cord. The cord wrapped around the work piece on the lathe just as it did with the pole lathe. As an assistant turned the wheel with a crank, the circular motion of the wheel was transferred by the drive cord to the work piece and made it spin. The great advantage of the wheel was that it provided continuous motion and therefore continuous power.

Pole lathes are seen on the bench at the left and rear of the room. A great wheel lathe is seen in the center and on the bench at the far right.

Finally, lathes were made in which a foot treadle's reciprocating motion (up and down) was transferred through a rod, called a pitman, to a heavy flywheel that was connected by a belt to the mandrel of the lathe. The function of the flywheel was to give constant motion to a part. By its moment of inertia, it opposed any sudden acceleration or deceleration. The mandrel or main spindle of the lathe was a shaft to which a work piece was attached to be turned. Eventually, flywheels and foot treadles were replaced by belted line-shafts and then electric motors, but that comes later.

Rose Engines

Rose engines, or "guilloching engines," as they were sometimes called, were developed in Europe sometime prior to the 15th century and were intended to cut fancy patterns or guilloches on wood or ivory. They were horizontal lathes powered by a hand-wheel from which leather belting, usually coupled in a figure-eight, passed to a flywheel and from the flywheel to a pulley mounted on the central shaft or mandrel. This meant that the mandrel moved at a low speed, as required for this kind of work. On the mandrel was fitted a large steel or iron wheel, called a "rosette," which had a waved pattern cut on its periphery. As the mandrel moved the rosette in a circular motion, the waved pattern pushed against a stationary follower, now called a "rubber," or "touch," and rocked the mandrel back and forth (i.e., towards the operator and then away).

In some machines, the mandrel had parallel journals, allowing it to move freely both left and right through its bearing. The rosette, then, was actually a cam that imparted a regular waved motion to the cutting tool or stylus. The mandrel could move both to and fro, and if the rosette also had shapes cut into its periphery, it could move right and left. By placing several rosettes in line, called a "barrel," the operator could cut a waved or looping line in a complete circle on a work piece, such as a die, and then switch to another rosette, cut another line that interlaced with the first, and so on. Rose engines evolved into complex machines with equally complex terminology for their various parts.

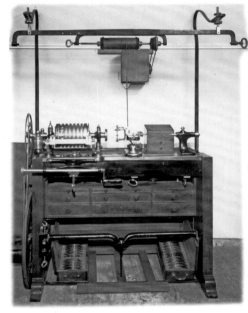

A Holtzapffel rose-engine lathe made in 1836. These lathes had not changed much since the early 1700s.

We know that several artisans were working with rose engines in cities in southern Germany during the latter half of the 16th century. Their work was collectively called "Kunstdrehen," meaning "art turning." These lathes were in use at least 100 years before Joseph Moxon wrote his *Mechanick Exercises, or the Doctrine of Handy-Works* in 1680. Chapter 24 of that work contains a rather confusing description of rose-engine work: "Rose-Work Turning, or Works of any other Figure, are performed by the same Rule and after the same Manner as Oval Work is made, only by changing the Guides, and using one whose outer edge is made with the Figure or several Figures you intend to have on your Work." He also added that "These Oval Engines, Swish Engines, and all other engines, are excellently well made by Mr. Thomas Oldfield at the sign of the Flower-de-luce, near the Savoy in the Stand, London." There are decorated ivory picture frames for miniature portraits of the wives of Henry VIII, exhibited at the Victoria and Albert Museum in London, which must have used rose-engine techniques for their ornamentation.[1]

The rose-engine lathe later evolved to cut metal and started to be used by jewelers and clock- and watch-makers. The famous watch-maker Abraham Louis Breguet used a rose engine to great effect on the backs of his pocket watches from 1775 onward, and Peter Fabergé used the effect, albeit covered by enamel, to decorate his famous jeweled eggs.[2] It was then a small step to start using these same machines to apply a rose pattern or guilloche to bank-note printing plates as a security feature. It is known that Applegath and Cowper used a rose-engine lathe made by Holtzapffel & Deyerlein for their essays for the Bank of England in 1819, and the 72-lobe rose-pattern guilloche may be attributed to this machine.[3]

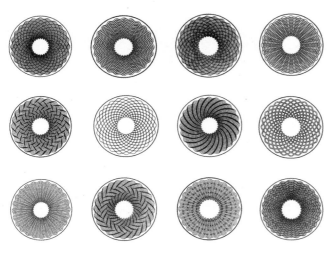

Various forms made by a rose-engine lathe using a single 24-lobe rosette.

There were limitations to the rose engine in its first form for bank-note work. The number of rose patterns which could be produced was limited to the geometry of the rosettes themselves. A 24-lobe rosette will only produce a "24-count" rose pattern and the height (or magnitude) of the rose pattern produced is the same as that of the rosette. Any change will require a new rosette, and to make the many different shapes of rosettes, the early manufacturers had to use saws and files—a difficult, protracted, and expensive operation. Holtzapffel & Company, an early manufacturer of rose engines, made a rosette-forming machine around 1840, but this was apparently the only one of its kind. By using various combinations of gears and cams, it could make a large number of differently contoured seven-inch diameter rosette wheels, but it was still a protracted process and the rosettes were only available from Holtzapffel & Company.[4]

A "barrel" of seven rosettes lined up on the mandrel of a Holtzapffel rose engine made in 1836. Note the different shapes on the peripheries of the rosettes.

The First Geometric Lathe

To overcome these costly and time-consuming problems, Asa Spencer came up with the brilliant design of his lathe. He used a single-lobe cam to rock the headstock but geared to the mandrel of the lathe with a gear ratio set by the operator. Hence, by having a gear ratio of 24:1, it produced an effective 24-count rose pattern; a 36:1 gear ratio gave an effective 36-count rose pattern; and so on. Gears were cheap and easy to make, and also prime numbers could be used to give rose patterns of prime-number count—an additional security feature. The single-lobe cam was actually a disc off-set on its shaft, and this off-set gave the size of amplitude of the rose pattern. The off-set was made by the adjustment of a screw, again under the control of the operator. This was the first true geometric lathe, and the significance of these modifications cannot be overstated. This concept of a single-lobe cam and variable rose-pattern count by gearing with variable amplitude was carried through in all later geometric lathes until their nemesis in the late 20th century.

The chronology of Asa Spencer's geometric lathe (with help from Jacob Perkins) is told in chapter 4. See also appendix D, a copy of the patent taken out by Jacob Perkins in England for the geometric lathe. Perkins was a co-inventor of the lathe but gave the primary credit to Asa Spencer, as he should have.

Cycloid Machines

Mathematicians and watch-makers are natural students of gear-shaped geometries. Even something as simple as a cycloid has a long history in mathematics. It was called the "Helen of geometers," since it caused so many quarrels among 16th-century mathematicians. Cycloids were first studied by Nicholas of Cusa in the middle of the 15th century and were later named by Galileo in 1599. The Danish astronomer Olaus Roemer investigated mechanical gears in 1674 and found that cog-wheels with epicycloidal teeth turned with minimum friction. Watch-makers of the 19th century, such as Asa Spencer, Christian Gobrecht, and Cyrus Durand, were used to working with stacked gear trains, and while they may not have understood the mathematics of their movements, they saw in those gears how to make lines curve in beautiful and complex shapes.

Since we will be using the term cycloids and epicycloids a lot, it may be helpful to review the terminology in a non-mathematical way. Suppose a diamond-pointed tool is put into a circular motion and cuts a circular line on a stationary plate. Now, if the plate is given a forward motion, the diamond point will cut a line that looks like this:

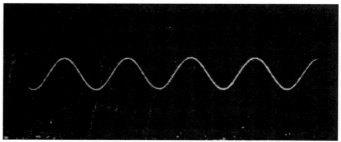

An open cycloidal line formed by two independent motions.

This line was produced by a point revolving around a moving center, or put another way, a cycloid is made by a point fixed on the periphery of a circle when the circle rolls in a straight line. The shape of the cycloid depends on the relative rate of speed of the two motions—the circular motion of the diamond point and the forward speed of the plate. If the forward motion of the plate is slowed down, the cycloids bunch up and may even touch, as in this figure:

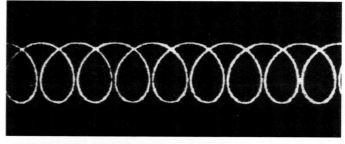

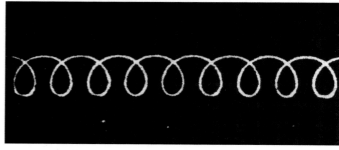

Contiguous cycloids made by slowing down the forward motion of the plate.

By repeating these lines and causing them to overlap each other, a lacelike effect can be produced, as shown here:

An epicycloid is a little more complex. It can be defined as a curve, resembling a series of arches, or petals, that is traced out

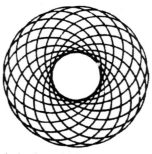

A simple cycloidal pattern made by a repetition of lines.

by a point on the circumference of a circle as that circle rolls around the outside of a second, larger circle.

The number of lobes or petals depends on the speed of the small circle (the "epicycle") as it rolls around the larger circle. By varying the speed of the epicycle, done by changing gear ratios, different numbers of epicycloids can be generated:

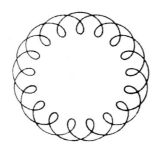

Epicycloids are the "petal-shaped lobes" traced out by the fixed point on the small circle as it rolls around the larger circle.

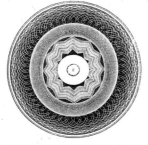

Geometric patterns are made by a combination of concentric cycloidal and wave ovals of the geometric lathe and the rose engine working on the same die.

The scientific study of how sun-and-planet gearing (also known as epicyclical gearing) generates geometric curves owes its origin to the Italian mathematician Count Gianbatrista Suardi. His beautifully illustrated book, *Nuovi Istromenti per la descrizione di diverse curve antiche e moderne . . .*, published in 1752, contains a description and engraved illustration of the "Geometric Pen" which he invented.[5]

The gears provided with this pen make it possible to produce 1,273 different figures, but only 20 are shown in the book. Suardi studied under Poleni at Padua University and became a well-known mathematician as well as an inventor of a number of instruments for making geometric curves. George Adams, the mathematical-instrument–maker to George III, published a work in London in 1791 entitled *Geometrical and Graphical Essays* which contains a description and illustration of the "Geometric Pen" invented by Count Suardi. William Ford Stanley published a work in 1866 entitled *Treatise on Mathematical Drawing Instruments* which went through at least eight editions, the last being published in 1925 under the new title *Mathematical Drawing and Measuring Instruments*. Stanley made several improvements to Suardi's "Geometric Pen" which greatly increased the number of figures it could make. Both the Adams and Stanley pens can be seen in the Science Museum in London.

Engine Turning for Bank Notes

In America beginning around 1814, Cyrus Durand made a series of increasingly complicated lathes for making ovals and similar patterns. These machines were really cycloidal engines and not true geometric lathes, but they were used by bank-note companies to make counterfeiting more difficult and ultimately lead to further improvements. Finally, after 10 years of experimenting with simpler lathes and seeing the great advantages that Asa Spencer's geometric had brought to Jacob Perkins, Cyrus invented his own version of what is really a geometric chuck. It depends on the epicyclical motion of the cutter in a similar way to the Suardi "Geometric Pen." He made several versions of the geometric chuck (1816, 1818, and 1823) and eventually gave one (an 1823 version) to the New York Historical Society.

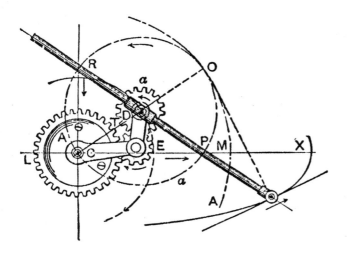

Suardi's "Geometric Pen," circa 1750.

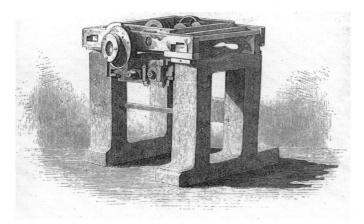

Asa Spencer's first geometric lathe, 1814.

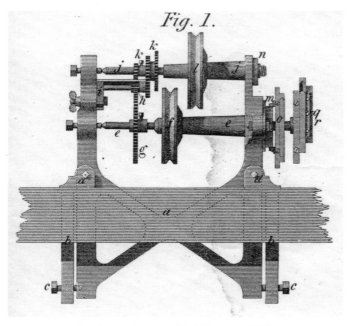

Fig. 1.

Asa Spencer's geometric lathe, circa 1819.

Cyrus Durand's geometric lathe of 1853. Note the foot-treadle.

It was said that after Asa Spencer died in 1847, Cyrus Durand was the only person in America that could operate the "geometric lathe." In 1851 he succeeded Spencer in setting up his own new lathe and operating it for the bank-note firm of Danforth, Wright & Company. It is not clear if this new lathe was a development of his epicyclical geometric chuck or if it took on the features of the original Spencer lathe. When Danforth, Wright & Company joined seven other bank-note companies to form the American Bank Note Company in 1858, Cyrus went with them and operated his lathe for the American Bank Note Company for about one year.

We see, then, that there were two broad traditions in the development of engine turning for bank-note work in the 19th century and one major development that belonged to the 20th century. The first was the development of the cycloidal machines, beginning with the "Geometric Pen" of Count Suardi, although it was never used on bank-note work. This approach culminated in the geometric chucks of Cyrus Durand (1814) and John Ibbotson (1819). These were sun-and-planet gears and were made to fit onto the mandrel of a standard lathe that had no cams. The second tradition is seen in the rose engines and the true geometric lathe made by Spencer and modified later by Chapman and Dickinson. The primary difference between these two traditions is the use of cams by Spencer. Both the rose engine and the geometric lathes had cams, could make rose patterns of variable count by gearing, and could vary the height of the rose "petals." Spencer's first lathe had but one cam and was somewhat primitive compared to the complex lathes of the 1890s that had seven cams and other attachments. The third tradition, harmonographs, were invented in the latter half of the 19th century, and the mathematics of harmonic geometries were explored by Lissajous and others, but their use on bank-note work did not take place until the latter half of the 20th century.

Cyrus Durand's 1823-version of his geometric chuck. Made of steel, brass and ivory, this was mechanically a major advance over the rose engine.

A different view of the Durand geometric chuck of 1823.

In England, a cycloidal machine was independently invented by John Holt Ibbetson in 1817. According to the research of Warren Greene Ogden Jr., Ibbetson was born in 1771, the youngest son of Dr. Ibbetson, the Archdeacon of St. Albans.[6] He resided in Chelsea, Middlesex, and died there on September 5, 1844, at the age of 73 years. His profession is unknown and he may have been a "gentleman," free to pursue his interests without the interference of work. His

first book, entitled *Specimens in Eccentric Circular Turning with practical Instructions for producing corresponding pieces in that Art*, was published for the author in 1817 by Holtzapffel & Deyerlein, Engine Manufacturers, London, and by Mr. Stewart, an Ivory Turner, also in London. This small book of 86 pages, 6 plates, and numerous illustrations did not list the author on its title page. That was corrected, however, when a reprint of the book was issued by the Architectural Library in London in 1818.

Ibbetson's second book is much more important to the history of the bank-note industry. Published in 1820, it was entitled *A Practical View of an Invention for the better protecting of Bank Notes against Forgery*. It was also a small book, with just 68 pages, but had the advantage of staying focused on the subject and without rambling off into philosophical discussions, as did many of the "scientific" books of that time. After a general discussion of the principles of bank-note security, Ibbetson mentions that Suardi's "Geometric Pen," in its simplest form, has the requisite ability to produce unique geometric figures that cannot be imitated by a skilled hand. He then states that he has constructed a machine which has a far greater number of adjustable settings than Suardi's pen and that it would take, by his calculations, "no less a period than 117,000,000,000,000,000 years to effect all the figures which might be produced from only twenty-four curves, supposing that ten figures were produced every minute." By my calculations, the total number of permutations that are possible with 24 different gear settings is 6.204484017 x 1,023, so I'm not sure how Ibbetson arrived at his number.

Ibbetson states that no one could possibly engrave even the simplest of these figures by hand and match the mathematical precision of the interlacing curves. He relates how Sir William Congreve, when he was one of the commissioners of the Bank of England's committee to examine the different proposals for bank-note security, had taken the famous engraver Mr. Branston to the shop of Mr. Stewart, the Ivory Turner, in Oxford Street and purchased his (Ibbetson's) book on *Eccentric Circular Turning*. After looking at the machine engraving in Ibbetson's book, Branston declared that he could imitate them. Ibbetson concluded that Branston was not able to copy the complex engravings because he had never shown them to anyone to prove his claim. Ibbetson also claimed that bank notes made with his machine engravings could easily be tested by the public to see if they were genuine. The engravings are so constructed as to be imprinted in detached parts and, in applying the test, the sides of the engravings which are opposite will perfectly coincide when brought into juxtaposition, line for line, and form perfect figures. To make the test even easier for the public, Ibbetson said he could print the scroll work on the left side of a note in black and the matching scroll work on the right side in red, so the public would only have to match red against black to test the genuine character of a note.

Ibbetson sent copies of his machine-engraved geometric figures to the Bank of England's Committee to demonstrate the security they offered. The committee, however, chose to adopt the bank's security plan as perfected by Messrs. Applegath and Cowper. Ibbetson then hoped to convince the country banks that they could avoid the forgery of their notes by adopting his system. Ogden says that "From Ibbetson's personal copy of his own two books, we may deduce that he was a careful and painstaking worker with the geometric chuck and the double eccentric chuck, both of which he made with his own hands."[7]

Ibbetson's geometric chuck, made by Holtzapffel & Company, circa 1819.

At present, there is no evidence that Ibbetson's geometric chuck was used by any of the bank-note companies in either England or Ireland. They apparently used rose engines to make cycloidal and epicyclical designs, primarily in the borders of notes. Ibbetson's work however did have great influence on the studies made by Henry Perigal Jr. Perigal took Ibbetson's chuck, fit it onto a mandrel of a regular lathe, and made it into a specialized machine, i.e., a geometric lathe. The configuration, however, was never particularly rigid enough to do good work. Ibbetson's chuck suffered the same problem—it was set too far away from the work piece and caused the cutter to wobble slightly. The theory was sound, but the machine's design needed further work.

The William Hartley geometric chuck was mounted vertically beneath a cutter on the head stock that remained stationary during its operation.

Another approach was the geometric chuck made by William Hartley, a mechanical engineer of Manchester, England. The chuck was further perfected by him during the period of 1860 to 1870. The only detailed explanation of the chuck that I have found is provided by Martin Matthews in his book on engine turning.[8] Paraphrasing Matthews, the chuck was composed of three stages, mounted one atop another, and each had its own slide, change wheels, and internal and external transmission wheels. "Three large gear wheels are arranged with the largest at the bottom, the first stage having 144 teeth, second stage 120 teeth, and finally the third stage 96 teeth . . ." William Hartley's "secret" lay in the method by which he generated the epicyclic motion for the second and third parts. This was achieved internally and therefore invisibly. It was accomplished by sinking the "sun" (32 teeth) and "planet" wheels (24 and 16 teeth) into the body of the great wheel (120 teeth). Not only was this very clever, but it afforded great rigidity of design and excluded dirt and debris."[9]

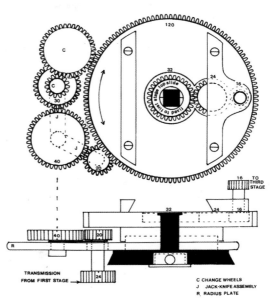

A diagram of the second part (middle section) of the William Hartley geometric chuck. When the largest wheel (120 teeth) moves, the planet gears (16 and 24 teeth) are given motion by circling the stationary sun gear (32 teeth), imparting motion to the upper (third stage) via gear 16. The same principle works in all stages.

An enlarged view of a Hartley four-part geometric chuck tracing out a pattern. Note the drive shaft leading up to the tool carriage.

A geometric design cut by the Hartley four-part geometric chuck.

This was an intelligent design that mystified Hartley's competitor (and some would say copyist) George Plant. The Hartley geometric chuck was given another improvement about 1877, when Hartley decided to add a fourth and utterly new motion to the cutter. He kept this improvement absolutely secret, even from his own family. The fourth motion consisted of moving the cutter by another gear train, one that was integrated with the motions of the other stages, but one that produced a regular wave change phased into their motion. This feature enabled the chuck to cut very complex overlapping designs.

The Hartley four-part geometric chuck would have been a very useful tool for the security printers of the day, but unfortunately it was kept secret and its mechanism was nearly lost forever. William Hartley died in September 1886, but his son, Alfred Hartley, sold the chuck to an amateur ornamental turner named Mr. Sidebottom in May 1897 for £180. Sidebottom studied the chuck for many years but failed to figure out its mechanism. He used it until his death in 1902. The chuck then passed to his son, who eventually sold it. The chuck was lost until Norman Tweedle, then the president of the Society of Ornamental Turners, tracked it down and bought it in 1952 from the daughter of the last (deceased) owner. Upon examination, the chuck was found to be missing its fourth part—the part that connected the gear train to the cutting tool. When the last owner was questioned about this part, she said that her father was so fond of the chuck that he wanted the fourth mechanism to be buried with him, and so it was. The fourth part was eventually reconstructed by Mr. Tweedle.

As a mechanical invention, it's hard to find any machine that exceeds the complexity of the geometric lathe. But for people with a mechanical turn of mind, the challenge of building such a lathe from scratch is pure delight. Charles Wesley Dickinson was that kind of man. Born in Newark, New Jersey, in 1822, he married in 1851 and started his own business the next year, specializing in the manufacture and repair of jeweler's equipment and engraving machines.[10] His success with the geometric lathe was recorded in this account:

> In 1862, when engaged in the manufacture of jewelers' tools, he received an order from Chicago parties for a geometric lathe. Without previous experiments he at once began the work and the efforts, aided by his inventive genius, were crowned with success, the result being the most perfect lathe of the kind ever produced. The original parties not fulfilling their contract, the lathe was patented and sold to the United Bank Note Company for $2,000, and on their failure, it was sold at Sheriff's sale for $4,500. The geometrical lathe thus brought to perfection, is used in the United States Treasury Department, and by all the principal bank note companies.[11]

George Rowden became a partner in the company in 1862 when it was located at 63 Hamilton Street in Newark, New Jersey. The company began with just one employee but grew to six employees in 1874 and had a weekly payroll of $125. By 1895 a geometric lathe cost about $5,000. C.W. Dickinson took his son, Charles Wesley Thompson Dickinson, as a full partner in the company about 1886, and he was the firm's general manager for more than 50 years.[12]

The geometric lathe the Dickinsons were making in the late 1890s had a mechanically shaped and sharpened cutting tool made of hardened steel that was held solidly fixed in a rest over the chuck. This cutting tool was therefore placed at the top of the machine. Below it, a die could be placed on "beds" (there were two of them) that moved forward or backward and right or left, as the operator desired. The several cams were linked to adjustable gears that moved at rates set by the operator. If a cam was geared to revolve four times while the chuck was revolving in a circle, then the combined motion would cut a line that had four waves or bulges in a circle. If that cam was taken "off gear," then the chuck would be the only part moving, and the cutting tool would cut a circle. If the cam was again linked to its gear, it would move the beds so the die was made to move back and forth as the chuck moved in a circle. The cams moved the beds, so it was possible to impart a very complex but regular movement to the beds by having several cams revolving at different rates. The cutting tool was passed through each line of the image about 20 times, cutting down about a thousandth of an inch deeper each pass. Then an adjustment was made so the cutting tool no longer went deeper with each pass, and the machine continued to trace the figure for another 50 times or so to cut out the burrs that may be down inside the incised lines. This was the basic mechanical concept of most of the late 19th-century geometric lathes. C.W. Dickinson, writing in 1895, said there were only three or four first-class operators of these lathes in the world, and they were all Americans. Not surprisingly, American dominance in this field ended shortly as European bank-note companies and governments bought geometric lathes from the two American manufacturers—Chapman and Dickinson—and their engravers became more proficient in lathe work.

W.H. Chapman began his business in Newark, New Jersey, in 1872 as a manufacturer of fine machinery. The next year, the city directory shows the company was then styled "Chapman and Lees," but this arrangement was short-lived and is not seen in subsequent directories. The company advertised that it made "geometrical engraving lathes, transfer presses for bank note engravers, and engraving machines," as well as rotary stamping presses for button-makers and a patent foot press for jewelers. The Chapman company never advertised it, but they also made lithographic presses.[13] Sometimes the name of the company appeared as "W.H. Chapman." The company name changed to "H.W. Chapman" in 1881 and was also sometimes given as "Herbert W. Chapman."[14]

The W.H. Chapman company produced a Cycloidal Engine for producing cycloidal patterns of loops, circles, and ellipses on the borders of bank notes. This machine was very substantial and, with the epicyclical head mounted on a cross-bar above the work table, it was capable of very accurate work and became a best-seller among Chapman's inventory. The regular Dickinson and Chapman geometric lathes which produced rose patterns were also capable of producing cycloidal work by a clever use of their cams. The French mathematician, Jules-Antoine Lissajous (1822–1880) had demonstrated that the sum of 2 sinusoidal movements in the x and y directions of the same frequency and 90 degrees out of phase with each other could produce a circle, ellipse, or other patterns. His work was originally applied to sound and water waves (1857) but found an application on the geometric lathe. Setting up the geometric lathe with equal counts on the x and y axes is analogous, and the rotation then of the work table produced the cycloidal patterns. However, the Chapman and Dickinson geometric lathes could only do cycloidal work on the circle and ellipse, and it required the separate Chapman Cycloidal Engine to do borders and straight-line work.

A Chapman cycloidal ruling machine.

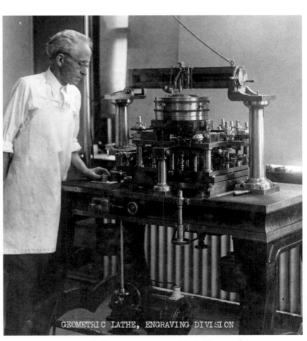

A Chapman geometric lathe
at the Bureau of Engraving and Printing in the 1940s.

increasingly to the Maschinenfabrik of Michael Kampf in Bad Homburg, West Germany. The Kampf machines offered capabilities not available on the earlier Chapman machines, such as a microletting device to produce relief engravings (letters or numbers) against a background of geometric-lathe work. Kampf dominated the geometric-lathe market until computer graphics and lasers supplanted them in the 1990s.

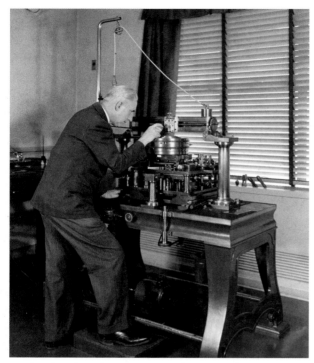

Another view of a similar Chapman geometric lathe used at the Bureau of Engraving and Printing, circa 1947.

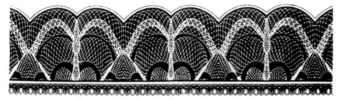

A geometric border formed by combining several sections of geometric (white-line) patterns.

A modern Guillochermaschine—a III Supra geometric lathe made by the Michael Kampf factory in Bad Homburg, West Germany.

Harmonographs, Campylographs, Fantasy Lathes, etc.

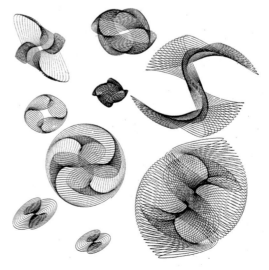

Harmonographic patterns made by Thomas De La Rue, Ltd. on their "fantasy lathe."

Both the Chapman and the Dickinson geometric lathes were produced in small numbers into the early part of the 20th century. The market for such machines was limited to security printers, and since the machines could be used for half a century or more, and very few bank-note companies were formed during the first half of the 20th century, the sale of new machines was correspondingly small. Companies that made geometric lathes had to diversify into other bank-note–engraving machinery, such as ruling machines, pantographs, and transfer presses. The Chapman company did this early in its history, and Dickinson far less so, but ultimately both companies failed for one reason or another. After World War II, the market for geometric lathes and other bank-note–engraving devices went

Harmonographs date from the middle of the 19th century. The firm of Tisley and Spiller in London made a demonstration model for use in classrooms about 1873. Harmonographs are mechanical devices that trace the resultant line made by two or more simple harmonic motions made by pendulums that are slowly dampened in their movement. A double-elliptical harmonograph made by S.C. Tisley in 1873 shows two pendulums fixed a short distance apart in a stand. The shaft of one of the pendulums has a flat table attached to the top. As the pendulum swings, the table is made to move in an oscillatory motion. The other pendulum has a pen attached in a right-angled holder at the top of its shaft, and this pen is held above the table of the first pendulum and pressed against it by a spring. When the pendulums are moving, both the table and the pen are also moving and tracing a series of Lissajous figures. This principle was used to make toys that were popular in many homes until the early 20th century.

The principle of the harmonograph was finally adapted for bank-note work by Vic Phelps, a geometric-lathe operator at Thomas De La Rue in England. His machine was called the "fantasy lathe," and the prototype was built in his garage about 1960 from the gears salvaged from a war-surplus bombsight and some angle iron. Eventually, this lathe was built by Westley-Finbow Engineering, and a copy sold for about £40,000 in 1980. Very few of these machines were built, but for a while, their use was quite popular on the bank notes produced by Thomas De La Rue.[15]

A $1 New Zealand note illustrating the "fantasy lathe" used to make the hollow tubes that extend from the Queen's right shoulder up to the denominational counter at the upper left.

The Campylograph was a machine built in the late 19th century for making rose patterns on dies of soft steel or polished copper. It is a cycloidal machine, similar to the "Geometric Pen" made by Count Suardi, but much more complicated. It is doubtful it was ever used by a bank-note company and seems more likely to have been a device for demonstrating gear trains and geometric curves.

Another device was the spirograph, a toy invented in 1962 by the British engineer Denys Fisher to make pen drawings of hypotrochoids and epitrochoids. The spirograph is a useful device to demonstrate how rose petals and other patterns can be made by the simple working of gears.

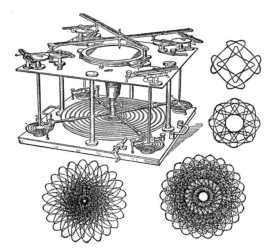

A Campylograph, circa 1900. The small crank on the bottom platform rotates the plate containing a multiple series of gears, which mesh with pinions on four radial arms and transfer their motion through four small but similar gear plates to vertical spindles (one at each corner) and to reversing gears on the upper platform. The faces of the gears on the upper platform have trammel pivots to carry the slotted bars that hold the tracing pen. The tracing table also turns in unison with the gear plate below. The number of loops in the figures is governed by the particular ring gear used. Specimens of the geometric patterns are shown beneath the machine.

A modern bank note made by Thomas De La Rue showing the security pattern made by their fantasy lathe, a modern version of the harmonographs of the previous century.

Pantographs

The pantograph is one of the most useful tools in bank-note engraving. It enlarges or reduces the size of virtually any graphic element, whether lettering, drawings, or numbers. The basic machine consists of four connected arms which form a parallelogram. One arm holds a sharp pointer in a set screw. A second arm holds a drawing implement, such as a pencil or pen. By moving the first arm carefully over each line of a drawing, the mechanical linkage between that arm and the second arm causes the drawing implement to duplicate the motion of the pointer and trace exactly the same design on a piece of paper or a metal plate. By changing the position of the set screws that lock the arms together, one can enlarge or reduce the size of the duplicate drawing.

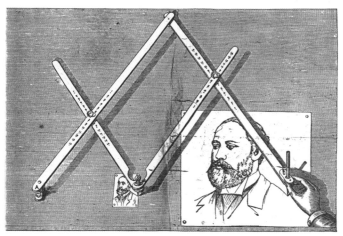

A simplified pantograph. Depending on the position of the set screws on the arms, the device enlarges or reduces the lines the pointer traces. This particular pantograph was sold as a toy for 25¢ in 1862, but it demonstrates the mechanical principles very well.

The pantograph was invented by a Jesuit priest named Christoph Scheiner while he was teaching mathematics and Hebrew at the University of Ingolstadt in Germany. Scheiner was born in Wald, near Mandelheim, in southwest Germany on July 25, 1571. He invented the pantograph sometime early in his career, probably about 1603, but did not publish his ideas until 1631.[16] Thomas Jefferson built a pantograph and used it at Monticello as a copy machine for his correspondence. When he wrote a letter, the drawing arm made an exact duplicate, saving him the time to copy the letter by hand. His machine is still on display at Monticello.

In bank-note companies, the pantograph was used to reduce drawings for vignettes and especially for reducing lettering and numbers to a small size. The counterfeit engraver could purchase a pantograph and duplicate the work of the original engraver, so small-sized lettering or the fine details of a vignette did very little to protect bank notes. When Jacob Perkins and his American friends were in London trying to win the Bank of England's prize money for a secure bank note, they engraved a particular note which Perkins had claimed would take a good engraver three-and-a-half years to make a copy that would fool the public, if indeed, one could be made at all. The note featured a head of Homer, repeated five times, a head of a woman engraved by Fairman and repeated four times, two pieces of geometric engraving made by Spencer's lathe, and eight ovals containing the Bank of England's charter in minute writing, which was done by a pantograph. Sir William Congreve gave the project to the engraver Robert Branson and his son, and they managed to copy it in 17 days. The pantograph made the small writing possible but did little to make the note secure against counterfeiting.

The pantograph has been modified many times. J.J. Hawkins of Boundenton, New Jersey, invented a pantograph and parallel-ruling machine and got it patented on May 17, 1803, but the patent was lost in the fire that destroyed the Patent Office in 1836, and no description of the device has been found.[17] About 1820 Bryan Donkin, one of Britain's great engineers, built a pantograph milling machine to enable Sir William Congreve to make his newly patented compound plates, as describe in chapter 4.[18] One of the security features of these plates was a combination of work done by the pantograph (scrolls, lettering, crescent and star designs, etc.) and work done by a Holtzapffel rose engine (parallel lines, waved lines, and background). In this machine, the work was done on a table that could be moved by hand in either of two directions. The belt drive turned the cutting tool at variable speeds from 2,000 to 7,000 rpm, depending on the type of metal being cut and the size of the tool.[19] The pantograph was also used to cut the irregular pattern of the two interlocking plates, and this was done so accurately that the two plates could be fitted together without any further filing or adjustments, and the lines of the cut were almost invisible. While the Bank of England did not print notes with the compound plates, several princes in India made their currency from such plates. In 1822 Cyrus Durand built a pantograph for reducing ovals in the borders of notes, possibly from a suggestion in the *Edinburgh Encyclopedia*.

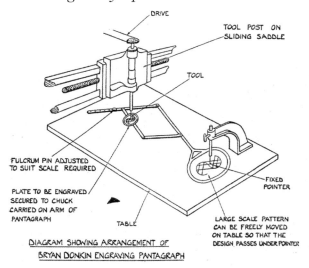

DIAGRAM SHOWING ARRANGEMENT OF
BRYAN DONKIN ENGRAVING PANTAGRAPH

Bryan Donkin's pantograph, circa 1820.

In America, the leading manufacturer of pantographs and ruling machines was the John Hope Company of Providence, Rhode Island. John Hope was born in Salford, Manchester, England, in 1820. He was raised in a textile community where cloth manufacturing and printing were the chief industries. His father and grandfather had engraved rolls for calico printing since 1780. His father, also named John Hope, founded a company for calico printing in 1810. When he was 14 years old, the young John Hope apprenticed in his father's shop and soon learned all the branches of the business. He and his brother came to the United States in 1847 at the urging of a friend who had known Hope in Manchester some years before. In 1854 he married Miss Emma Cordwell of Manchester. She came to the United States for the wedding and eventually bore eight children.

John and his brother Edmund set up business in Providence and built a machine shop in connection with their engraving business. It was in this shop that John Hope built the prototype of a pantograph that would soon become famous as the most accurate of its kind. It rapidly became the favorite pantograph in Canada, Japan, China, England, and America, where it was used in the Bureau of Engraving and Printing. The company's catalogue explained that it was designed to make cycloid ruling, tints for checks and bonds, lettering, numbers, etc. Other machines followed and became the principle source of income for this company. A ruling machine for making straight, waved, circular, and radiated lines was endorsed by all the leading bank-note houses. In 1890 the firm changed its name to the John Hope & Sons Engraving and Manufacturing Company. John Hope died on September 8, 1913, at his home at 221 Atlantic Avenue in Providence at the age of 92.

A John Hope ruling machine being operated at the Bureau of Engraving and Printing.

Another famous pantograph, used expressly for engraving, was the Francis Engraving Machine, invented by Allan Everett Francis of Garrettsville, Ohio. On March 15, 1881, Francis received U.S. Patent No. 238,882 for "new and useful improvements in engraving machines." The Francis pantograph could be adjusted to take varying thicknesses of objects. It could also engrave objects at different ratios. The machine also held a steel graver that cut into the surface of the metal just like a hand-held burin would. The graver was held in a swivel mount that allowed the point to be rotated in a circle as the graver followed a pattern. This gave a "bright cut," similar to professional hand engraving. The machine was used from the 1880s to about 1920.

Precision pantographs were more often made in Germany and England than in America. Those of Friedrich Deckel of Munich were especially well-built and are still in use today. Kulhmann started out in the late 1800s in Wilhelmshaven in a watch-maker's shop which was later converted to a precision-machine shop. Kulhmann began making pantographs in 1905. In England several companies made pantographs known for their rigidity and precision, including Alexander, Taylor Hobson, and Newing-Hall.

Two modern pantographs that were made by the Michael Kämpf Maschinenfabrik of West Germany sometime before 1975.

In modern pantographs, such as the Precision Engraving Machine Type B III made by the Michael Kämpf Company in West Germany, the entire "Lord's Prayer" of 242 letters and punctuation marks can be easily printed on a square die having side lengths of only 0.0148 inches. The type has perfectly sharp outlines, even when viewed under high magnification, because the height of the individual letters are all 0.0055 of an inch, the engraving depth is 0.004 inches, and the line thickness is kept at precisely 0.0055 inches. This was not a special machine made just to produce engraved type having microscopic precision, but a standard, commercial machine (pantograph) made for a wide variety of purposes in the 1960s. In America, only one company, Gorton of Racine, Wisconsin, made a heavy-duty precision pantograph. It also could engrave the "Lord's Prayer" on a small space. In fact, it was used to engrave the prayer on the point of a pin. A pin is a wire of about .005 inches in diameter. The heat from one light bulb shining on the surface of the engraving would expand the pantograph setting enough to obliterate the engraving.

Ruling Machines

Certain engravers, such as those doing landscapes, needed to make large numbers of closely spaced parallel lines to represent water or sky, or for cross-hatching, and it had often been the practice to use a metal rule with a straight edge to guide an etching needle as it cut through an etching ground. This method fails to space the lines at precise intervals and gives an amateurish look to the work. Wilson Lowry, an English engraver, solved the problem in 1790 by designing a ruling machine that allowed a steel-cutting tool or "pen" to move horizontally along a slide.[20] The slide was moved up or down by means of a screw that regulated the spacing between lines in precise intervals. Parallel lines made by this machine no longer had irregular spacing or a variable width. Lowry is said to have made his first ruling machine in wood, principally by his own hands.[21] Since a steel pen loses its sharp point rather quickly, Lowry replaced it with a diamond point in 1798. The diamond point allowed the engraver to cut finer lines than could be accomplished by any steel point. This was an actual cut diamond, rigidly mounted, so it needed no "sharpening" during the course of the work. Lowry continued to make improvements to his ruling machines, finally deciding that the use of a micrometer-screw to adjust the distances between lines was not accurate enough on account of the wearing down of the screw as it moved a heavy slide bar. As an alternative, Lowry adopted the method of fusing one wedge against another. Another innovation was the use of a carriage or tool assembly which held the cutting point rather than having it worked by hand. The carriage always presented the same edge of the cutter and formed a constant angle with the plate when passing over its surface. The carriage was also weighted to give equal pressure and was capable of being raised or lowered at pleasure, which allowed the engraver to break or interrupt the line which he was drawing.[22]

Lowry's pupil, Turrell, made further improvements. Instead of having a carriage to hold the cutter and move it over a stationary plate, Turrell made the cutter stationary and moved the plate beneath it by micrometer-screws on the *x-y* axes. This design, however, did not offer any significant advantage and was not a success.

In the ruling machine made by Percy Heath about 1836, the design allowed engravers to make lines that differed from each other so as to avoid the sterile rigidity of a strictly mechanical process, yet it produced a near resemblance to hand ruling. It was the first time that a machine combined the best of the two methods—retaining the perfect equality of distance between the lines and the uniformity of strength characteristic of machine-ruling, but making the lines look as if they were hand-ruled with the imperfections of human muscles and eyes. Mr. Heath was awarded the Silver Medal of the Society of Arts.[23]

In America, John James Baralet, working in Philadelphia, is said to have made the first ruling machine used by American engravers. Since he arrived in Philadelphia in 1795, his machine must have been made later than that. Imported ruling machines began to arrive, principally from London, after 1800. Baralet died in 1812, and there is no record that he ever took out a patent on his machine.

Christian Gobrecht, writing in 1842, when he was head of the engraving department at the U.S. Mint, gave the following history of his contributions to the development of the ruling machine:

> In the year 1810, I constructed a ruling machine so the platform in which the plate was laid to be ruled was made to move by an inclined plane, the ruler being stationary and the plate made to move under it. This machine was left in the hands of an engraver in Baltimore where I then resided. It has been very useful to him in ruling plates and he has worked with it for many years. This then is the first ruling machine that was ever made so far as I know, where the ruler was stationary and the platform on which the plate [rested] was made to move.[24]

Gobrecht moved to Philadelphia in 1811 and engaged in general engraving and die sinking. He joined the firm of Murray, Draper & Fairman in 1816 and worked with Asa Spencer, Jacob Perkins, and D.H. Mason, who were all mechanics either designing new engraving machines or improving old ones. Gobrecht invented a medal-engraving machine while at this company with the assistance of Spencer and Mason, and later he carried on a long debate about who did what and when.

William Rollinson invented a ruling machine in 1812 for making waved lines and used it to great advantage in making bank notes with his partner, W.S. Leney. Rollinson had come over from England in 1788, before Lowry had invented his ruling machine, but he soon acquired one and used it in 1804 when he invented a method of using a roulette inserted into the ruling machine to make the background on a portrait of Alexander Hamilton on copper.

Rollinson's waved-line ruling machine could not only make regularly spaced straight lines but also waved lines that were spaced very close together. By skillful operation, the waved lines could also be made to move closer to the adjacent line or further away from it, making it look like the ruling had been made by hand. This was similar to the effect achieved by Percy Heath's ruling machine in 1836 but differed from it by making lines of only one width. Heath's machine could make lines of variable widths. In the bank notes made by Rollinson and Leney, there is often found a vertical box or panel at the far-right side of the note. In this box, the waved pattern of lines move up from the bottom in a jagged shape like the lines made by a modern seismograph. Then they smooth out and become more like the moiré pattern seen in watered silk. At the far left side of the note is the same vertical box, but this time it is ruled differently by the same machine. Dunlap, in his *History of the Arts of Design*, says that Rollinson's ruling machine of 1812 "was a great improvement in bank-note engraving and caused a great sensation among engravers at the time."

Partington said in 1825 that "machines for ruling equidistant lines, both straight and waved, are now commonly made in London."[25] England certainly lead America in the development of this branch of mechanical engraving, but Americans soon caught up. W.L. Ormsby constructed a simpler machine and illustrated this in his book, *A Description of the Present System of Bank Note Engraving*, published in 1852.

Ruling machines have become more precise and accurate than anything the early engravers could possibly have imagined. Take for example the ruling machine designed and built by David W. Mann and Warren Greene Ogden Jr. for the British-American Bank Note Company of Ottawa, Canada, between 1938 and 1940. This machine was also used to produce the "grailling" that forms the background of George Washington's portrait on the U.S. $1 notes:

> . . . This grailling is made up of horizontal and vertical parallel ruled lines seven and one half thousandths of an inch apart. This is about the thickness of two sheets of writing paper, or, as the engraver says, "one hundred and twenty-eight lines to the inch." The accuracy required for the above ruling engine demands that the spacing from one line to its neighbor was not to vary more than forty millionths of an inch—an unheard of requirement in those days. This was accomplished with assistance from the U.S. Bureau of Standards, which furnished a certified standard length measure (a standard yard) calibrated to five millionths of an

inch at 62 [degrees] F. This measure was used to calibrate the master lead screw of the ruling engine which moved the ruling carriage 0.0075 inch space before ruling each line of the steel die.[26]

Grailling is a security device little known even to bank-note collectors. It is simply a ruled background against which a portrait or other engraving stands out in marked contrast. The assumption was that counterfeiters could not reproduce the ruling accurately, and their efforts to copy this background would be made immediately evident to even the casual observer. The human brain has a persistence of vision and notices even small errors in the otherwise smooth and even color of black lines in grailling. The ruling machine made by Mann and Ogden predated the era of photocopiers, but there was concern even then that the process cameras used in commercial lithography would have sufficient resolution to reproduce a grailling made by a standard ruling machine of lesser accuracy and precision.

Medallion-Engraving Machines

Also known as "medal engraving machines" and "image lathes," these devices copied the surface features of coins or medals to produce an engraving that appeared to be three-dimensional. This was done by having a tracing needle move horizontally across the coin or medal in lines that were about 1/200 of an inch apart. The tracing needle was mechanically linked to an engraving point that made a copy of the coin's image on a copper or soft-steel die. To get the three-dimensional effect on the engraved copy, the machine was designed to deflect the tracing needle and the engraving cutter in a vertical direction whenever the needle passed over a raised surface. The amount of deflection was proportional to the actual height of the three-dimensional surface the needle was passing over. On the part of a coin that was flat, there would be no deflection of the tracing needle, and all the lines would be spaced closely together at equal distances. When the tracing needle came across a raised feature, like the side of a nose in a human face, it would be moved vertically. If the feature on the coin stood 1/16 of an inch above the rest of the surface, the engraving point would be moved vertically 1/16 of an inch. This was repeated each time the tracing needle was moved back to a new starting point just 1/200 of an inch above the last trace. At each pass, the needle would be deflected proportionately as it moved across each point of elevation in the image.

As a result, the three-dimensional image of the coin would be represented on the engraving by lines that were spaced greater- or lesser-distances apart. The human eye is tricked into seeing these differently spaced lines as a three-dimensional image. This is the Gestalt theory of visual perception, which states that the brain recognizes figures and whole forms instead of just a collection of simple lines and curves. The finished engraving plays the optical trick on the brain. If the engraving showed only a small area of the image, say the flare of a single nostril, the lines would probably be meaningless. But if the engraving shows a larger area, the brain presumably sorts through its memory and matches up the form with that of a human nose and then anticipates the forms of the surrounding features and confirms them to be a human face in three dimensions.

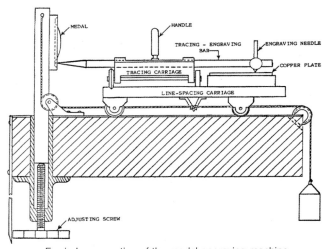

Frazier's conception of the medal-engraving machine described in the *Manuel du Tourneur* (1816).

There is some evidence that medallion-engraving machines were being made as early as 1775, but their operation was not described in print. The earliest description of a medal-copying machine is found in Bergeron's *Manuel du Tourneur*, published in Paris in 1816.[27] The description given there is quite good, and Arthur H. Frazier drew his conception of what the machine looked like and how it operated. This machine is said to have been made by Collard about 1805.

In the United States, Asa Spencer and Christian Gobrecht have both been credited with the independent invention of a medal-engraving machine. The priority of their work becomes clear in this comment made by Asa Spencer in 1842:

I will endeavor to give a plain and simple history of the whole affair. In the fall of 1816, I came to this city with Mr. Jacob Perkins, whose objective was in conjunction with Messrs. Murray, Fairman & Company to introduce into the art of bank note engraving, a new and original style of work, the production of a machine invented by me, and called the Geometric Lathe. Mr. Gobrecht was, at that time, employed in the same establishment, which afforded us frequent opportunities of conversing on subjects connected with the business. He talked much concerning ruling machines—had a great desire to possess one, and told me he had attempted to make one, to be moved by a screw, but that it failed from the imperfection of the screw. He thought, however, that by the aid of such means and implements that were then in my possession, he could be furnished with a screw of sufficient accuracy for the purpose. I undertook to assist him, but had not proceeded far when I became convinced, that the plan we were upon would not answer. Having, however, embarked in the enterprise, I was unwilling to give it up, and began immediately to study some other plan; when a modification of the wheel and axle, like that of the plating mill, was fixed upon by me. I then made known to Mr. Gobrecht, my entire want of faith in his old plan, and described to him my new one, in which I had the fullest confidence. He, however, was not pleased with it, and seemed loath to give up his own, but after consulting with Mr. Perkins, who gave a decided preference to my plan, and spoke in the highest terms of it, he became anxious to have the first machine on the new plan. I undertook it for him; my other engagements made it necessary, that I should get it up in the simplest form, and with the least amount of labor. I had previously to this, furnished Mr. Gobrecht, at his request, a very simple plan for ruling waved lines, taken from a movement in the Rose Engine, and easily attached to any ruling machine, consisting of an arm or lever, with a point or touch, as it is called in the Rose Engine, resting on a waved surface and kept in contact with it by a suitable weight or spring. This touch being connected with the slide which carries the etching point, and made to move over the waved surface or model, a vibratory motion thus caused was, by joints adjusted for this purpose, connected to the etching point.

Thus the machine was placed in Mr. Gobrecht's hands, with the exception, merely, of the waved surface or model, which was left for him to supply, to suit himself. This last appendage to the machine (taken from the Rose Engine) had not been in operation when he took it away. I have no recollection of having heard Mr. Gobrecht speaking of the machine afterwards.[28]

While Christian Gobrecht may well have made a simple ruling machine using a novel approach, it is clear from this letter that Spencer taught Gobrecht the basic mechanics of a waved-line ruling machine, made it for him (except for the rosette), and said little or nothing when Gobrecht implicitly took credit for what had been Spencer's design and work. In the debate that followed, Spencer stood on somewhat higher ethical ground than did Gobrecht and also had historical fact on his side. Gobrecht used the medal-engraving machine that Spencer built to produce a copy of the head of Tsar Alexander I of Russia, and this created some excitement among engravers who wanted to know how it was done. Gobrecht would not reveal how he made the engraving and watched as his fame grew.

This began to change when Spencer went to England in company with the Perkins group (1819) and took along an exact copy of the machine that he had made for himself. In London he used the machine for the first time with a waved model, a small rosette. Although the machine worked, it still had the distortion that had been seen in Gobrecht's machine. To continue the story, we can turn again to the letter that Spencer wrote in Philadelphia in 1842:

. . . The idea of changing the model immediately suggested itself. The waved model was removed, and a shilling [coin] put in its place, when a tolerable copy was at once produced. A distinguished machine-engraver tried the same experiment by my direction, at his place in Somerstown near London with great success. When I asked him how he had succeeded, his answer was "perfectly, it would not only copy the waved model, but any device I put under the touch."

During my stay in London, nothing was done to bring the art of medal engraving into notice. On my return to Philadelphia, I was the first to unveil the mystery [distortion] of medal ruling, but being deeply engaged in introducing improvements in bank note engraving, I gave no attention to it until about 1826 or '27, when thinking it might afford an additional security against counterfeiting, I put my machine a little in order for experimenting, and executed a large plate containing medals, a copy of which I herewith send you. The work was much admired. Impressions from the plate soon found their way to Europe, and excited to exertion the ingenious mechanicians of London and Paris. Mr. Saxton, of this city, also exercised his ingenuity on the subject. I do not perceive, however, in these specimens, a greater degree of perfection than in my own.[29]

Both Spencer and Joseph Saxton figured out, independently, that the problem with all existing medal engravers stemmed from the angle of the tracer. Spencer apparently solved the problem first, and Saxton was not far behind.

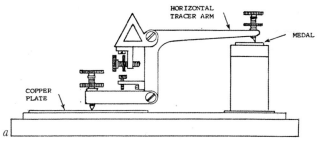

Frazier's conception of the Gobrecht medal-ruling machine of 1817.

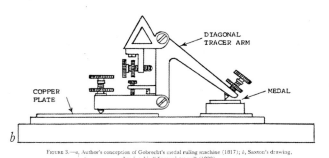

FIGURE 3.—a, Author's conception of Gobrecht's medal ruling machine (1817); b, Saxton's drawing, showing his "diagonal tracer" (1829).

Saxton's drawing showing his "diagonal tracer" (1829).

Joseph Saxton was born in Huntingdon, Pennsylvania, on March 22, 1790, the second of 11 children. He received a normal elementary-school education and began an apprenticeship at age 14 with a local watch-maker who also taught silversmithing and engraving. Saxton never engraved, but he did put to great use a curious and incredibly gifted mind. He moved to Philadelphia about 1809. In his early days he constructed an astronomical clock with a compensating pendulum and an escapement made by his own plan. He also constructed the town clock for the city of Philadelphia, which continues to the present day to chime the hours from the belfry of Independence Hall.

In Philadelphia Saxton became acquainted with Christian Gobrecht and learned about medal-engraving machines. He was not too impressed with the Gobrecht model and the distortion it produced, so he set about building his own medal-copying machine. He thought about various adjustments to his machine and experimented with it for almost 10 years. In August 1829, just a short time after he moved to London, Saxton figured out the problem and drew a sketch showing how he solved the mystery. That sketch is now in the archives of the Smithsonian Institution. It is likely that Asa Spencer beat Saxton to the solution by less than a year.

Impressions of the large plate of medals made by Spencer on his medal-engraving machine soon found their way to England and were shown to Angier M. Perkins, the son of Jacob Perkins, who in turn showed the plate to Mr. Bawtree, the chief engraver for the Bank of England. Bawtree thought the process had potential for making bank notes more secure against counterfeiting, so he showed it to Mr. Lacey, an employee of Perkins & Bacon, to see if he could make a medal-engraving machine like Spencer's. Lacey had no interest in trying this, so Bawtree next turned to R.B. Bate, an instrument-maker in London. Bate agreed to tackle the problem, but it soon fell to his son, John Bate, to continue the work. Bate had a rough idea how medal-engraving machines worked in general, but he needed the special tool or secret device that produced such excellent engravings for Spencer and Saxton. He approached Saxton and discussed the matter with him, offering him a share of the business if he would join him in a partnership and reveal his secrets. Saxton did not like the man and refused to reveal his secret. Bate held several other discussions with Saxton, gaining a little more information every time they talked. Eventually, Bate learned the secret of the "diagonal tracer," as Saxton called it, or possibly thought of the idea by himself. His last discussion with Saxton was in February 1832, at which time Bate claimed he had built an improved model, could do the work as well as anyone, and offered Saxton one more chance to form a partnership. Saxton refused, and Bate surprised everyone when he received British Patent No. 6,254 entitled "Machinery to Produce Imitations of Medals, Sculpture, etc." on October 9, 1832.

An acrimonious debate between John Bate and Joseph Saxton, conducted in newspapers and magazines, took several years to die down. The public generally sided with Saxton and recognized the priority of his claim but felt he was to blame for not having the good sense to protect his invention by requesting a patent. If one compares the drawing of the Bate machine with the drawing of the machine made by Saxton in 1829, one can see that the two are very similar in design, with the exception that Saxton's model has the diagonal tracer tilted downward at 45 degrees, and Bate's machine has it tilted upward 45 degrees.

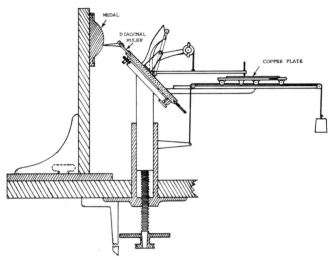

John Bate's medal-engraving machine (1832).

While Saxton and Bate were arguing the fine points of business ethics, some real businessmen were hard at work making medal engraving a profitable affair. In 1830 a French engineer named Achille Collas took the description of the medal-engraving machine in the *Manuel du Tourneur* and improved it so it was both simpler and more automatic. He was making very good engravings from medals by 1831. In 1832 Monsieur Collas met with an American businessman, Vincent Nolte, who had just formed a company named Lachevardière et Cie.[30] Nolte bought the Collas medal-engraving machine and all rights to its use. The Lachevardière company consisted of Nolte, the principal shareholder; Lachevardière, the manager; Paul Delroche, an historical painter; Henriquel Dupont, a famous engraver; Charles Lenormant, an historian; and Collas, who would operate the machine.[31] Their plan was to use the Collas machine to print a set of folio volumes to cover the entire history of numismatics from ancient Greece to modern times to be called the *Trésor de numismatique et de glyptique*. The series began in 1834, and subsequent volumes were

issued almost every year until 1858. The initial response was rather poor, so the Lachevardière company appealed to the French government to support the project, and they bought 350 sets of the 20-volume series, worth about £17,000.

When the English sales of the *Trésor de numismatique* did not go as well as hoped, Vincent Nolte went to England to work with the Keeper of Medals at the British Museum to start a similar project called *A Medallic Illustration of British History*. The British Museum required the House of Commons to give their assent to the plan, but during hearings held in that august body, John Bate said that the British government had no business giving the work to a French company, and that British machines (his) could do the job cheaper than the French. A heated argument erupted between Nolte and Bate, lasting for several months. Finally, a report on the hearings was released by the House of Commons on July 15, 1836, but it did not give authority to the British Museum to undertake the project.[32] Nolte, thoroughly disgusted with Bate, abandoned the effort and went back to France.

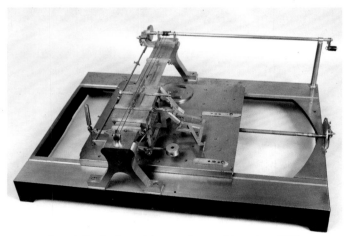

Joseph Saxton's medal-engraving machine, circa 1837.

The American machinist, James Bogardus, also contributed to medal-engraving technology. He was born in Catskill, New York, on March 14, 1800, and received a typical education at irregular intervals until he entered an apprenticeship with a local watch-maker. He was an outstanding student at this profession but also learned die sinking and engraving. After he completed his apprenticeship, he moved to New York and lived there for the rest of his life. The first evidence of his mechanical skill was a gold medal awarded to him by the American Institute of New York for an eight-day, three-wheeled chronometer, which he made in 1818. On March 2, 1820, he received a patent for a very complicated clock. The same year, he received a patent on May 25 for his first practical invention, a "ring flyer" used in spinning cotton. This was followed in 1831 by a patent for an eccentric sugar-grinding mill. These last two inventions made his fortune, but he continued to invent new machines and improve a number of old ones.

In 1836 Bogardus went to England and almost immediately accepted a public challenge to build a medal-engraving machine. His machine incorporated the diagonal tracer invented by Spencer and Saxton but had a few new features of its own. With this machine, he made a very accurate copy of a medal featuring the Greek goddess Ariadne, which came to the attention of Queen Victoria, who requested that Bogardus make a portrait of her on his new machine. Bogardus was also the first to address the problem of the damage that the diagonal tracer did to the surface of the medal or coins being copied. The fine point of the tracer made very fine scratches to the medallic surface, and every time it hit an existing scratch or pit in the medal, it left a blip on the engraved line in the copy. Bogardus first made a shellac cast of the medal or coin, smoothed out the imperfections, and used this cast to make his medal engraving, preventing any damage to the original.

The patent granted to John Bate to protect his medal-engraving machine was not as well written as it could have been, and a number of instrument-makers began to bring out their own versions of the machine in both England and Germany. The newer versions reached a zenith in the early to mid-1840s. Medallion engraving may have been touted by the American bank-note companies as a deterrent to counterfeiting, but actually only a few bank notes designed and printed in the 19th century had any medallion engraving.[33]

Transfer Presses

Jacob Perkins and George Murray took out a patent on January 25, 1813, with the title "Method of Impressing all Kinds of Die Work on Steel and Copper by Circular Dies." A drawing of the transfer press described in that patent has survived, but the patent itself was lost in the fire that destroyed the Patent Office in 1836.

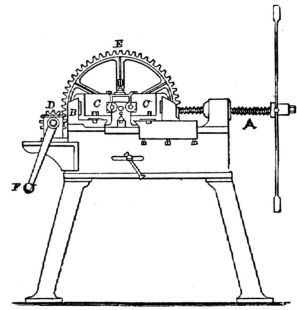

The Perkins-Murray transfer press of 1813.

Consequently, there are many unanswered questions about the history of this transfer press and the role that George Murray may have played in getting it built. As far as we know, George Murray was not mechanically oriented and probably had nothing to do with the design and construction of the press. It is more likely that he formed a working relationship with Perkins and may have given him financial support in return for joint ownership of the patent. It was this transfer press that Perkins and his associates took with them to London at the end of May 1819. It remained there and was used in engraving the "Penny Black" postage stamp and the borders of the notes of the country banks.

Perkins found the mechanical principles of presses to be very profitable. An example is his patented progressive-lever seal press. He patented (but did not invent) this toggle-joint lever press on February 27, 1819, and sold copies of it to offices that needed something better than a screw press to emboss their seals on important papers. In writing about this seal press, Perkins said "[one] is in use at the Mayor's [office] and another at the Philadelphia Insurance Office."[34] Perkins estimated that a force of 100 pounds exerted downward on the handle of the press would result in a pressure of 30,000 pounds on the seal. This mechanical principle was used in larger presses for a variety of purposes, such as the cutting, punching, and embossing of metal, expressing oil from nuts, operating the platen in presses, and compressing tobacco, wool, or cotton so they could be baled. In April 1819 Perkins and Gideon Fairman signed an agreement selling an exclusive right to General David Brydie Mitchell, a three-time governor of Georgia, to use a toggle-joint press for baling cotton on his plantation at Savannah, Georgia. They were paid $40,000 for this contract.

A major event in the development of the transfer press took place about 1824, when Cyrus Durand made a transfer press expressly for bank-note work. This was a compound-lever press but operated by different principles than did the one in Philadelphia, which was kept a secret.[35] Cyrus patented his transfer press on May 22, 1828, and like many other early patents, it was lost in the great fire that destroyed the Patent Office. Although other mechanics made transfer presses over the years, the Durand model became a standard in the industry, and even the presses made in the 1890s still show the basic design of the Durand model. If he had not independently invented a "geometric chuck" some years earlier, Durand would be famous today in the bank-note industry solely for his transfer press. It immediately replaced the slow and very awkward operation of the Perkins transfer press and helped tremendously to bring siderography to the forefront.

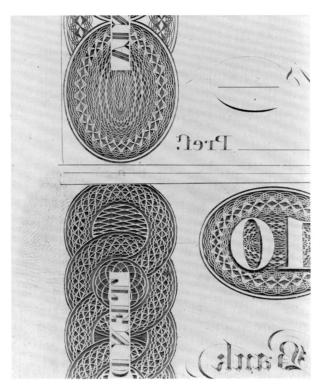

An enlarged view of a bank-note plate showing a geometric border that was abruptly truncated at the edge of the note. This was probably due to the use of a stock die that was too long for the intended space and not a mistake in transferring. Someone's fingerprint was left on the plate in printer's ink.

A transfer roller with two dies standing in relief. This roller would be used to impress the dies in a plate (intaglio).

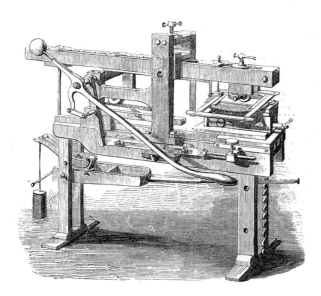

Cyrus Durand's transfer press of 1824. This was a revolutionary design that was quickly adopted by the industry.

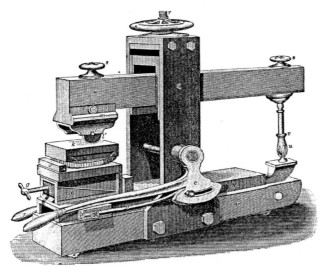

The Casilear-Tichenor transfer press.

James Bogardus, whom we met earlier in the discussion of medal-engraving machines, also made a transfer press during the early 1830s. None of his patents survived the fire at the Patent Office, so all we have now is anecdotal information about the machine, including the fact that it was a compound-lever press. The principle of the compound lever has been known since antiquity; in fact, there is a model of one in the Science Museum in London that was made in 1762 by George Adams, the instrument-maker to King George III.[36] In compound-lever machines there are two or more rigid beams acting on the same

fulcrum. Following the law of equilibrium, the length of the two beams that make up the effort arms give a high-mechanical advantage to the machine, allowing ordinary human-muscle power to exert several tons of pressure on a roll or die. Since we don't know the dimensions of the Bogardus press, we can't calculate the pressure it developed, but it was not unusual for a large transfer press to deliver more than 10 tons of pressure.

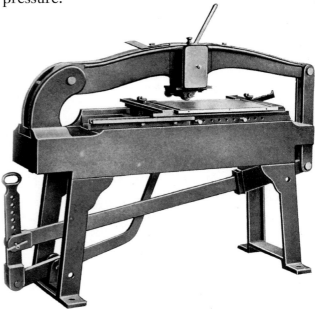

A transfer press brought into use in 1868. Manufacturer unknown.

A transfer press was built by R. Hoe & Company of New York City for the bank-note engraving firm of Rawdon, Wright & Hatch between 1832 and 1834. This is the earliest record of a company making a transfer press.[37] Always before, transfer presses were made individually by the firm that was going to use it. R. Hoe & Company typically kept the blueprints of everything they made, so it is likely that the company built other transfer presses for different bank-note companies as required. By July 1863, S.M. Clark, in charge of the Treasury Department's National Currency Bureau, had complained in a letter to the Comptroller of the Currency that:

I have now two transfer presses completed, and a third will be finished before it is needed . . . it will take a large number of transfer presses to supply the demand in a reasonable time. Indeed, there are not transfer presses enough now in existence in the United States to supply, in a year's time, the number of associations to whom certificates will have been issued by the 16th of September.

There are but two regular manufacturers of [transfer] presses in this country. They alone could not supply [transfer] presses enough in five years.

. . . The only way now left is to supply the transfer presses by private bargains with the different large machine shops in the northern cities.

. . . A greater difficulty, I apprehend, is to be found in obtaining transferrers in sufficient numbers to work the presses. There are not enough professional transferrers in the country to do the work in the time you desire it.

. . . I propose to overcome this when I have authority, by securing all the professional transferrers I can by making transferrers of such skillful and competent mechanics as I and by hiring calico printers' transferrers, whom I think I can easily educate to transfer notes.

Presses will cost from eight hundred (800) to twelve hundred (1200) dollars each—probably will average about one thousand dollars ($1,000). Transferrers will cost from one thousand (1,000) to two thousand (2,000) dollars per annum, depending upon their skill.[38]

One way around the problem was to contract the work to the private bank-note companies in New York. Another way was to build transfer presses that were bench-top machines. The Casilear & Tichenor compound-lever transfer press was designed by George W. Casilear and George Tichenor and was small enough to sit on a sturdy bench.

The transfer presses built by Chapman were also compound-lever machines of different sizes. The smaller press could exert a force of approximately 10,000 pounds per square inch, and the large presses were good for 35 tons. These presses were built of heavy steel and weighed several tons. They were operated by a "transfer man" or siderographer, and the pressure exerted

upon a transfer roll was regulated by either hand or foot. When the operating lever was pressed downward, the compound lever system forced the back end of the beam upward and the front end of the beam downward. The transfer roll was held in place in a carrier at the front end of the beam. There were two steel tracks, called "bearers," which were part of the transfer beam, and they held the mandrel or axle on which the transfer roll was fixed. To move the transfer roll back and forth, there was a large hand wheel, about six feet in diameter. When the operator moved this wheel in one direction or another, a pinion gear fastened to the axle of the wheel and geared into a straight-toothed bar (rack), which was part of the bed of the press, moved the transfer roll forward or backward in a horizontal plane and in direct proportion to the distance the hand wheel was moved. It was important to note that the heavy transfer beam that held the transfer roll did not move forward or backward. It moved up and down only. The bed of the press moved forward and backward, as described, and the pressure on the freely revolving transfer roll caused it to move precisely the same distance and direction as the moving bed.

A transfer press made by W.H. Chapman during the late 19th century.

Another view of a Chapman transfer press, about 1900.

Accuracy was everything in transferring designs. The transfer roll must be carefully centered over the image and aligned with registration marks so that work could be done at several different times and always match the previous image precisely. The position of two register points on the bed piece was accurately recorded by means of a low-power micrometer microscope and registered in a book kept for that purpose. The axels of the roll were then locked in the carrier by means of two set screws. To make sure the surface of the transfer roll was perfectly parallel with the surface of the die, and not tilted slightly at one end or the other, one screw was loosened and the other tightened. When these screws had set the roll in its correct position, auxiliary nuts were tightened to lock down the carrier. The bed piece or die was then raised up by turning a hand wheel or by means of a foot lever, so it met the roll under pressure. The bed of the press was then moved back and forth under the roll 10 times or more to make certain that the soft steel of the roll was pressed down into all the lines of the hard-steel die, steadily guided by a special parallel-motion arrangement. (In an opposite transfer, the roll was hardened and the bed piece was of soft steel.)

When everything was positioned correctly and locked down, the siderographer took the large wheel in his right hand and placed his left hand on the pressure lever. He gradually lowered the transfer roll until it contacted the die at a point just beyond the end of the engraved die farthest from him. A ratchet held the pressure lever in position. The pressure on the transfer roll was steadily increased while the operator moved the big hand wheel, and the bed of the press and its die moved backwards in a horizontal plane, permitting the roll to move over the engraved design on the bed piece. The hand wheel was then turned slowly in the opposite direction so the bed piece traveled in the opposite direction. If the press had been properly adjusted, each line would fall precisely the same place every time the direction was reversed. An experienced operator knew that the soft-steel transfer roll could be deformed by leaving the roll too long in one position over the hardened die and learned to avoid deformation by operating at a constant or nearly constant speed.

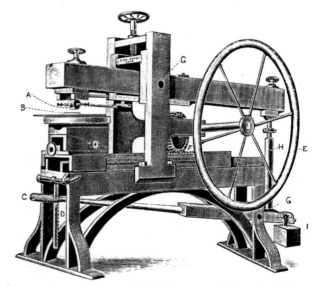

The parts of a transfer press. *(A)* Roll in carrier; *(B)* Die or bed piece; *(C)* Foot lever; *(D)* Rack to fasten down the lever; *(E)* Side wheel by which the bed of the press is moved back and forth; *(F)* Rack and pinion gear connecting the side wheel to the bed; *(G)* Fulcrum pins of the upper and lower levers; *(H)* Connecting rod between two levers; *(I)* Counter balance.

When a plate required renewing, it was again fixed upon the table in the same position as before by means of the micrometer microscope and the record of its previous position. This bed piece was moved back and forth under the hardened roller to deepen those parts of the impression which continuous printing had worn away. Before the micrometer microscope came into use, alignments were often made using simple tools and some ingenuity. One method was to engrave two small points on the plate and align them under magnification, with sharp pointers held rigidly in sleeves that screwed onto the of the roll on both sides of the roll. When measurements had to be made, the vernier caliper was sometimes used. The principle of the vernier scale was invented in 1631 by the French mathematician Pierre Vernier. It was incorporated in a measuring tool in 1848 by Jean-Louis Palmer and then steadily improved over the next century.

White-Line Engraving

In most bank-note work, white-line engraving was done by siderography and was slow work that required the talents of two or three people. White-line engravings are those in which white lines appear against a contrasting background. There were several ways to make white-line engravings, depending on the type of design needed. For example, a denomination figure was made one way and a fine-line geometric figure was made another way. When a geometric lathe was used to make an ornate figure, a special, thin die was used, usually about 1/16 of an inch thick and slightly longer in both directions than the design to be made. The figure cut by the geometric lathe was intaglio, or recessed below the surface of the die. All the lines were cut to the same depth. Next, the area lying just outside the geometric design was cut away by an engraver. Nothing inside the geometric figure was cut out. This die was then curved by a machine around a roll and hardened. This intaglio roll was then rolled back and forth over a bed piece. The bed piece, or "laydown" as it was later called, took up the design in relief, the black lines of the original figure becoming "white lines" in this operation, because they now stood above the surrounding surface. This relief roll was now used in the same manner as an ordinary roll in transferring the design. On the relief roll, the interstices (the

areas between the relief lines) were impressed below the surface of the plate. When the plate was inked, everything was covered with ink, but when the plate was wiped, only the interstices retained the ink. The relief lines were wiped clean of ink and would appear as "white lines" when the plate was printed.

It is easy to understand how white lines appear if you remember that the bed piece or laydown reverses the image cut by the lathe. The intaglio lines originally cut by the lathe are made to stand in relief, and it is the areas between those lines that sink below the surface of the plate. Diagrammatically, it looks like this:

An enlarged cross-section of a white-line die in different stages of progress. *(A)* This view shows a flat die in cross-section in which five lines have all been cut to the same depth by a geometric lathe; *(B)* This is the same die after it has been given to an engraver who cut away the metal outside the engraved area. Compare the two dies to see what has happened. The die is next curved to the periphery of a special transfer roll.

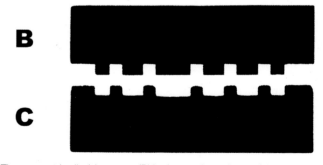

The geometric die (shown as *(B)* in the previous diagram) is now placed on a transfer press and rolled into a laydown, the black lines becoming white lines as shown in *(C)* (again in the previous diagram). The intaglio die has now been converted into a relief die.

Transfer rolls, dies, and plates were cleaned and coated with a moisture-resistant varnish, oil, or wax before they were stored in a bank-note company's vault. Since moisture can cause rust in steel and accelerates the tarnishing of copper, it was a common practice for engravers to coat their dies or plates at the end of each day so that nothing would sit overnight and become contaminated. Vaults were simply large storage rooms with strong doors and big padlocks. They never had the large steel doors one sees in bank vaults. Their protection came primarily from the night watchman who made frequent rounds throughout the building. During the daytime, padlocks with one-of-a-kind keyways did the job. Only one or two daytime employees had keys to open padlocks to special rooms, and they were responsible for keeping those keys chained to their clothes.

A modern transfer press made by Michael Kämpf, circa 1960s.

Steel and Copper

Steel and copper dies were to the bank-note engraver what canvas was to the painter. But not all steel was acceptable. The engraver had to begin his work on soft-steel dies. Soft steel must have a low carbon content, somewhere between 0.05% and 0.026% by weight. This steel has low-tensile strength but is easily malleable and very soft to the engraver's burin. If the steel is too tough, it can be treated by heat to make it softer. When a hard steel is heated to about 700-degrees Celsius for over 30 hours, it produces what is now called a "spheroid" structure. This is the softest and most ductile form of steel. Naturally, ferrous metallurgy had not progressed to this level of understanding when Perkins invented siderography. He had to experiment with different processes of hardening and softening steel, including steam. Steel that was available from local mills was usually low-carbon steel, anyway, so he had a foot-up on the processes without knowing it. When Perkins went to England in 1819, he found the steel mills there could make very low-carbon steel for him. One writer said that Perkins's steel plates were so popular that by September 1820, he (Perkins) had orders for nearly 1,000 steel bank-note plates.[39]

After the engraver was finished with a die, it had to be hardened before it was placed in the transfer press. Until the 1880s, this was done by a process called carbonizing or "case hardening." This was accomplished by placing the soft-steel die in a packing of carbonaceous materials, such as shoe leather, and subjecting it to elevated temperatures for a certain amount of time. This was a diffusion process in which carbon atoms from the packing materials moved into the outer layers of steel. A heating period of a few hours may produce a high-carbon layer about a millimeter thick. Later, at the Bureau of Engraving and Printing, the dies were placed in a liquid bath of molten sodium cyanide. The outer layer of steel absorbed both sodium and carbon, but the sodium had no real effect on the mechanical properties of the die. A faster and more modern method is to heat the die with an acetylene torch set with a fuel-rich flame, hardening and quenching repeatedly in a carbon-rich oil. The acetylene gas is a rich source of carbon since each molecule is composed of two carbon atoms and two hydrogen atoms.

Annealing is a softening process in which a steel die or roll is taken to a certain temperature and held there while the microcrystalline structure of the steel is changed. It helps to pack the steel object in iron filings so the carbon coming out of the steel is captured in the filings. Then, the die is removed from the furnace and allowed to cool by natural convection. There are different types of annealing for different types of steel, determined primarily by the carbon content. It is possible, therefore, to change a steel die from soft steel to hard steel and back again to soft steel. This is the principle behind siderography. Many small bank-note companies did not have the expertise or the equipment to do hardening and annealing, so they sent their work to a few companies that specialized in these services. The Kihn Brothers Bank Note Company, at 99 Beckman Street, New York, was a leader in this field.

Copper is a much softer material than steel, and consequently an engraved copper plate will wear down much more rapidly than one of steel. As with steel, annealing changes the grain structure of copper and can make it slightly harder or softer. However, this was not known until late in the 19th century and had no effect on the copper plate used by bank-note engravers. They were much more interested in the price and the "polish" of copper than its hardness. New, bright copper plate oxidizes naturally, and over time it takes on a brownish, dull cast, like an old penny. To restore the bright color, the engraver, or more likely his assistant, must take a pumice stone or some other fine abrasive and polish the plate until it shines. The other reason for polishing the plate is to make sure it is smooth and

perfectly flat. This was often a time-consuming process, especially on larger plates, so engravers were reluctant to do it and made it a job for apprentices. Alexander Anderson's diary mentions that a man called "the Swede" was paid $1.15 an hour to polish a copper plate about six inches square and $1.35 for one slightly larger. Today, we would just expose the oxidized plate to hydrogen gas. Hydrogen is a moderately strong reducing agent and would convert the dull cupric oxide back to a bright and shiny cuprous oxide.

After the Civil War, a number of companies were established to supply steel and copper plates to the bank-note industry. Sharp & Sons Steel and Copper Plate Company, established in 1871 at 13 Baxter Street in New York, was the largest manufacturer of steel and copper plate in the United States. The George A. Brooks Engraving Company in Philadelphia was another supplier of steel and copper plates, as was the Hawkins-Wilson Company at 712 Sansom Street. The growth of the steel- and copper-plate–engraving industry continued to expand. The U.S. Census Bureau began collecting statistics about the engraving industry in 1879 and reported these data in Table 229 of the 1910 Census. They showed that the number of engraving firms had increased from 55 in 1879 to 286 by 1899 and 316 in 1909, a 6-fold increase in only 30 years. Only a few of these firms actually engaged in security printing.

Chapter 15

Paper

"Invention"

Paper is one of the two or three most important inventions of all time and was a key element in the evolution of money. Since few people know much about paper, especially bank-note paper, it may be helpful to follow its development from the very beginning to the present technology. The purpose of the following history is to provide enough detail that anyone can follow the processes used in making paper and to show how little has changed between 2nd-century China and 19th-century America.

Bamboo shoots painted on thin, hand-made paper.

According to both Chinese tradition and the official history of the Han Dynasty, paper was invented by *Ts'ai Lun*, an official of the royal court in the walled city of Kuei-yang (now called Lei-yang) near Hengchow in Hunan Province in the year 105 AD. We know that Ts'ai Lun was a native of that city and that he was made a eunuch and began serving the imperial court about 75 AD. He was soon noticed for his intelligence and was chosen to be a member of the imperial guard. He rose through the ranks, and in 89 AD he was placed in charge of the office of military works. There, he set new standards by which the workmen made military arms and armor. He built a solid reputation as a loyal and exceptionally intelligent servant, and while he was still of middle age, he was elevated to the rank of imperial counselor to the Emperor Ho Ti.

Before Ts'ai Lun invented paper, most of the writing in China was made vertically on thin strips of bamboo, which were then sewn together into a tablet. An alternate method was to write on pieces of silk called *chih*. But since silk was too costly and bamboo was heavy and made for very bulky documents, these materials were not convenient to use. By 102 AD, one of the imperial consorts, a beautiful lady who was known for her interest in literature, asked some of the ambassadors at court to have their governments send *chih* as a tribute to the emperor. She may have used the term *chih* in a more general sense, meaning "writing material." It has been suggested that she may also have asked Ts'ai Lun to find out how *chih* was being made so he could set up a workshop and make even better *chih* for use in the palace, and that he was so smitten by her charms that he went willingly to the task. Whether that's true or not, it lends a certain romantic charm to the story.

Several scholars have pointed to evidence that local artisans had been experimenting with crude forms of paper for several years before Ts'ai Lun became interested in the subject, and it is increasingly the modern view that he did not invent paper so much as perfect an ongoing experimental process. Nevertheless, Ts'ai Lun was given credit for the invention, and the official history says that he made paper "from the bark of trees, remnants of hemp, cloth rags, and fishing nets." In 114 AD the Imperial Mother bestowed the title of "marquis" on Ts'ai Lun, ostensibly to reward his long and faithful service at the palace but more likely to honor his invention of paper. He was also awarded a yearly purse consisting of the taxes collected from three households, and he may have appreciated that even more than the title. The histories tell us, however, that Ts'ai Lun's loyalty to the throne was also his downfall. When the Empress To requested that he invent slanders against a certain member of the imperial family that she didn't like, he acceded to her wishes. When she died, her successor discovered that Ts'ai Lun had perpetrated the slanders and ordered him to report his involvement to the Minister of Justice so that he might be judged. Whether from shame or fear of his fate, Ts'ai Lun chose to drink poison instead, and he died in 121 AD.

Other than those brief details, we don't know much about Ts'ai Lun's life, and the historians never tell us exactly how he invented paper. Scholars have speculated that the first artisans that tried to make paper probably used second-hand materials, such as rags of old clothing and worn-out fish nets. Ts'ai Lun may have been the first to realize that tree bark, rope ends (hemp), and other organic materials could be added to the mix of vegetable fibers that eventually became paper. This greatly increased the supply of raw materials and made it possible to manufacture paper on a much larger scale using renewable resources.

There were two essential processes in making paper, and since these are closely linked and interdependent steps, they must have been conceived at virtually the same time. First, paper was made from vegetable fibers. To get these, one had to beat or macerate plants or materials made from plants, such as cloth or rope, until they were reduced to a fibrous form. The simplest way to do this at the time was to place the raw materials in a stone mortar with a small volume of water and pound them with a stone pestle or mallet until they became a fibrous pulp. In the

second process, the pulp was added to a suitable volume of clean water so the fibers floated to the surface, where they were collected on a flat, woven screen which retained them in a thin sheet and allowed the excess water to drain through the small open spaces of the screen. As the water drained away, the fibers matted together to form a sheet of paper.

As we will see later on, one can improve on the efficiency of these processes primarily by replacing human effort with mechanical devices that make paper much more rapidly and in a continuous web, but the basic steps that were used to make paper in ancient China were still in use in Europe and America at the beginning of the 18th century.

The mortar and pestle were used in China long before paper was invented, and they were adapted as simply the best tools available for macerating the raw materials used in making paper. The screen mold, however, was clearly a specialized tool designed specifically to recover the paper fibers floating on the surface of the water. The earliest molds were probably made from coarse woven cloth that was tied down tightly to a four-sided frame of bamboo. The early craftsmen may have held this type of mold in a vertical position and lowered it into a vat containing the water and fibers and then turned it to a horizontal position and lifted it out so the fibers were captured on the cloth.

A vatman capturing pulp on a mold.

Just as easily, they may have laid the molds on the ground or supported them horizontally on frames and then poured the fibrous pulp onto the woven cloth. In either case, the fibers would mat together as the water drained and evaporated, forming a sheet of paper on which the warp and woof of the cloth-support were impressed. Any mold that leaves an imprint of a woven support on the finished paper is said to be a "wove" mold. From the little that we know of ancient Chinese papers and what we can deduce by common sense, it seems likely that the first molds were of this "wove" type, that they were made of the simplest materials available, such as bamboo for the frame and cloth or possibly ramie ("China grass") for the woven support, and that they had no cross members or wooden slats to support the cloth.

The disadvantage of these simple molds probably occurred to craftsmen right away. Such molds had to be small so they could be handled easily, and the mold and its fibrous mat had to be placed in the sun for half an hour or longer to dry, so a craftsman could not make very much paper using just one mold. One could always increase production by using more molds, but the process remained inefficient as long as each mold had to be used to dry the paper. It probably didn't take long for someone to get the idea of making a mold from which they could remove the wet sheet of paper as soon as it was formed. This allowed them to reuse the mold to make paper continuously rather than at half-hour intervals. This "transfer mold" may have been the first important advance in paper-making.

The basic idea in building a transfer mold was to use a smooth yet firm material that would support the paper pulp and yet could also be removed from the frame. Bamboo answered these requirements nicely. A mold covering was made from very thin strips of bamboo which were placed side by side at close and very regular intervals and then laced or stitched together with thread made from silk, flax, horse hair, or camel hair. Because the individual strips of bamboo were laced or sewn together, the whole mat was flexible and could be rolled up by the worker using it. These mold coverings or mats were made to fit within a bamboo frame, and bamboo rods were sewn to the top and bottom of the frame to keep the paper pulp from spilling over the edges. When paper was formed on these mats, the individual bamboo strips left faint impressions, all running in one direction, known as "laid lines," and the stitches left even fainter impressions, running at right angles, known as "chain lines," from the chain stitching that goes over one strip of bamboo and under the next strip to hold everything together. In one example of paper from the Tang Dynasty, the laid lines number 23 to the inch, while the chain lines are spaced at intervals of approximately 1 inch. This shows that a laid-mold covering provided a more open network of support for the paper and one that would have drained water more rapidly than the earlier wove mold.

When a workman wanted to make a sheet of paper, he placed the flexible mold covering on the bamboo frame and dipped it into a vat of macerated pulp and water. He then brought them out horizontally, as was done with wove molds. The suspended fibers were kept on the laid-mold covering by bamboo rods at the top and bottom of the mat and by two sticks held at each end of it. Today, these are called "deckle sticks." When the worker was ready to "couch" the sheet of paper, meaning to lay it down to dry, he simply lifted the mold covering off the frame and carried it and the wet paper a short distance to where it could be dried. Paper was couched in different ways in different areas of China, and sometimes old methods were combined with newer techniques. Some workers couched paper on slanted wooden frames or boards to dry in the sun, while others stuck wet sheets to the slanted walls of a specially made oven. The sheet at the bottom of the stack rested on a flat board, and as each additional sheet of wet paper was placed on the stack, it helped to compress the sheets below. A heavy weight was placed on top of the stack to press out the excess water. It seems that as long as the paper was made from Asiatic fibers and was well sized, it was not necessary to place felts between the individual sheets. The sheet did not bond together, and they came out firm and unwrinkled.

Lichens that create "lichen glue."

Over the course of 1,000 years, the Chinese made many important advances in the technology of paper-making, but the names of the inventors and the specific dates of their work are lost. The Chinese did not have a patent system to protect inventors, and given the commercial advantages that an improved paper or a better ink might confer on a family specialized in its manufacture, it isn't surprising that they kept many of their processes secret. In fact, the first detailed description of paper-making in China was only a single chapter in a book that was published in 1637 AD.[1] Scientists have learned a few facts from chemical and microscopic analyses on some of the earliest specimens of paper, and oriental scholars continue to find ink recipes and references to paper-making in the ancient literature, but since the Chinese said so little about their technological achievements, researchers are often left to guess when certain advances took place.

The Chinese took a giant step forward when they invented sizing sometime in the 3rd century AD. Sizing helps to keep plant fibers floating in water until they can be captured on a mold. It also increases the bonding strength of the fibers, prevents sheets of paper from sticking together when they are stacked wet, and improves the ability of paper to hold ink. The earliest sizing was apparently made from lichens—small airy plants that grow on rocks and walls and are actually formed of a fungus and algae growing together. The sizing made from them is called "lichen glue," and the first workers to use sizing probably added it directly to the pulp. By the 5th century, paper-makers were adding a starch sizing to the pulp. Animal sizes, such as the gelatin extracted from cowhides, were probably not used until recent times owing to their greater cost. The early craftsmen soon learned that they didn't have to add the sizing directly to the pulp. They discovered that by dipping a finished sheet of paper in a vat of size, they could control the process better and improve the quality of their sized paper. For some purposes, though, the extra step of vat sizing the paper may not have been worth the additional effort, and pulp sizing was probably used for certain types of paper until recent times.

The use of fillers to "load" a paper is also noted on samples from the 3rd century AD and shows that even then workers were experimenting with various materials to improve their paper. Fillers usually increase the opacity of paper and improve its printing quality by reducing the penetration or "strike-through" of the ink. Chemical analyses have shown that some papers made in the 3rd century were first coated with gypsum (calcium sulfate) and then sized with lichen glue.

Trip hammers eventually replaced most of the mortars and pestles that were used to beat plant fibers into pulp. In the simplest of these, a heavy stone hammer was secured to one end of a beam, called the "tilt-bar," which pivoted on a shaft that ran horizontally through a vertical beam. The tilt-bar was operated by foot.

An early Chinese trip-hammer for macerating raw materials for making paper.

The mechanical advantage of this device increased the force of the hammer blows and sped up the maceration of the material in the mortar. As the demand for paper increased, trip hammers were made in increasingly larger sizes. Some of the largest were pivoted on cross beams much like a child's seesaw at a playground. On these, a worker walked back and forth on the tilt-bar to move its center of gravity towards one end or the other and force the hammer stone to alternately rise and fall.

Paper Money In China

Counterfeiting is almost as old as greed and larceny, so it shouldn't surprise anyone that paper money was counterfeited soon after it came into general use during the Southern Sung Dynasty in China. The earliest example we have of this crime occurred in the 11th century AD, but it's probably only a matter of time before some Chinese scholar discovers a court record or some other document that tells a similar story from an even earlier time.[2]

In the 11th century, everyone was having a difficult time with the heavy iron coins used in everyday transactions. This led people to deposit their coins in "proto-banks" and then use the receipts, which were like promissory notes, in making purchases. These were called *chiao-tzu*, meaning "exchange medium." During the reign of Chen-tung (980–1022 AD), the government gave 16 merchants a monopoly on their issuance. Although none of the notes have survived, we know from official records that they were printed from wood blocks on special paper in black, blue, and red ink. Usually one note represented one string of coins, and the merchants were allowed to charge a three-percent fee for supplying and handling the notes. Some of the merchants became greedy and charged far more than the allowed rate, which led to widespread complaints and many legal cases.

Finally, in 1023 AD, the government replaced the private merchants with a "Bureau of Exchange Medium" in the city of I-Chou, which is the modern city of Ch'eng-tu in Szechwan Province. The Chinese were then experimenting with other forms of paper money in different areas of the country, but the chiao-tzu was the first widely distributed paper currency to reach large-scale use.[3] The government issued the notes every other year, starting in 1023. By the time this counterfeiting story takes place, a little more than 150 years later, the total circulation was more than 70 million notes.

Chiang Hui— A 12th-Century Counterfeiter

Our counterfeiter was a professional wood-block cutter known as Chiang Hui. In those days, published material was printed from inked wood blocks on which the characters stood in relief and the surrounding wood had been cut away. As with other trades, young boys were apprenticed to learn the requisite skills before they became professionals, and no doubt Chiang Hui came up the same way. In a deposition he gave the court, Chiang did not tell us why he turned to counterfeiting the first time, but he does say it happened in 1177 AD when he made 450 sheets of *hui-tzu* notes. He may have been induced to cut the wood blocks and print the notes by T'ang Chung, a prefect or chief administrative officer who was indicted along with Chiang.

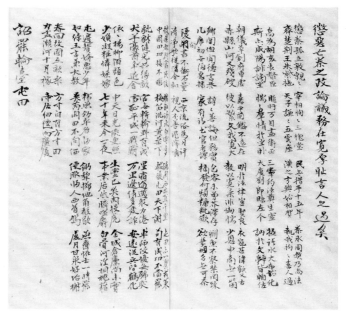

A Chinese woodblock-printed book.

Hui-tzu was the name given to the notes that replaced the chiao-tzu, but both notes were circulating at the time. We know from official records that the government printed hui-tzu from brass plates in a single color and probably over-printed the notes using wood blocks or dies with other colors for the seals, signatures, and denominations.[4] Chiang, however, cut his counterfeit plate in pear wood. The design of the note may have been very elaborate, as it took him 10 days to complete the work. As soon as his work was discovered and his identity as the counterfeiter became known to the government, he was arrested and sentenced to be tattooed as a soldier and exiled to a different prefecture. There, he was assigned to serve at the Wine Bureau, but rather than do this demeaning work, he hired a substitute and paid this man with money that he made legitimately by cutting wood-blocks for books.

Chiang's next adventure in crime came in 1180 or 1181 AD. Hearing that he was about to be arrested on suspicion that he had been involved in another counterfeiting case, Chiang sought refuge in the house of a local official and was hidden in a back room. Chiang's grandmother brought him food each day. The official soon asked him to make some counterfeit notes, and when Chiang hesitated to comply, the official made it clear that he would have his way or else send Chiang to prison, where he might well die. Fearing for his life, Chiang agreed to the plan.

The next day, when his grandmother came with food, Chiang explained his plight to her and asked her to help him get the special paper that would be needed. She made the necessary arrangements and even brought him a traced master copy of a hui-tzu note for 770 cash (made by another counterfeiter) and a block of pear wood for making the counterfeit plate. When Chiang was finished with the block, the grandmother then brought in paper for making 200 sheets of hui-tzu and the red, indigo blue, and brownish-black pigments for ink. Grandma was quite a help, constantly bringing in supplies and taking out the finished product.

According to the deposition, Chiang made another 150 sheets of hui-tzu during the last 10-day period of the 12th moon (1182 AD). Then, during the first 6 months of 1183 AD, he printed another 2,600-odd sheets. He usually printed 100 or 200 sheets at a time. On the 26th day of the 7th moon, Grandma came rushing in to tell Chiang that he must run away quickly, as police archers were all around the house looking for him. Chiang put up a ladder, climbed over the back wall, and ran to a pavilion behind the house, but there he was caught by the police and soon delivered to prison.

Chinese historians have not found any other court records related to this case, so we know very little about the technical details of Chiang's work. There is nothing to tell us how well the counterfeit notes were made, how they were passed, what impact they had on the local economy, how they were detected, or what became of Chiang and his grandmother. Most of the very old accounts of counterfeiting give few details that would be of interest to modern criminologists. It is not until the advent of newspapers and magazines that we begin to get detailed technical information about specific cases and their social impact.

The Spread of Paper-making

By the 8th century AD the Chinese had invented virtually all of the basic techniques in making paper and had kept them a secret from the rest of the world. That changed about 751 AD, when the Chinese fought a large battle in Turkestan on the banks of the Tharaz River. Among the Chinese taken as prisoners were a number of paper-makers who had been impressed into military service. When their professional skills were learned, they were induced to teach paper-making to their captors. This was done in the city of Samarkand (now in the sovereign state of Uzbekestan). At the time, the Chinese were using the bark of mulberry trees to make paper, and while this was not available to the Arabs, the area did have other resources that worked just as well. Both flax (linen) and hemp were abundant, and the region had numerous fresh-water canals for irrigation.

Mulberry Tree by Vincent van Gogh.

The Arabs modified the Chinese methods and made perfectly good paper. By placing linen rags in piles and saturating them with water, they started a natural fermentation that facilitated the breakdown of the material into a fibrous mass. This mass was boiled along with wood ashes, then placed in cloth bags and suspended in streams of fresh running water. The water removed the alkaline materials and any dirt that remained. The rags were then macerated by a trip-hammer until they reached a truly fibrous state and were ready for the vat.

From Samarkand, paper-making spread slowly to Baghdad and Damascus and eventually into Egypt and then on to Europe. It is interesting to note that paper money was introduced in Persia about 1292 AD by Sadr-al-Din, the minister of the emperor Geikhatu. This came about during a time when the Persians were suffering a great cattle plague and the treasury had been emptied by royal extravagance. Sadr-al-Din decided he too would issue paper money, called *chao*, after its Chinese model.[5] No plates of this currency can be found today, and we know of it only from official records.

This diffusion of paper-making took almost 500 years to go from Samarkand into Italy and beyond. It is told that Jean Montgolfier was taken prisoner by Saracens on the Second Crusade and forced to work in a paper mill in Damascus. When released, he is supposed to have returned to France and set up a paper mill in 1157 AD in the town of Vidalon, but there is no documentary evidence of this story and modern historians doubt its validity. There is good evidence for a paper mill in Fabriano, Italy, in 1276 AD, and for one at Bologna in 1293 AD. Marco Polo wrote about paper money that he had seen in China in 1298 AD. There were at least eight pre-Renaissance Europeans who traveled to China and saw paper money and wrote about it on their return. Marco Polo's description of paper money was the most comprehensive and most widely read of these accounts, but contrary to common belief, the basic processes of making paper were already in use in some parts of Europe when Polo returned home.[6]

European Improvements

Europeans soon began to improve on the old, essentially Chinese method of making paper. Instead of using a single trip hammer to macerate rags, Europeans began to make stamping mills that employed several hammers on a single long shaft. They operated those devices by water power, resulting in far-greater production rates.

It was a simple matter to divert water from a fast running stream onto a water-wheel that turned the shaft of the stamping mill. An unknown Dutchman, working in the latter half of the 17th century, used a windmill to turn the shaft of a cylinder beater to macerate rags.[7] This consisted of an oblong wooden tub, rounded at both ends, which contained a thick shaft fitted with iron knives. As the shaft turned, the knives cut apart and macerated rags against a stone or iron bed-plate set in the bottom of the tub. The rags were kept in constant motion by a backfall and by the rotation of the shaft and its knives. Because the machine was invented in Holland, it was called a "Hollander." This device was first described in a book written in 1682 by a German writer on mechanics.[8] Hollanders produced fibers faster than the old stamping mills, but the fibers had the disadvantage of being short, which made the paper weaker and less durable than the long-fibered paper of the old tradition.

A view of a 17th-century European paper mill. The pistolet is seen coming through the wall on the left and going into the vat. A vatman, a coucher, and a layboy are doing their jobs. Through the open door, a wooden-shaft beating machine driven by a water wheel outside can be seen.

Another European improvement was the charcoal heater, attached to a sidewall of the vat, usually at the back, so that the water and "stock" (fibers) could be heated. The heater, called the "pistolet" by the French, increased the evaporation of the water and allowed workmen to make more sheets of paper in a given time. To keep smoke out of the vat-house, the vat was usually placed against the side of the building in which a large hole in the wall allowed the heater, outside, to have a common surface with the vat and to transmit its heat directly through the wall. The stock was kept in constant motion and prevented from settling to the bottom of the vat by means of a simple paddle that was usually worked by a young apprentice.

In the most common procedures used in 18th-century American paper mills, a worker called a "vatman," stood in front of the vat on a platform and dipped a screen mold into the stock or pulp at an almost vertical angle.[9] When the mold was completely submerged, the vatman turned it to a horizontal position and lifted it out of the vat. He then shook the mold, first from right to left and then from front to back. This shaking caused the fibers to cross each other and mat together. This action made the sheet about as strong in one direction as in the other. It also drained water from the mold. The vatman then removed the wooden deckle. This left the moist sheet of paper on the mold. The mold was passed to another worker, called the "coucher," who laid the mold against an inclined board called the "asp" that allowed excess water to drain back into the vat. When the fibers of the sheet had reached the right stage of solidification—determined by a distinctive luster over its surface—the coucher turned the mold over and placed its sheet of paper on a woolen felt. If these operations were done correctly, the resulting sheet of paper was flat and unwrinkled. The vatman and coucher worked together to form a pile of 144 moist sheets of paper. Each sheet of paper was separated from the next by a felt that was cut slightly larger than the paper. The pile of felted paper consisted of 6 quires of 24 sheets each, making a total of 144 sheets. Such a pile was called a "post." When finished, the post was placed in a wooden screw press and the excess water was squeezed out. Screw presses of this type were very heavy, massive machines and were probably the most expensive items in a paper mill's inventory. When it was time to press the post, a bell was rung, and all the workers in the mill came to turn the screw by means of a long wooden lever. The lever was usually 16- to 20-feet long and 6 inches or so in diameter. A screw press with such a lever was powerful enough to compress a post two-feet high into a pile only six-inches high.

A paper mill for making paper by hand. The vatman is seen dipping a mold into a vat of dilute pulp to form a sheet of paper. To the right of the vatman is a screw press being loaded with alternating sheets of paper and felt. These will be pressed to remove excess water. Another screw press is seen in the background.

A drying loft. After excess water has been pressed out of the paper sheets, they are hung on slats in a ventilated drying loft. Note the ventilation slats on the left that have replaced windows.

When the pressing was completed, the individual sheets of paper were separated from their felts and stacked four or five sheets to a pile. Single sheets of paper wrinkle, but when stacked in "spurs," or piles of a few sheets, they dry smoothly and with no curling. The next stage was the drying loft, a room at the top of a building in which warm air could circulate among sheets of paper hung on wooden slats. The paper was hung in spurs on round or half-round wooden poles by using a device called a "T." This was simply a long handle topped by a short bar set at a right angle to the handle, much like a lawn rake. The T lifted the spur to the long slats near the ceiling of a loft and helped to drape them evenly over the slats.

Sizing

When dried, the paper was taken down and usually sized by dipping each sheet in a vat containing a solution of gelatin made from the hooves, hides, and horns of animals. While vat-sizing closed the pores of the linen and cotton paper and improved it considerably for writing, it was not as good for printing inks. John Ames of Springfield, Massachusetts, was granted a patent on September 1, 1832, for an improvement in sizing paper by machinery.[10] In his machine, paper in an endless web passed over and under several rollers, two of which were wetted by size. One roller applied size to the top surface of the paper, and the other roller applied it to the bottom surface. The rollers were wetted by size dripping from perforated pipes. Size flowed through these pipes in a continuous circuit. Ames was granted many patents that improved the dusting, washing, and sizing of paper.

Rags! Rags! Rags!

Linen has always been the material preferred for making bank-note paper. Cotton is also acceptable, but not as good. These materials were bought by paper mills to make paper of all sorts. Bank-note paper did not become a specialized item for some time. One of the earliest rag sellers was Benjamin Franklin.[11] Franklin's ledger shows that he sold to the Pennsylvania paper-maker Anthony Newhouse, between February 1741 and April 1749, about 25 tons of rags and also considerable quantities of alum and glue used in sizing paper. On the credit of those sales, Franklin bought "money paper" from Newhouse, which he probably used to print the Pennsylvania currency issue of 1744 and later those of Delaware. Franklin also dealt with Thomas Wilcox, who ran a paper mill at Chester, Pennsylvania, selling him about 23 tons of rags between 1740 and 1749. Franklin sold large quantities of rags to William Parks and about a dozen other mill operators. His standard charge was 1-1/2 pence for a pound of rags. Franklin was first and always a printer, but he was smart enough to establish himself in allied businesses, like rag supplies and paper trading. After he died on April 17, 1790, it was found that his estate was worth between $200,000 and $250,000—a large fortune in those days.

Rags were usually sold by ordinary citizens to rag collectors. John Keating, who established the first paper mill in New York in 1768, placed a typical advertisement in the *New York Journal* or *General Advertiser*, under the date of February 18, 1768. It read:

Ready Money for Clean Rags

May be had of John Keating, between

Burling's Slip and the Fly Market

In Queen Street

All those that really have the Welfare of their Country at Heart, are desired to consider seriously the importance of a Paper Manufactory to the Government, and how much Good they may do it by so small a Matter by saving only the Linen Rags, especially the fine ones that would be otherwise useless . . .

The Savings of Rags requires very little Time or Trouble, nothing is necessary than a Habit of Care and Attention to Preserve instead of throwing them away, when they become otherwise useless. A paper or linen bag for that Purpose should be hung up in some certain Place in every House,

and a little Care and Patience would soon, almost insensibly, Produce a Habit of Saving, that would have the desired Effect, and supply us with Paper at Home sufficient for our own use, without money, whereas now we are obliged to send Money abroad, not only to pay for the Paper at a high Price, but an Oppressive Duty upon it into the bargain.

Bleaching and the Gilpin Brothers

The supply of linen and cotton rags decreased almost every year, and these were the only two materials suitable for making bank-note paper at that time. Fortunately, science came to the rescue with the invention of chemical bleaching. To be fair, it was European science. Chlorine was discovered by the Swedish chemist Carl Wilhelm Scheele in 1774. He called it "dephlogistecated muriatic acid gas." That became more generally known as "oxymuriatic acid gas," from the mistaken belief that it contained oxygen. The manufacturers simply called it "bleaching gas." The gas was finally given its present name—Chlorine—by Humphry Davy in 1810. For quite a long time, paper mills had treated white or light-colored rags by laying them on grassy hillsides to bleach in the sun. Chemical bleaching was much quicker and did a better job. In this country, chlorine bleaching was first used by the Gilpin brothers in the summer of 1804 at their paper mill on the Brandywine River about two miles above Wilmington, Delaware.

Joshua and Thomas Gilpin were born in Philadelphia to a prosperous Quaker merchant named Thomas Gilpin and his wife, the former Lydia Fisher, of a well-known Quaker family.[12] Both boys were intelligent and received the best education that Philadelphia could offer. Joshua studied law but never entered the profession. Thomas is said to have had a more technically oriented mind. Their maternal grandfather, Joshua Fisher, had started a flour mill on Brandywine Creek in 1765, and later on his brother, Miers Fisher, gave his nephews this property to do with as they wished. Benjamin Franklin was a personal friend of Thomas Gilpin Sr., and they were both members of two clubs that collected books. As the Gilpin boys grew up, they came to know Franklin as an occasional visitor to their house. Franklin later suggested to Thomas Gilpin Jr. that he consider starting a paper mill on the land he had inherited. Benjamin Franklin once told J.P. Brissot de Warville that he had been instrumental in starting 18 paper mills, so it was not out of character that he advocated the construction of another.

Gilpins Mill by Thomas Doughty.

The first public notice of the Gilpin Mills was an advertisement placed in the *Delaware Courant* of May 12, 1787, appealing to the citizens to sell their rags. The first paper was made at the mills in June 1787. The enterprise began as a hand mill with a typical crew of three paper-makers that could make about five reams of paper a day. In her book, *Reminiscences of Wilmington*, Elizabeth Montgomery describes the mill in this way:

> Things here were on the most approved plan, and order and neatness presided. We will venture to describe one apartment in the old mill—a large sale on the lower floor, where more than thirty women were seated on high stools at a long table placed before the windows, each one having a knife to pick the moles from every sheet, and they were dressed becoming their occupation, with a clean apron as smooth as if an iron had just been rubbed over it. Not a cobweb marred these white walls, nor was dust allowed to soil the floors.
>
> Just above this, a large and modern stone building was occupied in the same way. Many departments were carried on in each of these houses. The stone house below was used for assorting and cutting rags, and another stone structure for extracting colors. In this, immense kettles were fixed in furnaces built of stone that seemed immovable.
>
> The boats often conveyed paper on the water from one mill to another, but it was generally taken in wagons to the Wilmington wharves. Large quantities of bank note paper were made. We have seen whole pieces of new silk handkerchiefs cut to mix with the rags, to designate its manufacture.[13]

In 1795, when he was 30 years old, Joshua Gilpin decided to take a "grand tour" of Europe. He stayed in England for nearly six years and made it a point to visit numerous paper and iron mills and pottery factories. His journals, numbering 62 volumes, show that he was a keen observer of European industrial processes. As a paper-mill owner, he was most interested in the new art of bleaching rags to make paper. He saw this process in paper mills in Scotland. He bought and read thoroughly an essay on bleaching by the French chemist Berthollet, and he wrote a long description of its methods to his brother.[14] In his final year in Europe, Joshua married Mary Dilworth (the daughter of a banker), from whom he acquired a fortune.

After Joshua Gilpin returned to Delaware in the autumn of 1801, he and his brother hired an English paper-maker named Lawrence Greatrake who assisted them in early experiments with making chlorine gas and in setting up a special room for bleaching rags. The Gilpins decided to use the process of an American inventor named Cyrus Austin, who had been granted a patent dated December 14, 1798, for bleaching rags.[15] From Joshua Gilpin's letters and technical notes, which have been recently discovered and transcribed by Sidney M. Edelstein, it appears that the patented process evolved chlorine gas by combining muriatic acid (hydrochloric acid) with the black oxide of manganese (manganese oxide) in a large retort and passing this gas into a chest or box containing washed rags.[16] Austin received $500 to license the use of his patent to the Gilpins for two years. The Brandywine Mill continued to prosper and soon specialized in bank-note paper, including that made for the Union Bank of Rhode Island, the Elkton Bank of Maryland, the State Bank of North Carolina, the Louisville branch of the State Bank of Kentucky, the United States Treasury, and others.[17] In 1816 Thomas sought the advice of Jacob Perkins in Philadelphia to perfect a new device for making watermarks in bank-note paper. Perkins apparently had more to do with that invention than Gilpin, for he was given a patent on the method on December 19, 1816. In this patent, an engraved plate bearing the watermark was transferred to a roller which was then used to impress the watermark in wet paper. The actual patent was lost during the fire that destroyed the Patent Office in 1836.

Joshua Gilpin made two tours of Europe, the second between 1811 and 1815, and became acquainted with Bryan Donkin, John Hall, John Whatman, and two men that were making paper by machine—Henry Fourdrinier and John Dickinson. These were important contacts because Joshua had in mind to learn how the paper-making machines operated so he could make one for the Brandywine Paper Mill. Industrial espionage of this type was common between America and Europe, and the Gilpin brothers had no qualms about their efforts.

Machine-made Paper

The history of mechanical paper-making begins with a frail and quarrelsome Frenchman named Nicholas Louis Robert. After spending nine years in the French Army, he went to Paris and became a clerk in the firm of Saint-Leger Didot, the famous publisher. Later, he was sent to work in a paper mill belonging to a relative of Didot. There, Robert was constantly offended by the undisciplined and vulgar behavior of the workmen. He sought escape by working on a model of a machine that would make paper automatically. The first model was made in 1797 and came to the attention of his employer, Monsieur Didot. The model did not work, however, so Didot took

Robert out of the paper mill and set him up in a flour mill where he could work in relative calm. Didot also provided technical assistants, but even then the model did not work. Finally, in 1798 Robert made a machine that successfully formed paper in a continuous sheet on an endless belt of woven wire and drained the excess water through the mesh. A patent was granted to Robert on January 18, 1799. Within a few months Robert began to quarrel with Didot and refused to work with him any further. He sold Didot his patent for 25,000 francs to be paid in installments. When Didot was late in making payments, Robert took back his patent in June of 1801.

A ruined paper mill shows
paper-making machinery exposed to the elements.

The Fourdrinier Machine

Seeing that he could not work with Robert, and the new machine would likely sit idle for years to come, Didot wrote to his brother-in-law, John Gamble, an English paper-maker, to raise money to make a machine that he promised would revolutionize the industry. Gamble found two London stationers, Henry and Sealy Fourdrinier, who eventually spent £60,000 on the project. A brilliant engineer, Bryan Donkin, set to work perfecting the machine and secured three patents for his improvements.[18,19] Donkin's final design had a woven-wire belt 5-feet wide and 27-feet long which traveled in a continuous path through the machine. Pulp was poured on the belt, and a side-to-side shaking motion was imparted to the belt to simulate the motions made by hand by a vatman in the old method of making paper. The shaking motion spread out the pulp and left a pad of paper of fairly even thickness across the web. Most of the water in the pulp drained through the mesh right away, and as the paper became firm enough, it was passed between a pair of rollers, one over the wire web and one under it. These rollers further consolidated the pulp into a sheet of paper and squeezed out the excess water. The paper was then taken up on a reel and carried away to be unwound and hung up to dry. An assistant placed a new reel on the machine and started the new paper winding on it.

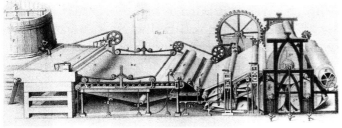

A Fourdrinier paper machine. Dilute pulp flows from a vat at the left and onto an endless wire mold. As the wire mold moves from left to right, the excess water drains through the mold and leaves a continuous sheet of paper. The paper is then transferred to couching rolls over an endless felt and then over steam-heated drying drums. Finally, it is rolled up on a paper reel at the right-hand end of the machine.

Henry Fourdrinier was suspicious of any visitor who came by his plant to see the new machine in action, and both Joshua Gilpin and Lawrence Greatrake failed to win his cooperation. Greatrake considered Fourdrinier to be "an arrogant, swearing low man, and not much esteemed here." Fourdrinier told him he would never consent to letting one of his machines leave England, but in fact, he had already begun to sell the machines at prices ranging from £715 to £1,040, depending on the number of vats used and the width of the belt. By 1814 Bryan Donkin had constructed 12 machines and sold them to various paper-makers. The Tsar of Russia visited England just after the War of 1812 and heard about the Fourdrinier

machine. He negotiated the purchase of two machines from Henry Fourdrinier, and these were sent to Russia and set up by Bryan Donkin's son at Peterhoff. In addition to their initial price, the Tsar was obligated to pay an annual royalty of £700 for 10 years. In fact, the Tsar never paid a penny for the machines. Finally, Fourdrinier went to Russia when he was over 70 years old to try to collect the money he was owed. He even got into the garden of the royal palace and accosted the Tsar face to face. The two men had a talk, but the Tsar's promises were not worth a rouble.[20] Because Henry Fourdrinier was so fearful of selling one of his machines to a competitor, neither Lawrence Greatrake nor Joshua Gilpin were ever successful in getting him to change his mind. It was not until 1827 that an English Fourdrinier machine was brought to America. The first Fourdrinier machine built in America was installed at the paper mill of Amos Hubbard, in Norwich, Connecticut, in 1829. It was built by Phelps & Spafford of South Windham, Connecticut.[21] The Gilpins, determined to automate their paper mill, decided to approach a different inventor that Joshua had met during his grand tour of Europe.

Dickinson's Cylinder Machine

The second type of machine for making paper was invented by John Dickinson. He was born March 29, 1782, the oldest son of Captain Thomas Dickinson of the Royal Navy.[22] John was well-educated and took an apprenticeship with a stationer in London. His first patent was granted on June 30, 1807, No. 3,056, for an improvement in cutting and placing paper on the reels of the Fourdrinier machine. In this design, he used a grooved cylinder revolving at high speed. Above this cylinder was set a spindle with circular knives that corresponded in position with the grooves in the cylinder. As the paper unwound from the reel, it passed between the roller and the knives and was cut to the desired width. Tongs then grabbed the paper and moved it forward to the transverse cutting apparatus. Dickinson also took out a second patent, No. 3,080, granted November 12, 1807, for an improved cannon-cartridge paper. In this patent he mixed wool with the linen rags used to make the paper casing for gunpowder charges. When the cannon was fired, the wool-and-linen mixture of the paper did not retain sparks and therefore didn't cause premature explosions when the next charge was loaded. This cartridge paper was used in the Peninsular Campaign and at Waterloo with much success and was adopted by the Board of Ordnance. Of course, it didn't hurt that Dickinson's father had been Superintendent of the Ordnance Transports at Woolwich.

John Dickinson.

Dickinson's most important patent, No. 3,191, dated January 19, 1809, was for a machine to make paper. One of the best descriptions of this machine is found in the *London Encyclopedia* of 1829, and to paraphrase that article, Dickinson made use of a hollow brass cylinder closed at each end but having a large hollow tube as its axis. The cylinder was covered with fine-woven wire that permitted water to flow through it. It was made to revolve in a vat of very diluted pulp, in which it was about two-thirds immersed. During the revolution of the cylinder, the water in the pulp vat flowed through the wire covering of the cylinder, into the interior, and flowed out through the hollow tube, each end of which passed through the sides of the vat in which the cylinder revolved. As the water of the pulp flowed through the surface of the cylinder, the fibers of the rags floating in the vat were deposited on the wire and thereby gradually formed the paper on every part of the cylinder during its immersion in the fluid pulp. An endless felt took the paper off the highest point of the cylinder. The felt was pressed against the cylinder by the pressure of a roller, technically called the "couching roll." The interior of the cylinder was acted on by two double-acting air pumps. The pumps drew air from the interior of the cylinder, producing a partial vacuum, which helped to draw water through the wire covering of the cylinder and promoted the adhesion of the pulp to that wire covering. The air that was exhausted from the interior of the cylinder was forced through a pipe into a receiver where it was condensed and then returned by a pipe to the top of the cylinder. There a continuous blast of compressed air helped to keep the consolidated pulp on the wire covering until it reached a point on the cylinder at which it was detached from the surface by a stream of compressed air that had taken a different route from the compressor. The elaborate system of compressed air was essential to the operation of the machine. Since the pulp was taken up on a wire-covered cylinder, the device was called a cylinder machine. By contrast, the Fourdrinier machine used an endless belt to convey the pulp through its operations.

Dickinson held many patents for minor improvements in his paper-making machines and played small roles in the development of related processes. His 1817 patent included the idea of drying machine-sized paper round a cylinder heated by steam revolving in the same direction as the paper, or by using several steam-heated cylinders in series. Thomas Bonsor Crompton was granted a patent on November 1, 1820, for drying cylinders to be added to a paper-making machine in a manner very similar to those in the

Dickinson patent. Dickinson took no action against Crompton, and eventually he used his own rolls without a patent. In January 1829 Dickinson was granted Patent No. 5,754 for passing water out of the formed paper by having it pass on an endless felt through several press rolls, one being given with the paper reversed so that both sides of the paper would be glazed alike. This began the whole process of calendaring.

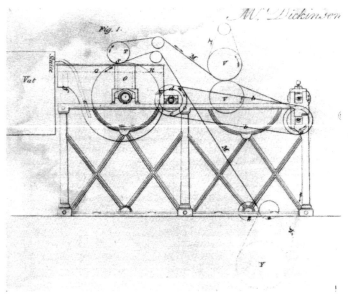

A drawing of a Dickinson cylinder paper machine. The cylinder was immersed in the dilute pulp to the level Q-R. The sheet formed on the cylinder's surface was transferred at S to the continuous felted belt, M.

Dickinson had allowed Greatrake to view his cylinder machine in operation and was happy to explain the complex parts of its interior. This allowed Greatrake to describe the machine in two similar letters that he sent to Joshua Gilpin, along with drawings. When Greatrake returned to America, he and the Gilpin brothers constructed a fully functional machine by 1817. The Gilpins patented their "invention" but purposely concealed details to make imitation difficult. The original patent was lost during the fire at the Patent Office in 1836. Fortunately, Lyman Weeks discovered that Thomas Gilpin had attached a copy of the patent and a drawing of the machine to a deposition he filed in 1833 for a lawsuit brought by John Ames of Massachusetts against the firm of Howard and Lothrop. In this way,

the specifications of the machine were preserved in court files.[23]

GILPIN PAPER MACHINE

A. *mesh cylinder revolving in a vat of rag pulp*
B. *felt covered roller to which pulp adheres*
C. *pulp being carried on felting to pressing rollers*
D. *pressing rollers; paper and felting separate*
E. *felting moving toward cylinder to pick up pulp*
F. *reel on which paper is wound after pressing*
G. *bucket wheel that raises water from trough into pulp vat*
H. *crank to tighten up felting*
I. *vat of rag pulp*
J. *spout that carries water from vat back to trough*
K. *trough containing water*
L. *agitator, or paddle that stirs pulp*

A drawing of a Gilpin paper machine made from the patent sketch and specifications. This was a cylinder machine of the Dickinson type, not a Fourdrinier. See full-size image on page 256.

A wide variety of sources have documented the industrial espionage of the Gilpin brothers and the manager of their paper mill, Lawrence Greatrake. The fact that British patents had no legal standing in America (and vice versa) was one of the problems that encouraged the theft of ideas. The affair with John Ames was another example of failed ethics.

John Ames operated a paper mill in Springfield, Massachusetts, and was frequently granted patents for small improvements he made to the machines used in paper mills. In March 1822 he went to the Gilpin paper mill with the intention of seeing their acclaimed cylinder machine. He was refused permission to enter the mill, but soon after, an employee of the mill named Hugh McFee received an invitation to meet "an unknown friend" at a local tavern. Ames met him there and took him to a locked room where he showed him a drawing of an automatic paper machine that he had constructed at his mill in Massachusetts. The machine that Ames had built was inferior to the Gilpin design, and Ames wanted to know how to improve it. When McFee refused to help him, Ames offered a handful of bank notes and promised to pay him even more money if he would help. When McFee still refused, Ames promised to move his family to Massachusetts and pay him a salary of $15 a week to work in the Springfield mill. When that tactic also failed, Ames tried to get McFee drunk, but he refused the glass of brandy and told Ames, "If I want a glass, I'll call for it and pay for it myself." McFee reported the attempted bribery to Greatrake, who in turn alerted Thomas Gilpin. Gilpin went to see Ames and rebuked him for trying to bribe McFee. But Ames persisted and eventually found a former employee of the Gilpin mill who gave him the information he needed. Within two months, Ames had patented a paper-making machine that was remarkably like the one Gilpin was using.

What goes around comes around, and 11 years after his trip to the Gilpin mill to bribe Hugh McFee, John Ames returned, seeking help in a suit he was bringing against the firm of Howard and Lothrop for infringing upon his patent and for hiring away his foreman. Thomas Gilpin refused to go to Boston to give testimony but did offer to testify in writing. A long list of questions was sent to Gilpin and McFee by the attorneys for Mr. Ames, and they answered them. The questionnaire was sent to Boston and read into the court records. That testimony gives a full account of the attempted bribery by John Ames, and the attached patent and drawing gave the specifications for the cylinder machine. It is unclear how this testimony helped Mr. Ames, but at least the proceedings preserved the patent drawing and specifications of the cylinder machine, which otherwise would have been lost to fire.

The Willcox Paper Mills

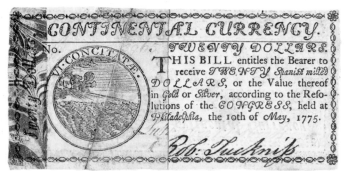

A $20 Continental bill.

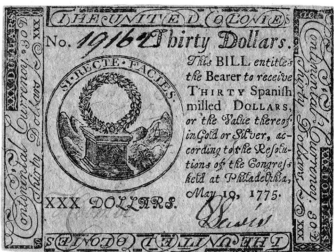

Notes of the first Continental bills authorized May 10, 1775.

American printers had long been dependent on imported paper, but this began to change in the 18th century as small paper mills were established throughout the eastern states. By the time of the American Revolution, there were 70 paper mills from the Carolinas to Massachusetts, but the demand for paper was greater than even these mills could meet. One of the most important of these mills, at least for the bank-note industry, was the one established on a one-acre tract in Chester County, Pennsylvania, during the autumn of 1729 by a recently arrived English paper-maker named Thomas Willcox and his partner, Thomas Brown.[24] This is believed to be the third paper mill built in America. It is said that the early production of the mill was fuller's pressboards, such as those used by clothiers to press cloth. A few years later, Benjamin Franklin played a role in getting the Willcox mill to make paper for colonial currency. Franklin was a friend of the family and a frequent visitor to their house and mill. Thomas gave up the mill to his son, Mark, in 1767. Mark is believed to have made paper for the first Continental bills, the first issue of which was authorized by Congress on May 10, 1775. By that time, the mill was known as "Ivy Mills."

The first two issues of Continental currency were printed on plain paper, owing to the emergency of their need, but in June 1775 Benjamin Franklin and others were appointed by Congress to form a committee "to get the proper plates engraved, to provide paper and agree with printers to print the bills." In October of that year, Congress authorized that "five millions of Continental dollars be immediately borrowed for the use of the United States at the annual interest of four per cent per annum . . ." The paper was made at Ivy Mills and delivered by wagon to Michael Hillegas, the newly elected treasurer, at Baltimore. The Journals of the Continental Congress contain the following record:

> In Congress, February 9, 1779. The Commissioners of Claims reported—That there is due to Mark Willcox for 46,946 sheets of paper for loan office certificates and bills of exchange a balance of 4,694 dollars. Ordered that said account be paid.

A sample of the paper made by Mark Willcox for the Bank of North America at this time and believed to be the same as used for the Loan Office certificates measures 12 by 18-1/2 inches. It is a thin paper, and each sheet contains the watermarks for six notes.

One of the interesting aspects of the congressional journals is that they record the precautions taken by Congress to have an official personally supervise the operations at Ivy Mills in making and transporting watermarked paper. In 1781 Robert Morris of the "National Bank" sent Joseph Pennell to "superintend the manufacture of ten thousand sheets of bank note paper at the mill of Mark Willcox." This was undoubtedly the first paper money used for bank notes of the United States. The next year Benjamin Dudley was given the same job. Dudley delivered the mill's paper to Franklin & Hall, the printers, and their successors, Hall & Sellers. In March 1786 General Percifor Frazer supervised the making of paper for new loan certificates; Robert Gilchrist was also an agent of the United States who performed these services. It was often the practice of the agent to keep a set of keys by which he could lock up certain parts of the mill at the end of the day.

By 1783 Mark Willcox realized that a stronger paper was needed for paper money, and he began using "Russia Sheeting" and Irish linen.[25] These were the main materials used in making bank-note paper until bleaching came into use at this mill in 1846. These kinds of linen often cost more than 50¢ a pound. Colored-silk fibers, especially red silk from handkerchiefs, were also used in making many different bank-note papers. The practice began in 1756 with the New Jersey currency dated June 22 of that year. The notes of Pennsylvania dated November 29, 1775, and the Continental currency of 1775 also contained silk fibers.[26] The price for these rags was not an important matter for the mill, as it was the common practice for the bank to pay for the rags and for any molds if the notes were to be watermarked. A local history carries the story further:

> Again, in the War of 1812, the Government was obliged to issue paper money, and again recourse was had to Ivy Mills to supply its necessities. At that time a distinctive paper, with colored silk shreds woven through it, was made for the Government's use, and the mill was guarded by the Government, to prevent the paper from leaking out into unlawful hands.[27]

The Willcox family made bank-note paper by hand until 1866, when it was finally discontinued.[28] However, they realized early on that mechanization was not only inevitable, but absolutely essential if they were to stay competitive. James M. Willcox built two paper mills, one in 1837 and another in 1845, at Glen Mills, about 2-1/2 miles from Ivy Mills, in which paper was made by Fourdrinier machines. Much of the machine-made paper was used for bank notes. After about 1830, the Willcox mills specialized in bank-note paper and began to get large government contracts. Most of the bonds of the United States were printed on plain, strong paper, but in 1843, when a national loan was approaching its maturity, Congress approved an issue of new notes. In July of that year, James M. Willcox supplied the Treasury Department with two classes of watermarked paper. One class consisted of large sheets for bonds and the other class was 35,000 sheets for Treasury Notes. In 1848 the president was granted authority to borrow $16 million, and this resulted in an order for 26,000 sheets of paper from the Willcox mills that was sent to Rawdon, Wright, Hatch & Edson in New York. Many large banks also used Willcox paper and placed orders for several thousand sheets at a time. It became a common practice at both Ivy Mills and Glen Mills to keep large stocks of plain bank-note paper in storage.

Not all bank notes were printed on paper of one size. The Bank of the United States, for example, had different sizes of notes for different denominations. The mill records show that Willcox sent 22,500 sheets for small-size notes and the same number for a larger denomination to this bank. In 1838 the Willcox mills won a contract with the state of New York to make paper for state-chartered banks. The engraving and printing of these notes was awarded to Rawdon, Wright & Hatch (New York), to Draper, Toppan, Longacre & Company (Philadelphia), to Danforth, Underwood & Company (New York), and to Hall, Packard & Cushman (Albany, New York). The comptroller of New York wanted the notes printed on both sides, so Willcox made a thicker and more-opaque paper to prevent the "strike through" of the ink from one side to the other. After this date, more and more notes were printed on both sides of the paper. Generally speaking, the banks in the southern states preferred thin bank-note paper, and those of the

northeastern states wanted thicker paper. The range in thickness made the paper weigh from 12 to 18 pounds per 1,000 sheets, each sheet making 8 notes.

When the first Demand Notes were authorized by Congress in July and August 1861, Secretary of the Treasury Salmon P. Chase asked J.M. Willcox & Sons to make paper of a heavier weight—20 pounds per 1,000 sheets—so the green ink on the back side of the notes would not strike through. The order required enough sheets to print $50 million of notes. That exceeded the capacity of the hand-made paper operations at Ivy Mills, so the entire order was made on Fourdrinier machines at Glen Mills. When the Legal Tender Notes were authorized by Congress on February 25, 1862, a thinner paper was chosen—18 pounds per 1,000 sheets—and that became the standard weight of government currency paper for some time.

Not only did the Willcox family play a major role in the financial aspects of the Union side of the Civil War, supporting the Treasury Department by supplying huge quantities of bank-note paper on short notice, but they also made paper for a number of foreign banks. In 1838 they made bank-note paper for Messrs. Everett & Batrtelle of New York, agents for the bank of "New Granada," which became Columbia. In 1839 they made 25,000 sheets of blue-tinted paper and 15,000 sheets of yellow paper for the notes of Greece, which were engraved and printed by the American Bank Note Company in New York. This was probably the earliest bank-note paper made in America for a foreign government.

Counterfeiting was constantly a problem for every part of the bank-note industry, including the paper-makers. One of the plans tried at Ivy Mills was to incorporate flakes of mica into the paper. Mica is familiar to all of us who collected minerals as kids, but it's actually not just one mineral but a group of similar minerals with over 30 members. They all have a layered, silicate structure which allows the crystals to be split into very thin sheets that are tough, usually transparent, chemically stable, and quite flexible. No one knows who first thought of using mica to make a distinctive paper for bank notes, but it occurs in notes printed as early as 1764. Mica was used in the colonial notes of New York, Pennsylvania, Delaware, Maryland, Virginia, and North Carolina, as well as in some Continental notes. Given these properties, it was probably added to the vat when making paper by hand and therefore occurs in a random pattern throughout the notes. Counterfeiters who made their own paper could easily buy mica and use it the same way as professional paper-makers.

The use of localized jute fibers was another method to make a distinctive bank-note paper on the Fourdrinier machine. James M. Willcox took out a patent on the process, No. 56,650, dated July 24, 1866, entitled "Safety Paper." He explained the history of his invention in a testimony before a congressional committee in May 1874:

> But at the end of the last administration, I made a contract with Mr. Boutwell. He was very anxious to have a special paper, but I knew of none except water-marked paper and plain bank paper. Our contract was commenced with paper of that kind. I afterward explained to him the nature of localized-fiber paper, which I told him had never been manufactured, and that I should have to undertake it as an experiment. . . . I then consulted manufactures of paper who assured that the thing could not be done. That it would be impossible to handle the long fiber, wet in such a condition to localize it in paper. Nevertheless, I had faith in it, and I had machinery made for the purpose of localizing the fiber in the paper. Such a thing had never been done before. The experiment succeeded. . . . This paper has now been in use for several years, and what it has done in the way of protecting Government issues from counterfeiting is for the judgment of this committee.
>
> . . . The nature of the fiber that was placed in this paper was kept a secret, but, under a resolution offered in the House by Mr. Dawes, requiring the Secretary of the Treasury to furnish a statement of what fiber was used, Mr. Boutwell divulged it. A short time after that the fiber, which before that time had remained a secret, was imitated.

A small paper mill was erected in the upper part of a building in New York, and an attempt to counterfeit the paper was made.

After identifying the once-secret fiber as jute, Willcox goes on to explain:[29]

> It [jute] has to be stripped from the bark and to be bleached and dyed, and it is so difficult a matter to dye it that I have found but two dyers in the United States who can accomplish it. . . . The use of jute for this purpose is a discovery of our own, in experimenting with it before recommending it to the Government. Mr. Boutwell adopted it, and four years' use of it as paper-material has shown that it is at least as good as silk. I regard it as being better, for the reason that, being a round fiber, the outlines are always distinct, whereas, where silk is used a soiled note merely takes a pinkish hue, and the outlines of the fiber are obliterated.[30]

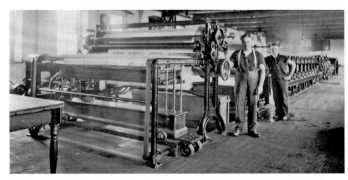

The machine room at Crane & Company, circa 1890s.

The government had originally requested in 1869 that both red- and blue-silk fibers be used for its Fractional Currency and for U.S. notes. For some reason, only short red-silk fibers were used, and then only for about six months. In September 1869 the government entered into a new contract with Willcox that required currency and bonds to have randomly distributed jute fibers and the Legal Tender issues to have the newly patented feature of a two- or three-inch–wide band of dark-blue–jute fibers. This latter feature was called "localized fiber." At some point, and I have not been able to determine the exact date, jute fibers were dyed in both blue and red colors, and the blue fibers greatly predominated.

One author has written that blue-jute fibers outnumbered the red fibers by approximately 1,000 to 1 but did not mention any research supporting this figure.[31] This contract was continued in force until September 1877, when the Treasury decided the existing stocks of paper at Glen Mills would last a long time and asked Willcox to temporarily stop making paper. In 1879, when the Treasury wanted to resume production, Willcox refused to make data available that would allow the government auditors to estimate a "just and equitable price" for his paper. Consequently, John Sherman, the secretary of the Treasury and a person who was suspicious of the Willcox firm, had the proposed contract put out on bid.

During the late 1870s Willcox had reduced his original contract price of the localized fiber paper from 75¢ a pound to 70¢ a pound. Given the importance of the contract, James M. Willcox went to Washington, D.C., to influence as many people as he could to accept his bid. This was a time when influence peddling has risen to high art, and Willcox was adept at giving dinners in swank restaurants and impressing officials with his knowledge and the family's long history in making paper. Other paper mills had sent their agents as well, and one of them was 26-year-old Winthrop Murray Crane from Crane & Company in Dalton, Massachusetts.[32]

The shipping room at Crane & Company's Government Mill. Note that one of the boxes is addressed to the "Honorable Secretary of the Treasury."

For the new contract, Willcox bid 61.4¢ a pound for one type of paper and 55.5¢ a pound for another type. Crane bid 40¢ a pound. According to the rules, the bids would be received on Monday, and a committee would decide on the winner the following Wednesday. But before the bids were officially opened, someone leaked the information that Hurlburt Manufacturing Company of North Manchester, Connecticut, had bid 39.75¢ a pound. Crane learned of the lower bid, and in the last hour before the bids were to be opened, he left a "going home" party at his hotel and literally ran to the Treasury Department to file a new bid of 38.9¢ a pound.[33] Having the lowest bid, Crane won the contract, but it was obvious that he had gotten specific knowledge of the Hurlburt bid in order to squeeze in a bid just under their price. This led to an immediate call for a congressional investigation and a disqualification of all bids. In a scathing letter written by Henry Hayward to H.L. Fairchild, secretary of the Treasury, dated May 30, 1897, Hayward implied that the Crane family had asked Senator Dawes to exert his influence on Secretary Sherman to give Crane & Company the contract, and in return, the senator would nominate the secretary for president at the upcoming Republican Convention in Chicago.[34] Hayward had a right to complain since he held a patent for the incorporation of imprinted or alternating colored-silk threads in bank notes, and the government had previously accepted that patent and promised him a contract only to have Secretary Sherman turn around and send samples of Hayward's distinctive paper to different paper-makers asking for fresh bids on "Hayward's patent." But politics aside, the real crime was allowing a second bid from Crane & Company, or as Hayward called it, "a thing unprecedented." At the hearing, which was held at the Treasury Department rather than before a congressional committee, the objections of the losers fell on deaf ears, and Winthrop M. Crane was given the contract. For the first time in nearly 100 years, the Willcox mills stopped making paper for the U.S. government.[35]

Watermarks

Before leaving the subject of the Willcox paper mills, it may be of interest to take up the subject of making molds to watermark paper. Watermarks, of course, are variations in the thickness of paper that will reproduce a figure, such as a portrait or an outline of a form or letters when the paper is held up to the light. According to Dard Hunter, the earliest use of watermarks occurred in Italy about the year 1282. In this country, the use of watermarks as a security device on bank-note paper dates from the time of the Revolutionary War, one of the first being the notes of Pennsylvania dated April 10, 1777. One of the few Americans skilled in making paper molds at this time was Nathan Sellers, and he soon dominated the trade.[36] Sellers kept elaborate records of the molds he made, listing the name of the person for whom he made the mold, the design of the watermark, its size, etc.[37]

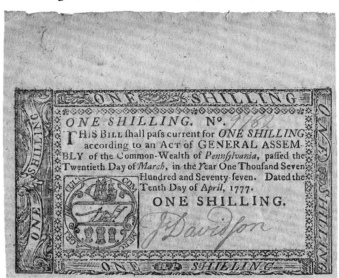

A one-shilling note of Pennsylvania, April 10, 1777.

Sellers was born November 27, 1751, in Darby, Pennsylvania, a fourth-generation American who could trace his genealogy back to his great-grandfather, who came to Philadelphia with William Penn in 1682. The Sellers in England had been weavers, so mold-making was not far removed from those skills. Although he was a Quaker and supposedly opposed to military service of any kind, he soon joined the American Army. In August 1776 paper-makers in Pennsylvania petitioned Congress to release Sellers from duty because of his unique ability to make molds for the paper mills. The Journals of the Continental Congress give the following report:

In Congress, August 26, 1776

A petition from sundry paper-makers was presented to Congress and read praying that Nathan Sellers an associator in Colonel Paschll's battalion and who has marched to New Jersey may be ordered to return home, to make and prepare suitable molds, washers & utensils for carrying on the paper manufactory. Resolved that the prayer of the petition be granted.

We don't know how Nathan Sellers learned to make molds. Probably, he saw molds that had been made in England and learned to copy them. Making molds is a very laborious and time-consuming process, but Sellers apparently had a keen understanding of mechanics and was able to invent new tools to improve the work. To make a laid mold, each successive wire had to be laid by hand on the frame of the mold and spaced accurately by hand-twisting the cross-wires and, in effect, sewing the wires in place. Brass wires had to be imported from England, but the diameter of the wire varied from reel to reel and sometimes it varied over the length of the wire in a single reel. To get the wire to an even 3/32-inch diameter, and to remove its curvature, the wire had to be drawn out on a "draw-bench." Sellers improved the design of this straightening board so greatly that the new board was copied and then patented in France about 1800. In fact, Sellers reinvented almost all the tools used in his craft. He retired from his business in 1817, suffering from bouts of vertigo, moved to a country home near his birthplace, and died there in 1830.

The Englishman, William Henry Smith, invented another process for making portrait watermarks as a security device for bank-note paper. These are called "light-and-shade" watermarks, and while they are more complicated to make, their use in modern notes has been popular. Basically, a portrait is drawn in a wax that is a 50/50 mixture of pure beeswax and common paraffin. This is done by using small cutting and gouging tools. Once the incised portrait is ready, it is covered with powdered graphite (plumbago) which gives a metallic surface to the wax. Then, an electrotype is made of the wax model. The electrotype has a thickness of about 1/32 of an inch, so it is backed by a quarter-inch of lead to make it rigid. The contours of the electrotype must be imparted to a woven brass-wire gauze that will eventually form the face or surface of the paper-making mold. The woven wire is made of small-diameter stock, running 48 to 60 wires to the inch. This impression is made by using burnishing tools. The finished mold shows delicate shading that could never be accomplished by the normal laid-wire technique. Dard Hunter gives a step-by-step procedure for making such molds and shows pictures of each stage of the process.[38]

Light-and-shade watermarks have only recently been incorporated into American currency but were often used in the currencies of a number of countries around the world. The paper mills using this type of watermarking were previously located only in England, France, Germany, Italy, and Russia. America's recent adoption of this security device represents a real shift in the bureau's thinking about currency design. It was a long-standing policy that changing our currency would only confuse the public and facilitate counterfeiting. This policy required that our federal bank notes should always have unchanging line-engraved portraits of high-artistic merit, combined with geometric-lathe work, green ink, and a distinctive cream-colored 24-pound sized paper with randomly distributed red and blue fibers, and that all denominations should be of the same size. That way, the image and feel of a real note would be "burned" into everyone's memory so thoroughly that even slight deviations of a counterfeit note would be noticed. But this was a naïve policy that failed to consider the fact that people do not spend much time inspecting bank notes when they receive them in normal business transactions. In fact, most people look very briefly

at the denomination number and take only a quick glance at the face of the bill in order to complete a transaction or make change. These quick glances are more impressions than inspections. Experience has shown that counterfeit notes which are made by photographic processes and printed on paper of approximately the same weight as real notes are often mistaken for the "real thing."

The U.S. government finally decided that our currency should incorporate security features which could not be photographed but could be instantly recognized by sight. There was real concern in Washington, D.C., that certain foreign governments which could legitimately buy highly sophisticated bank-note–printing equipment and which could afford to manufacture bank-note paper identical to the Crane & Company product might do just that. Perhaps they did. A number of exquisite counterfeits have shown up in the past few years, including a Canadian counterfeit of the U.S. $100 note, made with offset plates and printed (not embedded) red and blue security fibers. It took 2-1/2 years for the Secret Service to crack that case, during which more than $10 million worth of these counterfeits was detected. A Columbian counterfeit of the U.S. $100 note, first detected in 1981, had more than 100 minor varieties. Almost $36 million was detected by 1994. These notes were printed on real currency paper that had been bleached to remove the ink and then reprinted in a higher denomination. The Treasury has also detected a counterfeit $100 note originating in the Middle East called "the Super Dollar" because of its near-perfect imitation. A task force set up to investigate the Super Dollar counterfeits reported that the total amount in circulation was between $100 million and possibly billions of dollars, but no hard evidence has been released to the public to support that claim.[39]

Portals of England

The Portal family of Laverstoke, England, has made the currency paper for the Bank of England since 1725, a history of service not matched anywhere else. The family was Protestant, and like other Huguenots, they suffered at the hands of the French government. Henri Portal was born in Poitiers, in the south of France, in 1690, the year that the Massachusetts Bay Colony began its experiment with paper money. After a period of some trouble under Louis XIV, the head of the Portal family and his wife and children tried to escape, but several members of the family were killed, and only four children made it to safety in Holland. There, Henri attached himself to the Court of William of Orange and eventually made it to England, landing in Southampton in 1706.[40] They found work in a paper mill in 1706, and by 1711 Henri had purchased a small paper mill from a friend named William Heathcote. A few years later, he leased the nearby Laverstoke Mill, which had been a corn mill. His friend was the nephew of Sir Gilbert Heathcote, then the governor of the Bank of England, and it was through this connection that the superior quality of Portal's paper was brought to the attention of the bank and eventually adopted for its bank notes. Previously, from the time the Bank of England was founded in 1694, it had used the bank-note paper made by Mr. Rice Watkins at Sutton Mills in Berkshire.

Louis XIV, King of France, dining at court.

The bank-note paper made by the Portals was distinctive. It was very thin, crisp, somewhat transparent, and yet strong. It had a unique "feel" and made a distinctive rattling or crackling sound when new. The paper was made of linen and cotton rags, like other bank-note papers, but part of the material may have been made from the flax plant directly without first being split and made into linen. A different paper was made at Bere Mill, the first mill that Henri Portal had purchased, and that paper was sold only to the provincial banks. The paper for the Bank of England had an intricate scroll on the left side of the note. The crisp, hard paper used for the bank's notes soon became limp and soiled, but that was not as much a problem as might be thought, for the bank did not recirculate its notes. When they were turned in, new notes were issued in their place, and most of the notes in circulation looked new.[41]

Membrane Paper and Stuart Gwynn

The United States has had a mixed record of successes and failures in developing security features on its currency. The story of membrane paper was a little of both. The principals were an inventor named Dr. Stuart Gwynn of New York and a provost marshal, or special agent of the War Department, named Colonel Lafayette C. Baker, assigned to investigate Gwynn at the Treasury Department during the Civil War.

In a voluntary statement that Stuart Gwynn gave to Colonel Baker, he states that he was a consulting engineer, chemist, and inventor.[42] At the time of his arrest, Gwynn was 46 years old, and his family, a wife and five children, lived in Cortland township in Westchester, New York. He had been in Boston for most of the time since 1855 but considered New York City his residence since he had a room and business there. Gwynn was aware that the Treasury Department had advertised its interest in getting proposals from paper manufacturers for a distinctive bank-note paper. He wrote to the department in June or July 1862 to explain that he had invented a new kind of paper that offered protection against counterfeiting. He sent several letters to the Treasury Department, some including samples of his paper, but heard nothing from the department until October of that year.[43] At that time he received a telegram from Secretary Chase asking him to come to Washington, D.C., immediately.

Gwynn says he hesitated because he was heavily engaged in other matters, doing work for the railroads, working on a telegraphic instrument, a gas apparatus, etc., and making at least $5,000 a year with good prospects of increasing his income. After consulting with his partners, he went to Washington on two occasions and hammered out a contract to make bank-note paper for the Treasury Department. The contract was first written in a rough draft by Gwynn, then corrected for technical issues by S.M. Clark, the superintendent of the National Currency Bureau, then read and corrected for legal and administrative purposes by Edward Jordan, the Solicitor of the Treasury, and finally signed in duplicate by Secretary Chase.

Gwynn was given an office on the third floor of the Treasury Building and the use of the north attic room of the west wing to house 78 hydraulic presses. Gwynn said S.M. Clark then revealed to him a new "broad plan" that he envisioned to make the bank-note paper perfectly safe. This involved not only

Lafayette Baker.

Gwynn's new paper (membrane paper), but also a new way of engraving in which both face and back would be done "in the highest style of art by elaborate hand labor of artists of rare genius and skill, in lieu of the cheaper and common, though beautiful, mechanical product of lathe work." Clark wanted to add to the labor by making four impressions instead of the two used on postal currency. The two additional impressions being "an irremovable mordant, the manufacture of which is original and a secret with the department, then covered with bronze, which effectually prevents copies being made by the cheap and easily acquired process of photography."[44] Clark also wanted a new way of printing—dry printing by hydraulic presses, and new inks. Gwynn had originally told his partners in New York that his contract with the Treasury would require only a quarter of his time, but it was obvious that Clark's

new plan would require lots of experimentation to develop the new methods. This was a difficult period for Gwynn. In February 1863 he lost his two youngest daughters, one six and the other eight years old, within three weeks of each other. He was beset by so many problems at work that he decided to stay permanently in Washington and rented a furnished house in Georgetown which he shared with General Herman Haupt.[45]

Gwynn designed steam-driven hydraulic presses and had them manufactured by Woodruff and Beach in Hartford, Connecticut.[46] These weighed 11,000 pounds each and cost an average of $1,100 apiece. Similar presses and related hydraulic equipment, pulleys, and steam engines were made by Poole & Hunt of Baltimore, Maryland, and by Hayward, Bartlett & Company.[47,48] Thin bank-note paper was bought from P.W. Hudson of the Hudson & Cheney Paper Company of North Manchester, Connecticut, to make the membrane sheets. Gwynn made experiments to find a non-photographic ink for the paper. A report on these experiments states:

> He [Gwynn] made extensive experiments, but with all his scientific knowledge failed to produce an even non-photographic tint which that same scientific knowledge could not effectually remove. In the course of his experiments he discovered a method of tinting non-photographically, with a new and rare pigment, a fibre foreign to that used in the manufacture of paper, but which could be introduced into and mingled with it in such a manner that no reagent known to chemistry nor any method that he could devise, would remove its non-photographic property without at the same time removing the fibre itself. This was the origin of the so-called "spider legs" in the membrane paper, and which has been adapted as one of the distinctive characteristics of the National Paper now [1864] made in the Department.[49]

There were various technical problems with the large hydraulic presses, especially noticeable when the hydraulic cylinders ruptured under great pressure. The huge iron cylinders had pistons that compressed oil and sent it through pipes to a few special presses used for making the membrane paper. Gwynn was making progress in getting these problems under control when Lafayette Baker entered the scene.

Baker became involved when a suspicion arose about Charles Cornwell, an employee in the redemption department at the Treasury. Baker at that time was a provost marshal in the War Department and was investigating problems in the quartermaster's department. He was summoned to the Treasury by the secretary and told briefly that he would be reassigned to investigate certain problems in the National Currency Bureau. He began his investigation just a few days before Christmas 1863. Cornwell was soon detected stealing money and was arrested and placed in the Old Capitol Prison in Washington. Baker says $31,000 or $32,000 was taken from Cornwell, part of it in national currency and part in 5-20 bonds. Next, one G.A. Henderson, a warrant clerk in the Requisition Warrants department, was arrested on the suspicion of receiving valuable presents for giving priority to Treasury warrants for payment. The law required that all warrants be paid in the order in which they were received. The warrant clerk was ordered to be prosecuted, but for technical reasons, the prosecution was dropped. The Solicitor of the Treasury then turned his attention to Stuart Gwynn and Spencer M. Clark.

Baker raided Gwynn's office during his absence on January 6, 1864, and confiscated private letters, invoices, drawings, memoranda, specimens of printing, and miscellaneous notes. This was done without a search warrant and without authorization from any officer in the Treasury. Baker read through the evidence and quickly concluded that Gwynn and Spencer M. Clark were attempting to defraud the government by purchasing giant presses and other equipment under the color of government authority and then pocketing the money instead of sending it to the vendors. This was sufficient to get Gwynn thrown in prison. Secretary Chase naturally wanted a full report of Baker's investigation so Gwynn could be prosecuted. Baker was to have the report ready in a few days; instead, he took

three months to submit his charges. In a voluminous report, Baker laid out all the specifics of invoices that hadn't been paid to manufacturers and suppliers. He also claimed that Gwynn was damaging the Treasury Building by suspending a dead weight of nearly 200 tons from the girders of the north attic room of the west wing (the hydraulic press room) and causing damage to the exterior of the building by the use of a 100-ton dead weight suspended by pulleys over the cornice of the roof to increase the pressure put out by the hydraulic presses to print on membrane paper. On the basis of these charges, Gwynn was committed to the Old Capitol Prison where he remained for one month, although he was never officially charged with any crime and never permitted to see a lawyer. Normally, such heavy-handed procedures would be illegal and a cause for dismissal, but the war was not far away and Washington was under martial law. Baker could do pretty much what he wanted.

The Old Capitol Prison during the Civil War was overcrowded and dirty.[50] While Gwynn was confined there, Secretary Chase sent the Solicitor of the Treasury to interview him. Dr. Gwynn answered questions fully and protested that he was not guilty of any wrongdoing. Mr. Jordan reported his cooperation to Secretary Chase, who eventually ordered Gwynn's release.

The Old Capitol Prison.

On March 30, 1864, Dr. Gwynn commenced two suits in the U.S. District Court against Colonel Baker—one for arresting him without a warrant and the other for trespass in entering his rooms in Georgetown and at the Treasury to take private books and papers without a search warrant. A third suit was filed on April 4 for libel in causing false statements to be published in newspapers. Immediately after the first two suits were commenced, Colonel Baker wrote the Solicitor of the Treasury and asked if the department would assume responsibility for the arrest of Gwynn and for his (Baker's) proceedings in the case. When the solicitor said that he would have such protection as the facts in the case afforded him and that it must depend upon the law whether he was justified in what he had done, Baker replied with considerable hostility and threatened that if the department did not defend him, he would bring to light some very damaging facts.

Shakespeare got it right. "Oh what a tangled web we weave when first we practice to deceive." Baker began a quick investigation, taking as a confederate in this scheme a local actress. Together they interrogated a number of female employees in the printing division of the Currency Bureau and threatened most of them that they would be imprisoned in the Old Capitol Prison if they did not confess to acts of immorality and lascivious behavior with the superintendent or his associates. Their "confessions" were all written by the same hand and all concluded with the assurance that their statements were given "voluntarily and without duress, fear, or fee." These charges were given to an investigating committee of Congress, but the majority of that committee saw through Baker's lies. But crude as his tactics were, Baker may have outdone himself on one occasion:

> In one instance, with a barbarity rarely surpassed, he arrested a funeral procession, took from the coffin the corpse of a young lady, late an employee in the Treasury Department, charging that she died in an attempt to procure an abortion, the result of immorality in the Treasury Department. The case was examined by a justice of this city, and a post mortem examination held, which resulted in a decision that the young lady died of pulmonary consumption. The physicians reported that the post mortem examination afforded incontestable evidence of the unsullied virtue of the deceased.[51]

A popular theory of the time held that the bank-note companies in New York perceived a great threat to their future if Spencer Clark was successful in setting up the government's own currency bureau, and they were willing to do almost anything to get him out of the way. Colonel Baker may have been their agent provocateur. The evidence for this is more real than imagined. Under questioning by an investigating committee of Congress, Spencer Clark told that he had seen a report critical of his (Clark's) work in the Treasury that Colonel Baker had claimed to have written, but Clark says:

> I recognized the style of composition of the Vice President of one of the bank note companies in New York.
>
> Question: What was his name?
>
> Answer: Mr. Gavit, vice-president of the American Bank Note Company. I also thought I recognized the style of this Mr. Jewitt I have spoken of. Throughout the document there was a knowledge of technicalities and of the details of the trade, which is hardly to be supposed could be possessed by any other than an expert—which I supposed Colonel Baker to be.
>
> Question: Any other grounds for your inference?
>
> Answer: It has been frequently reported to me by men under me, that they had seen the presidents of these companies going in and out of Mr. Baker's office. I saw Mr. Hatch [George W. Hatch, president of the American Bank Note Company] coming off the steps of the office, as if he had come out of it. I cannot say he was in the office.[52]

Philo Durfee testified that in the autumn of 1863, Hatch had a conversation with him at the St. Nicholas Hotel in New York "in which he expressed the opinion that Mr. Clark could be bought out of the Treasury Department, and expressed his willingness to pay a large amount— a great deal more than Clark could make in Washington—if he would abandon his position and help break up the system of printing in the Treasury Department."[53] There was similar testimony by other witnesses. One of them, Edward Learned, president of the Mississippi and Ohio Railroad, replied: "I have known Clark for several years, Mr. Hatch, and the man who spends his time between his office, his family, and the microscope, and who is devoted to those things pretty much exclusively, is not a venal man, and I suppose you will permit me to say that though you have printed a great many bank notes, you have not printed enough to purchase S.M. Clark."[54]

As the curtain falls for the final time in this story, Dr. Stuart Gwynn is exonerated of his legal problems, Colonel Lafayette Baker is hissed as a simple-minded villain, and S.M Clark rides into retirement on a white horse, his honor and reputation unblemished. It was a good start for the bureau.

Originally, even before Stuart Gwynn was brought into the picture, the government had intended to use one distinctive paper for all the different types of currency. Gwynn and Clark, however, had decided to limit their risk by using it first on Fractional Currency to make certain they had solved the technical problems. Secretary Chase even had a law passed which made it illegal for anyone to possess a paper similar to the distinctive paper used by the government, and a different but similar law exists today. Over the next few years, the government played "musical chairs" with the colors and placement of fibers in their notes. Beginning in 1885, the use of distributed fibers was stopped, and notes had only two threads, each about an inch long, that were located on the right and left sides. In August 1886 this was changed so that one blue thread appeared near the center of each note. Two threads were used again from 1887 to 1891. In July 1891 another change placed a localized strip of red- and blue-silk fibers, perpendicular to the length of the note, on each side of the center portrait. No other changes were made in the fibers until small-size currency was introduced in 1929.

Recently, Fred L. Reed III discovered that many U.S. notes had been overprinted in small text with information that related to the specific patent used to protect the notes. He has written about the history of these patents and shown enlarged photographic views of the mention of these patents on various bank notes in several issues of the *Bank Note Reporter*, beginning about February 2009.[55] Some of these patents were inventions relating first to special inks and then to special papers or manufacturing techniques that the federal government had hoped would prevent counterfeiting or make it too difficult for men of average skill and experience. Reed argues convincingly that none of these patented ideas ever really protected our notes, and counterfeiting continued even as the notes became more technically difficult to imitate. It is the oldest story in counterfeiting—that whatever the invention, a way is soon found to imitate it. Experience has shown that even advanced technologies are available to men with money or to governments without honor.

Cotton began to rise over linen due to the embargo during the war.

World War I caused the British to place an embargo on the export of linen to the United States. By the Fall of 1914 the government authorized Crane & Company to substitute cotton for one-third of the linen normally used in bank-note paper. By January 1917 a further reduction in the linen content was required, and the new notes were printed on paper with a 50/50 ratio of cotton to linen. By 1918 U.S. currency was entirely cotton, and this continued until the 50/50 ratio was restored in March 1921. As linen became more readily available after the war, the currency was changed again, and linen was increased to 75%, and finally the transition was made to an all-linen paper in July 1922. By then, however, tests made at the Bureau of Standards showed that all-linen notes had inferior qualities for printing and durability, and in 1924 the government authorized the substitution of 25% cotton in combination with the linen.[56] This ratio was maintained up to the time of World War II, although experiments with different cotton-linen ratios continued without public notice. Such experiments are important to the Bureau of Engraving and Printing since the wearing qualities of paper are directly related to the average life-span of currency, and that determines the rate of redemption (replacing worn-out currency) and the cost of making paper money.

Crane & Company

Although Willcox & Sons had a long and reputable history of improving the paper used for currency through their experience and work ethic, it is another old firm, Crane & Company, that has made the greatest number of technical advances in this highly specialized field. The Crane family can trace its origins back to Henry Crane, who came over from England in 1648 and settled in an area that became the town of Milton, Massachusetts, in 1656.[57] His great-grandson, Stephen Crane, became the first paper-maker of the American Cranes. Stephen died during the Revolutionary War, but his mill sold a quantity of special currency-type paper to Paul Revere in 1775. All three sons of Stephen Crane learned the craft of making paper at the Milton Paper Mill, and one of them, Zenas Crane, went on to build his own mill in February 1801 near Dalton, Massachusetts, on a 14-acre plot of farmland that he bought for $194. The original two-story building had just one vat. Zenas, in turn, taught his son, Zenas Marshal Crane, the fundamentals of paper-making. In 1844, when Zenas Marshal Crane was 29 years old, he invented a distinctive bank-note paper in which parallel silk threads ran lengthwise through the notes. The number of threads corresponded with the denomination of the note, so one thread indicated a $1 note, two threads were on $2 notes, and three threads were on $3 notes, then a common denomination. This prevented anyone from "raising" one denomination to a higher one without showing a discrepancy between the denomination and the number of threads. It was more common in those days to raise a denomination than to counterfeit a complete bill. The banks that used this type of bank-note paper probably didn't need the protection on bills above $3. Bills of $5 and higher denominations were more carefully inspected, and a raised denomination was less likely to succeed in those notes.

Paper-drying buildings at Crane & Company, circa 1890s. Note the ventilation slats on the sides of the drying buildings.

In 1890 Crane & Company developed a new kind of bank-note paper using silk fibers instead of the longer silk threads. This came to the attention of the Greek government, which was then looking for some means to make their notes more difficult to counterfeit. Knowing that Crane made the bank-note paper used by the American Bank Note Company, the same company that engraved and printed Greek bank notes, Greece asked the American Bank Note Company if they would begin printing the Greek notes on the new silk-fiber paper. The executives at the American knew that they would need government approval to use that kind of paper, and they immediately asked for permission, pointing out that if the American Bank Note Company didn't get the contract, there was another bank-note company in Europe that stood ready to do the job. The U.S. government, however, refused permission to the American Bank Note Company to use a paper similar to the distinctive paper used for U.S. currency. But rather than give up, the American Bank Note Company set about finding a solution.

Planchettes

Planchettes solved the problem. They were small discs of paper in different colors that could be added to the bank-note paper in a random distribution during its manufacture. The discs had special identifying characteristics, some of which were secret, but all of which instantly revealed a counterfeit note. The American Bank Note Company made the planchettes and sent them to Crane & Company. The patent for this invention, No. 447,336, dated March 3, 1891, was assigned to James MacDonough, the president of the American Bank Note Company. It is a common practice to assign patents to the president of a company to keep control of the invention within the company. In this patent, McDonough explained that the planchettes were to be introduced into the paper pulp as it came from the vat onto the apron of the paper-making machine. The planchettes would be pumped through tubes or nozzles directly into the pulp. As with most patents, this one was written to give the greatest possible latitude to the company, describing the use of different shapes, colors, and sizes of planchettes, whether they were made from paper or some other material, and allowed for random distribution or localized placement within either plain paper or a distinctive safety paper. Following the example set by Greece, many other countries were soon using planchette paper for additional security. Printed planchettes made with micro-printing techniques were suggested by Fues (German Patent No. 422,294), and a number of European patents proposed different materials and shapes (e.g. tiny stars and triangles) for planchettes. In the 20th century, planchettes were made by the American Bank Note Company which fluoresced under ultraviolet light. Red planchettes fluoresced red, yellow planchettes fluoresced yellow, orchid planchettes did not fluoresce but contained blue and red fibers, and blue planchettes contained blue fibers.

Crane & Company has made many improvements in their paper-making machinery. One example was their Patent No. 537,753, dated April 16, 1895, which described an improved way to deliver silk fibers to the pulp on the apron of a paper-making machine used to make the distinctive paper of U.S. currency. A shaft, powered by a belt pulley, was placed on the paper-making machine, above the apron. There were 16 receptacles placed side-by-side along the length of the shaft, and these dipped into a special pulp vat containing silk fibers during one part of the shaft's revolution, delivering the pulp and silk fibers to the paper beneath the shaft on another part of its revolution.

An example of a note printed on planchette paper.

Making Paper

It may be of interest to follow some rags as they make their way through a typical paper mill in the late 19th century. First, there's cleaning, sorting, and cutting to be done. Rags were collected from all sorts of places, so it was usually necessary to put them into a dusting machine to shake loose the sand and dirt that may have come along with them. If the rags were collected in eastern cities, many of them would be contaminated by carbon soot and coal dust—things that weren't easily removed by household laundry. Those kinds of rags had to stay in the dusting machine for a longer time. Women then removed hooks, buttons, eyes, and things of that sort. Next, the rags were properly sorted, requiring a good eye and some experience. It's easy enough to sort by color, but then one had to sort each pile by the age and appearance of the individual rags to make sure the materials were similar and the fibers would receive the appropriate processing later on. Finally, after the sorting was finished, the rags had to be cut into the appropriate size to facilitate the digestion in the boiler and beating machines.

A rag cutter, or Hollander, is a machine in which revolving blades cut against a stationary bed knife. The more slowly the rags are fed into the machine, the longer they are exposed to the cutting action, and the shorter the pieces become. If small pieces are desired, then the rags are passed through the cutter two or three times. The knives have to be kept sharp, and this is one of the duties of the workers. If the knives get dull, they will tear the rags instead of cutting them, and some thread will be lost.

After the cutter, rags go back to the dusting machine to remove the dust produced by the cutter. The cleaned rags are then ready to go to the boiler. The boiling or "cooking" process dissolves or softens the non-cellulose part of the rags. Impurities, such as dyes, size, starch, dirt, grease, etc., are freed from the fibers. Now we get into a little chemistry. Soda ash (sodium carbonate) was added to the cooking solution to remove oil, grease, alcohol stains, inks, waxes, etc. from the rags. Caustic soda (sodium hydroxide), or more commonly lime, was added to the water for this function. Lime is a mild alkali and does minimum damage to the cellulose fibers. Either quicklime (calcium oxide) or hydrated lime (calcium hydroxide) was used. The solubility ratio of lime is 1:800 in cold water and 1:1,500 in boiling water. An excess amount of lime was thrown into the boiler. As part of the lime went into the solution and combined with non-cellulose materials, additional quantities of the lime dissolved to take its place, so the strength of the solution remained fairly constant. Cotton rags were cooked separately from the linen rags. Both cotton and the white- or cream-colored linen rags were cooked in a six-percent solution of lime. Quicklime was filtered through a screen before it was used to remove dirt, coal dust, splinters of wood, etc. Once the lime was added, "digestion" began. After an hour or so, steam was added to the boiler to increase the temperature, and the digestion continued for several more hours. When finished, the steam was vented and the boiler drained overnight. In the morning, the rags were removed and ready for washing.

The rags were sent back to the beater, or Hollander, but this time it was used as a washing machine. By adjusting the revolving roll of blades,

the rags were drawn into the machine by the revolving roll and partially disintegrated. Their impurities were mixed with the water and later removed with it. At this stage, the rags were called "half stuff." Huge amounts of water were necessary to thoroughly wash the half stuff.

Boiling rags at Crane & Company, circa 1890s.

The Hollander had to run for several hours to get to a clear effluent, and this sometimes took up to 100 gallons of water per pound of rag stock. That's one reason why paper-making mills were located on rivers or large streams.

The half stuff was not ready for bleaching. In the early part of the 19th century, chlorine gas was the bleaching agent, and this was made in large retorts that were usually placed outside the building and fed the gas through pipes into a "bleaching chest," a closed oblong tub that contained the half stuff. By the end of the century, mills had specialized equipment or used the beater as a washing machine. A solid bleach powder (calcium hypochlorite) had replaced the gas method. Bleaching was done for two reasons: first, to remove any impurities left in the half stuff from all the previous steps, and secondly, to whiten the linens and cotton. You need very white half stuff if you want to make white paper. Bleaching is an oxidation process, and to most laymen, oxidation "burns up" the impurities.

Bleach powder was added to water to make a bleaching liquor, and this was added to the half stuff in the Hollander. The bleaching continued for an hour or so, and the half stuff was then removed to a tub called the "drainer." The Hollander was washed out with fresh water. Fresh water was also added to the half stuff, and it remained soaking in the drainer for a full day or so. Sometimes the half stuff was sent back to the Hollander and circulated in fresh water for several hours before it was ready for paper-making.

Rag-beating vats at Crane & Company, circa 1900. Water quality was important in the days of hand-made paper, so most paper mills were located along streams.

Some mills had a machine called a "Jordan," after the name of its inventor, Joseph Jordan. The purpose of the Jordan was to "refine" the half stuff and free it from lumps. This was done by a horizontal conical plug that fitted into a stationary conical shell and was free to rotate inside it. Both plug and shell had metal bars attached along their length. The distance between the revolving and stationary bars was adjusted by moving the conical plug along its axis in the direction desired. Centrifugal force propelled the half stuff from the narrow end to the wide end of the machine, where it was heated by steam and then forced through a screen. This half stuff was now called "stock." Not every mill had a Jordan engine, but since it was invented about 1860, it is likely that Crane & Company acquired Jordans well before the turn of the century. The stock passed onto the traveling endless wire screen of a Fourdrinier machine. The Fourdrinier imparted a shaking motion to the web to shake out the water, which fell as a rain beneath the machine, and automatically felted the paper. A porous dandy roll pressed

the pulp and removed even more water, as did a pressure roll. The paper then passed through drying, sizing, and finishing steps, and was either cut to size or taken up on a reel. The Fourdrinier machines underwent a continuous evolution and became larger and more automated with time.

The paper-making procedures just described were common to both fine stationery and bank-note paper. Their purpose was to make a long-fibered, white paper of uniform strength and quality. Special procedures were used to make specific types of bank-note paper. A few of these have already been described, such as watermarks, the addition of mica to the paper, the random or localized distribution of dyed-silk or jute fibers, and changing the ratio of cotton to linen in the paper. But to stay ahead of counterfeiters, inventors often tried to make a "forgery-proof" paper, a kind of Holy Grail which they never found.

Sizing tanks in the basement of the Bureau of Engraving and Printing.

Peter Hannay, in his Patent No. 15,486, dated August 5, 1856, proposed making photographic bank notes. For example, he would photograph the president and cashier of a bank and print their pictures in relatively large size across the front of a bank note. Then, a copper-plate engraving of the words and denomination would be printed on top of the photograph and suitably varnished for protection. An engraver could not match the realistic detail of the photographs, and any attempt to alter the wording or denomination of the notes would be revealed by the damage done to the underlying photograph. This anticipated the later combination of photo-lithography and engraving, but unfortunately, it was too expensive for its time.

Leopold Eidlitz, in his Patent No. 27,116, dated February 14, 1860, proposed a photographic bank note similar to Hannay's but suffering from the same high cost of production. Photography offered a fidelity and richness of detail that even the best engravers would find difficult to match. However, most of the technical problems of using photography were not overcome until near the end of the century, and even then, photography remained a secondary art that merely assisted the engraver in his work. Well-executed, hand-engraved vignettes remained a standard for security throughout the industry.

Safety Papers

The technology of security printing also involved the development of safety papers for bank checks. This technology was quite different from the security problems faced by the intaglio engraver. Safety papers were intended to prevent alteration in the hand-written portions of a bank check or at least reveal any attempt to alter the writing. Alteration was usually accomplished by erasure and the substitution of new writing. To prevent erasure, indelible inks were developed, and chemicals were used in the paper that "fixed" writing inks so they could not be removed. Soft and absorbent papers were tried, but these generally proved to have poor wear qualities. Chemicals were also used that developed colors or stains when ink eradicators were used. Fugitive tints were often suggested for security printing, being used primarily for checks, drafts, and other non-currency documents. Patent No. 101,786, assigned to George F. Thomas Jr. on April 12, 1870, advocated the addition of an aniline dye from coal-tar derivation to the pulp. He believed that aniline dyes could be fixed to the paper by the addition of acetic acid but would be fugitive if any chemical was placed on the paper to remove ink. George La Monte and George Saxe were given Patent No. 123,782 on February 20, 1872, for a "figure-tinted" paper in which they proposed a tinted sizing. In their invention, a

Fourdrinier machine made white pulp in a continuous sheet in the normal manner. After the sheet passed over a number of heated cylinders for the purpose of drying, it descended and passed around a cylinder immerse in a tinted sizing, and rising, passed between a wooden and a brass roller by which all superfluous sizing was pressed out. The brass cylinder was engraved in relief with the desired figure that the operator wanted impressed on the finished paper. The raised portion of the roller would press out the most water and cause the absorption of the most color, thus leaving the parts of the paper adjacent to their action of a darker tint, while the depressed portions would retain more water and show a lighter tint. As long as the tint was fugitive, this protected the paper against erasures and ink eradicators.

Ink eradicators were known to 19th-century chemists and counterfeiters, especially in the form of ordinary bleach. Hot bleach was used to remove all the ink from notes as early as the Civil War. Other chemicals were discovered to be effective ink solvents later in the century. These included acids, alkalies, oxalates, bisulphates, hypochlorites, permanganate, hydrosulphites, and their combinations. Oxalic acid in combination with sodium (or calcium) hypochlorite was a common commercial-ink eradicator. The best chemical eradicator was a two-step method in which ink was removed by a dilute acidified permanganate solution followed by sodium bisulphate. These two chemicals avoided the problem created by the use of hypochlorites and other alkaline chemicals which destroyed the sizing of the paper and made it difficult to write over the eradicated area. The permanganate method actually left the paper better suited for writing. Ink eradicators worked far better on surface-printed solid colors than on intaglio-printed designs. Lithographic notes were especially vulnerable to solvents, and the denomination counters on the four corners of a note were sometimes removed so that new counters, cut from obsolete and worthless bank notes, could be pasted over the area. It didn't matter that the counters didn't match the wording on the note, since few people ever examined a note that carefully. Raising the denomination of a note by replacing the counters was one of the first tricks that Pete McCartney was taught in the early 1840s. He probably didn't know of any ink-eradicating chemicals at that time, but he may have tried to remove some of the ink of the counters by simple mechanical erasures.

A $1 note altered by the erasure of its original denomination to be replaced by a higher value.

It wasn't well known to the public, but one reason for making the denomination counters by white-line engraving was to protect against ink eradicators and erasures. Strong chemicals usually remove the sizing from a note, making it more difficult to print over the same area, and the same is true for erasures. When a denominational number was printed over an underlying design of geometric-lathe work, it became impossible to eliminate the number without effacing the lathe work.

Patents to prevent written instruments from alteration began as early as 1838 when Ebener Watson took out Patent No. 871, dated August 3. Although designed primarily for bank notes, Watson's ideas were a little ahead of his time by spelling out the denomination of the instrument in large outlined letters printed on top of a script statement. This meant that the outline of the large letters would be difficult to destroy without also destroying the underlying script. A great deal of meticulous labor would be required to change and then restore the printed script on the note. This principle became a basic defense against erasures and eradication as we will see in later patents.

Another approach to prevent alteration was to use a laminated paper much like the "triple paper" of Congreve's invention in 1819. This was the

subject of an American patent granted to Arthur Varnham of London on August 9, 1845 (U.S. Patent No. 4,143). Varnham required two different types of paper to be made simultaneously by hand in two different "assembly" lines, so that the rags of the first type were boiled, bleached, cut, washed, made into half stuff, and when added to the beating engine, dyed to a delicate color. The rags for the other paper were treated the same way, except when the half stuff was added to the beating machine, a resinous size was added along with a small amount of alum. This stuff was used to make the outer sheet of paper. By selecting rags of certain materials, it was possible to make a paper that had a "soft" texture. Varnham stated that his purpose was:

> . . . to protect the test or colored sheet from being tampered with by chemical agents employed to obliterate writings and to prevent the using of any sharp instrument or rubbers for scraping or erasing writing, and should any chemical agent be employed the test or colored sheet would be so changed as to alter conspicuously the former appearance of the paper, and the white, or delicate sheet, or sheets . . . would likewise be imbued with a stain or color produced by the action of those chemical agents on the test sheet.

There were, in fact, many patents granted to inventors which specified some kind of identifying material to be laminated between ordinary white outer papers. Howell, in Patent No. 28,370, invented a paper in which the center ply carried designs in metal foil. Carbon paper was proposed as a center ply by Brooks (Patent No. 210,089), and L.M. Crane proposed in 1867 using a thin layer of *gutta percha* as the center ply of a laminated safety paper (U.S. Patent No. 61,321). The *gutta percha* would soften under the heat of the drying cylinder and mix with the intermingling cellulose fibers to form an inseparable layer. The Frenchman, J.P. Olier, in his U.S. Patent No. 38,835, proposed using hemp as the central ply in a laminated safety paper.

Another tactic often used was to add fibers or other distinctive materials to the paper pulp or finish. Henry Hayward, then of Chicago, Illinois, received Patent No. 34,634, dated March 11, 1862, for his proposal to make paper on the Fourdrinier machine which would incorporate threads made of colored floss-silk within the substance of the paper. Several spools of differently colored thread could be used simultaneously on the Fourdrinier. The silk would impart greater strength to the paper and could be interwoven with the fibers of the pulp so that they could not be removed without tearing the surface of the paper and giving a telltale sign of alteration. Hayward proposed a different series of colors to represent the different denominations if used on bank notes. The colored threads would be visible to the naked eye when the note or bank check was held up to the light. This patent became the basis for a lawsuit against the federal government when distinctive fibers were later added to the paper used for U.S. currency without recognition or payment for Hayward's ideas. Willcox had a similar idea in his Patent No. 56,650, discussed elsewhere in this work, but it was not used for bank checks.

George La Monte, in U.S. Patent No. 121,946, dated December 19, 1871, proposed making a tinted paper for bank checks by adding a sensitive dye which was fugitive under the action of acids and alkalies. The dye was added to the size before the size was applied to the paper. The size thus acted as a shield, and the paper was protected externally, while a portion of the inner fibers remained white. If greater permanency of color was wanted, then the web had to pass through a vat of the fluid dye before entering the sizing vat. After that, the paper was dried and calendared in the usual way. This safety paper became a big success in the manufacture of bank checks, and La Monte made a fortune.[58]

Anthony C. Paquet, a die sinker and medalist of Philadelphia, took another approach which had limited success. His Patent No. 114,963 of May 13, 1871, used hardened-steel dies containing rotating figures, like a modern date stamp. Once a check had been written for a certain amount, the steel figures on the die could be rotated to show the same exact sum. This die was placed over the top surface of the check in a clear area, and a flat, hardened-steel die was placed beneath the check to act as a bed. When suitably compressed, the two dies embossed the paper check and left the amount of the check shown in "water-line," or translucent figures.

Ink-fixing has a long history of being used to prevent alteration. The early British Patent No. 4,131 issued in 1817 proposed steeping paper in soluble ferrocyanide. This chemical reacts with iron in an iron-glutamate ink to form Prussian Blue on the fibers on the paper. Prussian Blue is an insoluble pigment that resists acids and alkaline chemicals and can only be removed from paper by methods that readily show destruction. There followed a long list of patents, both British and American, that suggested either soluble or insoluble ferrocyanides for fixing inks, including Lewisburg (U.S. 53,081), Schreiber (U.S. 322,131), Hill (U.S. 330,894), Schlumberger (U.S. 443,116), Hoskins and Weis (U.S. 511,271), and Chmidt (U.S. 1,217,076). Thiocyanates were proposed in a number of mostly British patents for this purpose, as were tannin and tannic acid, and Phenanthroline, but none of these ideas came to much, and only the ferrocyanides remain commercially useful today.

Although it is economical to make safety papers having solid colors, it has been the practice for many years to print a security device, such as a fugitive colored ink, in a pattern that will make erasure more difficult for the counterfeiter. It is much easier to restore a solid color to an erased area of a bank check and match the color so precisely as to be undetectable than it is to restore a pattern or intricate design that will escape detection. And since the objective in security printing is to make forgery or counterfeiting too laborious to be profitable, a printed pattern, especially one that is intricate and difficult to reproduce, works to that end. Most patterns are printed in fugitive inks, and their chemistry is discussed in chapter 16.

Chapter 16

Ink

China and Ink

As with paper, we can understand ink better once we have seen how it was developed through the long march of Chinese history. The very beginning, of course, is more myth than material science and doesn't concern us. Throughout the T'ang dynasty (607–918 AD) and later, ink was made by combining a pigment (carbon soot) with a vehicle (animal glue). Carbon soot was obtained by the controlled burning of pine wood in long bamboo ovens covered with paper. Some of the ovens were as long as 100 feet. The best soot for making ink was taken from the end of the oven that was farthest from the fire. Soot collected much closer to the fire was unsuitable because it contained unwanted debris such as fly-ash, charcoal fragments, and tars. Other woods were tried, but pine gave the best soot. The almost exclusive use of pine trees for making soot lead to a deforestation of large areas of China during the first millennium.

A Chinese ink painting showing the street in front of a tea house.

By the 12th century, lampblack was being substituted for pine soot. Lampblack was made by burning oil at a wick and controlling the amount of oxygen present. The method was more expensive than burning pine but also more efficient in making soot. To make good quality lampblack, tung oil, vegetable-seed oil, linseed oil, bean oil, and sesame oil were used. The stronger the flame, the coarser was the soot. The particle size of the soot was very important to the quality of the ink. John Winter, in his recent experiments with a scanning electron microscope and samples of ink from ancient Chinese paintings, concludes that an oil lamp had a steady flame of fairly constant size and produced fairly uniform particles of soot, while a wood fire had a variable and flickering flame and produced a broad range of particle sizes. The smaller the average size of the soot particles, the better the ink.[1] Modern lampblack has particle sizes in a range from 50 to about 120 nanometers, with average sizes at about 90.

The Chinese used animal glue as the vehicle of their ink. Animal glues were made from the skins of cows, buffalo, pigs, donkeys, horses, camels, and mules. Fish glue was made from the scales and maw (jaws, throat, and gullet) and was considered the best material for making fine ink. To kill the unpleasant odor of the glue, a little camphor was added to the ink. If a colored ink was needed, the additives were usually minerals, such as gamboges, realgar, hematite, auxite, malachite, red lead, etc. Each ink-maker had his own recipes for making different inks, and during the course of several centuries, these recipes changed constantly. All of these materials were diluted in water, and that is an important difference between Chinese inks and those of European origin. Chinese inks are thin and water-based. European inks are oil-based, made from carbon black combined with linseed-oil varnish. A varnish is made by boiling down an oil, such as linseed or rosin, until it reaches a thicker and more suitable consistency.[2]

By the time Johannes Gutenberg invented printing with movable metal type in the 1450s, black ink was usually made from lampblack in linseed oil, and for a long time scholars thought this was part of the reason that Gutenberg's printing, after five centuries, still presents a glossy jet black against the intensely white linen pages of his books.[3] But in 1984, two physicists at the Crocker Nuclear Laboratory at the Davis Campus of the University of California analyzed ink specimens taken from Gutenberg's 42-line Bible, as well as some of his other works, and discovered that his jet black ink was based on a much different formula. By exposing ink specimens to a proton beam from a cyclotron, they excited molecules in the ink to fluoresce in the X-ray range. This technique causes each element to emit a characteristic spectrum, and the intensity of the radiation indicates its relative abundance. The physicists found that Gutenberg, who made his own ink, had used copper and lead for the pigments instead of lampblack. He may have been inspired to do this based on his knowledge of how artists used these pigments in oil paintings. Copper and lead are chemically stable for long periods, but the carbon in lampblack oxidizes to carbon monoxide and slowly evaporates. Unfortunately, Gutenberg kept his ink formula secret.[4]

The Gutenberg Bible.

American Ink

In America, the supply of ink from England was irregular, and the product was often of poor quality. These problems continued until Rogers and Fowle, of Boston, took matters into their own hands and started making good ink, supplying local printers between 1742 and 1750. The credit for setting up the first *regular* printing-ink manufacturing plant goes to Charles Johnson in Philadelphia.[5] He started his business on January 7, 1804, and had the misfortune to see the building burn to the ground within one year. Soon after, he rebuilt the plant on a much larger scale and gradually reduced the importation of ink from Germany and England. Charles Johnson retired and was succeeded by his son and eventually by his grandson, Charles Eneu Johnson. Horace Wade, a chemist and druggist of Rochester, New York, found that rosin oil, made from the sap of pine trees, could be substituted for linseed oil and would work just as well. In 1850 he sold his drug business, and two years later he started manufacturing ink in New York City. The famous house of C.W.H. Carter was started in Brooklyn, New York, in 1865 as a factory making lithographic varnish. After becoming successful as a manufacturer of writing ink, Carter also did business with the Bureau of Engraving and Printing as a supplier of burnt plate oils for steel-plate–printing inks and for dryers and pigments. Several other companies began manufacturing black and colored inks for printers during the middle and latter part of the 19th century, but since the market was very limited for steel- and copper-plate printing, few companies made specialized inks for this kind of work.

Titus Eddy & Sons

Titus Eddy & Sons was the exception. Titus was born on March 1, 1803, the son of an engraver named Isaac Eddy.[6] Titus was taught to engrave by his father, but he soon became more interested in the manufacture of ink. He was granted a patent in his father's name on December 31, 1823, for "an improvement in the art of pulverizing and grinding all kinds of drugs, minerals and plants by a machine called 'The Improved Pulverizing Engine'."[7] He bought a farm of some 125 acres near Troy, New York, in 1826 where he set up several buildings for making ink. In one, he installed furnaces of his own design to burn beef bones. Burnt bones can be pulverized to make "bone black," one of the five classes of carbon used as a pigment for making black ink. The manufacturing process changed over the years but usually started by boiling large, dense bones to remove the fat, then burning the bones in furnaces with little air, a process called "calcination," and finally pulverizing the material. This produced a useful form of carbon and a residual ash consisting of the mineral constituents of the bone—calcium phosphate, calcium carbonate, and calcium sulfate. In the latter part of the century, it was found that washing the bone black in acid dissolved out the calcium salts and left a superior product that produced a very deep black. Acid-treated bone black was often called "hard black" in the trade. Titus made a great secret out of his process, locking himself into a small room where he formulated his special black ink during a two-week period each year. He won the government's contract, and he and his son, James, made all the black ink used on government currency and other securities for more than half a century.[8] To keep his formula secret, Titus had only six employees, and none of these men knew the formula. The government paid well, and Titus's son made as much as $50,000 a year. After the turn of the century, other manufacturers began to make black ink that met government standards at a cheaper price. In 1908 James Eddy decided not to bid on the government's contract but continued to supply ink to some private engraving companies until 1925 or so.[9]

American ink formulas were often based on European traditions but sometimes substituted local materials for those used in the more exotic European recipes. Writing in 1852, Thomas Antisell noted that in copper-plate printing "the ink usually employed is a composition made of the stones of peaches and apricots, the bones of sheep, and ivory, all well burnt, and called 'Frankfort Black,' mixed with nut-oil that has been well boiled; the two being ground together on a marble slab, in the same manner as painters grind their colors."[10]

"Hard black" ink was made from the bones of animals, as well as other organic materials.

Ink Terminology

Until the beginning of the 20th century, chemists had few instruments for measuring the various working properties of plate inks and only a few books and technical papers to guide them in formulating better inks. That began to change around 1890, but it was still a common practice in the late 19th century for plate printers to judge the quality of inks by subjective and organoleptic methods; that is, by the look and feel of an ink and by experience. Engravers also kept notes about which pigments and varnishes made good black or colored inks, and they often specified which pigments they wanted. Over time, a specialized vocabulary was invented by ink-makers to describe the working qualities of inks, and this terminology continued to be used even after ink chemistry became a highly specialized field. Terms such as "short" and "long," referring to the flow of an ink, were quite common. If an ink could not be drawn out into a string between the fingers, but broke quickly, it was said to be "short." In the opposite manner, if the ink was easily drawn out between the fingers without breaking quickly, it was said to be "long." Intaglio inks needed to be long. The tack of an ink—its tendency to stick to a surface—was defined by the term "softness." A "soft" ink did not have good adhesion. "Livering" was the phenomenon observed when an ink was allowed to stand for a while and turned into a spongy mass. This was usually caused by the saponification of the fatty acids in the oil. Any ink that livered was not acceptable as a plate ink. In speaking about dry pigments, the term "body color" was often used. The body color often changed when a vehicle was mixed with the pigment. "Opacity," "color strength," "density," and "covering power" were often used interchangeably. "Bleeding" referred to the fact that certain pigments were not completely soluble in a chosen vehicle and would "run" when printed, blurring fine lines or even "striking through" the paper. A "tint" was a pigment that was lightened by mixing it with white, usually zinc white. "Fastness" referred to the ability of an ink to maintain its color strength when exposed to light. After 1900 or so, this parameter was tested in the lab by exposing inks to ultraviolet light in a specially made light box. "Oil absorption" is the old term that expressed how much oil in an ink would be absorbed by the pigment. This was given as a simple percentage and showed the weight in grams of oil per 100 grams of pigment. In plate inks, the components having the lowest oil absorption were preferred. If the oil absorption was too high, it could be corrected by adding more base, such as barytes or Paris white.

Ink chemistry is not always a simple and straightforward affair, especially when formulas have numerous components and each component has multiple qualities, some of which may be appropriate for an intended purpose, while others will not work well for that purpose. A wag once observed that it's easy to tell an ink chemist—he's the one with large patches of hair missing from his head. Black ink is a good example of the problems. We have seen that the particle size of the carbon is important, and ink made with small-size carbon particles will have greater color strength and last longer. On the other hand, gas blacks—very fine pigments made from a carefully controlled gas flame which are almost pure carbon of small-particle size—are not used in plate inks because they absorb too much oil and do not have the "body" to be easily wiped or polished. Carbon blacks and lampblacks suffer from the same defects and are not used in plate inks. Vine blacks, which were called "soft blacks" in the 19th-century trade, were made from grape-vine twigs, willow wood, wine yeast, fruit pits, etc. These organic materials were carbonized in the absence of air, washed with water to remove any soluble alkaline salts, then pulverized and acid-washed. They made excellent black pigments with good working qualities for plate inks. The so-called "mixed blacks" were combinations of vine blacks

and bone blacks and were commonly used in plate inks. It was a mixed black that Titus Eddy & Sons made for the U.S. government. "Ivory Black" was once made from ivory, but as the expense of ivory has increased so rapidly, it is now made from selected bones.

"An Elegant Man Seated under a Willow Tree." Willow wood and fruit pits were used to make "soft black" ink.

Green Anti-photographic Inks

As previously noted, several people were involved in the development of green currency ink, especially in the line that runs from Hunt to Matthews to Edson, and the less-important utility patents taken by Smillie and Eaton. Asahal Eaton took a slightly different approach by making a green tint that was printed over the whole note to protect it against photographic counterfeiting. He used "chromate of baryta," which he claimed to have invented to make a chromium oxide tint. Barytes was a commercial name for barium sulfate, a white mineral mined all over the world. It had low oil absorption and was milled to a finely divided powder. This meant that it wiped and polished easily on the plate. Barytes were especially good for making tints of the various chrome pigments, and as Eaton claimed, inks made with barytes were impervious to common reagents and could not easily be removed from the paper. Since the green tint was printed first, and black lettering and vignettes were then printed over top, the green tint was actually an "underprint." His patent, No. 38,298, dated April 28, 1863, was used on the $10 Legal Tender Notes (some, but not all, of Friedberg-95, and all F-95a and F-95b varieties). However, it would be easy enough to counterfeit such notes. One could photograph the note, losing the green tint and capturing only the black-ink lettering and vignettes, but then print the photograph on paper already tinted in a similar green. Tinted paper was of little value in protecting notes.

An enlargement of text printed over a tint found on the $10 Legal Tender Note. (Friedberg-95a.)

Another approach was taken somewhat earlier by Christopher Dicran Seropyan, who was born in Constantinople, Turkey, on August 16, 1825, and came to the United States with his parents while he was still young enough to learn English easily. Seropyan attended Yale and studied chemistry under the famous Professor Benjamin Silliman and John A. Porter, graduating in 1852. His academic career was typically eclectic for the time. During the summer of 1853, he assisted Professor Silliman Jr. in the mineralogical department of the Crystal Palace Exhibition. After graduation, he studied at the Yale Theological Seminary and was licensed to preach in July 1854. He began to study medicine in September of that year. He went to New York in January 1855, where he attended lectures at the College of Physicians and Surgeons. He returned to Yale in March 1856 to continue his study of medicine, and his MD was conferred by the College of Physicians and Surgeons in 1856.[11]

Seropyan became interested in bank-note inks in the mid-1850s, when the subject began to attract the efforts of several chemists in the United States to develop an "anti-counterfeiting" ink. This was a relatively easy subject for Seropyan, since he had considerable experience in mineralogy and had assisted Professors Dana and Silliman Jr. in the arrangement of the Mineral Cabinet at Yale College during the summer of 1854. Seropyan's experiments lead to his first patent, No. 14,069, granted on January 8, 1856, entitled "Method of Preventing Bank-Notes, Etc. From Being Counterfeited."[12] Seropyan used different oil-colored papers. He ground different coloring substances to a fine-particle size and then combined them with printer's varnish or boiled linseed oil. He then printed this colored varnish uniformly on blank bank-note paper by the standard lithographic process. As an alternative, he could take blank bank-note paper which was already tinted, sized or not, and print on its surface a thin film of the printer's varnish or boiled linseed oil. The varnish would then penetrate the paper, including any size, and protect the tint from being removed by a bleaching agent. By using different dry colors, he could make oil-colored paper that was red, pink, orange, yellow, green, gray, or a light shade of indigo. He then printed the graphic images on the note in an indigo ink that was made by the same use of printer's varnish or boiled linseed oil and ground very finely. This application of oil-colored paper, together with a fugitive ink, protected bank notes against counterfeiting by photographic processes, lithographic transfers, or the anastatic method. Any attempt at bleaching off certain parts of a bank note, such as the denomination counters, or any attempt to treat the note with potash for making a lithographic transfer, would simultaneously remove the fugitive ink on the rest of the note. In this and a subsequent patent, Seropyan used Proof notes of the City Bank of New Haven to illustrate his processes.

An example of a note printed on yellow paper.

In another patent, No. 17,473, granted on June 2, 1857, and entitled "Improvement to Prevent Counterfeiting Bank-Notes, Etc.," Seropyan copied many of the processes used in his earlier patent but used a tint that was less fugitive than the inks used to make the graphic designs on the note. Any attempt to remove the graphic parts, such as the vignettes or denominational counters, as by bleaching, potash, or other chemicals, would also affect the oil-colored tint and blur the background. This patent was assigned to William Cousland and J.D. Bald. Recently, Fred L. Reed III has written a detailed article which illustrates many of the obsolete bank notes and U.S. currency that were supposedly protected against counterfeiting by the use of patented ink formulas. As Reed shows in his article, special inks did not protect currency against the nimble mind of counterfeiters.[13]

An enlarged photo of a patent found on U.S. currency.

Seropyan left America in October 1858 and for 18 months continued his medical studies in Paris. In July 1860 he arrived at Constantinople and began his practice as a doctor. In February 1864 he married Miss Mugerdich, the daughter of an Armenian banker in Constantinople. His chemical knowledge was a service to the Turkish government, and he was soon appointed a member of

the Imperial Mining Council. He died of paralysis about the middle of May 1874.

By 1860 or so, there were two types of green plate ink. The more expensive of these two—chromium oxide—was used only on the highest grade of work, such as government currency. The other green ink, called "chrome green," was made by mechanically combining chrome yellow and Prussian blue without the addition of barytes. This gave a bright green. Other shades of green can be made by varying the ratio of chrome yellow with the Prussian blue. Lead chromate, which was called "chrome yellow," "Lemon yellow," or "canary yellow" in the trade, forms a variety of yellow pigments that make excellent plate inks. The color of inks made with chrome yellow can be varied from light to dark. If the manufacturing conditions are kept the same each time a batch is made—the amount of water, the length of stirring, and the temperature of the mixture—a particular hue can be duplicated. These inks have excellent lightfastness and brilliant hue.

In printing foreign bank notes during the 19th century, blue inks were especially successful. These were usually made from pigments called the "ferrocyanide blues," namely Prussian blue, Chinese blue, Milori blue, and bronze blue. They were first made by Heinrich Diesbach (called "the Prussian") in Berlin in 1704 and can be described as ferric ferrocyanides. Prussian blue is the darkest of these inks, Chinese blue is the lightest, and bronze blue has a metallic luster on drying. They are resistant to acids but vulnerable to alkalies. They were the first stable and lightfast blues available to paint and ink-makers. Previous blue pigments faded rather quickly and did not have the range of hues found in the ferric ferrocyanides. Another blue pigment called "Ultramarine blue" is made from the mineral lapis lazuli, found in Afghanistan, Tibet, China, and Siberia. This is a bright-blue lightfast pigment but very expensive. The first synthetic ultramarines were made by Jean Baptiste Guinet in France in 1822 and were mixtures of aluminum silicates, sodium carbonate, sodium sulfate, and charcoal. In fact, ultramarine is the most complex of any natural mineral pigment. The color of ultramarine inks varied from batch to batch and could be easily removed from paper by mineral acids.

Prussian blue, Milori blue, Chinese blue.

Chrome-yellow orange was another important pigment used on mostly foreign bank notes and some stock certificates and bonds. It was easily made by converting some of the lead chromate in chrome yellow into basic lead chromate by the addition of caustic soda. This produced a bright, soft pigment with good lightfastness and good working properties. The pigment was cheap to make, and that may have figured in its frequent use. The chrome pigments were often mixed with finely ground barytes to improve their working qualities.

Red inks were usually based on vermillion, the red sulfide of mercury. The natural pigment was not as good as the one manufactured artificially. One of the defects of vermillion ink was that it rubbed off paper much too easily, even when left to dry for a long time. For plate ink, vermillion pigments worked fairly well, but they were eventually replaced by lake colors based on less expensive forms of the pigment. Lake colors are organic dyes, but since they did not come into use until after 1895, they are beyond the scope of this book.

An 1882 National Bank Note with the brown back.

In painting, brown ink is a mixture of pigments that form the three primary colors—red, yellow, and blue. In printing, however, a different primary color set is used—cyan, magenta, yellow, and key black. In printing, brown is made from all the primaries, producing a muddy brown that is lightened with a white pigment. One sees quite a lot of brown in foreign bank notes and on bonds and corporate certificates because it makes a nice contrast to white or cream-colored paper and has good psychological qualities. In American currency, the Silver Certificates of 1878 and 1880 are printed with brown and black ink on their backs, and the issues of the 1882 National Bank

Notes are called "brownbacks" because of the brown ink used on their backs.

The smaller, private bank-note companies did not employ chemists to mix inks and did not have elaborate facilities for making pigments. Instead, they bought both black and colored inks from established ink-makers. If a designer or engraver wanted a particular color of ink, he would try to find the closest match available from the different manufacturers. Both the American Bank Note Company and the Bureau of Engraving and Printing had ink-making departments that bought pigments and oils for making their own inks. An article on "Color Formulas" that appeared in the *Essay-Proof Journal* gave the pigments and other ingredients used in bank-note inks during the 1850s.[14] There, such terms as "English Vermillion," "Trieste Vermillion," "Persian Red," "Venetian Red," and "Rose Pink" were names of pigments used in the trade. "Orange Mineral" mentioned in these formulas was a standard pigment, being one of the lead oxides, and was sometimes called "red lead," but it suffered from several working defects and was soon replaced by "chrome yellow orange."

A $2 note with a red tint.

White pigments were used to make tints of other pigments. A tint, by one definition, is a color that has been lightened with white. The white pigment that worked best in copper- and steel-plate inks was zinc white, a zinc oxide of the formula ZnO. It was made by heating zinc ore or pure zinc-metal grit in a retort that fed the evolved gas into a tube of very hot air and carbon monoxide. This precipitated zinc oxide in collecting chambers. The chambers farthest away from the retort gave the finest grade of zinc white. This pigment had good covering power and excellent working qualities. Lithopone was another pigment often used to make tints. It was a mixture of barium sulfate and zinc sulfide and was similar in covering power to zinc white. White lead had excellent covering power but inferior working qualities and was seldom used in plate inks.

Barytes are naturally occurring deposits of barium sulfate. They were used as a base that gave body to an ink made with other pigments. They had low covering power, so they didn't take away the color intensity of the primary pigment. They also had low oil absorption and could be added to a pigment having high oil or varnish absorption to improve this defect. They were chemically stable with all solvents, including acids. Because of its abundance, barytes were cheap and didn't add much to the cost of an ink. They were frequently found in plate-ink formulas because they improved the working qualities of the ink. "Blanc fixe" was the term given to artificially made barium sulfates that had a smaller average particle size than the barytes. The smaller particle size or "fine grain" was important since it reduced the abrasion on steel or copper printing plates.

Paris white, a very high grade of calcium carbonate, was another base similar to barytes. It also had low covering power and dried rather slowly. It was usually added to barytes in plate inks to improve the polishing of the plate. Aluminum hydrate, like Paris white, was added to inks to improve the polishing step of plate printing. It was also used to improve inks that did not grind smoothly.

Ink Mills

Colored inks have always been made by mixing dry colors, bases, and oils in large ink mills. Dry colors are insoluble metallic compounds derived from either natural sources or made synthetically. The earliest ink mills were the plate mills used in the 1830s. In those devices, two flat, circular grinding plates were mounted on a vertical spindle. One plate was fixed in position and the other revolved. On these plates were teeth whose cutting faces were arranged half in one direction and half in the opposite direction. Such devices took a long time to grind ink to a proper consistency. W.J. Stone, an engraver in Washington, D.C., designed a hand-cranked, single plate and muller type of ink mill in 1829 and published a description and drawing in *The Journal of the Franklin Institute*.[15] A muller is a flat, perfectly smooth grinder with a handle that is rotated in circles to grind a pigment on an oiled slab.

A Dodge ink mill from the 1890s made by the Kent Machine Works of New York.

Roller mills proved to be much more efficient, and several types were made using different principles of action. In the "Neal" mill, invented in 1860, the bottom roller revolved while the top roller stayed fixed. The "Kindon" mill was invented in 1873. It had two rollers moving in opposite direction, the upper roller being smaller than the one on bottom. This arrangement was supposed to facilitate the passage of material between the rollers. The three-roller mills that followed often had granite rolls. The "Dodge" mill is dated from the period just after the Civil War and used two cast-iron rollers, one on top of the other. The small roll was 4-inches in diameter and the larger roll 12-inches in diameter, and both rolls were 18-inches long. The dry colors were held in a hopper above the top roller. This hopper was lined with brass where it came into contact with the upper roller to reduce friction

and extend the life of the roller. An apron that could be brought into contact with the lower roller took off the ink when it was sufficiently ground. Dodge mills were made by the Kent Machine Works and by Charles Ross & Sons, both companies being located in Brooklyn, New York. The "Plymouth" three-roller mill, also made by the Kent Machine Works, was similar to the design of their earlier Dodge mill. Introduced about 1893, it featured water-cooled rollers, each being 9-inches in diameter and 24-inches long.

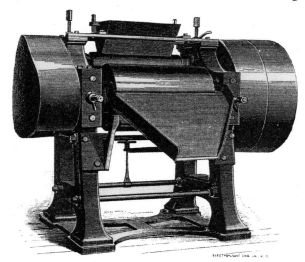

The Plymouth three-roller ink mill of the 1890s.

Like other equipment in the industry, there has been a continuous evolution in the design and efficiency of ink mills. By 1918 steel bearings replaced those made of bronze and reduced the heat generated by rolling friction. Rollers were bored through and had thinner walls, again reducing heat. Still, grinding inks was partly an art and partly a science in the 19th century. Plate printers were constantly complaining about the ink they worked with, and those complaints continued for 40 years or more, as can be seen in the letters to the editor of the *Plate Printer*, the official newspaper of the International Plate Printers' and Die Stampers' Union of North America. Some people think that intaglio inks have to be ground very fine so the pigment particles don't wear down the steel plates, but actually the opposite is true. Typographic inks are a different case, and they do have to be ground very fine so they will distribute evenly on the high-speed rollers.

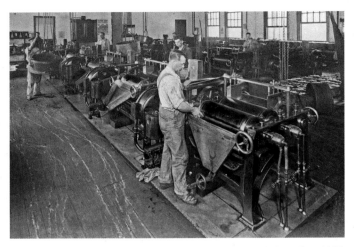

The ink-grinding room at the Bureau of Engraving and Printing, circa 1900. Note the belted power shaft at the right of the picture.

Plate oils are the vehicles used to make ink. Linseed oil makes the best plate oil and was found in the inks of both private bank-note companies and the Bureau of Engraving and Printing. All through the 19th century it was the common practice to burn linseed oil to make plate oils. In fact, most ink-makers sold "burnt plate oils" so small companies didn't have to make their own. In the early part of the century, linseed oil was put into an iron pot and heated. When the proper temperature was obtained, the oil was ignited by a red-hot poker. If the oil didn't ignite, it had to be heated for a longer time. If the oil ignited, it was then stirred as it burned. If stirred too rapidly, the flame would go out, but if stirred too slowly, the oil would not mix thoroughly, resulting in poor polymerization and oxidation.[16] The longer the oil was burnt, the greater its consistency became. Plate oils were usually sold in three consistencies—light, medium, and strong. Burning linseed oil for about 15 to 20 minutes produced a light oil; burning it for 25 to 45 minutes made a medium oil; and burning it for 2 to 3 hours yielded a heavy or strong oil. Those times, of course, were approximations and depended on the initial viscosity of the oil. Underwood and Sullivan discovered that burning was not necessary and that a superior oil could be made if the linseed oil was heated by gas, coal, or electricity. Their method required heating the oil to about 320-degrees Celsius and holding it there until the oil reached the desired viscosity. The advantage

of that process was that the linseed oil itself was not used as a fuel, and that reduced the loss of oil by burning. Plate oils made by controlled heating are transparent, lack the disagreeable odor of burnt oils, and have less carbon and a much lower percentage of free fatty acids.

Soy-bean oil is almost equal to linseed oil in making plate oils and varnishes. The working qualities are about the same in both products, but inks made from soy-bean oils are a little more greasy and sometimes require a drier to be mixed into the ink. Still, plate oils made from linseed oil were always preferred for the highest grade of work. Rosin oil does not have the same working qualities of linseed and soy bean oil, and consequently, it was used primarily for typographic inks.

Soy beans would sometimes be used instead of linseeds for making oil.

The word *varnish* refers to a vehicle, usually for a planographic ink (lithographic or offset), such as linseed oil which has been boiled long enough to reach a desired viscosity. The boiling thickens the oil by oxidative polymerization. Even well into the 19th century it was a common practice for ink-makers to burn raw linseed oil in a large pot for five minutes, then extinguish the flame by placing a lid on the pot. After stirring, several pieces of bread were held in the oil by tongs until the bread slices were toasted to a brown color but not burnt. This was supposed to remove grease from the oil. Occasionally, peeled onions were employed for the same purpose. No scientific reason for this practice has been discovered.[17] Heating changes the working characteristics of linseed oil quite readily, so it is important that the raw linseed oil is heated under carefully controlled conditions. Still, ink-making was considered an art rather than a science for a long time, and old practices were slow to change. The heating end-point for boiling linseed oil, to get the right "body," was determined by the threads or strings of the oil as it dripped from the stirring ladle. Other manufacturers wanted to see a certain length of thread when it was drawn out between the thumb and forefinger. Today, laboratory measurements of the molecular weight and viscosity have replaced the "art."

What dry colors and minerals did the bureau use for its inks? The only aniline colors were the reds, and they were limited in the 19th century to formulas for making inks for postage stamps. Chrome yellow was used for yellow inks and for mixing with other colors to get yellow tints. Prussian blue and ultramarine blues were used. Bone black, made from calcined animal bones, was the primary source of black, but not the only one. Green inks were made by mixing blues and yellows.

In 1908 the Ink Division of the Bureau of Engraving and Printing came under allegations of fraud and graft.[18] A Federal Grand Jury indicted Edwin Van Dyck, a chemist and ink-maker at the bureau, and Victor Gustav Bloede, the president of a company in Baltimore, Maryland, that sold black pigment to the bureau. Van Dyck and Bloede were charged with having an agreement in which Bloede was to pay Van Dyck a percentage of the money his company received from the government for the black dry color he furnished to the bureau. Van Dyck, in his position as chemist and ink-maker, had to analyze and certify the dry colors submitted by various manufacturers. It was charged that he fraudulently favored the Bloede company, and as a result of that conspiracy, he was paid by Bloede (over the course of several years) between $70,000 and $75,000.

Attorneys for the two men claimed that the indictments were technical matters and that the alleged fraud did not involve any loss of money to the bureau. They said the bureau had received the best dry color available and at a cost that was 10¢ less per pound that it had paid prior to the letting of the contract to the Bloede company. The allegation was made that when samples of hard black were received from various manufacturers, they went to Van Dyck, who analyzed them and then reported the results to a committee in charge of evaluating the bids. It was said that Van Dyck made certain that the hard black from the Bloede company was always given the highest test rating. The bureau purchased an average of 225,000 pounds a year of the hard-black color at a price of 45¢ a pound.

Mr. Bloede's attorney said the charges against his client involved no moral turpitude or fraudulent intent because he (Bloede) had purchased the formula for making hard black from Mr. Van Dyck, who had met with and won the consent of Secretary of the Treasury Gage and Assistant Secretary Vanderlip to show his formula, which he considered "his intellectual property," to Mr. Bloede. Everything, he said, was well known to the bureau, and there was no deception. In some recent cases, however, the court had ruled "that an employee of the government, who has a pecuniary interest in an article being purchased by the government, is technically guilty of conspiracy."

Van Dyck pleaded guilty to two of the four counts in the indictment and was fined $10,000. Victor Bloede was fined $5,000, and the remaining two counts against both men were dropped. Van Dyck went on to become the chief engineer for the firm of Ault & Wiborg, which for some years was the largest ink and dry-color supplier in the world. He retired from that position in 1935 and died peacefully at the age of 87 in 1953.[19]

Fugitive Inks

A fugitive ink is one that is not stable. The word *fugitive* comes to us from the Latin *fugitis*, the past participle of *fugere*, meaning to flee. Fugitive inks flee by fading or disappearing when bleached or acted upon by a chemical agent, such as an ink eradicator. The earliest fugitive inks were made with natural colors, such as Prussian blue, indigo, etc., but the discovery of coal-tar (aniline) dyes about 1870 revolutionized the use of fugitive inks. To the ink-maker of that period, the aniline colors were of poor quality because they did not make "fast" inks, but that is exactly the quality one needs for a fugitive ink. As mentioned in chapter 15, many inventors proposed safety papers, especially for hand-written documents, based on the use of a fugitive ink. Newton (British Patent No. 9,771 of 1843), Varnham (U.S. Patent No. 4,143), Lea (U.S. No. 38,231), Olier (U.S. No. 38,835), Jones (U.S. No. 54,834), Gibson (U.S. No. 41,118), and Kellogg (U.S. No. 77,887) are examples. Thomae (U.S. No. 101,786 of 1870) seems to have been the first in the United States to propose a safety paper based entirely on the use of aniline dyes. He suggested the dye be placed directly in the beater, but Willcox (U.S. No. 115,005) suggested the dye could be applied as a surface coating directly on finished paper. All of these inventors, including La Monte (U.S. No. 121,846 of 1871), wrote patents for solid colors. But since fugitive inks can be placed on paper by any printing method, they were soon printed in patterns or designs of intricate shapes. This improved their value as a security device, since it was much more difficult for a forger to restore a pattern, especially one of intricate shape, than an area of solid color. Fugitive inks can be printed on a lighter color of paper as a surface tint. Any attempt to erase or eradicate the writing would also bleach out or smear the underlying fugitive ink pattern, thus revealing a forgery.

Fugitive inks would ruin an entire note if an attempt was made to alter the lettering. This stamp had wavy security lines printed in fugitive ink along the stamp's center.

An important advance was made by the second patent of La Monte and Saxe (U.S. No. 123,782 of 1872). There, they colored the sizing to a desired tint and passed the paper while it was still moist with this colored sizing through a pair of rollers, one of which was wooden, the other which was made of brass and relief-engraved with the design they wanted to reproduce on the paper. The raised portion of the brass roller pressed out the most water and caused the adsorption of the most color. The depressed portions of the engraving compressed the paper less and left more water, imparting a lighter shade. The principle was simple: the greater the pressure, the deeper the color. This gave a light-and-dark shading to the pattern of the tint. The process was also explained in the patents issued to Madden (U.S. No. 1,666,031), Gailer (U.S. No. 1,692,645) and Samson (U.S. No. 2,403,461).

Chapter 17

Printing Presses

Early Presses

The roller press used by 19th-century bank-note printers evolved slowly over several centuries. Like most devices, the earliest forms are lost in antiquity, but we begin to see the basic mechanical principles in the oil and wine presses depicted on ancient Greek vases of the sixth century BC and in mural paintings of the first century AD, such as those from the ruins of Pompei.[1] These presses lead to the development of the direct-acting screw press in which a nut was wrenched down a threaded pole (screw) to push on a plate that squeezed oil out of seeds or wine out of grapes. By the time Conrad Saspach had built a printing press for Johannes Gutenberg in the middle of the 15th century, it was simply a modification of a press already well known to bookbinders, paper-makers, fullers, and others. We don't know specifically how Gutenberg designed his press, but he may have gotten some ideas from watching a draper's press-printing designs on cloth from engraved and inked copper plates. Gutenberg made small changes in the framework, the screw, and the platen of an existing press of the wine-making or paper-making type, and this was the birth of the roller-printing press.

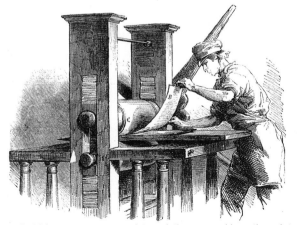

An early 19th-century copper-plate–printing press. Here, the printer is taking an impression from the plate. A heavy wooden frame and a long-handled gear wheel were common features.

The paper money printed during colonial times was done on the common press found in every printer's shop. The technology did not change for almost 150 years. These presses were built on heavy wooden frames. A bed held the engraved copper plate which was inked and then wiped by hand and moved under the platen. A bar attached to a screw lowered the platen to make the impression, but this was slow, strenuous work.

Another view of a hand-roller press for copper-plate printing. The gear wheel (spider) is attached to a pinion gear that rotates the rollers and moves the bed.

By 1813 George Clymer of Philadelphia had invented America's first all-iron hand press, known as the "Columbian." The most important feature of this press was its system of power-multiplying levers which could exert enormous pressure with just a light pull on the bar. Because of its high cost—$300 to $500 at a time when other presses cost $130 to $150—and the great weight of the press and the difficulty of repairing it, the Columbian was not popular and sales were poor. In May 1817 Clymer took his press to England where it was well-received and soon replaced the iron press designed by Charles, the 3rd Earl of Stanhope.[2]

The Perkins Press

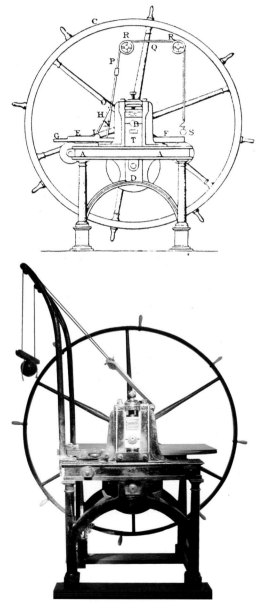

The copper-plate–printing press patented by Jacob Perkins and George Murray in 1813. It was taken to England in 1819. This press is now on display at the British Library.

The year 1813 was also important to the direct line of press inventions that became the backbone of the American bank-note industry. In that year, Jacob Perkins and George Murray were granted a patent on June 25 for a "method of impressing all kinds of die work on steel and copper by circular dies." Four days later, they were granted a patent for a "printing press for copper and steel engraving." Neither of these patents are available today. On December 15, 1836, a fire destroyed the U.S. Patent Office in Washington, D.C., burning 168 volumes of records and more than 9,000 patent drawings, including those describing these two new presses. Perkins and Murray did not set up a factory to make these presses, but others may have made the presses and paid a royalty to Murray, Draper, Fairman & Company.

The "spider press" was also now in use. Although this specialized hand-roller press was developed within a period of a few years, the actual mechanical principles for taking impressions were based on a long history of printing technology. Simply put, a copper or steel plate was engraved, then inked and wiped. The wiping removed all the ink on the surface of the plate, leaving only the ink lying in the engraved lines. Then, a piece of bank-note paper was dampened and laid on the plate. One or more pieces of cloth, called "felts" or "blankets," were placed on top of the paper. A roller turned by long radial handles (the "spider") moved the plate and paper on a bed traveling on anti-friction rollers. As the bed moved under the roller, the dampened paper was pressed against the plate so hard that it was forced down into the incised lines and picked up the ink. This left the ink standing up on the surface of the paper. Using this technique, extremely fine engraved lines could be printed, and that was a great advantage to the security of bank notes.

Eventually, iron replaced some of the parts in the hand-roller presses. Wooden presses with a substantial number of iron parts became common during the 1820s. Many wooden presses were constructed of solid mahogany. An anonymous chronicler writing in the *Engravers' Bulletin* said that most of the press planks were two-inch mahogany boards, topped with a thin plating of iron. Afterward came the iron wheels and frame, but wooden rollers were still used. Gradually, these rollers were eliminated, and about 1830 the all-metal press came into fashion.[3] Here's a description of the press depicted in Thomas Antisell's book, published in 1852:

> The rolling-press, which is employed in nearly every species of copper-plate printing, is divided into two parts, the body and the carriage. The body consists of two wooden cheeks, placed perpendicularly on a stand or foot, which sustains the whole press. From the foot, likewise, rise four other perpendicular pieces, joined by the cross of horizontal ones, which serve to sustain a smooth even plank or table, about four feet and a half long, two feet and a half broad, and an inch and a half thick. Into the cheeks go two wooden cylinders or rollers, about six inches in diameter, borne up at each end by the cheeks, whose ends, which are lessened to about two inches in diameter, and called trunnions, turn in the cheeks about two pieces of wood in the form of half moons, lined with polished iron to facilitate their motion. Lastly, to one of the trunnions of the upper roller is fastened a cross, consisting of two levers, or pieces of wood, traversing each other, the arms of which cross serve instead of the bar or handle of the letter-press, by turning the upper roller, and, when the plank is between the two rollers, giving the same motion to the under one, by drawing the plank forward and backward. . . .

Functionally, this press is no different from ones shown in engraved prints from the late 16th century, except for the use of iron parts. The roller press always sandwiches the printing plate between two rollers, and the bed is moved forwards and backwards by human effort in turning the pinion gear with handles called the "spider." Printing bank notes was exclusively a male occupation until the last quarter of the 19th century, and S.M. Clark, at the Bureau of Engraving and Printing, had much to do with the innovative use of female assistants at each hand-roller press.

D-Rollers

Jacob Perkins is generally credited with the invention of the D-roller, a vast improvement over the round roller previously used. In the D-roller, one side was flat, so the shape resembled the capital letter "D." This shape allowed the bed and plate to return to their original position after passing beneath the roller due to the tension of a counter-weight. This, in turn, saved time since the plate did not have to be picked up by hand and moved back to its original position on the other side of the roller. The advantages of the D-roller were immediately apparent, and it was soon found on all hand-roller presses.

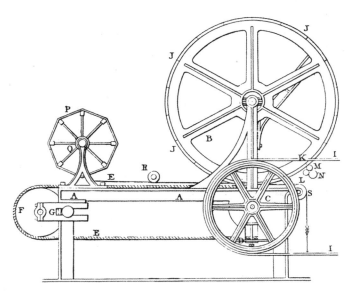

A steam-driven copper-plate–printing press invented by Jacob Perkins in 1819. It was a concept press rather than a practical machine but very advanced for its time.

(A) The cast-iron table of the press; (B) The cylinder to which the printing plates (J)(J)(J) are fixed by screws; (C) The lower cylinder or roller that gives the required pressure and motion to cylinder (B); (D) One of the adjusting screws; (E) The endless web or blanket; (F) The idler pulley and the adjustable bearing (G); (K) The inking roller for the plates (J); (M) (N) The distributing ink rollers; (P) The reel on which the endless sheet of paper is wound; (R) The doctor roller to guide the paper; (S) The roller over which the sheets pass after being printed.

A very advanced bank-note press was invented by Jacob Perkins in 1819.[4] The design was ahead of its time, somewhat like the model of a future car that one can see at auto shows. This was a steam-driven press, the second of its kind for bank-note work, and the first to have distributing ink rollers instead of hand inking with a brayer.[5] It also had an endless blanket web so that printers did not have to set new blankets for each plate, and a long reel of bank-note paper instead of individually cut sheets. These designs were the precursors of many of the automatic labor-saving features found on the web-fed presses used today in bank-note plants around the world. One of the disadvantages, of course, was the requirement for a boiler to make steam. Even if the boiler were placed outside a building to protect the printers, it would still be too expensive for all but the largest bank-note companies. Bank-note paper was still being made by hand in individual sheets, so the idea of a web-fed press was just too novel. Where would a company find large reels of bank-note paper? Still, the press is an amazing example of Perkins's inventive mind.

Composition Rollers

There were a number of printers who claim to have invented the composition roller, so it is difficult to assign this invention to any one person. The earliest rollers were made of wood turned on a lathe to make them perfectly round and fitted with a skin that was stitched on the inner side and glued down. In Joseph Moxon's day, it was a common practice to urinate on the rollers from time to time in the belief that drying urine would tighten the covering. The composition roller generally refers to a metal cylinder covered with canvas and treated with a composition of glue and treacle and usually other compounds. Treacle was a mixture of honey and molasses.

The credit for composition rollers is sometimes given to Adam Spears, a printer employed by the London printing house of Bently & Sons. Apparently, a cousin of Spears who worked at the Staffordshire potteries told him of a method by which the potters placed designs on earthenware with a mixture of glue and treacle. Spears experimented with the idea and succeeded in 1808 by making an inking ball of glue and molasses. He discussed his method with Bryan Donkin, who

patented a "polygonal printing machine" in 1813 which used a metal cylinder covered by canvas and coated with a composition of treacle and glue. Koenig, a manufacturer of presses, switched from using skin-covered rollers to composition rollers in 1814. The first rollers were imperfect and their molding left a ridge and there was usually great difficulty in removing the cylinder from its mold. These problems were solved, and seamless rollers were being made by 1840. Composition rollers were introduced in the United States by 1826.

By the end of the 19th century, the typical formula for the composition was 12-parts treacle, 8-parts glue, and 1-part Paris white. Another popular formula was 10-parts glue, 10-parts sugar, and 12-parts glycerin. The glue was heated in a kettle until it dissolved, and then the other parts were added and continued cooking for about an hour. Care was taken that the mixture never boiled. A stock or handle was placed in the cylindrical mold, and the inside walls of the molds were coated with a thin film of sperm oil, and the composition poured in slowly. This was allowed to stand for at least 12 hours, and then the stock and roller were removed. Once ink had dried on an old roller, it could be revived by taking it off the press, laying it flat on a board, and rubbing it gently with a worn brick dipped in cold water. This abraded the ink and washed it off.

Wetting Presses

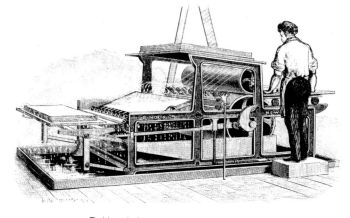

R. Hoe & Company's Paper Wetting Press.

Bank-note companies kept a number of specialized presses in operation, including lithographic and typographic machines. These were sometimes used for special types of work, such as printing checks, drafts, pay warrants, federal bonds, etc. The wetting presses, however, belonged to the bank-note printers and were used to dampen paper so that it became pliable and could be pressed more easily into the recessed lines of an intaglio plate to pick up the ink. They were used for this purpose until well into the 20th century, when dry-intaglio printing methods replaced the old wet-intaglio process.

Cyrus Durand's Press

During the period from 1815 to about the middle of the 1830s, early models of spider presses were made for bank-note companies by small machine shops and foundries. One famous inventor should be mentioned in this respect. Cyrus Durand was granted a patent on May 22, 1828, for an improved copper-plate–printing press. The only description we have of this press was a brief notice given in the *Journal of the Franklin Institute*.[6] This press consisted of a strong bench or table, perfectly flat, of wood or metal, on top of which were placed several rollers, up to six, mounted in an iron frame. The plank, or bed, like that of a common press, was placed on these rollers, and the printing plate was laid on the plank. The large rollers passed over the plate. Since the frame and the plank all moved together on the smaller rollers, the friction that ordinarily attended the operation of the common press was almost entirely removed, and the labor was greatly reduced. Durand claimed that impressions were made more perfectly on his new press. The cross or spider wheel of the common press remained the same.

Because of the heavy ink used in copper- and steel-plate printing, it was necessary to heat the printing plate before it was used. A warm plate softened the ink and made it flow more easily so it would completely fill the engraved lines. In most small shops, and especially when a plate was only going to be used for a short time, a charcoal brazier answered this purpose. Sometimes the plate was just set on top of the pot-bellied stove for awhile. When a plate was going to be used for a longer period of time, it was usually heated by an oil lamp placed below the bed piece. Angier Perkins, Jacob's son, invented a method for heating plates by pumping heated water or liquid metal through tubes to the plate. His patent covering this invention is No. 888, dated August 20, 1838. The Bureau of Engraving and Printing experimented with electrical stoves to heat their plates in 1887, using a model provided by the Sawyer-Man Electric Light Company of New York. To run an electric stove required a countershaft to belt its power to a drive pulley on a dynamo that connected to the stove. The bureau found it was simpler and less expensive to stay with the open flame of an oil lamp. After a power grid was set up in Washington, D.C., it was possible to electrify the bureau and do away with belted power drives.

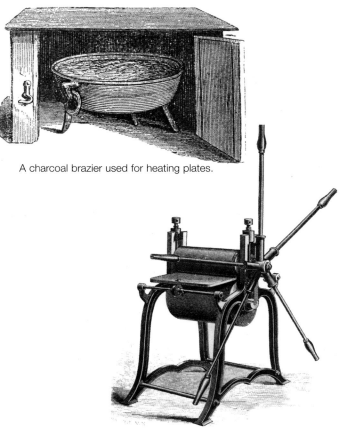

A charcoal brazier used for heating plates.

R. Hoe & Company's copper-plate press of 1867. This press was bought by the Bureau of Engraving and Printing in large numbers.

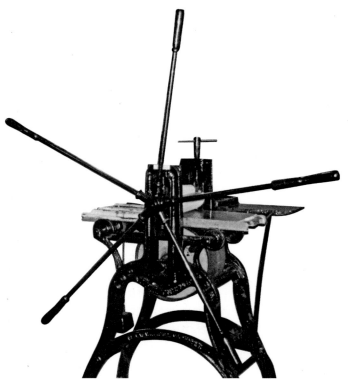

Quite a few 19th-century hand-roller presses can be found in museums today. This one can be seen at the Higgins Museum in Okojobi, Iowa.

In the mid-1830s, R. Hoe & Company of New York City began making hand-roller intaglio presses for copper- and steel-plate printing. Richard Hoe wrote the following letter to Thomas Jones on August 24, 1837:

> . . . I have also made an improvement in the copper plate press which is simply this—the applying [of] a friction roller under the journals of the under roll. I have never heard of this being done and have a model & drawings made which I send to your address.[7]

R. Hoe & Company became the largest-single manufacturer of spider presses in America, although these presses were never an important part of the company's work. When Congress authorized the Demand Notes in 1861 and the Legal Tender Notes in 1862, the three bank-note companies in New York City each ordered 50 Hoe spider presses to handle the workload, and these orders "were supplemented from time to time by lots of twenties and tens, as necessity

required."[8] When the government set up the National Currency Bureau, First Division, in the Treasury Department in the mid-1860s, they also bought spider presses from R. Hoe & Company. While the popularity of the spider press continued to grow, some inventors were beginning to look at the whole process of printing bank notes to find ways to mechanize hand operations and improve the speed of the work.

Robert Neale

In 1858 Robert Neale, a printer from Ohio, commissioned R. Hoe & Company to build a steam-powered copper-plate–printing press that he believed would be capable of printing bank notes. Here is Stephen Tucker's description of this machine:

> This was a large and expensive machine. The printing plate bed was attached to a pair of endless chains which carried it along horizontally with the printing plate face upwards under the impression cylinder and an inking apparatus, and returned it underneath with the printing plate face downwards, where the wiping and polishing operations were performed. The machine was tried and altered many times in the factory and printed ordinary work fairly well, but it never cleaned and polished the plate sufficiently well for first-class work.[9]

Neale was not satisfied by the performance of the press and decided to go back to the drawing board. He returned with a new design in 1876, and this time, to finance the improvements, he had the backing of a wealthy publisher, William S. Appleton. Tucker said the "arrangements for inking, wiping and polishing the plate were said to be very effective, and the machine was set to work in the offices of Messrs. D. Appleton & Co. in Brooklyn." The press came to the attention of officials at the Bureau of Engraving and Printing, and they immediately expressed their interest in seeing it tested for a period of some weeks.

At this point, Colonel Hoe was not willing to wait for the government to finish its tests, and being out some money on the project, he sued

Neale and Appleton. After investigating the case, Worthington and Heald, the attorneys for R. Hoe & Company, informed Colonel Hoe that "they had learned certain facts relative to the ownership of the plate printing machine which render further prosecution of the suit useless." Apparently, Messrs. Neale and Appleton had taken legal precautions to protect themselves against such suits. It was one of the few times that Colonel Hoe didn't get his way.

Invitations were sent out to interested parties to see the Neale-Appleton press in a demonstration test on November 23, 1878, at the machine shop of the Treasury Department. The results of the tests were good enough to warrant further trials at the Bureau of Engraving and Printing. On January 9, 1879, the two steam-powered presses then at the bureau—the Neale-Appleton and the Milligan Press—were given extensive trials, and their printing was compared to an equal volume of work done by the hand-roller presses. The printing of each type of press was judged by a committee of experts, and it was found that the steam-powered presses were suitable for printing certain classes of work in a satisfactory manner with a considerable savings to the government (the Milligan more so than the other). The government then contacted the owners of the power-plate presses and offered to construct five additional machines of each type at $500 per press and to pay royalties of $1 per 1,000 impressions. "Owing to a want of harmony between the owners of the Neale-Appleton press, the proposition was not accepted by them, and as they failed to operate the press that was then in the Bureau, it was finally dismantled, boxed, and stored for the owners."[10]

The Neale-Appleton press "was attended by one man, a plate printer, and by one boy. The inking in is done by the machine from a distributing roller. . . . The wiping cylinder is of flannel, covered by fine leather. This cylinder removes about 35 per cent of the ink, which is saved by 'doctors' . . . The motion of the wiping cylinder would soon dim the light tints since about 42 inches of the leather comes in rubbing contact with about each inch of the surface of the plate in use."[11] Except for the wiping operation, which needed to be improved or possibly re-invented, the machine had great potential. Unfortunately, the clash of personalities between the two entrepreneurs could not be fixed.

The Milligan Press

The Milligan press was invented by James Milligan of Brooklyn, New York, who said he was a "practical plate printer by trade."[12] He was granted Patent No. 180,490, called "Improvement in Plate-Printing Presses," on August 1, 1876. Its steam engine was rated at one horsepower, which was enough to move four plates, each 9 inches by 14 inches, around a square side frame by means of a chain or belt passing over pulleys. The chain was connected to the bed or plank by projecting studs or pins, so that as the chain moved around the frame of the press, the plates were also moved. The press was operated by a printer and two assistants. Usually, the assistants were females who earned $1.50 a day. Inking was done mechanically, and the printer then polished the plate by hand. Wiping was also done mechanically, and one of the assistants placed a sheet of paper on the plate. The plate was engraved with register markings so the paper could be placed accurately. The plate then moved through a set of pressure rollers which made the impression. A second assistant removed the printed sheet, and the plate continued on its circuit back to the inking roller. Four layers of felting with an aggregate thickness of at least 1/4 inch, interposed between the roller and the paper, allowed the plate to pass easily and smoothly under the roller without any perceptible jarring. The Milligan press was manufactured by the Gould and Eberhardt Iron Works of Newark, New Jersey, at a cost of $1,250 each.[13] The presses were owned by the government, but a royalty of $1 per 1,000 perfect sheets printed by each press was paid to the estate of the deceased inventor, Mrs. Elizabeth R. Milligan of Brooklyn, New York, and Mr. Charles F. Steele of Philadelphia. From 1879 through February 1888, these royalties amounted to $44,560.

There are four distinct operations in both hand-roller and steam-powered presses: (1) the inking of the plate by rolling to and fro an inking roller charged with ink from an inked slab; (2) the wiping of the plate by rubbing it with a thin muslin cloth; (3) the polishing of the plate by rubbing the hand over a cake of whiting and then over the plate until the ink is entirely removed from the surface and remains only in the engraved lines; and (4) the taking of the impression by having the inked plate face upwards on the plank of the press, placing the dampened paper on it, and forcing the plank and the plate under an iron roller covered with several layers of thick felting and adjusted to such a height as to force the paper down into the inked lines under considerable pressure.

In the Neale-Appleton press, all of these operations were done mechanically. In the Milligan press, however, the polishing step was done by hand, exactly as it was in the hand-roller press, but with the advantage that an assistant was assigned to perform this step and did not change to other jobs. The assistant naturally became proficient in polishing plates and turned out a better class of work. In every type of press, the wiping and polishing steps are critical to the perfection of the printing. If a plate is wiped too hard, some of the ink is wiped out of the engraved lines, causing the impression to lose "color," or contrast. This was a frequent problem with power-plate presses. If the pressure was too great, the ink was forced out of the lines of the plate, and a blurred or "mashed" impression was produced. The pressure of the impression roller could be adjusted by the printer to give a full and clear printing, but when this was necessary, it took several adjustments to find the one that worked best, and this was time consuming.

One nice feature about the Milligan press, and one that is rarely mentioned, was the concern of the inventor for the safety of the operators. Once the sheet of paper had been placed on the plate according to the register marks, the two passed under a blanket-roller. It was often necessary for the operator to pull the paper one way

or the other to prevent wrinkling, and the operator's fingers were occasionally caught by the blanket-roller and smashed. This happened even in the hand-roller presses, but in a power press the risks of serious injury was greater. Milligan solved the problem by providing a transparent shield, made of glass, which could be adjusted in height, to prevent the fingers from getting too close to the blanket-roller and still allow the paper to be observed and accurately guided.

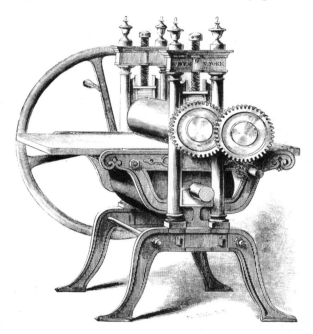

R. Hoe & Company's geared copper-plate–printing press.

The Milligan press, a steam-operated, semi-automatic plate-printing press used at the Bureau of Engraving and Printing in the 1880s.

The Homer Lee Press

The Homer Lee Steam-Powered Automatic Plate-Printing Press of the early 1880s. Note that this press printed from continuous reels of paper.

The Homer Lee rotary steel-plate press was named after its inventor, although it was said that Mr. Lee copied the design of the French press invented by Constant Alexis Guy, which he saw while studying art in Europe.[14,15] The Bureau of Engraving and Printing was interested in the Lee press, and in October 1880 they sent George W. Casilear, Thomas J. Sullivan, and Ward Morgan to observe it in operation in New York City. Mr. Lee was then printing the face and back plates of bank notes for a South American bank at his bank-note company. The committee reported that "The results from both plates was highly creditable. . . . The press is an automatic printing machine, performing all the operations necessary to the perfection of a print, including inking, wiping, polishing, and the making of the impressions, and needs only the attention of a pressman to adjust the press and keep it in running order, a 'feeder,' and a 'taker-off.'"[16] That model of the Homer Lee press was soon improved, and testing of the new machine began in 1883. The old model worked one plate attached to a flat block which was laid on the bed of the press, printed ten impressions per minute, and had a reciprocating motion. The newer model also worked one plate, but that plate was curved and attached to a cylinder which operated in a continuous circular motion and printed 20 impressions per minute.

The new-model press was found adequate to print several different classes of securities, including the internal-revenue stamps, all checks and drafts, the back of the U.S. notes, and the black-backs and tints of National Bank Notes.

The new model of the Homer Lee press worked well enough mechanically; however, it remained to be seen what quality of work it would produce under actual operating conditions. Secretary of the Treasury Charles J. Folger appointed seven men to a committee to run tests on the Lee press and make recommendations. Two of the committee members, William Earle and John R. White, were employees of the bureau. After a series of tests, the majority of the committee found that the Homer Lee press could execute the securities for which it was adapted at less expense that the Milligan, and they recommended the bureau waste no time in acquiring a number of these presses. The two men from the bureau did not concur with their opinion and thought the tests were not accurate and had been rigged in the favor of the Lee press. T.N. Burril, the Chief of the Bureau, wrote to Secretary Folger that the Lee press would not be acceptable to the bureau principally because of its automatic polishing of the plate, something that Mr. Burril believed that no machine could ever do with sufficient quality. Burril also noted that none of the private bank-note companies used the Lee press except for Mr. Lee's own company, the Homer Lee Bank Note Company. Nevertheless, Secretary Folger, on May 26, 1884, authorized the purchase of three additional Lee presses of the improved pattern, with a contract to pay royalties of $1 per 1,000 perfect sheets printed. For some unexplained reason, Homer Lee declined to sell the presses to the government or to accept the contract. The government tried again, very politely, to get him to reconsider their offer, but he never answered the letter. This appears to have been a clash of personalities between Homer Lee and Chief Burril. The chief's reluctance to use the Lee press may have angered Mr. Lee to the point that he over-reacted by refusing to even talk with the government.

A four-plank power-printing press used at the
Bureau of Engraving and Printing in the 1940s.

The Robertson Press

Meanwhile, a young inventor named Judah
Touro Robertson began a meteoric career in the
bank-note industry with his own steam-powered
plate-printing press and a constant stream of
improvements to that design. "Touro," as he was
called, was born March 7, 1841, in Philadelphia,
the son of Colonel William Howland Robertson,
who was aide-de-camp on General Andrew Jackson's staff during the Battle of Pensacola and was
later the American Consul at Havana, Cuba.[17]
Touro entered commerce in Havana briefly but
left to return to America to enter a preparatory
school. Upon graduation, he decided to follow
the sea and went on one of his father's ships
which sailed regularly between Havana and
Liverpool, England. Upon the death of his father
in December 1857, he came to New York at the
age of 17 to live with his guardian, Henry Jarvis
Raymond, the owner and first editor of the *New
York Times*. With the outbreak of the Civil War,
he enlisted in the 12th Regiment of New York
Volunteers for six months but was sent home
with an injury and never saw active service.
When he recovered from his injury in 1862,
he was induced to put some of his inheritance in
the newly formed Continental Bank Note
Company, founded and partly owned by W.L.
Ormsby in New York City. The company
suffered some reverses, and Touro decided it

would be necessary to learn the business and take
over its management or risk losing the money he
had invested.

"Panorama de la Habana."

Touro entered the Continental Bank Note
Company in January 1863 as secretary. He was
then 22 years old but had unbridled enthusiasm
and energy, and by quick successive steps he
became manager, general superintendent, and
vice-president of the company. He was a quick
learner and solved most of the company's production problems as quickly as they came to the
fore.[18] When the Continental Bank Note Company was consolidated with the American Bank
Note Company in January 1879, Touro was made
both a trustee and vice-president of the new company, positions which he held until his death on
January 5, 1900.[19]

Touro's first patent, No. 113,346, granted on
April 4, 1871, was entitled "Improvement in
Printing Presses," and described a printing press
having five copper or steel plates arranged radially on the surface of a circular table. These plates
were heated by steam or by lamps. As the table
moved, the printing plates were inked, wiped, and
polished by hand, and paper was also placed on
them by hand. The table moved in a continuous
circle, powered by a belt drive. The speed of the
circular motion was governed by gears that operated in synchrony with a cranking motion of a
power shaft. The motion of the power shaft was
also used to move the plates to and fro on the
table so they lined up and passed automatically
between D-rollers to make an impression on

paper. Touro tells us that the old-style hand-roller press was inefficient because it wasn't doing anything while the inking, wiping, polishing, and paper laying was being done. The design of his new press was intended to keep the assistants continuously occupied. Therefore, the actual printing was done much more rapidly. The press was named the "Robertson press" and was used only at the Continental Bank Note Company. Plate printers from the Bureau of Engraving and Printing who saw the press in operation spoke well of its efficiency and the quality of work it turned out.

In Patent No. 123,933, dated February 20, 1872, called "Improvement in Plate-Printing Machinery," Touro reduced the number of assistants needed for his presses by automating the wiping and polishing of plates. Various attempts had already been made to wipe and polish plates by machinery, but they had only limited success. Touro devised a new method by which cloth-covered sponge rubber pads were attached to arms that radiated from a revolving shaft and pressed down on the plates at a proper angle. These arms were of slightly different lengths, so the pad on the longest arm would wipe and polish the outer side of a plate, and another pad, on a slightly shorter arm, would do the same on a different area of the same plate, and finally a third pad on a still shorter arm would cover just the inner side of the plate. The cloth covering the elastic pads could be easily wound up when it became dirty.

A rather brief patent, No. 130,153, dated August 6, 1872, was termed "An Improvement in Printing Presses." The specifications describe a press for printing copper and steel plates or lithographic stones, and the principle feature is a method of regulating the pressure of the printing roller by means of adjustable spring-loaded roller bearings. The press may have been powered by a belt drive, but none is shown in the diagrams nor discussed in the text.

Touro was granted Patent No. 175,875 on April 11, 1876, called "Improvement in Coupon Bonds." This patent addressed the problem with coupon bonds that normally had their attached six-month coupons all printed in the same color and with the same lettering style. To prevent mistakes in identifying the coupons—such as tearing off a July coupon for a January coupon—and to prevent a counterfeiter from altering the amount of the coupons or their dates of payment, Touro proposed to print the different classes of coupons in different tints and to alternate between different lettering fonts.

Patent No. 181,597, dated August 29, 1876, was called "Improvement in Processes of Removing Ink." Touro explained that ink was used in a wasteful manner in plate printing, and only one gallon in ten used actually appeared on bank notes or bonds, which made printing more expensive than it should be. He also mentioned that the inking rollers and wiping rags were generally of woolen or cotton cloth, and sometimes of the fabric known as "Canton Flannel," which had a fleecy nap on one side that added fibrous material to the ink wiped from the plate. In some power presses, the wiping pads were cleaned by contact with similar materials or taken off by scrapers. This fibrous material made waste ink unsuitable for further use. To solve this problem, Touro proposed to save waste ink under water to prevent the formation of skins on the ink. He then passed the ink through a centrifuge to separate solid materials. He also suggested that wiping cloths be placed in the same centrifuge to remove their ink. He renovated the ink by grinding it in an ink mill or in a mixing machine.

Patent No. 541,985, entitled "Plate Printing Press," dates from July 2, 1895, while Touro was an officer of the American Bank Note Company. This patent relates to steam plate-printing presses, and its object was to "provide a means whereby plates of different sizes may be printed from on the same machine at the same time without incurring the danger of soiling the back of the sheet that is printed from the large plate with the dirt which may have been pickup from the small plate." To accomplish this, Touro's press had two printing or blanket rollers in combination with two or more movable beds for carrying the engraved plates, the beds and the blanket rollers being with such means and so arranged that one of the blanket rollers would engage only with certain of the movable beds, so as to print from their plates, while the other printing roller would engage only with the remaining movable beds to print from their plates. The patent was written to apply to the "Milligan press and that machine [as] diagrammed in the several drawings that form part of this patent." In Touro's design, only one inking mechanism and only one wiping mechanism were employed for the two blanket rollers. Each type of plate selected and started its own printing roller automatically by means of differentially disposed starting devices that activated differentially disposed engaging devices on the printing rollers.

In Patent No. 649,976, titled "Automatic Wiper and Polisher for Plate-Printing Presses," granted to Touro on November 19, 1895, an automatically operated wiper and polisher belt is shown which will thoroughly and effectively wipe and polish plates without wiping out the ink from engraved lines. This was a complex patent with the functioning of 40 different parts shown in the diagram.

Patent No. 590,114, called "Feeder Attachment for Printing Presses," dated September 14, 1897, and an improvement to that design called "Feeder for Printing Presses," granted the same date but with Patent No. 590,115, are complex patents with 11 pages of diagrams between them and detailed texts. They were intended to show the construction of a printing press with a feeder adapted to move transversely across the path of the line of feed and to reciprocate into and away from the delivery position while maintaining accurate registration of the paper.

Finally, Patent No. 592,664, called "Inking Device for the Plate-Printing Presses," granted to Touro on October 26, 1897, described an

inking fountain that released ink onto the surface of an inking roller which in turn inked an endless belt that revolves over and under three or more inking rollers of smaller size. The endless belt was pressed against the printing plate and delivered to it a uniform and thin film of ink. The diagram in this patent shows a rotary press, but the mechanisms could be used just as well on a flat-bed press.

Touro had a rich and full life in his 58 years. He married Miss Lucilda Sandford of New York City, and they had a son, William Jr., and a daughter, Jessie. Their son was connected with the American Bank Note Company. Touro died suddenly of heart disease at his residence, 21 East 56th Street in New York City, on January 5, 1900, and is buried in the family vault at the old North Laurel Hill Cemetery, alongside the Schuylkill River in Philadelphia.[20]

The old North Laurel Hill Cemetery.

Chapter 18

A Little Chemistry

The bank-note industry has always been concerned about any process that can reproduce a graphic design with sufficient accuracy to deceive the casual observer. That concern intensified when a number of technologies were developed during the 1840s, such as anastatic printing and photography. Lithography, then some 40 years old, seemed capable of further refinement, and photoengraving, with its unerring accuracy, seemed especially ominous. There was reason for concern.

A rare, early counterfeit made by photography.

Politypage

Beginning in April 1791, a French artist named Gingembre conceived the idea that an engraving in low relief on hardened steel could be transferred to a copper plate by the pressure of a screw press. The resulting copy on copper would be intaglio, and new copper plates could be made from the original steel-engraved plate whenever needed. Gingembre got a French engraver named Fiezinger to execute an engraving on steel and then make an intaglio copy on copper by his method, which came to be called "Politypage" or "le laminage." The method appeared to work so well that it was approved for making the plates for the 400-livre notes issued by a decree of November 21, 1792, for the assignats of the Republic Frânçaise. This note was designed by Nicholas-Marie Gatteaux and featured an eagle holding a staff with a liberty cap in the center vignette, symbolizing the immortality of freedom. It was engraved on steel by Alexander Tardieu, and the plate was then hardened. This was given to Monsieur Herlan who laid a copper plate on the steel plate and passed them through a roller press to make a copper-plate copy in relief. This copper plate was then placed with another, softer-copper plate and passed through the roller press to make an intaglio printing plate.

The assignats of 400 livre and 50 livre were polityped and printed in this fashion in 1793 and 1794. Unfortunately, the process did not work as well as expected. Copper, when strongly pressed, expands in both directions at a rate that is proportional to its annealing and its thickness. With these two assignats, there was such distortion that few of the notes were acceptable, and new copies of the master plate had to be made frequently. The method was renounced and never used again.[1]

Lithography

This $20 note was easily counterfeited due to the fact that it was a simple lithographic print.

The genuine note of the above counterfeit.

Lithography was used to print a great deal of the Confederate currency, stamps, and bonds and also played a minor role in counterfeiting. Lithography in the 1860s could not produce fine lines and left no ink standing above the surface of the paper, so the "feel" of the print was quite different. The look of lithographic notes was also decidedly inferior to currency printed by steel line engraving, but the Confederacy was in a hurry to start a war and had little time to prepare for a new currency. Lithography was the only viable option at the time. The description of lithography given here is based on discussions that August Dietz had with several printers, engravers, and transfer men who had worked for Hoyer & Ludwig or its successor, A. Hoen & Company. Dietz sought out these men for research on his book, *The Postal Service of the Confederate States of America*, published in 1929.[2]

The stone—Lithographic stones were always limestone and varied in color from a drab yellowish to gray and from soft to hard grades. The gray stone was preferred for engraving such work as required fine lines, and the different shops usually used this hard grade of stone for printing currency. The thickness of the stones varied from 1-1/2 to 3-1/2 inches.

Preparing the stone—After the surface of the stone had been ground level and polished, it was etched with a solution of gum Arabic and muriatic acid. Gum was the chief ingredient in preparing the stone and remained so throughout the printing process. The acid performed the etching, removing whatever fatty particles may still adhere after the grinding and polishing. The stone was next coated with a solution of lampblack, glycerin, sugar, and gum Arabic, spread evenly with a brush and fanned until dry.

The engraver now made a tracing—actual size—of the approved note design on a small sheet of gelatin. This tracing was then "scratched" into the gelatin with an engraving needle—practically a steel-pointed pencil. Blue chalk was then rubbed into the lines the engraver had scratched. The blue chalk remained in the lines of the design while the surface was cleaned by wiping. The gelatin tracing was then placed face down on the black-coated surface of the stone and held firmly in position by gluing down the four corners. It was then burnished thoroughly, which transferred the fine lines of the blue chalk from the gelatin onto the black ground. Removing the gelatin sheet, the engraver breathed upon the design, which caused the stone to "sweat," moistening the gum of the black coating, which in turn fastened the blue chalk of the design, so that after drying, it was firmly fixed, and the stone was ready for the engraving.

The engraving—The engraver used a steel needle and worked under a strong magnifying glass. The blue-chalk transfer carried the essential features of the design, while the fine working-out of contour and detail depended on the skill of the engraver. The process of "engraving" on stone was, in fact, a "scratching," since the engraving needle was drawn towards the artist. Every scratch of the needle, penetrating the ground, bared the surface of the stone, and thus the engraver proceeded until he had "scratched" the complete design. The design now appeared in reverse image in sharp white lines on a black background. The engraving was now finished.

A portrait created by lithography.

A few drops of linseed oil were next put on the engraving and rubbed into the scratched lines with the finger. The oil (fat) penetrated and adhered to the surface exposed by the engraving, while the black coating protected the unexposed areas.

Making the transfers—After treating the engraving with linseed oil, the black background was washed off with pure turpentine and water. The stone was then inked-in by means of a "dauber." This dauber was a block of wood, about three by six inches, covered by several layers of felt, and well-charged with very fatty black transfer ink. This inking was a vigorous pounding. The stone was kept well dampened during the operation. The transfer ink adhered to the lines of the design, finding its affinity in the linseed oil, while the remaining area of the stone was left clear.

After the original engraving had been charged with transfer ink, as described, and the stone was fanned dry, a small sheet of transfer paper was laid, coated-side down, on the stone, and the stone was drawn horizontally through a press which had a stationary scraper that pressed the transfer paper against the stone. Carefully removed from the stone, this print showed the original Proof of the engraving. These single prints were the transfers.

Transfer paper—Indian or Chinese paper was most extensively used. This very thin paper was coated with a composition of lump starch, dextrin, flour, gelatin, glycerin, and water, which was boiled to a paste in a double boiler before being applied to the paper with a sponge while hot. The first coat was allowed to dry by hanging the paper on lines, then a second coat was applied in the same manner.

The transfer stone—A number of impressions were now "pulled"—first the stone was dampened, transfer ink was applied with the dauber, the stone was fanned dry, and the impression was made. From these single prints, the best copies were selected for transferring to a secondary stone. This was called the transfer stone. This intermediary manipulation was necessary to produce multiple engravings on the stone. In the case of printing currency, a stone usually had "four-up," or four subjects on the stone, and would therefore print four notes to a sheet.

The press and the principle of impression—Hoyer & Ludwig's presses, both for transferring and printing, were of identical pattern but differing in size—the smaller for transferring, the larger for printing. They were built according to

Senefelder's specifications, and Senefelder was the original inventor of lithography in Germany. Ludwig's presses were built in Germany and imported many years before the Civil War.

The frame was constructed of cast iron, which was supported by four legs carrying a bed of heavy oak. The bed was raised from below by means of a lever when the impression was to be made, and was moved forward and backward, on a track, by means of cog-wheels turned with a handle, as one turns a hand-grindstone. The stone rested upon the bed.

An ad for Jacob Haehnlen's steam-powered lithographic and letter-press printing rooms.

Between the upright arms of the frame, located at the middle of the press, there was a strong cross-bar, which could be raised or lowered by a hand-screw located between the uprights. This cross-bar had a groove along its lower surface for the insertion of the "scraper." These scrapers were "rulers" of hard wood, approximately one inch in thickness, and of lengths to suit the varying widths of stones, with blunt but truly straight edges. These edges were spanned with a strip of leather the entire length of the "blade," turned up at the ends and tacked fast. No tacking was made along the blade. This strip of leather adjusted itself and clung after several preliminary "scrapes."

The printing—The process of lithographic printing was the same as that of pulling impressions from the secondary (transfer) stone, save that, instead of black fatty transfer ink, the less-fatty lithographic printing ink was used, and the regular bank-note paper took the place of transfer paper.

After the stone had been dampened, it was "rolled up" with color—a leather-covered roller taking the place of the dauber. The slightly dampened sheet of bank-note paper was carefully laid down upon the surface of the stone—guide lines (or dots) on the stone margins marked the position for the sheet. A layer of several sheets of paper was placed on top of this. Finally, a sheet of zinc or copper (or stretched leather) covered with tallow was added. The purpose of the tallow coating was to enable the stone, with the sheet to be printed, to pass smoothly under the tightly adjusted scraper, which exerted the required printing pressure, and to prevent the sheet from sliding or slipping on the stone.

Anastatic Printing

This process was first used by Senefelder in his experiments to develop chemical lithography in 1776. It was then re-invented in the early 1840s by a German named Baldemus, about whom we know almost nothing, and introduced in England by (Sir) William Siemens in 1844. In that year, Joseph Woods took out a patent on the process, but it did not become well known until Michael Faraday gave a lecture on it at the Royal Institution in 1845.[3] The anastatic process was designed to transfer any image or writing on paper that had been made with a saponaceous or fatty nature, such as common lithographic or printer's ink, onto a metallic plate, such as a copper-printing plate. If someone wanted to counterfeit a bank note, they began by soaking the note in a dilute solution of one-part nitric acid to eight-parts rain water, or distilled water. The note was soaked for a period that varied from 12 hours to 7 days, depending on the age of the note, for which no accurate rule can be given. Next, the back of the note was brushed with a solution of caustic potash (potassium hydroxide) and water. Then, a dilute solution of tartaric acid was prepared in a shallow dish, and the note was soaked in this solution. A reaction took place between the tartaric acid and the caustic potash, forming small crystals of potassium hydrogen tartrate, which in those days was called "cream of tartar." These crystals formed over the entire surface of the note except where there was ink. The counterfeiter then rolled a hard lithographic inking roller, charged with a small portion of lithographic ink, over the surface of the note. This laid down a new coating of ink over the old printed design and lettering. The superfluous ink was removed by a roller that was not charged with ink. The blank part of the note was still covered with the cream of tartar crystals, so these were removed by soaking the note in a dilute solution of nitric acid.

The original note was then blotted dry, placed on a prepared copper plate, and subjected to slight pressure. This transferred the original design and lettering of the real note to the copper plate. The plate was then washed in all directions by a sponge charged with very thick "gum water." Gum water is a solution of gum Arabic and water. The gum Arabic is an exudate collected from the bark of acacia trees. The gum water was used to make the non-image areas of the printing plate ink-repellant. This was called "desensitizing" the plate. Gum Arabic is more efficient at desensitizing a plate if it is combined with an acid, such as phosphoric acid.

The counterfeiter then "rubbed up" the plate, meaning to rub the plate with a linen rag charged with a mixture of lithographic printing ink and gum water. The ink stuck to the plate only where the original image was printed on the note. This process was very much like lithography except for the method of transferring the design to the metal plate. There were many disadvantages to the process, most of them limiting the number of impressions that could be printed. Because the original note was soaked in acids, it was destroyed. Therefore, if the counterfeiter wanted to counterfeit a $100 note with this method, he would have to get at least two good impressions in order to recover his investment.

Photolithography

One of the best descriptions of photolithography is that given by its inventor, J.W. Osbourne, in testimony he gave to a congressional committee in 1888. The following process is taken from his explanation:

That is a process in which we print from stone on a well-known press by well-known processes. Having first made a photographic negative, we take a sheet of paper and prepare that sheet with a solution of gelatine, dichromate of potash, and albumen, as in the case of my own process. That sheet of paper is dried in the dark. It is then a brilliant yellow with a glossy varnished surface. That sheet is exposed under the negative, in contact with it, and the light produces a change. It decomposes the dichromate of potash, an orange salt, and acts upon the organic matter, which, in this case, is the gelatine. It produces a visible photograph on the yellow paper. That photograph is of a chestnut brown color on a brilliant yellow surface. The sheet of paper is next inked all over by inverting it (face down) upon a stone or plate, which is rolled up with transfer ink and pulling through the press. When the sheet is taken off or lifted off the plate, it brings with it a homogenous covering of transfer ink all over it, obliterating the visible picture to a considerable extent. When it is so far advanced it is put with the paper side down floating upon hot water. The action of the hot water is that it penetrates through the paper and coagulates the albumen in the sheet, making it insoluble, and it finally softens and sells the gelatine.

In all those places where the light has acted the changed gelatine remains intact and dry. These portions of changed gelatine now hold the transfer ink solidly on their surface and the softened and swelled and gelatinized otherwise, has the ink upon a soft foundation. Now, by the application of a wet sponge and friction, you wash off all the ink from the places that are to become white and leave all the ink upon those places that represent the picture. That sheet now represents a black picture in transfer ink, which is dried and given to the lithographer. The lithographer, from that point on, strictly adheres to his own method. He damps that sheet again between damp papers, lays it face down upon a clean stone, pulls it through the press, damps the sheet again and pulls it through the press again, and finally takes it off. He has then transferred the ink from the delineations on the paper to the stone. That is then subjected to a lithographic preparation. It is etched and gummed, technically speaking, treated with an acid and with gum, the gum being an essential element. Then comes the printing. The printing is done by dampening the stone between each impression, inking it and printing it in the press.[4]

Osbourne went on to say that photolithography was capable of making 10,000 to 14,000 impressions per day in a hand-roller press and 15,000 in a steam press. He stated further that the usefulness of the method in counterfeiting would depend on the intricacies of the original note. While he was in London, he asked the Bank of England for permission to counterfeit one of their notes by photolithography and pass it. They refused permission, but he was sure that he could have done it quite easily since the Bank of England notes were simple in design and printed from a flat surface from an ordinary relief matrix in a type-press.

Electrotyping

Beginning about 1837 to 1839, several people independently discovered that an electrical current could be used to duplicate an engraving on copper. The process was first called "electro-typing," and that term continued in use until the end of the century. Alternate terms, such as "electrography," "electro-gilding," and "electro-plating," were also used, with "electro-plating" becoming the most common term in late 19th-century America. Thomas Spencer read a paper to the Liverpool Polytechnic Society describing experiments he had made in 1837 in which he made casts of coins and then casts in intaglio from the matrices thus formed. C.J. Jordan ran experiments in 1838 using "galvanism" to plate metals with copper, and Professor Jacobi of St. Petersburg, Russia, developed a method in 1837 and 1838 for duplicating engraved copper on steel plates. So successful was Jacobi's work that he was chosen to gild the iron dome of the Cathedral of St. Isaac at St. Petersburg. The dome weighed about 224 tons and was electro-gilded with 274 pounds of gold from melted ducat coins. The earliest electrotypes were made in voltaic batteries, and the objects to be plated were not connected to an external battery. Consequently, the batteries required days and sometimes weeks to deposit a sufficient amount of copper on the object being copied. Later, when self-contained batteries were made, such as those of Daniell, Bunsen, or Smee, the rate of electro-deposition was increased enormously, and objects could be copied in days or even hours.

The Cathedral of St. Isaac at St. Petersburg.

W.L. Ormsby was so concerned about the ability of electrotyping to make perfect copies of copper bank-note plates that he described the process in his book, published in 1852.[5] Helpful as this explanation might have been to the curious layman, it was also a guide to the counterfeiters. Ormsby wrote to the New England Bank Note Company and asked for a copy of the portrait of Jacob Perkins which he had engraved for that company in 1834. The company would not give him a copy on steel but did send him one on copper. Ormsby then had a "practical workman in this branch of business" make a duplicate electrotype of the portrait at the standard charge of $1.50. The portrait was reproduced in Ormsby's book.

Ormsby pointed out that bank-note engravers frequently sold their vignettes to the public. He went on to say that sometimes a failed bank-note company would auction off or sell their entire stock of such dies, citing the examples of Burton, Edmonds & Company and Durand & Company. Ormsby said it was no longer necessary to own a transfer press to make superb copies of bank-note vignettes or any part of a copper or steel bank-note plate, and "after properly filing and fitting the plates thus produced, [counterfeiters] may compose copper bank plates about as readily as printers can set up a form in type."[6] There is evidence in the form of newspaper advertisements that some companies did sell their stock dies and cuts when they went out of business, but I've not seen any proof of who bought that material. The failed companies may have advertised such sales but then restricted the material to well known and respected engravers from other companies. Ormsby goes on to suggest that stock-vignette dies were sold to the public by Woodruff & Hammond in Cincinnati, Terry Pelton & Company in Boston, the Boston Bank Note Company, and Hall, Packard & Company in Albany, but offers no proof as to whom the material was sold.

The method used in Ormsby's day to electrotype a plate was about the same as that described in an article published in *The American Journal of Science and Arts* in 1841.[7] The first step was to make a battery from an earthenware pot using plaster of Paris to make a porous divider that separates the pot into two chambers. One chamber held a solution of copper sulfate, and the other chamber held acidified water in which a bar of zinc was placed and connected by a metal strap that arched over to the other chamber and would be connected to the object to be copied. The next step was to take an impression of the plate by pressing it down on soft and bright sheet lead. When done under great pressure, the soft lead would be forced into the incised line of the copper plate, forming an exact copy of the engraving, even down to the thin lines. The sheet of lead now held the engraving in relief and reversed. This sheet of lead was immediately attached to the metal strap and immersed in the chamber holding the copper sulfate solution of the battery. The action was immediate, as a small electric current was generated by the dissimilar metals in their solutions. The copper sulfate was broken down by electrolysis to release copper, which was then attached to the lead sheet and coated it in copper. The copper-coated lead sheet could be separated into its different metals by holding the sheet in boiling water or over a heat source, such as a spirit lamp, causing the two metals to expand at different rates, resulting in their separation. The copper shell was too thin to be used directly in printing, so the side that stood out in relief had to be covered with a fusible metal or plaster to form a flat base that supported the other (intaglio) side.

The article mentions that Mr. Joseph Saxton of the United States Mint had made a similar battery and copied a daguerreotype plate, the picture being visible by the difference of polish in the (copper) deposit. Silliman said this was the strongest proof yet seen of the great delicacy of this process. It is not surprising that Saxton was working in two newly invented experimental technologies. He had a curious and facile mind, and he never hesitated to try something new.

Photoengraving

To quote from the Amstutz *Handbook*, the term "photoengraving" means to produce "a printing plate having images formed in relief upon a metal surface, these images being obtained by a series of photographic and chemical operations. There are two general classes of these engravings, known respectively as line plates and half-tone plates."[8] This discussion centers mainly on the use of photoengraving to produce line plates, since they were of the greatest concern to the bank-note industry.

The origins of this process go back to the experiments conducted in France during the 1820s by Joseph Nicéphore Niépce, and later by Louis Jacques Mandé Daguerre and William Henry Talbot. Each of these men made important discoveries concerning the sensitivity of certain chemicals to light. In the case of Joseph Niépce, his discovery came about almost accidentally. He was trying to improve the relatively new techniques for making lithographic prints. In his experiments, he discovered that bitumen, a kind of black tarry substance that bubbles up to the earth's surface in tar pits, changes when exposed to light. He began by etching a portrait of Cardinal Georges of Amboise, the Papal Minister to Louis XII, then coated the drawing with oil, so light would shine through it more easily. Next, he placed it on a pewter plate covered with a thin film of bitumen and exposed the plate to strong sunlight. The light, shining through the paper, "burned" an image into the bitumen, creating a nearly perfect copy of the original. Niépce then etched the image into the pewter with a brief wash of acetic acid, producing an intaglio printing surface. The pewter plate could then be used to print the image in the traditional print-making techniques of the day.

Joseph Nicéphore Niépce.

In 1827, following in the footsteps of his uncle, Niépce de St. Victor laid an asphalt ground upon a metallic plate. This was exposed under a positive print, the unaltered asphaltum was removed by lavender oil, and the plate was etched with acid. This was analogous to the process described by the elder Niépce to Daguerre when their co-partnership was formed for the purpose of perfecting the sun-pictures to which the name of daguerreotype was subsequently applied. It is almost certain that the elder Niépce had not merely the intention of making pictures but designed to use the process for the production of intaglio etchings. It seems the photographic industry lost sight of this intention in the wonderful success of Daguerr's process. A specimen of the nephew's photographic engraving effort is said to be in the possession of the French Photographic Society, and several of his asphalt photographs upon metallic plates are in the British Museum. By 1840 daguerreotype studios were being established in most of the major cities in the United States, and the process, which was cheap, became a mania across

Johannes Gutenberg.

America. Daguerre's process lasted well into the 1850s, and most of the pictures of the California gold fields were taken by daguerreotype cameras.

Niépce made two important contributions to the development of photoengraving: (1) the creation of a printing surface by the aid of photography; and (2) the production of printing plates by etching a photographic image on metal in the form of an acid resist.

A number of experimenters working in France brought us closer to photoengraving, but the next real advance was made by Fermin Gillot about 1850, when he patented a process for photoetching on zinc, in which the metal was sensitized by asphaltum, a principle Gillot had borrowed from Niépce. Etching is the process of using strong acid to cut into the unprotected parts of a metal surface to create a design in intaglio in the metal. The process that Gillot invented was later named "gillotage" in his honor. One of the first specimens of his process was a relief zinc etching of a line-engraved portrait of Johannes Gutenberg, which Gillot had drawn on lithographic stone. An impression of this litho drawing was transferred to a zinc plate, the transfer then rolled up with a lithographic ink and powdered with colophony [rosin] to give greater acid resistance to the design, after which the plate was etched in a bath of nitric acid. To give greater depth to the lines, they were again rolled up with litho ink, colophony powder added, and washed again with nitric acid. This process was sometimes repeated six to nine times. This was the true gillotage procedure, sometimes called the "French Etching Process." This became the first commercially successful photoengraving method, although it had a strong competitor in the Talbot method (described below). The etching of Gutenberg first appeared in a French photographic journal, *La Lumière*, in the issue of April 1, 1854, and lead to the introduction of relief etching on zinc plates in several European countries.

Gillot went on to form a company about 1864 that introduced photolithographic transfers on zinc for etching. His son, Charles Gillot, employed the dichromate albumen process in 1872 (invented in 1855 by Alphonse Poitevin) known as "ink top" on zinc plates with photographic negatives of the drawings to make direct photomechanical images intended for zinc etchings. The inked prints, after development, were dusted ("topped") with resin before etching.

Frederick Scott Archer certainly deserves recognition in this review for his invention of the Wet Collodion Process, which became the dominant photographic process between 1851 and 1880 and was one of the most important steps in the development of modern photoengraving. Just a decade ago, we celebrated the 150th anniversary of the first publication of his process in the March 1851 issue of *The Chemist*. Even so, few people know of his contributions.

Much of his early life is undocumented, but after his death, his wife, Fanny Archer, provided a few details. He was born in England in 1813. His parents died while he was still a child, and he was brought up by distant relatives and apprenticed to a bullion dealer and silversmith in London. There, he was constantly exposed to antique gems and coins from many different countries. He was an appraiser of coins for a time, which lead to his study of numismatics, and from that to sculpture. His friends helped him set up a studio in London where he sculpted the busts of many well-known people, including the Marquis of Northampton, William Smith of the National Portrait Gallery, and Lord Albert Conynghan.

A calotype of a Newhaven fisherboy.

To help him with his portrait sculpturing, Archer began to take photographs of his subjects. At that time, there were only two photographic processes, the daguerreotype and the calotype. The daguerreotype gave a superior picture but could not be reproduced. The calotype could be reproduced but suffered from the fact that it showed imperfections in the paper and often gave a print with uneven texture. Archer learned the calotype process but was unhappy with the results and tried to find a process that would combine the best of both daguerreotypes and calotypes. In the calotype process, light sensitive materials were coated onto glass plates by using albumen (egg whites) as a binder. Archer tried a number of substitutes without much success. Finally, in 1849 he made a breakthrough when he tried coating a glass plate with a solution of iodine in collodion and using the plate while it was still wet.

Collodion is a clear, viscous liquid obtained by dissolving nitrocellulose in ether and alcohol. Nitrocellulose (guncotton) is made by exposing cotton (cellulose) to any strong nitrating substance, such as nitric acid or ammonia. If the cotton is only partially nitrated, it is called "pyrocellulose" and is a favorite of beginning chemistry students who like to nitrate cotton balls in a beaker, dry them, and then ignite them one at a time in the palm of their hands. The cotton burns so quickly that one never feels much heat. However, if cotton is completely nitrated, it becomes a low-order explosive, and it was often used as a propellant in large naval canons.[9] In the form of collodion, it was used during the Crimean War (1854) because it dries quickly and forms a thin, clear film that serves well as a dressing to protect wounds.

A photomechanical print of Lake Como, Italy.

Archer made other discoveries that aided the development of photoengraving. In 1850 he published an article in *The Chemist* concerning the advantages of pyrogallic acid as a more powerful developer than gallic acid in photography. The main advantage of the Wet Collodion Process was that it afforded a photographic surface exceedingly well-adapted for line images. Daguerreotypes with their non-reproducible prints did not scare the bank-note industry. Calotypes were a different story, and the bank-note engravers knew it was only a matter of time before the industry would be seeing counterfeits made by photography. Crude photographic counterfeits showed up in the 1850s, but they were of poor quality, especially because of their false color. The Wet Collodion Process that Archer invented increased the threat dramatically and was the prime mover behind the efforts to find "non-photographic inks" for bank notes, such as the Patent Green Tint.

Like Archer, William Henry Fox Talbot was a man of many interests and talents. His interest in photography began in 1833 when he was sketching on the shores of Lake Como (Italy), and his ideas were put into action a year later when he made contact prints of leaves, lace, and other flat objects using paper that had been sensitized to light with silver chloride. As early as 1835, he made camera exposures on sensitized paper, four years before the introduction of the daguerreotype.

Talbot lost interest in photography for a short time, but when the daguerreotype was introduced, it re-kindled his interest, and he set to work on his own process. In 1841 he introduced his calotype process, in which paper sensitized with silver iodide was used both for camera exposures and to make positive prints from the negatives. This was a direct link between the daguerreotype and the Wet Collodion Process. Calotypes could be made for about one-tenth the cost of daguerreotype, helping to make photography affordable to the common man.

Talbot's principal contribution to photoengraving was his practical application of Antoine Becquerel's discovery in 1840 that dichromate gelatin becomes insoluble under the influence of light. The process patented by Talbot on October 29, 1852, (British Patent No. 565) involved the sensitization of a steel plate with dichromate gelatin, which was exposed under a positive print and the image developed by washing with water. The plate was then etched with a solution of platinum chloride, the insoluble gelatin image serving as an acid resist. He called this process "photoglyptic engraving." *Knight's American Mechanical Dictionary* (1881) gives this description of Talbot's process:

> A solution of 1 part gelatine to 40 parts water is mixed with 4 parts of a saturated solution of bichromate of potash. The mixture is floated over a plate, giving an exceedingly thin film, and allowed to dry in the dark. Being exposed in connection with a print in a frame to sunlight, its surface is strewed with finely powdered copal, which is melted by the aid of heat. The plate is then etched by a solution of the perchloride of platinum or perchloride of iron, which attacks only the parts unacted on by the light. When a sufficient depth is attained, the etching liquid and the ground are washed off, and the plate, after cleaning, is employed for printing.

Talbot tried to obtain even more-delicate detail by inserting two or more folds of black gauze between the positive print and the sensitized metal plate during the time of exposure. Actually, this use of a screen was an early attempt at making a halftone print. A halftone screen breaks the light rays so a plate is sensitized in a dotted pattern. The human eye, when viewing a dotted pattern at a distance, cannot resolve the individual dots of ink and is tricked into seeing the image as a continuous tonal picture in various shades of gray or black. This phenomenon was well known to artists familiar with pointillism, like Seurat. Talbot's experiments with the halftone process did not work well, but other scientists, principally Frederic Ives, developed it further and made it practical in 1878. Ives then invented the first crossline halftone process in 1885, which was improved and made a commercial success by Max and Louis Levy in 1895.[10]

After Talbot's invention of his "photoglyptic" engraving, which produced an intaglio plate suitable for reproducing line engravings, a number of people made contributions to photoengraving, but mainly in the development of halftone plates rather than line-engraved plates. No counterfeit notes were made by the halftone process during the 19th century, but counterfeiters became interested in photomechanical processes during the 1870s and began making plates by the Talbot process during that time. By the 1890s, photoengraving was sufficiently advanced that it was used by Baldwin Bredell and Arthur Taylor to make the plates for printing counterfeit $100 Silver Certificates of the series of 1891. The notes looked and felt authentic, causing the secretary of the Treasury, on the advice of experts from the

Bureau of Engraving and Printing, to call in all the $100 notes of that issue—$26 million. From the turn of the century onward, counterfeiting was done by camera. The development of the three-color process for making realistic color pictures from half-tone negatives, beginning in 1895, led the way for future counterfeiters.

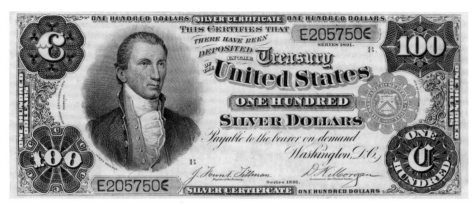

The $100 Silver Certificate, series 1891.

Secretary of the Treasury
Charles Foster,
1891–1893.

William Henry Fox Talbot.

Epilogue

(A Greek word that means the author gets to say things he may later regret.)

Counterfeiting

During the three centuries of "American" paper money covered in this book, there were many factors that influenced the design and technical protection of our currency. For the most part, changes in American currency have been a response to counterfeiting, and there has been a constant struggle between science and fraud.

Neither art nor technology had much effect on counterfeiting. It was said that engraving a note "in the highest order of the art" would solve the problem, but then engravers began to counterfeit. The geometric lathe was supposed to engrave designs so intricate and precise that no counterfeiter could possibly imitate them. But Henry Fox Talbot solved that problem with a lens and gelatin. The Patent Green Tint promised protection against photographic counterfeiting, but Frederic Eugene Ives developed panchromatic film. Distinctive paper was hailed as an answer to bogus notes, but amateur chemists learned how to bleach the ink off paper. Colored planchettes were put inside the paper, but equally clever men learned how to make their own bank-note paper, planchettes included. History shows an endless series of advances and reversals in the fight against fraud, and one is compelled to believe that human nature will produce counterfeiters till the end of humanity.

Did counterfeiting really matter? John Peter McCartney worked for years as a prolific counterfeiter, but he was never worth a million dollars at any one time. The same with Frederick Biebusch, with Brockway, Boyd, Ballard, and the whole Johnson family. Compared to the millions stolen by the robber barons of Wall Street, or the captains of industry who conspired to pay low wages and charge high prices, or the bankers who made usury a common word, or the tax cheats like the "Whiskey Ring," the money made by counterfeiters was never really significant. It was, to be certain, immoral and dishonest, and if left unchecked had the potential to undermine the confidence of the people in their paper money, but it never threatened our economy. In fact, the argument could be made that counterfeiting helped local economies by infusing money into businesses. People who have PhDs in economics can argue this point *ad infinitum* at cocktail parties anywhere in the world,

taking one side or the other, so the matter remains unsolved, as all good arguments must be.

Were our laws severe enough to suppress counterfeiting? The legal records of both England and Ireland show that people were hanged right and left and many others transported to Australia for engraving, printing, or even passing counterfeit notes. Yet counterfeiting grew steadily worse under the draconian punishment of English law. America, by contrast, hanged only a handful of men for counterfeiting. But this compares "apples to oranges" because our countries took different historical paths and developed different social norms and religious beliefs. The *desideratum* has always been to make the punishment fit the crime, and the Americans seem to have done a better job at this than the English. Counterfeiting, after all, is a property crime and did not justify a death sentence, especially in colonial court rooms where the standards of evidence were often primitive.

The End is Coming!

Whatever happened to bank notes engraved "in the highest order of the art?" They were killed by accountants with sharp pencils. The ones who said it would save money if notes were made in smaller sizes. The ones who said it would save money if portraits of dead presidents were used instead of all the fancy art. The ones who said it would save money if machines replaced real people. And the ones who said "all black is black," so let's save money by buying the cheaper black ink. And gradually the once-famous American bank-note industry was changed so it could print notes faster and cheaper. The accountants did not compromise. When that rational is carried to its logical end, paper money will be replaced by electronic-data–transfer cards, and finally even these will vanish, and all purchases and transactions will be done by machines that read finger prints or the pattern of retinal blood vessels. *Sic transit gloria mundi.*

It has been said that a country's bank notes are its "calling cards." A well-engraved note with an interesting design says something about the artistic taste of the country and the sophistication and cultural level of its people. Utilitarian notes, on the other hand, not only disappoint the discriminating public but also imply an intellectual dullness. Compare the notes of the European Union ("Euros") with the multicolored notes they replaced in France. The old notes of France celebrated the intellectual history of the country with vignettes of its scientists and philosophers. The national pride of France was apparent on its old notes, an unmistakable *esprit de corps*. The new Euros fail to inspire anyone in Europe. Their pictures hide from culture, history, philosophy, or even the human form. They celebrate the ordinary.

Many people are concerned that security and economy now dictate the design of bank notes and see that as a necessary evil inherited from two centuries of counterfeiting. Art and national symbolism are relegated to a much lower priority. The immediate challenge to bank-note designers and Treasury Departments is to find a compromise between these two very different criteria and make notes that are both practical and spirited. It will not be easy.

In the longer view, paper money is probably doomed, no matter how intricate the design, how technical the art. Monetary transactions in some distant future will probably be electronic, so Big Brother or a HAL 9000 can reduce lives to numbers. In the *reducio ad absurdum*, money may not exist at all. We may just say, "I want that," and Big Brother will figure out if we can have it.

But like the Roman *denarius* or the Greek *drachma*, which have long vanished from common use, paper money will undoubtedly live on in the private collections of future generations that appreciate not only the beauty of their notes but are intrigued as well by the story of the constant struggle between the engraver and the counterfeiter to produce those notes.

I hope this book will serve in some small way as an introduction to that struggle.

Appendix A

Memorial of Jacob Perkins on his Invention of
A Stereotype Steel Plate for Impressing Bank Notes 1806

To the Honorable The Senate and House of Representatives of the Commonwealth of Massachusetts in General Court assembled—

The Memorial of Jacob Perkins of Newburyport in the County of Essex Gentleman respectfully shewth—

That your memorialist has invented and made a Stereotype Plate of Steel for impressing Bank Bills, by a new method and upon a new principle. He formerly invented a method of impressing such bills upon the like principle, with distinct copper plates, for each different Bank, for which, he obtained a Patent under the seal of the United States. He has since improved that method, by making the said steel plate, which can be fixed with separate [sic] dies, also made of steel, for all the different denominations of bills and suited to the different styles of Banks; so that all the bills impressed with his plate, for whatever bank, will, in all the material parts, check and perfectly compare with each other. He has also secured to himself and his assigns the exclusive right of using this improvement, according to the laws of the United States.

Your memorialist has expended at least eight hundred days work of himself and his workmen, in making and perfecting his said steel plate, and was proceeding to avail himself of the fruits of his labour, by contracting with different banks for the use thereof, when he was much flattered to hear that the Legislature of the Commonwealth had, unsolicited by him, taken the subject into their wise consideration, and were contemplating to introduce this improvement into general use. He has understood the mode proposed for this purpose, by the bill now pending in the Honorable Court, and is willing to deliver up his said steel plate, with the necessary dies on or before the first day of July next, to the Treasurer of the Commonwealth for the purpose expressed in said bill.

This plate was intended and is equally well calculated for banks of other states, with the alteration only of a small part of the margin, but your memorialist understanding, that it is desired to have the bills of all banks in this State to differ in their shape and appearance from those of other States, will also agree, in case the said bill passes into a Law, not to use said plate for any Banks out of the State, but to make a new plate for those banks, which shall differ in its form and appearance from that now made, so that the bilvls of all Banks in this State can be readily and certainly distinguished from those of all others.

The plate is made of case-hardened steel, so that it can be used as much as may be necessary for fifty years, without any sensible change or deterioration. Your memorialist is also willing, in case such a law should be made, to print and impress all the bills required to be made in virtue thereof, at least as they can be properly executed on the reasonable demand of the banks in this State. He will perform all the above services on terms similar to those for which he has therebefore agreed with sundry banks, with the addition of a reasonable compensation for his said plate, which follow, Viz. 1st. He shall receive from each bank in full for printing and impressing their bills, at the rate of four dollars, for every hundred impressions or half sheets to be paid when the bills are delivered. 2nd. He shall receive from each bank, at the same time, the sum of forty dollars in full, for his said plate to indemnify him for the expenses and labour of making a new plate, which cannot be less than one thousand dollars. 3rd. In addition to the above compensation for his labour and expense, he shall receive for the use of his patent-right, by every bank whose Capital Stock actually paid in does not exceed one hundred thousand dollars, the sum of fifty dollars annually; by every bank whose Capital Stock so paid in is above one hundred thousand dollars and not exceeding the sum of two hundred thousand dollars, the sum of seventy dollars annually; and by every bank whose Capital Stock so paid in exceeds two hundred thousand dollars, the sum of ninety dollars annually. Those annual payments to commence . . . And the first payment to be made by each bank, in one year from the time when he begins to impress their respective bills, and to be continued by each bank until he or his assigns cease to have the exclusive right of using his said improvement. And if the Proprietors of any bank after their bills are so impressed by him, shall pay in more of their capital stock, so as to make the amount thereof fall into a higher class, according to the above distribution, such bank shall immediately thereafter pay the annual sum above fixed for such higher class. These annual payments to be properly and satisfactorily secured to the said Perkins, his executors, administrators and assigns, by each bank at the time of receiving their respective impressions.

Your memorialist presumes, that the paper, which is directed by the said bill to be furnished by the Treasurer will be provided at the expense of the Commonwealth, the cost to be repaid by the several banks, as they respectively call for the same. But if this should be thought improper or inexpedient, your memorialist is willing to advance the price thereof, if it should be necessary, according to the contracts therefore made by the Treasurer, the cost to be repaid to him, by each Bank as they respectively call for and use the same.

February 28th, 1806

Jacob Perkins

Appendix B
Jacob Perkins and the Massachusetts Act of 1809

Commonwealth of Massachusetts

In the Year of our Lord One Thousand Eight Hundred and Nine.

An Act requiring the several incorporated banks in this Commonwealth to adopt the Stereotype Steel Plate in certain cases; and for other purposes.

Whereas Jacob Perkins, of Newburyport, in the county of Essex, hath invented and completed certain Stereotype Steel Plates for the printing of bank bills, and hath obtained from the President of the United States a patent for the exclusive use of the same; and whereas the said Jacob Perkins hath given a bond with sureties in the penal sum of ten thousand dollars, to this Commonwealth, conditioned among other things, to print and impress with the said Plates, Bank Bills of the denomination of Two, Three, Four and Five Dollars, for the use of the several incorporated Banks in this Commonwealth, and to furnish Bank paper for the same of the best quality, upon the terms which are specified and contained in the said bond; and whereas the public good requires that the Bills of the several denominations aforesaid should be printed and impressed from the said Plates, in order to produce a uniformity in, and prevent the counterfeiting of the same:

Sect. 1. Be it enacted by the Senate and the House of Representatives in General Court assembled, and by the authority of the same, That from and after the first day of July next, no Bills of the denomination of Two, Three, Four, and Five Dollars, shall be issued or emitted by the President, Directors and Company of any Bank incorporated under the authority of the Legislature of this Commonwealth, unless the said Bills shall be printed and impressed from Stereotype Steel Plates; from which Plates original impressions of the Bills of the several denominations aforesaid are deposited in the office of the Secretary of this Commonwealth; nor unless the said Bills of the denomination of Five Dollars shall have on the back of the same, an impression from the Check Plates, one of the impressions from which is also deposited in the office of said Secretary of said Commonwealth.

Sect. 2. And be it further enacted, That the several incorporated Banks within this Commonwealth, which have heretofore issued their Bills in the names of the President and Directors of said Banks, shall, from and after the said first day of July next, issue all their Bills of the several denominations aforesaid, in the names of the President, Directors and Company of the said Banks; any thing in the respective Acts of incorporation of said Banks to the contrary notwithstanding.

Sect. 3. And be it further enacted, That from and after the said first day of July next, and during the pleasure of the Legislature after that time, the President, Directors and Company of all the Banks aforesaid, be, and the same hereby are authorized and empowered, to issue and emit Bills of the denomination of Two, Three, and Four Dollars, to the amount of fifteen per centum of their several capital stocks actually paid in; any thing in their respective Acts of incorporation, or any thing in an Act entitled "An Act to authorize the several Banks incorporated within this Commonwealth, to issue Bills of the denomination of One, Two, and Three Dollars," made and passed on the fifteenth day of June, in the year of our Lord one thousand eight hundred and five, to the contrary notwithstanding.

Sect. 4. And be it further enacted, That from and after the said first day of July next, no person shall pay, or receive in discharge of any contract or bargain, or for any valuable consideration whatever, any Bill or Bills issued by any Bank or Banking Company other than the Bank of the United States, or the several incorporated Banks in this Commonwealth, of any less denomination than Five Dollars, under a penalty of Twenty Dollars; to be recovered of the person so paying the same by action of debt, with cost of suit; or by indictment by the Grand Jury, in the Supreme Judicial Court, Court of Common Pleas, or the Municipal Court in the town of Boston, to the use of the person or persons who shall within one year thereafter sue or prosecute for the same; in which suit or prosecution the person who shall receive the same Bill or Bills may be admitted as a competent witness. And the Bill or Bills which shall be paid as aforesaid shall be forfeited to the use of the person or persons who shall sue or prosecute as aforesaid.

Sect. 5. And be it further enacted, That an Act entitled "An Act to prevent the circulation and currency of Bank Bills of a denomination less than Five Dollars," made and passed on the eighth day of March, in the year of our Lord one thousand eight hundred and two, be, and the same is hereby repealed.

Appendix C

The Prevention of Forgery Communicated to the
Society for the Encouragement of Arts, Manufactures & Commerce in 1819

By Perkins, Fairman and Heath

Sir:

The Society for the Encouragement of Arts, Manufactures, and Commerce having devoted so much of their valuable time to investigating the different methods proposed for the prevention of the forgery of Bank notes, we, the proprietors of the Siderographic art, believe that a full account of our plan (which has been in successful operation many years in America, and is now adopted by many banks in this country) will not be thought unworthy of their attention.

We will, in the first place state what we consider to be the grand basis of security in this plan, and secondly, the means of executing it. Although it is certainly not a new idea, that the greatest security which could possibly be afforded in preventing forgery would be that of employing a combination of the talents of the first-rate artists in fabricating a bank note plate and of having the notes always identically the same; yet we conceive the following plan to effect this object is entirely new. It is the power of reproducing and multiplying the works of the greatest artists, which constitute the strength of this system; it is the basis on which we build our hopes. The method of multiplying engravings is as follows:

A steel plate (the method of preparing which will be hereafter described), is engraved or etched in the usual way; it is then hardened. A cylinder of very soft steel, of from 2 to 3 inches in diameter, is made to roll backwards and forwards on the surface of the steel plate, until the whole of the impression from the engraving is seen on the cylinder in alto-relievo; after this cylinder has been hardened, it is made to roll backwards and forwards on a copper or soft steel plate, and a perfect facsimile of the original is produced of equal sharpness. The following calculations will show to what extent this system of preventing forgery may be carried.

Suppose 20 of the best historical and other engravers were employed, each to engrave a vignette; each vignette to occupy four square inches, and each artists to expend 6 months on his vignette; let those 20 vignettes be transferred to two steel plates, one for the front of the note, and the other for the back; the result will be, that one man (could such a one be found) would be occupied 10 years, or 20 men 6 months, to produce a note of equal goodness. Is it possible to suppose any thing better can be adopted, than to make it unprofitable to be engaged in such business? If a bank note plate can be made to cost 10,000£ (which would be the case, if 20 artists, whose time would be worth 1,000£ per annum, were engaged 6 months each), would it not be much less

likely to be initiated than one that would cost but 5 or 10£? If a bank plate can be made to contain the work of 20 of the best artists in the world, could another plate of equal goodness be made without employing the same artists? It is hardly to be presumed that 20 such artists would be engaged in making a spurious note; but admitting it possible, it would not be a facsimile, and might be easily distinguished from the true note, by anyone acquainted with the original. One of the peculiar features of the invention is, that any one may be furnished with a perfect facsimile of the whole or of any part of the original note; which will serve to identify the note is good: this is owing to the infinite number of impressions that may be obtained from the original engraving. Having shown that a plate may be made to cost 10,000£, we will undertake to prove that it is not incompatible with economy. To show the economy of this plan in its best light, we must be allowed to apply it to the best advantage, which would be by its being adopted by a bank whose daily consumption is not less than 25,000 notes.

Suppose the first steel plate costs 10,000£, the next 999 plates will only cost 10,000£: then 1,000 steel plates will amount to 20,000£. Each steel plate will print at least 150,000 impressions; of course 1,000 plates would furnish 150,000,000 of impressions, which is the number that would be wanted in 20 years, at 25,000 impressions per day. Now, the cost of impressions from steel plates would be (where the above number is wanted) one penny for 31-1/4 impressions; whereas, if copper plates were used, which cost only 3£ each plate, the number of impressions for a penny would be but 8, since a copper plate prints but 6,000 impressions before it is worn out.

Another very important consideration is, that steel plates admit of an improved method of printing, and when worked to the greatest advantage, will make a saving of 50 per cent; this saving, in 20 years, in printing the above number of notes would be 75,000£, which would not only pay the whole cost of making the plates, but leave a balance of 55,000£.

This system of making plates and of printing, will apply equally well to that of ornamenting standard works, particularly Bibles, prayer books, primers, catechisms, spelling books, natural history, and philosophy. In proportion to the number wanted, will be the advantage of adopting this plan. It is often the case in this country, that from 4 to 6 copper plates are worn out in one edition, and not half the impressions perfect. A hardened steel plate will print more proof impressions than the above number of copper plates can furnish, even of common impressions. This fact is demonstrated by the plates Nos. XXXIX and XL, accompanying this communication. The impressions from plate No. XXXIX, are of the first impressions taken from the plate. The impressions, plate No. XL, were taken after 35,000 impressions had been taken from it.

This plate will also show the practicability of identity. The four medallions by inspection will be found to be perfectly the same, line for line and dot for dot. By examining the machine engraving, particularly the chain, the two styles of work, viz. copper plate and letter-press printing will be seen beautifully combined. This is effected by the process of transferring and re-transferring. This kind of engraving is extremely difficult to imitate. This machine, which is denominated the geometrical lathe, was invented in America by Mr. Asa Spencer. Its powers for producing variety are equaled only by the kaleidoscope; but for beautiful patterns it surpasses every thing of the kind. It has one of the peculiarities of the kaleidoscope, viz. that the turning of a screw, like the turning of the kaleidoscope, produces an entire new pattern, which was never before seen, and perhaps would never be seen again. This pattern however may be perpetuated by the transferring process. We are now printing from a plate of the most delicate work, which has already printed above 100,000 impressions, and is yet sound. We cannot yet say, how long a hardened steel plate will last, having never printed more than 500,000 impressions from the same plate: it should however, be observed, that this plate consisted principally of writing, or work quite as strong. It may also be observed, that the impressions are yet good. The manufacture of printed calicoes, ribbons, etc., as well as of earthenware, may be much improved by adopting this system; and we are happy to say that experiments are soon to be made thereof. This improvement in engraving will apply to about one quarter of the present number of plates used. The others must necessarily be of copper, as a sufficient number of impressions would not be wanted to defray the expense of a steel plate. Not less than a number of impressions which would wear out three copper plates would warrant the making a steel plate. But such is the number of subjects to which this art will apply, and the great inducement to publishers to embellish their works, where large editions are wanted, which they now can do in consequence of its economy, that instead of the demand of engravers being lessened, it will be very much enhanced.

The use of fine and delicate engraving for Bank notes, has been objected to, in consequence of the difficulty of printing on such highly sized paper. But this objection is entirely got over by our method of printing in the water leaf, and sizing after printing. This improvement has a triple advantage, that of producing beautiful impressions, having on its surface, after printing, a better size, and preventing the ink from being so easily transferred.

In order to describe the method of preparing and hardening the steel plate and dies, the following particulars are necessary:

In order to decarbonate the surfaces of cast steel plates, cylinders, or dies, by which they are rendered much softer and fitter for receiving either transferred or engraved designs, we use pure iron filings, divested of all foreign or extraneous matters . . . The stratum of decarbonated steel should not be too thick for transferring fine and delicate engravings; for instance, not more than three times the depth of the engraving: but for other purposes the surface of the steel may be decarbonated to any required thickness.

To decarbonate it to a proper thickness for fine engravings, it is to be exposed for four hours in a white heat, enclosed in a cast iron box, with a well closed lid. The sides of the cast iron box are made at least three quarters of an inch in thickness; and at least a thickness of half an inch of pure iron filings should cover or surround the cast steel surface to be decarbonated. The box is to be suffered to cool very slowly, which may be effected by shutting off all access of air to the furnace, and covering it with a layer six or seven inches in thickness, of fine cinders. Each side of the steel plate, cylinder, or die, must be equally decarbonated, to prevent it from springing or warping in hardening. It is also found that the safest way to heat the plates, cylinders, or dies, is by placing them in a vertical position.

The best cast steel is preferred to any other sort of steel for the purpose of making plates, cylinders, circular or other dies; and more especially, when such plates, cylinders, or dies are intended to be decarbonated. For the reason given above, the steel is decarbonated, solely for the purpose of rendering it sufficiently soft for receiving any impression intended to be made thereon; it is therefore necessary that, after any piece of steel has been so decarbonated, whether it be in the shape of a plate, or a cylinder, or a die, it should, previously to being printed from, be again carbonated, or re-converted into steel capable of being hardened. In order, therefore, to effect this carbonization, or re-conversion into steel, the following process is employed:—a suitable quantity of leather is to be converted into charcoal by the well-known method of exposing it to a red heat in an iron retort, for a sufficient length of time; or, until most of the evaporable matter is driven off the leather. Having thus prepared the charcoal, it is reduced to a very fine powder; then take a box made of cast iron, of sufficient dimensions to receive the plate, cylinder, or die, which is to be re-converted into steel, so as that the intermediate space between the sides of the said box, and the plate, cylinder, or die, may be about one inch. This box is to be filled with the powdered charcoal, and having covered it with a well fitting lid, let it be placed in a furnace similar to those used for melting brass, when the heat must be gradually increased until the box is somewhat above a red heat; it must be suffered to remain in that state till all the evaporable matter is driven off from the charcoal. Then, remove the lid from the box, and immerse the plate, cylinder, or die, into the powdered charcoal; taking care to place it as nearly in the middle as possible, so that it may be surrounded on all sides by a stratum of the powder, or nearly an uniform thickness. The lid being replaced, the box, with the plate, cylinder, or die, must remain in the degree of heat before described, for from three to five hours, according to the thickness of the plate, cylinder, or die so exposed. Three hours are sufficient for a plate of half an inch in thickness; and five hours when the steel is one inch and a half in thickness. After the plate, cylinder, or die has been thus exposed to the fire for a sufficient length of time, take it from the box and immediately plunge it into cold water. It is important here to observe, that it is found by experience that the plates or other pieces of steel when plunged into cold water, are least liable to be warped or bent when they are held in a vertical position, or made to enter the water in the direction of their length. If a piece of steel, heated to a proper degree for hardening, be plunged into water, and suffered to remain there until it becomes cold, it is found by experience to be very liable to crack or break; and, in many cases, it would be found too hard for the operation it was intended to perform. If the steel cracks or breaks, it is spoiled. In order to render it fit for use, should it happen, not to be broken in the hardening, it is the common practice to heat the steel again, in order to reduce or lower its temper, as it is technically called. The degree of heat to which it is now exposed determines the future degree of hardness, or the temper, and this is indicated by a change of color upon the surface of the steel. During this heating a succession of shades is produced from a very pale straw color to a deep blue. It is found, however, by long experience, that on plunging the heated steel into cold water, and suffering it to remain there no longer than is sufficient for lowering the temperature of the steel to the same degree as that to which a hard piece of steel must have been raised, in order to temper it in the common way; it not only produces the same degree of hardness in the steel, but, what is of much more importance, almost entirely does away the risk or liability of its cracking or breaking. It is impossible to communicate by words, or to describe the criterion by which we can judge of, or determine, when the steel has arrived at the proper degree of temperature, after being plunged into cold water; it can only be learned by actual observation, as the workman must be guided entirely by the kind of hissing or singing noise,

which the heated steel produces in the water while cooling. From the moment of its being first plunged into the water, a varying sound will be observed; and it is at a certain tone before the noise ceases, that the effect to be produced is known. The only direction which can be given, whereby the experimentalist can be benefited, are as follow: namely, to take a piece of steel which has already been hardened by remaining in the water till cold; and, by the common method of again heating it, to let it be brought to the pale yellow, or straw color, which indicates the desired temper of the steel plate to be hardened by the above process; as soon as he discovers this color to be produced, to dip the steel into water and attend carefully to the hissing, or, as some call it, singing noise, which it occasions; he will then be better able, and with fewer experiments, to judge of the precise time at which the steel should be taken out. It is not meant to be understood that the temper indicated by a straw color, is that to which the steel plate, cylinder, or die, should be ultimately reduced; because it would then be found too hard; but merely that the temperature which would produce that color, is that by which the peculiar sound would be occasioned when the steel should be withdrawn from the water for the first time. Immediately on withdrawing it from the water, the steel plate, cylinder, or die, must be laid upon, or held over a fire, and heated uniformly, until its temperature is raised to that degree at which tallow would be decomposed; or, in other words, until smoke is perceived to rise from the surface of the steel plate, cylinder, or die, after having been rubbed with tallow. The steel plate, cylinder, or die, must be again plunged into water, and kept there until the sound becomes somewhat weaker than before. It is then to be taken out, and heated a second time to the same degree, by the same rule of smoking tallow as before; and the third time plunged into water, till the sound becomes again weaker than the last. Expose it a third time to the fire as before; and, for the last time, return it into the water and cool it; after it is cooled, clean the surface of the steel plate, cylinder, or die; and, by heating it over the fire, the temper must be finally reduced by bringing on a brown, or such other lighter or darker shade of color, as may best suit the quality of the steel, or the purpose to which it is to be applied.

(This letter was published in the Society's Journal, *volume 38, 1820, in the section called the Polite Arts.)*

Appendix D
Final Report of the Commissioners Appointed for
Inquiring Into the Mode of Preventing the Forgery of Bank Notes

(Taken from the London Times, *February 22, 1820, page 3, column 3.)*

To His Majesty, George the Fourth, King of the United Kingdom of Great Britain and Ireland. Since we had the honour of explaining to your Majesty the course of our proceedings, a longer interval has elapsed than we had anticipated as likely to occur. This has arisen partly from our wish to have some experiments tried, with a view to the improvement of that plan, which we then stated ourselves to have selected, and partly from our anxiety to give the fullest and most deliberate consideration to another plan, of great ingenuity, and exhibiting specimens of beautiful work, which had formerly been suggested to use, and the particulars of which have upon several occasions, and within a recent period, been laid before us: this plan, however, after much consideration, we do not find to possess such merit as would make it proper for us to recommend its adoption, in preference to that which we had first selected.

With respect to the paper, we are of opinion that it will not be advisable to make an alteration in that which is now used by the Bank.

Upon the whole, we have ventured to recommend for adoption by the Bank the plan brought forward by Messrs. Applegath and Cowper, which was originally submitted to the Directors a short time only before the appointment of this Commission, and received immediate encouragement from them; and upon which some improvements have since been made. The Directors have readily complied with this recommendation, and the necessary machines are in a state of great forwardness.

We humbly conceive that your Majesty, for obvious reasons, would not wish us to enter upon any detailed explanation of the particulars of this plan. The objects which we have kept in view, in making the selection upon which we have determined, have been to enable the Bank to ensure to the public a regular supply of their notes in sufficient quantity to meet the daily demand, and to have those notes executed in such a manner, as shall render them fit for general circulation amongst all classes of society, whilst at the same time very considerable obstacles are opposed in the art of any person who might be disposed to engage in forging them. And we humbly submit to your Majesty our opinion that those objects will be attained by the adoption of the note formed by the machines submitted to our view by Messrs. Applegath and Cowper.

We cannot but be aware, that no form of a note can possibly be contrived that may not be successfully imitated by some artist of superior talents; we hope, however, and we believe, that no man capable of forging the note which we recommend can be in such distressed circumstances as to feel any inclination to place himself in danger of the ignominious punishment which awaits a crime so hurtful to public credit and to the community at large.

All which is humbly submitted to your Majesty's consideration and judgment.

Jos. Banks   Wm. H. Wollaston

Jer. Harman   Wm. Courtenay

Wm. Congreve   Charles Hatchett

Davies Gilbert

Appendix E
Directors of the Bureau of Engraving and Printing from 1862 to 1921

Name	Title	Date of Appointment
Spencer M. Clark	Chief	August 22, 1862
George B. McCartee	Chief	March 18, 1869
Henry C. Jewell	Chief	February 21, 1876
Edward McPherson	Chief	May 1, 1877
O.H. Irish	Chief	October 1, 1878
Thomas J. Sullivan	Acting Chief	January 28, 1883
Truman N. Burrill	Chief	April 1, 1883
Edward O. Graves	Acting Chief	May 20, 1885
Edward O. Graves	Chief	June 1, 1885
William M. Meredith	Chief	July 1, 1889
Claude M. Johnson	Chief	July 1, 1893
Claude M. Johnson	Director	July 1, 1896
Thomas J. Sullivan	Acting Director	May 11, 1900
William M. Meredith	Director	November 24, 1900
Thomas J. Sullivan	Director	July 1, 1906
Joseph E. Ralph	Director	May 11, 1908
Frank E. Ferguson	Acting Director	October 15, 1917
James L. Wilmeth	Director	December 10, 1917

Appendix F
Superintendents of the Engraving Division at the Bureau of Engraving and Printing

No.	Name	Title	Term of Office
1.	John A. O'Neill	Supt.	April 28, 1885 to December 15, 1889
2.	George W. Casilear	Supt.	*See note*
3.	George W. Casilear	Supt.	December 13, 1889 to October 31, 1893
4.	Thomas F. Morris	Chief	November 1, 1893 to July 1, 1897
5.	John R. Hill	Chief	July 1, 1897 to February 14, 1913
6.	George W. Rose Jr.	Supt.	February 19, 1913 to March 31, 1922
7.	John T. Guilfoyle	Supt.	April 1, 1922 to July 15, 1924
8.	H. Preston Dawson	Supt.	July 16, 1924 to July 1, 1926
9.	Edward E. Myers	Supt.	July 1, 1926 to January 11, 1933
10.	Edward M. Weeks	Supt.	February 23, 1933 to December 16, 1935
11.	Joachim C. Benzing	Supt.	January 10, 1936 to August 1943

Note: George Washington Casilear was called to the National Currency Bureau on December 1, 1862. In December 1864, he was Custodian and served as Acting Superintendent of Engraving between 1869 and 1877. On December 13, 1889, he was appointed Superintendent of the Engraving Division at $4,000 a year. He held this position until he retired on October 30, 1893, at the age of 68 years. He then took a long vacation in the south of France.

Appendix G
Departmental Employee Numbers at the Bureau of Engraving and Printing, 1921

Department	Number
Director's Office	4
Assistant Director's Office	4
Chief Clerk's Office	60
Purchasing Agent	34
Superintendent Of Orders	10
Division Assignments & Reviews	18
Cost Accounting Office	10
Mechanical Expert & Designer	3
Experimental Engineer	2
Engineer of Tests	3
Custodian of Dies, Rolls, & Plates	8
Medical Office	8
Stock Room	1
Federal Reserve Vault	8
Superintendent of Work	2
Telephone Exchange	5
Guide Force	11
Watch Division	38
Disbursing Office	7
Engraving Division	253

Department	Number
Wetting Division	323
Printing Division	230
Numbering Division	507
Examining Division	1,328
Surface Division	429
Binding Division	179
Stamp Perforating Division	197
Stamp Gumming Division	67
Stamp Book & Coil Division	106
Stamp Packing	26
Vault Division	23
Engineering & Machine Division	492
Ink Making Division	30
Watch Division	77
Office Foreman, Building, & Cleaning	330
Garage	37
Apprentices to Plate Printers	15
Plate Printers	846
Printers' Assistants	1,638
Total	**7,369**

Appendix H
Secretaries of the Treasury 1789 to 1901

Secretary	Date Served	President
Alexander Hamilton[1]	September 11, 1789 to January 31, 1795	George Washington
Oliver Wolcott Jr.	February 3, 1795 to March 3, 1797	George Washington
	March 4, 1797 to December 31, 1800	John Adams
Samuel Dexter[2]	January 1, 1801 to March 3, 1801	John Adams
	March 4, 1801 to May 6, 1801	Thomas Jefferson
Albert Gallatin[3]	May 4, 1801 to March 3, 1809	Thomas Jefferson
	March 4, 1809 to February 9, 1814	James Madison
George W. Campbell	February 9, 1814 to September 26, 1814	James Madison
Alexander J. Dallas	October 6, 1814 to October 21, 1816	James Madison

chart continued on next page

Appendix H *continued*
Secretaries of the Treasury 1789 to 1901

Secretary	Date Served	President
William H. Crawford[4]	October 22, 1816 to March 3, 1817	James Madison
	March 4, 1817 to March 3, 1825	James Monroe
Richard Rush	March 7, 1825 to March 3, 1829	J.Q. Adams
Samuel D. Ingham	March 6, 1829 to June 20, 1831	Andrew Jackson
Louis McLane	August 8, 1831 to May 29, 1833	Andrew Jackson
William J. Duane	May 29, 1833 to September 23, 1833	Andrew Jackson
Roger B. Taney	September 23, 1833 to June 24, 1834	Andrew Jackson
Levi Woodbury	July 1, 1834 to March 3, 1837	Andrew Jackson
	March 4, 1837 to March 3, 1841	Martin Van Buren
Thomas Ewing	March 5, 1841 to April 4, 1841	W.H. Harrison
	April 5, 1841 to September 11, 1841	John Tyler
Walter Forward	September 13, 1841 to March 1, 1843	John Tyler
John C. Spencer	March 8, 1843 to May 2, 1844	John Tyler
George M. Bibb	July 4, 1844 to March 3, 1845	John Tyler
	March 4, 1845 to March 7, 1845	James K. Polk
Robert J. Walker[5]	March 8, 1845 to March 3, 1849	James K. Polk
	March 4, 1849 to March 5, 1849	Zachary Taylor
William M. Meredith[6]	March 8, 1849 to July 9, 1850	Zachary Taylor
	July 10, 1850 to July 22, 1850	Millard Fillmore
Thomas Corwin	July 23, 1850 to March 3, 1853	Millard Fillmore
	March 4, 1853 to March 6, 1853	Franklin Pierce
James Guthrie	March 7, 1853 to March 3, 1857	Franklin Pierce
	March 4, 1857 to March 6, 1857	James Buchanan
Howell Cobb[7]	March 7, 1857 to December 8, 1860	James Buchanan
Philip F. Thomas	December 12, 1860 to January 14, 1861	James Buchanan
John A. Dix	January 15, 1861 to March 3, 1861	James Buchanan
	March 4, 1861 to March 6, 1861	Abraham Lincoln
Salmon P. Chase[8]	March 7, 1861 to June 30, 1864	Abraham Lincoln
William P. Fessenden[9]	July 5, 1864 to March 3, 1865	Abraham Lincoln
Hugh McCulloch[10]	March 9, 1865 to April 15, 1865	Abraham Lincoln
	April 15, 1865 to March 3, 1869	Andrew Johnson
George S. Boutwell	March 12, 1869 to March 16, 1873	Ulysses S. Grant
William A. Richardson	March 17, 1873 to June 3, 1874	Ulysses S. Grant
Benjamin H. Bristow	June 4, 1874 to June 20, 1876	Ulysses S. Grant
Lot M. Morrill	July 7, 1876 to March 3, 1877	Ulysses S. Grant
	March 4, 1877 to March 9, 1877	Rutherford B. Hayes
John Sherman	March 10, 1877 to March 3, 1881	Rutherford B. Hayes

chart continued on next page

Appendix H *continued*
Secretaries of the Treasury 1789 to 1901

Secretary	Date Served	President
William Windom[11]	March 8, 1881 to September 19, 1881	James A. Garfield
	September 20, 1881 to November 13, 1881	Chester A. Arthur
Charles J. Folger	November 14, 1881 to September 4, 1884	Chester A. Arthur
Walter Q. Gresham	September 25, 1884 to October 30, 1884	Chester A. Arthur
Hugh McCulloch	October 31, 1884 to March 3, 1885	Chester A. Arthur
	March 4, 1885 to March 7, 1885	Grover Cleveland
Daniel Manning[12]	March 8, 1885 to March 31, 1887	Grover Cleveland
Charles S. Fairchild	April 1, 1887 to March 3, 1889	Grover Cleveland
	March 4, 1889 to March 6, 1889	Benjamin Harrison
William Windom	March 7, 1889 to January 29, 1891	Benjamin Harrison
Charles Foster	February 25, 1891 to March 3, 1893	Benjamin Harrison
	March 4, 1893 to March 6, 1893	Grover Cleveland
John G. Carlisle	March 7, 1893 to March 3, 1897	Grover Cleveland
	March 4, 1897 to March 5, 1897	William McKinley
Lyman J. Gage	March 6, 1897 to September 14, 1901	William McKinley

Appendix I
Comptrollers of the Currency

Name	Appointed	State
Hugh McCulloch	May 9, 1863	Indiana
Freeman Clark	March 21, 1864	New York
Hiland R. Hulburd	July 24, 1866	Ohio
John Jay Knox	April 24, 1872	Minnesota
Henry W. Cannon	May 12, 1884	Minnesota
William L. Trenholm	April 20, 1886	South Carolina
Edward S. Lacey	May 1, 1889	Michigan
A. Barton Hepburn	August 2, 1892	New York
James H. Eckels	April 26, 1893	Illinois
Charles G. Dawes	January 1, 1898	Ohio

Appendix J
Bank-Note and Security-Printing Patents from 1790 to Date

The U.S. Patent and Trademark Office burned to the ground on December 15, 1836. All of their records were in temporary storage while a more fire-proof building was being erected. The temporary storage was next to a fire station, but the weather was so cold that the firemen were unable to get the frozen pumps and hoses to work. All patents and trademarks issued from July 1790 until July 1836 were lost, estimated to be a total of about 9,957. The copies of patents kept by their inventors have been used to reconstruct about 2,800 originals. The following "unknown" patents have never been recovered. The abstracts are my own descriptions.

Patent No. Unknown. Bank Note Check Plate to prevent counterfeiting. Issued to Jacob Perkins. March 19, 1799.

Patent No. Unknown. Improvement in the art of engraving. Issued to J. Hutton and Gideon Fairman. January 8, 1802.

Patent No. Unknown. Pentagraph and parallel ruler. Issued to J.J. Hawkins. May 17, 1803.

Patent No. Unknown. Mode of preventing counterfeits. Issued to George Murray. February 13, 1810.

Patent No. Unknown. Mode of putting on the ink in copper-plate printing. Issued to Andrew Maverick. April 17, 1810.

Patent No. Unknown. Method of preventing counterfeits. Issued to Jacob Perkins. June 16, 1810.

Patent No. Unknown. Improvement on circular dies. Issued to Jacob Perkins and George Murray. June 25, 1813.

Patent No. Unknown. Printing press. Issued to Jacob Perkins. June 29, 1813.

Patent No. Unknown. Printing on the back of bank notes. Issued to John Kneas. April 28, 1815.

Patent No. Unknown. Graphic plates for bank notes. Issued to John Meer. July 1, 1815.

Patent No. Unknown. Etching the end pieces of bank notes. Issued to Henry S. Tanner. July 1, 1815.

Patent No. Unknown. To prevent forgery of bank notes. Issued to Abel Brewster. July 15, 1816.

Patent No. Unknown. Watermarking paper. Issued to Jacob Perkins. December 18, 1816.

Patent No. Unknown. Making paper. Issued to Thomas Gilpin. December 24, 1816.

Patent No. Unknown. Making bank notes. Issued to George Murray. March 23, 1822.

Patent No. Unknown. Making metallic plates for engraving. Issued to David H. Mason. May 17, 1822.

Patent No. Unknown. Mode of making bank notes. Issued to James P. Puglia. August 13, 1822.

Patent No. Unknown. Making paper for bank bills. Issued to Richard Willcox. September 19, 1823.

Patent No. Unknown. To prevent forgeries of bank notes. Issued to Nathaniel Sylvester. July 12, 1824.

Patent No. Unknown. Blanks for checks, drafts, bills of exchange, etc. Issued to T. Atwater and Nathaniel Jocelyn. June 11, 1827.

Patent No. Unknown. Blanks for checks, drafts, etc. Issued to James Atwater. August 18, 1827.

The following patents were issued after 1836.

Patent No. 320. "Mode of Printing and Drawing Checks to Prevent Counterfeit Alterations." Checks are printed with a safety bar to prevent alteration to the written amount. There is a four-part alphanumeric code specific to each depositor, and a master list of signatures kept at the bank which is arranged by the code numbers. One page of text, no drawings.
Issued to John Dainty of Philadelphia, Pennsylvania. July 31, 1837.

Patent No. 394. "Mode of Regulating the Temperature of Inking Rollers and Ink Used Therewith in the Inking Apparatus of Printing Presses." A reservoir of hot or cold water is allowed to flow into the interior of a hollow metal inking drum to adjust the temperature of the ink on the exterior surface. 1-1/4 pages of text, 2 drawings.
Issued to Eliphaz Weston Arnold of Boston. September 21, 1837.

Patent No. 871. "Mode of Protecting Notes, Checks, &c. from Alteration." A design for banknotes and other securities in which the denomination of the bank note is engraved in large letters across the face of the note and any text, such as the name of the bank, officials' names, dates, etc. are engraved between these large numbers, but not over them. In the case of "ONE" or "TWO" dollar notes, one of the letters would contain engraved writing curved to fit inside the letter. 1/2 page of text, 3 drawing figures.
Issued to Ebenezer Watson of Albany, New York. August 3, 1838.

Patent No. 888. "Mode of Heating Buildings and Evaporating Fluids." This invention describes a furnace consisting of two chambers. A fire maintained in one chamber heats a coil of drawn metal tubing containing an expandable fluid in the other chamber. The tubing circulates throughout a building for heating. In lines 66–101, the inventor explains how this may be used to heat printing plates instead of the prior method of using a charcoal grate. 1-1/2 pages of text, 1 sheet of drawings.
Issued to Angier March Perkins (son of Jacob Perkins) of Great Coram Street, London, England. August 20, 1838.
Note: One half of the patent rights were assigned to Merritt Moore Robinson.

Patent No. 2,894. "An Ellipsograph to Draw or Copy Ellipses and Adjusting and Proportioning All Figures To Any Given

Ellipse." Six pages of text, two pages of figures.

Issued to Luman Carpenter of Oswego, New York. December 31, 1842.

Note: Not to be confused with the much earlier patent X2894.

Patent No. 2,912. "Allen's New Engraving Machine." A mode of engraving flat, round, or cylindrical surfaces by means of a graver moving in a sliding frame regulated by a point tracing a pattern. Has the function of a pantograph but does not operate the same way as regular pantographs.

Issued to Ethan Allen of Norwich, Connecticut. January 16, 1843.

Patent No. 4,143. "Improvement in the Manufacture of Paper for Notes, Checks, &c." The inventor called this product a "Safety and Protective Paper." It was to be made of a delicate colored "test paper" combined with another sheet of lighter or different color, so that any attempt to erase writing by use of a rubber or a chemical agent would destroy or deface the other sheet and make obvious the attempt to alter the document. 1-1/2 pages of text, no drawings.

Issued to Arthur Varnham, stationer, of the Strand, London, England. August 9, 1845.

Patent No. 5,155. "Bank Note Engraving." Describes a method for protecting bank notes, checks, etc., by engraving a ground on the paper by means of a roulette consisting of a hardened-steel cylindrical die containing the letters of a word. The roulette is held in a handle and is free to rotate. This device is then mounted in a ruling machine and passes back and forth over the document. Since the roulette is free to rotate, it is likely to start each line with a different letter of its word. One page of text, one drawing sheet of one figure.

Issued to Benjamin Chambers of Washington, D.C. June 12, 1847.

Patent No. 7,786. "Copper and Steel-Plate Printing Press." Five improvements in the design of a bank-note spider press are described. Two pages of text, two pages of figures.

Issued to E.C. Middleton, Edward Nevers, and Robert Neale, all of Ohio. November 19, 1850.

Note: Edward Nevers became a counterfeiter. Robert Neale went on to patent the Neale-Appoleton Press.

Patent No. 7,959. "Producing An Improved Watermark by Using a New and Much Improved Paper Mold." Describes a method by which the conventional practice of forming a watermark by bending wires to form an image and threading such wires in and out of the laid or woven wires of the paper mold is replaced by a new mold made by stamping or forming a design by impressing a die on the mold backing. Seven pages of text, three pages of drawing figures.

Issued to William Brewer of Malcolm Place, Clapham, County of Surrey, England, and John Smith of Southville, South Lambeth, Surrey, England. March 4, 1851.

Note: Warning—Although tediously explained, the patent is difficult to understand.

Patent No. 10,575. "Table to Hold Bank Notes When Cut." Background: The only method heretofore practiced in the trimming and cutting of the vast number of bank notes is by means of common shears. The notes are usually printed four on a sheet, requiring at least thirteen distinct and accurate clips of the shears—so that the most brisk and experienced cutters are able to trim only from 700 to 1,000 sheets per day, and are constantly liable to cut off too much or too little of the margins of the notes and hardly

ever cutting them with a uniform and desirable accuracy. In this invention, a table is provided with depressible needles mounted on thumb screws and there are clamps to hold notes in place. Fifty to a hundred sheets of banknotes can be mounted on the table at one time. A T-square mounted at the top of the table is moved as necessary to allow a knife to cut the note margins vertically, and then the sheets are moved so the same operation can take place horizontally. The inventor claims he is able to cut from 5,000 to 7,000 sheets per day, leaving the edges perfectly accurate and smooth. 1-1/4 pages of text, 1 page of drawings.

Issued to Frank G. Johnson of Brooklyn, New York. February 28, 1854.

Note: Surprisingly, this invention does not seem to have been adopted in the early Treasury Department First Currency Division, where ladies with shears were still cutting notes by hand.

Patent No. 14,069. "Method of Preventing Bank-Notes, &c., from being Counterfeited." Describes a method of using "oil-colored" paper for bank notes and printing them with indigo ink, which is equally or more fugitive than the color of the paper itself. Any attempt to copy the bank note by the photographic process, by transferring on lithographic stone, or by anastatic printing, will fail for the reasons explained in the patent. 1-1/4 pages of text, 1 page of 4 figures.

Issued to Christopher D. Seropyan of New Haven, Connecticut. January 8, 1856.

Patent No. 15,486. "Improved Blank for Bank Notes, Bills, &c." Describes a method to prevent counterfeiting of bank notes and other forms of value by first printing a photograph on blank bank note paper and then printing the form of the note (words, scroll work, etc.) over the photograph. One page of text, one sheet of drawings.

Issued to Peter Hannay of Washington, D.C. August 5, 1856.

Patent No. 17,319. "Printing in Colors." Describes a method of printing in bands of different colors in accurate registry with no overlapping of the colors. 1-1/2 pages of text, 1 sheet of drawings.

Issued to William Croome of New York. May 19, 1857.

Patent No. 17,473. "Improvement to Prevent Counterfeiting Bank Notes, etc." Describes a method of using tinted or colored paper for bank notes, and printing the other parts of them—i.e., the obligatory and the ornamental parts—with an ink which is equally or more fugitive than the tint or color of the paper. In order to alter or copy an original note, the tint or the color of the paper must be first removed without disturbing the vignettes and lettering. One page of text, one page of three figures.

Issued to Christopher D. Seropyan of New York. January 2, 1857.

Note: Assigned to William Cousland and J. D. Bald (banknote printers). See Seropyan's earlier patent, No. 14,069.

Patent No. 17,688. "Improvement In Printing Inks." Describes an anti-photographic and chemically stable bank-note ink made with chromium sesquioxide and ordinary printers' varnish.

Issued to George Matthews of Montreal, Canada East. June 30, 1857.

Note: The patent rights were later purchased by Tracy Edson of the American Bank Note Company, New York.

Patent No. 18,668. "Improvement in the Preparation of Engraved Metal Plates for Printing." Describes the preparation of iridium and the method of electroplating it on copper plates to increase their hardness and prolong their usefulness. 2 pages.

Issued to John Montgomery Batchelder of Cambridge, Massachusetts, and Luther L. Smith of New York. No drawings. November 24, 1857.

Patent No. 19,046. "Shears for Cutting Bank Notes, &c." Describes a paper cutter very similar to one you can find in any office supply store today. 1-1/2 pages of text, 1 page of 5 figures.

Issued to Stephen P. Ruggles of Boston, Massachusetts. January 5, 1858.

Patent No. 24,341. "Method of Printing Bank Notes." The inventor uses two or more plates, which he calls "primary plates," each of which is cut into two or more pieces which are so proportioned and fitted together, that by taking a piece of each plate and putting the pieces together by "tongue and groove or dowel joints," they are made to form practically one plate which he calls a "combination plate." On one of the "primary plates" he engraves the "tint-work," and on the other what is known as the "face-work." The tint-work and the face-work are printed in different colors by using "primary" and "combination" plates, each bearing a different color of ink, and each set held together in a chase. Two pages of text, one page of ten figures.

Issued to Alfred Tichenor of Newark, New Jersey. June 7, 1859.

Note: Alfred Tichenor became a leading transfer operator at the BEP in its early years.

Patent No. 27,116. "Improvement in Photographic Bank Notes." Describes a method of photographically printing bank notes on paper having a movable or variable watermark. The majority of the design (vignette, etc.) would be in the form of a photograph. One page of text, no drawings.

Issued to Leopold Eidlitz of New York. February 11, 1860.

Patent No. 27,857. "Improvement in the Manufacture of Bank-Notes." Proposed using two or more layers or sheets of paper in which the back side of the note is imprinted with an image that shows through the front side and forms an integral but faint part of the design of the face of the note. The two sheets are cemented together so they cannot be separated. One page of text, one page of four figures.

Issued to Augustus C. Carey of Lynn, Massachusetts. April 10, 1860.

Patent No. 28,370. "Safety Paper." Describes the application of a colorless metal in foil or in powder form between the laminae of thin paper, to designate the character or denomination of each particular bank note or other security. The method requires the printing of the denomination by type on a thin strip of gauze or paper, using a mordant to assure the ink adheres to the gauze or paper. This strip is then inserted as the middle ply of a three ply roll of bank note paper. 1-1/2 pages of text, no drawings.

Issued to Martin A. Howell Jr. of Ottawa, La Salle County, Illinois. May 22, 1860.

Patent No. 30,488. "Style of Engraving Bank Notes, &c." Describes a first-time combination of "machine work" (geometric and cycloidal lathe work with waved line and rosette work) in repetition of the title and ornamental work on a bank note or other security. 1-1/2 pages of text, 1 page of several drawing figures.

Issued to James MacDonough of New York. October 23, 1860.

Patent No. 31,820. "Improvement in Bank Notes to Prevent Alteration." Proposes the design of bank notes in which all of the printing, engraving, and writing on a bank note be embodied within the outline of a numeral designating the denomination of the note. One page of text, one page of three figures.

Issued to John Murdock of New York. March 26, 1861.

Note: This method is considered to be aesthetically unpleasing.

Patent No. 33,526. "Improvement in Apparatus for Printing Bank Notes." Describes an apparatus for printing bank notes in two or more colors in perfect registry. This method uses a chase to hold the plate. A bank note is cut to the exact size of the plate and placed in the chase. This prevents lateral or endwise movement of the paper. The bank-note paper is not wetted, but printed "dry" to avoid shrinkage. 1-1/2 pages of text, 1 page of figures.

Issued to Jabez W. Hayes of Newark, New Jersey. October 22, 1861.

Patent No. 34,634. "Improvement in Safety Paper." Embedding continuous threads of different-colored silk in bank-note paper made on the Fourdrinier machine to prevent counterfeiting. 1-1/2 pages of text, 1 page of 6 figures.

Issued to Henry Hayward of Chicago, Illinois. March 11, 1862.

Patent No. 37,235. "Engraving Machine." Describes the construction and operation of an engraving machine very similar to a pantograph but capable of varying the proportions of a drawing or pattern as well as its scale. 2-1/2 pages of text, 1 page of 3 drawings.

Issued to Joseph S. Ives of Monrisania, New York. December 23, 1862.

Patent No. 37,561. "Improvement in Bank Notes." Preventing the alteration or "raising" of bank notes by having either (1) engraved lines radiating from the denominational counters in the upper corners of the note to the same number in a column of numbers vertically placed in the center of the note, drawing one's attention to the match between the numbers, or (2) a circle in the middle of the note with lines radiating from each side of the inner surface to a matching number in a column running vertically in the circle. One page of text, one page of five figures.

Issued to John M. Batchelder of Cambridge, Massachusetts. February 3, 1863.

Patent No. 37,984. "Improved Green Ink." The inventor claims that the green ink used in steel plate and other printing is composed of the anhydrous oxide of chromium, and due to the hardness of its particles, wears down the printing plates or other printing surfaces very rapidly. His solution is to make a different chromium salt, combined with asbestos, to reduce wear. Since the chromium is the source of the coloring of the ink, he recommends using greater or lesser amounts of it to lighten or darken the color of the ink. He obtains his chromium salt by dissolving the hydrated oxide of chromium (Chromium III, or Cr_2O_3) in hydrochloric acid and evaporating the solution, washing and drying the compound thus obtained and reducing it to an impalpable powder by trituration (grinding it). One page of text, no drawings.

Issued to George Smillie of New York. March 24, 1863.

Note: George Smillie was a renowned bank note engraver.

Patent No. 38,231. "Device to Prevent Counterfeiting Bank Notes, &c." Inventor proposes to print or stain or otherwise produce a ground tint, ground design, or incorporated color in a graduated shade, commencing with a fainter color at one edge or corner of the note and gradually increasing or changing in depth, true shade color or intensity to another side or corner. Another form consists in passing from a darker shade at the edges to a lighter one in the middle, or conversely. In another protective measure, he intends to print the portraits, vignettes, scenes, devices, &c., constituting the ornamental work, with a fugitive tint or color; but the obligatory part, including the dies, words, lettering, numerals, ciphers, figures, lettering, and denomination in one or more permanent colors. Two pages of text, no drawings.

Issued to M. Carey Lea of Philadelphia, Pennsylvania. April 21, 1863.

Patent No. 38,297. "Improved Chrome Compound." The inventor discovered the general chemical reactions for making the chromites of zinc, iron, manganese, copper, &c. in 1857. In this patent, he explains how to make the "chromite of baryta (given here as $BaOCr_2O_3$) and claims the chemical can be used advantageously as a printing or tinting material. One page of text, no drawings.

Issued to Asahel K. Eaton of New York, New York. April 28, 1863.

Note: See the following patent.

Patent No. 38,298. "Improvement in Ink for Printing Bank Notes, &c." Addition of the "chromite of baryta" to the green ink for plate printing bank notes, &c.

Issued to Asahel K. Eaton of New York. April 28, 1863.

Note: This patent was used by the government in an attempt to prevent counterfeiting by photography, but such notes were counterfeited extensively and the use of the patented ink was discontinued.

Patent No. 38,335. "A Mode of Preventing the Counterfeiting of Bank-Notes, &c." This patent proposes that a vignette or design on a bank note be reproduced by photolithography and reduced to about 1/5 the original size and printed again in a clear space on the note. The inventor believes this reduced vignette would be too difficult to engrave and could not be reproduced by a counterfeiter photographically since it was printed in non-photographic inks on the original note. He also suggests printing the reduced vignette in a stereoscopic view, requiring stereoscopic glasses to see in registry. 1-1/4 pages of text, 1 page of 5 figures.

Issued to Isaac Rehn of Philadelphia. April 28, 1863.

Patent No. 38,835. "Improvement in Safety Paper." Describes a three-ply paper in which the center ply is a fugitive color and the outer plies are charged with magnesium silicate (talc) or other minerals such as magnesia, magnesite, alumina, &c., to make them soft and improve the visibility of a watermark. 1-1/2 pages of text, no drawings.

Issued to Joseph P. Olier of Paris, France. June 9, 1863.

Patent No. 40,839. "Improvement in Compositions for Bank Note and Other Inks." Describes a bank-note ink made from a combination of stannic acid (peroxide of tin) and a small amount of chromium, forming a "mineral lake." The inventor discusses several other chemical reactions that replace the chromium oxide with an oxide of gold, uranium, copper, lead, cobalt, nickel, iron, manganese, or cerium. The inventor claims that the use of inks made by these methods cannot be removed from paper by any known solvent or reagent that will not also remove the ordinary black printers' ink, thus revealing an attempt at alteration. One page of text, no drawings.

Issued to Thomas Sterry Hunt of Montreal, Canada East. December 6, 1863.

Patent No. 41,118. "Improvement in Postage and Other Stamps." Printing postage and revenue stamps in fugitive ink to prevent erasure of cancellation marks and the reuse of the stamps. One page of text, no drawings.

Issued to Abram J. Gibson of Worcester, Massachusetts. January 5, 1864.

Note: Assigned to Edward Livermore of New York and Jonathan Luther of Worcester.

Patent No. 41,724. "Improvement in Plates for Printing Bank Notes." The inventor explains the difficulty of transferring the designs on hardened steel rollers to flat bank-note plates. It was the common practice in his day to make a compound plate by welding or casting a steel surface on an iron backing. The inventor claims that is the reverse of what was needed and proposes the manufacture of plates for engraving composed of a layer of iron forming the face and steel the back of the plate. One page of text, no drawings.

Issued to Alfred Sellers of New York, New York. February 23, 1864.

Patent No. 47,744. "Improvement in Bank Note Engraving." The inventor advocates the prevention of counterfeiting by using designs on bank notes made by his "design hammer" which makes lines from small dots of uniform size and circular designs made by the repetition of figures, numbers, or words to form concentric circles. 1-1/2 pages of text, 2 pages of drawings.

Issued to Waterman Lily Ormsby of New York. May 16, 1865.

Note: See the following patent.

Patent No. 47,745. "Apparatus for Engraving Metallic Plates." Describes a machine for impressing a design on a metallic plate by means of a blow from a "design hammer" which is precisely controlled and adjusted to place the design at any desired location on the plate. The inventor explains that one method of impressing a design on a plate uses a die laid on the plate and then struck by a hammer. That method often resulted in an imperfect impression and the die was sometimes misplaced on the plate. He proposes making the die a part of the hammer to get an even impression. Two pages of text, two pages of drawings of four figures.

Issued to Waterman Lily Ormsby of Jersey City, New Jersey. May 16, 1865.

Note: Ormsby's method did not replace the traditional use of a transfer press.

Patent No. 53,081. "Improved Paper for Postage-Stamps." This describes a safety paper in which "prussiate of potash" (potassium ferrocyanide) and oxalic acid, a mordant, separately or mixed, are added to paper to permanently discolor the paper if an alkaline agent is used to remove cancellation ink. The discoloration is rapid and gives such a deep tint that the attempted fraud is easily recognized. One page of text, no drawings.

Issued to Henry Loewenberg of New York, New York. March 6, 1866.

Note: The inventor does not mention that when potassium ferrocyanide is mixed with an acid, hydrogen cyanide is produced, which is extremely toxic.

Patent No. 54,759. "Improvement in Pantographic Machines." Describes a pantograph with several novel features. One is a transparent tracer, consisting of a glass with a dot on its surface, to be used instead of a metallic tracer. When tracing from a paper sketch, a metallic tracer would obscure a portion of the line to be followed. The machine is capable of producing copies of the same size as the pattern; also, of producing copies either smaller or larger than the pattern, but preserving the relative proportions; and of producing copies with any selected part of the outlines out of proportion; and of producing a series of parallel lines by means of a ruler which is made to advance over the pattern by the action of a pawl and ratchet. The diamond pointer can be given independent movements while the plate is being moved beneath. This latter feature is particularly helpful in bank-note work to expand a letter or figure in width or length in order to occupy a given surface therewith. 2-1/2 pages of text, 3 pages of figures.

Issued to Edward Oldham, New York. May 15, 1866.

Patent No. 54,834. "Improvement in Manufacturing Bank Notes." Background: The inventor first explains the disadvantages of sizing bank-note paper before printing on it. "Sized paper is robbed of a portion of its strength each time it is damped for the purpose of printing; second, the inks do not enter into the fiber of the paper, but lie upon the surface, and hence may be easily softened or removed for the purpose of counterfeiting or altering from one denomination to another; third, upon sized papers it is impossible to use some of the most brilliant and valuable colors, because, owing to their softness and lack of adhesiveness, they are liable to rub off or be changed by moisture, unless they enter into the fiber of the paper; fourth, owing to the contraction and expansion of sized paper it is impossible to obtain a perfect register in printing with various colors at successive operation; fifth, counterfeiting bank notes has usually been effected by subjecting the ink on the note to the action of an alkaline solution and then transferring the point upon the plate to be engraved, and this has been greatly facilitated by the exposure of the ink upon the outside of the glazing." Abstract: The inventor proposes that printing upon the paper should be done while it is in an unsized or only partially sized condition, so that the ink will come into actual contact with and to some extent penetrate the fiber of the paper. After printing, the glutinous size is applied in the ordinary manner. He recommends Russian isinglass for the size. 1-1/8 pages of text, 2 claims, no drawings.

Issued to George T. Jones of Cincinnati, Ohio. May 15, 1866.
Note: See the following patent.

Patent No. 54,835. "Mode of Preparing Bank Notes to Prevent Counterfeiting." The inventor proposes printing bank-note designs in colored or fugitive inks on unsized paper and covering the printed matter with a transparent film of sized pulp for the reasons given in the previous patent. 1-plus pages of text, no drawings.

Issued to George T. Jones of Cincinnati, Ohio. May 15, 1866.

Patent No. 56,650. "Safety Paper." Bank note and safety paper made with localized distinctive fibers which are intermingled into the pulp while it is being formed on the wire of the Fourdrinier machine. 3-1/2 pages of text, no drawings.

Issued to James M. Willcox of Glen Mills, Pennsylvania. July 24, 1866.
Note: The Willcox family is famous for setting up one of the earliest paper mills in America and furnishing bank-note paper to the government. Richard Willcox received a patent for making bank-note paper in 1823.

Patent No. 59,281. "Improvement in the Manufacture of Paper." The inventor proposes making a safety paper by adding metallic powders to the pulp during its manufacture. The powdered metals may also be cemented to the surface of paper by first coating the paper with India rubber dissolved in benzene. When the benzene evaporates, a thin film of the rubber remains on the surface and forms an adhesive base for the metallic powders. Finally, that sheet is covered with another layer of pulp. Several alternate methods are discussed. One page of text, no drawings.

Issued to Taliaferro P. Shaffner of Louisville, Kentucky. October 17, 1866.
Note: This patent has no real advantage for use in making bank notes, but it appears to represent the first attempt to incorporate metallic

powders into paper, a technology that would become important in later years for magnetic authentication of bank notes and other technologies.

Patent No. 61,321. "Improvement in Safety Paper." The inventor describes a method of making a safety paper for valued documents by incorporating strips of gutta percha into the paper pulp which will soften under the heat of the drying cylinder and fuse with the fibers of the paper so the strips nor any part of them can be removed. One page of text, one sheet of three figures.

Issued to L.M. Crane of Ballston, New York. January 22, 1867.

Patent No. 66,337. "Mode of Detecting Counterfeited Bank Notes, &c." The inventor describes a method for detecting counterfeit notes by comparison of proffered notes with portions of real notes printed on white paper from authentic BEP dies. The Treasury Department gave permission to the inventor to cut their dies in halves or to cut out sections, such as vignettes, and print them in a book. One page of text, one sheet of drawings of two figures.

Issued to Laban Heath of Boston, Massachusetts. July 2, 1867.

Patent No. 66,500. "Process for Manufacturing Bank Notes, &c." The inventor describes a combination of surface and plate printing to prevent counterfeiting or alteration of bank notes. He also recommends printing directly on the paper before sizing, so as to cause the ink to penetrate the paper. He then requires covering the printed impressions with a coating of size to permeate the body of the paper and add strength and prevent the transferring of letters (as by anastatic printing). Additionally he requires the use of anti-photographic inks. 1-1/2 pages of text, 6 claims, no drawings.

Issued to George T. Jones of Cincinnati, Ohio. July 9, 1867.
Note: See also patent Nos. 54,834 and 54,835.

Patent No. 71,663. "Improved Sizing for Bank Note Paper." Describes an improved sizing for bank note paper, consisting of equal parts of gum-dragon and albumen, sodium chloride, sodium carbonate, and silica. The inventor claims that out of the five or six colors the note may contain, at least two of them will become fugitive and will float off in solution when a counterfeiter soaks a note in an alkaline solution to soften it. One page of text, no drawings.

Issued to John M. Sturgeon of New York. December 3, 1867.

Patent No. 74,878. "Improvement in cleaning cloths used by banknote engravers." Describes the use of refined coal-tar light oils, benzole, or naptha to remove the gums and coloring matter left in the cloths used by bank-note printers. The cloths are then subjected to steam in an appropriate vessel and may be further treated with soaps or alkalies. One page of text, no drawings.

Issued to Haydn M. Baker of New York. February 25, 1868.

Patent No. 81,339. "Improved Self-Cementing Bands for Holding Bank Notes, Papers, &c." The inventor provides strips of stout paper or other flexible materials, such as thin leather, parchment, or muslin, with an adhesive coating at each end, united by pressure of one adhesive surface upon the other after the band has been folded around a package. The adhesive he recommends is India rubber dissolved in benzene, naptha, or an analogous solvent. One page of text, one sheet of drawings of 6 figures.

Issued to Elijah M. Carrington of New York, New York. August 25, 1868.

Patent No. 84,341. "Method of Preventing the Alteration of Numbers on Bonds, &c." This invention consists of printing the numbers on bonds, notes, or other securities, in brackets, or other peculiar forms, leaving no room for adding an additional number on either side of the figures composing the number; and in order to prevent the alteration of the numbers, or the removal of the parentheses or other marks, the inventor proposes to print the whole on a finely-engraved background of scroll-lathe work, or any other printed matter, the groundwork of which shall be printed in fugitive colors or inks. One page of text, one drawing sheet of one figure.

Issued to George W. Casilear of the BEP, Washington, D.C. November 24, 1868.

Note: This patent was adopted by the U.S. Government in printing the serial numbers on the Legal Tender "Rainbow notes" of 1869.

Patent No. 84,606. "Mode of Preventing the Counterfeiting of Bank Notes, &c." Describes a method using well-grained wood of walnut, ash, chestnut, or a similar wood, or an electrotype made from such wood, for a bank-note plate to prevent counterfeiting since the natural pattern of the grain would be too difficult to reproduce by mechanical or hand engraving. Several variations of the method are discussed and reference is made to "Beerized wood" as described in the inventor's Patent No. 78,565. Two pages of text, one drawing sheet of one figure.

Issued to Sigismund Beer of New York, New York. December 1, 1868.

Patent No. 92,593. "Improvement in Printing Revenue-Stamps, &c., in Two or More Colors." Is described for printing stamps or other security documents in two or more colors at one impression by the use of two united plates having specific areas holding different colors of ink, one fugitive and one indelible. One page of text, one drawing sheet of four figures.

Issued to John Earle and Alfred B. Steel, both of Philadelphia, Pennsylvania. July 13, 1869.

Patent No. 95,626. "Improvement in Inks for Printing Revenue, Postage and Other Stamps, so as to Secure Greater Safety and Prevent Frauds." Describes a number of formulae for making fugitive inks from metallic salts and from vegetable dyes to imprint postage stamps that will reveal attempts to remove cancellation marks. For the basis ink, the metallic salts can be made from copper, nickel, or cobalt, and are mixed with pigments of light tint, such as chrome-yellow. In one of his recipes, the inventor likes to mix copper acetate (verdigris) with chrome-yellow in the ratio of 15:1 respectively, then add flake-white to give the ink body, and then "rub up" with boiled oil to make a very sensitive ink. Although most stamps of that time, whether revenue or postage, were printed in only one color, the inventor thinks additional colors would have advantages and suggests vegetable colors might form the basis ink. He reports success with litmus and logwood, by treating those with a small quantity of acid, either a vegetable or mineral acid, so as to change their colors to bright red, then mixing the ink with flake-white, and "rubbing it up" with boiled oil. The vegetable-color ink and the metallic salt ink should be printed by successive applications. One page of text, no drawings.

Issued to Thomas Antisell of Washington, D.C. October 5, 1869.

Patent No. 99,757. "Improvement in Bank Notes, Bonds, Revenue Stamps, &c." This improvement consists in ruling, in an ornamental design, a ground tint of fugitive ink over the otherwise blank portion of the paper reserved for and intended to receive signatures, dates, or other obligatory printing. The use of any acid or alkaline agent to remove the writing will also remove the ruled lines. The inventor claims the lace-work ground design is made possible by means of an improved attachment to ruling machines that he patented (Patent No. 99,758 of February 15, 1870). One

page of text, one drawing sheet.

Issued to George W. Casilear of the BEP, Washington, D.C. February 15, 1870.

Note: James Duthie, also of the BEP, appealed successfully to the U.S. Patent Office to be acknowledged as the true inventor of this idea and alleged interference from Casilear's application. See the Patent Office Official Gazette for March 19, 1872, pp. 255 and 256. This reference is now available on the internet using search terms such as "Decisions of the Commissioner of Patents 1872," and "page 255."

Patent No. 99,758. "Improvement in Ruling Machines." This improvement consists in providing a ruling machine with a device for producing a waved line or lines, with one pen or set of pens. A ruling machine using this device enabled the inventor to print the lace-work ground tint described in the previous patent. 1 page of text, 1 drawing sheet of 16 figures.

Issued to George W. Casilear of the BEP, Washington, D.C. February 15, 1870.

Patent No. 101,170. "Improvement in Inks for Printing Stamps, Drafts, and Checks." This invention is intended to prevent the erasure or removal of the signatures, amounts, cancellation marks and other written portions on bank notes, bonds, checks, drafts, deed, mortgages, wills, revenue or postage stamps, etc., by printing with a fugitive ink containing orchil. The inventor claims success with the follow recipe: zinc white or Paris white, six parts; magnesia, one part; beeswax, one part; printers' varnish, three parts; turpentine, one part; orchil, two parts. Tints or designs printed in this ink are changed in color or entirely destroyed if acted upon by the acids or alklies used by counterfeiters. One page of text, no drawings.

Issued to John P. Simonds of New York, New York. March 22, 1870.

Note: The parent compound, Orcinol, is made from specific lichens. This is then converted to a violet dye-stuff called Orchil by exposure to ammonia and air. Urine was the source of ammonia owing to its universal availability.

Patent No. 101,786. "Improvement in Paper for Checks, Drafts, Notes, &c." This invention consists in the addition of aniline or other coloring-matter or dye, to paper while it is in the pulp stage of manufacturing. Such materials are fugitive on the application of any solution which removes the various inks or writing-fluids ordinarily used. Coal tar derivatives may be mixed with acetic acid (vinegar) to make a fugitive tint deeper or lighter and more or less permanent. One page of text, no drawings.

Issued to George F. Thomae Jr. of Brooklyn, New York. April 12, 1870.

Patent No. 104,554. "Improvement in Printing Ink." This invention consists of the combination of "patent drier" with glycerin and boiled molasses to produce a vehicle for a fugitive ink. This combination permits the ink to dry so far as to lose all gummy or stickiness which would be inconsistent with its use on securities, yet has sufficient body and permanence as to permit normal printing operations without smearing, blurring or being defaced. One page, no drawings.

Issued to George W. Casilear of the BEP, Washington, D.C. June 21, 1870.

Patent No. 104,862. "Improved Compound for Printers' Ink." This invention consists in a compound made by adding prussiate of potash (potassium ferrocyanide) to ordinary printers' ink in a ratio of about 100 parts of the printers' ink to 5–20 parts of prussiate of potash. This is then used as a writing ink to express the value or the current numbers of documents. If an attempt is made to erase the writing by use of a chemical, such as oxalic acid, nitric acid, or potash, then the writing is changed immediately and the fraud is detected. One page of text, no drawings.

Issued to Henry Loewenberg of New York, New York. June 28, 1870.

Note: A previous and similar patent by the same inventor is No. 53,081.

Patent No. 113,346. "Improvement in Printing Presses." Describes a printing press consisting of a circular table that carries a series of plates, arranged radially, that are presented in succession to printing rollers that are arranged tangentially to the table. It may be supplied with steam-pipes or furnished with lamps for heating the plates, if required. The printing rollers are of the form known as "D-rollers." The table's movements are powered by a shaft rotated by a steam-powered belt. The table has a forward and backward motion so that each impression made can be removed and the plate inked and cleaned, and again supplied with paper before it is in turn again presented to the printing-rollers. This was the first mechanically operated bank-note printing press, although some helpers were needed to assist in its operation. 1-1/2 pages of text, 1 drawing page with 2 figures.

Issued to Judah Touro Robertson of the Continental Bank Note Company of New York City, New York. April 4, 1871.

Patent No. 114,963. "Improvement in Bank Checks, &c." A steel frame holding removable figures is used to print the amount of a bank check in an open space on the check so that it matches the written amount, preventing alteration. The action of the die, which is not inked, compresses the paper of the check, leaving a translucent impression in what is known as "water-line." One page of text, one drawing sheet of five figures.

Issued to Anthony C. Paquet of Philadelphia, Pennsylvania. May 16, 1871.

Patent No. 115,005. "Improvement in Paper for Bank Notes, Bonds, &c." This invention consists of a "chameleon paper" containing two chemically sensitive tints, one of which is sensitive to acids and the other to alkalies and ammonia. The use of these chemicals to erase or alter printing on security documents would be revealed by color changes in the print.

Issued to James M. Willcox of Glen Mills, Pennsylvania. May 16, 1871.

Patent No. 119,599. "Improvement in Bank Notes." Describes a method of preventing the alteration of bank notes, checks, and other documents of value by perforating the paper of these documents with the original figures or dates. 1-3/4 pages of text, 1 drawing sheet of 7 figures.

Issued to John Gibson Jr. of Albany, New York. October 3, 1871.

Patent No. 121,946. "Improvement in Colored Paper." This invention consists of adding a desired tint to the sizing used during the manufacture of paper. As the paper passes through the sizing vat in a continuous web it is duly colored as well as sized, and is ready for drying and calendaring. The tint should be of a fugitive color to reveal any attempt to alter printing by acids or alkalies. One page of text, no drawings.

Issued to George La Monte, George G. Saxe, and Charles Clayton, all of New York, New York. December 19, 1871.

Note: See the following patent.

Patent No. 123,782. "Improvement in Figure-Tinted Paper." Describes how a safety paper is made with different shades of tinting. This is accomplished by passing paper through a tinted

sizing and then between two rollers, one of which is brass and carries engraved figures in relief. The raised portion of the brass roller (i.e. the figures) will press out more water and cause the absorption of more color. This leaves the paper with light and dark shades of tint and makes the figures or designs more prominent. One page of text, no drawings.

Issued to George La Monte and George G. Saxe, both of New York, New York. February 20, 1872.

Patent No. 123,933. "Improvement in Plate-Printing Machinery." Background: The inventor was concerned with the automation of plate-printing presses for security printing. It was the usual practice in those days to distribute the ink over the plate with a roller and then wipe off the superfluous ink with a cloth and subsequently polish the plate by the naked hand of the printer. There had been some experiments to perform this operation by machinery, but they had either failed to clean the plate sufficiently or polished it too much, removing the ink from the incised lines. Abstract: The inventor designed a machine for wiping and polishing plates by means of elastic pads of sponge India rubber covered with cloth and placed on arms radiating from a revolving shaft. All of the operating surfaces could be regulated in the pressure they exerted on the plate. After the pads had left the plate in their rotation, they pass over a cleaning roller and scraper, or over a stationary wiping-pad furnished with a movable covering-cloth. A printing press would have two of these machines attached to them, of which one, to wipe the ink, should have the pads covered with twilled muslin or cloth, and the other, to be used as a polisher, should have chamois or other similar covering. The polishing pads are automatically dusted with whiting. 1-1/2 pages of text, 1 drawing sheet of 2 figures.

Issued to Judah Touro Robertson of the Continental Bank Note Company of New York, New York. February 20, 1872.

Note: The invention was generally lauded for its efficiency and design, but it was ultimately objected to for adding too much machinery to replace a part of the printer's job.

Patent No. 124,905. "Improvement in photo-engraving on metals." This invention consists of subjecting a finely polished plate of pure silver to the action of iodine until a film of silver iodide is formed. The inventor then exposes the plate to the action of light in the camera obscura, or under a photographic negative, until a faint image of the object is formed. The plate is then submitted to the action of electrotype-battery (copper solution) until a well-defined image of the object in copper is formed, the cupreous deposit attaching itself only to those parts of the plate which were rendered conductors of electricity by the action of light, while the unexposed parts will remain non-conductors. The plate is then dried and an etching solution is poured on it, composed of sulfuric acid and "nitrate of potash" (potassium nitrate). This solution immediately attacks the exposed portions of the silver surface, while the cupreous deposit from the electrotype-bath is not affected. After etching to the required depth, the copper deposited on the plate may be readily removed by aqua regia, which will not act on the silver plate, leaving a finely etched image in the silver plate. The same operations could be carried out on steel or copper, using different acids and etchants. One page of text, no drawings.

Issued to William Alphonso McGill and Robert Granville Pine, both of Memphis, Tennessee. March 19, 1872.

Note: Although not a bank-note patent as such, the method of photographically producing an image on a metal surface would later become an important feature in counterfeiting.

Patent No. 125,550. "Improvement in Bank Notes, Bonds, Revenue-Stamps, &c." Making checks from a sized paper on which a ruling engine has laid down a ground work of fluid writing ink. The ground will be of the same chemical properties as the writing on the check, and therefore one cannot be removed without removing the other. The use of acids to remove the ground would also remove the size and prevent other writing ink lines from being ruled again over the same place. One page of text, one page of four figures.

Issued to James Duthie of New York. April 9, 1872.
Note: See the note on No. 99,757.

Patent No. 130,153. "Improvement in Printing Presses." This patent deals with various mechanical improvements in the regulation of the pressure-roller in plate printing presses. One page of text, one drawing sheet of two figures.

Issued to Judah Touro Robertson of the Continental Bank Note Company of New York, New York. August 6, 1872.

Patent No. 138,613. "Improvement in the Methods of Engraving Bank Note Plates." This invention consists of engraving the English alphabet in couplets, such as AA, BB, CC, etc., on soft steel plates, in any style desired—plain, ornamental, or script— then hardening the plates, and finally transferring these couplets to the periphery of soft steel rolls and hardening them. These alphabet rolls can then be used to engrave names and titles on bank note plates by using a combination of the rolls in an appropriate succession. The inventor gives as an example the printing of the word "Washington." First he would choose the roll having the alphabet with W as its initial letter and A as its second letter; he then rolls into the plate the couplet W A; then takes the alphabet with the initial letter A, and select the couplet A S. By repeating these operations, he eventually transfers all the letters of the word. An advantage of using such rolls is the even spacing it gives to the letters. One page of text, one drawing sheet of four figures.

Issued to George W. Casilear of the BEP, Washington, D.C. May 6, 1873.
Note: See the following patent.

Patent No. 138,614. "Improvement in the Methods of Engraving Bank Note Plates." Background: Prior to this invention, the usual way of engraving names and titles upon plates for printing bank notes, &c., was to cut the same by hand with the customary tools. Where a large number of plates were required, having different names and titles, the saving of time and money in their production becomes a matter of great importance. Abstract: The inventor does not lay any claim to the broad idea of transferring letters or characters from a plate to a roll and back to a plate, nor to the use of "engraving rollers," but does claims as new the use of alphabetical rolls in couplets as describes in his Patent No. 138,613, issued on this same date. One page of text, one page of several figures.

Issued to George W. Casilear of the BEP, Washington, D.C. May 6, 1873.

Patent No. 162,677. "Improvement in Plate-Printing Presses." This invention relates to plate-printing machines and presents a number of mechanically technical improvements in various parts of the press. One needs a rather high level of mechanical skills to fully comprehend these descriptions. 5 pages of text, 4 drawing sheets of 13 figures.

Issued to Robert Neale of Brooklyn, New York. April 27, 1875.
Note: See No. 189,377.

Patent No. 167,223. "Improvement in Safety-Papers." This invention describes a safety paper for revenue and postage stamps in which the surface of the paper is covered with a woven fabric, or with a warp of fragile open texture and meshes, or the warp secured to and embedded in the body of the paper during the process of manufacture, or afterward by uniting the two under pressure. The natural moisture of the pulp, or the dampening of the sheet after manufacture, serving to sufficiently moisten and soften the starch or gluten in the textile covering, or the sizing of the paper, to produce a perfect union of the fabric and paper when pressed and dried and calendared. After the paper has been printed, any effort to erase any of the printing or writing by the use of a knife will result in the destruction of the lace-work or fabric covering. The use of an acid or other chemical reagent to erase printing will be obvious because the woven fabric or warp readily and quickly absorbs, by capillary attraction, any fluid coming in contact with it, separating from the underlying paper and exposing the attempted fraud. One-plus pages of text, one drawing sheet of three figures.

Issued to George W. Casilear of the BEP, Washington, D.C. August 31, 1875.

Patent No. 172,721. "Improvement in Processes of Extracting Printers' Ink from Rags." A new process for extracting printer's ink from wiping rags. The dried ink is first softened in linseed oil and then expressed by a wringer. The rags are then immersed in turpentine, sent through a wringer, placed in an alkaline bath, rinsed in water, soaked in dilute sulfuric or muriatic (hydrochloric) acid, rinsed in water and dried. The inventor claims that the ink that falls back into the linseed oil and the turpentine is suitable for use again in printing. One page of text, no drawings.

Issued to Louis H.G. Ehrhardt of Philadelphia, Pennsylvania. January 25, 1876.

Patent No. 175,875. "Improvement in Coupon Bonds." Background: The coupons attached to a bond were necessarily of rather small size, making it necessary to use small type and compress the printing. Another disadvantage was that the entire series of coupons presented a generally uniform appearance, which prevented one coupon being selected or separated from the others without special examination. Abstract: The object of this invention is to separate the six-months coupons with which bonds are usually printed into separate and distinct classes, which can be readily recognized, so that a mere glance will be sufficient to distinguish a January from a July coupon. This is to be done by separating the coupons into different classes based on color or tint. For example, the January coupons could be tinted red and the July coupons tinted a buff color. One page of text, no drawings.

Issued to Judah Touro Robertson of the Continental Bank Note Company, New York, New York. April 11, 1876.

Patent No. 177,896. "Improvement in Processes for Producing Safety-Paper." Describes a process for surface-coloring the pulp web in a Fourdrinier machine that leaves the color in diffused spots or irregularly-waved lines. The method is intended to provide a safeguard against alteration in railroad tickets, bank bills, checks, &c., but does not explain how the invention would be superior to other methods.

Issued to William E. Syms of Holyoke, Massachusetts. May 23, 1876.

Patent No. 180,490. "Improvement in Plate-Printing Presses." Describes a plate-printing press consisting of a four-way slide-frame (table) in which the plank or bed is moved progressively and allowed to pause at the four corners to permit the inking, polishing, laying-on, and taking-off operations to be performed. By employing four separate beds, these operations are performed simultaneously by different operatives upon different plates, greatly accelerating the printing process.

Issued to James Milligan of New York, New York. August 1, 1876.

Note: In a report made by the BEP in 1888, it is stated that the Government owns 18 Milligan steam-powered presses and pays a royalty of $1 per 1,000 impressions for their use.

Patent No. 181,597. "Improvement in Processes of Renovating Waste Ink." Background: In plate printing, the inking rollers and the wiping-rags are generally of woolen or cotton cloth, and sometimes of the fabric known as "Canton Flannel," which has a fleecy nap on one side. Consequently, the waste ink wiped from the plates contains fibrous matter which renders it unfit for further use. Also, the boiled oil with which the ink is mixed causes it quickly to form a skin on the surface when exposed to the air, and this, too, renders ink unfit for reuse. Abstract: The inventor takes recovered ink and immediately covers it with water to prevent the formation of skin. When a sufficient quantity of ink has been collected, it is run through a centrifugal machine to separate the fibrous matter and any solid impurities. The recovered ink is then ready for reuse. One page of text, no drawings.

Issued to Judah Touro Robertson of the Continental Bank Note Company, New York, New York. August 29, 1876.

Patent No. 189,377. "Improvement in Devices for Wiping and Polishing Engraved Plates." The inventor had previously designed a cylinder of leather to wipe and polish engraved plates (Patent No. 162,677). Subsequently, it was found that intaglio ink has such a tenacious character that the force required to wipe it from a plate causes the leather cylinder to deform. The inventor addresses that problem in this patent. An improved device consists of a series of bars arranged in a cylindrical form, each covered by leather, which are adjusted by set to move closer to or farther from the inked plate. One-plus pages of text, one drawing sheet of four figures.

Issued to Robert Neale of New York, New York. April 10, 1877.

Patent No. 193,097. "Improvement in plate printing presses." In this design, the bed for the plate is carried around a quadrangular frame by means of an endless chain passing around wheels, and the plate-bed or plank is stopped periodically for the successive operations of wiping, polishing, and supplying the sheet, and during the successive movements, the sheet is printed, the impression removed, and then the plate is inked for the next cycle. 2-1/2 pages of text, 2 pages of figures.

Issued to James Milligan of Brooklyn, New York. July 17, 1877.

Patent No. 193,221. "Improvement in Bank Checks." This invention is intended to prevent the alteration of bank checks by the use of "detective numbers." Checks are manufactured which have a small stub or coupon at each end. The serial number of the check is recorded on each coupon, but a "detective number" is printed on the second or right-hand coupon. This number is concealed from view by a cemented seal flap and overprinted by fugitive ink to reveal any attempt at tampering and to make the flap opaque. When the check is presented at the bank, the detective number revealed must match records kept at the bank and also match the serial number of the check. 2-1/2 pages of text, 1 drawing sheet with 15 figures.

Issued to Franklin W. Brooks of New York, New York. July 17, 1877.

Note: There is no explanation of how checks could be mailed to a distant payee and provide this protection without a long delay in mailing the check back to the issuing bank. See also No. 202,515.

Patent No. 193,805. "Improvement in Hard-Metal Types." Background: Prior to this invention, it had not been customary to manufacture movable type from hard metal, owing to the many difficulties attending the process and the great expense.

The electrotype was used instead, but did not compare well. To correct this problem, the inventor proposes the following solution—Abstract: To produce movable type in hard metal, it is first necessary to engrave the design upon steel, and then taking up the design on the periphery of a decarbonized (soft) roller, hardening the same, and rolling the design, now in relief, into a suitable plate or strip of hard metal, such as steel or brass. At this point the design is incapable of being used in surface printing because it is sunk below the surface (intaglio) of the hard metal. To bring the design into relief, the inventor would use a routing machine to cut away the surrounding metal. This produces a type that to all practical purposes gives as good a result as steel-plate engraving. One-plus pages of text, two sheets of drawings with several figures each.

Issued to George W. Casilear of the BEP, Washington, D.C. August 7, 1877.

Patent No. 202,515. "Improvement in Blanks for Bank-Checks." This is very similar to Patent No. 193,221 to prevent the alteration of written bank checks by using concealed "detective numbers" matched to bank records, except that the inventor now proposes the use of children, or other cheap labor, to manufacture the blank checks. Two pages of text, two drawing sheets of six figures.

Issued to Franklin W. Brooks of New York, New York. April 16, 1878.

Note: Assigned to Edward J. Brooks of New York, New York.

Patent No. 210,116. "Improvement in Plate-Printing Machines." Background: In plate printing, it is necessary to impart a certain movement to the wiper to remove superfluous ink from the plate, and this movement is neither circular nor rectilinear, but is a compound curvilinear motion, reciprocating in the direction of the length and width of the plate. It is also well known that the wipers must be frequently changed to produce good work. Abstract: To obtain the compound movement referred to, the inventor employs a printing-cylinder, upon which the plate is fixed; and to avoid the frequent change of wipers, he employs traveling wipers, of any desired length, moving from one roller under the reciprocating tension devices over the printing-cylinder; and from thence to and around a second roller upon which they are wound. There is also a system for adjusting the pressure of the wiper-cloth upon the plate. The diameter of the printing-cylinder may be varied to carry two or more engraved plates, by means of which a number of impressions may be taken at every revolution of the cylinder. 2-1/2 pages of text, 2 pages of drawing sheets with 3 figures.

Issued to Constant Alexis Guy of Paris, France. November 19, 1878.

Note: This is believed to be the press studied by Homer Lee while he was in France and later used as a model for his automatic press.

Patent No. 210,497. "Improvement in the Manufacture of Paper for Bank-Notes, Bonds, Checks, &c." This invention consists of a safety paper of two or more distinctive and possibly anti-photographic colors by combining the different colored inks with fibers (silk, jute, etc.). One page of text, no drawings.

Issued to George W. Casilear of the BEP, Washington, D.C. December 3, 1878.

Patent No. 238,882. "Engraving-Machine." The inventor's improvements relate generally to an engraving machine employing a pantograph to which are connected the tracer and the graving-tool, and more particularly to the means for facing the tool properly and the lever for operating the tool; to the construction of the tracer-arm and the means for adjusting the tracer; to the bed and supports of the machine, and the means for adjusting the pantograph and the work. 1-3/4 pages of text, 3 drawing sheets of 4 figures.

Issued to Allan Everett Francis of Garrettsville, Ohio. March 15, 1881.

Patent No. 241,021. "Process of Producing Engraved Plates." This process prepares a printing plate from a photographic negative by first producing a relief film from the negative and then engraving such plate by means of a pantograph or equivalent device, direct from such relief film, for the purpose of printing either with the typographic press or with the plate-press. 1-1/2 pages of text, 1 page of drawings.

Issued to Alfred Jones of Yonkers, New York. May 3, 1881.

Patent No. 225,279. "Preparation of Bank Note Paper." Describes processes for making bank note paper having embedded threads of strips of silk or other material that run lengthwise across the note and are differently colored in whole or at intervals. The inventor would, for example, use a single thread for small denominations and two or more threads for larger denominations. For smaller denominations, the thread might have one colored space for 1 dollar notes, two colored spaces for $2 notes, etc. In another proposal, he would use an orange strip to indicate a basic number, and intervals of blue spots to indicate how many times the basic number is to be multiplied to match the printed denomination counter. Additionally, the threads can be chemically treated prior to their introduction into the pulp so that the use of certain chemical reagents in an attempt to alter the color of the strips would, in fact, produce a change in color or some other effect. Two pages of text, one drawing sheet of three figures.

Issued to Henry Hayward of New York, New York. March 9, 1880.

Note: One disadvantage to this scheme, which the inventor acknowledges, is that the sequence of colored spaces on the strips would not be remembered by the general public and would be of help only to merchants and bank tellers. Finally, the inventor is naive in believing that the chemicals employed in the treatment of the threads would be kept a secret by the government.

Patent No. 245,970. "Plate-Printing Press." The inventor describes several improvements to one of his previously designed steam-powered plate-printing presses. His object is to print bank notes in particular without the use of whiting as a polishing material. 6 pages of text, 5 pages of drawings with 13 figures.

Issued to Robert Neale of Brooklyn, New York. August 23, 1881.

Patent No. 272,878. "Plate Printing and Embossing Machine." This invention relates to many improvements on the machinery for plate printing which were patented by the inventor under No. 216,273 and No. 221,461. One of the salient points of this invention consists of the combination of a rocking printing block with the horizontally-sliding and vertically-movable die, with an actuating mechanism so that when the printing-block and the die are in contact with the paper between them, and the block is rocked, the die is made to slide thereby, and to thus transfer to the paper the color or colors in the order in which they are applied to the lower face of the die, the paper also sharing in the sliding motion of the die. 6-1/2 pages of text, 4 drawing sheets of 16 figures, 19 claims.

Issued to Edward Hewitt of New York, New York. February 27, 1883.

Note: Minnie Hewitt was the administratrix of the deceased Edward.

Patent No. 282,106. "Manufacture of Yellow-fibered Paper for Bank Notes, Check, &c." This invention consists of subjecting raw jute, raw linen (flax), silk, wool, feathers, or hair, to the action of 10–50 parts dilute nitric acid at a specific gravity of 1.368 to 100 parts of water, and exposing the fibrous mass for 12 to 48 hours in the bath, then washing it until the water no longer shows any yellow color, and then adding the mass to paper pulp just before it goes into the Fourdrinier machine. The inventor claims that the yellow fibers, although barely visible in the finished paper, give it superb protection against chemical agents and photography. On being photographed, the fibers turn black. One page of text, no drawings.

Issued to Eduard Musil of Vienna, Austria. July 31, 1883.

Patent No. 307,956. "Manufacture of Bank Notes and Paper Therefore of Asbestos." The inventor claims that paper made from palmetto fibers is fully equal to India paper and far superior to any good quality of paper in use for printing bank notes. Therefore, he proposes making a paper by adding asbestos to prevent destruction by fire, with palmetto or hemp fibers to impart greater strength. He also proposes the addition of different colored silk fibers to paper pulp to indicate different denominations. For example, he would use green fibers to indicate $1; orange to indicate $2; blue to indicate $5; scarlet to indicate $10; any two of these colors for $20 notes, and for notes of $50, $100, and above, a combination of three colors according to any prearranged plan. One page of text, no drawings.

Issued to George T. Jones of Cincinnati, Ohio. November 11, 1884.

Patent No. 330,894. "Safety Paper for Checks, Drafts, &c." The inventor makes a safety paper mixing the ferro-cyanide of manganese and the hydrated peroxide of iron with a paper pulp, either in pulp vat or sizing vat. The ferro-cyanide of manganese is turned blue by most acids and brown by caustic alkalies so that any attempt to erase writing will discolor the paper. 1/2 page of text, no drawings.

Issued to Frederick M. Hill of New York, New York. November 24, 1885.

Note: The following patent is very similar.

Patent No. 443,116. "White Safety-Paper." The inventor describes a method of making a white safety paper that will produce blue or brown spots if acted upon by acids or "chloride of lime" (calcium hypochlorite, or bleaching powder). He does this by impregnating pulp with various resinous compounds of metallic salts, such as ferro-cyanide of tin or ferro-cyanide of manganese, mixed with a resin compound of molybdenum salt or a resin compound of cadmium oxide and a resinated sulfide of zinc. The amounts of each ingredient per unit weight of pulp are given as well as the basic chemistry of how to make the resinous compounds. Two pages of text, no drawings, three claims.

Issued to Albert Schlumberger of Paris, France. December 23, 1890.

Patent No. 447,336. "Distinctive Paper." Planchets are defined by the inventor as small pieces of different shapes of colored paper, or other suitable material, cut or punched out of the matrix. The planchets may be of oval, square, or round shape, or of any geometrical or fanciful shape, such as a star, cross, diamond, etc. To achieve greater variety, different colored planchets and those of different shapes may be mixed together within the pulp to form a great number of distinctive safety papers showing a random distribution, or they may be added to the paper at a later stage of its manufacture to give a localized distribution. 1-1/2 pages of text, 1 drawing sheet of 3 figures, 7 claims.

Issued to James Macdonough of the American Bank Note Company of New York, New York. March 3, 1891.

Note: The story of the invention of planchets is told in chapter 17.

Patent No. 481,770. "Safety Paper." A method of making safety paper for bank notes, bank checks, &c., in which designs on one side are printed in exact registry with the same design on the other side of the paper. These designs are printed in two or more colors, but in reverse sequence on the two sides of the note, so that reflected light produces all the colors, but transmitted light produces only the compound color resulting from the mixture of all the colors employed. 1-1/2 pages of text, 1 drawing sheet of 2 figures, 4 claims.

Issued to Albert Schlumberger, Paris, France. August 30, 1892.
Note: French Patent No. 213,226 dated May 22, 1891.

Patent No. 491,858. "Process of Making Safety-Paper." The inventor describes a safety-paper made by first dying "splash fibers" with permanent colors such as indigo, madder, alizarine, chrome-yellow, etc., and adding a mordant to paper pulp and making a paper from the mix. The fibers in the paper are then acted upon by reagents which modify the dye in them. The resultant paper appears splotched with white areas against a colored background and usually contains red and blue fibers. This was sometimes called "Granite Paper" in America. One-plus pages of text, no drawings, three claims.

Issued to Albert Schlumberger of Paris, France. February 14, 1898.
Note: French Patent No. 213,285 issued May 6, 1891.

Patent No. 537,753. "Machine for Supplying Silk Fiber to Paper." Background: Previously it had been the practice to add silk or other fibers to paper while it was in the Fourdrinier machine by arranging a vat above the web with a series of spouts or tubes projecting down close to the moving web. These spouts were controlled by cocks, but the material supplied to the paper was not uniform or at regular intervals. To correct this problem, the inventor designed a device especially for supplying silk fibers to paper used by the U.S. Government in making currency. Abstract: The primary part of the device consists of a trough or vat mounted transversely over a moving apron carrying the pulp. This vat holds the silk fibers mixed with a suitable amount of pulp to enable it to flow onto the moving web of paper below. Running through the vat is a shaft, rotated by a belt drive. A series of 16 receptacles on wheels are mounted on this shaft. As they revolve in the vat, the receptacles dip up a certain amount of material and deliver it to the paper traveling beneath. This provides a means to deliver silk fibers directly to the paper in a localized and continuous manner. 1-3/4 pages of text, 2 drawing sheets of 6 figures, 5 claims.

Issued to Winthrop M. Crane and William S. Warren, both of Dalton, Massachusetts. April 16, 1895.
Note: Assigned to Crane & Company of Dalton, Massachusetts.

Patent No. 538,625. "Safety-Paper." Describes a safety paper in which fast ink colors are printed in some areas and fugitive ink colors are printed in adjacent areas with near perfect registry. It would be extremely difficult, if not impossible, to erase written or printed material and restore the exact tint or tints of the background(s). One page of text, one drawing sheet of one figure, two claims.

Issued to Judah Touro Robertson of the Continental Bank Note Company, New York, New York. April 30, 1895.

Patent No. 541,985. "Plate-Printing Press." This invention relates to steam-powered plate printing presses, and its object is to provide the means by which plates of different sizes may be printed from at the same time without incurring the danger of soiling the back of the sheet printed from the large plate with the dirt which may have been picked up from the small plate. Another object is to use plates of different characters, demanding different treatment as regards pressure, &c. For this purpose there are two printing or blanket rollers, in combination with two or more movable beds, for carrying the engraved plates, the beds and the blanket-rollers being provided with such means and so arranged that one of the blanket-rollers shall engage only with certain of the movable beds, so as to print from their plates, while the other print-roller shall engage only with the remaining movable beds to print from their plates. Three pages of text, two drawing sheets of five figures, nine claims.

Issued to Judah Touro Robertson of the Continental Bank Note Company of New York, New York. July 2, 1895.

Patent No. 549,976. "Automatic Wiper and Polisher for Plate-printing Press." Given that automatic wipers and polishers on plate-printing presses operate with such pressure that they often, if not always, wipe out the ink from the engraved lines of a plate, the inventor attempts to correct that problem with novel designs for new equipment. First, the wipers and polishers (which are duplicates of each other) are mounted on shafts parallel with the shaft of the plate-cylinder and journaled in bearings that are adjustable to or from the plate-cylinder. Smaller auxiliary rollers are located on opposite sides of the main rollers; driving rollers are mounted upon shafts also parallel with the plate-cylinder; and tension-rollers act on the belt drive powering the other rollers. An endless wiper and polishing belts are mounted on and extend around the trains of rollers just described and are interposed between the main rollers and the plate-cylinder. Cleaning pads mounted on the frame press rags against the wiping and polishing belts to remove the ink. Two pages of text, one drawing sheet of one figure, three claims.

Issued to Judah Touro Robertson of the Continental Bank Note Company of New York, New York. November 19, 1895.

Patent No. 590,114. "Feeder Attachment for Printing-presses." For illustration, this patent shows the feeder attached to a rotary-plate printing-press provided with two plates adapted to be run at 10 or more revolutions per minute. Running at such speed, it would be physically impossible for an operator, or even two operators, to feed such a press, especially in cases requiring careful registration or attention to shrinkage in dampened paper. The inventor proposes several improvements in feeder devices to allow such rapid operations. 5 pages of text, 4 sheets of 12 drawings, 19 claims.

Issued to Judah Touro Robertson of the Continental Bank Note Company of New York, New York. September 14, 1897.

Patent No. 590,115. "Feeder for Printing-Presses." In his Patent No. 590,114, the inventor proposed a series of independently-movable feeder-boards adapted to travel transversely across the path of the delivery-line of feed to the press, it being necessary that the housing supporting the plate and impression rollers should be cut away or recessed to permit of this transverse movement. However, this cutting away of the housing has been found in some instances to materially weaken the structure, and it is to do away with the necessity for this cutting or recessing of the housing that this present improvement is designed. 7-1/2 pages of text, 7 drawing sheets of 17 figures, 26 claims.

Issued to Judah Touro Robertson of the Continental Bank Note Company of New York, New York. September 14, 1897.

Patent No. 592,664. "Inking Device for Plate-Printing Presses." This invention relates to an improvement in automatic inking devices that apply ink from a suitable ink fountain or hopper to a roller which transfers the ink to an inking-belt, which in turn, as it revolves, deposits the ink upon the face of the engraved plates in a thin film and by means of a series of three rollers forces it fully into the engraved lines. This is intended for use on a rotary press, but slight alterations can be made to the device to enable it to be used on flat-bed presses. 1-1/4 pages of text, 1 drawing sheet of 1 figure, 3 claims.

Issued to Judah Touro Robertson of the Continental Bank Note Company of New York, New York. October 26, 1897.

Patent No. 595,281. "Safety Paper." Describes a safety paper made for checks, tickets, etc., with alternating groups of both fast and fugitive microscopic lines of complementary colors so closely spaced that they leave an impression of a color different from either of the two actual colors, and using these lines as a background over which words, writing, numbers, etc. can be printed. 1-3/4 pages of text, 1 drawing sheet of 8 figures, 7 claims.

Issued to John C. Yetter of Chicago, Illinois. December 7, 1897.

Patent No. 776,470. "Safety Composite-Color Print." Describes how a combination of colors and patterns in a multi-colored ground can make reproduction by photo-mechanical means extremely difficult. The inventor suggests a multi-colored ground of printing colors such as white lead, naphthol-yellow, yellowish cosin, rhodamine-pink, and Capri-blue. Upon this ground a design can be printed in a mixture of two or more of the ground colors so it cannot be separated from the ground photo-mechanically because of the spectral similarity of the ground colors. 4-1/2 pages of text, 1 drawing sheet of 7 figures, 44 claims.

Issued to Frederick E. Ives of Weehawken, New Jersey. November 29, 1904.

Patent No. 776,515. "Safety Composite-Color Print." Describes a process for making a safety composite design on paper comprised of well-differentiated lines of different hues printed so that the lines cross and interweave. The different colors of ink must have similar spectral absorption so they cannot be separated photographically. The following colors of ink have similar spectral absorption and can be used for these prints: (1) Rhodamine Pink and Methyl Blue; (2) Capri Blue and Methyl Blue; (3) Capri Blue and Victoria Green; (4) Brilliant Yellow and Victoria Green; (5) Eosine Red and Methyl Violet; (6) Eosine Red and Naphthol Orange; (7) Rhodamine Pink and Methyl Violet.

Issued to Frederic E. Ives of Weehawken, New Jersey. December 6, 1904.

Patent No. 1,002,600. "Means for Detecting Counterfeit Bank Notes, Bonds, Coupons, and the Like." Describes the use of a lined ground-work on which are printed letters or figures in the same tint as the ground-work but at angles with the imprinted lines. Suspected counterfeit notes, or notes in general, can be viewed under a glass screen having upon it equally-spaced lines at angles with the lines of the letters or figures hidden in the groundwork. The glass screen is made of a color that will make visible the imprinted letters or figures. 1-1/2 pages of text, 1 drawing sheet of 3 figures, 3 claims.

Issued to Edward Robert Morris and Alfred Edwin Bawtree of 9 and 10 Fenchurch Street, London, England. September 5, 1911.

Patent No. 1,299,484. "Intaglio Print." Describes a method of intaglio printing in which two plates are used, the first one laying down an invisible or nearly invisible line of ink, say in a cross-hatching or other type of ground, or in figures, or both, and the second plate using bold colors to superimpose security features such as vignettes, machine borders, script, etc. When an attempt is made to transfer the ink on a note to glass, for counterfeiting,

the resulting plate made from the glass will contain not only the engraved recesses of the 1st plate printing, but also the engraved recesses of the "artistic" or 2nd plate printing, forming a confused mess. 3-1/4 pages of text, 1 drawing sheet of 2 figures, 3 claims.

Issued to Homer Lee of the Homer Lee Banknote Company of New York, New York. April 8, 1919.

Patent No. 1,457,805. "Safety-Tint Paper." Describes a bank-note paper, or other negotiable documents, in which the safety tint consists of a repeating scroll of fine-line Rose Engine work or pantograph work, but which is made to look hand-engraved because certain lines are wider than others. This makes it extremely difficult for a counterfeiter to duplicate the design by using a pantograph or rose engine. Additional security is provided by using anti-photographic ink colors in the loops formed by the geometrical designs, and having some of these colors overlap at the intersections of the loops. Three-pluspages of text, one drawing sheet of two figures, nine claims.

Issued to Daniel E. Woodhull of the American Bank Note Company of New York, New York. June 5, 1923.

Note: Assigned to the American Bank Note Company of New York, New York.

Patent No. 1,539,202. "Intaglio-Printing Machine." This invention relates to doctor operating gear for wiping ink from sheets on printing cylinders and describes a mechanism by which the lift of the doctor may be varied according to the speed of the cylinder. Three pages of text, two drawing sheets of four figures, eight claims.

Issued to Malcolm Owen of London, England. May 26, 1925.

Patent No. 1,692,645. "Safety Paper." This invention consists of a paper impregnated with a color dye and having a surface design and text matter in the form of words, etc., in register on opposite faces of the paper, consisting of compressed particles of the dye coloring. Another procedure produces a paper colored distinctively on both sides with text and designs which appear in the form of a second tone of the same dye color. 1-1/2 pages of text, 1 drawing sheet of 4 figures, 9 claims.

Issued to Louis Gailer of New York, New York. November 20, 1928.

Note: Assigned to E.E. Lloyd Paper Company of Chicago, Illinois.

Patent No. 1,929,828. "Fraud-Preventing Paper." Intended for use in the manufacture of paper for bank notes, bonds, checks, and the like, this patent describes the use of micro-metallic geometric forms incorporated into the paper which pass transversely through the note or check in certain predetermined spatial relationships to the denominational figures. This seems poorly thought out, since a distinctive paper would have to be made for each denomination of currency, requiring additional steps in the selection of currency paper when printing various denominations of notes. 1-1/2 pages of text, 1 page of drawings.

Issued to John Schlitz of Leavensworth, Kansas. October 10, 1933.

Patent No. 1,938,543. A safety paper of a certain color having "detecting-fibers" dispersed throughout and intermingled with the fibers of the paper, said "detecting fibers" having previously been treated with a chemically sensitive substance whereby said fibers are the same color as the finished paper and normally indistinguishable from the paper, but will change their color and become distinguishable when treated by certain chemicals used to remove ink from paper. 1-1/2 pages of text, no drawings.

Issued to Justus C. Sanburn of Springfield, Massachusetts. December 5, 1933.

Note: Assigned to the Srathmore Paper Company of Springfield, Massachusetts.

Patent No. 2,116,374. "Method of Making Safety Inks." A patent for making inks that contain both a water-soluble pigment and an insoluble pigment. Requires the mixing of two different ink types. 2-1/2 pages of text. No drawings.

Issued to Arthur A. Wittnebel of New Rochelle, New York. May 3, 1938.

Note: Assigned to the American Bank Note Company.

Patent No. 2,143,406. "Paper for Security Documents and Process of Manufacture thereof." This patent describes the method of laying a continuous flexible filament into the web of paper as it is being formed. This filament is coated with an electrically-conductive, extremely thin metallic film. Two pages of text, one page of six figures.

Issued to Stanley Beaumont Chamberlain of London, England. January 10, 1939.

Patent No. 2,208,652. "Safety Papers." A safety paper in which identification marks, such as figures or words, are incorporated into the paper and are made of certain organic derivatives of cellulose (such as cellulose acetate) are visible. Any attempt to remove these identification marks will be evident, or will not succeed. Three pages of text.

Issued to William Whitehead of Cumberland, Maryland. July 23, 1940.

Note: Assigned to the Celanese Corporation of America.

Patent No. 2,659,305. "Multicolor Rotary Intaglio, Letterpess, and Offset Press." The first of the Giori banknote presses. This patent describes a multi-color, rotary press capable of executing intaglio, letterpress and offset printing. Seven pages of text, five pages of figures.

Issued to Gualttero Giori of Buenos Aires, Argentina. November 17, 1953.

Patent No. 3,088,841. "Safety Inks and Documents." Safety inks which make checks sensitive to attempted alteration by the fact that they are bleachable, water-soluble, containing lower alcohols and lower ketones (those containing not more than eight carbon atoms per molecule). These inks are used to print a background of elements, such as words or figures, in the area of the check in which a cash amount is written.

Issued to Clifford D. Guerlin of River Vale, New Jersey. March 1, 1960.

Note: Assigned to the American Bank Note Company of New York.

Patent No. 3,400,003. "Safety Inks and Documents." Another safety ink for checks, invented by Guerlin. This ink has a vehicle consisting of glycerin, sorbitol, and water, and a coloring matter made of a dye that is soluble in the lower alcohols and lower ketones.

Issued to Clifford D. Guerlin of River Vale, New Jersey. August 9, 1966.

Note: Assigned to the American Bank Note Company.

Patent No. 3,822,644. "Apparatus for Maintaining Registry between the Plates of a Multiple Plate Cylinder Press and Sheets supplied thereto." A problem arises when operating a multiple-plate cylinder press, where it is necessary to have each of the several plates on the cylinder in perfect registry with one another for the sheets to pass through the press in registry. This invention addresses that problem with a novel sheet-stop mechanism that automatically adjusts the speed of the mechanical drive to keep the sheets in registry.

Issued to Chauncey Foote Jr. and others. July 9, 1974.

Note: Assigned to the American Bank Note Company.

Patent No. 3,880,706. "Security Paper Containing Fused Thermoplastic Material Distributed in a Regular Pattern." Security paper containing fused thermoplastic material distributed in a regular pattern. The thermoplastic materials include polyethylene, polyamides, and polyvinylchlorides. When heated to a certain temperature, the thermoplastic materials fuse to surrounding cellulose fibers and cannot be delaminated. The dots of thermoplastic materials are easily visible by either transmitted or reflected light. 4-plus pages of text, 3 pages of 8 figures, 16 claims.

Issued to Harold Malcolm Gordon Williams of Sedlescombe, Sussex, England. April 29, 1975.

Patent No. 3,886,083. "Safety Inks and Documents." A safety ink having essentially the same constituents as that of Guerlin's Patent No. 3,088,841, with the addition of a fluorescent pigment which is non-bleachable, insoluble in water, and no more than slightly soluble in the lower alcohols and lower ketones. Any attempt at erasure will partly remove the fluorescent pigment, changing the color and fluorescent intensity of the background when viewed by UV light.

Issued to Herbert Laxer of Franklin Square, New York. May 27, 1975.

Note: Assigned to the American Bank Note Company of New York.

Patent No. 3,980,990. "Ferromagnetic Currency Validator." An improved ferromagnetic currency validator which permits hand-held operation. Three pages of text, six pages of circuitry diagrams.

Issued to Arthur A. Berube of Methune, Massachusetts. September 14, 1976.

Patent No. 4,010,293. "Ink Incorporating Optically Variaable Thin Film Flakes." Describes a multilayered thin film interference structure which can be pulverized and dispersed in the vehicle of the ink to provide a color shift between two distinct colors when viewed in incident light at two different angles. 11 claims, 3 pages of drawings.

Issued to Roger W. Phillips, Thomas Mayer, and Gary S. Ash. March 1, 1977.

Note: Assigned to Flex Products, Inc.

Patent No. 4,036,130. "Intaglio Printing Plate Manufacture." An intaglio printing plate is prepared by coating a copper-plate–engraved plate having a superficial chromium layer with an ink-accepting material such as a hardenable epoxy or acrylic resin, an enamel varnish, or a chemically or electrolytically deposited metal, and removing said layer from the non-grooved parts by treatment in a ball-grinding machine. The ink-accepting material remaining in the grooves forms concave recesses suitable for wet offset printing with the precision, complexity, and fineness of a copper-plate design. Nine claims, two drawing figures.

Issued to Gualtiero Giori of Lonay, Switzerland. July 19, 1977.

Note: Assigned to De La Rue Giori S.A., Switzerland.

Patent No. 4,056,056. "Rotary Printing Press." A combined rotary printing press comprises an offset printer and a direct plate printer arranged in tandem. The offset printer comprises a transfer cylinder, a plurality of plate cylinders for applying an image to the transfer cylinder, and an impression cylinder. The direct plate printer comprises a plate cylinder, inking means, and a further impression cylinder. Paper handling means comprise a conveyor drum for feeding paper to the transfer cylinder in proper registration and means for conveying paper from the transfer cylinder of the offset printer to the impression cylinder of the direct plate printer. The impression cylinders of the offset printer and the direct plate printer are adjustable independently of one another and independently of the paper handling means so that each can be independently adjusted to provide the pressure desired without disturbing the paper registration. Four pages of text, three pages of figures.

Issued to Gualtiero Giori of Lonay, Switzerland. November 1, 1977.

Patent No. 4,066,280. "Documents of Value Printed to Prevent Counterfeiting." To prevent copying of bank notes with the aid of modern color copiers, this patent describes an ink containing a specularly reflective coloring material, for example, powdered aluminum. The modern color copiers depend upon a color analysis of the light absorbed by various parts of a document, and do not reproduce true colors when they encounter specular reflections from the surface of the document being copied. A specular reflection on the surface of the document being copied results in a product from the color copier which does not faithfully follow the colors on the original document, and hence is readily distinguishable from an original. 2-1/2 pages of text, 3 pages of 11 drawings.

Issued to Anthony LaCapria of Brooklyn, New York. January 3, 1978.

Patent No. 4,183,989. "Security Papers." A security paper which contains a security device, e.g. a strip, thread, or planchette having at least two machine-verifiable security features thereon, one of which is a magnetic material, which may be magnetically coded or printed in a predetermined pattern on the device, and a second of which is a luminescent material, an X-ray absorbent, or a metal. The provision of several features on one device provides a large increase in document security. Seven pages of text, no drawings.

Issued to Alan J. Tooth of Whitchurch, England. January 15, 1980.

Patent No. 4,186,943. "Security Devices." Describes bank notes or other documents of value incorporating an optical authentication device in the form of a strip, or thread, disposed within the thickness of the paper, and having known characteristics of spectral reflectance and transmittance. This strip has superimposed windows that reveal an underlying thin film dichroic material. These windows may be arranged along the strip at regular intervals or in a predetermined pattern. When viewed in white light, the spectral reflectance of the thin film material can vary with the angle at which it is viewed, so that part of the spectrum which is strongly reflected changes as the note is tilted in relation to the direction of the illuminating light. This patent is widely used on Bank of England and other British colonial notes. 2-1/2 pages of text, 2 pages of 8 drawings.

Issued to Peter D. Lee of Hertford, England. February 5, 1980.
Note: Assigned to the Bank of England, London, England.

Patent No. 4,215,170. "Metallization Process." In carrying out this process, an extremely thin coat (substantially less than the wavelength of light) of metallic particles is deposited on a transfer agent. A thin coat of varnish is applied to either the substrate or the transfer agent, the substrate and the transfer agent are laminated together and the varnish is cured. The metallic particles will become absorbed within the varnish and the substrate and varnish are then separated. The substrate is provided with a highly polished specular metallic finish, which may be used in a variety of ways to provide security to documents of value. 3-3/4 pages of text, 3 pages of 9 drawings, 17 claims.

Issued to D. Entique Vilaprinyo Oliva of Barcelona, Spain. July 29, 1980.

Patent No. 4,224,095. "Method of Making a Plate Cylinder for a Web Printing Press." Giori patents are generally too long and too complex to describe briefly. Nine claims, three drawing figures.

Issued to Gualtiero Giorio of Lonay, Switzerland. September 23, 1980.
Note: Assigned to De La Rue Giori S.A., Lausanne, Switzerland. See the patent online at the U.S. Patent and Trademark Office's website (http://www.uspto.gov/) for description.

Patent No. 4,240,347. "Banknote Intaglio Printing Press." This press includes improved mechanism for removing excess ink from the printing plate. The press includes a main frame which supports a plate cylinder, a pressure cylinder vertically above the plate cylinder and a scraper blade which engages one side of the plate cylinder and removes most of the excess ink. A first auxiliary carriage at one side of the main frame supports an ink supply mechanism and receptacles for receiving surplus ink removed by the scraper blade. A second auxiliary carriage, at the opposite side of the main frame, supports two wiping webs, their supply and take-up reels, and the driving and control mechanism for the webs and their reels. The wiping webs remove any residue of excess ink on the plate. Each auxiliary carriage is lockable in an operating position abutting the main frame, and is movable to a retracted position spaced from the main frame without disturbing the setting of any adjustable element. 9-1/2 pages of text, 15 pages of 32 drawings, 17 claims.

Issued to Robert H. Hazelton of the Bronx, New York and John J. Kimball of Huntington Station, New York. December 23, 1980.
Note: Assigned to the American Bank Note Company of New York.

Patent No. 4,420,515. "Metallization Process for Protecting Documents of Value." A process for preventing the counterfeiting of valuable documents through the use of photography, photocopying techniques, or other methods. The process includes laminating an extremely thin metallic film to the substrate of the valuable document before the document is printed with the area of the metallic film being small in comparison to the area of the document. The metallic film can be located anywhere on the face of the document and a "latent image" is embossed on the metallic film when the document is printed. Embossing the latent image on the metallic film, rather than on the document substrate, provides many advantages not possible in the prior art. A photocopy of a document containing the embossed metallic film does not include the latent image and a color photocopy will be different in color than the original document. Therefore, a lay observer can readily differentiate between a genuine document and a counterfeit document. 3-plus pages of text, 1 drawing, 5 claims.

Issued to Maurice A. Amon of New York, New York, and Haim Bretler of Lausanne, Switzerland. December 13, 1983.
Note: Assigned to Sicpa Holding, S.A. of Glarus, Switzerland.

Patent No. 4,437,935. "Method and Apparatus for Providing Security Features in Paper." A security device is integrally combined with the fibers of the paper in a paper-making process. A carrier web of water-dispersible fibers carrying the security element is brought into contact with the paper stock during the paper-making process. The carrier web becomes rapidly dispersed upon contact with the wet stock, leaving the security element firmly attached to the paper fibers in the stock. In one embodiment, the security element comprises a plastic diffraction grating structure. In a further embodiment, the carrier web comprises an open porous structure for enhancing intermixing with the paper stock.

2 pages of text, 4 pages of 10 drawings, 2 claims.

Issued to Frederick G. Crane Jr. of Dalton, Massachusetts. March 20, 1984.

Note: Assigned to Crane & Company of Dalton, Massachusetts.

Patent No. 4,441,423. "Collect-Printing Unit for Security Printing for use in a Rotary Printing Press." The patent is confined to security printing in dry-offset mode and for use in a rotary printing press. 2-1/2 pages of text, 1 drawing.

Issued to Albrecht J. Germann of Wurzburg, Federal Republic of Germany. April 10, 1984.

Note: Assigned to Koenig & Bauer Aktiengesellschaft of Wurzburg.

Patent No. 4,442,170. "Security Document with Security Features in the form of Luminescing Substances." Not particularly relevant to bank-note security, but worth obtaining for those who are interested in the background of photoluminescent rare earth compounds in security printing. 4-1/2 pages of text, 2 drawings, 16 claims.

Issued to Wittich Jaule, Gerhard Schwenk, and Gerhard Tenzel of Munich, Federal Republic of Germany. April 10, 1984.

Patent No. 4,462,867. "Paper Incorporating A Partially Embedded Strip." This patent describes a method of forming a security paper by depositing paper fibers onto a support surface from a furnish by drainage, laying a strip having fiber-deposition blocking regions and fiber-deposition permitting regions onto the deposited fibers and continuing deposition to form a paper having the strip partially embedded in the paper and partially exposed. 4-1/2 pages of text, 10 drawings, 9 claims.

Issued to James S. Fuller of Platford, England. July 31, 1984.

Note: Assigned to Portals Limited, Hampshire, England.

Patent No. 4,509,424. "Convertible, Multicolor, Rotary Printing Press." This press is used for printing the safety background of bank notes. It is designed to print such multicolor backgrounds by the "Orlof" method or by offset. 2-plus pages, 2 drawings, 3 claims.

Issued to Albrecht J. Germann of Wurzburg, Federal Republic of Germany. April 9, 1985.

Patent No. 4,516,496. "Copperplate Engraving Machine for Printing Paper Currency." Another Giori invention. This direct plate printing or copper-plate machine consists of a plate carrier cylinder with at least one engraved or etched plate provided with cuts corresponding to the elements of a main design and shallower, finer cuts corresponding to the elements of a safety background. This machine assures a perfect register between the reliefs of the various color areas obtained on the color selector cylinders of hard material. Due to the presence of hard surface material on the color selector cylinder, there is no limit as to the fineness of the safety background elements. 2-1/4 pages of text, 1 drawing, 1 claim.

Issued to Gualtiero Giori of Lonay, Switzerland. May 14, 1985.

Note: Assigned to De La Rue Giori, S.A. of Switzerland.

Patent No. 4,524,276. "Apparatus for Detecting A Security Thread Embedded in a Paper-like Material." This device is intended for the optical detection of security threads by infrared radiation. The apparatus consists of an infrared radiation source and two infrared radiation detectors. Each detector is fitted with an optical filter, and each filter has a different infrared transmission characteristic. Therefore, the two detectors operate in different ranges of the infrared spectrum. This gives the apparatus the ability to detect security threads and determine what they are made of. 5 pages of text, 5 drawings, 11 claims.

Issued to Ko Ohtombe of Tokyo, Japan. June 18, 1985.

Note: Assigned to Tokyo Shibaura Denki Kabushiki Kaisha of Kawasaki, Japan.

Patent No. 4,534,398. "Security Paper." This patent relates to a security paper incorporating counterfeit deterrent, optical variable devices that display their optically active properties in reflectance when there are changes in the angle of incident light with respect to the eye of the viewer. The devices are applied by means of a carrier paper and a base web format during the paper-making process. An embedment roll presses the device within the base web while the base web fibers are unconsolidated and pliable. 2-1/2 pages of text, 4 pages of 8 drawings, 11 claims.

Issued to Timothy T. Crane of Windsor, Massachusetts. August 13, 1985.

Note: Assigned to Crane & Company of Dalton, Massachusetts.

Patent No. 4,552,617. "Security Features in Paper." Security features for authentication of currency paper are incorporated within the paper during the paper-making process. Various codes are incorporated within the paper for viewing by means of transmitted light. In one embodiment, the identifying indicia is microprinted on thin strips of a carrier material which dissolves during the dewatering and drying stage of the paper-making process. The microprinted indicia remains intact and is readable by means of transmitted light yet is neither legible nor reproducible with reflected light. 2-1/2 pages of text, 3 pages of 9 drawings, 9 claims.

Issued to Timothy T. Crane of Windsor, Massachusetts. November 12, 1985.

Note: Assigned to Crane & Company of Dalton, Massachusetts.

Patent No. 4,584,939. "Compound Rotary Printing Machine." This machine comprises an indirect printing device, a drying device, a sheet transfer and turning device actuated according to requirements, and an intaglio printing machine. It permits of printing—in a single pass—through the press a simultaneous recto-verso printing, name on one side according to the color collecting printing method, an image with juxtaposed colors, and on the other side according to the offset printing method an image with superposed colors and designs, notably for creating safety backgrounds on bank notes, and after drying and, if necessary, turning the sheets, an image printed by intaglio printing on one of the sides, notably for creating a main design on the bank note. The multicolor printing on the side receiving the image with juxtaposed colors may be completed in the press by a monochrome wet offset printing. A register control device may be incorporated between the sheet transfer and turning device and the intaglio printing machine. Five pages of text, three pages of five drawings, eight claims.

Issued to Gualtiero Giori of Lonay, Switzerland. April 29, 1986.

Note: Assigned to De La Rue Giori, S.A., Switzerland.

Patent No. 4,604,961. "Intaglio Printing Machine." This press is designed to properly supply ink to a plate surface, decreasing ink consumption and improving wiping performance. 3-plus pages of text, 3 pages of 7 drawings, 5 claims.

Issued to Ieyasu Ichikawa et. al. of Matsudo, Japan. August 12, 1986.

Note: Assigned to Komori Printing Machinery Company, Ltd. of Tokyo, Japan.

Patent No. 4,652,015. "Security Paper for Currency and Banknotes." Security devices in the form of metalized plastic films are incorporated within a security paper, such as bank notes and other valuable documents during the paper-making process for viewing solely by means of transmitted light. The devices comprise printing of extreme fine line clarity and high opacity such that legibility is possible by means of transmitted light while remaining completely indiscernible under reflected light. 2-1/2 pages of text, 3 pages of 8 drawings, 4 claims.

Issued to Timothy T. Crane of Windsor, Massachusetts. March 24, 1987.

Note: Assigned to Crane & Company of Dalton, Massachusetts.

Patent No. 4,705,300. "Thin Film Optically Variable Article and Method having Gold to Green Color Shift for Currency Authentication." Eight claims, three pages of drawings.

Issued to Peter H. Berning and Roger W. Phillips. November 10, 1987.

Note: Assigned to Optical Coating Laboratory, Inc. Continued under Patent No. 6,246,523.

Patent No. 4,761,205. "Security Paper for Currency and Banknotes."

Issued to Timothy T. Crane of Windsor, Massachusetts. August 2, 1988.

Note: Assigned to Crane & Company of Dalton, Massachusetts. Similar to Patent No. 4,652,015.

Patent No. 4,892,336. "Antifalsification Document Having A Security Thread Embedded Therein and a Method for Producing the Same." This security thread is transparent and has a printed pattern on one side and, on the opposite side, a lenticular structure coordinated with the printed pattern. Such threads change their appearance when the viewing angle changes. To produce the security threads, a transparent film impressed with the desired lenticular relief is directed to a printing apparatus in exact register via guide elements having a relief structure that is negative with respect to the film impression, and then divided in a cutting apparatus into individual threads. 4-1/2 pages of text, 4 pages of 4 drawings, 22 claims.

Issued to Wittich Kaule of Emmering, Federal Republic of Germany et. al. January 9, 1990.

Note: Assigned to GAO (Gesellschaft fuer Automation und Organisation) mBH, Munich, Federal Republic of Germany.

Patent No. 4,897,300. "Security Paper." This invention relates to a security paper having a security thread embedded therein, running from edge to edge that is printed with luminescent colors in such a way that they are invisible in normal lighting. The luminescent colors are provided along the security thread in successive overlapping portions which, when the colors are excited, have a length recognizable to the naked eye and show characteristic mixed fluorescences in the overlapping areas. 2-3/4 pages of text, 1 page of 4 drawings, 15 claims.

Issued to Michael Boehm of Heimstettem, Federal Republic of Germany. January 30, 1990.

Note: Assigned to GAO (Gesellschaft fuer Automation und Organisation) mbH, Munich, Federal Republic of Germany.

Patent No. 4,915,371. "Device for Sorting and Stacking Paper Securities, Notably Banknotes." This device separates and stacks bank notes that are provided with a distinguishing mark to be guided into a horizontal stacking magazine. Eight claims, four drawing sheets.

Issued to Brian Quinton of Lausanne, Switzerland. April 10, 1990.

Note: Assigned to De La Rue Giori S.A., Switzerland.

Patent No. 4,921,280. "Security fibers and Other Materials Made Luminescent by a Dyeing Process, Processes for their Manufacture and their Applications." This invention relates to security fibers and other allied materials made luminescent by a dyeing process employing rare-earth compounds and their application to fiduciary documents and other materials requiring authentication. 2-1/2 pages of text, no drawings, 5 claims.

Issued to Michael Jalon of Paris, France. May 1, 1990.

Patent No. 4,941,687. "Security Paper for Currency and Bank Notes." A metallized plastic strip containing security indicia is incorporated within currency paper to deter counterfeiting. The plastic strip is made difficult to detect under reflected light by selective pigmentation to match the currency inks. The presence of the security indicia is verified by detection under transmitted light. 1-3/4 pages of text, 4 pages of drawings, 8 claims.

Issued to Timothy T. Crane of Dalton, Massachusetts. July 17, 1990.

Note: Assigned to Crane & Company of Dalton, Massachusetts.

Patent No. 4,943,093. "Security Paper for Bank Notes and the Like." This invention relates to a currency paper in which is incorporated a strip or thread of not more than 5 mm width, which is flexible, water-impermeable substrate with a layer of metal on one or both sides of the substrate. On one side of the strip or thread, there is a continuous metal path along its length in which metal-free portions constitute between 10% and 50% of the area of the strip. These metal-free portions provide a repeating pattern, design, indicia or the like. 6-1/4 pages of text, including a background history of the art, 5 pages of drawings, 28 claims.

Issued to Raymond J. Melling of Overton and Malcolm R.M. Knight of Basingstroke, both of the United Kingdom. July 24, 1990.

Note: Assigned to Portals Limited, Basingstoke, United Kingdom.

Patent No. 4,966.628. "Security Document Printing Ink." This patent relates to a printing ink for the printing of security documents, such as bank notes, by the method of engraved steel die printing, wherein the volatile solvents comprise at most 15%, referred to the total weight of the ink, of one or more volatile organic substances, and wherein the volatile matter may further contain water. These inks reply to the new environmental requirements and have still better wiping characteristics on the printing cylinders or plates. They allow document printing without interleaving. This moves the art from the so called "trichloroethylene wiping intaglio printing inks" of the past to the newer "waterwiping technology" using intaglio inks which can easily be removed from the PVC wiping roller without highly toxic solvents such as the chlorinated hydrocarbons. 6 pages of text, no drawings, 17 claims.

Issued to Albaert Amon of Lausanne, Switzerland, and Anton Bleikolm, Pierre Degott, Olivier Rozumek, and Haim Bretler, all of Switzerland. October 30, 1990.

Patent No. 5,002,636. "Security Paper for Currency and Bank Notes." Very similar to the Crane Patent No. 4,941,687, given above.

Issued to Timothy T. Crane of Dalton, Massachusetts. March 26, 1991.

Patent No. 5,007,339. "Convertible Multicolor Printing Machine, Especially for the Printing of Banknotes." 3-1/2 pages of text, 4 pages of 4 drawings.

Issued to Albrecht J. Germann of Wurzburg, Germany. April 16, 1991.

Note: An improvement over the rotary press described in Patent No. 4,509,424 of April 9, 1985, by the same inventor.

Patent No. 5,009,156. "Multi-color Rotary Printing Machine for Simultaneous Recto-verso Printing." Another modification of the inventor's press designs. See Patent No. 5,007,339, given above. 2-1/2 pages of text, 1 page of 1 drawing.

Issued to Albrecht J. Germann of Wurzburg, Germany. April 23, 1991.

Patent No. 5,063,163. "Method of Detecting Counterfeit Paper Currency." A method of detecting illegitimate paper currency by detecting the starch content therein that exceeds the amount in genuine currency. A colorless iodine solution is applied to the suspect note. In genuine currency there will be no change in the color of the solution. In illegitimate currency paper, the applied solution will change to a black coloration.

Issued to Dov Carmeli, Tampa, Florida. November 5, 1991.

Patent No. 5,062,360. "Combined Rotary Web-fed Printing Machine, Especially for the printing of Securities." This rotary web-fed printing press has three successively arranged printing units, namely one offset and two intaglio printing units which are all of a similar design to sheet-fed printing units. All of these combined, rotary, web-fed presses make it possible to print securities, especially bank notes, in one operation, with a safety background which can be made by an indirect printing process, such as offset, and with a main design made by intaglio printing. 8-1/2 pages of text, 9 pages of drawings, 16 claims.

Issued to Albrecht J. Germann, Hans B. Bolza-Schunemann, Johannes G. Schaede, all of Wurzburg, and Joachim A. H. Lapp, of Margetshochheim, Germany. November 5, 1991.

Patent No. 5,074,596. "Currency Paper, especially Bank Note, with a Safety Design and the Process for Producing It." The safety design printed on a currency paper is composed on the one hand, of a basic design with parallel lines (10, 20, 30) extending in a specific direction, with a plurality of interruptions, by means of which regions in the form of letters are marked out, and of a plurality of line segments (1, 11, 21) which fill these regions. A plurality of groups (R to Z) of letters located next to one another respectively form a word. Within each group, all the line segments are parallel to one another, but from word to word the directions of the respective line segments differ from one another, so that there is a plurality of words with line segments inclined differently in relation to the direction of the basic-design lines. Mutually adjacent successive lines of the basic design and mutually adjacent successive line segments have alternately different colors, preferably three different colors being represented in an attempt to reproduce a currency paper with a multi-color safety design of this type by means of a color copier, the line segments crossing the sensing direction at a relatively large angle, above all approximately at a right angle, are reproduced more broadly and more diffusely than the line segments and lines extending approximately in the sensing direction, so that, as a result of this line spread, the corresponding words, inconspicuous in the safety design of the genuine currency paper at a fleeting glance become clearly visible. Nine claims, nine drawing sheets.

Issued to Castgagnoli Rinaldo, Lausanne, Italy. December 24, 1991.

Note: Assigned to Thomas de la Rue, Giori, S.A.

Patent No. 5,093,184. "Security Paper with Metallic Patterned Elongated Security Element." This invention is concerned with enhancing the security of currency paper and checks. It describes a security strip which is more difficult to counterfeit than the present bank notes containing windowed threads. 5-plus pages of text, 4 pages of drawings, 21 claims.

Issued to David J. Edwards of Overton, United Kingdom. March 3, 1992.

Note: Assigned to Portals Limited, Hampshire, United Kingdom.

Patent No. 5,096,038. "Thread Detector Assembly." Describes a thread detector assembly for detecting an activated, elongate thread which is incorporated within a sheet of paper. 2-1/2 pages of text, 4 pages of drawings.

Issued to Michael Potter and David C. Reeves, both of Hampshire, England. March 17, 1992.

Patent No. 5,136,942. "Web-Fed Printing Machine for Recto-Verso Printing, Especially of Banknotes." A modification of the press designs invented by the ever prolific Albrecht J. Germann of Wurzburg, Germany. See U.S. Patents Nos. 4,441,423; 4,509,424; 5,007,339; 5,009,156; and 5,062,360, all of which are referenced above. 4-plus pages of text, pages of drawings, 8 claims.

Issued to Albrecht J. Germann of Wurzburg, Germany. August 11, 1992.

Note: Assigned to De La Rue Giori, S.A. of Lausanne, Switzerland.

Patent No. 5,151,607. "Currency Verification Device Including Ferrous Oxide Detection." Describes an automatic verification device for currency and other security paper containing an embedded security thread. It first determines the presence of the thread within the paper and then assures that the thread is not present on the paper surface. The device is in the form of a stand-alone currency insertion unit similar to a credit card reader and includes a metal detection circuit to verify the presence of the embedded metal thread. Photo detectors within the unit detect the presence of reflected light off either or both currency surfaces. The currency is verified when the metal is detected and there is no reflection off either surface of the currency paper. 3-1/2 pages of text, 3 pages of drawings, 13 claims.

Issued to Timothy T. Crane of Dalton, Massachusetts, and Richard A. Menelly of Burlington, Connecticut. September 29, 1992.

Patent No. 5,261,954. "Authenticatable Security Paper and Authenticating Composition Therefor." A security paper authenticating system comprises, in combination, a security paper carrying both starch and an iodate salt, typically potassium iodate, and an authenticating composition comprising an acidic solution of an iodide salt, typically potassium iodide, the system being such that on applying the authenticating composition to authentic security paper, as by a pen, brush, or stamp pad, iodine is generated and a characteristic starch-iodine coloration is produced. The authenticating composition is preferably aqueous or part-aqueous, and is preferably made acidic by means of a weak organic acid such as tartaric acid. The authenticating composition preferably also contains an antioxidant such as ascorbic acid. The invention extends to the paper and the authenticating composition individually. 20 claims, no drawings.

Issued to Peter Collins, High Wycombe, England. November 16, 1993.

Note: Assigned to the Wiggins Teape Group Ltd., Hampshire, England.

Patent No. 5,308,992. "Currency Paper and Banknote Verification Device." A photodiode and a phototransistor are positioned on opposite sides of a bank note subject to verification for authenticity under transmitted light. A logic circuit determines the presence or absence of the security feature and correspondingly provides visual or audible indication thereof. The photodiode, phototransistor, and related circuitry are arranged within an enclosure that is attached to a currency receiving device, such as a cash register. 5 pages of text, 6 pages of drawings, 21 claims.

Issued to Timothy T. Crane of Dalton, Massachusetts, Robert J. Danek of Andover, Connecticut, Steven K. Harbaugh of Castro Valley, California, and Richard A. Menelly of Burlington, Connecticut. May 3, 1994.

Patent No. 5,324,567. "Ink Composition and Components Thereof." Raman-active compounds such as polydiacetylenes are provided in the form of particles whose maximum dimension is 40mm. They can be formulated into inks, for the purpose of printing on security documents which are thus readily capable of authentication. The Raman spectra of chemical compounds have been used for many years as a means of identification. Raman spectra arise when laser light incident upon a sample of the material is scattered. The scattered light includes light of the laser wavelength, plus, at much lower intensity, light of additional wavelengths which are characteristic of the compound. The additional light appears at frequencies which are shifted from that of the laser beam by amounts equal to the frequencies of collective vibrations of the atoms in the compound. The frequencies are determined by the masses of the atoms comprising the material and the forces which hold them together. As these are almost always unique for every chemical compound, the Raman spectrum is often used as its fingerprint. In this way, the compound may be identified in various conditions, for example as a crystal, in solution, as a powder, and in mixtures with other compounds. 5-1/2 pages of text, no drawings.

Issued to Robert Bratchley of Berkshire, Nicholas O. Nugent of Hampshire, and Linda S. Ellis of Wolverhampton, all of England. June 28, 1994.

Note: Assigned to Thomas de la Rue and Company, London, England.

Patent No. 5,388,862. "Security Articles." A bank note includes a security element which is visually detectable in transmitted light to display portions which transmit light and portions which are opaque, the security element including a plurality of layers that include a light-transmitting support layer and two or more series of opaque regions. The arrangement of the opaque regions is such that at certain parts of the security element the regions overlap to prevent light transmission and elsewhere along its length the opaque regions do not overlap or only partially overlap such that light transmission through the security element occurs. Abstract, 2 pages of drawings, description, 35 claims.

Issued to David Edwards of Basingstoke, Great Britain. February 14, 1995.

Note: Assigned to Portals.

Patent No. 5,393,099. "Anti-Counterfeiting Laminated Currency and Method of Making the Same." This invention pertains to a method of producing an anti-counterfeiting document or currency which acts and feels like existing paper currencies. The method of the invention laminates two sheets of currency paper on each side of a thin durable substrate film, thereby forming a durable currency which maintains a paper-like feel. The currency so made exhibits unique and powerful anti-counterfeiting features compared to those presently available. Such currency also lasts significantly longer than conventional "paper" currency. 25 claims, 1 drawing sheet.

Issued to Salvatore F. D'Amato, Monmouth Beach, New Jersey. February 28, 1995.

Note: Assigned to American Bank Note Holographics, Inc., Elmsford, New York.

Patent No. 5,393,556. "Composition and Method for Detecting Counterfeit Paper Currency." A composition for detecting the starch content in counterfeit currency comprising an aqueous-alcohol solution of iodine and acetic acid, and method of applying same to paper currency genuine or counterfeit. In other embodiments, phenolthalien and bromine are included. Five claims, no drawing.

Issued to Camille Romano, 10964 S.W. 71st Lane, Miami, Florida 33173. February 28, 1995.

Patent No. 5,440,601. "Counting Station for Counting the Notes of Value, in Particular Banknotes, of a Banderoled Pack of Notes." The counting station has a transporting section (26) on which the banderoled packs of notes (P) are moved at certain intervals uniformly past the rotating counting disk (1a, 1a') of a note-counting device (1, 1') fixedly installed on this transporting section. Downstream of the transporting section (2b) there is a diverter (9) with two further transporting sections (2c, 2d), of which one receives packs of notes having the correct number of notes of value and the other receives packs of notes having the incorrect number of notes of value. 11 claims, 5 drawing sheets.

Issued to Rumwalt Kühfuss of Lausanne, Switzerland. August 8, 1995.

Note: Assigned to De La Rue Giori, S.A., Lausanne, Switzerland.

Patent No. 5,449,200. "Security Paper with Color Mark." A security paper is provided for incorporation in a security document. The paper includes a resinous substrate sheet on which indicia are printed. Paper sheets are laminated on either side of the resinous substrate sheet using a suitable adhesive. In the laminated security paper, the indicia printed on the substrate sheet are undetectable when viewed in reflected light, but become apparent when viewed in transmitted light within the visible spectrum. A method for manufacturing the security paper is also provided. 10 pages of text, 4 pages of drawings, 46 claims.

Issued to Dragisa Andric and Borislav Stojanovic, both of Montreal, Canada. September 12, 1995.

Note: Assigned to Domtar, Inc. of West Montreal, Canada.

Patent No. 5,465,301. "Security Threads." A security thread for use in bank notes and the like, includes a substrate having a coating on one or both sides, the coating containing a thermochromic material selected from pigments and dyestuffs which changes from colored to colorless when the temperature of the pigment or dyestuff is changed to the activation temperature. The thermochromic material may be colored when the temperature is below the activation temperature and become colorless when the material is at the activation temperature or above. 6-1/4 pages of text, 1 page of 4 drawings, 63 claims.

Issued to Richard B. Jotcham of Wiltshire, and Gerald S. Payne of Bath, both of the United Kingdom. November 7, 1995.

Patent No. 5,486,022. "Security Threads Having at least Two Security Detection Features." A security device for incorporation into currency paper or other documents of value, consisting of a plastic thread or ribbon having a repeating pattern of a metal region following a non-conducting region. Both regions are imprinted with metal indicia. 3-1/2 pages of text, 1 page of drawings, 10 claims.

Issued to Timothy T. Crane of Windsor, Massachusetts. January 23, 1996.

Note: Assigned to Crane & Company of Dalton, Massachusetts.

Patent No. 5,618,378. "Apparatus for Applying Images, Particularly Security Images to Banknotes." A security or other image, for example a hologram, is applied to a moving stock, e.g. bank-note sheets, by carrying the images in the form of transfers on a web which is moved at the same speed as the stock during application but at a lower speed between application steps, so as to allow relatively close spacing of the images on the web. The web is retracted following each application to compensate for distance traveled during acceleration and deceleration during each cycle. The images are transferred by pressure cylinders which press the images on to adhesive patches provided on the stock at predetermined positions by application rolls. 4-1/2 pages of text, 4 pages of drawings, 28 claims.

Issued to Michal J. Cahill of Coventry, England. April 8, 1997.

Note: Assigned to Molins PLC, London, England.

Patent No. 5,618,630. "Cross-laminated Multilayer Film Structure for use in the Production of Banknotes or the Like." The film substrate includes layers of high-density polyethylene in certain orientations that provide good folding, tearing resistance, and printing characteristics when laminated by certain adhesive resins. 4-1/2 pages of text.

Issued to Gordon L. Benoit et. al. April 8, 1997.

Note: Assigned to Mobil Oil Corporation.

Patent No. 5,631,039. "Security Thread, A Film and a Method of Manufacture of a Security Thread." A magnetic metal is deposited on a film of polymeric substrate as the substrate passes through a solution containing the magnetic metal and a preparatory operation is carried out on a surface of the substrate prior to immersion in the solution. This results in the magnetic metal being deposited on the substrate in a specific pattern and provides both a visually discernable security feature and a magnetically detectable security feature. 7-1/2 pages of text, 2 pages of drawings, 23 claims.

Issued to Malcolm R.M. Knight and Duncan H. Reid, both of Basingstoke, and Jeffrey A. Harrison of Hawarden, all of the United Kingdom. May 20, 1997.

Patent No. 5,660,919. "Sheet for Security Documents Having High Printability and High Handling Resistance." This invention concerns paper sheets for bank notes or other valuable securities that can be imprinted by offset printing and/or by intaglio printing. It relates to a composition for surface treatment of or for impregnating the face of a paper sheet in such manner as to simultaneously confer to it the properties of good imprintability and resistance to the effects of circulation. The properties are found when the surface is treated with a composition containing one mineral filler selected from the kaolins or silicas, and one elastomeric binder selected from a group of aqueous dispersions of polyurethanes, acrylate copolymers, carboxylated styrenebutadiene copolymer, or polymers in which one of the monomers is acrylonitrile or isoprene or neoprene, or their mixtures. Polyurethan seems preferable. These coatings will not affect a watermark, if one is used. 4-plus pages of text, 1 page of drawings, 20 claims.

Issued to Antoine Vallee of Charavines, France, and Christophe Halope of Voiron, France. August 26, 1997.

Note: Assigned to Arjo Wiggins S.A., Paris, France.

Patent No. 5,662,735. "Chemical Solution for Detecting Counterfeit Paper Currency." This invention relates to a solution for detecting counterfeit paper currency. The solution contains iodine at a concentration of from 0.005 to 3 grams/liter and one or more solvents selected from the groups consisting of alcohols,

ketones, polyalcohols, esters, ethers, or mixtures thereof of solvents belonging to the same group or to several groups of these solvents. The solvent, if miscible with water, contains distilled water in a ratio of from 99:1 to 1:99 parts by volume. If not miscible in water, the solvent is saturated with distilled water at a temperature of 20 degrees C. The solution is preferably contained in ballpoint pens, fountain pens or other similar dispensers which are then used to countersign the paper currency. A counterfeit currency will cause a visible line to appear on the currency in about one minute. However, in the case of genuine paper currency, the drawn line of solution does not change color and disappears completely from the countersigned currency. 23 claims, no drawings.

Issued to Piergiorgio Pifferi of Bologna, Italy. September 2, 1997.

Patent No. 5,698,333. "Multilayer film structures for use in the production of banknotes or the like." A laminated multilayer film substrate for use in the production of bank notes includes a first layer comprises (a) a first layer having inner and outer sides, comprising at least about 50 weight percent of a high density polyethylene having a density of at least about 0.94, said first layer being oriented in the transverse direction (TD) to a degree which is at least three times greater than the degree of orientation present in the machine direction (MD); . . . 36 claims, no drawings.

Issued to Gordon L. Benoit, Victor, New York, and Vander Velden, Macedon, New York. December 16, 1997.

Note: Assigned to the Mobil Oil Corporation.

Patent No. 5,915,731. "Embossing of Banknotes or the Like with Security Devices." A security document such as a bank note (40) is provided which has a transparent portion (42) of plastics material which includes a security device (50). The region (44) surrounding the transparent portion (42) and preferably all the remaining part of the banknote (40) is printed with indicia. The security device (50) includes regions (52, 54, 56 and 58) of embossed lines extending at different angles to each other defining different shapes that are visible to a greater or lesser extent upon transmission and reflection of light as the note is tilted, rotated or viewed from different angles relative to a light source. The embossed lines in some of the regions (52 and 54) are finer than coarser and deeper and more widely spaced lines in the other regions (56 and 58). The coarser, deeper lines are of such a thickness and width to be detected by touch in addition to being visible by the naked eye. There is also provided a method of and apparatus for producing a banknote with a security device in accordance with the invention in which the transparent portion of the note is embossed during an intaglio printing process. 27 claims, 5 drawing sheets.

Issued to Wayne Kevin Jackson of Reservoir, Australia. June 29, 1999.

Note: Assigned to the Reserve Bank of Australia, Craigieburn, Australia.

Patent No. 5,935,696. "Multilayer Film Structures for use in the Production of Banknotes or the Like." A laminated multilayer film substrate for use in the production of bank notes having an oriented polypropylene layer and at least one high density polyethylene layer on each side of the oriented polypropylene layer. The resultant films exhibit good embossability, dead-fold characteristics, and other properties, making them highly suited for the production of bank notes and other security documents. 16 claims, no drawings.

Issued to Gordon L. Benoit of Victor, New York, and Rudolf W. Van der Velden of Farmington, New York. August 10, 1999.

Note: Assigned to the Mobil Oil Corporation, Fairfax, Virginia. This patent is similar to Nos. 5,618,630, 5,698,333, and 5,716,695, all by Benoit et. al.

Patent No. 6,063,176. "Bright Metallic Intaglio Ink Composition." A two-part metallic ink composition for intaglio printing is provided which produces bright and shiny ink deposits when printed. The two parts of the ink are stored separately from each other and mixed together either immediately or within a predetermined time period prior to use. The first part comprises varnish in the amount of 60–85%, wax in the amount of 6–15% and solvent in the amount of 6–25%, by weight. These three constituents of the first part are heated together until the wax has just completely melted, stirred and cooled to room temperature. The resultant mixture, which appears physically as a gelled varnish (vehicle), advantageously permits the formulation of a bright metallic intaglio ink without the use of an extender. The second part comprises metallic pigment. About 1 part by weight of the first part and about 0.5–2.0 parts by weight of the second part are mixed together to form the composition. Preferably, the metallic pigment is pre-wetted with about 2–4% solvent, so as to form a bread crumb-type consistency, before it is mixed with the first part to prevent dusting (i.e. the escape of pigment into the environment) and to assist in the mixing of the two components. The first part may comprise a drier in the amount of 0.4–2.0% by weight. The particle size of the pigment is preferably less than about 18 microns. To produce the brightest reflective appearance the printed ink composition deposit is heated, immediately following printing, to about 65–75 degrees C. for a period of about one second. Background: In the security printing industry a major concern is presented by the use of color photocopiers by counterfeiters to produce counterfeit documents from security documents. One means of alleviating such counterfeiting would be to incorporate into a security document areas of bright metallic printing because a color photocopier is unable to accurately reproduce such printing due to certain known inherent limitations of color photocopiers themselves (bright gold surfaces are reproduced as yellow and bright silver surfaces are reproduced as grey). However, to date, all attempts in the industry to produce a metallic intaglio ink which will successfully print a long-lasting metallic image having a bright and shiny appearance, have failed. 15 claims, no drawings.

Issued to Eric A. Lyen of 67 Amberwood Crescent, Nepean, Ontario, Canada K2E 7C2. May 16, 2000.

Patent No. 6,089,614. "Security Device." A security device comprises a substrate (1) having a viewing region (3) which is provided on one side with first indicia (7) and on the other side with second indicia (9) overlying the first indicia. The substrate carries an obscuring material (10) aligned with the second indicia (9) so as to prevent at least the second indicia from being viewed from the one side of the substrate under reflected radiation. The substrate is sufficiently transparent while the obscuring material permits the passage of sufficient transmitted radiation to allow the second indicia (9) to be viewed from the one side of the substrate under transmission conditions. 46 claims, 4 drawing sheets.

Issued to Paul Howland of Hants, Kenneth John Drinkwater, and Brian William Holmes, both of Surrey, all of the United Kingdom. July 18, 2000.

Patent No. 6,098,546. "Method and Device for Security Printing." For security printing of documents, in particular bank notes, by printing a sheet or web using intaglio technology, an ink image is applied to transfer rollers (6) using rotary screen printing technology, said ink image is transferred from the transfer rollers to one or more intaglio plates which are provided with engravings and are fixed in or on the shell of a plate cylinder, and the ink present in the engravings of the intaglio plates is transferred to a sheet or web pressed against the plate cylinder (1) by a counter pressure cylinder (8). Two claims, two drawings.

Issued to Karel Johan Schell of Voorstraat 60, NI-2201 HX Noordwijk, Netherlands. April 8, 2000.

Patent No. 6,101,939. "Rotary Printing Machine for Security Papers." The web-fed or sheet-fed printing machine for security papers, in particular bank notes, possesses a principal printing group. It further has an additional, independent printing group (20) placed upstream of the principal printing group in the feed direction of the paper and allowing a pattern in at least one predetermined color to be printed over the entire width of the paper before the paper passes into the principal printing group. Seven claims, one drawing sheet.

Issued to Fausto Giori of Lausanne, Switzerland, and Johannes Schaede of Wurzburg, Germany. August 15, 2000.

Note: Assigned to De la Rue Giori S.A., Lausanne, Italy.

Patent No. 6,243,204. "Color Shifting Thin Film Pigments." A color shifting multilayer interference film is provided which may be used to produce flakes for use in colorants having color shifting properties. The flakes can be interspersed into liquid media such as paints or inks which can subsequently be applied to objects or papers to achieve color variations upon shift in angle of incident light or upon shifts in viewing angle. 29 claims, 6 drawing sheets.

Issued to Richard A. Bradley Jr. of Santa Rosa and Matthew R. Witzman of Rohnert Park, both of California. June 5, 2001.

Patent No. 6,270,610. "Method for preparing multilayer film structures for use in the production of banknotes or the like." Nine claims, no drawings.

Issued to Gordon L. Benoit, Victor, New York, and Vander Velden, Macedon, New York. August 7, 2001.

Note: An improvement, but essentially the same techniques as described in Patent No. 5,698,333 by the same inventors.

Patent No. 6,471,248. "Banknotes Incorporating Security Devices." A security document (1) such as a bank note, is formed from a sheet-like substrate (10) of clear plastic material with layers (13, 14, 15, 16) of opacifying ink applied to the surfaces (11, 12) of the substrate (10). The security document (1) includes a security device (20) which is at least partially obscured by the layers (13, 14) of opacifying ink on a flat surface (11) of the substrate (10). The layers (15, 16) on the second surface (12) of the substrate (10) are applied in such a manner so as to leave a "half-window" area uncovered by opacifying ink through which the security device (20) is visible for one side of the document (1). The security device (20) may extend transversely outside the half-window area and be visible in transmission, enabling a different contrasting effect to be observed from both sides of the document. Background: In Australian Patent Specification No. AU-A-87665/82 there is disclosed a security document and a method of producing a security document, in which opacifying coatings of ink are applied to both sides of a sheet-like substrate formed from a clear plastics film. The security document may be produced with some areas to which no opacifying coating is applied on both sides of the clear plastics substrate. These clear, transparent areas are known as "windows" and are particularly suitable for incorporating security devices, for example diffraction gratings, optically variable devices, and embossed images, which can be inspected in the transparent areas or windows from both sides of the security document. However, a security device, such as a diffraction grating, in a window generally has the same appearance when viewed from both sides of the security document. It is therefore desirable to provide a security document which incorporates a security device that presents a different appearance from opposite sides of the document.

Issued to Bruce Hardwick of Wandong, Wayne Kevin Jackson of Reservoir, Paul Zientek of North Carlton, and Cameron Rex Hibbert of Churchill, all of Australia. October 29, 2002.

Note: Assigned to Secrency Pty Ltd. of Victoria, Australia.

Patent No. 7,883,762. "Double sided printed security document." This invention concerns a security document comprising as security element against recto/verso copying, indicia present on both sides and capable of being viewed under reflected lighting and forming an image capable of being viewed under transmitted light. The invention is characterized in that said indicia comprise lines and form said image with 3D effect. 14 claims, 1 drawing.

Issued to Pierre Doublet of Saint-Brice, France. February 8, 2011.

Note: Assigned to Arjowiggins Security, Paris, France.

Patent No. 8,064,632. "Interference Security Image Structure." An interference filter having a plurality of layers and a spectrum as a function of angle of observation is combined with a metameric element adjacent the interference filter and appearing to have a same color as the interference filter at at least one angle of observation and a contrasting color as said interference filter at least one other angle of observation. A plurality of interference filter layers, including a metallic layer, can be provided on a support structure for the layers. The support structure is then adapted to allow the layers to be seen from a top and a bottom side, with the layers being adapted to have different spectra as a function of angle of observation in reflection and transmission. 20 claims, 6 drawings.

Issued to Bill Baloukas and Ludvik Martinu, both of Montreal, Canada. November 22, 2011.

Note: Assigned to Corporation de l'Ecole Polytechnique de Montf, Montreal, Quebec, Canada.

Patent No. 8,230,786. "Method of Manufacturing An Engraved Plate." Abstract: A method of manufacturing an engraved plate used in intaglio printing, said plate being engraved by a tool, for example a laser beam, characterized in that the engraving tool used data from a depth-map, based on a three-dimensional raster image of the document to be printed. Background: Traditionally, the manufacture of intaglio plates is a long and complex process, which begins with the hand engraving of a steel or copper plate, making a copy of this first plate, adding by chemical engraving other elements, making several plastic imprints of this final original plate, welding them together, and going through an important number of galvanic bathes to obtain the final product, being the intaglio printing plate to be mounted on the machine. The whole process of plate manufacturing can take several months, and is therefore very long and costly. The present invention is based on the use of a depth-map, which is a computer file, which contains a three-dimensional raster image of the engraving, on the use of a plate as a workpiece to be engraved and on a tool receiving a depth-map information.

Issued to Fausto Giori of Lausanne, Dirk Dauw of Vinzel, Jacques Perrier of Commugny, and Laurent Mathys of Plan-les-Ouate, all of Switzerland. July 31, 2012.

Note: Assigned to KBA-Giori S.A., Lausanne, Switzerland.

Patent No. EP 1400353 A1. "Intaglio Printing Machine." A rotary web-fed printing machine for printing securities, on a substrate, consisting of at least a plate cylinder (1) supporting at least one printing plate (2) and inked by inking units, and an impression cylinder (3), both cylinders (2, 3) forming a printing nip through which the substrate (4) passes during the impression operation. It further comprises a wiping system (21, 22) for wiping the ink on the plate cylinder and a high energy beam drying system (14) to dry the print.

Issued to Johannes Georg Schaede. March 24, 2004.

Note: Assigned to Kba-Giori, S.A.

Appendix K

Aliases Used by Counterfeiters
(Based on U.S. Secret Service Records, Court Records, and Newspapers)

Real name	Occupation	Aliases
Adams, Thomas	Engraver	Thomas A. Lewis
Alexander, William	Dealer	William Lyons
Ashton, Charles K.	Forger	Harris Smith
Ballard, Benjamin F.	Dealer	Charles Marshall
		George McBride
		Charles Reid
		Benjamin F. Newell
		Peen
Ballard, George	Dealer	George Hill
Ballard, Thomas	Engraver	Thomas Avery
		Thomas Weston
		Tom Davis
		John Davis
		Tom Reed
Boyd, Benjamin	Engraver	Billy Wilson
		B.F. Wilson
		Charles Mitchell
Bridge, John	Dealer	"Hoosier Bill"
		"Hoosier Brown"
		Eli Brown
Brockway, William E.	Major	E.W. Spencer
	Capitalist	"Long Bill"
Brockway, Mrs. William E.	Wife	Mrs. Gilbert
Brown, Mary A.	Dealer	Mary Henderson
	Wife of Billy Brown	"Mother Brown"
	Mother of Billy Brown	
Charles, Salem	Engraver	Charles Hill
		J.W. Murphy
		James H. Wilson
Cole, Henry C.	Capitalist	"Big Dutch"
		Dutch Harvey
Cluff, William	Mid-level	Frank Bennett
	Capitalist	
Congdon, Charles Timothy	Printer	Charles Conklin
	Dealer	
Congdon, Henry T.	Printer	Tom Congdon
		Harrison Bentline
		"The Grand Duke"
Conners, Michael	Dealer	Michael Brady
Courtney, James	Capitalist	"Little Jimmy"
		James Brunnel
		Charles Harwood
		James L. Courtney

chart continued on next page

Appendix K *continued*

Aliases Used by Counterfeiters
(Based on U.S. Secret Service Records, Court Records, and Newspapers)

Real name	Occupation	Aliases
Cowsden, Jeremiah	Engraver	John Colburn
	Forger	A.P. Miller
Davis, John	Shover	Philip Leiberman
		Henry Leiberman
		Henry Schmidt
Deetjen, Anthony	Engraver	Anthony Decker
		A. Rose
Doyle, James B.	Capitalist	Foster
		Grace
		Baker
Dressler, Washington	Printer	W.H. Rogers
	Dealer	
Driggs, Nelson	Capitalist	David Downs
		J.L. Watson
		Captain Jones
		Captain Nelson
		George Baker
		J.T. King
		Dr. John King
		W.E. Jones
		William Jones
		J.F. Belden
		John Candle
		Mr. Carroll
		Lewis Nelson
		Nelson D. Riggs
Ellison, Charles	Engraver	Kale Ellis
		George Pintwater
Finch, Oscar		Lucas McGlue
		Lucas McGhee
Ganzer, Richard P.	Dealer	Rudolph Meyer
George, Will	Shover	Joe Smith
Gray, James	Shover	John Pettingal
Guletin, G.	Dealer	"Terrarossa"
Guyon, Henry (Jim)	Dealer	Henry Clinton
	Engraver ?	J. Dusenberry
		Jim Hank
		Jim Hamilton
Hale, Thomas (Tom)	Capitalist	"Cranky Tom"
Harrison, Henry	Dealer	Thomas Congdon
		Charles Conklin
Harrison, Dennis	Dealer	"Dashing Charley"
		Tom Clifford

chart continued on next page

Appendix K *continued*

Aliases Used by Counterfeiters
(Based on U.S. Secret Service Records, Court Records, and Newspapers)

Real name	Occupation	Aliases
Harrison, Dennis		Harry Ferrin
		Henry Ferrin
Henry, Edward	Raiser	Edward Rondell
Hogan, Thomas	Shover	"Black Jack"
Holmes, Henry	Dealer	Hank Hall
		"Little Henry"
		Harry Hall
Hooper, Samuel	Shover	"Lone Sam"
Johnson Sr., John	Engraver	Charles Davis
Johnson, Charles	Engraver	Cyrus Davis
Johnson, Thomas Ira	Engraver	James Reed
Locke, Joseph	Dealer	"Gopher Bill"
Mack, Mrs. M.T.	Counterfeit	Mrs. Tinsa MacMillan
	Stamp Dealer	
Martin, Isaac	Green Goods	Martin Farrall
	Game	W.A. Newman
McCartney, John Peter	Engraver	Joe Woods
	Capitalist	Charles Lang
		Robert L. Wilmer
		Professor Joseph Woods
		Andrew Long
		Captain Judd
		Pete McCartney
		Thomas McCartney
		Mr. Warren
		Carter Ward
		Wilman Judd
		George Zandt
		John Clark
		J.G. Swan
		Thomas Raddish
		Thomas Myers
		Thomas Riley
McCartney, Levi	Shover	Robert Rankin
		John Ogle
		John Douglas
		"The Hoosier"
		Joe Rogers
McQuirk, James H.	Dealer	James Cobin
Menges, Clinton	Dealer	J.G. Hamilton
Northerman, George	Engraver	Gordon C. Montrose
Norton, Charles	Engraver	Philander Nobel
Novak, Moses	Dealer	H. Frankel

chart continued on next page

Appendix K *continued*

Aliases Used by Counterfeiters
(Based on U.S. Secret Service Records, Court Records, and Newspapers)

Real name	Occupation	Aliases
O'Connor, Margaret	Shover	Ann Berry
Ogle, Miles	Engraver	George W. Ogle
		J.F. Oglesby
		George W. Wilson
		James Graham
Ogle, John	Shover	Tom Hayes
		Robert M. Rankin
		George Irwin
		John Oney
Ott, Julia	Wife of Jacob	Annie Lenhart
Rittenhouse, James K.	Dealer	James K. Kincaid
Robinson, William H.	Dealer	"Gopher Bill"
Shafer, Augustus	?	William Lang
Sheriden, Walter	Forger	Charles Ralston
		Keene
Shotwell, Theodore	Dealer	Tom King
Smith, Sidney	Engraver	"Baldy"
Stadtfeld, Charles	Dealer	Charley Belden
		Thomas Miller
Stadtfeld Family, the old	Dealers	"The Beldens"
Stadtfeld Family, the old*	Dealers	"The Schafers"
Stadtfeld, Nicholas	Dealer	Peter Marsh
Straille, Charles	Raiser	Hiram Lepper
Sullivan, Percy B.	Raiser	S.M. Allen
		S.W. Woodson
Thompson, Robert	Capitalist	Dr. J.H. Roberts
Thompson, William H.	Dealer	"One-Eyed Thompson"
	Raiser	
Trout, Mrs.	Wife of John B. Trout	Mrs. Young
Ulrich, Charles	Engraver	James Winell
		"Dutch Charlie"
Van de Linden, C.A.	Capitalist	Augustine Lettaril
Walters, Charles	Dealer	Henry Boland
		Walter Scott
Warburton	Capitalist	"Bristol Bill"
		Henry Parker
Ward, Fred	Shover	Fred Harris
Warfield, Eugene	Shover	Joseph E. Graham
Wendelken, George	Dealer	"Dutch George"
White, Irvine	Engraver	George Irvine White
		G.J. White
		George White
		Charles White

(while in Clinton, Illinois)

Endnotes

Chapter 1

1. This may be the Captain John Blackwell who was born before 1630 in Mortlake, Surrey, England. That person was appointed the rank of captain in 1650 for his services in the Parliamentary Army. In America he was the Deputy Governor of Pennsylvania from December 18, 1688, to January 2, 1690.

2. Anonymous. "A Model for Erecting a Bank of Credit, With a Discourse in Explanation thereof. Adapted to the Use of any Trading Countrey, where there is a Scarcity of Moneys: More Especially for His Majesties Plantations in America." London, England: 1688. Reprinted in Boston, Massachusetts: 1714.

   There is a copy in the Library of the Massachusetts Historical Society. The pamphlet is also reprinted in *Tracts Relating to the Currency of the Massachusetts Bay, 1682–1720*, by Andrew McFarland Davis. It is clear that banks originated in Europe and that some of them pre-dated the Massachusetts Bank by a considerable time. The Bank of Venice can trace its origins to 1171, although bank bills were not issued until much later. The Bank of Amsterdam was founded in 1609 and was modeled after that of Venice. *The Analectic Magazine*. "Historic Sketch of the Principal Banking Companies of Europe." December 1819. pp. 433–442.

3. John Blackwell (?). "Some Additional Considerations Addressed unto the Worshipful Elisha Hutchinson, Esq., By a Gentleman that had not seen the forgoing Letter." Boston, Massachusetts: 1691. J. Hammond Trumbull attributed this pamphlet to Captain Blackwell. A copy of the pamphlet is in the collections of the Boston Athenaeum.

4. Letter from Deputy Governor Danforth to Sir H. Ashurst. April 1, 1690. Quoted in Thomas Hutchinson's *The History of the Colony and Province of Massachusetts-Bay*. Volume 1. Mayo edition, 1936. p. 337.

5. Peter Earle's *The Treasure of the Concepcion* gives the most accurate and detailed information yet published about the Phips expedition to Hispaniola and his recovery of the treasure. This wreck yielded the greatest amount of treasure recovered from any sunken ship until the 20th century. During the past 50 years, there have been several well-financed attempts to find this wreck, including one lead by Jacques Cousteau in the summer of 1968, but all failed until it was rediscovered on November 30, 1978, by Burt Weber Jr. on Half Moon Reef, using a custom-designed, hand-held cesium magnetometer. Weber and his fellow divers found that Phipps had recovered most of the treasure.

6. Thomas Hutchinson. *The History of the Colony and Province of Massachusetts-Bay*. Volume I. Mayo edition, 1936. Footnote on p. 336. The best biography of Sir William Phips is by Cotton Mather, *q.v.*

7. Major Walley's narrative journal was published on November 27, 1690, and appears as a nine-pageappendix in Volume I of *Hutchinson's History*. A different view of the expedition is given by Baron de Lahontan in his *Nouveaux Voyages* (*q.v.*), Letter XX, dated January 12, 1691. He exaggerated the number of English killed but generally presents an accurate account. Ernest Myrand collected 19 separate, first-hand accounts of the Phips expedition in his book, *Sir William Phips devant Quebec: Histoire d'un Siege*, published in Quebec in 1893. Benjamin Church wrote prolifically on the history of the French and Indian wars, and his book, *The History of the Eastern Expeditions of 1689, 1690, 1692, 1696, and 1704, against the Indians and French*, published in 1867, was the most popular early work on the subject and was based on the stories told by the author's father, who was a participant.

8. The original drafts of the authorization and the draft of the bills are in the collections of the Massachusetts Historical Society.

9. Cotton Mather. *The Life of Sir William Phips*. New York, New York: Covici-Friede, 1929. p. 90.

10. *Ibid.* p. 89. Normally, there are 20 shillings to a pound.

11. The definitive biography on Coney is Hermann Frederick Clark's *John Coney, Silversmith, 1655–1722*. New York, New York: Da Capo Press, 1971. For its genealogy of the Coney family, the author drew on *Ancestors and Descendants of John Coney* by Mary Lovering Holman.

12. Patricia E. Kane. *John Hull and Robert Sanderson, First Masters of New England Silver*. Volume 1, Chapter 4. pp. 113 and 114, footnote no. 2, and pp. 125 and 126. Kane found evidence in the Boston tax lists suggesting Coney's apprenticeship to Jeremiah Dummer. That alone is not a compelling argument, but it does strengthen the evidence for a Dummer-Coney connection.

13. Goodell. *Acts and Resolves*. Volume VII. p. 747. An article in the *Collectors Club Philatelist* for April 1938, p. 86, lists the payment to Coney as being in the unpublished archives of Massachusetts, volume 1, pp. 238, 320, and 360.

14. David M. Stauffer. *American Engravers Upon Copper and Steel*. Part I (Biographical Sketches). p. 54.

15. Clarke and Foote's *Jeremiah Dummer* is the best biography of this craftsman. See the bibliography for a complete citation.

16. Abridgements of these patents can be found in the (British) *Printing Historical Society's Printing Patents*. pp. 69, 70, 79, and 80.

17. Rollo G. Silver. *The American Printer, 1787–1825*. p. 10. Quoting from Milton W. Hamilton's *The Country Printer*. p. 45.

Chapter 2

1. The first notes of Vermont, bearing a date of February 1781, were inscribed "State of Vermont," but actual statehood did not come until March 4, 1791, owing to the fact that both New York and New Hampshire claimed part of Vermont's land. The issue was resolved in court.

2. Thomas M. Halsey, editor. *The Diary of Samuel Sewell, 1674–1729*. New York, New York: Farrar, Straus and Giroux, 1973. p. 511.

   Samuel Sewell was born in Hampshire, England, in 1652. He came to America as a Puritan but soon developed more secular interests than was normal. He studied at Harvard College and began writing a diary while there. His *Diary*, which covered almost 57 years, gives a rare view of Colonial life during this period. He married Hannah Hull, the daughter of John Hull, the goldsmith mentioned elsewhere in this book.

3. *Boston Weekly News-Letter*. July 31, 1704, no. 15. p. 2, col. 1. The actual proclamation was issued at the Council Chamber in Boston on July 24, 1704. Sewall, in his *Diary*, under the date of July 24, also mentioned the "Proclamation is issued out against the Forgers of the Bills, Etc."

4. Peregrine is a French and Middle English word that means "pilgrim," or a person who journeys to a foreign land. Peregrine White was born

aboard the Mayflower in the Provincetown Harbor to William and Susanna White on November 20, 1620. As the first Pilgrim baby born in the New World, he became esteemed in the community. It came as a particularly shocking and sad development when his son and grandson were arrested for counterfeiting. Peregrine White Jr. was born in 1660 in Marshfield, Massachusetts, and died there November 20, 1727. He was a blacksmith, as was his son, Benoni White, who was born in Weymouth on January 26, 1686.

Virginia Dare was born in Roanoke Colony in what is now North Carolina on August 18, 1587. We know this because John White, Virginia's grandfather and the leader of the colony, went back to England to get assistance and while there gave the information about her birth. When he returned exactly three years later, the colonists had disappeared.

5. The announcement of the gang's arrest appeared in the *Boston Weekly News-Letter* of July 31, 1704: "Several Persons who were Actors and Contrivers in attempting to Counterfeit the 20s. Bills of Credit on this Province, Thereby to Cheat and Cousen Her Majesties Good Subjects, are now in Prison, *viz.* Peregrine White and Benoni White, Black-smiths, John Brewer, Carpenter, and Daniel Amos, Wine-cooper. By the Examination taken, it do's not appear that there had been the Value of One Hundred Pounds of the said Counterfeit Bills Made or Issued, and their Plate and Press is Seized, which it's hoped will put a Full Stop to the further Progress of that Wicked Practice. Thomas Odell one of the principal Actors in that Villany & Cousenage, and also Infamous for his making & uttering of base Money, absconds and is fled from Justice. Whosoever shall discover and cause him to be apprehended that he may be brought to answer for his Crimes aforesaid, will be well rewarded for his pains. And 'tis said the greatest loss in this matter will fall upon N Hampshire in the said Odell be not taken, he having carried most of his Counterfeit Bills into that Province."

6. It's a distinction worth noting that while Fenton and Pierce were counterfeiters because they made notes that were fakes, neither were engravers and merely erased denominational figures on notes and replaced them with higher values.

7. *Cf.* Kenneth Scott. *Counterfeiting in Colonial America.* New York, New York: Oxford University Press, 1957. pp. 28–31. This chapter draws heavily on Scott's work and that of Richard L. Bowen, *q.v.*

8. Apparently, Odell escaped while imprisoned at Castle William, the fortress built on Castle Island in Boston Harbor to defend against attack from the sea. See the warrant referenced in the *Massachusetts Archives*, Lib. LXXI. f. 474.

9. Province of Massachusetts Bay, Province Laws (1704 and 1705), volume I, Chapter VIII. p. 556.

10. A word about dates. Most of the early colonists regarded March 25 as the beginning of the new calendar year. Therefore, you will sometimes see dates in January, February, and March written in a two year format, such as March 1, 1710–11. The first year is the old style of dating, and the second year is the new or current calendar date.

11. The deposition given by Nicholas Campe is quoted in full in Richard L. Bowen's *Rhode Island Colonial Money and Its Counterfeiting, 1647–1726*, pp. 72–75. Bowen states the original document is in the Superior Court Clerk's Office, Drawer 1722M-1723, September, Newport, Rhode Island.

12. Robert Lippincott was born December 12, 1685, in Shrewsbury, Monmouth County, New Jersey. He died in Barbados on April 2, 1718. No genealogical records have been found for Freelove (Lawton) Lippincott.

13. Quoted from the *Bill of Indictment*, published in General Court of Trials, Newport County (1691–1724), volume I. p. 205.

14. *Ibid.* p. 211.

15. *Boston Weekly News-Letter.* No. 724, February 16, 1719. p. 2, col. 2; Felt's *Historical Account of Massachusetts' Currency*, p. 72. Felt states that "Jeremiah Dummer, agent in London, had been instructed by Massachusetts to look after one Bryan, an Engraver on Tower Hill, who had assisted Woddin to counterfeit the Province Bills. Mr. Dummer employed an ingenious man to wait on Bryan, who told him that Woddin had carried the copper plate to Boston."

16. *Boston Weekly News-Letter.* No. 2005, Thursday, August 19, 1742. p. 1, cols. 1 and 2.

17. Owen Sullivan remains one of the most colorful figures in the history of counterfeiting. His story is well told by Kenneth Scott in his book, *Counterfeiting in Colonial America.* New York, New York: Oxford University Press, 1957. Sullivan was obstinate to the end, and on the gallows he turned to the people and said, "I cannot help smiling as 'tis the nature of the beast."

18. *The Life and Confession of Herman Rosencrantz, Etc.* Philadelphia, Pennsylvania: Published by the author, printed by James Chatin and sold by him. 8 pages of text and a final page listing the 17 confederates who helped him pass counterfeit bills.

19. He probably married Grace Kitchel (1757–1818).

20. *New York Times.* Sunday, January 6, 2000.

21. Monroe D. Conway. *The Life of Thomas Paine.* Volume I. p. 102. Paine's accusations are quoted in Eric Newman's *The Early Paper Money of America*, Bicentennial edition. p. 19.

22. William Dunlap. *History of the Art of Design.* Volume I, 1834. 1st edition. p. 156.

23. *Ibid.* Footnote on p. 11.

24. Some authors have said that the first notes using Franklin's nature printing techniques were the 1737 issue of New Jersey.

25. Eric P. Newman. "Nature Printing on Colonial and Continental Currency." *Numismatist.* Volume 77 (1964). pp. 147–154, 299–305, 457–465, and 613–623.

Chapter 3

1. The best account of the Harrison bank-note–engraving dynasty is the article by William J. Harrison entitled "Some Notes on the Harrison Family of Engravers," published in the *Essay-Proof Journal*, volume 3, no. 4, October 1946, pp. 195–203. The author was the great-great-grandson of William Harrison Sr. and had access to many family records. David McNeely Stauffer has brief biographical notes on 10 of the Harrisons in his *American Engravers Upon Copper and Steel*. Scharf and Westcott's *History of Philadelphia* gives only two sentences to the Harrisons and manages to mistake Samuel Harrison for his older brother, Charles. W.S. Barber made no mention at all of the Harrisons in his *American Engravers*, even though he wrote the book while he lived in Philadelphia and mentions other engravers, even bank-note engravers, of that period who were working in the city.

2. The Bank of the United States was created largely through the efforts of Alexander Hamilton while he was secretary of the Treasury. Congress had directed him to study the problem of public credit and his report of

December 13, 1790, outlines the measures he thought should be taken, including the establishment of a new "National Bank." That idea became the federally chartered Bank of the United States. Its charter was the subject of much controversy. The Constitutional Convention of 1787 did not expressly grant Congress the right to charter corporations, but on the other hand, it didn't expressly deny Congress that right, and so the issue was still open for debate when Congress wanted to create a national bank. The proposed legislation to create the bank took the form of a 20-year charter. Thomas Jefferson, James Madison, and General John J. Knox, the secretary of war, were in favor of it. President George Washington, who was initially against the charter, finally decided to accept Hamilton's views and pushed the charter through Congress. The bank was capitalized by the sale of stock and branch offices opened in many cities.

3. The Bank of North America was founded by Robert Morris in Philadelphia in 1781 and opened a branch in New York City in 1782. It continued for many years as the most prominent of the several large banks in the United States and was the first attempt at creating a "central bank" like the Bank of England. Markham states that this bank had 700 clients by 1783, and its weekly receipts and payments totaled $1 million. Jerry W. Markham. *A Financial History of the United States.* Volume I. Amonk, New York: M.E. Sharpe, 2002.

4. The original receipt is in the Dreer Collection at the Historical Society of Pennsylvania. Apparently he charged the bank $5 for the copper plate itself, $100 for engraving the plate, and $5 for "working the plate," which may refer to the preparations that leveled and smoothed the surface of a rough plate. Post notes were payable only after a stated time. In this they were different from the ordinary Demand Notes that were payable upon presentation. Some post notes had engraved denominations while others had blank spaces so the value could be written in. Some post notes were payable only at the issuing bank, while others were payable at a branch office or at both.

5. William Harrison Sr.'s obituary was published in Poulson's *Daily Advertiser* in Philadelphia, October 18, 1803. Both Stauffer and the article in the *Essay-Proof Journal* for October 1946 reprinted the obituary. Philadelphia lost many of its citizens to frequent epidemics of yellow fever. The outbreak that started in July 1793 was the first major epidemic of the disease in the United States. During the next 4 months it killed nearly 5,000 people and orphaned nearly 200 children. We know now that the disease is spread by the female mosquito of a particular species, but physicians in the 1790s had no idea what caused the disease, and the standard treatment was to bleed patients and to give them strong purges, cathartics, and emetics. The epidemic that lasted from August to November 1797 killed 1,292 people. The next year, more than 3,600 died from this scourge, even though thousands of people fled from the city. Yellow fever struck Philadelphia again in 1802, 1803, 1805, 1819, and 1853. There were fewer and less-severe outbreaks of yellow fever in Philadelphia after 1800 because the city cleaned up the streets in that year and built the first major municipal water system in the nation. That did away with the need to store rainwater in barrels, which were a convenient breeding ground for mosquitoes.

These statistics are from several sources, but see especially J.H. Powell's *Bring Out Your Dead: The Great Plague of Yellow Fever in Philadelphia in 1793.* Philadelphia, Pennsylvania: University of Pennsylvania Press, 1993.

6. The "sc" following a person's name is an abbreviation for the Latin word *sculpsit*, meaning "engraver." The term derives from the verb *sculpere*, to carve or engrave. Some engravers signed as "sculp.," others as "sculpsit.," and frequently as "sc." The Latin verb *incidit*, meaning "to incise" or cut," is abbreviated "incid.," and sometimes as "inc.," both forms denoting the engraver.

7. Some of the bank-note work of William Harrison Jr. can be seen in Haxby's *Standard Catalog of United States Obsolete Bank Notes 1782–1866.* Examples include the Farmers Bank of the State of Delaware (Dover branch), the Bank of Delaware, the Farmers and Mechanics Bank of Laurel, Delaware, the Franklin Bank of Alexandria, District of Columbia (1817–1820), the Merchants Bank of Alexandria (all notes dated 1815), the Central Bank of Georgetown & Washington (1817–1820), the Bank of Georgetown, the Union Bank of Georgetown (of which only two counterfeits are shown), and of course, his first work for the State Bank at Trenton. An unidentified "Harrison" is imprinted on some of the notes of the Trenton Banking Company, and since some of these notes are so similar to the notes of the State Bank at Trenton, it is very likely that William Harrison Jr. engraved them as well. In Pennsylvania, William engraved and his brother Charles Peter Harrison printed some of the notes issued by the Farmer's Bank of Lancaster, all of which are dated 1815. Other examples of William Jr.'s work for the Pennsylvania banks are the Northwestern Bank of Pennsylvania, the Farmers & Mechanics' Bank of Fayette County (at New Salem), and the Farmers and Mechanics' Bank of Pittsburgh (1814–1818). This list is by no means comprehensive, but the illustrated notes should give a good idea of Harrison's style and design preferences.

8. The Ohio banks include the Owl Creek Bank of Mount Vernon, the Bank of New Philadelphia, the Farmers Bank of New Salem, the Jefferson Bank of New Salem, the Practical Farmers Bank of Springfield, and the German Bank of Wooster. The only Pennsylvania bank listed in the Haxby catalog and attributed to these Harrisons is the Farmers and Mechanics Bank of Pittsburgh.

9. Sam Bass Warner Jr. *The Private City: Philadelphia in Three Periods of Its Growth.* Philadelphia, Pennsylvania: The University of Pennsylvania Press, 1987. pp. 7, 17, 52.

10. James Mease, MD. *The Picture of Philadelphia.* Philadelphia, Pennsylvania: B & T Kitre, 1811.

This edition was reprinted in 1970 by the Arno Press in New York based on a copy in the library of the State Historical Society of Wisconsin. It makes no mention of any bank-note companies.

11. Harry B. Weiss. *The Growth of the Graphic Arts in Philadelphia 1663–1820.* New York, New York: The New York Public Library, 19—. Table on pp. 82 and 83. H. Glen Brown and Meade O. Brown. *A Directory of the Book-Arts and Book Trade in Philadelphia in 1820 Including Printers and Engravers.* New York, New York: New York Public Library, 1950.

12. Anker Smith had been a pupil of the elder James Heath as well as the historical engraver to King George III, George IV, and finally William IV. James Heath engraved the first notes of the Bank of North America, perhaps before 1790, and so began a rather curious circular link between himself, his pupil Smith, Smith's pupil Murray, and later on, Murray's business associate Jacob Perkins and his partner James Heath Jr. Anker Smith (1759–1819) was elected to the Royal Academy in 1797.

13. The Liberty Boys, also known as the Sons of Liberty, were a political group of American patriots who opposed the British government's treatment of the colonies. After the French and Indian War, the Crown found that its treasury was nearly depleted, and to restore it, they sought to impose a series of taxes on the colonists. The Stamp Act of 1765 was especially resented. Some of the Liberty Boys carried out violent acts, such as the burning of the HMS *Gaspé* in 1772. Some notable patriots were members of the Sons of Liberty, including Paul Revere, Patrick Henry, John Adams, Samuel Adams, and Benedict Arnold.

14. William Dunlap. *History of the Rise and Progress of the Arts of Design in the United States.* pp. 285 and 286.

15. Little is known about John Draper's early life. Aside from the plates in Ree's *Cyclopedia*, no engravings have been found signed by him, and it is likely that his professional life was devoted entirely to letter engraving on bank notes. Cemetery records indicate he was 86 years old when he was buried in 1865, putting his date of birth at about 1778. William H. Griffiths's *Story of the American Bank Note Company* says Draper was 24 years old when he began engraving for the *Cyclopedia* in 1794. That would put his date of birth at about 1770, which seems more likely. He became Robert Scot's assistant and pupil, but the exact year is not known. Scot was appointed chief engraver for the newly established U.S. Mint at Philadelphia on November 20, 1793, and he held that position until his death in 1823. Griffiths says that Draper joined Scot in 1803 but gives no documentary evidence. Draper was a member of several bank-note companies through the years, including Fairman, Draper & Company (1822 and 1823); Fairman, Draper, Underwood & Company (1823–1827); Draper, Toppan, Longacre & Company (1835–1845); Draper & Company (1845–1850); and Draper, Welch & Company (1850–1853). After 1853 John Draper remained in retirement until his death on February 10, 1865. His inventory, filed eight days after his death, shows an estate in excess of $150,000. His will left most of his money to his four sons (Edmund, Robert, Henry, and George), his sisters (Hannah Richardson and Rachel Evans), and his daughter (Emma Eliot Speakman). He is now buried next to two of his sons in Lawnview Cemetery in Rockledge, Pennsylvania.

16. These notes are shown in the Haxby *Standard Catalogue* under DC-385, the Bank of Washington (volume 1, p. 212). Since the notes were issued during the period the bank was an "association" (1809 and 1810), and John Draper is assumed to be the engraver since his name is imprinted on the note, this is the earliest bank-note work attributed to him. During the bank's charter period, beginning in 1811, the notes were printed by Murray, Draper & Fairman. I have not seen the association notes of this bank to verify the Draper imprint.

17. The notes are shown in Haxby under PA-430, the Farmers & Mechanics Bank (volume 4, p. 2,081). These notes were issued while the bank initially operated as an uncharted association (1807–1809). After the bank was chartered, notes printed in 1810 and later are imprinted Murray, Draper & Fairman. I have not seen the association notes of this bank to verify the Murray imprint.

18. This imprint appears on Proof notes of the Marine Bank of Baltimore, Maryland. One of these notes is shown in Haxby under MD-90 (volume 1, p. 663). The note was issued while the bank operated as an unchartered association (1810).

19. Abel Brewster said he was born in "Preston, Connecticut, of Benjamin and Elisabeth Brewster, on the 6th day of February, 1776." He continued: "When about 14 years of age, I went apprentice to my brother Walter, in Canterbury, to the Clock, Watch, Jewellery [sic] and Silversmith business, and continued with him till I was 18,—when he gave up the trade and entered Dartmouth College, leaving me with a power of attorney to carry on the business for him." (*A Brief Memoire of Abel Brewster, Written by Himself.*)

20. Archibald Binny was born near Edinburgh, Scotland, about 1762 and apprenticed to John Baine in the type-founding business sometime around 1787. He and his family came to the United States in 1795 after he had problems with the Scottish government for supporting annual parliaments and universal suffrage. James Ronaldson was also born near Edinburgh in 1769, and he followed his father in the baking business. He came to America in 1794 and opened a biscuit bakery in Philadelphia. After Ronaldson's bakery burned in 1796, Binny talked

him into a joint partnership in the type-founding business, with Binny as the senior partner. In 1806 they bought the French-made foundry equipment that Benjamin Franklin had purchased for his grandson, Benjamin Franklin Bache. Ronaldson was out of the country when Binny bought an interest in Murray, Draper & Brewster. Binny's investment may have been made with his own money, though, as he had considerable wealth. When Binny retired from his type foundry in August 1815, he sold his half of the company to his partner for $62,000. Binny never took an active role in the management of operations of Murray, Draper & Fairman. He seems to have been only an investor. The legal papers that would have protected Binny's investment have not been found. A search for those papers might be a worthwhile project of a future student of the industry.

21. This description is found in a footnote on pages 10 and 11 of Abel Brewster's *An Appeal to Banks in Particular, and the Public in General*, published in 1815. The use of circular cut-outs which were separately inked in a color different from the rest of the plate and fitted back into the plate is very similar to the "compound plate" that Sir William Congreve patented in England in 1819. John Holt Ibbetson claimed Congreve had stolen the concept from his work. It is doubtful that either Congreve or Ibbetson had heard of Murray and Draper's plan.

22. The short title of this pamphlet is *A Plan for Producing an Uniformity in the Ornamental Parts of Bank or other Bills*. The American Antiquarian Society has a copy.

23. *Ibid.* p. 5.

24. Brewster says David H. Mason "came to Hartford sometime in the winter season of 1807–08, while I was engaged with my said plan for bills, and did sundry small jobs of copper-plate printing, for Mr. [Abner] Reed with whom he had a younger brother [William] living as an apprentice." According to other statements made by Brewster, Mason had learned copper-plate printing in New York City before going to Hartford. Stauffer says Mason is listed in the Philadelphia directories from 1805 to 1818 as a "music engraver." In 1816 he engraved some bank-note vignettes for Murray, Draper, Fairman & Company, but very little bank-note work is attributed to him. He died sometime after 1830.

25. A good example of his paranoia is this passage on page 12 from *A Brief Memoire of Abel Brewster, Written by Himself*: "About the first of September last, I received a quarter cask of Madeira wine from New York, through the hand of an agent in this city, which came to my possession professedly sealed up, but actually left open. In this, it is believed, was an attempt to produce my death by secret and slow poisoning. Unsuspicious of the fact, I persisted in the use of it till it brought me to the very brink of the grave, from which situation I am now laboring to rise."

26. The enmity between Murray and Brewster continued long after Brewster left the company. When Brewster published and distributed several hundred copies of his 1815 pamphlet, Murray was outraged and sued Brewster for libel in the Circuit Court at New Haven, Connecticut. The suit appears on the *Docket Book* for April 13, 1816, but the case continued in court for a full year, starting before Judge Brookhoist Livingston and ending finally with Judge Pierpont Edwards in the April term of 1817. These judges found the pamphlet was not libelous, but Brewster said legal expenses still came to about $1,500. These two documents are to be found in the general case files of the U.S. Circuit Court, District of Connecticut, Unnumbered April Term, Record Group 21, in the National Archives, New England Region.

27. David Fairman was born in Fairfield County, Connecticut, in 1782 and died in Philadelphia on August 19, 1815, about a year after he joined his brother at Murray, Draper & Fairman. Abel Brewster says that David Fairman had visited Jacob Perkins in Newburyport and subsequently

wrote a pamphlet while in Boston, entitled *Philotecnus*, in which he criticized Perkins's bank-note security designs. This pamphlet would be of great interest to students of the industry, but it remains elusive. It is not listed in the National Union Catalog or in Early American Imprints, does not show up in the Research Libraries Information Network (RLIN) database, and is not known to the Library of Congress, the American Antiquarian Society, the Boston Public Library, or the British Library.

28. Anonymous. *Memoire of Charles Toppan*. It is likely that this memoire was written by Robert Noxon Toppan, Charles Toppan's son, and a person who had an interest in the role his father played in the development of bank-note engraving. He also had access to family letters and records. There is a copy of the memoire in the library of the University of Pennsylvania (call number HG 350, N48, 1880a).

29. Robert Noxon Toppan. "A Hundred Years of Bank Note Engraving in the United States." p. 7.

30. The article appears in the *Port Folio*, volume 6, number 3, dated September 1815, on pages 308 and 309, with one illustration of a specimen note. This particular issue is very difficult to find, but the Library Company of Philadelphia has a copy. The white-line engraving shown in the specimen note, which seems to be the principal safeguard against counterfeiting, may have been done using a pantograph. This process is described in chapter 14 of this book.

31. Francis Kearny was born July 23, 1785, in Perth Amboy, New Jersey, the sixth son of Michael and Elizabeth (Lawrence) Kearny. His father was a merchant in New York, and his mother was a sister of Captain Lawrence of the U.S. Navy. Kearny studied drawing at the Columbian Academy of Painting in New York City, and at 18 he was placed with Peter R. Maverick of New York City to study engraving. As soon as he came of age, Kearny opened his own studio. His business card describes him as a "historical engraver." His principal work at this time was in making bookplates. He went to Philadelphia in 1810 and spent the rest of his professional life there. He engraved some of the plates for the *Analectic Magazine*, the *Casket*, and Godey's *Lady's Book*. In 1829, when John Pendleton went to Philadelphia to establish a commercial lithograph house in that city with Cephas Childs, Kearny became a member of the firm, which was then known as Pendleton, Kearny & Childs. He died in Perth Amboy on September 1, 1837, at the age of 52, and is buried at St. Peter's Church.

32. Most references give 1816 or 1817 as the date this company was established, but that is clearly wrong, as one can see on the bank-note specimen illustrated in the 1815 *Port Folio* article mentioned in note 30. That specimen note is imprinted with the company's name and their "TK & T" logo.

33. Scharf and Westcott. *History of Philadelphia, 1609–1884*. p. 1,045.
    I have not been able to confirm Barralet's work on copper-plate inks. His work may have been of a personal, experimental nature and never written up for the professional literature.

34. Abel Brewster. *An Appeal to Banks in Particular and the Public in General*. p. 26.
    Writing about David H. Mason and Christian Gobrecht, Brewster says, "The two former persons were of Murray's own choice; they had been some time under my instruction—one in the art of making dies, and the other one of using them. They were both in the company's employ—one at twelve hundred, and the other at fifteen hundred dollars a year." It isn't clear from the passage which of the two salaries belonged to Gobrecht, but since he was the one making the dies, which requires greater skill, it is logical that he was paid the larger salary.

Chapter 4

1. John J. Currier. *The History of Newburyport, Massachusetts, 1764–1905*. Volume II. pp. 360–362.

2. The definitive and only complete biography of Jacob Perkins is Grenville and Dorothy Bathe's, *Jacob Perkins: His Inventions, His Times, & His Contemporaries*. Philadelphia, Pennsylvania: The Historical Society of Pennsylvania, 1943.

3. Perkins used the term "stereotype" to indicate that a master-printing plate, containing many permanent design elements and some removable dies, could be used to print an endless variety of bank notes simply by removing certain dies, such as those that printed the name of a bank, the name of a town, state, denomination, etc., and substituting other dies having different wording. He borrowed this term from the printing trade where it had long been used to denote a process for making solid plates that were made up of separate designs or printing types. The first such plates were made in Scotland about 1728 by William Ged, a goldsmith. He set up a page of movable type, locked in a frame called a "form," and then turned this upside-down and laid it in a pan of gypsum or "plaster of Paris," or some other semi-liquid substance, just as it was drying. When it was dried completely, he removed the form from its gypsum cast and, using this as a matrix, poured molten type metal into the cast letters, forming one solid plate of lead type. These solid plates of type could be used again and again to print pages for a book. Such plates were called "stereo-types." Stereotyping was not used in general practice until it was improved by Charles Mahon, the third Earl of Stanhope, an eccentric but ingenious nobleman born in London in 1753. He is better known as the inventor of a printing press which bears his name. Through the years, many famous people made improvements to the stereotyping process, including Augustus Applegath, Sir Marc Isambard Brunel, and Sir William Congreve.

4. Perkins described his Stereotype Steel Plates in a pamphlet he published in Newburyport, Massachusetts, on January 1, 1806, entitled "The Permanent Stereotype Steel Plate, With Observations on its Importance and An Explanation of its Construction and Uses." He published a somewhat more-detailed description of the "standard check plate" and gave instructions on its use in a seven-page brochure entitled "Perkins' Bank Bill Test. Together with the Standard Check Plate," which was published in Newburyport in 1809. The check plate is further described in a petition that Perkins addressed to the General Court of Massachusetts dated February 28, 1806. The American Antiquarian Society has originals of both pamphlets.

5. James Akin was born in Charleston, South Carolina, in 1777 and died in Philadelphia, Pennsylvania, on July 18, 1846. Currier, in his *History of Newburyport, Massachusetts*, states that Akin was a clerk for several years in the State Department at Philadelphia under Timothy Pickering. In an advertisement published in the *Newburyport Herald* of April 27, 1804, Akin states that ". . . having completed [his] professional studies in London under an eminent master . . . Specimens may be seen in his possession which will testify [to] his abilities, and more particularly in BANK WORK, having executed the business for several banks in the Southern states, he therefore solicits the attention of the Banks in New England, as there appears at present to exist a want for the security of bills." Akin had been an engraver even before he went to England, as he was one of the engravers who signed their names to an announcement placed by Jacob Perkins in various newspapers in March 1799 concerning his invention of the Stereotype Check Plate. It is also believed that Akin worked with William Harrison Jr. in producing the U.S. Naval Commission certificates in 1798 and 1799. Akin worked in Salem and Newburyport from 1804 to 1808, saying that yellow fever had exiled him from Philadelphia. In 1811 his office was located at No. 22 Mulberry Street (now Arch Street) in Philadelphia. In addition to his

bank-note work, he painted portraits in water colors, furnished designs for book-plates, and engraved satirical cartoons. During his later years, he had an apothecary shop where he sold drugs and medicines. His wife engraved certificates for at least one social organization. Apparently, Akin did not sign any vignettes he engraved for bank notes, as none have been attributed to him.

6. Bathes. *op. cit.* p. 25. The Bathes attribute this quotation to Currier's *History of Newburyport, Massachusetts*, but this appears to be incorrect as a thorough search of both volumes of that work fails to locate the statement.

7. Marthurin Jousse's *La Fidele Ouverture de l'Art de Serrurier*, published in La Flèche (western France) in 1627 and never reprinted, is generally considered to be the earliest work in Europe to give a clear, thorough, and practical description of how to harden and temper steel. Chapters 64 to 68 of the book, which deal specifically with the hardening of steel, have been translated and published in Cyril Stanley Smith's *Sources for the History of the Science of Steel, 1532–1786*. Another work that also explained the conversion of iron to steel and changes in the hardness of steel was Rene de Réaumur's *L'Art de Convertir le Fer Forgé en ACCIER ET L'Art d'Adoucir le Fer Fondu*, published in Paris in 1722. A modern translation by Anneliese Sisco has been published as *Réannur's Memoirs on Steel and Iron*. Chicago, Illinois: University of Chicago Press, 1956.

8. George Escol Sellers was the grandson of Nathan Sellers, who established the family business of making wire-paper molds. His maternal grandfather was the famous portrait painter and museum builder Charles Willson Peale. George was born in Philadelphia on November 26, 1808. When he was 75 years old, Sellers began writing a series of articles for the *American Machinist* magazine, recounting his long life in engineering. These articles were published from 1884 to 1895 and include several mentions of Perkins and the early bank-note industry in Philadelphia. Eugene S. Ferguson, then Curator of Engineering in the Museum of History and Technology at the Smithsonian, collated and edited these articles and other material from unpublished sources in a volume entitled *Early Engineering Reminiscences (1815–40) of George Escol Sellers*. This volume was published in 1965 by the Smithsonian Institution as United States National Museum Bulletin No. 238. George Escol Sellers died January 1, 1899.

9. Eugene S. Ferguson. *Early Engineering Reminiscences (1815-40) of George Escol Sellers*. p. 14.

10. Clarence W. Brazer relates an interesting story about the short life of copper plates. Writing in the *Collectors' Club Philatelist* for October 1943, he says that the famous bank-note firm of Rawdon, Wright, Hatch & Edson put out an advertisement in July 1853 in which they guaranteed "3000 good impressions from a copper plate." Within six months they had to change the wording, reducing the number of copper-plate impressions guaranteed to only "2,000 before and 1,500 after retouching." See the *Collectors' Club Philatelist* for January 1939, p. 38, for the full text of the advertisement.

11. These invoices form a part of the *Perkins Papers* at the Phillips Library of the Peabody Essex Museum in Salem, Massachusetts.

12. Abraham was born on May 4, 1768, at Newburyport. He married Elizabeth Knapp on December 14, 1794. He was quite different from his brother Jacob, being noted for his common sense and honesty. When Jacob ran up several bills he could not pay, Abraham took on the debt and eventually paid it off over a number of years.

13. The only known photograph of this building appears in Genville and Dorothy Bathe's *Jacob Perkins, His Inventions, His Times & His Contemporaries, q.v.* See plate VIII following page 33 in that work. The address of the house given in Bathe is No. 14 Fruit Street, but the Massachusetts Historical Commission has the address at 16–18 Fruit Street as of 1980. The house was built in the Federal style and has almost 8,000 square feet of living space on the three floors. This "Mansion house" was appraised at $3,000 in the inventory of the estate of Abraham Perkins filed in Probate Records in June 1840. His total estate was valued at $20,461.54, which means he died a moderately wealthy man by the standards of the time. Though difficult times made it necessary for Abraham to sell the large house at one point, he later bought it back and lived there until he died. The building used for printing paper money was apparently appraised at only $400. Fruit Street was so named because it had been cut through a fruit orchard in 1801. The owner of the orchard in his transfer of land to the city had stipulated that all of the dwellings built there must be of three stories, and for that reason Jacob Perkins had to build a three-story printing plant. Since the plant had glass windows on all three floors, it is likely that the printing plates were stored in strong boxes or a vault at the end of each workday and a night watchman kept the building secure.

14. Gene Hessler. *The Comprehensive Catalog of U.S. Paper Money*. 5th edition. Port Clinton, Ohio: BNR Press, 1992. pp. 55–58.

15. Charles Wye Williams's *Considerations on the Alarming Increase of Forgery . . . etc.*, was printed in London in 1818 and ran 190 pages, rather long to be called a pamphlet but technically still that. It was addressed to the Bank of England's "Commissioners appointed to inquire into the Remedy for the Prevention of Forgeries." Sir William Congreve was one of the commissioners.

16. The statement was made by J.T. Barber Beaumont in his communication to the Bank of England, part of which was printed in the *Report of the Committee of the Society of Arts, Etc.* London, England: 1818, p. 14. The full statement read: "An apprentice to a writing engraver of two years standing, by three or four days work, is able to copy a Bank Note plate, so that ordinary judges cannot tell the genuine from the spurious. There are not less than 10,000 persons in this country who are able to engrave successful imitations of Bank of England Notes, and nine-tenths of these are in needy, and many of the in distress circumstances. It is, therefore, not surprising, if amongst so many who are competent to relieve their necessities by these forgeries, some should be desperate enough to commit them."

17. Quoted from Virginia Hewett and John Keyworth's *As Good As Gold: 300 Years of British Bank Note Design*. London, England: British Museum Publications, 1987. p. 57.

18. Charles Theodosius Heath was the second (and illegitimate) son of James Heath, the Royal Academician. He was born in 1785 and died on November 18, 1848. He was probably the author of the long article on siderography which was published in the *Journal of the Society of Arts* in 1820. Charles and his brother George Heath actively promoted the business of Perkins and Fairman after they set up in London, and for a time the firm was known as Perkins, Fairman & Heath. George Heath put money into the firm but took no active part in its management. Although Charles was an engraver, like his father, there is no evidence that he engraved any bank-note vignettes for the company. The elder and junior Heath often get mixed up. Griffiths, in his work *The Story of the American Bank Note Company*, writing about the notes of the Bank of North America, mistakes Charles Heath for his father (p. 19). It was the elder Heath (James) who engraved those notes. It helps to read George W. Smith's *James Heath, Engraver to Kings and Tutor to Many*, privately published by the author in 1989, and the biographical notes in *The National Dictionary of Biography*.

19. The Society of Arts is the short name of The Society for the Encouragement of Arts, Manufactures and Commerce, and is usually known as "The Royal Society of Arts." It was founded by William Shipley in 1754, and its membership grew rapidly, reaching 2,500 by 1762. The society gave awards for outstanding inventions, whether they came from poor workmen or rich noblemen. At first these awards were from 10 to 50 guineas, but later they became either silver or gold medals.

20. John Chessborough Dyer was born in Stonington Point, Connecticut, on November 15, 1780, the son of Captain Nathaniel Dyer of the Rhode Island Navy. He was wealthy by inheritance and by his own success as a businessman in Boston. He was well educated and had a fascination for mechanical inventions, especially those that he thought he could promote to both his and the public's advantage. He first became acquainted with Jacob Perkins in 1809, when Perkins had just improved his machine for making nails. Dyer soon patented the nail machine in his own name in England in 1810. He also took out a British patent for Perkins's invention of copper-plate printing and his 1810 patent for preventing counterfeits. Dyer took out these and other patents to protect the business rights and the priority of the machines they advanced, but fully credited Jacob Perkins as the inventor in each patent. He first visited England in 1802 and soon became the equivalent of a modern-day business promoter, representing other American inventors as well. Fulton sent him specifications and drawings of his steamboat in 1811, and Dyer was eventually successful in getting this invention accepted in England. He moved to England permanently in 1811 and established his residence in Manchester in 1816, where he was one of the founders of the *Manchester Guardian* newspaper in 1821. He was also one of the original directors of the Bank of Manchester until that bank came to a disastrous end by fraud, and he lost no less than £98,000. Dyer worked tirelessly to promote the Perkins system in England. In 1819 he published a pamphlet entitled "Specimens and Descriptions of Perkins' and Fairman's Patent Siderographic Plan to Prevent Forgery." He died at Manchester on May 3, 1871, at the age of 90.

21. Apparently the Commissioners of the Bank of England chose to forget that Dyer had failed in a series of experiments that he oversaw at the bank beginning in 1811. In that year he submitted specimens of some notes printed by Abraham Perkins for the New England banks by the patented stereotype process. The bank was very interested in those notes, but when they were given to J.H. Harper, the bank's new superintendent of engraving and printing, he succeeded in a short time in making a good copy on a copper plate, and for that reason, the bank officially turned down the "American" process. The bank had always insisted that any plan of bank-note security must provide a design that could not be copied by another engraver so expertly that the two notes could not be told apart. The bank's officials did, however, remain interested, and the following year they asked Dyer to teach the engraving department how to make and print steel plates. In May 1813 Harper reported that to engrave steel plates took four times as long as would be spent on identical copper plates and that half the steel plates became too brittle in the hardening process and broke. He said also that blemishes had appeared in the unengraved areas of the plates, due probably to oxidation of the steel, and that he was only able to print 35,000 impressions from one plate. These failures may have been the fault of Dyer's supervision. As Mackenzie has pointed out, Dyer may have been an expert in some branches of mechanics, but he was not an engraver, and he was not Jacob Perkins. A.D. Mackenzie. *The Bank of England Note*. pp. 56 and 57.

22. Sir William Congreve was born in Staffordshire on May 20, 1772, and died in Toulouse, France, on May 16, 1828, just four days short of his 56th birthday. He was a member of Parliament from Plymouth from 1818 until his death. His pamphlets include (1) "Of the Impracticability of the Resumption of Cash Payments," published in 1819; (2) "Principles on which it Appears that a more Perfect System of Currency may be formed either in the Precious or Non-Precious Metals," also published in 1819; and (3) "An Analysis of the True Principles of Security Against Forgery . . ." published in 1820. His patents include No. 4404 (inlaid metals for currency plates), granted in 1819; No. 4521 (compound plates for color printing), granted in 1820; and No. 4898 (printing and embossing at one impression), granted in 1824.

23. Augustus Applegath was born June 17, 1788, near the parish of Stepney in west Kent, England. His father had been a ship's captain for the East India Company and later traded with his own ships, making a small fortune and then losing it through unwise speculations. Augustus had a good education and later studied to be a medical doctor. His interest in mechanics, however, proved too powerful, and he left medicine to enter the printing trade. After his work for the Bank of England, he apparently worked alone. He built his own rotary printing presses and repaired and improved the Koenig and Bauer newspaper presses for the *Times*, including eight-feeders and nine-feeders. One of his large presses was on view at the Great Exhibition, and he was privileged to show its operation to Queen Victoria. He died at Dartford, in west Kent, on February 9, 1871, at age 84. W.T. Berry. "Augustus Applegath." *Printing Historical Society Journal*. No. 2, 1966. pp. 49–57.

24. Edward Cowper was born in 1790 and died in 1852. A.D. Mackenzie, in *The Bank of England Note*, states that the museum collections of the Bank of England hold a letter written by Cowper in which he diagrams in a very simple way the printing press that he and Applegath used at the bank to print notes. Mackenzie states that the press printed the back of the note in perfect registry with the front design, but in a reversed impression. Cowper has two patents that relate indirectly to bank-note printing: No. 3974, of January 10, 1816, which describes printing with curved stereotype plates; and No. 4194, of January 7, 1818, which describes "an improved method of distributing and applying the ink or color to the surfaces of the types, stereotype plates . . . etc."

25. Congreve's Patent No. 4404 of November 1, 1819, describes "an improved method of inlaying or combining different metals or other hard substances applicable to various useful purposes."

26. I can find no patent for Congreve's triple paper, but Dard Hunter had the original and unique folio volume that Congreve submitted to the Bank Committee in 1818. Hunter says the volume measured 8-1/8 by 13 inches and contained 62 pages with 12 pages of manuscript in Congreve's hand. There were 36 specimens of water-marked bank-note paper made by Congreve or made for him by John Portal, and each example is described by the inventor. For a detailed account of triple paper, including photographs of the watermarks, see Dard Hunter's *Papermaking. op. cit.*

27. Jacob Perkins had two sons, both of whom were with him in England. The eldest, Ebenezer Greenleaf Perkins, born on December 29, 1797, went to England with his father on the *Telegraph* in 1819, but little is known about him and it cannot be determined from the available evidence if he had any experience at engraving. Given his young age and the considerable artistry of the engraving, it is doubtful, but remotely possible, that he was the engraver. He suffered from an unknown disease and had to return to Newburyport sometime before 1820. He lived there as an invalid until his death on January 20, 1842. The second son, Angier March Perkins, was born August 21, 1799, and did not go to England until November 1821, when he went over with his mother and three sisters on the *Electra*, arriving in England just before Christmas. This late date means he could not have been the son that engraved the head of Homer unless he had done it sometime earlier while he was still in America. Writing his memoirs in 1877, Angier remembers his arrival in London and said that "I was twenty-one years of age and went at once into the employment of my father and his

partners and was engaged for the next eight years in manufacturing banknotes, dies and plates. During the latter part of the time I taught other partners to do the work I was engaged upon and my services in the firm became unnecessary and I found myself obliged to obtain other business." When he left the company about 1830, he became an engineer working in steam engineering, like his father, and this does not suggest that he had acquired any engraving skills. The son who engraved the head of Homer is still a mystery.

28. Frederick George Hall. *History of the Bank of Ireland.* Footnote 1 on p. 123.

29. John Oldham entered the service of the Bank of England in 1837 and continued making improvements in the presses and numbering devices for several years. His system of heating buildings, which he initiated at the Bank of Ireland and subsequently at the Bank of England, is described in the *Civil Engineer and Architect's Journal,* 1839, p. 96. He died at his home on Montagu Street, Russell Square, on February 14, 1840. It is said he left a family of 17 children. His eldest son, Thomas Oldham, succeeded to his father's position at the Bank of England. In 1842 he published a paper, "On the Introduction of Letterpress Printing for Numbering and Dating the Notes of the Bank of England," in the *Proceedings of the Institution of Civil Engineers,* 1842, p. 166, and the following year he published "A Description of the Automatic Balance at the Bank of England, Invented by W. Cotton," *Ibid.,* 1843, p. 121. Thomas Oldham (Jr.) died at Brussels on November 7, 1851.

30. Rowland Hill was born at Kiddeminster on December 3, 1795. His intellectual gifts were recognized at an early age, but his decision to end his formal education and become a teacher at age 12 was both arrogant and a serious mistake, for he was self-educated after that and his knowledge and ignorance became a strange mixture. He learned mathematics and became a good astronomer and an expert trigonometric land-surveyor. He is said to have excelled in mental arithmetic but ruined his health with strange dietary experiments. He started the Hazelwood School for Boys, which became famous and attracted students from many different countries. His many inventions and long service with the post office are beyond the scope of this book. In 1857 he was made a Fellow of the Royal Society and in 1860 a Knight Commander of the Order of the Bath (KCB). He died on August 27, 1879, at his home in Hampstead and was buried in Westminster Abbey.

31. Frederick Augustus Heath was born in 1810 and died May 7, 1878. As well as the "penny black," Frederick Heath engraved the five-shilling coin stamp of New South Wales issued in 1861 and the small half-penny red stamp of Great Britain in 1870. Some of the company records of Perkins, Bacon & Petch are to be found in Edward Denny Bacon's *The Line Engraved Postage Stamps of Great Britain Printed by Perkins, Bacon and Company.* This work, published in two volumes in 1920, is the most-complete history of the company.

32. Jacob Perkins excelled as an engineer during his life, but the Institution of Civil Engineers made no comment on his death. In fact, no obituary appeared until 1865 and 1866, when The Proceedings of the Institution of Civil Engineers published, under the title of "Memoires," a fairly comprehensive account of Perkins's life. The indexes of the (London) *Times* make no mention of Perkins' death in 1849. The *Boston Courier* published an obituary notice on August 27, 1849 (p. 2, col. 1), and the *Newburyport Herald* published a longer obituary that was written by George Lunt, a lawyer who also grew up in Newburyport. The *Scientific American* magazine published a long obituary in the issue of September 8, and the *Farmer and Mechanic* magazine published another on October 11. The Patent Office Report of 1849 devoted three pages of small type to a review of Perkins's life. It concluded in these words: "A simple and unostentatious notice of the demise of this remarkable man is all the tribute that the public press has yet paid to his memory. The merits of our ingenious countryman deserve more; he passed quietly away from the scene of his labors, but has left his mark upon the age. *Monumentum auer perennius.*" (I have erected a monument more permanent.)

Chapter 5

1. Both documents are part of the small collection of papers concerning George Murray at the Historical Society of Pennsylvania. The promissory note to Matthew Cary is numbered "590" and dated November 27, 1821. The judgment against Murray is not numbered. It was dated February 12, 1822, and entered in the records of the Supreme Court for the Eastern District of Pennsylvania, March 14, 1822. The first payment for that judgment was not due for two years, so it is unlikely that Murray ever repaid a penny.

2. An advertisement was placed in the *Aurora General Advertiser* of November 11, 1822: "The co-partnership of Murray, Fairman & Company has been dissolved in consequence of the death of George Murray. The surviving partners, jointly with Asa Spencer, will continue to carry out the Engraving and Printing of Bank Notes, under the name of Fairman, Draper, Underwood & Co., and from the arrangements that have been made, they will be enabled to execute the work in a manner superior to any that have heretofore been done. (signed) Fairman, Draper, Underwood & Co."

3. Charles Toppan married Laura Ann Noxon on July 17, 1826. She was the daughter of Dr. Robert Noxon of Poughkeepsie, New York. They had six children: (1) Charles Fairman Toppan, born June 13, 1827, died July 28, 1852; (2) Robert Noxon Toppan, born October 20, 1829, died May 20, 1832; (3) Harriette Rogers Toppan, born July 8, 1834, died in Florence, Italy, February 1903; (4) Robert Noxon Toppan, born in Philadelphia, Pennsylvania, October 17, 1836, died May 10, 1901; (5) Edward Toppan, born April 28, 1840, died December 1846; and (6) Frederic Toppan, born October 1, 1843, death unknown. It is believed that Charles Toppan visited England and France for one or two years in the 1820s before he married.

   This data is taken from Daniel Langdon Tappan's, *Tappan–Toppan Genealogy, Descendants of Abraham Toppan of Newburyport, Massachusetts.* Arlington, Massachusetts: Privately printed by the author, 1915. Only 200 copies were printed.

4. Gideon Fairman died at his home at 326 Chestnut Street in Philadelphia on Sunday afternoon, March 18, 1827. An obituary appears in *Poulson's Daily American Advertiser,* March 20, 1827, p. 3. According to Dunlap, Fairman was ruined financially by the "insane speculation" of George Murray, but he gives no specific examples of these financial failures.

5. Extracts from J.B. Longacre's diary of 1825 were published in the *Pennsylvania Magazine of History and Biography,* XXIX, April 1905, pp. 134–142.

6. These two brothers worked together as an independent bank-note company and as agents for the following firms: (1) Fairman, Draper, Underwood & Company [1823–1829]; (2) Balch, Stiles & Company [1829 and 1830]; (3) Draper, Underwood, Bald & Spencer [1830–1840]; (4) and Rawdon, Clark & Company of Albany, New York [1833 and 1834].

7. His death is listed briefly in the *Wabash Atlas* of July 4, 1849, p. 2, and he was buried in Greenbush Cemetery in Lafayette. Four of his eight children were sons, but none of them ever became bank-note engravers. There is an inventory of his estate on file with the Tippecanoe County Historical Association dated February 5, 1851, which shows a net worth of only $5,694. His widow lived on for another 52 years, dying in Oxford, Indiana, on March 18, 1901.

8. The Census of 1850 shows he was the owner of real estate valued at $7,500. 10 years later he had property valued at $30,000 and his personal wealth was $40,000.

9. Henry E. Saulnier was born in Philadelphia on January 6, 1811, and died at Ivy Mills in Delaware County, Pennsylvania, on March 13, 1907. He was both a script and letter engraver. He married in Philadelphia on November 15, 1838, to Harriet Ann Scott, who was born in Philadelphia in January 1816.

10. Mezzotint is a process by which a smooth copper plate is textured by a tool called a "rocker." The rocker has a serrated blade that cuts small furrows in the plate. On the cross cut, the plate is given a rough texture that will print entirely black if inked. The engraver can now use scrapers and burnishers to polish certain areas that he wants to show lighter when printed. The rough areas retain more ink and print darker while the more-polished areas retain less ink and will print lighter or even white. With practice, it is possible to achieve a full-tonal range and even to make fine lines.

11. The letter to Joseph Willcox is quoted, in part, by Clarence W. Brazer in an article in the *Collectors' Club Philatelist*, volume 17, (July 1938), p. 191, and again in the *Essay-Proof Journal* of April 1947, volume 4, no. 2I, p. 75.

12. John Sartain. *Reminiscences of a Very Old Man, 1808–1897*.

13. William Shakespeare. *Julius Caesar*. Act 4, Scene 3, lines 218–222.

Chapter 6

1. Stauffer says Leney was of Scottish descent, being the son of Alexander and Susana Leney. In the biography of Leney written by Robert W. Reid, MD, and Charles Rollinson, his great-grandson, Leney's Scottish descent is mentioned only briefly. Dunlap, who actually knew him and spent time with Leney after he retired, says he was English.

2. Stauffer, writing in 1907, says that Leney's account books were then in the possession of Mr. W.C. Crane of New York.

3. James A. Haxby. *Standard Catalog of United States Obsolete Bank Notes, 1782–1866*. Four volumes. Iola, Wisconsin: Krause Publications, 1988. Referred to as "Haxby."

4. This circular is now in the collections of the New York Public Library.

5. The best comprehensive and well-researched biography of Peter Maverick and his family is Stephen DeWitt Stephens's *The Mavericks, American Engravers*, published by Rutgers University Press in 1950. William Dunlap, in his *Rise and Progress of the Art of Design in the United States*, published in 1834, also provides interesting data about Maverick and Asher B. Durand, as does David McNeely Stauffer in his monumental work, *American Engravers upon Copper and Steel*, published in 1907.

6. Peter Rushton Maverick was born April 11, 1755. He married Ann Reynolds on July 4, 1772. She died in August 1787. Peter R. Maverick then married her sister, Rebecca, in 1788. He died in New York City on December 12, 1811.

7. This print formed the frontispiece of *The Holy Bible, Abridged*, published in New York in 1790 by Hodge, Allen & Campbell.

8. Gandolfi was 52 years old when he left Italy with his mistress and voyaged to America in April 1816. His memoir of the trip, *Viaggio agli Stati Uniti*, was written in Milan in 1822, six years after he returned to Italy.

The account was passed down through the family but disappeared in the Allied bombing of Bologna in 1944. A handwritten copy of the account was found and has been translated by Antonia Franklin and Mimi Cozort and published by Yale University Press as *Mauro in America*.

9. Colonel Trumbull brought Mr. Neal over from England to print the Durand engraving. Trumbull believed there were no printers in America capable of printing as well as Mr. Neal.

10. The honor of making the first lithographic prints in the United States goes to Bass Otis (1782–1861), a self-taught portrait engraver who lived in Philadelphia. His lithographic prints were first published in the *Analectic Magazine* for July 1819.

11. A long list of the engravings by Asher B. Durand is to be found in David McNeely Stauffer's *American Engravers Upon Copper and Steel*, volume II, pp. 96–117. For a description of numerous small-subject plates, bank notes, business cards, etc., see (Anonymous pamphlet), "Catalogue of the Engraved Work of Asher B. Durand Exhibited at the Grolier Club, New York, April, 1895."

12. Several of Durand's original drawings for bank notes can be seen at the New York Public Library in the Print Room.

13. "Kindred Spirits" passed to William Cullen Bryant's daughter, Julia, who donated the painting to the New York Public Library in 1904. The Library sold the painting to Walmart-heiress Alice Walton in a Sotheby auction in May 2005 for an estimated price of $35 million.

14. His father, John Durand, did not die until 1813, when he was crushed by a tree that he had chopped down in the woods behind his home.

15. "Cyrus Durand." *Illustrated Magazine of Art*. Volume III, 1854. pp. 237–270. The detailed, and often personal, information within the article suggests it was written by Asher Durand. It is the single-best biography of Cyrus.

16. The *Edinburgh Encyclopedia* was a monumental project started in 1808 by Sir David Brewster, an optical physicist of some renown, who had previously published the *Edinburgh Magazine* for about six years. His ambition was to publish an encyclopedia that was scientifically accurate and up-to-date. Previous encyclopedias had been arranged haphazardly with articles written by amateurs. The *Edinburgh* was published in several volumes over a number of years. A complete set is now extremely rare. Even the Library of Congress does not have one. The volume or volumes bought by Cyrus Durand had been reprinted about 1820. I was never able to find the volume containing the article on the pantograph.

17. These companies were (1) Fairman, Draper & Company, in Philadelphia, but later in the year they became Fairman, Draper, Underwood & Company; (2) Charles Toppan, in Philadelphia; (3) Peter Maverick in New York; (4) Durand & Wright in New York; and (5) Abner Reed and Samuel Stiles in Hartford, Connecticut.

18. Alan A. Siegel. *Out of Our Past*. p. 90.

19. *Ibid*. pp. 90 and 91.

20. Fourier Transform Infrared Spectroscopy (FTIR) would be the technology of choice since it can analyze an almost microscopic area of a surface film, such as ink, and identify most of the chemical constituents. If the "Red Letter" contained a mineral pigment, another instrumental technique might be necessary, such as Energy-Dispersive X-ray Analysis.

21. See House of Representatives, Report 150, Printing of United States Notes, pp. 218 and 219, and a thumbnail biography of George Baldwin in the January 1939 issue of *The Collectors' Club Philatelist*, p. 30.

22. Griffiths. *The Story of the American Bank Note Company*. p. 37.

23. Albert Durand's last will and testament and the inventory of his estate are recorded in the New Jersey State Archives as No. 17296G, dated June 21, 1871. No children are mentioned in the will.

24. Much of the biographical material about Tracy R. Edson and his family is taken from Jarvis Bonesteel Edson's *Edsons in England and America* and *Genealogy of the Edsons*, and from Tracy Edson's obituary in the New York Times, November 30, 1881, p. 5. Another source is the legal battle that was fought over the last will and testament of the Edson sisters. This contains interesting facts about their family life.

    "Margaret B. Edson, individually and as Executrix of the Last Will and Testament of Marmont B. Edson, deceased, vs. John A. Bartow, Charles S. Fairchild and John E. Parsons, as Executors of the Last Will and Testament of Mary A. Edson, deceased, and others." pp. 90–179.

    The Supreme Court of New York, City and County, (and attached) cases heard in the Court of Appeals, pp. 1–31, 1–36, 3–23, 1–4, and 1–3.

    These documents are available online in a read-only format.

25. William Jarvis Edson was born in the town of Lanesborough, Massachusetts, on February 23, 1786. He married on March 26, 1809, in Fly Creek, New York, to Mary (called "Polly") Fairchild, daughter of Abijah and Sarah Fairchild of Sugar Loaf Valley, Orange County, New York. He died in Utica, New York, at 88 Fayette Street on October 1, 1848. Polly died in New York City on December 24, 1873. They had five children: (1) Tracy Robinson, born December 12, 1809, at Fly Creek, New York, died November 29, 1881, in New York City; (2) Clement Massilon, a lawyer, born August 14, 1811, at Exeter, New York, death unknown; (3) Marmount Bryan, born April 12, 1813, at Fly Creek, died April 21, 1892; (4) Mary Augusta, born February 1, 1819, in Oxford, Chenango County, New York, died May 20, 1890, in New York City, leaving an estate valued at $700,000; and (5) Susan Maria, born April 9, 1826, in Oneota, Otsego County, New York, died June 13, 1885, leaving an estate valued at $1,000,000.

26. In 1839 Clarence Brazer, then editor of the *Collectors' Club Philatelist*, assumed that Tracy Edson was an engraver, based in part on the fact that James M. Willcox of the Ivy Mills paper company had done business with him. Brazer may also have read Edson's obituary published in the *Boston Evening Transcript* on November 30, 1881, which erroneously informed readers that Edson had been "one of the most prominent engravers of New York City." There is no hard evidence that Tracy Edson ever engraved vignettes or lettering for any bank-note companies. On the contrary, there is considerable evidence that he was always engaged in administrative duties only.

Chapter 7

1. Foster Wild Rice. "Antecedents of the American Bank Note Company of 1858." New York, New York: American Bank Note Company, 1961. p. 10. 27 pages.

2. Chromium sesquioxide, now more commonly called chromium III oxide, is a hard compound that was discovered in 1838 by two French chemists who worked out a method for manufacturing it as a pigment for inks and paints. It is not easily attacked by acids or bases, especially when present in ink on paper.

    Chaplin Eastaugh and Siddel. *The Pigment Compendium: A Dictionary of Historical Pigments*. Oxford, England: Butterworth-Heinemann, 2004. p. 391.

3. James Douglas. "Obituary Notice of Thomas Sterry Hunt." Read before the American Philosophical Society, April 1, 1898. p. 84.

    The article has its own pagination in most reprints (such as Google's online version) and the letter from Workman to Hunt is on p. 25. The reply from Hunt is on pp. 26 and 27.

4. Letter of Thomas Sterry Hunt to William Workman. *op. cit.*

5. Fred L. Reed, III. "More Light Shed on Counterfeit Deterence." *Bank Note Reporter*. Part 40. December 2008. pp. 50–56. "Feds Roll Out 'Rainbows' with Extra Security." *Bank Note Reporter*. Part 41. November 2008. pp. 44–64.

    These articles were printed as a continuing series entitled "Shades of Blue and Gray."

6. "American Bank Note Company *vs.* Tracy R. Edson." *The Reports of Cases Argued and Determined in the Supreme Court of the State of New York, 1870*. pp. 388–397.

    This report is available online in a read-only format (except for those with Google accounts).

7. *Printed by order of the House of Representatives during the Second Session of the Thirty-Eighth Congress, 1864–65*. 15 volumes. Washington, D.C.: Government Printing Office, 1865.

8. Jarvis Bonesteel Edson. *Edsons in England and America and Genealogy of the Edson*. p. 362.

    Reproduces the letter that Tracy Edson wrote to his sister, Susan, dated July 4, 1861, from Washington, D.C., in which he mentions his attempts to get the government contracts for engraving and printing government loans.

9. Gene Hessler. *An Illustrated History of U.S. Loans, 1775–1898*. Port Clinton, Ohio: BNR Press, 1998. p. 13.

10. "Trophy of Steel Plates for Treasury Notes of the Confederate States." *The World* (New York City newspaper). April 26, 1861.

    This article is quoted in full in W.L. Ormsby's *Cycloidal Configurations, or, The Harvest of Counterfeiters*, p. 11.

11. "The Treason of the New York Bank Note Companies." *The Evening Star* (Washington, D.C.). May 8, 1874. p. 1, col. 5. "Developments in the Banknote Printing Monopoly Investigation—Who Printed the Confederate Paper Money." *San Francisco Bulletin* (San Francisco, California). Friday, May 8, 1874. p. 2, col. 4. (Taken from the *New York Herald*).

12. Quoted from a restricted document of the American Bank Note Company titled "Detection and Recognition of Fraudulent Securities." No date, no author.

13. "Potecting a Monopoly." *New York Times*. September 1, 1884. p. 8.

14. The corporate papers of the Kendall Bank Note Company include (1) The Annual Report for 1880, File No. 1162; and (2) the Annual Report for 1881, also File No. 1162. The first Trustees were George H. Kendall, Llewellyn Starkey, both of New York City, and Charles Burnham of South Orange, New Jersey. By October 1889 there had been a reorganization of the company under the name of the New York Bank Note Company, and the new officers were Russell Sage, president, a miserly multimillionaire who died at age 90 with a fortune of $150 million; George J. Gould, vice-president and son of Jay Gould the wealthy financier; George P. Sheldon, who made his fortune as head of the Phenix Fire Insurance Company, secretary; and George H. Kendall, treasurer. George A. Field, a second cousin of Mr. Kendall, was the vice-president.

15. This report is reprinted in whole from *Investigation of Financial and Monetary Conditions in the United States, House Resolution Nos 429 and 504*. Before a House Subcommittee on Banking and Currency, Washington, D.C.: Government Printing Office, 1913. pp. 2203 and 2204. Also published as *Money Trust Investigation*, by Henry Mac-Morran, 1913.

16. "Stock Exchange Attacked by Signs." *New York Times*. May 21, 1911. p. 6, col. 1.

17. The Stilwell bribery case is detailed in the following reports of the *New York Times*: (1) "A Talk by Telephone." April 2, 1913. p. 2, cols. 3 and 4; (2) "Stilwell Accused of Bribe Offer." April 2, 1913. p. 1, col. 8 and p. 2, cols. 1–4; (3) "To Try Stilwell in Senate April 8." April 3, 1913. p.2, col. 3; (4) "The Kendall Charges." April 3, 1913. p.12, col. 3; (5) "To Hear Kendall Charges." April 4, 1913. p. 2, col. 6; (6) "Stilwell Charges Ready on Monday." April 5, 1913. p. 4, col. 5; (7) "Support for Kendall." April 6, 1913. p. 10, col. 2; (7) "Stilwell Disowns Bribe Telegram." April 9, 1913. p.5, col. 2; (8) "Field Backs Bribe Story of Kendall." April 10, 1913. p. 2, cols. 3 and 4; (9) "Stilwell Fails to Shake Accuser." April 11, 1913. p.3, cols. 1 and 2; (10) "Stilwell Denial In, Senate Now to Act." April 12, 1913. p. 5, cols. 1 and 2; (11) "Plans in Stilwell Case." April 13, 1913. p. 13, col. 2; (12) "Senate Stops Work to Try Stilwell." April 14, 1913. p. 10, col. 1; (13) "Stilwell's Friends Fear To-Day's Vote." April 15, 1913. p. 20, cols. 3 and 4; (14) "Clears Stilwell on Bribe Charge." April 16, 1913. p. 1, col. 8; (15) "The Stilwell Senators." April 17, 1913. p. 10, col. 2; (16) "Prosecution of Stilwell." April 18, 1913. p. 1, col. 2; (17) "Stilwell's Last Chance." April 22, 1913. p.1, col. 2; (18) "Stilwell Breaks Silence." April 24, 1913. p. 13, col. 2; (19) "To Confer Over Stilwell." April 27, 1913. p.12, col. 5; (20) "Stilwell Guilty of Asking Bribe, Jurors Find A Verdict Against State Senator in 2 Hours and 13 Minutes." May 25, 1913.

   Stilwell died at the age of 76 while awaiting sentencing for another charge of bribery.

18. "George Kendall Dies in Hotel Here." *New York Times*. April 25, 1924. p. 17, col. 3. Kendall left the New York Bank Note Company to Miss Ethel Graham Allon, his private secretary for 20 years and the treasurer of the company. The company at that time was considered to be worth $1,000,000. Many people were surprised that George left only $125,000 to his widow, Mrs. Hattie L. Kendall, $100,000 to his daughter, Mrs. Muriel Kendall Bellamore, and $10,000 in trust to his grandson, David Kendall Bellamore. George said that Miss Allon knew as much about the operations of the company as he did. Nevertheless, the company was soon closed.

19. "The Bond-Printing Scandal in Virginia. Mr. Kendall's Statement [illegible] Obligations to a Bank-Note Company for Money Advanced for Political Purposes." *The Sun* (Baltimore, Maryland). April 26, 1882. p. 4, col. 6.

20. "Charges Against a Banknote Company." *New York Times*. October 31, 1902. p. 1, col. 6.

21. *A Little Inside History on How the Government Treated the Bank Note Contract and the Encouragement Given to Canadian Investment Together With Hansard Report on the Subject by Mr. Foster, Mr. Charles Tupper, Mr. Craig, M. P. and Sir Hibbert Tupper*. Ottawa, Canada: British-American Bank Note Company, 1897.

   This document is available online and is part of the Public Archives of Canada in the public domain.

22. "Plant For 2,500 Men Moves to the Bronx." *New York Times*. November 21, 1908. p. 1, col. 5.

23. "Completing Plans for Immense Plant of American Bank Note Company." *New York Times*. May 23, 1909. p. 14, cols. 5–7.

Chapter 8

1. A number of corporate papers of the National Bank Note Company are on file with the Municipal Archives of New York City, including: (1) a Certificate of the Payment of Capital Stock, dated November 29, 1861, no. 1859; (2) an Amended Certificate of Incorporation, dated November 2, 1874, no. 1859; (3) an Amended Certificate of Incorporation, dated February 4, 1879; (4) an Amended Certificate of Incorporation, dated February 11, 1880; (5) a Certificate of Paid-Up Stock, dated January 26, 1882, no. 1880; (6) an Original Certificate of the National Bank Note Company, filed and recorded July 13, 1904, no. 1880; (7) a Certificate of Amendment of the Certificate of Incorporation, dated February 9, 1953.

2. James Macdonough explained in a letter that "Mr. Chase, while secretary of the Treasury, instituted the system whereby the two companies [National Bank Note and Continental Bank Note] were compelled to use the dies and rolls belonging to each other, containing the material which had been selected for the notes, bonds, postage currency, etc."

   See the full text of the letter in "Competing Printers Allowed to Use the Same Dies and Rolls." *Essay-Proof Journal*. Volume 30, no. 1, Winter 1973. pp. 30 and 31.

3. "Bank Note Counterfeiting—Slander Suit." *New York Times*. March 23, 1858. p. 2.

   "Ormsby vs. Douglas." *New York Times*. March 26, 1858. p. 2, cols. 4 and 5.

   The court's decision to uphold the judgment against Ormsby is reported in "Waterman L. Ormsby v. Benjamin Douglas." *Reports of Cases of the Court of Appeals* (New York). Volume XXXVII. pp. 477–486.

4. Alexander C. Wilson was the first president. Edward E. Dunbar and William D. Wilson (Alexander's brother) were salesmen. Judah Touro Robertson was secretary until November 30, 1863, when he became General Superintendent. On December 9, 1863, at an Annual Meeting of the Stockholders, the president and treasurer were reelected. The office of vice-president was then created and given to William D. Wilson, and a Mr. Russell was elected secretary. Mr. Dunbar was president in September 1866, and the trustees were Alfred Edwards, William D. Wilson, Mr. Moore, Silas M. Stilwell, and Homer Stuart. William D. Wilson was president for a time, but at the Annual Meeting on December 3, 1866, all trustees were reelected. President Dunbar resigned January 23, 1867, and Silas M. Stillwell was elected president. At the time of the consolidation with the American Bank Note Company in 1878, the officers were Homer H. Stuart, president, and Jared K. Meyers, secretary.

   These notes were taken from the *Collectors' Club Philatelist*. January 1941. p. 27.

5. Alexander C. Wilson was the first assistant to the editor of the *New York Times*, starting with that paper on September 18, 1851, and continuing with them for several years. The editor of the *Times* was Henry Jarvis Raymond. Mr. Raymond was also the legal guardian of Judah Touro Robertson, who worked at the *Times* briefly and was persuaded by Mr. Raymond to invest some of his money in the Continental Bank Note Company. Because Alexander C. Wilson was Robertson's uncle, and also worked at the *Times*, there is a connection between the two men and the involvement of the Wilson brothers in the bank-note company. Alex C. Wilson left the *Times* to become president of the Continental Bank Note Company. He was probably the son of General James Jefferson Wilson, U.S. Senator from New Jersey.

6. The full text of the contract was reprinted in Thomas F. Morris Jr.'s article, "The First National Bank Notes." *Essay-Proof Journal.* Whole No. 80, 1963. pp. 168–172.

7. Albert Philip Cohen. "The Fenian Movement in the United States: Its Philatelic and Numismatic Aspects." *Essay-Proof Journal.* Whole No. 80, 1963. pp. 147–156.

8. The information in this paragraph was discovered by the late Sol Altman in an article entitled "The New United States Stamp Contract." *The American Journal of Philately.* March 20, 1877. Reprinted in the *Essay-Proof Journal.* Whole No. 77, 1963. p. 20.

9. His middle name is correctly spelled "Lily," without the double "l" that one sees frequently. There are no known photographs or drawings of the man. He married first Julia Ann Brainard on November 22, 1830, in New York, and later Amelia Willcoxson.

10. The cylinder scene engraved on the 1847 Colt Army Pistol was suggested by a former Texas Ranger named Captain Samuel H. Walker, a person who helped Samuel Colt win a government contract. Ormsby was assigned to engrave the scene based on Walker's recollection of the "Hays Fight" in 1844, when 15 Rangers defeated a Comanche war party of 80 braves, killing half of them. Ormsby had never seen a Texas Ranger, so he engraved them dressed as U.S. dragoons. According to a Texan legend, Captain Walker died later in action, with two Colt revolvers in his hands.

11. These notes were apparently first listed by Gordon L. Harris in his book, *New York State Script and Private Issues,* 2001, p. 115, and referenced also in Q. David Bowers's *Obsolete Paper Money Issued by Banks in the United States 1782–1866,* Atlanta, Georgia: Whitman Publishing, LLC, 2006, p. 278. Haxby often did not list notes in his catalog if they did not have the word "bank" or "banking" in their titles, so the absence of Manhattan Association notes may have been intentional if he thought they were scrip or some other form of money.

12. George Peyton, an exchange broker in New York City, had the assistance of Rawdon, Wright, Hatch, & Edson in writing a 45-page pamphlet in 1856 entitled *How to Detect Counterfeit Bank Notes, or An Illustrated Treatise on the Detection of Counterfeit, Altered and Spurious Bank Notes, with Original Bank Note Plates and Designs by Rawdon, Wright, Hatch & Edson . . . .*This work, however, lacks the clarity and authority of Ormsby's writing and pales in comparison with his book on technical information. Tomasko offers an interesting point in saying that Ormsby's work was "a polemic against the bank note industry," and an effort to impress government officials. I see nothing wrong with those objectives and applaud Ormsby for his attack.

13. Quoted from Ormsby's letter to Secretary Boutwell, dated March 1870. The letter is part of Record Group 318, Records of the Bureau of Engraving and Printing, Entry 3A. "Official and Miscellaneous Letters Received, M–Z, 1870." A rubber stamp indicates it was received at the bureau on April 5, 1870. National Archives, College Park, Maryland.

14. Clark's letter can be found in the House of Representatives, *Executive Document No. 50,* titled "Printing Department of the Treasury Department," dated February 6, 1865, p. 9. It is also available in Record Group 318, Finding Aid NC 47, Entry #5, (press copies of official and miscellaneous letters sent 1862–1912), volume 1, pp. 756–760.

15. Both Q. David Bowers and I have dug through the archives of the County Clerk and Clerk of the Supreme Court at the New York Court House and the Court Reporters in law libraries to locate the legal papers about Ormsby. Q. David Bowers. *Obsolete Paper Money Issued by Banks in the United States 1782–1866.* pp. 294–304. Robert McCabe. "Waterman Lily Ormsby and the Continental Bank Note Company." *Paper Money.* March/April 2001. pp. 163–170. *New York Times.* March 23, 1858. p. 2, col. 4; March 26, 1858. p.2, cols. 4 and 5.

16. There are many court papers for this case, though most of them are not important. The Judgment Roll, 29 pages, was filed on July 30, 1859. Photocopies of this document can be purchased from the County Clerk and Clerk of the Supreme Court, New York County Court House, as Index No. 877/1859.

17. Dunbar's letter, dated February 10, 1867, is part of a file entitled *Applications and Recommendations for Positions in the Washington, D.C. Office of the Treasury Department, 1830–1910.* National Archives, College Park, Maryland, Record Group 56, Entry No. 210. The file is marked "Washington, April 6, '67."

   For the full text of the letter, see Robert McCabe's "Waterman Lily Ormsby and the Continental Bank Note Company." *Essay-Proof Journal.* March/April 2001. p. 168. "Counterfeiting and Some Jerseymen." *The Evening Journal* (Jersey City, New Jersey). May 24, 1867. p. 3.

18. This letter from Ormsby is found in Record Group 318, Records of the Bureau of Engraving and Printing, Entry 3A, "Official and Miscellaneous Letters Received, M–Z, 1870." National Archives, College Park, Maryland.

Chapter 9

1. Schmidt was a general engraver who came to New Orleans from Baden, Germany, about 1840 and became the local agent for Rawdon, Wright, Hatch & Edson, one of the predecessors of the American Bank Note Company. When the war broke out, Schmidt changed the name of the company to the Southern Bank Note Company. He is listed as "Henry Schmidt" in the 1850 Census and as S. Schmidt in the 1860 Census. Memminger's correspondence refers to him as "Samuel Schmidt." His real name, according to biographical dictionaries, was Solomon Schmidt. He was active in New Orleans until at least 1870.

2. Raphael P. Thian. *Correspondence to the Treasury Department of the Confederate States of America, 1861–1865.* Washington, D.C.: 1879. pp. 5 and 6.

3. August Dietz. *The Postal Service of the Confederate States of America.* Richmond, Virginia: Dietz Printing Company, 1929. p. 96

4. *Ibid.* pp. 172–174. Dietz got this story from a 1921 issue of the *Richmond Times-Dispatch* but didn't give an exact citation.

5. Much of what we know about Blanton Duncan's role in the Confederate Treasury was found by Douglas Ball. "Representing Nothing on God's Earth Now." *The Bank Note Reporter.* September 1978.

6. Several of the principals in these printing firms demanded to be paid in gold coin, knowing full well the inflation rate of Confederate dollars. Printers and other workers, however, were generally paid in Confederate money. An exception was that Keatinge, an Englishman, and his group of English printers all had contracts that stipulated they were to be paid in gold.

7. The old brick building was built by slaves in record time. It was burned down by General Sherman's forces just two days short of its first-year anniversary. Since the war, it has been used many times as a warehouse and sometimes as an assembly plant. It is presently a Publix grocery store. The building now has a second story. It was placed on the National Registry of Historic Places in 1979. The history of the building and several photographs are to be found in *The State* (newspaper) of Columbia, South Carolina, in the "Neighbors" section, for Thursday, September 4, 2003. The history of Evans & Cogswell and the

operations of this plant are described in George D. Terry's *Carolina Folk: The Cradle of a Southern Tradition*, published in Columbia, South Carolina, by the University of South Carolina Press, 1985. There is also a photograph of the original burned-out building, taken sometime after the Civil War, on the Google website "CSA Printing Plant."

8. Allan's report to Memminger was discovered in 1950 by Sidney C. Kerksis, who described his search in an article entitled "A Newly Discovered Confederate Treasury Note: The $10 Manouvrier." *The Numismatist*. September 1952.

9. Quoted from John Hodge, a Confederate lithographer, in Miles Raisig's "Memoirs of a C.S.A. Treasury Note Lithographer." *The Numismatist*. No. 8, August 1951. pp. 840 and 841.

10. Phillip H. Chase. *Confederate Treasury Notes: The Paper Money of the Confederate States of America, 1861–1865*. Philadelphia, Pennsylvania: Published by the author, 1947. footnote on p. 11.

11. Judith Ann Benner. *Fraudulent Finance: Counterfeiting and the Confederate States, 1861–1865*. Waco, Texas: 1970. p. 39.

12. *Richmond's Daily Dispatch*. February 28; March 3, 4, 6, 11, 12, 14, and 27; April 4 and 7, 1862.

13. *Richmond's Daily Dispatch*. February 28; March 3, 4, 6, 11, 12, 14, and 27; April 4 and 7, 1862.

14. Raphael P. Thian. *Correspondence of the Treasury Department of the Confederate States of America, 1861–1865*. Washington, D.C.: 1879. pp. 596 and 597.

15. Douglas B. Ball. *Financial Failure and Confederate Defeat*. p. 116.

16. Thian. *op. cit.* p. 231.

17. According to Arlie Slabaugh, only one Confederate note, the 50-cent fractional note engraved by Archer & Daly, was authorized to be printed with engraved signatures. Alie Slabaugh. *Confederate States Paper Money*. Racine, Wisconsin: 1961. p. 40.

18. Richard Cecil Todd. *Confederate Finance*. Athens, Georgia: University of Georgia Press, 1954. p. 2.

19. Charles W. Ramsdell. *Behind the lines in the Southern Confederacy*. Baton Rouge, Louisiana: Louisiana State University Press, 1944. p. 85.

20. Robert G. Kean. *Inside the Confederate Government: The Diary of Robert Garlick Hill Kean*. Baton Rouge, Louisiana: Louisiana State University Press, 1993. pp. 213 and 214.

Chapter 10

1. Counterfeiters are naturally drawn to locations which are remote and offer a degree of security. Dunham, settled in the mid-1790s, provided those criteria by offering good farmland surrounded by a rough terrain with no incoming roads. Travelers going to Dunham had to walk or ride horses over this terrain to get there. Counterfeiting became an established business in the early 1800s. *Histoire de Dunham* (several authors). Quebec, Canada: Les Ateliers Jacques Gaudet Ltée, 1967. p. 39.

2. Catherine M. Day. *Pioneers of the Eastern Townships*. Montreal, Canada: John Lovell, 1863. p. 117.

3. *George III, 2nd Session, 5th Provincial Parliament*. Chapter IV.

4. George A. Thompson Jr. "Counterfeiter's Jargon of the 1820's." *American Speech*. Duke University Press: Volume 71, no. 3, (Autumn 1996). pp. 334 and 335.

In current usage, "boodle" means "money gotten illegally, especially through graft. . . ." In the mid-19th century, the term referred to a package or roll of counterfeit money. Until recently, that meaning had been first known from the *National Police Gazette* of 1845. Now, it is realized that the word had a vogue in New York City newspapers in the mid-1820s:

"Severence told him that he was going to Canada, and should bring back with him a boodle [a cant term for a bundle of counterfeit bills]." *Commercial Advertiser*. March 15, 1822. p. 2, col. 3.

"The Mayor asked witness if Ann took out with her when walking, the boodle [slang word for a bundle of forged notes.] Here, A.C. [Ann Carter, the defendant] laughed and said to the Mayor, I see your honor is up to the slang.'" *New York Statesman*. June 21, 1823. p. 2, col. 4.

There are several theories about the slang use of "cogniac" and its evolution into "coniackers," meaning counterfeiters. One of these theories suggests that the word originated in Lower Canada and came from the observation that only counterfeiters had enough money to buy cogniac. Honest people had to settle for lesser spirits. The only support for this theory is that most of the counterfeiters in Lower Canada lived along "Cogniac Street" in Dunham, and they were relatively well off. The word *snags* seems to have been limited to the northeastern United States and its origin is unknown.

5. Stephen Burroughs. *Memoirs of the Notorious Stephen Burroughs*. Boston, Massachusetts: Charles Gaylord, 1835. 374 pages.

6. "Counterfeiters." *Weekly Wanderer*. Randolph, Vermont: July 27, 1807. p. 3, cols. 2 and 3.

7. Untitled paragraph in *Poulson's American Daily Advertiser*. Philadelphia, Pennsylvania: October 26, 1807. p. 3, col. 3. Quoting from the Canadian paper, *The Courant*. October 12, 1807.

8. "Serious Trifling." *New York Weekly Museum*. New York, New York: April 8, 1809. p. 3, col. 2.

9. "Stephen Burroughs." *The Balance & State Journal*. Albany, New York: June 25, 1811. p. 207, col. 2.

10. Untitled paragraph in the *Jamestown Journal*. Jamestown, New York: August 7, 1833. p. 3, col. 1.

11. "Counterfeiters." *Salem Gazette*. Salem, Massachusetts: October 6, 1807. p. 3, col. 1. Quoting from the *Dartmouth Gazette* of unknown date.

12. "Counterfeiters." *Vermont Republican and American Yeoman*. Windsor, Vermont: September 4, 1820. p. 2, col. 4.

13. "Counterfeiters." *Farmers' Cabinet*. Amherst, New Hampshire: August 26, 1820. p. 3, col. 1. Quoting from the *Columbian*. New York, New York.

14. William Stuart. *Sketches of the Life of William Stuart, The First and Most Celebrated Counterfeiter of Connecticut*. Bridgeport, Connecticut: Published by the author, 1854. p. 42.

"Slab City" refers to Frelighsburg, in the Eastern Townships, and "Crane and Staples" refers to William Crane, an engraver, and probably George Staples, another counterfeiter who lived in the area.

15. "Counterfeiters Detected." *New Hampshire Patriot*. Concord, New Hampshire: July 13, 1813. p. 1, col. 3.

16. "Counterfeiting Upon A Wholesale Scale." *Vermont Gazette*. Bennington, Vermont: July 18, 1820. p. 2, col. 5.

17. "The Boston Bankers." Typescript of the memoir by Charles Whittlesey (1808–1886) dated 1857 in Seriers V (Writings), Sub-series C, Folder 169, in the Western Reserve Historical Society, Cleveland, Ohio.

18. Untitled paragraph in *The New York Daily Advertiser*. New York, New York: May 13, 1828. p. 1, col. 3.

19. "Escape of Prisoners." *The Eastern Argus*. Portland, Maine: November 30, 1830. p. 2, col. 5. Quoting from *The Register* of Norristown, Pennsylvania.

20. "Counterfeiters Caught." *Niles' Register*. Baltimore, Maryland: September 7, 1833. pp. 29 and 30. Quoting from the *New Hampshire Statesman*. Concord, New Hampshire: August 24, 1833.

21. Heather Darch. "Living on Easy Street: The Counterfeiters of Missisquoi County." (Parts 1 and 2). Township Heritage WebMagazine. Available online.

22. "Counterfeiters in Canada." *Woodstock Observer*. Woodstock, Vermont: March 14, 1820. p. 2, col. 4.

23. "Apprehension of the Canadian Counterfeiters." *The National Gazette*. Philadelphia, Pennsylvania: August 20, 1833. p. 1.

24. Untitled paragraph in the *Saratoga Sentinel*. Saratoga Springs, New York: September 17, 1833. p. 3, col. 3. Quoting from the *Montreal Gazette*. September 7, 1833.

25. *Second Annual Report of the Board of Managers of the Association of Banks for the Suppression of Counterfeiting*. Boston, Massachusetts: William A. Hall, 1855. pp. 21 and 23.

26. "Counterfeiter Arrested." *New York Commercial Advertiser*. New York, New York: October 14, 1833. p. 3, col. 4.

27. For an earlier history of James Stewart, see "Counterfeiter." *New York Gazette*. New York, New York: January 17, 1812. p. 2, col. 3.

28. "Counterfeiters Taken." *The Baltimore Patriot*. Baltimore, Maryland: February 17, 1834. p. 3, col. 1.

29. "The Prevention of Counterfeiting." *The Sun*. Baltimore, Maryland: February 2, 1855. p. 1, col. 2.

30. Undated letter of E. Wells of Bakersfield, Vermont, to Mrs. Ruby G. Moore. Volume 107-2-2. Missisquoi Historical Society Archives, Musée de Missisquoi, Quebec Province, Canada.

31. "Counterfeiters Detected." *The Reporter*. Brattleborough, Vermont: September 9, 1809. p. 3, col. 2.

32. "Counterfeiters." *New-York Gazette*. New York, New York: January 17, 1812. p. 2, col. 3.

33. "Seneca Page." *American Watchman and Delaware Republican*. Wilmington, Delaware: April 14, 1812. p. 3, col. 1.

34. "One Hundred and Fifty Dollars Reward." *American and Commercial Daily Advertiser*. Baltimore, Maryland: June 3, 1815. p. 4, col. 2.

35. Untitled paragraph in *The Columbian*. New York, New York: August 23, 1816. p. 2, col. 2.

36. Undated letter of E. Wells of Bakersfield, Vermont, to Mrs. Ruby G. Moore. Volume 107-2-2. Missisquoi Historical Society Archives, Musée de Missisquoi, Quebec Province, Canada.

37. Darch. *op. cit*. Part 2.

38. "Counterfeiters." *New York Spectator*. New York, New York: January 28, 1825. p. 1, col. 3.

39. "Death of the Honorable Seneca Paige." *The Albany Evening Journal*. November 12, 1856. p. 2.

40. "Counterfeiters Discovered." *New York Spectator*. New York, New York: May 1, 1848. p. 4, col. 5.

41. *Second Annual Report of the Board of Managers of the Association of Banks for the Suppression of Counterfeiting*. Boston, Massachusetts: William A. Hall, 1855. p. 26. Quoted from the *Montreal Gazette*. October 30, 1854.

42. At the time this manuscript went to press, the *Bedford Gazette* for 1816 was not available. However, several newspapers in Pennsylvania and elsewhere copied the *Bedford Gazette* article verbatim. "History of A Gang of Counterfeiters." *The Ohio Repository*. Canton, Ohio: May 2, 1816. p. 1, cols. 2, 3, and 4.

43. "Counterfeiters." *Lancaster Journal*. Lancaster, Pennsylvania: March 13, 1816. p. 3.

44. Aside from Philander Noble and "Tabitha," the confessions identified Davis Lewis, James Smith, Cela Cole, Robert Allison, James Rowley, Joseph Osburn, David Jones, and a few others. With the exception of David Lewis, none of these names appear in other newspapers from 1810 through 1825. David Lewis was known for his many daring escapes from local jails. He was finally caught and tried for robbing a wealthy traveler in October 1819. He was convicted and sentenced to prison, but he was later pardoned by the governor in consequence of his giving information to the guards of a conspiracy to break the jail.

45. "A Distinguished Counterfeiter." *Plain Dealer*. Cleveland, Ohio: August 31, 1846. p. 2.

46. All of the partners (the "Boston Bankers," as they were euphemistically called) were counterfeiters. Taylor was a lawyer and considered to be an educated and wealthy man. Colonel Ashley started his career in counterfeiting in Vermont, but when "hard pressed," he fled to "Slab City" (Frelighsburg) in Canada and then moved to Boston, Ohio, in 1822. He was arrested at his home in Boston in 1837 and between $9,000 and $10,000 of counterfeit bills on the non-existent Mechanics' Bank of Toronto was found. "Arrest of A Gang of Counterfeiters." *Columbian Register*. New Haven, Connecticut: August 12, 1837. p. 2.

Ashley died in the Ohio Penitentiary in 1838. William Latta (sometimes spelled "Lather") was still shoving the "queer" with Perry Randolph in 1853. *Trenton State Gazette*. Trenton, New Jersey: August 4, 1853. p. 2, col. 4.

Dan Brown was arrested at age 18 for passing counterfeit notes in Lorain County, Ohio, but was released on a technicality of the law. Abraham Holmes, one of the "stockholders" of the enterprise, fled Boston as a fugitive from justice but returned in 1837 and died soon after with "consumption." General L.V. Bierce. *Historical Reminiscences of Summit County*. Akron, Ohio: T. & H.G. Canfield, 1864. p. 43; "The Boston Bankers." A 4-page typed transcription of Charles Whittlesey's account of 1857. Series V, Sub-Series C, Folder 169, Western Reserve Historical Society.

47. "Counterfeiters Taken." *The Phenix Gazette*. Alexandria, D.C.: February 21, 1831. p. 7, col. 2.

   This article mentions that four persons were captured, two of them being "David and James Brown."

48. Untitled paragraph in the *Rhode Island American and Province Gazette*. Province, Rhode Island: July 4, 1826. p. 2, col. 4; "Counterfeiters." *American Mercury*. Hartford, Connecticut: July 18, 1826. p. 2, col. 6.

49. Samuel A. Lane. *Fifty Years and Over of Akron and Summit County*. Akron, Ohio: Beacon Press, 1892. p. 882.

   Ex-Sheriff Lane knew Jim Brown personally. After retiring and becoming a newspaper publisher, he wrote a series of reports about the Brown family and their associates in a little paper called *The Buzzard* (1837 and 1838). These reports brought attention to the various members of the Brown gang but did little to curb their activities. Stephen Mihm. *A Nation of Counterfeiters*. pp. 188 and 189, 194.

   The evidence that Reuben Moses counterfeited the notes of the United States Bank is found in "The United States vs. Reuben Moses." *Reports of the Circuit Court of the United States, Third Circuit* (Eastern Pennsylvania). 4 Wash, CCR 726.

50. Lane. *Ibid.* p. 879

51. Lane. *Ibid.*

52. "Bold Villany." *New Bedford Mercury*. New Bedford, Massachusetts: February 2, 1838. p. 2, col. 4.

53. "Forgers and Counterfeiters Arrested." *Philadelphia Inquirer*. Philadelphia, Pennsylvania: April 28, 1841. p. 2, col. 7; "The Late Forgeries." *Public Ledger*. Philadelphia, Pennsylvania: April 26, 1841. p. 2, col. 7.

54. Lane. *Ibid.* p. 882.

55. Lane. *Ibid.* p. 883.

56. Lane. *Ibid.* p. 884; "The Akron Counterfeiters." *Cleveland Daily Plain Dealer*. Cleveland, Ohio: February 12, 1846. p. 2, col. 2.

57. Lane. *Ibid. op. cit.*

58. Lane. *Ibid.* p. 886.

59. "An Old Offender." *Cleveland Daily Plain Dealer*. Cleveland, Ohio: June 27, 1865. p. 1, col. 6; "Death of the Noted Jim Brown." *Cleveland Daily Plain Dealer*. Cleveland, Ohio: December 14, 1865. p. 3, col. 2.

60. Lane. *Ibid.* p. 891.

61. "The United States of America vs. Lyman Parkes alias James Wilson." *New York Spectator*. New York, New York: April 27, 1835. p. 3, col. 3.

   This is a report of the proceedings of the Circuit Court of the Eastern District of Pennsylvania. A similar report is found in "Trial of Wilson, the Counterfeiter." *Alexandria Gazette*. Alexandria, Virginia: April 28, 1835. p. 2.

62. Henry L. Boles. *History of DeKalb County*. Chicago, Illinois: O.P. Bassett, 1858. pp. 451 and 452; Professor Lewis M. Gross. *Past and Present of DeKalb County*. Chicago, Illinois: Pioneer Press, 1907. pp. 184 and 185.

   The discovery of Gleason's counterfeit money is told in "Century-Old Genoa Hotel May Be Razed." *Rockford Morning Star*. Rockford, Illinois: September 3, 1939. p. 5, col. 4.

   After a confederate squealed on Gleason in Chicago, officers went to Genoa and surrounded Gleason's cabin and waited till he came to the door at daybreak. Gleason invited them in and made them breakfast and then invited them out back to show them his cornfield. As they approached the cornfield, he ran into it and soon outdistanced the officers. He stayed gone for several years and then came back and married.

63. Boies. *op. cit.* p. 453.

64. The 1850 Federal Census shows Turner S. Wing, born about 1815 in Canada, living in Mayfield, DeKalb County, Illinois (the nearest post office was Sycamore, Illinois). He married Mary Lyonson on May 20, 1877, in DeKalb County (she was born about 1822), and had a son named Turner Wing, age 17.

   In 1860 a Turner G. Wing, possibly a brother of Turner S. Wing and living in Sycamore, DeKalb County, is shown as having been born in Dunham, Quebec, on March 31, 1818. His parents were listed as "Jason" Ward Wing and Sarah E. Perrigo. His wife was born Agnes Galbrath. His children included two daughters, Auistatia, age 15, and Ida F., age 10, and a son, Turner G. Wing Jr., age 6. Turner G. Wing died on December 8, 1899, in Ogden, Boone County, Iowa.

   Further proof that these were the sons and grandsons of the infamous Wing family of counterfeiters is found in the Cemetery List of the 14 headstones in the Wing family in Dunham: Sarah ("Sally") Perrigo, wife of (Jason) Ward Wing, died March 8, 1865, age 65 years; Ward Wing, born May 24, 1777, died February 25, 1863, was the son of Captain Thomas and Phebe Ward Wing; Ward's brother, Turner Wing, was born November 16, 1768, died January 26, 1832, age 63 years.

65. All the county court records for Cumberland County Illinois were destroyed in a fire in 1885. Consequently, documentation is lacking on some details of Pete McCartney's family, but in his last trial (1879), Pete stated that he and his family moved to Neoga when he was about seven years old (1831?). The standard story that Pete was born in 1824 is probably based on his recollections and is likely true. I have found no data that unequivocally indicates the names of his parents or siblings, except for a brother, Levi. His father was probably named John McCartney, as that name appears in a U.S. Federal Census Non-Population Schedule for 1870, showing that a John McCartney owned a farm in Neoga. This could not have been John Peter because he was on the run in 1870. We know that Pete had three daughters, one of whom may have been named Emily. One intriguing possibility is that Pete may have been related to Daniel McCartney, a farmer, born January 15, 1768, in Rockingham County, Virginia. Daniel married Sarah Price (sometimes called "Sally") in 1795, and they moved to Lawrence County, Ohio, about 1807. Most of this branch of the McCartneys moved again in late 1837 to Coles County, Illinois. Cumberland County was created out of Coles County in 1843. Daniel is said to have died in Neoga Township, Cumberland County, on August 11, 1847. In the 1830 Census, Daniel had sons named Peter, John, and Vincent (but no Levi) and two daughters. Other children (Hannah, William, Andrew, and Sarah) were already married and living on their own. Our Pete McCartney is probably related to the Daniel McCartney family in some way, but his age rules him out as a son. There are numerous McCartneys in the Census records for Coles and Cumberland Counties from 1820 through 1850, so this is a rich field for research.

   There is nothing related to John Peter McCartney in *Portrait and Biographical Album, Coles County, Illinois*. Chicago, Illinois: Chapman Brothers, 1887. He is also absent from *Counties of Cumberland, Jasper and Richland, Illinois, Historical and Biographical*. Illinois: F.A. Battey & Co., 1884. There are several Land Purchase Records for Illinois in the name of Peter McCartney, but the dates of these purchases are too early to be connected with John Peter McCartney.

66. This story has been told in several sources, but one of the earliest is John S. Dye's *The Government Blue Book*, p. 47. Dye gave the best account of Pete McCartney's life, but it has been nearly equaled by the exhaustive research of Thomas F. Eagen in "Pete McCartney, Counterfeiter." *Paper Money*. January/February 1993 and March/April 1993.

67. "Shoving the queer" is a phrase that is used often in this book. Shoving is self-explanatory, but "queer" requires some background. It is believed to have entered the English language in the 16th century and is related to the German word *quer*, meaning "diagonally or transverse," which came to mean "strange," "unusual," "out of alignment," something suspicious, or "not quite right." The British have long used the word to indicate insolvency. If a person was bankrupt, he was said to be in "Queer Street," which might have originated in Carey Street off Chancery Lane in London which housed the bankruptcy courts. In American criminal slang, it meant counterfeit money and was used both as an adjective and a noun.

68. The Johnston family of counterfeiters is difficult to trace. The best information comes from Dye's *The Government Blue Book*, p. 71. Dye identifies Charles Rhodes Johnston, born in the late 1790s, as the patriarch of the counterfeiting Johnstons. His son, George Johnston Sr., had (1) a son named Charles Rhodes Johnston II, born May 19, 1850, who married Eva Boone in July, 1870. He died in Decatur, Illinois, on October 24, 1931; (2) a son named William Rhodes Johnston, born about 1855; (3) a son named George Johnston Jr., born about 1863; (4) a son named Ira Johnston, born about 1865; (5) a daughter named Ida Johnston, born about 1860, and (6) a daughter named Lizzie Johnston, also born about 1860. Newspaper accounts of the Johnston family also mention an Elijah Johnston, who was about 18 years old in 1864, but this is probably Elijah Johnson (different spelling), a counterfeiter who is mentioned in the *Description and Information of Criminals*, p. 70, at the National Archives. The ancestral home was about 2 to 3 miles south of Indianapolis. "City News—Important Arrests." *St. Louis Democrat*. St. Louis, Missouri: August 5, 1864.

69. Monroe Achman was born about 1821 in Ohio. He was living in Lake Logan, Hocking County, Ohio, in the Federal Census of 1850, and was married to Abigail Achman.

70. Dye. p. 48.

71. "The Recent Arrest of Counterfeiters." *Missouri Democrat*. St. Louis, Missouri: August 8, 1864. p. 2, col. 2.
    These men were all members of the Sleight-Frisby gang, consisting of Louis Sleight, John Frisby, James Vezey, William Homer, John Brown, and Charlie Stadtfeld. Sleight, the leader of the gang, lived in St. Louis but spent much of his time in Nauvoo, Illinois. James Vezey, a farmer, lived about seven miles from St. Louis. William Homer, a "shover," lived at No. 443 Broadway, St. Louis. He was also a business agent for the rest of the gang. John Brown also lived in St. Louis but travelled extensively. "Grand Haul of Counterfeiters." *New York Times*. August 11, 1864.

72. "City News—Important Arrests." *St. Louis Democrat*. St. Louis, Missouri: August 5, 1864.
    Gives a good description of the plates, dies, lithographic stones, and paper found during the raid by Colonel Baker. "Grand Haul of Counterfeiters." *New York Times*. August 11, 1864.

73. "Arrest of Counterfeiters." *Indianapolis Daily Journal*. Indianapolis, Indiana: August 4, 1864. p. 3.
    Unfortunately, this article does not name the two Johnston men arrested. The article confuses the Johnstons with the Johnsons. From other evidence, we know the men arrested were definitely Johnstons.

74. None of the Johnstons were received at the Old Capitol Prison during August 1864. This is also true for anyone named Johnson. *Morning Reports of Prisoners at Old Capitol Prison, Washington*. Volume 1, Record Group 393. p. 234. National Archives, College Park, Maryland.

75. "Arrival of Counterfeiters at Washington." *Cincinnati Daily Enquirer*. Cincinnati, Ohio: August 8, 1864. p. 3, cols. 5 and 6.
    Colonel Baker told a newspaper reporter that one of the counterfeiters had jumped from the train while it was moving and was killed—meaning, of course, Pete McCartney.

76. "Important Arrest of Counterfeiters—Capture of Plates, Press and Money." *Cincinnati Daily Enquirer*. Cincinnati, Ohio: August 6, 1864. p. 3.
    Charles Burnell, known as "Little Jimmy," was briefly associated with Charles Ulrich and was a counterfeiter for most of his life. Louis Dollman, originally from Cincinnati, was a counterfeiter and burglar and was hunted down by Chief of Police Laurence Harrigan of St. Louis. Harrigan once missed catching Dollman by only a minute or so but found that he (Dollman) had left $540,000 of counterfeit money behind, along with a press, plates, and other material. Harrigan caught him a little later. A pistol battle ensured and Dollman was hit by a bullet to the forehead and died instantly. "A Noted Chief of Police." *Denver Post*. Denver, Colorado: June 5, 1898. p. 5.
    Peter McCue is a mystery, unless the prisoner was Lucas McGlue, an alias for Oscar Finch. William Minzer is not otherwise mentioned in 19th-century newspapers.

77. "An Arrest in East St. Louis." *Missouri Republican*. St. Louis, Missouri: January 8, 1866; "The Conflict of Authority in East St. Louis—Mayor Bowman's Statement." *Missouri Republican*. St. Louis, Missouri: January 11, 1866. (page and column missing.)
    Joe Wood had in his possession $11,000 in counterfeit compound-interest notes and $5,000 in good money when arrested. "Miscellaneous." *Albany Evening Journal*. Albany, New York: p. 2, col. 3.

78. "Arrest of Counterfeiters." *Illinois Daily State Journal*. Springfield, Illinois: August 25, 1866. p. 4, col. 1.
    Pete McCartney was using the alias of William Wilson, and his brother Levi was going under the name of John Douglas. Marshal Rittenhouse found $30,000 in counterfeit U.S. Treasury Notes on the men plus a large lot of bogus fractional currency. A large press, boxed up, and the engraved plates of the notes were found in a warehouse at Mantoon, but it was believed by some that the actual work was done in Champaign, Illinois.

79. "Singular Escape of Prisoners from the County Jail." *Illinois Daily State Journal*. Springfield, Illinois: October 18, 1866. p. 4, cols. 2 and 3; "Interview with Pete McCartney." *Illinois State Register*. Springfield, Illinois: March 22, 1879. p. 4, col. 2.
    Almost 13 years later, Pete's explanation of his escape exonerates the Sheriff and implies that Martha, Pete's wife, brought the keys to the jail doors. It does not explain where she got the keys.

80. Samuel Felker and Colonel Wood were snakes in the grass—unscrupulous, cunning, and devious. Felker was especially outrageous. He had a long history of manipulating, exploiting, and violating the rights of others.
    For a description of his rogue behavior, see George P. Burnham's *Memoirs of the United States Secret Service*, pp. 136–143; and H.C. Whitley's *In It*, pp. 305–307.
    For his role in attempting to murder the detective Allan Pinkerton, see "Alan Pinkerton." *New York Times*. August 5, 1869; and "The Pinkerton Conspiracy." *New York Times*. August 24, 1869.

81. "Shoving the Queer—Descent Upon a Den of Counterfeiters." *Louisville Courier-Journal*. Louisville, Kentucky: November 5, 1870. p. 4, col. 2. The article contains some factual errors. John Carter and his wife were actually Mr. and Mrs. Pete McCartney, so the party numbered three instead of five people; "The Counterfeiters." *Louisville Courier-Journal*.

November 13, 1870. p. 4, col. 2. The person named as "Fred Leebush" in this article is actually Frederick Biebusch.

82. "Report of Operative John Eagan." Register of Reports. Volume 5. November 1870. p. 75. Record Group 87, *Records of the United States Secret Service*, National Archives, College Park, Maryland.

83. "Capture of A Counterfeiter." *Cincinnati Daily Gazette*. Cincinnati, Ohio: November 22, 1870. p. 2. The person named Ira Johnson in the article was actually Charles Johnson; "Testimony of the Police Officers." *Cincinnati Daily Gazette*. December 1, 1870. p. 1.

84. "A Counterfeit Plate Case Before the United States Court." *The Cincinnati Commercial*. Cincinnati, Ohio: May 4, 1871. p. 6, col. 6.

85. "A Big Haul." *Decatur Republican*. Decatur, Illinois: December 15, 1870. p. 1.

86. George Albert Mason was a large bully and a dangerous man with an unpredictable bent for violence. Born in England, he came to America just before the Civil War and joined the Confederate Army. It was said that he was the moving spirit behind a plot to kidnap President Abraham Lincoln after the war, but was detected, arrested, court-martialed, and sentenced to imprisonment for life, only to be pardoned by President Ulysses S. Grant and deported. He moved to Canada and began a criminal career in which he was arrested almost 50 times for assault, drunk and disorderly conduct, assault with a dangerous weapon, burglary, perjury, libel, bribery, theft, etc. His counterfeiting case is reported in: "A Counterfeiter's Sentence." *New York Tribune*. New York, New York: May 10, 1875. p. 2, col. 3; "The Mason Counterfeiting Case." *New York Herald*. April 14, 1875. p. 5, cols. 1 and 2.

A history of his criminal life is found in (1) "George Albert Mason." *Daily Inter Ocean*. Chicago, Illinois: May 15, 1875. p. 5, col. 5; (2) "The Convicted Counterfeiter Mason." *New York Herald*. New York, New York: May 9, 1875. p. 7; (3) "An Offender With A History." *Cleveland Leader*. Cleveland, Ohio: March 26, 1875. p. 3, col. 1; (4) "A Counterfeiter's Career." *New York Times*. January 14, 1883; and (5) "The Counterfeiter Mason." *The Manitoba Daily Free Press*. Winnipig, Canada: March 13, 1883. Drummond. *True Detective Stories*. pp. 174–176.

87. "Desperate Affray." *Daily Inter Ocean*. Chicago, Illinois; December 13, 1874. p. 5, col. 4; "A Thieves' Battle." *Daily Inter Ocean*. December 14, 1874. p. 5, col. 6.

88. Dye. *op. cit.* p. 59.

89. Thomas F. Eagan. "Pete McCartney, Counterfeiter." (Part 2). *Paper Money*. March/April 1993. p. 45.

90. Dye. *op. cit.* p. 60.

This source contains a copy of the letter from Solicitor Bluford Wilson to George H. Williams, Attorney General, to dismiss Mr. Duckworth from the Secret Service.

91. "How McCartney Escaped." *Austin Daily Democratic Statesman*. Austin, Texas: June 8, 1875. p. 3, col. 2.

92. "Arrests." *Bankers' Magazine & Statistical Register*. Volume 31. December 1876. p. 484.

93. Secret Service operative Estes G. Rathborne saw an account of the arrest of Lang and Boland in the *Cincinnati Commercial* and, believing one of them to be Pete McCartney, sent an encrypted telegram to Chief James J. Brooks, instructing him to go immediately to Richmond and identify the prisoners. Charles Lang turned out to be Pete McCartney after all. His long-time accomplice, Henry Boland, also

went by the aliases of Walter Scott and Charles Walters, but his real name was probably Shepherd. We know so little about him because he never spoke once arrested.

The story of these arrests is well documented in Dye, pp. 62–64; "Counterfeiters Sentenced." *New York Times*. December 2, 1876.

94. "Jake," born Jacob McCartney about 1827, is listed in the 1870 Federal Census as living in Neoga, Illinois, with wife Emily and two sons ages five and six. "The Coney People." *Daily Illinois State Journal*. Springfield, Illinois: March 22, 1879. p. 4, cols. 2 and 3. This article gives a detailed record of the evidence against Dr. Mason; "Pete McCartney's Revenge." *Chicago Daily Tribune*. Chicago, Illinois: March 22, 1879. p. 2.

95. "The Twenty-Dollar Plate." *Chicago Daily Tribune*. Chicago, Illinois: February 15, 1879. p. 5; "A Valuable Find." *Daily Illinois State Register*. Springfield, Illinois: February 15, 1879. p.4, col. 5.

96. "The Coney People." *op. cit.*

97. "A Clever Counterfeiter." *The Daily Picayune*. New Orleans, Louisiana: February 19, 1888. p. 8, col. 2.

This article gives a detailed report on the mistakes that Pete made in pasting up a $1 Silver Certificate with a vignette of Martha Washington to a $50 note of George Washington. This is evidence that Pete's skills had declined considerably during his time in prison. "Pete McCartney Again." *The Daily Picayune*. March 11, 1888. p. 6, col. 6; "Pete McCartney." *The Daily Picayune*. June 3, 1888. p. 8, col. 1.

98. "Pete McCartney Is No More." *The Daily Inter Ocean*. Chicago, Illinois: October 22, 1890. p. 1.

99. The 1850 Federal Census of Poughkeepsie, Dutchess County, New York, shows Peter J. Ballard, age 49, a cabinet-maker, and his wife Elisa Ballard, age 47, keeping house. Thomas Ballard was then age 10, George was age 2, but another brother, Albert, age 7, is not listed in subsequent censuses or in other sources and probably died at an early age.

100. The 1870 Federal Census for the 22nd Ward, New York City, shows a Thomas Ballard, age 30, carriage painter, and his wife, Julia, age 20, both born in New York State. Julia and her parents were born in Hanover, New York. In the 1880 Federal Census, the Ballard family shows a daughter, Minnie, age 8, living with them. The family living right above them was that of Henry Avery, a tailor, born in Hanover, and his daughter, Amelia, age 36, also born in Hanover. Since we know from other sources that Tom married an Avery from Hanover, it is very likely that Julia's father and sister were living just above her and Tom. Tom often used the alias "Tom Avery."

101. Dye. *op. cit.* pp. 31 and 32.

102. "Arrests of Counterfeiters." *New York Times*. October 27, 1871. p. 5, col. 3. The arrest of several counterfeit shovers (David Kirkbride, Stephen Paine, etc.) eventually leading to the capture of Thomas Ballard is detailed in this article. This article also reports some testimony given by John Ballard. A list of the evidence is given in Dye, *op. cit.* p. 33.

103. "The Counterfeiters." *Buffalo Commercial Advertiser*. Buffalo, New York: October 13, 1874. p. 3, col. 1; and October 14, 1874. p. 3, col. 2; Dye. *op. cit.* pp. 37 and 38.

A more detailed list of the evidence is found in "Description and Information of Criminals." Volume unknown. p. 8. Record Group 87, *Records of the United States Secret Service*, National Archives, College Park, Maryland; *The United States vs. Thomas Ballard*. Northern District of New York, Criminal. A case file of 29 indictments and the

Record of Conviction filed on January 19, 1875. This case file is available from National Archives, Northeast Region, New York, New York.

104. "The Escaped Ludlow Street Jail Prisoners." *New York Times*. November 17, 1871.

So many prisoners escaped from the Ludlow Street Jail that it was often called the "Ludlow Street Hotel" and the "Ludlow Alimony Club," the latter name earned by the fact that it housed so many men who hadn't paid alimony to their ex-wives. The jail was understaffed and the guards poorly paid, making them easily bought. It became a revolving door for some of the prisoners with money.

105. "Important Discoveries." *Buffalo Commercial Advertiser*. Buffalo, New York: October 10, 1874. p. 3, col. 1.

106. "Ballard, the Counterfeiter." *New York Times*. December 25, 1874.

107. The wife of Benjamin Franklin Ballard, who had given her name as Julia Ann Elizabeth Britton during her examination in Buffalo, changed her story in testimony at trial in Albany. She then explained that her maiden name was Booker, and the name of her first husband was Britton, to whom she married in 1856; he died, and about 1869 she married Benjamin in Ohio. She was arrested in Davenport, Ohio, for having in her possession a valise containing $5,000 in counterfeit money, and she was served a term of imprisonment. "Tom Ballard." *Albany Evening Journal*. Albany, New York: January 21, 1875. p. 3.

108. "A Counterfeiter's Offer." *New York Times*. September 2, 1877.

109. "Tom Ballard, the King of Counterfeiters, Attempted Suicide Again At the Albany Penitentiary." *The Times*. Troy, New York: April 24, 1879. p. 3, col. 1.

110. "A King of Counterfeiters." *New York Times*. July 1, 1887. p. 1.

111. *Ibid.*

112. "State Contract To An Ex-Convict." *New York Times*. July 9, 1893.

113. This information is taken from Fred's Death Certificate issued by the City of St. Louis Health Department (No. 1635). The 1860 Federal Census shows he is listed as a "horse dealer," with wife Fredricka, born in Prussia in 1826, and children Mina, Matilda, and Fred. The 1880 Census shows Fred has told the census taker to list his occupation as "Prisoner." His children in 1880 are "Minnie," age 30; Frederick, age 23; Amanda, age 20; and William, age 15.

114. Dye. *op. cit.* p. 95.

115. The Marshals Service was created by the Judiciary Act of 1789, and hundreds of their men were spread throughout the country and became the bulwark against counterfeiting. U.S. Marshals in the 19th century had little communication with the government, and so they were given wide latitude in figuring out the law and how to enforce it.

116. "The Biebusch Gang." *The Rockford Morning Star*. Rockford, Illinois: November 25, 1905. p. 16.

This is part of a series of articles written by Captain Patrick D. Tyrrell, formerly of the U.S. Secret Service, and syndicated in a number of newspapers throughout the country.

117. "State vs. Biebusch." *Reports of Cases Argued and Determined in the Supreme Court of the State of Missouri*. Volume XXXII. (32 Missouri 276). St. Louis, Missouri: George Knapp & Co., 1863. p. 275.

118. A good example is found in "Fred Biebusch." *Daily Missouri Republican*. St. Louis, Missouri: February 16, 1858. p. 3, col. 5. There, a witness against Fred failed to appear at a hearing, and when captured the next day, he explained that he had received a letter from some of Fred's friends warning that if he gave testimony against Fred, he would be "dispatched."

119. Of the several prisoners sent by Colonel Baker to Washington, only Fred Biebusch was received at the Old Capitol Prison. *Morning Reports of Prisoners at Old Capitol Prison, Washington*. Volume 1. p. 240. Record Group 393, National Archives (this was previously listed as Volume 311-A, p. 240). Biebusch was received on August 14, 1864. The other prisoners may have been placed in other jails to prevent over-crowding in the Old Capitol Prison. After serving a few months in the prison, Fred's lawyer sent a petition for pardon to President Abraham Lincoln, arguing that Fred was convicted on insufficient evidence, had been a model prisoner, and was of old age and poor health. Lincoln considered the request and granted the pardon. "One of Grant's Pets." *Chicago Sunday Times*. Chicago, Illinois: November 12, 1876. p. 7.

120. Dye. *op. cit.* p. 97.

121. William Shelly was an engraver of great skill, living usually in St. Louis, and who, at various times, worked for nearly a dozen counterfeiters. At the time Biebusch was arrested, Shelly was at Fred's house but escaped. He left St. Louis and headed east, settling in Greenpoint, Long Island, where he assumed the name of Charles Cooper and found employment as an engraver for the Singer Sewing Machine Co. He lived at the corner of Graham and Van Cott avenues in Greenpoint. He went to work for Bill Gurney engraving a set of plates for the new 15-cent fractional currency. He was arrested on Sunday morning, September 18, 1870, in New York, with a full set of plates, comprising front, back, and seal, for printing the currency. He was held in default of a $10,000 bail. He was a shrewd man and realized that his only chance to leave prison was to agree to testify against Biebusch.

"History of A Counterfeiter." *National Aegis*. Worcester, Massachusetts: September 24, 1870. p. 4, col. 3; "Queer." *Cincinnati Daily Enquirer*. October 18, 1874. p. 1, cols. 5 and 6.

122. The 1850 Federal Census shows Nathaniel Kinsey Jr. single, age 21, and living at home with his parents (Nathaniel and Ruthanna). His occupation is listed as "engraver."

123. Edward Nevers was one of three men granted Patent No. 7,786 on November 19, 1850, for an improvement in copper and steel-plate–printing presses. At the time Nevers lived in Cincinnati, Ohio. He is identified as a "notorious counterfeiter" by M.H. Mott in his *History of the Regulators of Northern Indiana*. Indianapolis, Indiana: Indianapolis Journal Company, 1859.

Mott says on page 53 that Nevers's shop was raided just recently and counterfeiting supplies were found.

124. This letter is dated January 25, 1865, marked No. 124, and filed in the "Register of Letters Received by the Solicitor of the Treasury," Record Group 206, *Records of the Treasury Department*, National Archives, College Park, Maryland.

125. The 1860 Federal Census shows that Maria A. Boyd, a widow, age 52, had a family consisting of a son John Boyd, age 29, a bookkeeper; a

daughter Frances C. Boyd, age 16; and a son Benjamin Boyd, age 26, a "steel engraver."

126. Achman is the correct name of this family, not "Ackerman" or "Ackaman." In the 1850 Federal Census, the family is found at Lake Logan, Ohio. Almiranda, five years old, is spelled "Almander" and the last name is shown as "Ackaman," both wrong. The Illinois marriage records show that Pete McCartney's bride signed her name as "Martha Ann Achman" on October 19, 1864. Michigan marriage records show that Benjamin E. Boyd's bride signed her name as "Almiranda Achman" on October 22, 1867, in St. Clair, Michigan. It's clear that the 1850 Census taker misspelled the family's name. John B. Trout, who started his criminal career in the 1850s, was sentenced in 1867 to the Indiana prison at Michigan City for counterfeiting. He was taken out of prison in 1870 to testify as an expert witness about the Johnson family. "Mysteries of Counterfeiting." *Cincinnati Daily Enquirer*. April 8, 1870. p. 2, col. 5.

Knowing he was going to die while in prison, he made his own coffin. However, he was pardoned on December 20, 1870, by President Ulysses S. Grant, who then revoked the pardon but reissued another on February 5, 1872. Trout died out of prison in 1872.

127. Dye. *op. cit.* p. 81.

128. Boyd made many of his plates using a "skeleton plate." The part of the plate he wanted to erase, such as the name of a bank, was "hammered up" from the back side of the plate then filed down on the front side to make a level, clean field. This process is described by John Ballard, when he was a witness against Joshua Miner at his (Miner's) trial: ". . . there is a process of driving up the letters which give the name of the bank, so that they may be filed down and new names engraved, and printed from as counterfeits on the other banks; the twenty-dollar plate which is here had been filed down in this way at least twenty-eight times, the Farmers and Manufacturers Bank of Poughkeepsie being the last counterfeit." Dye. *op. cit.* p. 34.

Boyd probably learned how to make skeleton plates when he worked with Pete McCartney, who is believed to have invented the method.

129. The best account of the raids on Boyd and Driggs is to be found in "The Lincoln Tomb Raiders," by Patrick Tyrell, *The Evening Star*, Washington, D.C., June 18, 1905, p. 18; Dye. *op. cit.* pp. 82 and 83; "Sinuous Sinners." *Daily Inter Ocean*. Chicago, Illinois: January 20, 1876. p. 2; "Queer Ben Boyd—A Famous Counterfeiter." *Indianapolis Sentinel*. Indianapolis, Indiana: January 21, 1876. p.5.

130. In the 1840 Federal Census there is a single male named Nelson Driggs listed in the town of Freeport, Harrison County, Ohio. That census did not reveal any other information on him. In 1850 he opened a store in Moorefield, about four miles east of Freeport. The following year he put in a "nice lot of goods" in a house which he rented to a partner to whom he paid a wage to sell the items. In March 1852 Driggs sold all his store goods on both sides of the street to Holloway and Parson. *Biographical Record, Harrison County, Ohio*. Chicago, Illinois: J.H. Beers & Co., 1891. pp. 109 and 452.

The 1850 Federal Census shows Nelson living with the Guthrie family in Freeport and a 17-year-old girl named "Phoebe Driggs." His relationship with Phoebe is not presently known. Samuel H. Guthrie, the head of the household, was married to Rebecca, who was the sister of Nelson Driggs, which explains why Nelson was living in that household. Rebecca was born about 1812. Nelson's real-estate value was listed as $20,000.

131. "Over Thirty Thousand Dollars' Worth of Counterfeit and Altered Money Seized." *New York Times*. February 20, 1855. Copied from the *Chicago Tribune*. February 16, 1855.

See also the untitled paragraph in the *Alexandria Gazette and Virginia Advertiser*. February 22, 1855. p. 2. This source says that the great body of the spurious notes consisted of genuine notes altered from $1 to $5, $10, $20, and $50. That's a lot of cutting and pasting.

132. "Over $5,000 Spurious Money Seized—Counterfeit Plates Secured." *Cleveland Plain Dealer*. June 29, 1857. p. 2, col. 6. Copied from the *St. Louis Republican*. June 24, 1857.

133. According to Thomas Gregg's *History of Hancock County, Illinois*, 1880, Lewis Sleight was born on March 2, 1819, in New Jersey. He moved to St. Louis, Missouri, when he was 16, and he resided there for 16 years. He then moved to Navoo, Illinois, where he was captain of a ferry boat that ran from that place to Montrose, Iowa. He ran the ferry from 1851 until his death on June 2, 1872. He was married in 1842 to Sarah Frisby, and they had three children.

While in Nauvoo, John Frisby's brother was killed during a fight on a boat. Both Sleight and Frisby were arrested for counterfeiting during the Civil War and sent to Washington to grace the halls of the Old Capitol Prison. John Frisby bought a hotel in Jersey City that became a hiding place and rendezvous for counterfeiters. Later, he went to live in the state of Wisconsin.

134. I am indebted to Daniel Stadtfeld for this information.

135. Driggs reportedly spent $4,000 trying to get a Presidential pardon. The Treasury Department was suspicious and sent an investigator to the prison to see if Driggs was really as sick as the Warden claimed. The investigator found Driggs "jovial," talkative, and in good health. "The Driggs Pardon Matter." *Decatur Daily Review*. Decatur, Illinois: March 23, 1893. p. 2, cols. 1 and 2.

136. "Counterfeiters Detected." *Wheeling Daily Register*. Wheeling, West Virginia: p. 1, col. 5.

137. According to Daniel Stadtfeld, Nicholas and Barbara Stadtfeld and all the little Stadtfelds came from Mehren, Rheinland, Prussia. Most of the children were born in Mehren, but Charles was born in Gillenfeld, nearby. Barbara's maiden name (taken from the Roman Catholic birth records) was Morsch or Marsch, possibly Von Marsch.

138. A good account is given in "Like A Dime Novel." *Cleveland Plain Dealer*. November 17, 1890. p. 5; and "An Important Capture." *The Daily Inter Ocean*. Chicago, Illinois: July 20, 1889. p. 3.

After Jim Guyon escaped from Dayton, he disappeared. Daniel Stadtfeld believes the Secret Service tracked him to Corinth, Mississippi, but then lost all trace of him. As late as 1901, he had not been found. "Bold Counterfeiters." *The Sunday Globe*. Washington, D.C.: August 4, 1901. p. 2, cols. 3–5.

139. He is buried in the Woodland Cemetery, Dayton, Ohio, in Section 110, Lot No. 2982.

140. Although his production is believed to have been low, Charles W. Hill was one of the very best counterfeit engravers of the 19th century, as witness his "Webster head" $10 note. His home was at Bethel, Connecticut, about 60 miles northeast of New York City. Secret Service agents estimated his age at "about 65 years" when he was arrested in 1894. His social relations and past history are given in *Descriptions and Information of Criminals*, volume 3, p. 205, and his description and arrest record is given in Volume 8, p. 135 of the same work, both of which are available at National Archives, College Park, Maryland.

141. "Mystery in Immense Legacy." *Rockford Daily Republic*. Rockford, Illinois: May 4, 1903. p. 6, cols. 3 and 4; "Crook's Fortune." *The Daily*

Herald. Biloxi, Mississippi: December 10, 1902. p. 1; "Estate of Charles Hill." *The Standard*. Ogden, Utah: December 9, 1902.

Gertrude had two daughters: the first, Grace, was on the New York vaudeville stage as "Baby Doll," married a MacDonald, and had two children: Ralph and Gertrude. Gertrude MacDonald married George Lemuel Lovejoy Jr. of California. In 1927 they had a son named George L. Lovejoy, to whom I am indebted for this information [letter of July 27, 2012, and private phone conversations]. Gertrude Driggs's second daughter was named Florence. A newspaper article of the time states that these two daughters (Grace and Florence) took the name "the Morrison Sisters" in their song-and-dance vaudeville routine. The family's address was given as 687 3rd Avenue, New York. Mrs. Gertrude Driggs also said, in court testimony, that her daughter, Grace, was born in 1888, which would make Nelson a father at age 78, which is possible but not likely. A review of the medical data shows the oldest father in Great Britain was 78, and fathers older than 65 are rare in America. It would also make Mrs. Driggs a mother at about age 38. This raises the possibility that Grace was a "love child," but it is even more likely that Gertrude Driggs lied about her daughter's age and date of birth. "Great Legal Fight Over A Fortune." *Boston Globe*. July 20, 1903. p. 3, cols. 3–6.

142. "People vs. Driggs." *The Pacific Reporter*. Volume 108. St. Paul, Wisconsin: West Publishing Co., 1884. pp. 62–64. Available on-line.

143. Most of the family is buried in Woodmere Cemetery in Detroit, Michigan, in Section G, Lot 128. There is no burial marker for John Johnson, and he may be buried in Canada. Census records indicate he was born in New York. Agnes, his wife, was born in 1820, according to her tombstone, and Census records indicate she was born in Pennsylvania. She was buried at Woodmere on February 25, 1908. Charles Johnson died in the Ohio Penitentiary in Columbus, Ohio, in mid-April 1900. He was buried at Woodmere on April 23 of that year. Edward Johnson, born in Kentucky in 1848, had no tombstone but was buried at Woodmere on November 11, 1937. Henry D. Johnson, also called "Dave," was born in September 1859 and died in 1945. He is buried next to his wife, Emily W. Johnson, and their daughter, Irene. Emily Johnson (nee Wetherald) was born in Canada in 1852 and was buried in Woodmere on July 10, 1916. Irene Johnson, born 1885, was buried on October 4, 1898, at the age of 13 years and 6 months. Josephine Johnson, known as "Jessie," was born in Kentucky about 1848 and died on December 20, 1896. She was buried elsewhere before interment at Woodmere and has no tombstone. Georgia Johnson, known as "Georgie," was born in 1850 and was buried February 10, 1941. She is named "Georgie F. Bayliss" on her tombstone. Her husband, Captain Frank L. Bayliss, died November 26, 1888, age 36 years. The other members of the Johnson family were buried elsewhere and have not been located. This information is from the tombstones and cemetery records. Charles Johnson's obituary appears in "Died in Prison; End of A Fraud." *Plain Dealer*. Cleveland, Ohio: April 29, 1900. p. 4, col. 4.

144. Thomas Carter's account of his search for Charles Johnson is given in "Mrs. Johnson Sure of Her Freedom." *Detroit Journal*. Detroit, Michigan: August 18. p. 1, cols. 1 and 2.

145. *Memoirs of a Great Detective: Incidents in the Life of John Wilson Murray*. Chapter XXX. New York, New York: Baker & Taylor, 1904. pp. 167–182.

146. "Three Noted Men Behind the Bars." p. 1, cols. 1 and 2; "The Johnsons Are Well-Known Criminals." p. 1, col. 2; "Dave Johnson's Clever." p. 1, col. 3; "Dave Johnson's Home." p. 1, col. 3. All these articles were in the *Detroit Journal*. August 15, 1898.

147. The Johnsons and the Weatheralds were related by the marriage of David Johnson to Emily Weatherald on May 31, 1880. Emily, born in 1852 in Toronto, was the daughter of Joseph J. and Sarah Wetherald. Joseph J. Wetherald was born in Guelph, Ontario. He died November 2, 1896. Sarah ("Janey"?) Wetherald was born in 1817 in England and died June 3, 1895.

148. "Johnson's Bail Fixed at $5,000." *Detroit Journal*. August 17, 1898. p. 3, col. 5; "The Johnson Family Crooked Away Back." *Detroit Journal*. August 17, 1898. p. 3, col. 5; "Mrs. Bayless is Decidedly Angry." *Detroit Journal*. August 18, 1898. p. 3, cols. 5 and 6; "Rejected the Offer." *Detroit Journal*. August 19, 1898. p. 3, col. 3; "Chapter Closed in the Johnson Case." *Detroit Journal*. August 23, 1898. p. 3, col. 6; "Ed Johnson Smooth as Silk." *Detroit Journal*. August 25, 1898. p. 3, col. 6; "The Great John Webb." *Detroit Journal*. August 31, 1898. p. 3, col. 3.

149. "The Johnson Family is Well Rounded-Up." *Detroit Journal*. August 16, 1898. p. 3, cols. 2–4; "Dave Johnson was Exceedingly Pious." *Detroit Journal*. August 16, 1898. p. 3, col. 5.

150. "The Johnsons Get 9 Years in Prison." *Detroit Journal*. December 22, 1898. p. 3, col. 5.

151. There is a six-page, double-spaced, typed indictment of Edward Johnson, Criminal Case No. 4524, for the Eastern District of Michigan, which contains photographs of the 1891 Silver Certificate ("Windom Head Two") counterfeited by Edward, a typed three-page True Bill of the sentence imposed by the Judge, also No. 4524, a six-page typed indictment of Charles Johnson, Case No. 4525, with two photographs of the Windom $2 Silver Certificate, a six-page typed indictment of David H. Johnson, Case No. 4522, with photographs of the Hancock $2 Silver Certificate, a six-page typed True Bill sentencing David Johnson to nine years of hard labor, and various docket and secondary records of the court, all in Record Group 21 (Records of the District Courts of the United States), at National Archives, Great Lakes Regional Office, Chicago, Illinois.

152. *Descriptions and Information of Criminals, 1863–1906*. Volume 21A. pp. 469–471. Record Group 87, National Archives, College Park, Maryland; John S. Dye. *The Government Blue Book*. pp. 70–77.

153. Dye. *op. cit.* p. 72.

154. In this case, Dabb's Photograph Rooms at 174 Liberty Street was honored with the work. The Secret Service had been taking photographs of counterfeiters and other criminals for several years, and many of these pictures can be seen in the various volumes of *Description and Information of Criminals*, Record Group 87, National Archives, College Park, Maryland. A much smaller collection can be found at a few of the larger Police Departments around the country.

155. National Archives, College Park, Maryland, has documents for seven cases against Miles Ogle for the February Term of 1877, for the U.S. District Court, Western District of Pennsylvania, cases 11–17, numbering 61 pages in total. No record appears to exist for the October 1871 arrest, and there are no court dockets to locate records of the 1871 arrest. Miles Ogle was also tried in U.S. District under the name George W. Wilson in 1870, and the records for that case are filed under *U.S. vs. George W. Wilson*, Case 2, for the October 1870 term, U.S. District Court, Western District of Pennsylvania (13 pages).

156. "Troublesome Counterfeiters." *Cincinnati Daily Gazette*. August 16, 1877. p. 8. Mentions the shooting at Cairo.

157. "Rearrest of An Escaped Prisoner—Counterfeiters Broken Up." *The Sun*. Baltimore, Maryland: March 14, 1873. p. 1, col. 7.

158. "Robert Rankin." *Cincinnati Daily Gazette*. June 4, 1878. p. 3.

159. Untitled paragraph in *The Sun*. Baltimore, Maryland: July 9, 1898. p. 10, col. 2.

160. "Death of A Noted Counterfeiter." *Cleveland Plain Dealer*. March 13, 1886. p. 4, col. 5; "Death of Miner, the Counterfeiter." *New York Herald-Tribune*. March 13, 1886. p. 5, col. 4.

161. "The Queer Men." *New York Herald*. October 27, 1871. p. 10, col. 1.

162. Dye. *op. cit.* p. 8. 6 printing presses, 2 transfer presses, 19 sets of steel plates. A ruling machine, ink colors (pigments), a $1,000 U.S. Treasury Note of the new issue, stock for making the pink-fibered government paper, and counterfeit bills representing $60,000 were captured. Additionally, 14 men were implicated as members of Miner's gang and were either charged or watched carefully by the Secret Service. The agents also went to the house of Lewelly Williams, a printer, at 438 West 54th Street, and found counterfeit plates ranging from 50 cents to $10. They found $1,500 in 50-cent currency stuffed into an old sofa, and several presses, inks, and paper were found in the house.

163. The other escapees were James Quimby of Philadelphia and William Brown of Cincinnati. Quimby had already served three years in the New Jersey State Prison for counterfeiting. Only a week before, he had been sentenced to five-years imprisonment in the Kings County Penitentiary for the same crime. Brown was a "shover" and petty thief. His father and mother were then both in prison for dealing in counterfeit. For the apprehension of Ballard, Colonel Whiteley offered a reward of $1,000. "The Escaped Ludlow Street Jail Prisoners." *New York Times*. November 17, 1871.

164. Reports on the trial are to be found in "Counterfeiting." *New York Herald*. December 13, 1871. p. 8, cols. 1 and 2; "Counterfeiting." *New York Herald*. December 15, 1871. p. 8, cols. 4 and 5; "Counterfeiting." *New York Herald*. December 19, 1871. p. 8, cols. 5 and 6; "The Miner Trial." *New York Herald-Tribune*. December 19, 1871. p. 2, cols. 2 and 3; "Counterfeiting." *New York Herald*. December 20, 1871. p. 11; "Counterfeiting." *New York Herald*. December 21, 1871. p. 8, col. 4; "Counterfeiting." *New York Herald*. December 22, 1871. p. 11, col. 6; "Counterfeiting." *New York Herald-Tribune*. December 23, 1871. p. 7, col. 1; "Acquittal of Miner, the Alleged Counterfeiter." *New York Herald*. December 28, 1871. p. 6, col. 4.

165. John testified that he had known Miner for four years; testified that he recognized the counterfeit plates in evidence; described the Rivington Street plant and said he had full charge of the operations there for the past three years, turning out about $10,000 a month; recognized Mr. Hinman and told how he once participated in an exchange of $10,000 from Hinman to Miner to Bill Gurney. Dye. *op. cit.* p. 34.

166. "An Old Counterfeiter Dead." *New York Herald*. March 13, 1886. p. 9, col. 5.

167. Biographical data for Charles H. Smith can be found in "Description and Information of Criminals," in Record Group 87, volume 8, pp. 47 and 48, *Records of the United States Secret Service*, National Archives, College Park, Maryland.

168. Two case files are held at National Archives in New York (A261 #5414 and #5415) for *U.S. vs. Charles H. Smith*). Both were filed in the U.S. District Court for the Eastern District of New York on October 19, 1883. These files contain indictments only. If there are any memoranda about his examination before the U.S. Commissioner, they are probably in the files of the Department of Justice, an area I have not searched. The NARA at College Park has two pages devoted to Mr. Smith in the "Description and Information of Criminals," Volume 1, p. 47, in Record Group 87. That entry was made on October 23, 1880. There is a photograph of him in Album Volume 4, p. 318, also in RG 87. According to an archivist, volumes in the DIC have been re-numbered. Bloom, in his excellent book, *Money of Their Own*, mistakes William H. Smith for Charles H. Smith on p. 116, but he gets the name right in all other passages.

169. "Smith The Counterfeiter." *Brooklyn Eagle*. September 13, 1897.
    Sidney Smith's arrest record and biographical data are found in "Description and Information of Criminals," Record Group 87, volume 31, p. 109, *Records of the United States Secret Service*, National Archives, College Park, Maryland; *New York Times*. August 29, 1895. p. 13, col. 7. The National Archives in New York holds case files on Sidney Smith and Abbie L. Smith. The title of the case is *United States vs. Wm. E. Brockway, alias E.W. Spencer, Orlando E. Bradford, Abbie L. Smith and William E. Wagner*. Sidney Smith was placed on trial April 2, 1896, but a *nolle prosequi* was filed, as he gave state's evidence and was cooperative with the investigation; "Dr. Bradford Confesses." *New York Times*. October 31, 1895. p. 1, col. 3.

170. The first mention of the arrests is to be found in "A Nest of Counterfeiters." *Brooklyn Eagle*. September 23, 1893. p. 10, col. 3. A smaller article appeared in "Italian Counterfeiter Held." *New York Tribune*. September 24, 1893. p. 20, col. 4; "Delnoce is An Expert." *Brooklyn Daily Eagle*. September 24, 1893. p. 24, col. 2; "Delnoce Convicted." *Brooklyn Daily Eagle*. April 5, 1894. p. 10, col. 2. An article on Delnoce's work in Argentina appears in "Counterfeiters in the Tolls." *Galveston Daily News*. September 17, 1893. p. 3, col. 5. A photo and biographical data are found in "Description and Information of Criminals." Volume unknown. pp. 297 and 298. Record Group 87, *Records of the United States Secret Service*, National Archives, College Park, Maryland. A case file at the National Archives in New York is missing from their records. The log sheet shows this case file contained an indictment, an arraignment, a Conviction Paper, several motions before the court, including the granting of an order for arrested judgment and a denial of a motion for the discharge of property. This case file may be misplaced or stolen.

171. "Brockway's Talent." *The Evening Star*. Washington, D.C.: August 27, 1895. p. 8, col. 6. Taken from the *Boston Globe*.
    This article covers only a short period of Brockway's life, but gives the most accurate picture of his character and early family background.

172. Murray T. Bloom, in *Money of Their Own*, said the proprietor of the printing shop was named Deacon Olmstead, but Bowen and Neal gave it as "Ezra Becker," and a contemporary newspaper account said the proprietor was Frederick Gorham. A check of the 1849 New Haven City Directory shows that Frederick P. Gorham is the correct name.

173. Bloom has written that Elizabeth H. Thompson, a co-author of *Benjamin Silliman, 1794–1864, Pathfinder in American Science*, couldn't find Brockway's name in any of the known lists of Silliman's students at Yale, but since Silliman didn't list non-matriculating students, Brockway could have been one of them. Bloom. *op. cit.* Footnote on p. 108.

174. Margaret Welsh may have been her actual name or an alias assumed by Hannah Seymour. She may also have been a previous marriage to Mr. Seymour. Hannah had been the wife of one Charles Weatherby, alias "Specks," who was sent to State Prison for an unknown crime. At that point, Hannah became the partner of William Brockway. Because counterfeiters choose a life of secrecy, they sometimes skip on the civilities such as marriage. By late 1867, while Brockway and his wife were under investigation for their involvement with the seven-thirty bond counterfeits, it was discovered that Mrs. Spencer's (Brockway's) maiden name was Seymour.

175. "Counterfeiters in the Employ of the Government." *New York Times*. June 28, 1867. p. 4, col. 5.

176. Patrick H. Reason was described in several news articles as a first-class engraver. It was sensational news that he was a negro, or dark mulatto, appearing to be in his mid-forties, and married to a young wife who was white. He was awarded the prize for the finest specimen of engraving at the Centennial at Philadelphia in 1876, an event in which engravers from all parts of the world took part. He was also adept at painting miniatures, portraits, and landscapes. His eyesight did not diminish with age and he had no need for glasses right up until his death on August 11, 1898. He was buried at Lake View Cemetery. "United States Commissioner's Office—Nov. 22, Before Commissioner Osborn." *New York Tribune*. November 23, 1866. p. 2, col. 5; "New York City, The Courts, Charge of Engraving Counterfeit Plates." *New York Herald*. April 28, 1868. p. 7, col. 1; "New York City, The Courts, United States vs. Patrick Reason." *New York Herald*. May 5, 1868. p. 4, col. 3.

177. "Law Reports, United States Circuit Court, Southern District. The Counterfeiters Sentenced Before Judge Shipman." *New York Times*. July 2, 1867. p. 2, cols. 1–3.

178. Atkinson was pardoned by President Lyndon B. Johnson in early November 1868 for the usual reason of the prisoner's advanced age and the need to provide for his family. Untitled new item in the *Providence Evening Press*. Providence, Rhode Island: November 3, 1868. p. 4, col. 1. President Johnson pardoned more counterfeiters than any other president in history.

179. National Archives in New York has two case files (A261 #5414 and #5415) for *United States vs. Charles H. Smith*, both of which were filed in the U.S. District Court for the Eastern District of New York on October 19, 1883. There are no transcripts in these case files. The National Archives at College Park, Maryland, has two pages on Mr. Smith in the *Description and Information of Criminals*, volume 1, p. 47, in Record Group 87. That entry was made on October 23, 1880. There is a photograph of Charles H. Smith in the DIC Album, volume 4, p. 318, RG 87. An indictment against Smith, alleging that he assisted in the theft of certain plates from the U.S. Bureau of Engraving and Printing, was discharged on a writ of *certiorari* because the indictment used the misspelling of "Charles Smythie." "Charles H. Smith Discharged." *Brooklyn Eagle*. Brooklyn, New York: June 1, 1882. p. 4.

180. The Secret Service believed Charles H. Smith had made the plates for printing the following notes: (1) the $100 national-currency note (1st charter period) of the Second National Bank of Wilkes Barre, Pennsylvania; (2) a $100 note of the Pittsburgh National Bank; (3) a $100 note of the Pittsfield National Bank in Pittsfield, Massachusetts; (4) a $100 note of a national bank in Boston; (5) a $100 note of the Mechanics' National Bank in New Bedford, Massachusetts; (6) a $100 note on the National Exchange Bank in Baltimore, Maryland;

(7) and a $100 Compound Interest Treasury Note at six percent (Act of March 3, 1863).

181. One of the functions of the Redemption Bureau, which operated within the Treasury Department, was to check off the serial number of every soiled or damaged note returned by the national banks for replacement. When multiple notes appeared with the same serial number, it was obvious that the notes had been counterfeited and some of these were sent to the U.S. Secret Service to examine further to see if they could determine the likely engraver.

182. "Interesting Suits Against Brokers." *The Springfield Republican*. Springfield, Massachusetts: October 5, 1870. p. 5; "The Suit Against Jay Cooke & Co.—Motion for Attachment." *New York Times*. November 24, 1870; "Proceedings in U.S. Courts, The United States *vs.* Jay Cooke and Others." *The Internal Revenue Record and Customs Journal*. Volume 13. New York, New York: W.C. & F.P. Church. 1871. pp. 4–7. The jury found a verdict for the plaintiff for $23,650.88.

183. "The Seven-Thirty Counterfeiters Arrested." *New York Herald*. November 23, 1867. p. 4.

184. A short version of this story shows that the principals were two printers at the Bureau of Engraving and Printing: Eli Langdon, the father, and Edwin Langdon, his son. One Holmes gave them lead sheets and they made the lead impressions from the genuine plates and gave the lead impressions back to Holmes. All were prosecuted, but the government stumbled badly on this case. None of the counterfeiters was punished. The Solicitor of the Treasury (Jordan) agreed not to use the counterfeit plates as evidence against Holmes if he would give them up and promise never to engage in counterfeiting again. Eli Langdon turned State's evidence and was dismissed. And Edwin Langdon, the guiltiest of them all, died before sentencing.

This information is abstracted from L.C. Baker's *History of the United States Secret Service*, pp. 381 and 382.

185. "The Counterfeit Bonds." *New York Times*. November 23, 1967.

186. A.L. Drummond. *True Detective Stories*. Chicago, Illinois: M.A. Donahue & Co., 1909. p. 185.

187. Media is only three miles or so from Glen Mills, Pennsylvania, the location of the Wilcox Paper Mill, so it is likely that the fiber paper stolen at Media was made by the Wilcox company.

188. These were not the 7-30 bonds that Charles H. Smith had counterfeited earlier. These bonds, authorized by the Act of March 3, 1863, carried an interest set at 6%, payable semi-annually, and they could be redeemed at face value at the end of 17 years or on July 1, 1881. The statement put out by Secretary of the Treasury Folger concerning these bonds called them the "six percents of 1881."

189. "J.B. Doyle Arrested." *The Rockford Journal*. Rockford, Illinois: October 30, 1880. p. 2. James B. Doyle was born in April 1830 in Belfast, Maine, the son of James Doyle and Amelia Brown. He moved to Bradford, Stark County, Illinois, and married Betsy A. Foster, the daughter of Nathaniel B. Foster, a long-time counterfeiter and fellow resident of Bradford.

190. Drummond. *op. cit.* p. 195.

191. A search of the archives in Record Group 87 at College Park, Maryland, failed to turn up a written confession by Smith. It is possible that the confession was used in court and became a part of the government's

192. "Brockway's Release—He Surrenders the Plates from Which the $250,000 of Bogus Government Bonds Were Printed." *New York Herald*. November 30, 1880. p. 8, cols. 3 and 4.

193. George Casilear's testimony is given in "Doyle's Counterfeit Bonds." *New York Times*. October 31, 1880. p. 5, col. 5.

  Other articles in the *New York Times* are: "A Counterfeiter's Defense." May 20, 1881. p. 2, col. 6; "The Counterfeit Bond Case." June 4, 1881. p. 5, col. 5; "James B. Doyle Convicted." June 5, 1881. p. 1, col. 6; "Doyle, the Counterfeiter, Convicted." June 7, 1881. p. 2, col. 7; "The Counterfeiter Doyle." May 21, 1882. p. 1, col. 4; "Doyle's Suspended Sentence." May 23, 1882. p. 5, col. 5; "The Doyle Bonds All Safe." May 28, 1882. p. 10, col. 6; "The Counterfeit Bond Mystery." June 5, 1882. p. 1, col. 2.

  Other articles in the *Chicago Tribune* are: "The Doyle Case." March 14, 1882. p. 7, col. 1; "Items." May 2, 1882. p. 7, col. 4; "James B. Doyle." May 3, 1882. page unknown, col. 4; "James B. Doyle." May 4, 1882. p. 12, col. 3 and 4; "The Courts." May 5, 1882. p. 12, col. 1; "Counterfeit Bonds." May 6, 1882. p. 16, cols. 4–6; "The Doyle Case." May 7, 1882. p. 10, col. 5; "The Doyle Bond-Forgery Case." May 9, 1882. p. 7, cols. 4 and 5; "The Courts." May 10, 1882. p. 12, col. 1; "The Courts." May 11, 1882. p. 12, col. 1; "Delay for Doyle." May 21, 1882. p. 9, cols. 3 and 4.

194. "Doyle's Bonds and Plate." *New York Times*. July 9, 1882. p. 1, col. 7, and p. 2, cols. 1 and 2. This lengthy article contains the full text of Homer Lee's report.

195. Nathaniel D. Foster was born in Bradford, Illinois, about 1843. Both his father and sister served prison terms for counterfeiting. He was arrested in Springfield, Illinois, in 1868 for counterfeiting but was never brought to trial. Lewis Martin, an engraver, was indicted in 1875 by the U.S. District Court in Western Pennsylvania for conspiracy with Henry Maxey for selling counterfeit $500 Treasury Notes of the series of 1869. He worked with "Englishman Moore," a noted counterfeiter, and was the engraver of the $100 Compound Interest Treasury Note in which "Hank" Holmes was interested. He was an associate of Theodore Shotwell (alias Tom King), who died in 1883 in Greenland, Colorado. After Shotwell's death, Foster pretended to be the husband of Shotwell's sister, Mrs. Blakely.

196. "Brockway Caught Again." *New York Herald-Tribune*. November 12, 1883. p. 1, col. 1.

197. Sidney Smith, known as "baldy" to his friends, was born in 1857. He was arrested in New York by Operatives Callaghan and Esquivell of the Secret Service on August 5, 1895. He was indicted in New York on October 9, 1895, on the charge of possessing "a part of a metallic plate in imitation of a security of a foreign government" (Canada). On October 23, 1895, he was indicted in New Jersey for manufacturing counterfeit $500 U.S. Gold Certificates and $100 Bank of Montreal notes, and for having in his possession imitations of the distinctive fibre paper adopted by the U.S. Government.

  This information comes from *Description and Information of Criminals*. Volume 31. p. 109; and Volume 7. pp. 986 and 1087. Record Group 87. Notes on his trial are in Volume 5. p. 227 (a *nolle prosequi*).

198. A photograph of Abbie L. Smith is shown in Volume 10, p. 110, of *Description and Information of Criminals*, Record Group 87, and additional information is given in Volume 8, p. 633, and in Volume 7, p. 818, of the same series. In court testimony, she said the following about her history: "My maiden name was Bailey, and I was born at Bangor, Maine. My maternal grandfather, Adrian L. Ellis, was a figure

in his time as a litterateur, and his biography is part of the history of the State of Maine. One of my sisters Lillian, wife of Hiram M. Jones of 118 High Street, Brooklyn. . . . I married Gideon C. Smith, traveling salesman. Two years ago, each of us sued for divorce on the ground of abandonment in Massachusetts. . . . Now I have to say it, but Dr. Bradford was the son of my father's sister." (Making him her cousin.) Taken from the article "Bradford Their Leader." *New York Times*. August 7, 1895. p. 8.

199. The criminal indictments in this case were titled *The United States vs. William E. Brockway, alias E. W. Spencer, Orlando E. Bradford, Abbie L. Smith, and William E. Wagner*. They were the first case called of the January Term, 1896 (criminal docket 2, p. 151, no. 1). The four indictments were filed January 22, 1896. There were seven additional indictments filed against these individuals on October 16, 1895, but only #3 through #7 are available on microfilm. These indictments are available from the Northeast Regional Office of the National Archives, New York.

200. "Chief Hazen's Great Capture." *New York Herald*. August 7, 1895. p. 5.

201. "Dr. Bradford Confesses." *The New York Times*. October 31, 1895. p. 1.

202. *Ibid.*

203. The final years of Brockway's life were unknown until Murray Bloom traced his movements. Bloom. *op. cit.* pp. 136–138.

204. The passenger list of the *Ticonderoga* does not show anyone named Ulrich arriving in October 1853. This information was provided by the Immigrant Ships Transcribers Guild, which checks passenger lists. Congress enacted legislation (3 Stat. 489) in 1819 to require the captains of all arriving ships to submit a list of all passengers to the collector of customs in the district in which the ship arrived. The absence of Ulrich's name on the *Ticonderoga*'s passenger list was the first clue that he was fast and loose with his biographical information.

205. I cannot confirm that Ulrich served in the Crimea with the Light Brigade or any other unit of the British army. The British Library stated that the Light Brigade was made up of parts of different regiments. In 1854 the Brigade was comprised of the 4th and 13th Light Dragoons, 17th Lancers, and the 8th and 11th Hussars. Checking the War Office records of these regiments, I found no mention of Charles Ulrich. I also checked the records of the Militia, which was a voluntary, part-time force for home defense, but found no listing for Ulrich. Ulrich gave another account of his army service in which he said he served in the "royal rifle brigade" as a draughtsman and received an honorable discharge at the end of the war. ["Charles Ulrich, the Counterfeiter." *The Massachusetts Weekly Spyk*. June 26, 1868. p. 2, col. 3.] There was no "royal rifle brigade," as such, and again the War Office records do not show anyone named Ulrich being discharged. There are other reasons to doubt Ulrich's veracity. Effie Cole, the German-speaking wife of Henry C. Cole, and a close friend of Ulrich for several years, told a reporter for the *New York Sun*: "He [Ulrich] had to fly to England in 1853, when 18 years old, for a charge of forgery, not that he feared the draft." ["A Counterfeiter's Career." *San Francisco Bulletin*. February 8, 1879. p. 4, col. 6.]

206. *Fifth Annual Report of the Association of Banks for the Suppression of Counterfeiting*. Boston, Massachusetts: William A. Hallk, 1857. pp. 15 and 16.

  This record shows that "Carl [sic] Frederick Ulrich (engraver) five years three months S.P." [State Prison.] Page 16 says: "Carl Frederick Ulrich engraved a two-dollar plate on the 'Rockville Bank, Conn.' He is a German from England, a young man, and a fine workman."

207. "The Great Counterfeiter." *New York Times*. June 21, 1868. p. 3, col. 6.

208. Dye. *op. cit.* p. 22. "A Dangerous Counterfeiter Rearrested." *Cincinnati Daily Gazette*. February 4, 1868. p. 1.

209. A case file of the U.S. Circuit Court of Cincinnati, Ohio, contains a three-page indictment of Charles Ulrich for counterfeiting, dated April 29, 1867. The file, numbered 331 in Record Group 21 (Records of the U.S. District Courts), is available from the National Archives at their Great Lakes Regional Office. There are at least 10 other records dated 1868 which continue the original indictment through to the final judgment, all in Record Group 21. "An Alleged Counterfeiter's Revelations." *New York Times*. April 15, 1867. p. 1, col. 2; "A Counterfeiter Pleads Guilty and is Sentenced to 20 Years' Imprisonment." *New York Times*. June 18, 1868. p. 5, col. 1; and "The Great Counterfeiter." *New York Times*. June 21, 1868. p. 3, col. 6.

210. Henry C. Cole purchased the press used by Ott from James Quigg on the corner of Seventh and Sansom streets in Philadelphia. Roller presses were quite common, but transfer presses were a different story. Bench-top transfer presses were occasionally made by a rogue machinist.

211. Most of the material about Ulrich, and especially that concerning his work with Henry Cole and Jacob Ott, comes from Dye. *op. cit.* pp. 9–29, and is based on the monthly reports of Secret Service agents.

212. "Two Important Arrests." *New York Times*. January 19, 1879; "The Counterfeiting Game. Important Arrests." *New York Times*. January 21, 1879; "Startling Disclosures Made by the Engraver Ulrich." *New York Herald*. January 31, 1879. p. 9.

213. Charles O. Brockway was a forger, check fraud artist, and sometime counterfeiter. He is often mistaken for William E. Brockway, but the two were not related. Charles Brockway was born in New Hampshire in 1838. He was convicted in Columbia County, New York, on February 18, 1861, of forgery and sentenced to Clinton Prison for two years and three months. He served several terms of imprisonment, including 1 year at the Worchester, Massachusetts, jail, 2 years at the South Boston jail for forgery of horse car tickets, 4-1/2 years at Sing Sing for forgery of a check for $11,000, and 15 years at Albany Penitentiary in New York for manufacturing counterfeit money (but pardoned through the influence of William P. Wood after serving 18 months).

    Some of his exploits are detailed in *Description and Information of Criminals*. Volume 2. p. 49; and Volume 3. pp. 310–314. Record Group 87, National Archives, College Park, Maryland. "A Forger's Gang Caught: Charles O. Brockway and His Men Outwitted." *New York Times*. August 17, 1880. His wife, Caroline Brockway, sued Abner C. Newcomb, a United States Deputy Marshal. "Law Reports." *New York Times*. August 17, 1867. p. 3, col. 2.

214. It became unlawful for U.S. citizens to possess counterfeit notes by the Act of March 4, 1909, titled "An Act to Amend and Consolidate the Acts Respecting Copyright." Sections 25 and 34 of this Act, as amended, later became sections 101 and 110, respectively, of Title 17 of the United States Code by the Act of July 30, 1947 (61 Stat. 652). Several paper-money collectors have federal counterfeit notes in their collections today but have to be careful to maintain their secrecy.

215. "Pen and Counterfeits." *New York Times*. April 5, 1891. p. 10, col. 7; "Ninger's Dangerous Pen." *New York Times*. April 3, 1896. p. 8, col. 4. "He Sketched Bad Bills." *New York Times*. April 12, 1896. p. 1, col. 2; the most detailed article is "Real Jim the Penman." *Buffalo Morning Express*. Buffalo, New York: July 29, 1900. pp. 4 and 5.

216. Bloom. *op. cit.* p. 40

217. "Clever With His Pens." *New York Times*. May 17, 1892. p. 8, col. 2.

218. Ninger's confession is recounted in part by William P. Hazen in *Daily Reports of the United States Secret Service Agents*. April 1, 1896. *et. seq.* Record Group 87, National Archives, College Park, Maryland. See also the reports of G. Raymond Bragg of the same date.

219. He gave his age as 74 during testimony at his trial, yet 7 years later, when he would have been 81, he told hospital employees that he was 90. One is more likely to tell the truth when in court and more likely to inflate their age when they want to win sympathy, as from nurses in a hospital.

220. *Description and Information of Criminals*. Volume 3. p. 135. Record Group 87, NARA, College Park, Maryland. His arrest record is found in Volume 5, p. 324, and his social history in Volume 3, p. 205, RG 87.

221. "Charged with Being a Counterfeiter." *New York Times*. August 3, 1894. p. 7, col. 1; "The Arrest of Hoyt and Massey." *New York Times*. August 4, 1894. p. 9, col. 1; "His Life Counterfeit, Too." *New York Times*. August 5, 1894; "Thousands in Counterfeits." *New York Times*. August 7, 1894; "Russell B. Hoyt," *New York Times*. January 15, 1899.

222. "Thousands in Counterfeits." *New York Times*. August 7, 1894. p. 8

223. "Lorenzo Hoyt Confesses." *New York Times*. August 15, 1894. p. 9.

224. "Thousands in Counterfeits." *op. cit.*

Chapter 11

1. This Secret Service should not be confused with the Secret Service that was formed within the War Department during the Civil War to investigate espionage and frauds against the War Department. That Secret Service was semi-officially named the National Detective Police and was headed by Colonel Lafayette C. Baker. Baker preferred to use the title "U.S. Secret Service" for his work, but that title was never officially recognized. Baker did investigate the National Currency Bureau, but he also engaged in bribery, false reports, and unlawful intimidation to support his claims in that investigation. He also took credit for the capture of some large gangs of counterfeiters early in his career. He was, however, a disgrace to the War Department and many of his recommendations were not accepted. Allan Pinketon also used the title "U.S. Secret Service" for his agency at the end of the Civil War, but again, his small and short-lived network of spies had no official right to use the title.

2. The agency became an official division of the Treasury Department by an act of Congress approved August 3, 1882 (22 U.S. Statutes at Large, p. 230).

3. U.S. Congress, House of Representatives, H.R. 2395, amending Title 18 of the United States Code, entitled "Crimes and Criminal Procedures," signed July 16, 1951. House Bill 2395 restated the existing Secret Service authority in a permanent act and also gave the agency two new powers: (1) the authority to execute search warrants, and (2) the authority to carry firearms. Before this bill was passed, it was always necessary to rely on U.S. marshals to execute arrest warrants. Agents have always carried firearms, but their authority to do so was an implied authority based on their general arrest and enforcement powers. This bill gave them specific authority to carry and use firearms.

4. Abraham Lincoln was one of the lawyers on the Manny defense team, but Wood's affidavit cleared him of having any knowledge of Watson's deceit.

5. Edwin McMaster Stanton was born in Steubenville, Ohio, on December 19, 1814, and died in Washington, D.C., on December 24, 1869. After graduating from Kenyon College in 1833, he entered the practice of law in Cadiz, Ohio, until 1847, when he moved to Pittsburgh, Pennsylvania. In 1856 he moved to Washington and had a large practice before the Supreme Court. He defended General Daniel Sickles, who was tried on a charge of murdering his wife's lover, Philip Barton Key, the son of Francis Scott Key. Stanton got Sickles acquitted by using the insanity defense for the first time in U.S. legal history. He was made the U.S. Attorney General in December 1860 and held that office for about 75 days, when he took over the War Department on the death of former Secretary Simon Cameron. He didn't like President Abraham Lincoln calling him "the original gorilla," but he was very effective in managing the huge War Department. Lincoln acknowledged Stanton's abilities, but whenever necessary he would "plow around him." At Lincoln's death, it was reportedly Stanton who said "Now he belongs to the ages." Stanton held on to his position of secretary of war under the administration of President Andrew Johnson. His relations with that president were not good, and Johnson tried to remove him from office. Stanton barricaded himself in his office, and the radicals in Congress sought to impeach Johnson for violating the Tenure of Office Act. The following year he was appointed to the Supreme Court by President Ulysses S. Grant, but he died four days after being confirmed by the Senate and before he could assume his seat. He is buried in Washington in the Oak Hill Cemetery. $1 Treasury Notes, also called "Coin Notes," of the series 1890 and 1891, have portraits of Stanton on their backs. He is also shown on the 50-cent notes of the fourth issue of U.S. fractional currency. The obituary of William P. Wood in the Washington *Evening Star* of March 21, 1903, said that "Colonel Wood was probably nearer to Edwin M. Stanton than any other man. Wood was the last man who ever saw Stanton alive, and their final interview was a stormy one."

6. Curtis Carroll Davis. "The Craftiest of Men: William P. Wood and the Establishment of the United States Secret Service." *Maryland Historical Magazine.* Volume 83, no. 2, Summer 1988. p. 113.

7. David R. Johnson. *Illegal Tender*. Washington, D.C.: Smithsonian Institution Press, 1995. p. 71.
    Johnson raises an interesting question about McCulloch's actual role in creating the agency. In a letter that Solicitor of the Treasury Bludord Wilson wrote to Secretary Bristow, he mentions that "I have not been able to find any written order from any of your predecessors creating the Division [Secret Service] . . ." and concluded that Solicitor Jordan had established the Secret Service after oral consultation with McCulloch. Johnson wonders why McCulloch took so long to create the Secret Service and why he did not seek either President Andrew Johnson's or congressional approval for the agency. See also Solicitor Bluford Wilson's letter to Secretary of the Treasury Benjamin Bristow, July 27, 1874, in *Secretary of the Treasury, Letters Received from the Secret Service*, Record Group 20, National Archives, College Park, Maryland.

8. Norman Ansley. "The United States Secret Service. An Administrative History." *The Journal of Criminal Law, Criminology, and Police Science.* Volume 47, no. 1, (May–June 1956). Footnote 12 on p. 94.

9. Quoted from the article "Counterfeiters in the Employ of the Government." *New York Times.* June 28, 1867. p. 4, col. 5.

10. *Op. cit.*

11. Chief Wood's letter was published in the *New York Times* on Tuesday, July 2, 1867. p. 2, col. 7.

12. Mason's trial is described in the following articles, all in the *New York Times*: "Examination of G.A. Mason for Counterfeiting." March 25, 1875. p. 2; "The Convicted Counterfeiter." April 18, 1875. p. 2; "The Convicted Counterfeiter." May 9, 1875. p. 10; "A Counterfeiter's Career." January 14, 1883.

13. A report on Wood's pamphlets and charges are found in the *Cincinnati Commercial Tribune.* August 4, 1869. p. 1, col. 2.

14. "Wood's Mind." *Cleveland Leader.* July 16, 1883. p. 1, col. 2.

15. "A Forgotten Sleuth is Honored at Last." *New York Times.* May 29, 2001.

16. "Col. Wm P. Wood Dead." *The Evening Star* (Washington, D.C.). March 21, 1903. p. 8, col. 2.

17. "The Work of the Secret Service Detectives." *New York Times.* January 11, 1872. p. 3, col. 2.

18. These statistics for the number of total arrests for counterfeiting are relative numbers based on a 10% sampling of the data shown in *Descriptions and Information of Criminals*. See table 5.1 in David R. Johnson's *Illegal Tender*. pp. 130 and 131.

19. This particular typewriter was invented by Christopher L. Sholes and was made in partnership with the Glidden Company and distributed by the Remington Arms Company. It was an ornate machine, enclosed in a heavy black iron frame covered by elaborate designs in gold filigree. The first commercially successful typewriter was the Remington No. 2, made in 1878. A picture of the Sholes-Glidden-Remington typewriter is shown in the August 10, 1872 issue of the *Scientific American*.

20. David R. Johnson. *op. cit.* p. 96.

21. For a good review of the role President Ulysses S. Grant played in the defense of his personal secretary in the Whiskey Ring Scandal, see the article "Grant, Babcock and the Whiskey Ring," by Timothy Rives in *Prologue Magazine*, volume 32, no. 3, Fall 2000. This magazine has been published quarterly for more than 40 years by the National Archives and Records Administration. Mr. Rives, an archivist at NARA's Central Plains Regional Office in Kansas City, Missouri, used previously unknown archival materials to tell his story.

22. Walter S. Bowen and Harry Edward Neal. *The United States Secret Service.* p. 182.

23. James J. Brooks died of heart failure at his home at 1848 Bluff Street in Pittsburgh. An obituary appeared in the *New York Times* for October 12, 1895. p. 5.

24. John P. Brooks died of "apoplexy" at his home at 247 Walnut Street, Newark, New Jersey. An obituary appeared in the *New York Times* on October 24, 1893. p. 4.

25. Johnson. *op. cit.* pp. 111 and 112.

26. Johnson. *op. cit.* p. 113.

27. Walter S. Brown and Harry Edward Neal. *The United States Secret Service.* p. 182.

28. Andrew Lewis Drummond. *True Detective Stories.* New York, New York: G.W. Dillingham Company, 1909. 327 pages, 5 plates.

29. In the summer of 1894, Mrs. Cleveland and her children were vacationing at their summer home near Buzzard's Bay in Massachusetts when she was warned that the Secret Service had learned of a plot to kidnap her and the children. She contacted Chief Hazen and asked that he assign three agents to their home to protect the family. He complied without notifying the president or Congress. Philip H. Melanson and Peter F. Stevens. *The Secret Service: The Hidden History of an Enigmatic Agency*. New York, New York: Carroll & Graf, Publishers, 2002. p. 24.

30. This line was inserted into the Sundry Civil Expenses Act of 1907. The president (and other officials) are now protected by Title 18 of the U.S. Code, Section 3056 (a) (1), entitled "Powers, Authorities, and Duties of the United States Secret Service." This authorized Secret Service agents to carry firearms and to make arrests without warrants.

31. *New York Times*. August 20, 1909. p. 1.

32. William P. Wood resigned his office. In spite of his many violations of law and ethics, he was never tried for any crimes. Charles Hill, using the alias James H. Walker, worked for William P. Wood before going on to a lucrative career as a counterfeit engraver. Sam Felker, an agent in the Chicago office for a time, took part in several criminal endeavors. Charles E. Anchisi, an ex-operative, was arrested in San Francisco in 1881 for counterfeiting. W.J. Edick was convicted of conspiracy in a plot to counterfeit in 1927, and Abraham Bolden was found guilty in 1964 for trying to sell a secret government file to an accused counterfeiter for $50,000.

Chapter 12

1. Ronald L. Horstman. "The First Greenbacks of the Civil War." *Paper Money*. Whole No. 135, May/June 1988. pp. 69–72.

   Until recently, the only surviving, complete note from this series was a $50 denomination that sold at the American Numismatic Association Convention in 1970 at a bid of $10,000. In 1981, with the sale of the Alexandre Vattemare collection, other notes from this series became available to researchers. Apparently, these notes were given to Mr. Vattemare by Secretary of the Treasury Salmon P. Chase in late 1862 with the request that they be used for public education. Instead, Vattemare kept the notes in his personal collection

2. The following excerpt from a letter written by President Abraham Lincoln to his friend, Colonel Taylor, gives a glimpse of the history behind the "legal tender" argument: "My dear Colonel Dick. I have long determined to make public the origin of the greenback and tell the world that it is Dick Taylor's creation. You had already been friendly to me and when troublous times fell on us, and my shoulder, though broad and willing were weak, and myself surrounded by such circumstances and such people that I knew not whom to trust, then I said in my extremity, 'I will send for Colonel Taylor, he will know what to do.' I think it was in January, 1862, on or about the 16th, that I did so. You came and I said to you, 'What can we do?' Said you: 'Why not issue Treasury Notes bearing no interest, printed on the best banking paper? Issue enough to pay off the army expenses and declare it legal tender.' Chase thought it a hazardous thing, but we finally accomplished it, and gave the people of this republic the greatest blessing they ever had—their own paper to pay their own debts." (Quoted from Emil Ludwig's *Lincoln*. Boston, Massachusetts: Little Brown & Company, 1930. pp. 448 and 449.)

3. Quoted from Bray Hammond's "The North's Empty Purse, 1861–1862." *The American Historical Review*. Volume LXVII, no. 1, October 1961. p. 2.

4. This legislation is known as "Act of Congress," *Statutes at Large*, volume 12, 37th Congress, Session II, Chapter 33, pp. 345–348.

5. In this case (75 U.S. 603 [1869]), a "certain Mrs. Hepburn" signed a promissory note to Henry Griswold on June 20, 1860, for $11,250 payable on February 20, 1862. At that time the only legal tender in the United States was gold or silver coin. Owing to the exigencies of the Civil War, Mrs. Hepburn could not pay the note, and suit was brought by Mr. Griswold in March 1864 in the Louisiana Chancery Court. Consequently, Mrs. Hepburn paid the principal and interest in the form of U.S. notes. The Chancery Court accepted that settlement and the form of payment. Mr. Griswold did not want to accept U.S. notes and brought suit in the Court of Errors in Kentucky. That court reversed judgment and said U.S. notes were not legal tender for private debts at the time the loan was made. This case was then taken to the Supreme Court, where Salmon P. Chase was the Chief Justice. In a 4–3 decision, the court upheld the decision of the Court of Errors.

6. The Confederate bank-note companies faced the same problem and hired many clerks to sign notes, but curiously, Memminger was unable to get authorization from the Confederate Congress to replace the signers and go to facsimile signatures.

7. These suggestions that Clark made to Secretary Chase, and other interesting stories, are found in "Origin of the Division, " in the House of Representatives 38th Congress, 2nd Session, *Executive Document No. 50*, entitled "Printing Bureau of the Treasury Department," February 4, 1865, p. 3.

8. *Ibid*. The American Bank Note Company of New York was employed to make the original dies for seals of three sizes. The Treasury said the seals were satisfactorily executed and paid for, as evidenced by bills on file. But the bank-note company refused to surrender these dies to the government though they had been formally demanded. After about a year, Spencer Clark was sent to New York to demand the dies, and he met with George W. Hatch, the president of the American Bank Note Company, and John Gavit, the vice-president. They adamantly refused to surrender the original dies but offered to sell the government duplicate dies at $10 each. Apparently, they expected to sell such dies as long as the government needed them. Clark bought one set of dies, took them to Washington, D.C., and had his transfer department make additional duplicates as needed. This is an early example of the hostility that existed between the New York bank-note companies and Clark.

9. "Origin of the Division." *op. cit.* p. 7.

10. The Act of July 11, 1862, considered the organic act that created the Bureau of Engraving and Printing, reads as follows:

    "Section 2.—And be it further enacted that the Secretary of the Treasury be, and is hereby, authorized in case he shall think it inexpedient to procure said notes, or any part thereof, to be engraved and printed by contract, to cause the said notes, or any part thereof, to be engraved, printed and executed in such forms he shall prescribe, at the Treasury Department in Washington, and under his direction, and he is hereby empowered to purchase and provide all the machinery and materials and to employ such persons and appoint such officers as may be necessary for this purpose." (Statutes at Large, volume 12, p. 532).

11. The idea was first proposed by W.L. Ormsby in Part III of his book, *A Description of the Present System of Bank Note Engraving*, published in 1852. On page 80 of that work, Ormsby describes a "new plan: for bank note designs. . . . The whole surface of the Bill should be covered with one unbroken and inseparable design, with the lettering so interwoven by the hand of the Artist, as to form an integral part of the design. If this be done, then the security against imitation or alteration will be exactly in proportion to the ingenuity of the design, the talent of the Artist, and the amount of labor bestowed upon it. The forger will be obliged to encounter all the difficulty in imitating, which the Artist experienced in constructing." There is no evidence that Clark got his ideas from reading this book, but since he was in the bank-note profession, it is very likely that he owned a copy and adopted those ideas

to his own use. The problem with Ormsby's plan is its failure to understand that what the hand can draw, the camera can copy. In the early 1850s, photographic technology was still in its infancy, so Ormsby may be forgiven for his oversight.

12. *Ibid*. pp. 9 and 10.

13. The official history of the Bureau of Engraving and Printing states that the Act of July 17, 1862, often cited in numismatic literature as the authorization for the printing of postal currency, in fact makes no mention of postal currency at all.

14. For the year ending June 30, 1863, the government paid the American Bank Note Company $595,024.76 and the National Bank Note Company $859,416.26 for printing notes, bonds, and fractional currency. There was no breakdown of the data to show how much was paid for printing just the fractional currency. That same year, the government paid the Adams Express Company $28,076.81 for transportation of the incomplete currency, bonds, and notes from New York and Philadelphia to Washington, D.C. This data is taken from the tables in "Money Paid to Bank Note Companies, etc.," in House of Representatives *Executive Document No. 188*, 41st Congress, 2nd Session, dated March 14, 1870.

15. See the *New York Herald* for a history of the strike, printed Tuesday, August 3, 1869, p. 8. A brief history of the beginning of the strike is found in the (Washington, D.C.) *Evening Star* of Thursday, August 5, 1869, p. 2, col. 2.

16. (Washington, D.C.) *Evening Star*. Tuesday, August 17, 1869. p. 1, col. 4.

17. *Ibid*. Saturday, August 14, 1869. p. 1, col. 4.

18. *Ibid*. Monday, September 6, 1869. p. 2, col. 1.

19. A doubtful story about J.F.E. Prud'homme was told by his friend and fellow engraver, Augustine L. Helms. According to Helms, the Prud'homme family owned a sugar plantation in Haiti until a revolt by slaves took place under the leadership of Touissant l'Ouverture. Prud'homme, his wife, and his baby daughter, with some other white planters and slave holders, escaped in the night in a small sailing vessel of which Prud'homme was the captain. A cyclone dismantled the ship which eventually was sighted, and the passengers were brought to a U.S. port. *Collector's Club Philatelist*. No. 4, October 1942. p. 248.

20. His obituary appeared in the (Washington) *Evening Star* for June 27, 1892.

21. U.S. Senate Committee Report No. 273, entitled *United States Securities*, dated March 3, 1869, pp. 236–242.

22. This "life-sized" work is said by some to be one of the finest in American portrait engraving. It took Gugler almost three years to complete the portrait, working out of a modest wooden cottage in Egg Harbor, New Jersey. The plate measured 30 by 23 inches, with Lincoln's head alone being 10 by 7-1/2 inches wide. The plate was commissioned by the artist John H. Littlefield and is based on his painting of Lincoln. Littlefield and Gugler had worked together at the Treasury Department and were close friends when Littlefield finished his painting. Littlefield was given a small part in the design of the portrait's engraving and filed for a copyright on the work under his own name on November 27, 1869. The finished plate was valued at $10,000. Henry Gugler joined his sons, Julius and Robert, to found the firm of H. Gugler & Sons in Milwaukee in 1878. That company had the plate and lent it to Alfred Jones, who was then working as an independent engraver with the American Bank Note Company, to use as a model to engrave the die for the four-cent stamp of 1890. Somehow, the plate got out of the control of the Gugler company, and by 1899 it was in a private collection. In 1920 the plate was offered for sale by a Philadelphia antiques dealer and was purchased by Alfred E. Harris, then president of the Gugler Lithographic Company in Milwaukee. In October 1966 the plate was presented by John B. Harris, then president of the Gugler company, to the Milwaukee Historical Society.

23. *New York Times*. Wednesday, May 16, 1878. p. 1.

24. Most of this data is taken from "New Building for Bureau of Engraving and Printing," *House of Representatives Report No. 134*, 62nd Congress, 1st Session, August 8, 1911.

25. The letter is dated February 14, 1890, and is found as pages 72–79 in Volume 142 of the outgoing correspondence files of the Bureau of Engraving and Printing at National Archives, College Park, Maryland. The letter, eight pages long, is typed double-spaced.

26. This letter is dated August 9, 1887, and is found in Volume 437, pages unknown, in the outgoing correspondence files of the Bureau of Engraving and Printing at National Archives, College Park, Maryland. The letter, signed by Edward O. Graves, Chief of the Bureau, is typed double-spaced.

27. "Marcus Wickliffe Baldwin, Bank Note Engraver." *Essay-Proof Journal*. No. 46, April 1955. pp. 79–84.

28. "Death of Sophia Holmes." *New York Times*. October 12, 1900. p. 1.

29. *Printing Bureau of the Treasury Department Report*. House of Representatives, Executive Document No. 50, 38th Congress, 2nd Session, pp. 56 and 57.

30. *Ibid*. p. 57.

31. *Ibid*.

32. *Ibid*. pp. 57 and 58.

33. The Schureman case was chronicled in two Washington, D.C., newspapers: (1) the *Evening Star* for September 13, 1869. p. 4, col. 4; September 16, 1869. p. 4, col. 5; September 17, 1869. p. 4, col. 4; September 18, 1869. p. 4, col. 3; September 20, 1869. p. 4, col. 4; September 21, 1869. p. 1, col. 7; September 23, 1869. p. 4, col. 5; September 24, 1869. p. 4, col. 3; October 11, 1869. p. 4, col. 3; November 19, 1869. p. 4, col. 5; December 7, 1869. p. 4, col. 5; and December 8, 11, 13, and 30. p. 1, col. 3. (2) *The Daily National Intelligencer* for September 22, 1869. p. 4, cols. 2 and 3; September 23, 1869. p. 4, col. 4; and September 24, 1869. p. 4, col. 4.

34. Reported in *Printing of United States Notes and Other Securities*, Report No. 150, House of Representatives, 43rd Congress, 2nd Session, February 16, 1875, p. 435.

35. Seth Johnson should not be confused with James J. Johnson, who was a clerk in the stamp department of the Sub-Treasury in New York. James J. Johnson embezzled a large sum of money from that office, perhaps as much as $185,000. In the middle of August 1872 he took a two-week leave of absence. At the end of his leave, he did not return to work, and when his superiors conducted an audit of his office, they found that he had embezzled the money. When he was found, he disclosed that he had taken the money over a period of 18 months and spent it all buying shares of stock. His stock speculations fizzled, and he lost all his money, leaving his family almost entirely destitute. When government documents refer to the "Johnson-Marden defalcations," they mean Seth Johnson. Accounts of James J. Johnson's antics can

be found in: *New York Times*. September 21, 1872. p. 5; *New York Herald*. December 3, 1872. p. 5, col. 3.

36. The newspapers of the day contain numerous articles about the Halleck-Ottman defalcation. Some of the more accessible are: *New York Times*. August 8, 1875. p. 7; *Ibid*. "Notes from the Capital." March 11, 1876; "Notes from the Capital." April 3, 1877; "The Ottman Compromise." June 2, 1883; "The Ottman Compromise." June 3, 1883; "Events in Washington." June 6, 1883; "Ottman Compromise." June 8, 1883. p. 4, col. 4; "The Ottman Compromise." June 11, 1883; "National Capital Topics." March 16, 1884; and the *Washington Chronicle* on several dates during the period of August 8 through the 20, 1875. A good summary article appears in "Frauds, Thefts, Defalcations and Gross Irregularities in the Treasury Department," in *The Political Reformation of 1884, A Democratic Campaign Book, 1884–1888*, published by the Democratic Party National Committee, pp. 153 and 154.

37. The union can trace its history back to the plate-printers associations that appeared in the Philadelphia and Washington, D.C., areas shortly after the Civil War. Seeking an alliance with a national labor organization, most of these locals affiliated with the Knights of Labor during the 1880s. In 1892 several affiliated and unaffiliated locals met in Boston and organized officially as the National Steel and Copper Plate Printers of the United States of America. In 1898 the national union affiliated with the American Federation of Labor. The union was a powerful force in negotiations over hand-roller press work and related matters at the Bureau of Engraving and Printing. In 1901 the union changed its name to the International Steel and Copper Plate Printers' Union of North America, and in 1920 it became the International Plate Printers' and Die Stampers Union of North America. This union merged in 1925 with the International Steel and Copper Plate Engravers League. The Constitution of the union dates from 1900. The *Proceedings* are only available for the period of 1925 to 1927. The union's official journal was called *The Plate Printer*, a monthly newspaper than ran from 1902 to the last edition on August 12, 1932. The Library of Congress has a small collection of that newspaper. The union changed its name in 1930 to the International Plate Printers, Die Stampers and Engravers' Union of North America. It was located in Ottawa, Canada, for a time, and more recently in Bensalem, Pennsylvania, but I've lost track of it. One occasionally hears of something called "the Canadian Plate Printer," but I am unable to find any such publication at any of the major Canadian libraries and conclude that previous references to the journal were in error and derive from the temporary location of the union in Canada. The decision made by the IPPDSEU to stop printing *The Plate Printer* in 1932 is verified by *Bulletin No. 618*, issued by the Bureau of Labor Statistics of the U.S. Department of Labor (1936). T.V. Powderly was the Grand Master of the Knights of Labor during much of the time that this union had influence at the bureau. His correspondence files are located in the Department of Archives and Manuscripts at the Catholic University of America in Washington, D.C. This is a very large collection which had not been indexed when I tried to find relevant material in 1994. Somewhere in those files there should be a wealth of information about the working conditions and negotiations at the BEP. I could only devote one day to the search, and although I had a research assistant helping me, we were not able to find the BEP files.

38. *Hand-Roller vs. Power Presses*. Hearings Before the Senate Committee on Printing, 62nd Congress, January 29–February 14, 1912, on Senate Bill 4239. 190 pages with index.

39. *Washington Post*. Friday, March 31, 1911. p. 6, col. 3. A review of the women's labor union movement.

40. *Washington Post*. Wednesday, August 31, 1904. p. 34, col. 6.

41. Mary Mitchell. *Chronicles of Georgetown Life, 1865–1900*. Santa Ana, California: Seven Oaks Press, 1986. p. 62.

42. His Last Will and Testament is registered as No. 80 in Folio 349, filed September 13, 1912, in the Register of Wills, Washington, D.C. I am indebted to Ms. Connie Jean Casilear, a descendant, for some of the information used in this biographical note. Most of the information known about George W. Casilear comes from an article in the *Collectors' Club Philatelist*, volume 28, no. 2, April 1, 1949, p. 139, which was based on information provided by Isabel Casilear Green, who was George's daughter and was listed in the 1880 Census as "Belle," aged 8, and in the 1900 Census as Isabell, born in September 1871, and then 28 years old.

43. Paul S. Casilear is listed in some biographical dictionaries as a "bank note engraver," but this is inconsistent with his own testimony in U.S. Senate Committee Report No. 272, "*United States Securities*," of March 3, 1869, pp. 200–202, where he states he was a superintendent of the Printing and Numbering Department at the American Bank Note Company, circa 1861 and 1862, and then went to the Continental Bank Note Company in June 1863, where he was the superintendent of the Printing Department before joining the Bureau of Engraving and Printing. According to the 1860 Census, he lived at 60 Blecker Street in Washington, D.C., and was born about 1818.

44. Thomas D. Gannawy. "The Government's Money Laundry, How Old Paper Notes are Washed." *Scientific American Supplement*. Volume 70, November 5, 1910. p. 298.

   Additional facts on washing currency is found in *History of the Bureau of Engraving and Printing, 1862–1962*, published by the Government Printing Office, Washington, D.C., 1962, pp. 76–79. A somewhat different story is given in "To Lauder Old Bills," *New York Times*, July 4, 1911, p. 1, col. 2. There, it was reported that a Philadelphia woman washed and ironed a dirty dollar bill so neatly that it was believed to be counterfeit when presented at her bank. This led to an investigation by Treasury officials and the conclusion that laundering would save them money.

45. This study group consisted of Mr. C.S. Pearce of the treasurer's office, who was chairman; Mr. Burgess Smith, a chemist for the BEP.; Mr. George Lee of the secretary of the Treasury's office; Mr. C.C. Pusey, the assistant treasurer at Baltimore; and Mr. L.R. Acton, a paper expert in Washington, D.C.

Chapter 13

1. Harry L. Chorlton. "Bank Note Etching on Steel." *Essay-Proof Journal*. April 1948. pp. 79–82.

2. Chorlton. *op. cit.*

3. A series of articles on engraving, taken from the notes of G.F.C. Smillie, Chief Engraver at the Bureau of Engraving and Printing, were edited by Clarence Brazer and published under the title "Picture Engraving" in the *Collectors' Club Philatelist*, July 1948, p. 63, and the *Essay-Proof Journal*, January 1949, p. 3, and April 1951, pp. 77–80.

4. Partington. *op. cit.*

5. An opposing view was given by C. John Ferreri, writing in the journal *Paper Money*. He suggested that the earliest historical vignettes on American paper money may have been the naval-battle scenes and machinery depicted on the notes of the New York Manufacturing Company, which later became the Phenix Bank of New York. Those notes are known from Proof sheets. The company was incorporated in 1812,

and one of the notes, according to Ferreri, shows a faint trace of a hand-written date of 1813, which is consistent with the other facts. Although Ferreri doesn't state this in the article, the imprint on the notes, under strong magnification, looks to be "Lenney & Rollinson," a company founded in 1811. Battle scenes of the War of 1812 are found on notes of the Jefferson Bank of New Salem, Ohio, dating from 1817, so it is likely that bank-note engravers were beginning to place historical vignettes on notes about this period (1810–1820). C. John Ferreri. *Paper Money*. Whole No. 157, January/February 1992. pp. 5–9.

6. Julian Blanchard. "Signed Vignettes on Obsolete Bank Notes." *Essay-Proof Journal*. Volume 2, Whole No. 6, April 1945. pp. 77–80.

Chapter 14

1. John Ferguson and Roger Davies. "A Survey of Tudor and Early Jacobian Rose Turning." *Bulletin of the Society of Ornamental Turners*. Volume 17, no. 83, Autumn 1990. pp. 133–144.

2. Breguet watches are probably the most fabulous and treasured watches in the world. Among the famous owners have been Marie Antoinette, Louis XVI, Napoleon Bonaparte, the Empress Josephine, Tsar Alexander I of Russia, George Washington, Queen Victoria, Sir Winston Churchill, Artur Rubenstein, Sergei Rachmaninoff, and Selim III, Sultan of the Ottoman Empire.

3. The Holtzapffel family lived in the Alsace region of eastern France, in Strasbourg, a major port on the Rhine River. Jean-Jacques Holtzapffel immigrated to England in 1784 and went into business for himself in 1792. In 1794 he started the firm of Holtzapffel of London, making rose-engine lathes. He died in London on April 6, 1835. His son, Charles Holtzapffel, was born in London on December 28, 1805. Like his father, he was a "tourneur" and technical writer. His major work, *Turning and Mechanical Manipulation*, is probably the single-most important work in the English language about the lathe and its accessories. It was intended to be a work of several volumes, but Charles died on April 11, 1847, at age 41, before he had finished his manuscript. His son, John Jacob Holtzapffel, wrote volumes IV (1879) and V (1884) of the series. A sixth volume was planned but never written. The Holtzapffel family built over 2,300 rose-engine lathes in three generations. In 1804 J.G. Deyerlein was brought into the company, but this was a rather difficult partnership, and it ended in 1827 when Charles Holtzapffel became of legal age and associated with his father. From 1828 onward the company was known simply as "Holtzapffel & Company." An obituary of Charles Holtzapffel appeared in the magazine *Artizan* for April 1847. This obituary was reprinted in the *Bulletin of the Society of Ornamental Turners*, volume VIII, no. 39, September 1968, pp. 105 and 106.

4. John Edward and George Popplewell. "The Holtzapffel Rosette Forming Machine in the Science Museum." *Bulletin of the Society of Ornamental Turners*. Volume 17, no. 85, September 1991. pp. 236–242.

5. This is a rare book not found in the Library of Congress. A copy can be found in the library of George Washington University in Washington, D.C. Apparently, no English translation is available.

6. Sidney George Abell, John Leggat, and Warren Greene Ogden Jr. *A Bibliography of the Art of Turning and Lathe and Machine Tool History*. 3rd edition. North Andover, Massachusetts: Museum of Ornamental Turning, 1987.

   This is the best single-volume bibliography on the rose engine and geometric lathe in English and should be required reading for any serious student of Engine Turning.

7. Ogden. *Ibid.* p. 53, note no. 161.

8. Martin Matthews. *Engine Turning, 1680–1980, The Tools and Techniques*. Privately printed in England.

9. Martin Matthews. *Ibid.* p.153.

10. The family begins, for our purposes, with Philemon, born May 31, 1784, who married Hetty Paradise, who was born September 26, 1792, and died S eptember 18, 1856. Philemon moved to Springfield, New Jersey, where he was a justice of the peace for many years. He was a founder of the Methodist Episcopal Church there. He died December 24, 1856. This couple had six children, of which Charles Wesley Dickinson was the fifth, born November 23, 1822. Charles Wesley married Maria Thompson on March 25, 1851. They lived in Belleville, New Jersey, and raised eight children. Charles Wesley Thompson Dickinson was their last child, born January 25, 1865, married June 7, 1887, to Annie Ellis, who was born in 1822 and died in 1884. Apparently Philemon Dickinson, born March 11, 1820, and married to Mary E. Roll De Camp on March 14, 1842, was the Philemon that became the foreman of the transfer department of the American Bank Note Company. This makes Philemon the slightly older brother of Charles Wesley Dickinson. Charles W. Dickinson's Essex County Estate Papers are recorded as docket 6221.

11. Quoted from William F. Ford's *The Industrial Interests of Newark, New Jersey*. 1874. pp. 62 and 63.

12. Charles Wesley Thompson Dickinson was born January 25, 1865, and died in Belleville, New Jersey, on October 4, 1937, age 72. He married Annie K. Ellis on June 7, 1887. His will, dated May 22, 1911, leaving his estate to his wife, was probated 27 years later in 1938—Essex County Docket No. 6221. They had three children: Wesley, born March 26, 1889, died in infancy; Charles Ellis, born September 3, 1890, married Katherine Hepp on October, 1919; and Leroy Thompson Dickinson, born March 26, 1898.

13. A lithographic press (for bank-note work) that once belonged to the Canadian Bank Note Company was given to the Canada Science and Technology Museum in Ottawa. It is clearly marked as manufactured by W.H. Chapman.

14. The following biographical note was printed in *The Passaic Valley, New Jersey, in Three Centuries*, edited by John Whitehead and privately printed. Quoting verbatim: "Herbert W. Chapman was one of the foremost inventors of the country. He was the son of William Chapman and Ann White, and was born in Nottinghamshire, England, April 26, 1847. There, in the schools of Redford, he received his education. He was a scientific machinist and mechanical genius of the highest order, learning his trade in Sheffield, Yorkshire, England, and thoroughly mastering every detail of it, by the time he was twenty-one. When twenty-two years old, he came to America and settled in Newark, New Jersey, where he remained until his death. For thirty years he devoted his skill and genius to perfecting inventions and constructing special machinery. In January, 1872, he engaged in business for himself at No. 11 Mechanic Street, whence he removed in 1880 to the present site of the establishment at Nos. 227, 229, and 231 Mulberry Street. In 1876, Mr. Chapman produced and patented his celebrated bank-note engraving machine, which are in daily use in the great bank-note and engraving concerns in the large cities at home and abroad as well as in the treasury departments of the United States, England, Germany and Mexico. He introduced in 1885, his rotary fed press, and also patented his foot press for jewelers, silversmiths, and sheet metal workers. This press is particularly adapted to the economical use of expensive tools and is in use by many large manufacturers. Mr. Chapman also produced engraving machines for calico and satinet printers, special and dead center lathes, stamping presses, and many other useful appliances, and built up a large and substantial trade throughout the world. He was a

man of acknowledged ability, not only as inventor, but also in executive and business capacities, and achieved remarkable success and a wide reputation. He was a Republican and member of the Newark Board of Trade and the Newark Yacht Club, and actively identified with the community. He died in January, 1899.

"On September 5, 1871, he married Miss Esther E. Hattersley, who survived him. They had eight children: Harry (deceased), Bertha, Agnes (wife of Roger M. Dowley), Gertrude, William H., George E., Walter W., and Ester H. Since Mr. Chapman's death, the business has been successfully conducted by his widow [and] their eldest son, William H., who had received an excellent training under his father and had given evidence of marked inventive genius."

15. I am indebted to Nicholas Edwards for this information. At the time he was the president of the Society of Ornamental Turners in England. He is a retired mechanical engineer who likes complicated mechanisms and is therefore at ease in operating and maintaining his three ornamental lathes: one is a Holtzapffel rose engine which belongs to the Society, a second is a Thomas De La Rue Fantasy Lathe, and the last is a modern Michael Kampf machine.

16. The full title of the book is *Pantographice Christophori Scheiner, e Societeate Jesu Germano-Sueni, Pantographice seu, Ars delineandi res queasiest per parallelogram mum lineare seu cauum, mechanicium, mobile: liabellis duobus explicate & demonstratienibus geometricis illustrate, quorum prior epipedographicen, sine planorum, posterior stereographicen, seu solidorum aspectabilium viuam imitatienem atque protectionism edocet. Pantographice seu, Ars delinendi res queasiest per parallelogram mum lineare seu cauum, mechanism, mobile. Ars nova delineandi.* It was published in Rome in 1631 and is 108 pages with illustrations. There is a copy in the Library of Congress, Call Number TJ181.9.S34 1631, but I haven't found any English translation. A good explanation of the history of the invention and a thorough discussion of how it works is found in G. Pellehn's *Der Pantograph, 1603–1903*, published in Berlin in 1903. Again, there is no English translation.

17. The patent is listed in *The Pantentee's Manual, q.v.* 1830. p. 62.

18. Bryan Donkin (1768–1855) had a remarkably productive career. He perfected the Fourdrinier paper-making machine while working as an apprentice for his brother-in-law, John Hall; invented a composition roller for printing; set up the world's first canning factory for vacuum packing perishable foodstuffs in iron cans sealed by tin solder; and invented the steel writing pen.

19. The illustration and mechanical data are taken from D.M. Henshaw's article, "Donkin Pantagraph Engraving Machine with Rose Engine." *Transactions of the Newcomen Society.* Volume XV, 1934 and 1935. British Library Shelfmark Ac.4313.e. pp. 77–83.

20. Wilson Lowry was born in Whitehaven, England, on January 24, 1762, the son of a provincial portrait painter. He took some elementary lessons in engraving, but it was not an apprenticeship. At 18, he went to London and was encouraged by William Blizard, the surgeon, to learn medicine and practice surgery. For four years he attended medical lectures and made hospital rounds, but he never pursued surgery, which he enjoyed. Although he did some landscape engraving, it was primarily as an engraver of architecture and mechanism that he showed distinction. About 1790 he made a ruling machine, which he first employed upon a plate of Stuart's "Athens." In 1801 he invented an instrument for making elliptical curves, and in 1806 another for making perspective drawings. These were described and highly praised by John Landseer in his lectures at the Royal institutions. In 1800, when Dr. Ree's celebrated *Cyclopaedia* was proposed, Lowry was engaged to execute the plates, and this was his chief occupation during the next 20 years. As

the result of his profound knowledge of geometry and the laws of mechanics, combined with an unfailing accuracy of eye and hand, Lowry's engravings are of unparalleled beauty in their particular class. Ree's *Cyclopaedia* contains some of his finest representations of machinery. Lowry died at his house in Great Titchfield Street, London, after a lingering illness on June 23, 1824.

21. The primary source is *The Annual Biography and Obituary*, published in London from 1817 through 1837 by Longman, Hurst, Rees, Orme and Brown. Volume 9 (1825) carries an obituary of Lowry, mentioning his invention of the ruling machine, pp. 96–100. The essential facts are also given in Basil Hunnisett's *Steel Engraved Book Illustrations in England*, p. 46.

22. "Engravers' Ruling Machine." *Transaction of the Society of the Arts.* Volume 51. London, England: 1837. pp. 25–36.

The article is concerned mainly with the ruling machine invented by Mr. Percy Heath, for which he won the Society's Silver Medal, but also contains a fairly thorough history of the ruling machines invented in England.

23. *Transactions of the Society of Arts.* Volume 51. 1837. p. 25.

24. This is the first paragraph of a seven-paragraph statement in the possession of the Historical Society of Pennsylvania.

25. C.F. Partington. *The Mechanics' Library, or Book of Trades.* London, England: Sherwood, Gilbert & Piper, 1825. p. 70. Also published in *The Franklin Journal and American Mechanics' Magazine.* Volume II, no. 3, September 1826. p. 165.

26. This quotation is taken from Sydney George Abell, John Leggat, and Warren Greene Ogden Jr.'s *A Bibliography of the Art of Turning and Lathe and Machine Tool History.* 3rd edition. North Andover, Massachusetts: Museum of Ornamental Turning Ltd., 1987. p. 59, note no. 180.

27. Louis-Eloy Bergeron was not the real author of the *Manuel du Tourneur*. We know now, thanks to the research of Warren G. Ogden Jr., that the real author was Louis-George-Issac Salivet, a lawyer and a prominent man of letters who was born in Paris in 1737. Salivet was apparently sensitive about being associated with this kind of mundane art, and he asked his friend, L.E. Bergeron, to pose as the author. The work is a classic and is so often referred to as simply "Bergeron" that it often makes no sense to cite the real author now.

28. Quoted from Asa Spencer's letter to the editors of the *American Journal of Science and Arts.* Volume XLIV, April 1843. pp. 1–12. The communication was entitled "Vindication of claims to certain Inventions and Improvements in the Graphic Arts."

29. Spencer. *op. cit.* p. 2.

30. Vincent Nolte's *Memorial of Facts Connected with the History of Medallic Engraving and the Process of M. Collas*, published in London in 1838, gives a defensive but detailed account of the competition with Bate and contains a letter from Saxton to Nolte concerning the affair.

31. Reproducing three-dimensional objects seems to have been a specialty of M. Collas. In 1846 he invented a machine that used a pantograph to make proportionally larger or smaller duplicates of any sculpture. He based his ideas on the ancient Greek and Roman technique called "pointing." Artists of that period made large or small duplicates of sculptured objects by taking exact measurements of the original and proportionally increasing or decreasing them on a model that sat next to the original. Collas did the same thing but used a pantograph system to transfer the curving lines of a sculpture to a larger or smaller model

that had already been roughly prepared to look like the original. Auguste Rodin was one sculptor who used the Collas technology to make both enlarged- and reduced-size copies of his work. Robert Sobleszek. "Sculpture as the Sum of its Profiles: Françoise Willeme and Photosculpture in France, 1859–1868." *The Art Bulletin.* Volume 62, no. 4, December 1980. pp. 617–630.

32. "Report of the Select Committee of the House of Commons on the British Museum." London, England: July 14, 1836.

33. The only publication I have found that contains a list of bank notes with medallion engraving is an attachment of actual notes added to a translation of Pierre Hamelin Bergeron's *Manuel du Tourneur*, volume II, 2nd edition, printed by Andres & Prentiss in Boston in 1849, pp. 424–437. This work is entitled *Description of the Image Lathe (Tour À Portraits) or Self-Directing Lathe for Turning, by one continuous operation, Irregular Forms, such as Medals, or Intaglios, or various other Articles.* Apparently, the only copy with this attachment of notes is in the Historical Society of Pennsylvania. I have surveyed other major libraries and cannot find such an attachment. This attachment consists of 33 notes, some of which had their corners cut off or were cut on the end in a wavy line. The printers of these notes include Murray, Draper, Fairman & Company; Draper, Underwood, Bald & Spencer; and Underwood, Bald & Spencer. The earliest of these companies was Murray, Draper, Fairman & Co., so it would appear that they owned the medallion lathe and it was transferred to the successor companies in Philadelphia. It should be an interesting project for bank-note collectors to identify other notes with medallion engraving, if there are any, and to see if they were printed only in Philadelphia, or elsewhere.

34. Perkins's reference to the "Philadelphia Insurance Office" almost certainly meant the company known as The Philadelphia Contributorship for the Insurance of Houses from Loss by Fire, founded in 1752. This company was still in existence in 1987 and had a seal press on display in their lobby which their records indicate was purchased from Samuel Merrick and John Agnew in 1831. This press, however, is exactly the same one illustrated by the Bathes in their scholarly work, *Jacob Perkins, His Inventions, His Times, & His Contemporaries.* This press has no name plate to indicate the manufacturer. An identical seal press was sold to the Mutual Assurance Company in May 1830, and it has a plate stamped with the name Merrick and Agnew. Samuel Vaughan Merrick bought out the fire-engine manufacturing company that had been set up in Philadelphia by Perkins and his brother-in-law, Joshua Bacon. Perkins left the company's control in the hands of Bacon, and Bacon apparently sold it to Merrick and Agnew in 1825, the year they started business together. They dissolved their business in 1836, Merrick devoting himself to the manufacture of steam engines and Agnew becoming a leading builder of fire engines. It is likely that Merrick also bought the rights to sell the remaining stock of seal presses left over from Perkins, or to manufacture them, and that he sold one of these presses to the Philadelphia Contributorship in 1831. A photograph of the seal press is also to be found in Anthony Garvan and Carol Wojtowicz's *Catalogue of the Green Tree Collection.* Philadelphia, Pennsylvania: The Mutual Assurance Company, 1977. p. 28. Personal correspondence with Carol Wojtowicz, Curator and Archivist, June 22 and July 1, 1987.

35. Jacob Perkins had apparently made a large and rather complicated transfer press that was used in the bank-note plant of Murray, Draper, Fairman & Company in Philadelphia for a few years. The design of this transfer press was kept secret but apparently consisted of a bean that was so large it required a hole in the floor so it could move up and down without hitting the floor. There are vague references to this machine in the literature, but no detailed description of the press appears.

36. The Science Museum inventory number is 1927-1102.

37. Stephen D. Tucker. *History of R. Hoe & Company.* p. 14.

38. U.S. Congress, House of Representatives, Report No. 140, (38th Congress, 1st Session), entitled Treasury Department, Washington, D.C.: June 30, 1864, p. 229, Appendix B, letter from S.M. Clark to the Comptroller of the Currency, dated July 7, 1863.

39. *The London Journal.* September 1820. p. 384.

Chapter 15

1. Sung Ying-Hsing. *T'ien-Kung K'ai-Wu, Chinese Technology in the Seventeenth Century.* Translated by E-tu Zen Sun and Shiou-Chuan Sun. University Park, Pennsylvania: Pennsylvania State University Press, 1966.

   This work contains many drawings of Chinese paper-making activities.

2. Robert McCabe. "An Early Counterfeiting Case in China." *Paper Money.* Volume XL, number 5, September–October 2001. p. 308.

3. Lien-Sheng Yang. *Money and Credit in China, A Short History.* pp. 52 and 53.

4. Lien-Sheng Yang. "The Form of the Paper Note *Hui-tzu* of the Southern Sung Dynasty." *Studies in Chinese Institutional History.* pp. 216–224.

5. Karl Jahn. "Paper Currency in Iran." *Journal of Asian History.* Volume 4, no. 2, 1970. pp. 101–135. An English translation of *Das iranische Papergeld. Ein eitrag zur Kultur und Wirtschaftsgeschicte Irans in der Mongolenzeit. ArchivOrientaini.* Volume X, (1938). pp. 308–340.

6. Dard Hunter. *Papermaking, The History and Technique of an Ancient Craft.* pp. 473 and 474.

7. Henk Voorn. "On the invention of the Hollander Beater." The Papermaker. Volume 25, no. 2, 1956. pp. 1–9.

8. *Närrische Weissheit und Weise Narrheit: oder Ein Hundert so Politscheals husicalische, Mechanische und Mercan-tilische Concepten und Propositionen.* Frankfurt, Germany: Johann Joaachim Becker, 1682.

   The earliest engraved depiction of the beating machine is to be found in a book titled *Volkständige Mühlen Bankuns*, written by Leonhardt Christoph Sturm and published in Augsberg in 1718. Sturm's work contains a good cross-sectional drawing of a Hollander, and this is reproduced in Vroon's article on page 5.

9. Based on the descriptions given in Ebenezer Stedman's manuscript diary, he was born in Dorchester, Massachusetts, on November 11, 1808. In 1816 he and his father, a local paper-maker, went to Kentucky to work in a paper mill in Lexington. Stedman's diary is the most complete account of early-American paper-making. Chapter 12 of this work mentions that Stedman worked as a lay-boy in a mill that made the bank-note paper for the state of Kentucky, though the description of his job is brief. He complained that the paper was made entirely of linen and was very thin and difficult to handle. Francis L.S. Dugan and Jacqueline P. Bull, editors. *Bluegrass Craftsman, Being the Reminiscences of Ebenezer Hiram Stedman, Papermaker, 1808–1885.* Kentucky: University of Kentucky Press, 1959.

10. Like most of the early U.S. patents, this one was lost in the fire at the Patent Office in December 1836. The text of the patent, however, is to be found in the *Journal of the Franklin Institute*, volume XI, no. 3, March 1833, pp. 178 and 179.

11. We have George Simpson Eddy to thank for his detailed account of Franklin's dealings with the paper mills in the Middle Colonies. *Account Books Kept by Benjamin Franklin, Ledger "D," 1739–1747, with notes*. New York, New York: Columbia University Press, 1928. 2 volumes. There are two copies at the Library of Congress.

12. Dard Hunter says the Gilpin family was "of Norman origin, and prior to the sixteenth century the name was De Gaylpyn. The first member of this family to leave England was Joseph Gilpin, who sailed for America in 1698 to assume ownership of lands that had been granted to him by William Penn." Dard Hunter. *Papermaking in Pioneer America*. Philadelphia, Pennsylvania: University of Pennsylvania Press, 1952. p. 82.

13. Quoted from William Bond Wheelwright's "The Gilpins of Wilmington." *The Paper-maker*. Volume 10, Number 1, 1941.

14. The full title is "Essay on the New Method of Bleaching by Means of Oxygenated Muriatic Acid, with the Account of the Nature, Preparation, and Properties of that Acid, and its Application to several other Useful Purposes in the Arts." This small volume was published in Edinburgh in 1790. Gilpin also read *The Art of Bleaching* by Pajot des Charmes in a translation by W. Nicholson and commented on its methods to his brother.

15. The U.S. Patent Office has no copy of this patent. Apparently, it was lost in the fire of December 15, 1836. The little that we know of the patent is described in Sidney M. Edelstein's article "Papermaker Joshua Gilpin introduces the Chemical Approach to Papermaking in the United States." *The Paper-maker*. Volume 30 (September), 1961. pp. 3–12. See also the long article on bleaching in James Cutbush's *The American Artist's Manuel*, which dates from 1814 and describes several methods of bleaching.

16. Edelstein. *op. cit.*

17. The scrapbook is entitled "Collections of Bank Note Paper and Checks Collected by Thomas Gilpin of Kenemere at the Brandywine Mills, Delaware," and is part of the Gilpin Collections at the Historical Society of Pennsylvania, Philadelphia, Pennsylvania.

18. Bryan Donkin, the son of a prosperous surveyor and land agent, was born on March 22, 1768, at the family home at Sandoe, a small village in Northumberland, England. As a child, he showed remarkable mechanical ability, making a thermometer and some ingenious toys. After working four years for his father as a land surveyor, he began a three-year apprenticeship in engineering. Soon he opened his own factory, and in 1802 he became involved with John Gamble and the Fourdrinier brothers in building a paper-making machine.

19. Patent No. 2487 was granted on April 20, 1801. A second patent, no. 2708, was granted on June 7, 1803, and the patent for a continuous paper machine, no. 2951, was granted on July 24, 1806.

20. R.H. Capperton. "The Invention and Development of the Endless Wire, or Fourdrinier's Paper Machine." *The Paper-maker*. Volume 23, no. 1, 1954. p. 10.

21. Dard Hunter. *Papermaking. op. cit.* p. 357.

22. The best biography of John Dickinson, and also a well-written history of the company he founded, is Joan Evans's *The Endless Web*. London, England: Jonathan Cape, 1955.

23. The case was Ames *vs.* Howard and Lothrop (Case No. 36), which started in the October term of 1833 of the U.S. Circuit Court for Massachusetts, but concluded in the October term of 1835. The case files are in four file boxes numbered 83, 84, 85, and 86, in Record Group 21. The Final Record Book (FRB), giving the final disposition of the case, is on microfilm for the U.S. Circuit Court—1790–1911 (box No. 11-9) and is found there in Volume 21, pp. 236–249. The depositions of Thomas Gilpin and Hugh McFee are in Box 85, Folder 10. Attached to this deposition is a single sheet with a drawing of "John Ames Improvement on Making Paper," dated September 1, 1832, and a second drawing dated (in pencil) 1822. There are several other larger drawings of the same, located in Box 86, Folders 11 and 12, National Archives, Northeast Region, Waltham, Massachusetts.

24. Joseph Willcox. *Ivy Mills, 1729–1860*. Printed for private circulation by the author. Baltimore, Maryland: Lucas Brothers, Inc., 1911.
    Most of this work was published at various times in the records of the American Catholic Historical Society.

25. Linen is a cloth made from either flax or hemp. Irish linens are almost always made from the flax plant and are much softer than the hemp linen made in eastern-European countries. Hemp linen, or "Russia Sheeting," is stronger and coarser.

26. These notes had randomly distributed red-silk fibers, meaning the fibers were placed in the vat along with the stock (pulp). Zenas Crane is generally considered to be the first person to place parallel silk fibers in notes in 1844.

27. John Hill Martin. *The History of Chester (and its Vicinity), Delaware County in Pennsylvania, with Genealogical Sketches of Some Old Families*. Philadelphia, Pennsylvania: W.H. Pile & Sons, 1877. 530 pages.

28. The business correspondence of the Willcox mills is available on microfilm from the Historical Society of Pennsylvania. Many of these letters are from bank-note companies and are a good source of addresses and the names of partners.

29. Jute is a fiber taken from the bark of several species of plants that are grown primarily in the Ganges Valley of India. The fibers are six-to-ten feet in length, but only the butts were used for this distinctive bank-note paper. The better-quality jute is used to make burlap sacks, and the poorer grades are used to make rope, twine, carpet backing, and gunny sacks. Jute has been known to western commerce only since 1830.

30. These comments are quoted from the testimony of James M. Willcox in *Printing of United States Notes and other Securities*, Report No. 150, House of Representatives, 43rd Congress, 2nd Session, February 16, 1875, pp. 230–240.

31. Byron N. Rooks. *Our Paper Currency*. Portland, Oregon: Rutherford & Smith, 1891. pp. 16 and 17.
    I can't find an explanation in the literature for the predominance of blue fibers in our paper currency, but it was probably a chemical problem to dye the jute fibers red.

32. Winthrop Murray Crane was the son of Zenas Marshall Crane and Louise Fanny Laflin. Winthrop was born in Dalton, Massachusetts, on April 23, 1853. He attended both public and private schools before entering his father's company to learn paper-making. He entered politics, becoming Lieutenant Governor of Massachusetts from 1897 to

1899, then Governor of Massachusetts from 1900 to 1902. Theodore Roosevelt appointed him secretary of the Treasury in 1902, but he declined and became a senator of Massachusetts from 1904 to 1913. He died in Dalton on October 2, 1920, leaving an estate of $8,800,000 divided among 117 beneficiaries. He held $252,000 in common stock of the American Bank Note Company at the time of his death.

33. This story is told in the official history of Crane & Company. Wadsworth R. Pierce. *The First 175 Years of Crane Papermaking*. North Adams, Massachusetts: Excelsior Printing Co., 1977. pp. 29 and 30. The Crane history takes the position that Winthrop merely "outmaneuvered his older experienced competitors" in the bidding. Considering that such tactics were commonplace in Washington, D.C., at the time, that may be a fair assessment.

34. This letter is reproduced in *Distinctive Paper for United States Banks*, Senate Document No. 134, 55th Congress, 3rd Session, (February 1899).

35. The Willcox family and business history can be summarized this way: Thomas Willcox died on November 11, 1779, at the age of 90 years. His son, Mark, inherited Ivy Mills in 1767. In 1808 Mark gave his eldest son, Joseph, one-third interest in the profits of the business, and in 1811 he gave one-third interest to his son, John. Joseph had a short life, dying in January 1815, after which John supervised the operations of the mill until he died in July 1826. Following John's death, his brother James M. Wilcox (new spelling) assumed the management of the mill. When Mark Willcox died on February 17, 1827, James inherited the mill. The last lot of watermarked bank-note paper made at Ivy Mills was 100,000 sheets for the Bank of Montreal in 1861. Thereafter, all bank-note paper was made at Glenn Mills until the company lost the government contract in 1879.

36. John W. Maxson Jr. "Nathan Sellers, America's First Large-Scale Maker of Paper Molds." *The Paper-maker*. Volume 29, no. 1, (1960). pp. 1–15.
   Sellers is also mentioned frequently in Joseph Willcox's *Ivy Mills, 1729–1866*, and a long and detailed description of his inventions is found in George Escol Seller's *Early Engineering Reminiscences (1815–40)*, edited by Eugene S. Ferguson.

37. This data is presented in two ledgers. The first ledger covers the period from 1776 to 1815, and the second ledger runs from 1815 to 1824. Both of these ledgers are in the collections of the library of the American Philosophical Society in Philadelphia and are available on microfilm.

38. Dard Hunter. *op. cit.* Dover edition. pp. 297–307.

39. Information derived from *Counterfeit U.S. Currency Abroad, Issues and U.S. Deterrence Efforts*. Washington, D.C.: General Accounting Office, February 1996, Appendix IV, "Three Case Examples of High-Quality Counterfeits," pp. 36–39.

40. A family tradition portrays a much more romantic and daring escape. In that story, Henri and his brother hid themselves in an empty wine cask and were shipped to England on the high seas. This is now regarded as a fanciful tale. Elliott Harrison. "The Portals: Papermakers to the Bank of England." *The Paper-maker*. Volume 22, February 1953. pp. 38–42.

41. The primary source for the history of Portals is Sir William Portal's *The Story of Portals, Limited, of Laverstoke, Makers of Good Paper for over Two Hundred Years, 1719–1925*. This may be difficult to find since the Library of Congress does not own a copy.

42. Almost all the information we have on Gwynn is to be found in testimony and reports given by Colonel Baker and S.M. Clark before a committee of the House of Representatives investigating charges of corruption and immorality with the currency bureau of the Treasury Department. House of Representatives Report No. 140, 35th Congress, 1st Session, June 30, 1864. Exhibit CC, being the report of Colonel Baker on Stuart Gwynn, pp. 387–404, is especially interesting.

43. A thorough search of the correspondence files of the Treasury Department and the Bureau of Engraving and Printing has failed to locate Dr. Gwynn's letters.

44. In this context, a mordant is a colloidal substance used to set dyes. Some natural dyes will not adhere to paper, but if a mordant is placed on the paper first, it creates bonds between the dye and the cellulose fibers, allowing the dye to "set." Common mordants are alum, chrome, copper sulfate, iron, tin, etc. It would be interesting if a chemist analyzed a specimen of fractional currency having the bronze feature to see what mordant was used. This was a secret process with the National Currency Bureau and there is no detailed record in the literature of the mordant used.

45. General Herman Haupt (1817–1905) was Chief of Military Railroads for the Union Army during the Civil War. He was, by profession, a civil and mechanical engineer and the first to develop a rational method of truss analysis. He was a good roommate for Stuart Gwynn since they were both inventors and mechanical engineers.

46. The Woodruff & Beach Iron Works (Samuel Woodruff and H.B. Beach) was the first company in Hartford to become involved with steam technology, and during the 1840s and 1850s, it was the largest producer of steam engines, boilers, and heavy machinery in New England. During the Civil War, it produced marine engines for the U.S. Navy. Despite the good reputation it enjoyed, the company went out of business in 1871.

47. Founded in 1851, Poole & Hunt was the largest and most prominent iron foundry and machinery shop in Baltimore. Among the many specimens of their workmanship are the columns of the dome of the U.S. Capitol in Washington, D.C., iron tanks and machinery for paper mills, gearing and shafting for cotton mills, and the 12-inch disappearing gun carriages for our coastal defenses.

48. The fact that this company also made hydraulic presses for Dr. Gwynn is found in a letter from Spencer M. Clark to the secretary of the Treasury, reproduced in "Additional Papers Relative to the Printing Division of the Currency Bureau of the Treasury Department," *Executive Document No. 64*, House of Representatives, 38th Congress, 2nd Session, February 13, 1865, pp. 16–18. This company was located in Baltimore, Maryland, and had originally started out in 1840 as Hayward & Friend, stove manufacturers, eventually expanding into foundry, heavy machinery, erection, and the engineering field. Their company records, now at the Smithsonian Institution, date only from 1882, so they are of no use in documenting their work for Stuart Gwynn.

49. (Letter of S.M. Clark to the Honorable Salmon P. Chase, Secretary of the Treasury.) House of Representatives, 38th Congress, 2nd Session, Executive Document No. 50, *Printing Bureau of the Treasury Department*, February 4, 1865, p. 19.

50. The Old Capitol Prison got its name from the fact that the British burned the original capitol during the War of 1812, forcing Congress to lease this building and meet there from December 1815 until the present capitol was rebuilt in 1825. The three-story prison was originally a tavern built around 1800. Because the federal government had no

prisons at this time, it used local prisons wherever necessary. Federal prisoners were incarcerated at the Old Capitol Prison along with both Union and Confederate soldiers.

51. House of Representatives, 38th Congress, 1st Session, Report No. 140, entitled *Treasury Department*, April 30, 1864, p. 16.

52. *Ibid.* pp. 120 and 121.

53. *Ibid.* p. 9.

54. *Ibid.* p. 158.

55. Fred L. Reed III. *Bank Note Reporter.* February–May 2009.

56. A 25% linen content was found to be the optimum ratio in a series of experiments carried out by the Bureau of Standards in 1925 and 1926. These experiments produced a bank-note paper that had 100% greater folding endurance than the paper previously supplied to the public. Merle B. Shaw and George W. Bicking. "Research on the Production of Currency Paper in the Bureau of Standards Experimental Paper Mill." *Technical Papers of the Bureau of Standards.* Volume 21, (June 1926). pp. 89–108.

57. Wadsworth R. Pierce. *The First 175 Years of Crane Papermaking.* North Adams, Massachusetts. September 1977. 77 pages.

58. "George La Monte Dies." *New York Times.* October 20, 1913. p. 7, col. 4.

Chapter 16

1. John Winter. "Preliminary Investigations on Chinese Ink in Far Eastern Paintings." *Advances in Chemistry.* Series 138 (1975). p. 221; R.N. Schwab, *et al.* "Cyclotron Analysis of the Ink in the 42-line Bible." *Papers of the Bibliographical Society of America.* Series 77 (1983). pp. 285–315; R.N. Schwab, *et al.* "New Evidence on the Printing of the Gutenberg Bible: The Inks in the Doheny Copy." *Papers of the Bibliographical Society of America.* Series 79 (1985). pp. 375–410.

2. An excellent review of Chinese inks is found in Lily Chia-Jen Kecske's *A Study of Chinese Inkmaking: Historical, Technical and Aesthetic,* submitted as a Master's Thesis at the University of Chicago, Illinois, March 1981.

3. Linseed oil is made by pressing the seeds of the flax plant in a large screw press or hydraulic press. The blue and white flowers of the plant mature into bolls that contain 10 seeds each. Flax is grown also for the fiber, which is spun into thread to make linen cloth, and since linen cuttings are the primary material for making bank-note paper, the security-printing industry, until recent times, was very much dependent on this plant.

4. Richard N. Schwab and Thomas A. Cahill. "Gutenberg's Ink and Paper." *Archeometry.* Volume 26, no. 1 (1984). pp. 3–14.

5. Charles Johnson ran the company until he retired on March 2, 1827. He died on April 15, 1840, at the age of 68. His son, Charles Johnson Jr., continued the business for 17 years until he retired in favor of his son, Charles Eneu Johnson, who greatly expanded the company until his death in 1897. The company made a wide variety of colored lithographic and typographic inks, burnt linseed oils, dry pigments, and solvents. The company did business until the late 1950s.

6. Isaac Eddy was born on February 17, 1777, in Weathersfield, Vermont. He was apparently self-taught in the engraving field, and in 1814 he bought the first printing plant in New Hampshire at Dresden, near Hanover. There, he engraved plates for the historical *Vermont Bible,* which now reposes in the museum at Dartmouth College. He died in Waterford, New York, on July 25, 1847.

7. The original Letters Patent signed by President James Monroe and Secretary of State John Quincy Adams is in the Eddy Family Records at the Rensselaer County Historical Society of Troy, New York. The patent itself was lost when the Patent Office burned in 1836.

8. I have not been able to find a contract in the Treasury Department records at the National Archives, but the *Times Record* (newspaper) of Troy, New York, owns a copy of a letter written by S.M. Clark, the Superintendent of the National Currency Bureau, dated October 20, 1862, addressed to Titus Eddy & Sons, which states, in part: "You will please send as soon as possible six barrels of best 'B' Black, one barrel of best calcined Lamp Black, together with your bill for the same."

9. Some of the business correspondence of Titus Eddy & Sons is now owned by private collectors. The *Essay-Proof Journal* for July 1953 reported that Dr. Julian Blanchard exhibited a lot of the Titus Eddy correspondence at a chapter meeting of the Essay-Proof Society in New York that year. The Rensselaer County Historical Society has a collection of the company's business letters (less than 100) with such firms as the Western Bank Note & Engraving Company; Tiemann's Color & White Lead Works; Hill, Bradley & Co.; Tiffany & Co.; The Diamond Ink Co., etc.

10. Thomas Antisell. *Handbook of the Useful Arts.* New York, New York: G.P. Putnam, 1852. 692 pages, illustrated.

11. These notes are derived from the *Statistics of the Class of 1852, Yale University* and the *Yale Obituary Record.*

12. A well-written explanation of the 1856 patent, but applicable also to the patent of 1857, is to be found in the article "Seropyan's Patent Bank Bills." *Boston Evening Transcript.* Tuesday, May 20, 1856. p. 1, col. 2. This article was written by Professors Benjamin Silliman Sr. and Jr., and by James D. Dana and John Torrey.

13. Fred L. Reed III. "Feds Look to Second Anti-photographic Ink." *The Bank Note Reporter.* Volume 36, no. 10, October 2008. pp. 38–54.

14. "Color Formulas For Bank Notes, Bonds, and Certificates." *Essay-Proof Journal.* No. 6, 1945. p. 76. Continued in No. 46, April 1955. pp. 94–96. The ink formulas were written by hand on legal-size paper that was found in a Brooklyn, New York, house formerly occupied by Mr. Cassin of the American Bank Note Company, who died about 1933. The formulas were once the property of Rawdon, Wright, Hatch & Edson and cover the period from 1849 to about 1858.

15. W.J. Stone. "Description of a Machine for Grinding Painters' Colours, Printing ink, &c." *Journal of the Franklin Institute.* Volume III, no. 4, April 1829. pp. 244 and 245

16. Norman Underwood and Thomas V. Sullivan. *The Chemistry and Technology of Printing Inks.* New York, New York: D. Van Nostrand Company, 1915. pp. 93–95.

    The authors were, respectively, the chief and assistant chief of the Ink-Making Division of the Bureau of Engraving and Printing.

17. Carlton Ellis. *Printing Inks, Their Chemistry and Technology*. New York, New York: Reinhold Publishing, 1940. p. 47.

18. *Washington Post*. Tuesday, January 7, 1908. p. 1, cols. 1 and 2.

19. Obituary printed in the *Syracuse Herald Journal*. Monday, August 17, 1953. p. 2, col. 1.

Chapter 17

1. Henry Meier. "The Origin of the Printing and Roller Press." *The Print Collector's Quarterly*. Volume 28, no. 1, (February 1941). pp. 8–55.
   Several of the earliest lever and screw presses depicted in ancient and medieval art are reproduced in this work.

2. Stephen O. Saxe. *American Iron Hand Presses*. New Castle, Delaware: Oak Knoll Books, 1991. 108 pages. A thorough history of the subject

3. Anonymous. "Old Style Plate Presses." *Engravers' Bulletin*. 1915. pp. 340–343.

4. This drawing is from Peter Barlow's *Manufactures and Machinery of Great Britain (to which is Prefixed an Introductory View of the Principles of Manufactures by Charles Babbage Forming a Portion of the Encyclpaedia Metropolitana)*. London, England: Baldwin Cradock, 1836. pp. 85–324 in the *Encyclopaedia Metropolitana*. A rare book.

5. Thomas Oldham, when he was in charge of the printing department for the Bank of Ireland, powered one of his flat-bed presses by an eight-horsepower steam engine, becoming the first to use steam (1812) for this purpose.

6. *Journal of the Franklin Institute*. Volume IV, no. 2, August 1829. p. 72.

7. Quoted in Frank E. Comparato's *Chronicles of Genius and Folly*. Culver City, California: Labyrinthos, 1979. p. 690.
   This is a history of R. Hoe & Company.

8. Stephen D. Tucker. *History of R. Hoe & Company*. Typed manuscript in the Library of Congress, Microfilm Shelf No. 36317, Call Number Z249. H7T8, p. 91.

9. *Ibid*. p. 81.

10. "Report on Operation of Milligan Presses." Appendix E. U.S. Senate Report No. 2064, 50th Congress, 2nd Session, February 15, 1889, p. 133.

11. Quoted from a report made by John S. Craig and Ward Morgan of the Bureau of Engraving and Printing to John B. McCartee, the Chief of the Bureau, dated January 17, 1876, concerning their observations of the Neale-Appleton press at work in New York City. This report is "Schedule C" in House of Representatives Executive Report No. 224, entitled "Plate Printing by Steam-powered Presses, dated July 18, 1882, pp. 22–23.

12. James Milligan was chief printer at the Franklin Engraving and Printing Company when it was founded in 1877. Later, he went to the Bureau of Engraving and Printing and was a foreman plate printer. He died in 1884, leaving his interest in the Milligan Press to his wife and daughter.

13. This information is contained in a letter from Edward O. Graves, the chief of the Bureau of Engraving and Printing, to Mr. L.J. Wall, the vice-president of the August Gast Bank Note Company in St. Louis, Missouri, dated October 25, 1887. This letter is on page 249 of volume 437 of "Letters Sent," Record Group 87, National Archives, College Park, Maryland. The Gould Machine Company was started in Newark, New Jersey, in 1833 by Ezra Gould in a tiny machine shop only 16-feet by 16-feet. Ezra Gould was one of the finest mechanics of his day and also possessed considerable skill as an inventor. He is credited with designing and building the first shaping machine and one of the earliest gear-cutting machines made in America. In 1877 Gould formed a partnership with Ulrich Eberhardt. The firm manufactured Gould's gear cutters and shapers and sold the machines around the world. The company also made Milligan Presses for the Canadian Bank Note Company and for other governments, as well as transfer presses for the Bureau of Engraving and Printing and some private bank-note companies. Gould retired in 1890 at the age of 81. The company is now known as the Gould & Eberhardt Gear Machinery Corporation in Webster, Massachusetts.

14. The "Guy" press was patented in the United States in 1878, U.S. Patent No. 210,116.

15. Homer Lee was born in Mansfield, Ohio, on May 18, 1856, the son of an engraver. He was taught engraving by his father and was apprenticed to a steel engraver in New York City. His master died before his apprenticeship was over, and so Lee started an engraving business called "Homer Lee & Company." This was successful, and he founded the Homer Lee Bank Note Company in 1881. This company merged with the Franklin Bank Note Company in 1897 and became known as the Franklin-Lee Bank Note Company. Mr. Lee died on January 25, 1923, at the age of 73. An obituary appeared in the *New York Times* on January 26, 1923, p. 17, col. 3.

16. Quoted from "Report on the Lee Press." Appendix D. U.S. Senate Report No. 2604, 50th Congress, 2nd Session, February 15, 1889. p. 130.

17. It would appear that he was named after Judah Touro (1775–1854), the famous Jewish philanthropist. During the war with England in 1812, Judah Touro fought as a volunteer under General Andrew Jackson. In the Battle of New Orleans, January 1, 1815, he was severely wounded and his heroism won the admiration and respect of Jackson's staff. After the war, Touro made a fortune and gave virtually all of it away to both Jewish and non-Jewish causes.

18. Robertson kept a diary of the operations of the Continental Bank Note Company, covering the period from 1862 to 1867. Julian Blanchard had the diary and presumably owned it in the early 1950s when he brought it to a meeting of the New York chapter of the Essay-Proof Society and read part of it to the audience concerning the trials and tribulations of the beginning of the Continental Bank Note Company. Thomas F. Morris Jr. wrote a brief article containing the diary entries from March 8, 1863, through December 27, 1863, which was published as "Touro Robertson and His Early Connection with the Continental Bank Note Company," in the *Essay-Proof Journal*, Whole No. 81, 1964, pp. 24–28. It is probable that Morris either bought the diary from Blanchard or owned it all along. The diary ends with the entry for December 27, and nothing more is stated about the business until it resumes in 1866. Apparently, nothing more has been written about the diary, and I am unable to find its present owner.

19. Most of the biographical information about Judah Touro Robertson was collected by Thomas F. Morris Jr., and published in *Collectors' Club Philatelist*, volume 20, no. 1, January 1941, pp. 30–32. An obituary appeared in the *New York Times* on Saturday, January 6, 1900, p. 7, col. 5.

20. The interment records of the North Laurel Hill Cemetery in Philadelphia show that (1) Charles Laughlin Robertson, who died at age 8, was buried in the family vault on March 2, 1847; (2) Ogden Robertson, "brought from Bremen, Europe," who died at age 20, was buried on October 19, 1848; (3) The remains of an infant, "brought from

Havana," no sex given, belonging to William H. Robertson, was buried on December 21, 1855; (4) William H. Robertson of Havana, Cuba (who was Judah Touro Robertson's father), died at age 70 and was buried at Laurel Hill on June 23, 1857; (5) Inez F. Robertson, who was probably a daughter of Judah T. Robertson, died at age 2 months and was buried December 23, 1889; (6) Elizabeth Edna Robertson, Judah's daughter, of Lakewood, New Jersey, died at age 25 years and 5 months in early May 1894; (7) Maria Elizabeth Robertson, of Spring Lake, New Jersey, died at age 58 and was buried in July 1905. Her relationship to Judah Touro Robertson is unknown; (8) William Touro Robertson, Judah's son, of Oakland, California, was buried on June 5, 1917. He died at age 46; (9) Jessie S. Robertson, Judah's daughter, of Hollywood, Florida, was buried there on December 4, 1942. She was 72 years of age when she died.

Chapter 18

1. Monsieur A.G. Camus, a member of the French Institute, read a memoir to the society on March 17, 1798, entitled "Histoire et Procédés du Polytypage et de la Stéréotypie." This memoir was printed in Paris and published by Baudoir in November 1801. Parts of the memoir were translated into English in a letter written by F.E. Guilot, ex-director of Assignats, and sent to the editor of the *Literary Gazette* of London where it was published in Nos. 190 and 191 in 1820. The Guilot letter was reprinted in the *London Journal of Arts and Sciences*, volume 1, no. IV, pp. 383–388. The history of the Politypage process is also given by Basil Hunnisett in *Engraved on Steel: The History of Picture Production Using Steel Plates*. Cambridge: University Press, 1998.

2. Permission to quote passages from this work was kindly given by the Dietz Press in Petersburg, Virginia.

3. F.W. Stoyle. "Michael Faraday and Anastatic Printing." *The British Ink Maker*. 1965.
   Joseph Woods was granted British Patent No. 10,219, dated December 6, 1844, entitled "Improvements in producing and multiplying copies of designs and impressions of printed or written surfaces." Woods died of cholera in 1849, and after his death Rudolf Appel claimed to have invented the process while he was in Germany working as an employee of Baldemus. The early history of the process is outlined in Geoffrey Wakerman's "Anastatic Printing for Sir Thomas Phillipps," published in the *Journal of the Printing Historical Society*, no. 5, 1969, pp. 24–40.

4. Taken from Senate Report No. 2604, 50th Congress, 2nd Session, Committee on Finance, dated February 15, 1880, pp. 49 and 50.

5. W.L. Ormsby. *A description of the Present System of Bank Note Engraving*. 1852. pp. 44–46.

6. *Ibid.* p. 46.

7. The article is "Electrography or the Electrotype," and appears in *The American Journal of Science and Arts*, volume XL, April 1841, pp. 157–164. It was apparently written by Professor Benjamin Silliman Jr. and is a revision of Thomas Spencer's article, "Instructions for the Multiplication of Works of Art in Metal by Voltaic Electricity," which was published as Part IV of Griffin's *Scientific Miscellany*, Glasgow, 1840. Silliman added notes on the chemistry of the battery.

8. Noah Steiner Amstutz. *Amstutz's Handbook of Photoengraving*. Chicago, Illinois: The Inland Printing Company, 1907.
   See page 11 which begins a section on the preliminaries. This book is a revision of the second edition of Harry Jenkins' *Manual of Photoengraving*, published in 1896. Amstutz was head of the research department at the Inland Printing Company, then the largest photoengraving company in America.

9. The story is often told in chemistry books that guncotton was invented in 1846 by a Swiss chemist named Christian Friedrich Schonbein. As Schonbein was working in the kitchen of his home in Basle, he accidentally spilled some nitric acid on a kitchen table. He reached for a nearby cloth, a cotton apron, and wiped up the spill. He hung the apron on the door of his stove to dry it, and when it was completely dried, there was a flash as it exploded.

10. I have omitted any further details of the history of halftone photoengraving since it is not relevant to the bank-note industry, but for anyone interested in the subject, I suggest they read about the work of the Austrian printer Paul Pretch in developing his "photogalvanography" process (British Patent No. 2,373 of November 9, 1854); Max Levy's invention of a special-ruling machine and his patented halftone process (U.S. Patent No. 492,333 of February 21, 1893); the work of Karl Klic in developing rotogravure (1878); the work of William Kurtz in developing a three-color halftone relief printing process (U.S. Patent No. 498,396 of May 30, 1893); and the work of Louis Levy in developing an etching machine (U.S. Patent No. 627,430 of June 20, 1899). Those men made the greatest advances in the art and science of photomechanics, but there were many others who made lesser but still significant advances, including Berchtold (1855); Swan (1865); Egloffstein (1865); Avet (1866); Kossuth (1866); Leggo (1869); Placet (1874); Petit (1878); Horgan (1880); Meisenbach (1882); Garside (1883); Borland (1883); Ives, for his development of color photographic film; and Levy (1886).

Appendix H

1. Alexander Hamilton's portrait is seen on the following U.S. currency:

   (1) $20 U.S. notes, series 1869, 1875, and 1880

   (2) $1,000 Gold Certificates, series 1870, 1875, 1882, and 1907

   (3) $1,000 Federal Reserve Notes, series 1918

   (4) $10 Silver Certificates, series 1933 and 1934A

   (5) $10 Federal Reserve Notes, series 1928, 1929, et. seq.

   (6) $10 National Bank Notes, series 1929

   (7) $10 Gold Certificates, series 1928

2. Samuel Dexter's portrait is seen on the 50-cent Fractional Currency notes, fourth issue.

3. Albert Gallatin's portrait is seen on the $500 U.S. notes, series 1862 and 1863.

4. William H. Crawford's portrait is seen on the 50-cent Fractional Currency notes, fifth issue.

5. Robert Walker's portrait is seen on the 25-cent Fractional Currency notes, fifth issue.

6. William M. Meredith's portrait is seen on the 10-cent Fractional Currency notes, fifth issue.

7. Howell Cobb's portrait is seen on the $500 interest-bearing Treasury Notes issued by the Act of December 23, 1857.

8. Salmon P. Chase's portrait is seen on the following U.S. currency:

   (1) $1 U.S. notes of 1862

(2) $10 Compound Interest Treasury Notes, Act of March 3, 1863

(3) $50 interest-bearing Treasury Notes (six percent, two years), 1861

(4) $1,000 Interest-Bearing Notes (five percent, two years), Act of March 3, 1863

(5) $10,000 Federal Reserve Notes, series 1918, 1928, and 1934

(6) $10,000 Gold Certificates, series 1928 and 1934

9. William P. Fessenden's portrait is seen on the 25-cent Fractional Currency notes, third issue.

10. Hugh McCulloch's portrait is seen on the $20 National Bank Notes of the third-charter period.

11. William Windom's portrait is seen on the $2 Silver Certificates, series 1891.

12. Daniel Manning's portrait is seen on the $20 Silver Certificates, series 1886 and 1891.

Glossary

Many of these definitions and historical facts were taken from the 1881-edition of *Knight's American Mechanical Dictionary*, the 1869-edition of the *American Bond Detector*, the 1852 *Appleton's Mechanics' Magazine and Engineering Journal*, numerous issues of the *London Journal of Arts and Sciences* (especially in 1820), the *Franklin Journal and American Mechanics' Magazine* (1826 and 1827), the *Journal of the Franklin Institute* (1828–1839), scattered issues of the *American Journal of Science and Arts* (1829–1841), the 1825-edition of C.F. Partington's *The Engraver's Complete Guide*, and notes taken over the years from many other books and journals.

A

Acanthus leaves—The *Acanthus* plant, indigenous to the Mediterranean area, has scalloped leaves which were often stylized and appeared in Greek and Roman art, especially in the decoration of Corinthian columns, friezes, and panels. By medieval times, it was associated with long life. The stylized leaves were sometimes used by artists, especially engravers, to surround vignettes or decorate counters on paper money.

Acid resist—An acid-proof protective coating applied to metal plates prior to etching an engraved image with acid. An example is an engraving on a zinc plate made with fatty ink. When the plate is washed with hydrochloric acid, the fatty ink acts as an acid resist and is protected from the corrosive effects of the acid. The non-image areas of the plate are eaten away by the acid, leaving the image intact and in relief. Asphaltum is also an acid resist.

Adhesion / Cohesion—For all inks, two properties—adhesion and cohesion—are very important. Adhesion refers to the power of an ink to stick to a different material, e.g. paper. Cohesion refers to an ink's ability to hold together. Printing is physically possible because an ink is more likely to adhere to a different material than to itself. It is the vehicle of an ink that supplies its adhesion and cohesion.

Adsorption—(1) The penetration of ink into the surface of the paper by capillary attraction between the ink vehicle and the paper fibers. (2) The physical adhesion of gum arabic to a lithographic stone or metal plate, believed to be caused by the presence of carboxyl groups in the material. Compare with *Adhesion / Cohesion*.

Alum—There are two chemicals called alum. Aluminum potassium sulfate was used in ancient China and in Western Europe from the mid-15th century to harden the gelatin size placed on paper. In the 19th century, a simpler alum (aluminum sulfate) was made by treating either bauxite or China Clay (kaolin) with sulfuric acid. Alum was combined with rosin sizing to improve the print qualities of paper. Bank-note paper was sized to give it "stiffness," to make it resistant to moisture, and to prevent "bleed through." Modern chemistry has found that hydrated forms of aluminum ions form cross-linkages with gelatin molecules, and aluminum salts can then attach to cellulose fibers.

Anastatic Printing—Patented by the Englishman Joseph Woods in 1844 but actually first used by Sennefelder in tests he made to develop the first lithographic process in 1776.

Anastatic printing is a reproduction process which copies a text which has already been printed in ink. It does not matter how old the text or graphic is. The method can copy fine-line engravings, but these are reproduced as a letterpress or flat surface printing and do not have the feel of an intaglio print. Since the original is destroyed by acid and only a few impressions can be made, the process had little potential for counterfeiting; nevertheless, anastatic printing concerned the bank-note industry and helped push the development of colored inks for bank notes.

Aniline dyes—William Henry Perkins discovered Mauve, a purple dye, in 1856. It was the first of a series of dyestuffs that now number in the hundreds. Inks made from coal-tar derivatives (the aniline inks) played only a small role in security printing during the 19th century. Because the aniline inks are easily dissolved in water or most chemicals, they were used primarily as fugitive inks in postage stamps, revenue stamps, and safety papers for bank checks. Aniline inks are usually not very permanent and have low values for light fastness, making them unsuitable for bank-note inks.

Annealing—To soften a hardened die, it is surrounded with iron filings, placed in a furnace, and brought to the required temperature. This removes the carbon from the surface of the die. The die is then allowed to cool to room temperature.

Aqua Fortis—This "strong water," as it was called in alchemy, is a corrosive solution of nitric acid in water. It was used in etching copper or brass.

Aqua Regia—This is the Latin name for "Royal Water," so-called because it was able to dissolve the "royal" metals gold and platinum. It cannot dissolve tantalum, iridium, and some other metals, so it ain't all that royal. The mixture is made by combining concentrated nitric acid and concentrated hydrochloric acid, usually in a ratio of 1:3 by volume. It was used by engravers as an etchant. This mixture of acids was first made by the Persian alchemist Abu Musa Jabir around the year 800 AD.

Aspect ratio—The aspect ratio of a bank note is found by dividing its width by its height and expressing the ratio as a decimal. For modern American notes, which are 6.14 inches x 2.61 inches, the aspect ratio is 2.35. In the older "large size" notes, which were 7.42 inches x 3.125 inches, the aspect ratio was 2.37. While the actual sizes of our national currency have changed, the aspect ratio has remained the same. In many other American notes, such as the interest-bearing Treasury Notes of the 1812 to 1860 era, where the rectangular shape of notes is shortened and they approach a square shape, the aspect ratio is different.

Asphaltum—The word is from the Late Latin and is transformed eventually into the English term "asphalt." It is a sticky, black, and highly viscous liquid or semi-solid material that is present in most crude petroleum and also occurs in natural deposits such as oil seeps. Asphaltum (then called "Bitumen of Judea") played an important role in the early development of photography because it was a material that hardened slowly when exposed to light. Joseph Niepce used this principle in 1822 when he coated a glass plate with a solution of asphaltum and let it dry. He then placed a paper engraving of Pope Pius VII face down on the glass plate and exposed it to direct sunlight. The paper had been oiled to make it nearly transparent. After several hours of exposure, Niepce found that the sunlight passing through the clear portions of the engraving had hardened the asphaltum to the glass, but those parts shadowed by the lines of the engraving remained soluble. When washed with oil of lavender, the unhardened asphaltum dissolved away, leaving a clear, fine-lined image. This first photograph was subsequently destroyed, but Niepce went on to make other contact-print photographs by this method. The term "Bitumen of Judea" dates back to ancient Egyptian times, and the term *asphaltum* is from more-recent Greek times, but the two terms are often used incorrectly among engravers and printers in the 18th and 19th century. Asphaltum is part of some etching grounds.

Assignats—One may wonder what relevance a discussion of a foreign currency has to a text on American paper money, but a history of this currency can serve as a good model of what happens when a country adopts a fiat currency. In 1791 the French government confiscated land from aristocrats and issued paper notes called "assignats" which paid interest on the properties. Land was auctioned off in exchange for these notes and inflation rose to 13,000% by 1795. The assignats became virtually worthless and public confidence in the money evaporated. Napoleon replaced the assignats with the gold Franc, and this ushered in a century of prosperity for the French. When the Socialists came to power in the 1930s, they removed the gold backing of the currency and France went back to a fiat money. In a dozen or so years, the Franc lost 90% of its value. Fiat money is not backed by reserves of gold or silver. Its acceptance depends on the faith of the public. The problem with this system is that the issuing authority can print as much money as its wants, and many governments, ours included, lack the restraint needed to keep a currency at a steady value. Governments like to print more money when revenues fail to keep up with its expenditures. As the money supply increases, the purchasing power of the currency decreases. This is inflation, and our Founding Fathers understood the concept very well. Thomas Jefferson warned us in 1791 that "banking institutions are more dangerous to our liberties than standing armies," meaning that we had allowed private banks to take control over the issuing of our currencies, and abuses of this power had damaged our economy. See *fiat money*.

B

Backing-up—Removing a hollow or mark from the face of a plate by blows from the peen of a hammer applied to the back, the face being laid on an anvil or stake. This mode is used by engravers in obliterating lines too deep to be treated by the scraper or burnisher. Also called "knocking-up."

Banking—Raising a wall of wax around an etching on a die to form an embankment to hold the acid used in biting-in. See *biting-in*.

Beating-Engine—(1) A machine having a revolving cylinder with sharp blades operating against a concave surface similarly armed, to cut rags into *stuff* for paper-pulp. Two or more of such engines are employed—a *washer* operates coarsely upon the stuff; a *finisher* completes the work. The first brings the material to *half-stuff*, in which condition it is

bleached; hence the terms "half-stuff engine," and "Stuff engine." (2) The machine in which cotton or other fibers are beaten to rid them of dust and to loosen them so that it may make a *bat* suitable for other operations in due course.

Bedpiece—Either a die or a plate, whether copper or steel, that is intended for use in a transfer press. The design on a hardened steel die may be transferred to a soft steel roll, in which case the flat die is the "bedpiece" in the press. Similarly, the design on a hardened steel roll may be transferred to a specific area or position on a soft steel plate, in which case the plate is locked down in the bed of the transfer press and becomes the "bedpiece." The word was in common usage among engravers in the 19th century but seems now to be archaic. Special bedpieces used in making white-line engravings were called "laydowns." See *white-line engraving*.

Binder—A heavy-bodied drying oil or resin which is added to an ink to bind the pigment to the paper.

Biting-in—Eating away soft steel or copper by the corrosive action of an acid. An etching point or burin is used to cut a line or a design through a ground and expose the underlying steel. When this is finished, a wall or barricade of wax is raised around the design to hold in a dilute acid. For a copper plate, the preferred etchant is one part nitrous acid to five parts water. For a steel plate, the etchant is one part pyroligneous acid, one part nitric acid, and six parts water. When a sufficient depth is attained for the lighter tints of the etching, the acid is removed and the surface washed and allowed to drain. The parts having sufficient depth are now "stopped out" by a varnish of Brunswick-black laid on with a camel-hair brush. When the varnish is dry, another biting-in will deepen the lines of the parts not "stopped out," and when these parts are deep enough for the second tint, the varnish is removed, the plate dried, etc. This is repeated as many times as necessary. The wall of wax is then removed, the surface of the plate is cleaned with turpentine, and the plate is sent to the printer for a Proof impression.

Bitumen—Bitumen is a mixture of organic liquids, primarily highly condensed polycyclic aromatic hydrocarbons that form a viscous, black, sticky, and flammable material. Bitumen is a part of the asphaltum mentioned above. It is chemically distinct from tar. Most geologist believe that bitumen is formed from ancient microscopic algae that grew in lakes and oceans and were deposited by gravity in the mud at the bottom of those bodies of water and were subsequently subjected to heat and pressure which transformed them into their present form. Bitumen is also a light-sensitive material and was used in early photography. It was also a waterproofing material often used as a mortar between stones in constructing buildings and as a waterproof sealant on the roofs of buildings. There is some evidence that the use of bitumen on the buildings of Carthage caused it to burn completely in 146 BC at the hands of the Roman army. See *asphaltum*.

Blankets—Blankets, also called *felts*, are made of high-grade wool cloth, which is white. Blankets were used in the intaglio press where they were placed between the two rollers and on top of the paper to be impressed. Their function is to soften the strong pressure of the rollers and to distribute the pressure over the entire surface of the plate. Usually, three or four blankets were used. Virgin blankets are not used until they have been run through the press many times to compress the cloth and make its texture like felt. Hence, the process is named *felting*. New blankets are still too soft to make good impressions, especially if the engraving has fine lines or dotted lines. In modern times, oil cloth has replaced wool as the material of choice since it offers several advantages.

Bleaching—The use of strong oxidizers to break down the fine particles of extraneous organic materials that adhere to the cellulose and linen fibers in bank-note paper, giving them a yellowish cast. Bleaches whiten the paper by this chemical action.

Bleeding—The spreading or running of a pigment by the action of a solvent, such as water or an oil. If an engraving is printed in an ink that bleeds, the lines will not be distinct. Bleeding through is a similar phenomenon in which an ink printed on one side of a note "bleeds" through to the other side.

Bodied Linseed Oil—Linseed oil that has been thickened by heating it until the desired viscosity has been achieved.

Boodle—A slang term, first used in the American criminal underground and then later enjoyed as vogue among the New York newspapers in the 1820s. A "boodle" was a package or roll of counterfeit paper money. Numerous examples of its use are found in George A. Thompson Jr.'s paper "Counterfeit Jargon of the 1820's," in *American Speech*, volume 71, no. 3, (Autumn 1996), pp. 334 and 335. A "boodle carrier" was a member of a two man team that went around a town passing counterfeit notes. The two men were supposed to act as if they were strangers to each other. The "boodle-carrier" gave one note at a time to the "shover," who made a trifling purchase, got his change in good money, met the "boodle-carrier" secretly, gave him the good change, and was given another bill. This way, if the "shover" was caught, the "boodle" remained safe.

Brazier—Small iron containers, often basket-shaped, that hold burning coal. In early times, a brazier was sometimes used to heat printing plates or warm dies. In intaglio printing, the brazier is placed beneath the iron bed of a hand-roller press to warm the plates and in turn to warm the thick ink that is laid on with a dabber. Since braziers burned organic materials and had no way to exhaust the smoke, they increased the carbon monoxide levels in closed rooms. The Sawyer-Man Electric Light Company of New York placed a dynamo and electric stoves in the Bureau of Engraving and Printing in 1887, solving some of the problems the bureau was having with sooty air and carbon monoxide.

Bronzing—The application of a finely pulverized bronze powder to an area of a bank note or bond that contains a mordant to "fix" the bronze to the fibers of the paper. Figures and letters were sometimes printed in drying-oil and then dusted with bronze powder. Bronzing was hated by the plate printers for its abrasion of the plates and difficulty in printing. One frequently sees a bronze ring around a portrait vignette on fractional currency.

Brown Backs—A name given to the $5 notes of the series of 1882 National Bank Notes, Second Charter Period, First Issue. The backs of these notes were printed in brown ink, hence the name "brown backs." The Chief of the Bureau of Engraving and Printing, Edward O. Graves, criticized the "cheap and open design" of the geometric-lathe work on the backs of the notes. Compared to the previous issue of 1875 (First Charter Period), which was printed in two colors and featured a beautifully engraved vignette called "The Landing of Columbus," the brown backs were dull and unimaginative. The face of the notes featured a portrait of James A. Garfield, the 20th president, who was assassinated after only 6 months and 15 days in office.

Burin—Another name for a graver. These are tools used for engraving or chasing metals or other materials, such as fine hardwoods. They are made of steel which, for cutting other steels, is tempered to a "pale straw" color, the first color that appears in "drawing the temper." Burins are made of different shapes. Those intended for line engraving are square or rhomboidal in their cross-section, and the end is sharpened by grinding it off obliquely. The bottom of the burin is called the *belly* and is angular for line engraving. For engraving lettering it is frequently rounded or flat, and for heavy work it is without a handle and is driven by a hammer. There is a special burin for stipple engraving.

Burnisher—A tool used by the engraver to eliminate cuts, scratches, layout lines, dots, dents, or other superficial blemishes, and to tone down lines that were cut too deeply. The engraver's burnisher is made of steel, elliptical in cross-section, and comes to a dull point. This steel point is usually mounted in a wooden handles. If a burnisher does not efface the problem to the engraver's satisfaction, it may be necessary to go deeper into the metal surface using a scraper. The burnisher was also used by craftsmen to make watermarks in wire. See *scraper*.

C

Calendering—In the paper industry, calandaring is a finishing process by which paper is passed through a series of metal rollers under pressure. This gives the surface texture of the paper a flat, smooth, glazed, or polished texture, depending on variables such as pressure, temperature, moisture content, paper composition, and the type of coating or glaze. The rolls are usually made of chilled iron or steel. At the microscopic level, paper surfaces are a tangle of loose cellulose fibers. The heavy pressure of a calendar roll presses these fibers down against the body of the paper and compresses the surface.

Calipers—A tool resembling a pair of dividers or ice tongs used in making corrections on an intaglio plate. By opening the calipers and placing one tip in the center of the area to be corrected on the front of the plate or die, the other end of the calipers will come down automatically on the corresponding position on the back of the plate, leaving a small shallow mark. When the damaged area on the front of the plate is corrected by scraping down past the offending lines, an indentation will be found on the corresponding location on the back of the plate, and this can be "knocked-up" with a hammer to give a smooth appearance to the area on the front. The smooth area can then be re-engraved.

Cam—The projecting part of a rotating wheel or shaft that strikes a lever or follower at one or more points on its circular path, translating rotary movement into a reciprocating movement. The rosettes of a rose engine are cams.

Cellulose—Until very recent times, bank-note papers were always made of cellulose, whether cotton or linen or other plant fibers were used. Cellulose is important in the plant world as it combines with other carbohydrates to give rigidity to cell walls. It is a structural polysaccharide derived from beta-glucose. It forms a straight-chain polymer of beta-d-glucopyranose units (called residues) which form microfibrils that consists of 2,000 to 14,000 residues that crystallize as a stack of flat ribbon-like structures. Hydrogen bonds are the important structural glue that keeps the strands in their place and make the substance insoluble in water and in aqueous solutions. Paper is made by collecting cellulose fibers in water (pulp) and then compressing the individual fibers into a mat or sheet.

Chromium Plating—Hexavalent chromium is an exceptionally hard metal which can be electroplated onto steel bank-note plates to improve their resistance to abrasion and corrosion. However, chromium plating was not generally used until the 1920s at the Bureau of Engraving and Printing and then later at other bank-note companies.

Chemicograph—This was a "house" term used by S. Straker & Sons in London during the American Civil War. It probably refers to an early form of the electrotyping process. It was used to print the backs of certain Confederate currency. See *electrotype*.

Colophony—A translucent, brittle substance produced from natural pine oleoresins. Also called Pine Rosin. It is used in varnishes and inks and on the bows of stringed instruments. Rosins and resins are the same thing. See *resins*.

Color—A term used in line engraving to designate the brightness or contrast created when a line is cut deeper or wider so it holds more ink and will print as a darker or more-vivid black. If an image is cut with lines that are too shallow and fine, the resulting print may be said to lack sufficient color. It is the depth, width, and spacing of lines that give the depth of color by holding more ink in a given area of an image.

Couching—To take a sheet of paper off the mould and lay it out to dry. There were many different ways to couch paper. In China some workers would place the sheets of wet paper on the slanted sides of special stone ovens; others merely laid the sheets on the grass. In Europe, when paper was not made using Asiatic fibers and was often made without sizing, it was necessary to place felts between the individual sheets. The person doing this work is called the "coucher." Couching was common work in bank-note paper plants well into the 19th century.

Counter—An Arabic or Roman numerical figure that represents the denomination of a bank note, often placed within an engraved geometrical shield or escutcheon and printed in a contrasting ink. The counters are usually placed at the four corners of a note, but many variations are found. Ornate counters were believed to make counterfeiting more difficult.

Cycloid—As a wheel travels in a straight line, a fixed point on the circumference of that wheel will trace a familiar curve known as a cycloid.

Cycloidal Engine—An instrument used by engravers in making what is called *machine work* upon the plates for bank notes, checks, etc. The lines have a general cycloidal form, being generated by a point revolving around a moving center, or, what amounts to the same, are cut by a graver-point to which a revolution is imparted, the plate traversing below in a straight line, a waved line, a circle, ellipse, or other figure. The line is thus compounded of two movements, and a wavy or complex interlacing figure of absolute regularity is produced as a guard against counterfeiting; it being impossible to produce such work by any means other than such a tool. [This definition was written before photography came into its own.]

D

Daguerreotype—The photographic process invented and then further developed by Daguerre during the years 1824 to 1839, resulting in the use of the camera for the exposure of a silver or silvered plate, sensitized by exposure to fumes of iodine in a dark chamber. The latent image was developed by fumes of mercury and fixed by sodium hypo sulfite. In 1829 Daguerre was joined in his experiments by Niepce, who had been experimenting for 15 years with an allied process in which a plate coated with asphaltum was exposed in a camera and the image developed by dissolving away the unalloyed portions by oil of lavender. Niepce died in 1833, Daguerre in 1851. The Daguerreotype camera was used by some bank-note engravers to take a photograph of a subject in the size he wanted to engrave, transferring the impression to a gelatin film, and tracing the outline of the impression with a sharp-pointed etching tool. The traced outline was then filled with red chalk and placed on a die under pressure, leaving a rough impression which the engraver filled out with a burin. This procedure was done later with a tin-type photograph. See *asphaltum*.

Dandy-roller—A sieve-roller beneath which the web of paper pulp passes and by which it is compacted and partially drained of its water. That is its primary function, but it may be used for *water-marking* the paper. The paper passes through the dandy-roller and to the first pair of pressing-rollers.

Daniell's Battery—The double-fluid battery invented by John Frederick Daniell, FRS, who received the Copley medal from the Royal Society in 1837 for this invention. It consists of a jar of glass or earthenware in which fits a plate of copper bent into a cylindrical form. Within the copper is a porous cup containing the zinc. The liquids used are a saturated solution of copper sulfate in the outer cell and of sulfuric acid in the inner cell or porous cup. To the copper a perforated shelf or jacket is often attached for holding crystals of copper sulfate so that the solution may be kept at the point of saturation. Such batteries were used in the earliest electroplating processes.

Desensitize—The non-image areas of a lithographic stone or zinc plate must be treated chemically to make them water-receptive and ink-repellent. These treated areas are said to be *desensitized*. The best desensitizing agent is acidified gum arabic. This material does not actually react chemically with the stone or metal plate but is adsorbed on the surface. When a pressman "washes off the gum," he removes a good amount of the gum, but a thin film of absorbed gum remains, and it is this film that desensitizes the non-image areas. See *gum arabic*.

Die—A small square piece of steel which varied in size and thickness according to the needs of the engraver. To prepare a die, the engraver made a drawing or took a photograph and reduced it by the Daguerreotype camera to the size he wanted to engrave. He then traced the outline of the reduced impression by placing over it a thin sheet of gelatin and using a fine etching tool. When the tracing was complete, he filled the lines with red chalk. He then took a polished die, heated it slightly, and applied an etching ground made of asphaltum, burgundy-pitch, and beeswax. The die was then held over a gas jet or a wax taper until the surface was black. After the die cooled, it was ready to receive the red chalk tracing, which was placed on the die reversed and then subjected to the pressure of the roller press. The gelatin was removed and the outline, as traced in red, was observed on the ground. All this work was done on soft steel. The engraver then used his burin to engrave the outline through the ground and onto the steel. After the engraving was finished, a proof impression was made on India paper on the hand-roller press. If approved by the superintendent of the department, the die was then hardened by packing it in some form of carbon (leather, bone charcoal, etc.) and placing it in a muffle furnace.

Die Sinking—In bank-note companies, die sinking was a term referring to the making of a medal, such as the head of a famous person, that would be used in medallion engraving and placed on a note for added security. See *medallion lathe*.

D-Roller—The D-roller was an important improvement in the evolution of the hand-roller plate press. It had one flat side and allowed the bed and plate to return by a counterweight after passing beneath the periphery of the roller. The D-roller is said to have been invented by Jacob Perkins.

Driers—Substances which accelerate the rate at which oxygen is absorbed into an oil, varnish, or vehicle, drying it out. Driers are usually organic salts of lead, manganese, or cobalt, such as lead acetate, manganese sulfate, or cobalt chloride. Iron, cerium, and zirconium can also be used, but they are less efficient. The drying time of an ink is important. If inks dry too fast, they may dry on the plate and give poor impressions. If they dry too slowly, they may cause the varnish to penetrate the paper and result in poor binding of the pigment when the ink finally dries. By adding more or less drier, a good balance can be reached. Driers come in liquid and paste form. The paste is considered the better form, especially for inks that are to be kept stiff, because it does not thin the ink as does the liquid form.

Drying Room—A special room, often in the loft of a building or on an upper floor, in which printed bank notes or other papers are hung on thin slats of wood or cords to dry. Drying rooms were usually heated, especially during the winter. Drying rooms were necessary during the period when our currency was printed by the "wet intaglio" method. Intaglio inks take a considerable time to dry by evaporation.

E

Electroplating—Electroplating is the method of applying a metallic coating to another material. The basic technology was developed before the discovery of electrons and a clear understanding of the chemical reactions involved. A modern explanation of electroplating theory begins with four basic definitions:

1) A Cathode: the negative electrode in electrolysis, where negative electrons are created and positive ions are discharged. The cathode is the object that is going to be plated, such as a bank-note plate.

(2) An Anode: the positive electrode in the electrolysis, where negative ions are discharged and positive ions are created. It is made of the same material as the plating metal.

(3) An Electrolyte: a conducting medium where the flow of current is seen as the flow of matter. The electrolyte is an aqueous solution of an acid, a base, or a salt.

(4) Direct Current: the electricity that passes from the anode to the cathode. In early years, it was supplied by a Smee, Danielle, or Bunsen battery.

As the direct current passes from the anode through the electrolyte, it brings positive ions of the plating metal to the cathode. It is then joined with negative electrons created by the cathode and transforms into the metal coating. The metal coating bonds to the cathode and thus the electroplating process is complete.

Electrotype—A copy, usually in copper, of a form or type. An electrotype is superior to a stereotype, as copper is harder and more durable than type-metal, and the plates take less room in storage. A page of the type is covered with wax, which is driven into the interstices by powerful pressure. The face of the wax mold is covered with plumbago to give it a metallic surface to which the metal will adhere. The positive pole of a battery is attached to the mold, and the negative pole to a copper plate, and both are placed in a bath of copper sulfate in solution. The copper is deposited on the face of the mold in a thin film, which increases in thickness as the process continues. After this *shell* attains the thickness of a heavy sheet of paper, the mold is removed from the bath and the shell detached and strengthened by a backing of type-metal. This process is called *backing-up*. As type-metal will not readily adhere to copper, the back of the shell is coated with tin, and the shell is then placed face downward on a plate, by which it is suspended over a bath of molten type-metal. When it has attained the requisite heat, a quantity of the type-metal is dipped up and floated over the back of the shell. When cold, the plate is reduced to an even thickness by a planning machine. For printing, it is mounted on a wooden backing. Another method of obtaining electrotype plates from letter-press forms uses a mold of gutta-percha brushed with graphite and then immersed in the electroplating bath. Gutta-percha is also used for obtaining intaglio molds and then cameo impressions from woodcuts for printing. Electrotyping was used in a few cases of early counterfeiting.

Emulsion—A mixture of two immiscible or unblendable substances, such as butter, mayonnaise, or an intaglio emulsion ink. Emulsions are stable colloidal suspensions consisting of an immiscible liquid held in another liquid by a substance called an emulsifier. During the 19th century it was found that intaglio inks could be improved for certain press operations and stability if certain materials were added to the ink. Intaglio and copper-plate inks became increasingly complex.

As resins and other chemicals were added to intaglio inks, separation of the dispersed phase from the continuous phase became a problem until it was discovered that surfactants (soaps) could be used to achieve long-term stability.

Epicycloid and such—An epicycloid is a curve generated by a point on the circumference of a movable circle which rolls on the inside or outside of the circumference of a fixed circle. It is very different than a simple cycloid, which is made when a circle travels in a straight line and any fixed point on its circumference forms a familiar arch-like curve. In epicycloids, the curves traced by a fixed point on a wheel rolling on the inside of a moving circle is called a hypotrochoid, and the curves traced by a fixed point on a wheel rolling on the outside of a moving circle is called a epitrocoid. There are also prolate cycloids and curtate cycloids. These can only be understood by taking hallucinogenic drugs.

Etching—An engraving executed by a pointed tool and acid upon a soft-steel die or plate previously covered with an etching ground. An etching ground is also frequently called a "varnish." The ground is then smoked with a gas jet or a candle until it is uniformly black. Lines are cut through the ground with a burin to expose the metal of the plate. Acid is then applied which eats into the exposed areas. The longer the plate is exposed to the acid, the deeper the bite and therefore the stronger the line. Different depths are achieved by covering some lines with acid impervious varnish (called "stop-out") and biting other lines a second or third time. The art is believed to have originated in Germany, judging by its name *etzen*; but the earliest known practitioners were Albert Dürer, a German, and Agostino Veneziano and Parninegiano, Italians, contemporaries of Dürer. In recent times, James Smillie, Christian Rost, and William J. Brown did masterful work in etching bank-note plates.

Etching Ground—Although different formulas were used, a common etching ground consisted of four parts asphaltum, twp parts burgundy-pitch, and one part beeswax. These ingredients were melted, combined, and allowed to cool to the point where they could be tied up in a silk rag. The silk rag was then rubbed over a soft steel die to give a thin but uniform film of ground to the surface. See *die*.

Etchants—Acids that eat away or corrode the soft steel or copper exposed by the etching point. Nitric acid was used for copper, and both nitric acid and pyroligneous acid were used for steel.

F

Fecit—The third-person singular present indicative of *facio*, a Latin infinitive meaning "to make," "to construct." Small inscriptions at the bottom of bank-note vignettes sometimes have this word before the engraver's last name, indicating that he engraved the vignette or painting. See *sculpsit*.

Felt—Woolen blankets used for packing around the printing rollers in an intaglio press. In paper-making, felts were sometimes placed between the wet sheets of paper as they were taken off the mould. See *blankets*.

Fiat Money—*Fiat*, in Latin, was the third-person present subjunctive of the infinitive *fiori*, meaning "to become," and therefore *fiat* means "let it be done." Borrowed from the Latin, it means, as an English noun, "an arbitrary order or decree." Fiat money, therefore, has an arbitrary origin and does not represent a certain amount of precious metals. It is printed by the government, or by a sovereign, and is accepted by the consent of the people. Fiat money, which is usually paper notes, cannot be exchanged for coins of precious metal or for bullion. Governments are free to print as much fiat money as they wish, but increasing the money supply decreases its purchasing power, creating inflation. When inflation goes too far, and the public loses confidence in its money, a condition called "hyperinflation" takes over, and the government has to print more and more money. The United States has managed to avoid hyperinflation by switching between a fiat money and a gold standard over the past 200-odd years. Americans had a fixed gold standard between 1785 and 1861. We then switched to a fiat currency (the "greenbacks") that lasted from 1862 until 1879, then switched again to a fixed gold standard from 1880 until 1914. Most of the world's currencies are fiat money. See *gold standard*.

Fiber Paper—A bond or bank-note paper that has distinctive short fibers distributed either randomly or in a regular pattern. The purpose of using fibers is to make counterfeiting more difficult. The fibers are added to the paper while it is in the pulp stage and cannot be removed from the finished paper without leaving obvious signs of tampering. Jute, silk, and synthetic fibers have been used for this purpose.

Free-Banking Period—The period between 1837 and 1863, when several states allowed banks to be organized and operated with virtually no regulation. These banks issued their own bank notes, leading to a wildering variety of notes. Notes were typically discounted in value when presented for payment at different banks depending on the reputation of the issuing bank and its location. Notes of distant banks, especially those in rural locations, were discounted more heavily. The period came to an end during the Civil War, when the government decided to issue its own currency and to tax notes issued by private banks. See *Wildcat banking*.

Fugitive Ink—An ink that is easily dissolved when exposed to a solvent. If the background of a figure or letter is printed in a fugitive ink, any attempt to remove the figure or the letter by using a solvent will also remove the background, giving evidence of tampering. Fugitive inks were used more in stamp designs than on currency.

Furnish—A term for all the materials (except water) which go into the paper-making machine.

G

Gelatin—Common gelatin is translucent, solid, colorless, tasteless, and odorless. It is made from the prolonged boiling of connective tissue, such as skin, hides, tendons, ligaments, cartilage, and bones of animals, mostly pigs and cows. When made from certain membranes in fish, it is called *isinglass*. Gelatin is an irreversibly hydrolyzed form of collagen and is classed as animal protein. It played an important role in early photography. In a jelly form it is called *size* and is used as a coating for bank-note paper to give it stiffness and improve the printing characteristics of the paper. Since animal sizing undergoes putrification rather quickly, alum was added to the tub to reduce the smell and prolong the usefulness of the size. Without alum, secondary amines form, and one of them, called "putrecine," is well known for making people vomit.

Geometric Lathe—Like the cycloidal engine, the geometrical lathe is used for making complicated patterns of interlacing lines to form an additional guard against counterfeiting. It is adapted for more-delicate and minute work than the cycloidal engine, and is the means by which the stars, rosettes, and ornamental tablets, escutcheons, and borders are produced around the denominational figures of a bank note. A graver whose normal motion is in a curve is made by the motion of the plate to form a waved line with any character of convolutions; this is crossed by one of somewhat varying character, and this by a third, and so on, forming an interlacing but regular pattern. If the plate moves in a direct line, this pattern will have a general straight direction, but if the plate is moved in a circle, a circular pattern of interlacing lines will be the result. By cams and other devices the general trend of the figure may be made to fill a circle, ellipse, shield, or tablet of any form. Fair examples of the work may be seen on the face and back of the "greenbacks" of the United States, and it will be seen that the spaces and escutcheons consist of a series of concentric designs. Machines of this character are very costly and possessed by few establishments, including the Treasury Department and the major bank-note companies in New York, for instance. The difficulty of counterfeiting is much increased by the use of this machine.

Glazing—Early American bank notes were usually printed on ordinary writing paper. Our forefathers did not want their writing paper to have nearly perfect smoothness and high gloss. It would have been very difficult to write on such papers with a quill pen, which requires some resistance from the surface of the paper to draw the ink from the quill. Yet, handmade paper that has been sized and dried is still too rough to make a good writing paper. Therefore, to reach a happy medium, paper was often glazed by polishing it with a stone such as agate or onyx or by rubbing it with a polished piece of glass. Such work was usually done by women. By the 17th century it was common to glaze paper with a heavy metal glazing hammer that was operated by a mill's waterwheel. This was replaced by a glazing press which passed paper between two metal drums that were turned by a gear and exerted the necessary pressure. These calendaring machines were probably of Dutch origin. See *calendering*.

Gold Standard—This was a commitment by participating countries to fix the prices of their domestic currencies in terms of a specified amount of gold. In 1834 the United States fixed the price of gold at $20.67 per ounce and it remained at that price until 1933.

Grailling—An area, usually in the background behind a portrait vignette, that has been ruled with very closely spaced lines, like the one behind George Washington on our $1 notes. This was a security feature since counterfeiters usually could not copy the grailling without having the lines "fill in," giving evidence of their work.

Graver—A burin or hand-held cutting tool used by an engraver of metals. See *burin*.

Gresham's Law—The principle that "good money drives bad money out of circulation." The principle was known even in ancient times but is named after Sir Thomas Gresham, a financier in Tudor times and the founder of the Royal Exchange. He wrote to Queen Elizabeth in 1558 that "all your fine gold was convayd ought of this your realm," meaning that foreigners had taken English gold coins out of the country. The principle is most easily understood in the context of metal coins. If the circulating currency consists of gold coins and coins of a base metal, the public will horde the gold coins, knowing that they always retain their value, and transact their business in the base metal coins. In other words, "the bad money drives out the good."

Guilloche—An ornate geometrical pattern of lines made by engine turning for the purpose of making it extremely difficult, if not impossible, to duplicate by hand, thereby giving additional security to bank notes and other valuable documents. The earliest use of guilloching appears on watch cases made by a rose engine in 1624. Rose engines, geometric lathes, and cycloidal engines have all been used to make guilloches.

Gum arabic—Also known as acacia gum, this carbohydrate polymer is collected as exudates from cuts made on the branches of a sub-Saharan tree, *Acacia senegal*. The exudate is a complex mixture of low-molecular–weight polysaccharides and high-molecular–weight glycoproteins. Gum arabic was first used as a plate desensitizer by Alois Senefelder, the inventor of lithography, and in 200 years nothing better has been found to serve this function. It is a hydrophilic material that repels ink from the non-image areas of a lithographic stone or zinc plate. Gum arabic is so named because it consists of calcium, potassium, and magnesium ions with arabic acid, a high-molecular–weight carbohydrate that contains carboxyl groups (-COOH). It is these carboxyl groups that are responsible for the adsorption to a metal or stone surface. See *desensitize*.

Gum water—A solution of water and gum arabic, usually acidified with phosphoric acid, used to *desensitize* the non-image areas of a metal plate, such as zinc, in lithographic or anastatic printing. See *anastatic printing*, *desensitize*, and *gum arabic*.

Gutta percha—Natural latex obtained from *Palaquium gutta* and several other species of evergreen trees that grow in East Asia. It was first made known in 1843 by Dr. Montgomery, a surgeon in the British Army stationed in India. He was rewarded by the London Society of Arts with a gold medal. Latex is obtained by natives making incisions in the appropriate trees and collecting a juice in bowls or coconut shells. This juice consolidates within a few minutes after being drawn and is then molded by hand into oblong bricks. It was much used in the 19th century in electrotyping and making molds for electroplating. Gutta percha was also proposed for use in making an improved bank-note paper by adding threads or strips of the pulp during manufacture, the claim being that the heat from the drying cylinder in the paper-making machine would fuse the gutta percha to the fibers of the paper and make them inseparable. A Letter of Patent No. 61,321 was granted to L.M. Crane of Ballston, New York, on January 22, 1867, for this purpose. We know gutta percha today as the covering of golf balls.

H

Hardening—A soft-steel die is hardened by placing it in a closed crucible that has been packed with animal charcoal and taken to a red heat in a furnace, then removed and allowed to cool. This process deposits carbon atoms on the surface of the steel. The carbon migrates down into the steel a few microns. This is called "case hardening." Cyanide liquids replaced the old Perkins crucibles used in hardening steel at the Bureau of Engraving and Printing in the 1880s.

Harmonographs—Devices which cut or trace complex patterns, called Lissajous figures, which are the result of two or more simple harmonic motions. Typically, the devices use pendulums whose motions decay by the force of gravity. The design of the double elliptical harmonograph became the principle on which the Thomas De La Rue "Fantasy Lathe" was built. *See chapter 16.*

Hatching—Parallel lines which are cut close together in an engraving with the aim of giving an effect, en masse, of a gray or dark tone. The lines may be intersected by other parallel lines, a technique known as cross-hatching, or they may be over-hatched. Parallel marks made with a dry point were used on geographical maps to represent water.

Hypotrocloidal—See *Epicycloids and such.*

I

Ink Mill—To reduce the size of the pigment particles intended for an ink, the raw pigment is mixed with a vehicle by stirring. This mixture is then added to an ink mill. There, a thin film is forced between steel rollers turning at various speeds and clearances. These rollers break the pigment into minute particles that become saturated with the vehicle. Driers, binders, and other modifiers can be added during this process.

Intaglio Press—A broad term for the hand-roller press used in printing engraved plates. The Dutch, Germans, and Italians have contended for the honor of the invention of this press, but it is usually attributed to the Italian sculptor and goldsmith Tomasso Finiguera, a Florentine who was working in the 1460s. The first intaglio presses were probably operated by the pressure of a screw. The rolling press is said to have been invented in 1545. Wooden presses gave way to iron presses, and the D-roller was another major improvement. Hand-roller presses were eventually replaced by steam-powered presses, which were replaced in turn by electric-motor presses. Modern web presses are very large, complex machines with multiple impression cylinders, rollers, inking fountains, doctor blades, wiping units, photocell monitors, and computer controls to coordinate the functioning of all the parts.

J

Jute Fibers—A long, soft, shiny, white to brown fiber made from certain plants. It is second only to cotton in the volume produced and the variety of its uses. Because it is made from both the cellulose of the plant and lignin, it is called a ligno-cellulosic fiber. Fabric woven from jute threads is called "burlap" in the United States. Red and blue jute fibers were used by the Wilcox paper mills to form a distinctive band ("localized fibers") in the paper used for bank notes. It was replaced in U.S. currency by silk about 1880.

K

Koniacker—(also spelled "coniacker" and "coneyacker") A slang term used in both the United States and Canada for a dealer in counterfeit money. The origin of the term is found in a road named "Cogniac Street" that splits off Highway 213 just north of Freighsburg in Missisqoi County, just above the Vermont state line, running northeast to the village of East Dunham. It was along this street that several persons lived and engaged in engraving and printing counterfeit notes. Americans, such as the infamous William Stuart, made trips to this area to buy counterfeit notes. The people on Cogniac Street became known as "coniackers," and the term was soon used to mean any counterfeiters. The earliest use of the term in print appears to be an explanation offered in the *Commercial Advertiser*, 26 January, 1827, page 2, column 3: "It is, we believe, solely a police term, and signifies a dealer in counterfeit money." The early slang dictionaries do not document the origin of the term, although Farmer and Henley (1905) suggest "coniack" is a play on the word *coin*, meaning money, and *hack*, meaning to mutilate. An alternate theory is that "coniacker" comes from the practice of buying the most expensive bottle of brandy a tavern might have (cognac) in order to cash a large bill.

L

Lake—The lake pigments are made by precipitating some organic coloring matter, usually a coal-tar dye, upon some suitable mineral base, such as barites. The term "lake" has its origin in the Italian word *lacca*, which was the term used by the old Italian dyers to designate the scum that accumulates at the top of the vats when dyeing with lac dye. Tin and aluminum oxides were used to fix the color on cloth, and the scum consisted of these colored oxides. The Italian *lacca* evolved into the English term "lake" to designate a mineral salt colored by a dye. Many lake pigments are fugitive, because the dyes involved are unstable when exposed to light. Most of the lake pigments have fascinating histories. Carmine Lake, also called crimson lake, was originally produced from the cochineal insect, native to Central and South America. After the Spanish conquered the Aztec Empire, they encountered warriors garbed in an unknown crimson color. Cochineal became the second most valuable export from the New World, after silver, and the Spanish dyers guarded the secret of its production for centuries.

Legal Tender—Originally, this was a legally valid currency that could be offered in payment of a debt and that a creditor must accept. The courts have addressed this issue several times and a newer definition makes legal tender "a payment, that by law, cannot be refused in settlement of a debt denominated in the same currency." There are many exceptions to this definition. A merchant, for example, does not have to accept a large denomination note if it is his stated policy (posted by a sign that is clearly visible to the public) not to do so.

Letter-press Printing—The ordinary printing by raised type. Also called relief printing. The ink on the paper is a flat film and is not raised. The opposite effect is found with intaglio printing, where the printed image leaves ink raised above the surface of the paper and can be felt by touch.

Linen Paper—The use of linen paper in Europe appears to have originated in Germany, about the 11th or 12th century, the exact date being undeterminable. There was a German paper mill at Nuremberg in 1396, one in England in 1343, in France in 1314, and in Italy in 1367. Linen paper, however, is known from much older dates. John Tate had a mill at Stevenage, England, in 1496, but the manufacture was much increased by Spielman in 1588. Whatman's mill was established at Maidstone in 1770. In modern times, linen is usually combined with cotton to make bank-note paper.

Linseed Oil—The oil that is pressed or extracted from flax seeds. It is the most widely used vegetable drying oil and is the main ingredient of printing-ink vehicles. See *bodied linseed oil*.

Lithography—The design is drawn or transferred to the polished, or grained, flat surface of a stone, usually Bavarian limestone, with a greasy crayon or ink. The design is chemically fixed on the stone with a weak solution of acid and gum arabic. In printing, the stone is flooded with water which is absorbed everywhere except where repelled by the greasy ink. Oil-based printer's ink is then rolled on the stone, which is repelled in turn by the water soaked areas and accepted only by the drawn design. A piece of paper is laid on the stone and it is run through the press with light pressure, the final print showing neither a raised nor embossed quality but lying entirely on the surface of the paper. The design may be divided among several stones, properly registered, to produce, through multiple printings, a lithograph in more than one color. A transfer lithograph (French *autographie*) employs the same technique, but the design is drawn on special transfer paper and is later mechanically transferred to the stone. A zincograph is the same technique but employing a zinc plate rather than a stone.

Lissajous Figures—A family of figures produced by the interaction of two sinusoidal curves, the axis of which are at right angles to each other. This is another way of saying they are the patterns formed when two vibrations along perpendicular lines are superimposed. These figures were first studied by the American mathematician Nathaniel Bowditch in 1815 and later in much greater detail, independently, by Jules Antoine Lissajous in 1857. The mathematics of these figures is of interest to geometric-lathe operators. By changing the a/b ratio in a simple parametric equation, they can create ellipses, parabolas, straight lines, and complex figures based on such geometries. This has allowed computer graphics to replace the geometric lathe on bank-note designs.

Livering—The solidifying of printing inks when stored. It is caused by chemical reactions between the ingredients. The solution to this problem is to reformulate the ink to avoid "incompatible" ingredients.

M

Medallion Lathe—A mechanical engraving device that moves a tracing needle horizontally across a coin or medal in lines that are spaced very closely. The tracing needle is mechanically linked to an engraving point that reproduces the portrait or image by making the lines have a greater or lesser separation in direct proportion to the height of the parts of the image that lie above the surface of the coin or medal. The machines of Asa Spencer (1817), Christian Gobrecht (1818), Achille Collas (1830), and Joseph Saxton (1829) are all improvements upon an apparatus originally described in a French work, the *Manuel de Tourneur*, published in Paris in 1816. The machine patented by John Bate (1832) is considered to be a modification of the Saxton machine based on ideas Bate took unethically from discussions with Saxton. The medallion-engraving machine can be linked to a pantograph to reduce the size of the engraved picture, making it suitable for use on bank notes as an additional deterrent against counterfeiting.

Metameric Inks and Optically Variable Inks—No, these weren't available in the 19th century, but there is so much confusion about these two types of ink that a brief discussion is warranted. Metamerism is the principle by which two inks that have matching colors under one set of light conditions may appear quite differently under a different set of light conditions. This has to do with the physiology of the human eye and the fact that we have only three color receptors (cone cells) so that all colors are reduced to sensory quantities, called the tristimulus values. Each cone cell reacts to the cumulative energy from a broad range of wavelengths. Surface colors may appear differently depending on the product of the spectral reflectance curve of the material and the spectral emittance curve of the light source shining on it. In incandescent light, two socks may appear to be black, but when you walk into a room lighted by fluorescent lamps, one of them may be dark blue. Incandescent and fluorescent lights have different wavelength distributions and these interact with the differences in the spectral reflectance curves of the two different sock colors. Therefore, one can print the figure "20" in a mesmeric ink on a design feature that is printed on a bank note in a metamerically matching ink. Under ordinary light, a person will not see the "20" figure, but under a red filter, it becomes readily visible. Optically variable inks, also called "color-shifting inks," are made by adding microscopic flakes from a thin-film coating that is ground up to form particles that are usually less than 10 microns in diameter. Inks made this way shift their color when observed at a 45-degree angle. This is a different physical phenomenon from metamerism.

Mica Flakes—The micas are a group of transparent silicate minerals, such as muscovite, that cleave into thin sheets. The sheets can be broken easily into small flakes. These flakes were sometimes added to paper during its manufacture, especially in colonial times, to give additional security to paper money. Such flakes were visible to the naked eye in the finished paper but did not detract from its appearance. Mica is a tough mineral and does not wear down easily. Since the mineral was readily available to anyone, its value as a security device was limited.

Mill—(1) A cameo impression made on a soft-steel roller from an engraved die on a hardened-steel roller. This soft steel die, or "mill," is then hardened and used to impress other rollers or a bank-note plate. See *bed piece*. (2) A common 19th century American term for a counterfeiting factory. (3) A term for a grinding device used to reduce the size of dry pigment particles for making ink.

Mollette—A metal template used in a geometric lathe to guide a cutter or milling machine in making lettering or simple designs that will stand in relief against a contrasting intaglio background. The mollette is usually quite a bit larger than the letters or designs to be printed, so a pantograph is used to reduce the letters or designs to the correct size. See *pantograph.*

Mordant—(1) A chemical that can be added to paper, fabric, or leather to "fix" a dye on cellulose or linen fibers. Without a mordant, the dye would soon wash out. (2) A chemical, such as an acid or ferric chloride, which "bites" or eats into a metal surface. Intaglio prints are made by covering a thin metal plate, called a die, with a protective ground, then drawing through the ground with a sharp metal point. This exposes the metal surface below the ground. The die is then immersed in a mordant that eats away some of the exposed metal and creates the outline of the image.

N

Non-Newtonian Fluids—Intaglio inks are non-Newtonian fluids because their viscosity varies with the shear rate. If the viscosity decreases with increasing shear rate, the fluids are called "shear-thinning." If the viscosity increases as the shear rate increases, the fluids are called "shear-thickening." A Newtonian fluid, such as water, continues to flow regardless of the forces acting on it.

O

Overprints—A figure or word printed on a finished note, usually in a contrasting color to the rest of the note. This was believed to add additional security to the note, but any counterfeiter could easily duplicate an overprint note. Sometimes, notes of a branch office were overprinted to indicate a different location.

P

Pantograph—A device for enlarging or reducing a drawing or lettering. Its invention is attributed to Christopher Scheiner, a Jesuit priest, in 1603. It has since undergone many modifications and improvements. A simple pantograph consists of four metallic rulers which are connected by metal pins to form the shape of a parallelogram. A drawing is placed on a table and the outline of the impression is traced by a point connected to one of the rulers of the pantograph. According to the way the rulers have been set, the tracing is either enlarged or reduced and is drawn on a clean sheet of paper by a pencil or pen. An alternate, primarily British spelling is "pentagraph."

Patent Green Tint—A green anti-photographic, chemically stable bank-note ink made with chromium sesquioxide. The ink was invented by Thomas Sterry Hunt, who then sold the patent rights to George Matthews. Mr. Matthews sold the American patent rights to Tracy Edson, for use at the American Bank Note Company in the United States. Matthews still held the Canadian patent rights and subsequently leased them to George Bull Burland for use in the British-American Bank Note Company in Montreal. The American Bank Note Company printed the "greenbacks" with this ink and started a tradition in American currency that has lasted for more than 140 years.

Photoengraving—The process of transferring an image photographically to a plate which is then etched for printing. The basic technology of photoengraving began with the experiments of a Frenchman, Joseph Niepce, about 1813, and resulted in the first permanent photograph in 1826. Niepce coated a copper plate with a photosensitive asphaltum and placed on it an etched drawing of a portrait. He then exposed the surface of the plate to bright sunlight. This light hardened the asphaltum in the open, unprotected areas, while the protected areas, being the lines covered by the ink drawing, were not affected. These protected lines were developed in oil of lavender and white petroleum to create an image on the copper plate. This image was then etched into the plate, and from the intaglio image, prints were made on a copper-plate press. There were many technical developments over the years, the most important of which are taken up in chapter 16. Photoengraving, which is a real danger to security printing, began to develop around 1891 and 1892. See *asphaltum.*

Photolithography—Any of several processes for transferring an image onto a lithographic stone. Photolithography was seldom used in producing bank notes, although the technical developments in photoengraving and photolithography were closely followed by the bank-note industry for fear that these processes might enable counterfeiters to duplicate the fine line engraving used in currency, especially that of the geometric lathe.

Pigments—Pigments are the solid particles that give color to an ink. Inorganic pigments are usually made by the precipitation of two chemicals mixed together, such as lead acetate and sodium bichromate to make chrome yellows. The solid residue that is left after the solution if poured off becomes the pigment. The pigment is then washed, filtered, dried, and poured into drums. Some pigments require a little more chemistry, such as the iron blues. There, a ferrous salt solution is mixed with a sodium ferrocyanide solution, forming a white precipitate of ferrous ferrocyanide. That needs to be oxidized in an acid solution by sodium chlorate before you have a pigment. To make the chrome greens, one mixes the chrome yellows with the iron blues. Pigments are not simply taken from a drum and added to a vehicle to make an ink. The size of the pigment particles is usually much too large to do that, so pigments must first be ground in an ink mill. Organic pigments require much more complex chemistries that are beyond the scope of this book.

Planchettes—Small discs of colored paper added to the pulp of bank-note paper to form a distinctive safeguard against counterfeiting. Planchettes were developed by the American Bank Note Company and most of them were either red or blue. Modern planchettes sometimes fluoresce under UV light.

Planographic Printing—Planographic printing means printing from a flat surface, as opposed to a raised surface (as in relief printing) or an incised surface (as in intaglio printing). The process utilizes the property that water will not mix with oil or grease. Lithography and offset lithography are examples.

Plumbago—An old name for graphite. Plumbago was given its name from the supposition that *plumbum* (lead) was its base.

This turned out to be a mistake, as it is a form of carbon and has nothing at all to do with lead. The substance is used in electrotyping and in making devices for watermarks.

Polymerization—A process of bonding monomers, or "single unit" molecules, to form larger molecules called "polymers." Some of these reactions are simple and need only heat to drive them. Other polymers require many different steps for synthesis. A good example of polymerization is found in the heating of linseed oil to make a printer's varnish. The heat causes individual molecules to bond to each other so they form polymers, changing some of the physical properties of the linseed oil, such as viscosity, or "body." Cellulose is a natural polymer made from glucose monomers (a sugar).

Proofs—A Proof is a trial printing. Plate or die Proofs were made at different stages of the construction of a bank-note plate so the engravers or others could see if corrections were necessary. Proofs were usually made on cardboard or India paper using a small press called a "proofing press." In a large bank-note company, such as the American Bank Note Company, engravers normally worked on several different plates at any one time. These plates or dies were sometimes stored in a vault to allow the engraver to work on other plates of higher priority. When conditions permitted, a plate might be taken from the vault, cleaned, and a Proof "pulled" to see what remained to be finished.

Pyroligneous Acid—Also called "wood vinegar," it is an acid produced from the dry, destructive distillation of wood. Its principal components are acetic acid and methanol. Wood is burned slowly in an airless chamber of firebricks or iron so that it is reduced to charcoal, rather than to carbon dioxide, water vapor, and ash. A device within the chamber collects and cools the vapors. The condensate consists of pyroligneous acid and a tarry substance. The earliest pyroligneous acid works were established in 1813 in Glasgow, Scotland. Pyroligneous acid one part, nitric acid one part, and six parts of water are combined to make an etchant for steel plates. The English engraver Charles Warren is credited with the discovery of this etchant.

Q

Quenching Vats—After a die, roll, or plate has been hardened, it is handled by tongs and allowed to cool in the air before it is dipped in a quenching vat containing brine or an oil having a high flash point. The purpose of quenching, of course, is to cool down the metal object still further without cracking it or causing too much shrinkage. A die that cracks on being quenched has to be discarded. 19th-century workmen could estimate the temperature of a plate by its color after it was removed from a furnace.

Queer—A term used frequently in the 19th-century criminal subculture to refer to counterfeit money. The *Oxford English Dictionary* cites "queer" for counterfeit paper money as early as 1812 and 1821. To "shove the queer" means to pass counterfeit money, and the term was used in America as early as 1847. "Queer" is listed in George Washington Matsell's *Vocabulum*, America's first dictionary of criminal slang, published in 1859. Matsell was a chief of police in New York City. A "queersman" was a counterfeiter in the broadest sense. Although the term was much used in the public media

to refer to counterfeit notes, it is never found in the formal charges of court documents. See *Koniacker*.

R

Redemption Bureau—A department of the Treasury, created by Section 24 of the National Currency Act of June 3, 1864, which accepted torn, mutilated, worn-out, or partially burned paper money issued by the government and sent to the bureau by national banks for replacement with new or almost new notes of equal value.

Re-entering—The deepening of lines by a burin, either in repairing a plate or for perfecting an engraving. Since wear is not even on a plate that has been printing many times, typically only the fine lines need to be re-entered when repairing a plate. Engraved lines are V-shaped in cross-section. As a plate wears down, the depth of the "V" is also cut down, resulting in thinner and thinner lines, so the image loses tone.

Relief Etching—An etching that leaves the image, whether line or character, standing above the rest of the matrix. The image areas are usually covered by an acid resist. The etchant (acid) eats away the unprotected areas, leaving the image standing above the rest of the matrix.

Relief Printing—"Relief" means that the printing surface, such as a letter or a line, stands above the matrix (plate or block) in which that letter or line was cut or cast. Usually the matrix is a wood block in which the lines or characters to be printed are drawn on the flat surface of the matrix and the surrounding material is cut away by knives or gouges so that only the lines or characters are left standing in relief. When inked, only the areas standing in relief will print on paper. The areas between the lines or characters will be left unlinked and will not print. The ink is printed on the paper as a flat film.

Resins—A viscous liquid hydrocarbon secretion of many plants, particularly coniferous trees, used for varnishes and vehicles in printer's inks. Most resins contain volatile fluid terpenes. Resin and rosin were synonymous terms.

Roll—A die of cylindrical form with a center shaft to fit into the holding assembly on a transfer press. Rolls were used in transferring steel-die engravings for bank-note printing. The design is first engraved on a die of soft steel, which is then hardened and placed on the bed of a transfer press. A roll of soft steel is locked into the jaw of the press and rolled back and forth, under great pressure, to "take up" the design in cameo. The roll is then hardened and, at the appropriate time, is placed back in the transfer press, locked in its jaws, and rocked back and forth, again under great pressure, to transfer the design to a bank-note plate. Nothing is left to chance in these operations, and the precise alignment of the die and the roll, or the roll and a plate, is made possible by very small dots made on their surfaces which are guides to the operator. He uses a strong glass, usually a jeweler's loupe, to align the dots and make sure that incised lines do not overlap or extend into areas where they should not go. A hardened roll is kept in storage by the bank-note company and may be used again on other plates.

Rose engine—An early ornamental turning lathe which was soon adapted for engraving complex figures on metal and is therefore of interest to bank-note students. Rose engines are lathes which have a device or devices for reciprocating the headstock both to and from the operator and can also move the headstock longitudinally in line with the bed, and can do this either one movement at a time or both. The name "Rose Engine" comes from the use of "rosettes," which are rotating wheels that have a pattern machined on their periphery. As they rotate, the rosettes impart a movement to a follower (called a "touch" in American usage, or a "rubber" in British usage) which is pressed against the rosette. The rosettes therefore act as a cam and cause the entire mandrel assembly and headstock to rock upon a pivoting point as the engine rotates. The combination of motions is relayed to a diamond or hard steel point which cuts a series of geometric figures on a soft steel or copper plate. The plate can then be hardened and transferred in the usual way to make the ornate figures seen on bank notes.

Roulette—A hand-held device, similar in appearance to a thick writing pen, but in place of the nib there is a U-shaped device that holds a wheel on an axle. The wheel is made of soft steel and engraved with letters to form a sentence or phrase on the periphery. The wheel is then hardened by the usual method used in bank-note engraving and mounted in the device. The wheel can be run across a soft-steel bank-note plate, or on an oblong die, to leave its impression of lettering. The roulette can be mounted in a ruling machine to give straight, evenly spaced lines of print on a soft-steel bank-note plate or die. William Rollinson mounted a roulette in a ruling machine to engrave a background of waved lines on a plate of Alexander Hamilton in 1805, creating quite a sensation among American engravers. Benjamin Chamber of Washington, D.C. patented a roulette on June 12, 1847, as Patent No. 5,155.

Ruling Machine—A machine that allows an engraver to place parallel lines at equal distances apart with great accuracy. The lines may be either straight or wavy in various degrees. Many of the early machinists made ruling engines, such as Wilson Lowry, Asa Spencer, Christian Gobrecht, David Mason, Joseph Saxon, W.L. Ormsby, Percy Heath, etc. Lowry also introduced the diamond-cutting point in engravers' ruling machines. Modern ruling machines are capable of ruling glass diffraction gratings several thousand lines per inch, but the limit in 19th-century ruling machines for metal engraving was about 100 lines per inch. 19th-century machines adjusted the spacing between lines by means of a screw turned by a geared crank on the side. To achieve accuracy, it was necessary to make screws with external threads of great precision.

S

Scraper—A special tool for gouging out engraved lines on the surface of a die or plate. The area is then rubbed with an engraver's stone to leave a smooth, rounded depression. This depression is then hammered out from the reverse side of the die with a special hammer or punch. If the scraped area is large, calipers are used to carefully mark the limits of the area on the backside of the die to be hammered. After burnishing and polishing, the area is ready to be re-engraved. See *calipers*.

Sculpsit—A Latin term meaning "he (or she) engraved it." Abbreviated "Sc." or "Sculp." Like *fecit*, it is sometimes seen in a small inscription at the bottom of a bank-note vignette, followed by the last name of the engraver, indicating that he engraved the piece. See *fecit*.

Security Fibers—The idea of using various materials added to paper pulp to make a distinctive finished paper for bills of credit appeared as early as 1764 when mica flakes were added to the paper of the notes of six different colonies and in some Continental notes. James Wilcox received a patent in 1866 for making paper with a localized band of jute fibers. The Legal Tender Notes of 1869 contained randomly distributed jute fibers.

Security Threads—A security thread is a strip of material placed either on the surface of a bank note or document, or embedded within the paper and visible when the note or document is held up to the light. Zenas Crane invented a bank-note paper in 1844 that used parallel silk threads running throughout the note. In 1935 Stanley Chamberlain invented a security thread made of one of the cellulose esters or ethers, such as cellulose acetate, coated with a very thin, electrically-conductive metal, such as gold or silver, and assigned the patent to Portals, Ltd., a British company. In modern notes, security threads are now high-technology security devices, usually serpentined or woven into the paper, giving a "windowed" effect, and often display a micro-printed text on their highly reflective metalized surfaces.

Seigniorage—Simply put, this is the difference between the value of money and the cost to produce it. It may take only a few cents to print a $100 bill, but its value in all transactions is far greater. Seigniorage is therefore a form of revenue for a government and can be used to finance a portion of their expenditures without having to collect taxes. When a government or national bank issues notes, the seigniorage becomes an interest-free loan that the holders of the currency (the public) make to the issuer (the government). Theoretically, the issuer must buy back the currency at face value when it is worn out, and this negates the revenue (seigniorage) earned when the currency was put into circulation. Actually, the issuer of the notes can make investments with seigniorage revenue and keep the profits (if there are any) when it buys back the worn-out notes. Looked at another way, seigniorage revenue is a form of tax paid by the holders of the currency and redistributes wealth to the issuer. See *fiat money*.

Shinplasters—"Shinplasters" was a derogatory name given to fractional currency or merchant's scrip. According to the *Oxford English Dictionary*, the term refers to the poor quality of paper used to print such notes. During the Civil War, both armies are said to have used shinplasters during the winter. With a bit of starch and some water, these notes could be used to make paper-maché-like plasters to be fitted under socks or stuffed into shoes or boots to warm the shins. John Russell Bartlett's *Dictionary of Americanisms*, published in 1849, defines a shinplaster as "A cant term for a bank-note, or any paper money." It probably came into use in 1837, when the banks suspended specie payment and paper money became depreciated in value. Shinplasters were also called "shinnies" during the Civil War and after.

Short Ink—An ink which possesses a buttery consistency and breaks off with short strings when it is drawn out between the fingers.

Shovers—People who knowingly pass counterfeit money. They usually make small purchases and pay with large denomination bills so they can receive a substantial amount of genuine money in change. The shovers usually worked on a percentage basis and split their earnings with a "boodle-carrier." Most of the "counterfeiters" mentioned in early newspapers were actually just shovers. Many shovers were women, since they were less suspicious than men. After the 1870s, many of the middlemen in the counterfeiting business in New York used Italians, German Jews, Poles, or other foreigners to "shove the queer." They were told that if they were caught, they should speak only in their native tongues, so lawyers could argue that they did not understand English and therefore could not recognize counterfeits from real money. See *boodle*.

Siderogaphy—The system invented by Jacob Perkins about 1817 in which an engraving made on soft steel is hardened, then taken up on a roll of soft steel by use of a transfer press. The roll is then hardened and used to transfer the impression to a bank-note plate of soft steel. There are two distinct technologies involved in this process. First, Perkins had to learn how to harden soft steel and then do the reverse. Secondly, he had to build a transfer press capable of rocking a steel roll back and forth over a die or a bank-note plate using great pressure and very precise accuracy. The first technology—the case hardening of soft steel and the annealing of hard steel—were already known to European craftsmen. The second technology—building a transfer press—was without precedent and entirely due to his mechanical genius. A transfer press makes white-line engraving possible, and as long as the bank-note companies had the only transfer presses, the white-line engravings on bank notes could not be duplicated by a counterfeiter. See *hardening*, *roll*, *transfer press*, and *white-line engraving*.

Size or Sizing—In making bank-note paper during the 19th century, gelatin or starch size was added to paper by dipping sheets in a tub. This "tub sizing" was one of the most difficult processes in paper-making and resulted in a lot of spoilage. The purpose of sizing is to close the pores in paper, making the surface of the paper resistant to moisture and preventing the "feathering" effect and "bleed through" when it is printed. Sizing also makes the paper stiffer. Paper can also be sized by adding a sizing agent to the stuff in the vat. This method is called "engine-sizing." See *gelatin*.

"Snags"—An early 19th-century American slang word for counterfeit bank notes. The origin of the word is unknown.

Spider Press—Another name for the common hand-roller press. The term is derived from the resemblance between the radial lines of a spider's web in nature and the spokes of the wheel that turns the rollers on such a press.

Spirographs—A type of cyclical machine that makes hypotrocloidal and epitroicloidal figures. Like the Geometric Pen of Count Suardi, it works by gears alone. There are no cams. The device was invented in 1962 and is a toy used to make geometric curves. Not used in bank-note or other security printing. Spirographs can be used to make figures that resemble Lissajous curves, but they differ by being bounded by circles whereas Lissajous curves always occur within square boundaries.

Star-Wheel Press—A hand-roller press with four or more spokes at the end of the shaft that turns the rollers. It is more a term of British usage than American. See *spider press*.

Stipple Engraving—A form of engraving in which dots are made instead of lines, and these are closer, deeper, and larger, in accordance with the depth of color desired. This mode of engraving originated in 1769 with Jacob Bylaert of London and was practiced in France during the last part of the 18th century, but did not arrive at its greatest excellence until the early part of the 19th century. The art is greatly admired for the softness and beauty of its finish in representing flesh and statuary. Bartolozzi is said to have brought it to perfection. Scenes and portraits are made through a ground on the plate, and then bit-in by acid. Afterward they are modified, deepened, and enlarged by the action of a burin whose belly is concave so as to present the point more vertically to the face of the plate than usual in line engraving, where the belly is slightly convex. The acid makes little pits in the plate, which hold the ink when printing. There is very little, if any, stipple engraving in bank-note work.

Stop-Out—Any chemical, including water, which stops the action of an acid "biting" or enlarging lines cut into the exposed bare metal of an etching plate. Jacques Callot perfected the technique of using multiple "stoppings-out" to achieve subtle differences in light and shade.

T

Tack—The adhesiveness of an ink for another surface. It is the "stickiness" or pull observed when tapping the ink out onto a piece of paper.

Thixotropic inks—Thixotrophy is a physical property of certain colloidal gels which enables them to become fluid under conditions of shear or pressure. When the shear or pressure is stopped, the fluid returns to a solid state. Ballpoint inks are sometimes thixotropic, meaning they are a "solid" in the pen's reservoir, but become liquid when the ballpoint revolves and places shearing forces on the ink.

Tint—A tint of any color is made by adding white lead or some other white mineral, such as titanium dioxide, to the original color. This lightens the color. A bank note can be printed on a tinted paper in which the color is uniform throughout the whole surface. In such cases, the dye is added to the pulp in the vat and mixed by machine to get an even distribution.

Tint Plate—A plate that lays down a second color to a bank note. Normally, in printing U.S. currency, the first color printed is green, and the "tint plate," coming next, lays down any other color. Tint engraving refers to the engraving of the tint plate. Tint also refers in a general sense to any color. See *Patent Green Tint*.

Tooling—In the 19th-century practice, a finished bank-note plate usually had to be "tooled" by special machines to restore the correct dimensions of the plate and to flatten the surface. Hammering out depressions or badly cut lines can appreciably alter the precise dimensions of a plate by thinning the hammered area and pushing metal in all directions.

Cutting the plate to a precise dimension is one example of tooling. Any deviations in the thickness of a plate had to be corrected so that plates would print correctly in a four-plank flat-bed power press, such as the Milligan press. All of these corrective processes are termed "machine tooling."

Transfer Press—A special press invented by Jacob Perkins for use in his *siderographic* system of intaglio bank-note printing. The press was later much improved by Cyrus Durand, who used a compound-lever system. A hardened-steel die is locked into an adjustable bed-plate of the press. A soft steel *roll* is placed above the die. Both the die and the roll have been given small marks at their edges so that the operator, using a jeweler's loupe, can align the two pieces perfectly. The die and roller being then brought forcibly together, the roller is made to revolve over the die, and the metal of the roll is pressed into all the engraved lines of the die, forming a relief or cameo impression of the engraving on the roll. The roll is then hardened and is ready for delivering an impression to a bank note plate. The pressure of the roller upon the plate in the transferring machine is given by a system of compound levers and is regulated by the pressure upon a foot lever, or by a hand lever. This rolling is repeated several times by rocking the roll back and forth until the steel of the roll has insinuated itself fully into every line of the die, whether heavy or light. The larger machines can give a pressure of 35 tons. Small transfer presses were also built which could fit easily on top of a bench. They delivered much less pressure, usually about 8 tons, so repeated rolling was necessary. See *intaglio*, *roll*, and *siderography*.

Triple-Paper—A kind of bank-note paper invented by Sir William Congreve. It was made in three layers with the first layer being a thin white paper, over which was added a lightly colored paper with a watermark, and finally this was overlaid by another thin white paper. The three-layers of paper were subjected to enough pressure to form an inseparable sheet. When held up to the light, a person could see the light tint of the middle layer and its watermark. The watermarks were very elaborate and difficult to make. The middle sheet could also be made of several colored strips of paper. These features made the triple-paper very difficult to imitate. Congreve had proposed the use of this paper to the Bank of England, but for reasons never fully given, the bank rejected the paper.

Trocloidal—See *epicycloidal and such*.

V

Vatman—One of three workmen assigned to a paper-making vat. The vatman stands on a platform in front of the vat, holding a mould firmly by its two narrow sides. Around this mould is a removable deckle, or frame, which acts as a little fence around the edges. The vatman plunges the mould perpendicularly into the fibrous liquid substance, and when it is well submerged, he turns it face upwards and lifts it horizontally out of the vat. By this action, the mould is completely and evenly covered by the macerated linen and cotton, and the stock not needed for the particular thickness of the paper being made is allowed to run over the sides of the mould and back into the vat to be used again. The vatman then shakes the newly formed sheet on the mould from side to side and then from back to front. These motions cross and matt the fibers, making the paper equally strong in both directions and at the same time expelling excess water from the mould. The wires of the mould retain the fibers but allow the water to drain through as in a sieve. The vatman then removes the deckle, which leaves the sheet of paper sharply cut along the edges of the mould, and then passes the mould to the "coucher." This completes one full cycle of the vatman's work.

Varnish—(1) In many inks, the vehicle consists only of linseed oil which has been "bodied," meaning polymerized, by heating until the desired viscosity has been achieved. This bodied oil was called "varnish." In the oldest methods of making varnish, the raw linseed oil was heated in a pot, ignited, and allowed to burn for five minutes or so. The flames were extinguished by a close-fitting lid, after which stale bread was introduced by tongs and stirred around in the oil until the bread was browned but not burnt. This was supposed to remove "grease" from the oil. Peeled onions were also used for this purpose. (2) Another name for an etching ground. (3) A compound, such as "Brunswick Black" used to "stop out" the action of an etchant while it is "biting-in." See *bodied linseed oil* and *etching ground*.

Vehicle—The liquid portion of an ink that holds and carries the pigment and provides workability or press-drying properties and binds the pigment to the paper after the ink has dried.

Vignette—A portrait or scene used on the face of bank notes. Some portrait vignettes are placed within an engraved oval frame in the center of a note, but there are no formal esthetic rules that dictate the design or placement of a vignette. A vignette was used to increase the security of a bank note in the belief that low-skilled engravers could not match the artistry of professionals. Counterfeiters were fond of buying up obsolete notes from "broken banks" so they could cut out the original vignettes and paste them on counterfeit notes. Such vignettes were usually run through a calendering press to thin the paper so the pasted vignette would not be so readily noticeable. Pete McCartney did this sort of "cut and paste" counterfeiting while he was in Canada. See *calendering*.

Viscosity—19th-century definition: The resistance to flow of an oil, varnish, or ink, caused by internal friction between the particles comprising them. Low-viscosity fluids pour easily and quickly. High-viscosity fluids pour slowly. Intaglio inks have higher viscosity than letterpress inks. Viscosity became important when power presses replaced the hand-roller presses. Power presses operate at higher speeds, so a thinner, softer, and lower-viscosity ink was required.

W

Wiping—In all intaglio printing methods, the plate is wiped after it has been inked. The white lines of a print will not appear clean unless this is done very thoroughly. Wiping was traditionally done by hand using muslin cloths. After this was finished and the plate appeared clean, it was wiped again by placing whiting on the palm of the hand and wiping in alternate directions. Wiping was an art, and those that did it successfully got better impressions from their plates. The earliest attempts at mechanical wiping were not successful and it took several years to improve the method. Even on the flat-bed power presses, plate printers preferred hand wiping to mechanical wiping.

White-Line Engraving—An engraving in which white lines appear against a contrasting background. There are several ways to make white-line engravings, depending on the type of design needed. For example, a denomination figure is made one way and a fine-line geometric figure is made another way. When a geometric lathe is used to make an ornate figure, a special thin die is used, usually about 1/16 of an inch thick and slightly longer in both directions than the design to be made. The figure cut by the geometric lathe is intaglio, or recessed below the surface of the die. All the lines are cut to the same depth. Next, the area lying just outside the geometric design is cut away. Nothing inside the geometric figure is cut out. This die is then curved by a machine around a roll and hardened. This intaglio roll is then rolled back and forth over a bed piece. The bed piece, or "laydown" as it was later called, takes up the design in relief, the black lines of the original figure becoming "white lines" in this operation, because they now stand above the surrounding surface. This relief roll is now used in the same manner as an ordinary roll in transferring the design. On the relief roll, the interstices (the areas between the relief lines) are impressed below the surface of the plate. When the plate is inked, everything is covered with ink, but when the plate is wiped, only the interstices retain the ink. The relief lines are wiped clean of ink and will appear as "white lines" when the plate is printed. It is easy to understand how white lines appear if you remember that the bed piece or laydown reverses the image cut by the lathe. The intaglio lines originally cut by the lathe are made to stand in relief, and it is the areas between those lines that are now sunk below the surface of the plate.

Whiting—(1) Before the days of photography, the surface of a steel die was sometimes coated with a white-chalk paint, called "whiting," and a scene or portrait was drawn by hand upon it. The engraver then followed this outline with his burin, modifying it as necessary. (2) Whiting was also the name for a white-chalk powder that the plate printers put on their hands to do the final wiping of an inked plate before printing. Chalk comes from the decomposition of plankton. Plankton concentrate calcium from sea water, taking it from the normal 0.4% to about 40% concentration. When plankton die, their bodies accumulate on sea floors in large volumes of sediment and their calcium shells are transformed into calcium carbonate. In the 19th century, chalk was usually removed from ground deposits by axes. This chalk was pulverized into a fine powder in a ball mill to remove fine dirt and impurities such as quartz and feldspar. "Soft" chalk

was preferred in the printing trade and was washed several times while it was being pulverized.

Wildcat Banking—This term is generally understood to mean the period (1837 to about 1863) and the practice in which banks were not regulated by Federal law and could issue their own notes. Theoretically, a bank was obligated to back up its notes with some kind of specie, either gold or silver coins, which would be exchanged for their notes on demand. Unscrupulous bankers realized that if they located their banks in remote areas, or as it was said, "where the wildcats lived," then it would be more difficult for customers to redeem notes for coins, and the bankers wouldn't have to keep as much specie on hand. Thus there would be more profit as fewer notes would ever actually be redeemed. Michigan bankers of this period are often cited as particularly unscrupulous because some of them opened banks only to collect deposits before vanishing. Worthless notes issued by these remotely located banks were termed "wildcat notes." Although the term "wildcat banking" is often used as a synonym for "free banking," this is not technically correct. Not all banks during the free-banking period were operated unscrupulously. "Wildcat banking" should be used only to indicate those banks that were operated with intent to defraud the public. See *free-banking period*.

X

Xylographic—Pertaining to or designating wood engraving. Wood engraving was often used in the 19th century to illustrate magazines and books and was used to a very limited scale in printing merchant's scrip, including their early fractional notes. Wood engraving was used in China to make the printing plates for the earliest paper money and also the earliest counterfeiting. Waterman Lily Ormsby did xylographic printing before turning to the more lucrative business of bank-note engraving.

Y

Yield Value—The yield value is technically the minimum amount of shear stress required to initiate the flow of ink. This is a rheological parameter that is only important in modern ink chemistry. It was not used in the 19th-century ink labs.

Bibliography

Books and Pamphlets

Altman, Sol. *U.S. Designers & Engravers of Banknotes and Stamps.* Unpublished manuscript in the New York Public Library, 1961.

American Bond and Currency Detector Company. *The American Bond Detector and complete History of the United States Government Securities.* Washington, D.C.: American Bond and Currency Detector Company, 1869.

Amstutz, Noah Steiner. *Amstutz' Hand-Book of Photoengraving.* Chicago, Illinois: Inland Printing Company, 1907.

Enlargement and revision of the 2nd edition of Harry Jenkins' *Manual of Photoengraving*, 1896.

Andersen, Gunnar. *Banknotes: Principles and Aesthetics in Security Graphics.* Translated from the original Danish. Copenhagen, Denmark: Danmarks National Bank, 1975.

Anonymous. *The Book of Trades, or Library of the Useful Arts.* London, England: London Tabart & Company, 1804. Reprinted by Jacob Johnson, 1807. Reprinted by Dover Books, 1992.

Anonymous. *The History of a Little Frenchman and His Notes. Rags! Rags! Rags!* Philadelphia, Pennsylvania: Edward Earle. Published by the author, 1815.

Apps, E.A. *Printing Ink Technology.* London, England: Leonard Hill Books, Ltd., 1961.

Association of Banks for the Suppression of Counterfeiting. *Annual Reports of the Board of Managers (1854–1865).* Boston, Massachusetts: The Association.

Baker, General La Fayette Curry. *History of the United States Secret Service.* Philadelphia, Pennsylvania: Privately printed by L.C. Baker, 1867. Bowie, Maryland: Reprinted by Heritage Books, 1992. New York, New York: Reprinted by Ams Press, 1973.

Baker, General La Fayette Curry. *Official Report of L.C. Backer, U.S.A., to Salmon C. Chase, Secretary of the Treasury, in the Case of Stuart Gwynn and S. M. Clarke: Also, the Minority Report of the Treasury Investigating Committee, with Accompanying Documents.* New York, New York: Henry A. Oliver, 1864.

Baker, W.S. *American Engravers and Their Works.* Philadelphia, Pennsylvania: Gebbie & Barrie, 1875.

Ball, Douglas B. *Financial Failure and Confederate Defeat.* Urbana, Illinois: University of Illinois Press, 1991.

Bankers' Magazine and Statistical Review, The. *Acts of Congress Relating to Loans and the Currency from 1842 to 1864 Inclusive.* New York, New York: The Bankers' Magazine and Statistical Review, 1864.

Barger, M. Susan and William B. White. *The Daguerreotype: Nineteenth-Century Technology and Modern Science.* Baltimore, Maryland: The Johns Hopkins University Press, 1991.

Bathe, Grenville and Dorothy. *Jacob Perkins, His Inventions, His Times, and His Contemporaries.* Philadelphia, Pennsylvania: The Historical Society of Pennsylvania, 1943.

Baudin, Robert. *Confessions of a Promiscuous Counterfeiter.* New York, New York: Harcourt Brace Jovanovich, Inc., 1977.

Baxter, James H. *Printing Postage Stamps by Line Engraving.* Reprint. Lawrence, Massachusetts: Quarterman Publications, Inc., 1981. Originally published by the American Philatelic Society based on serialized articles by Baxter that had been published in *The American Philatelist*, 1939.

Bazley, Thomas Sebastian. *Index to the Geometric Chuck: A Treatise upon the Description, in the Lathe, of Simple and Compound Epitrochoidal or "Geometric" Curves.* London, England: Waterlow and Sons, 1875. Published for the author in a single edition of 150 copies.

Belknap, Henry Wyckoff. *Artists and Craftsmen of Essex County, Massachusetts.* Salem, Massachusetts: Essex Institute, 1927.

Bender, Klaus W. *Moneymakers—The Secret World of Banknote Printing.* New York, New York: Wiley-VHC. Originally published in German, 2006.

Benner, Judith Ann. *Fraudulent Finance: Counterfeiting and the Confederate States, 1861–1865.* Hill Junior College Monograph No. 3. Hillsboro, Texas: Hill Junior College, 1970.

Bennett, Professor Lyman. *Observations upon the Method of Bank Note Manufacture, with Unerring Rules for the Detection of Counterfeit and Spurious Paper Currency of all Kinds.* Chicago, Illinois: Tribune Print, 1864.

Bloom, Murray Teigh. *Money of Their Own.* Port Clinton, Ohio: BNR Press, 1982.

Bloom, Murray Teigh. *The Brotherhood of Money. The Secret World of Banknote Printers.* Port Clinton, Ohio: BNR Press, 1983.

Bloom, Murray Teigh. *The Man Who Stole Portugal.* New York, New York: Charles Scriabners.

Bloy, Colin H. *A History of Printing Ink, Balls and Rollers, 1440–1850.* London, England: The Wynkyn de Worde Society, 1967.

Boggs, Winthrop S. *Ten Decades Ago, 1840–1850. A Study of the Work of Rawdon, Wright, Hatch and Edson of New York City.* State College, Pennsylvania: The American Philatelic Society, 1949.

Bowen, Francis. *American Political Economy. Including Structures on the Management of the Currency and the Finances since 1861.* New York, New York: Charles Scribner's Sons, 1870. New York, New York: Reprinted by Greenwood Press, 1969.

Bowen, Richard LeBaron. *Rhode Island Colonial Money and Its Counterfeiting, 1647–1726.* Providence, Rhode Island: The Rhode Island Society of Colonial Wars, 1942.

Bowen, Walter S. and Harry Edward Neal. *The United States Secret Service.* Philadelphia, Pennsylvania: Chilton Company, 1960.

Bowers, Q. David. *Obsolete Paper Money Issued by Banks in the United States 1782–1866.* Atlanta, Georgia: Whitman Publishing, LLC, 2007.

Bradbury, Henry. *Nature-Printing: Its Origin and Objects.* London, England: Bradbury and Evans. A lecture delivered at the Royal Institution of Great Britain, Friday, May 11, 1855, 1856.

Bradbury, Henry. *On the Security and Manufacture of Bank Notes.* London, England: Bradbury and Evans. A lecture delivered at the Royal Institution of Great Britain, May 9, 1856, 1856.

Brett, George W. *The Giori Press. A Comprehensive Study of Current Stamp Production at the Bureau of Engraving and Printing.* West Somerville, Massachusetts: Bureau Issues Association, Inc., 1961.

Brewster, Abel. *A Brief Memoir of Abel Brewster, Written by Himself, to Which are Added a Picture of Hartford, and the Form of a Will Lately Made by the Narrator.* Hartford, Connecticut: Folsom & Hurlbut. Published by the author, 1832.

Brewster, Abel. *A Plan for Producing an Uniformity in the Ornamental Part of Bank or other Bills*. Philadelphia, Pennsylvania: Privately printed, 1810.

Brewster, Abel. *An Appeal to Banks in Particular, and the Public in General*. Hartford, Connecticut: Sheldon & Goodwin. Published by the Author, 1815.

Brigham, Clarence S. *Paul Revere's Engravings*. New York, New York: Atheneum Press, 1969.

Brock, Leslie V. *The Currency of the American Colonies, 1700–1704. A Study in Colonial Finance and Imperial Relations*. New York, New York: Arno Press, 1975.

Byatt, Derrick. *Promises to Pay: The First Three Hundred Years of the Bank of England Notes*. London, England: Spink, 1994.

Buckland-Wright, John. *Etching and Engraving: Technique and the Modern Trend*. London, England: Studio Limited, 1953. New York, New York: Reprinted by Dover Publications, 1973.

Burnham, Captain George P. *Memoirs of the United States Secret Service*. Boston, Massachusetts: Laban Heath, 1872.

Byrnes, Thomas F. *Professional Criminals of America*. New York, New York: Cassell & Company, Ltd, 1886.

Carothers, Neil. *Fractional Money*. New York, New York: John Wiley & Sons, Inc., 1930.

Cazort, Mimi. *Mauro in America: An Italian Artist Visit's the New World*. New Haven, Massachusetts: Yale University Press, 2003.

Clarke, Hermann F. and Henry W. Foote. *Jeremiah Dummer, Colonial Craftsman & Merchant, 1645–1718*. Boston, Massachusetts: Houghton Mifflin Company, 1935. New York, New York: Reprinted by Da Capo Press, 1970.

Clarke, M. St. Clair and D.A. Hall. Compilers. *Legislative and Documentary History of the Bank of the United States: Including the Original Bank of North America*. Washington, D.C: Gales and Seaton, 1832. New York, New York: Reprinted by Augustus M. Kelly, 1967.

Collins, John. *The Art of Engraving on Metal, Wood and Stone*. Burlington, New Jersey: Published by the author, 1838.

Collins, M. Thomas. *Counterfeit Currency. How to Really Make Money*. Port Townsend, Washington: Loompanics Unlimited, 1990.

Comparato, Frank E. *Chronicles of Genius and Folly. R. Hoe and Company and the Printing Press as a Service to Democracy*. Culver City, California: Labyrinthos, 1979.

Compiler. *Laws of the United States Relating to Currency, Finance and Banking, from 1789 to 1891*. New York, New York: Ginn and Company, 1891. New York, New York: Reprinted by Greenwood Press, 1968.

Congreve, Sir William. *An Analysis of the True Principles of Security against Forgery*. London, England: T. Egerton. 2nd edition, 1820.

Coudert, Louis L. *Security Printing*. New York, New York: American Bank Note Company. (1929).

Coudert, Louis L. *The Romance of Intaglio Bank Notes*. New York, New York: The American Bank Note Company. 2nd edition.1925.

Cummings, Thomas S. *Historic Annals of the National Academy of Design . . . &tc*. Philadelphia, Pennsylvania: George W. Childs, 1865. New York, New York: Reprinted by Da Capo Press for the Kennedy Galleries, 1969.

Currier, John J. *The History of Newburyport, Massachusetts, 1764–1905*. Newburyport, Massachusetts: Privately printed, 1906. Somersworth, New Hampshire: Reprinted in two volumes by the New Hampshire Publishing Company, 1977.

Cutbush, James. *The American Artist's Manual, or Dictionary of Practical Knowledge in the Application of Philosophy to the Arts and Manufactures*. Philadelphia, Pennsylvania: Johnson, Waner & Fisher, 1814.

Davis, Andrew McFarland. *The Origin of the National Banking System*. Washington, D.C.: U.S. Government Printing Office, 1910 edition. Published as volume 5, no. 1, of Publications of the National Monetary Commission.

Davis, Andrew McFarland. Editor. *Tracts Relating to the Currency of the Massachusetts Bay, 1682–1720*. Boston, Massachusetts: Houghton, Mifflin & Company, 1902.

deFraine, H. G. *Servant of the House. Life in the Old Bank of England*. London, England: Constable, 1960.

deFraine, H.G. *The St. Luke's Printing House of the Bank of England*. London, England: The St. Luke's Printing Works, 1931.

Devinne Jr., Warren D. *Technological Change and Electrification in the Printing Industry, 1880–1930*. Research Memorandum 84-8(m). Oak Ridge, Tennessee: The Institute for Energy Analysis, Oak Ridge Associated Universities, 1985.

Dewey, Davis Rich. *Financial History of the United States*. 8th edition. New York, New York: Longmans, Green & Company, 1922.

Dewey, Davis Rich. *State Banking Before the Civil War*. National Monetary Commission. Washington, D.C.: Government Printing Office, 1910.

Dillistin, William H. *A Descriptive History of National Bank Notes, 1865–1935*. Person, New Jersey: Published by the author, 1956.

Dillistin, William H. *Bank Note Reporters and Counterfeit Detectors, 1826–1866*. New York, New York: The American Numismatic Society, 1949.

Domett, Henry W. *A History of the Bank of New York, 1784–1884*. New York, New York: The Riverside Press, 1884. New York, New York: Reprinted by Greenwood Press, 1969.

Drummond, A.L. *True Detective Stories*. New York, New York: G.W. Dillingham Co., 1909. Chicago, Illinois: MA. Donohue & Company, 1909.

Dumbar, Charles F. *Chapters on the Theory and History of Banking.* New York, New York: G.P. Putnam's Sons, 1897.

Dunne, Gerald T. *Monetary Decisions of the Supreme Court.* New Brunswick, New Jersey: Rutgers University Press, 1960.

Durand, John. *The Life and Times of A.B. Durand.* New York, New York: Charles Scribner's Sons, 1894.

Durand, Roger H. *Interesting Notes About Allegorical Representations.* Rehoboth, Massachusetts: R.H. Durand & Co., 1994.

Durand, Roger H. *Interesting Notes About Vignettes.* Rehoboth, Massachusetts: R.H. Durand & Co., 1995.

Durand, Roger H. *Interesting Notes About Vignettes II.* Rehoboth, Massachusetts: R.H. Durand & Co., 1996.

Durand, Roger H. *Interesting Notes About Vignettes III.* Rehoboth, Massachusetts: R.H. Durand & Co., 2001.

Dwiggins, William Anderson. *Towards A Reform of the Paper Currency, particularly in point of its Design.* New York, New York: Published by the author for the Limited Editions Club, 1932.

Dye, John S. *The Government Blue Book. A Complete History of the Lives of all the Great Counterfeiters, Criminal Engravers and Plate Printers.* Philadelphia, Pennsylvania: Dye's Government Counterfeit Detector, 1880.

Dyson, Anthony. *Etching and Engraving: Technique and Tradition.* New York, New York: Longman, Inc., 1986.

Dyson, Anthony. *Pictures to Print. The Nineteenth-Century Engraving Trade.* London, England: Farrand Press, 1984.

Edson, Tracy R. *A New Security for Protecting Bank Notes from Alterations and Photographic Counterfeits, by the Use of the Patent Green Tint.* New York, New York: W.H. Arthur & Company, 1858.

Elliot, William. *The Patentee's Manual; Containing a List of Patents Granted by the United States for the Encouragement of Arts & Sciences, Alphabetically Arranged, from 1790 to 1830.* Washington, D.C.: S.A. Elliot, 1830.

Ellis, Carleton. *Printing Inks, Their Chemistry and Technology.* New York, New York: Reinhold Publishing Company, 1940.

Ehrlich, George. *Technology and the Arts: A Study of the Interaction of technological Growth and Nineteenth-Century American Pictorial Art.* Urbana, Illinois: University of Illinois. Dotoral Dissertation, 1960.

Evans, Joan. *The Endless Web: John Dickinson & Company, Lt., 1804–1954.* London, England: Cape Publishing, 1955. New York, New York: Reprinted by Greenwood Press, 1978.

Faithorne, William. *The Art of Graveing and Etching.* London, England: Published by the author. 1662. Revised edition. 1702. New York, New York: Reprinted by Da Capo Press, 1970.

Felt, Joseph Barlow. *Historical Account of Massachusetts Currency.* Boston, Massachusetts: Published by the author, 1839. New York, New York: Reprinted by Burt Franklin, 1968.

Fenstermaker, J. Van. *The Development of American Commercial Banking: 1782–1837.* Kent, Ohio: Kent State University, Bureau of Economic and Business Research, 1965.

Ferber, Linda S. Editor. *Kindred Spirits. Asher B. Durand and the American Landscape.* New York, New York: Brooklyn Museum of Art, 2007. London, England: Printed by D. Giles, Ltd.

Ferguson, Eugene S. Editor. *Early Engineering Reminiscences (1815–40) of George Escol Sellers.* Washington, D.C.: Smithsonian Institution, 1965.

Franklin, Benjamin. *A Modest Inquiry into the Nature and Necessity of a Paper Currency.* Written in Philadelphia, Pennsylvania, and dated April 3, 1729.

Friedman, Milton. *Money Mischief: Episodes in Monetary History.* New York, New York: Harcourt Brace Jovanovich, 1992.

Friedman, Milton and Anna J. Schwartz. *A Monetary History of the United States, 1867–1960.* Princeton, New Jersey: Princeton University Press, 1963.

Gibbons, J.S. *The Banks of New-York, Their Dealers, The Clearing House, and The Panic of 1857.* New York, New York: D. Appleton & Company, 1859. New York, New York: Reprinted by Greenwood Press, 1968.

Gillingham, Harrold E. *Counterfeiting in Colonial Pennsylvania.* New York, New York: The American Numismatic Society, 1939.

Glaser, Lynn. *Counterfeiting in America. The History of an American Way to Wealth.* Philadelphia, Pennsylvania: Clinton Books, 1960. New York, New York: Reprinted by Clarkson Potter, Inc., 1968.

Godfrey, John Munro. *Monetary Expansion in the Confederacy.* Published as a doctoral dissertation at the University of Georgia, 1976. New York, New York: Reprinted by the Arno Press, 1978.

Golembe, Carter H. *State Banks and the Economic Development of the West, 1830–1844.* Doctoral Thesis, Columbia University, 1952.

Goodwin, Jason. *Greenback: The Almighty Dollar and its Invention in America.* New York, New York: Henry Hold and Company, 2003.

Gordon, Armistead C. *Congressional Currency: An Outline of the Federal Money System.* New York, New York: G.P. Putnam's Sons, 1895.

Gouge, William M. *A Short History of Paper Money and Banking in the United States. Including an Account of Provincial and Continental Paper Money to Which is Prefixed An Inquiry into the Principles of the System, with Considerations of Its Effects on Morals and Happiness.* Philadelphia, Pennsylvania: T.W. Ustick, 1833. New York, New York: Reprinted by Augustus M. Kelly, 1968.

Gouge, William M. *The Curse of Paper Money and Banking. A Short History of Banking in the United States of America, with an Account of Its Ruinous Effects on Landowners, Farmers, Traders, and on all the Industrious Classes of the Community.* London, England: Mills, Jowett and Mills, 1833. New York, New York: Reprinted by Greenwood Press, 1968.

Griffiths, William H. *The Story of the American Bank Note Company.* New York, New York: American Bank Note Company, 1959.

Groce, George C. and David H. Wallace. The New York Historical Society's *Dictionary of Artists in America, 1564–1860.* New Haven, Massachusetts: Yale University Press, 1957.

Hall, Frederick George. *History of the Bank of Ireland.* Dublin, Ireland: Hodges, Figgis and Company, Ltd, 1949.

Hansard, T.C. *Typographia: An Historical Sketch of the Origin and Progress of the Art of Printing.* London, England: Baldwin, Cradock and Joy, 1825.

Hartsuch, Paul J. *Chemistry for the Graphic Arts.* Pittsburgh, Pennsylvania: Graphic Arts Technical Foundation, 1979.

Harris, Elizabeth M. *Experimental Graphic Processes in England 1800–1859.* Reprinted from various issues of the *Journal of the Printing Historical Society,* 1968.

Harris, Elizabeth M. *Sir William Congreve and his Compound Plate Printing.* Washington, D.C.: Smithsonian Institution Press, 1967.

Hasluck, Paul N. Editor. *Engraving Metals.* Philadelphia, Pennsylvania: David McKay, Publisher, 1912.

Hass, Paul E. *Machines vs. Engraving. A Discourse on the Degeneracy of the Engraving Business by Present Day Methods.* New York, New York: Hass Bank Note Engraving Company. (1914).

Hasse Jr., William F. *A History of Money and Banking in Connecticut.* New Haven, Connecticut: Privately published by the author, 1957.

Haxby, James A. *Standard Catalogue of United States Obsolete Bank Notes, 1782–1866.* Iola, Wisconsin: Krause Publications, Inc., 1988.

Heath, Laban. *Heath's Infallible Counterfeit Detector at Sight.* Boston, Massachusetts: Laban Heath, 1864.

Heinz, Bernard. *Nathaniel Jocelyn: Puritan, Painter, Inventor.* Volume 29, no. 2. New Haven, Connecticut: Journal of the New Haven Colony Historical Society. Summer, 1983.

Hepburn, Alonzo Barton. *A History of Currency in the United States.* New York, New York: The Macmillan Company. Revised edition, 1924.

Herbert, Luke. *The Engraver's and Mechanic's Encyclopedia, Comprehending Practical Illustrations of the Machinery and Processes Employed in Every Description of Manufacture of the British Empire.* London, England: Thomas Kelly, 1837.

Hessler, Gene. *The Comprehensive Catalog of U.S. Paper Money. All United States Federal Currency since 1812.* Port Clinton, Ohio: BNR Press. 5th edition, 1992.

Hessler, Gene. *The Engraver's Line.* Port Clinton, Ohio: BNR Press, 1993.

Hessler, Gene. *The International Engraver's Line.* Cincinnati, Ohio: Published by the author, 2005.

Hessler, Gene. *U.S. Essay, Proof and Specimen Notes.* Port Clinton, Ohio: BNR Press, 1979.

Hewitt, Virginia H. *Beauty and the Bank Note: Images of Women on Paper Money.* British Museum Press, 1995.

Hewitt, Virginia H. *The Banker's Art.* London, England: British Museum Press, 1995.

Hewitt, Virginia H. and J.M. Keyworth. *As Good as Gold. 300 Years of British Bank Note Design.* London, England: British Museum Publications, Ltd, 1987.

Hildreth, R. *Banks, Banking, and Paper Currencies.* New York, New York: Reprinted by Greenwood Press, 1968.

Hill, Esquire, Clement H. *Argument of Mr. C. H. Hill, Assistant Attorney General, at the Trial of Hiram C. Whitley, Richard Harrington, and Arthur B. Williams, for Conspiracy in the Criminal Court of the District of Columbia, November 16, 1874.* Washington, D.C.: The Government Printing Office, 1874.

Hind, Arthur Mayger. *A History of Engraving and Etching, from the 15th Century to the Year 1914.* New York, New York: Houghton Mifflin Company, 1923. New York, New York: Reprinted by Dover Publications, 1963.

Holtzapfel, John Jacob. *The Principles and Practice of Ornamental or Complex Turning.* New York, New York: Dover Publications, 1973. London, England: Originally published by Holtzapfel & Company, as the last of the five volume work entitled *Turning and Mechanical Manipulation Intended as a Work of General Reference and Practical Instruction on the Lathe, and the Various Mechanical Pursuits followed by Amateurs,* 1894.

Houseman, Lorna. *The House that Thomas Built. The Story of De La Rue.* London, England: Chatto and Windus, 1968.

Hunnisett, Basil. *Engraved on Steel: The History of Picture Production Using Steel Plates.* Cambridge, Massachusetts: University Press, 1997.

Hunter, Dard. *Papermaking in Pioneer America.* Philadelphia, Pennsylvania: University of Pennsylvania, 1952.

Hunter, Dard. *Papermaking, the History and Technique of an Ancient Craft.* New York, New York: Dover Publications, 1978.

Hutchinson, Thomas. *The History of the Colony and Province of Massachusetts Bay.* Lawrence Shaw Mayo edition. Boston, Massachusetts: Harvard University Press, 1936.

Ibbetson, John Holt. *A Brief Account of Ibbetson's Geometric Chuck, Manufactured by Holtapfel & Company with a Selection of Specimens Illustrative of some of Its Powers*. London, England: Published by the author, 1833.

Ibbetson, John Holt. *A Practical View of An Invention for the better Protecting Bank Notes against Forgery. Illustrated by Various Specimens*. London, England: Published by the author, 1820.

Ibbetson, John Holt. *Specimens in Eccentric Circular Turning, with Practical Instructions for Producing Corresponding Pieces in the Art. Illustrated by Copper Plate Engravings, and Cuts referring to and Explaining the Different Figures to be Executed*. London, England: Longman, Orme, Brown, Green, and Longman. (3rd edition, 1851).

Jeffries Bank Note Company. Unnumbered (20 page) pamphlet. Los Angles: Jeffries Bank Note Company.

Johnson, David. *Illegal Tender: Counterfeiting and the Secret Service in the Nineteenth Century*. Washington, D.C.: Smithsonian Institution Press, 1995.

Kampf Graphische Maschinen. Instruction Manual and related sales brochures for a geometric lathe called the Guillochiermaschine A III "Supra" and several sophisticated pantographs, medallion ruling machines and transfer presses. Maschienenfabrik of Michael Kampf, K.G., Bad Homburg, v.d.H.

Kane, Patricia E. *John Hull and Robert Sanderson. First Masters of New England Silver*. Doctoral dissertation at Yale University, 1987.

Kecskes, Lily Chia-Jen. *A Study of Chinese Inkmaking: Historical, Technical and Aesthetic*. Chicago, Illinois: University of Chicago, unpublished M.A. Thesis, 1981.

Keyes, Harold. *Tales of the Secret Service*. Cleveland, Ohio: Britton-Gardner Printing Company, 1927.

Kisch, Sir Cecil H. *The Portuguese Bank Note Case. The Story and Solution of a Financial Perplexity*. London, England: Macmillan & Company, 1932.

Knight, Edward H. *Knight's American Mechanical Dictionary*. New York, New York: Hurd and Houghton, 1877.

Knox, John Jay. *United States Notes. A History of the Various Issues of Paper Money by the Government of the United States*. New York, New York: Charles Scribner, 1885.

Kranister, Willibald. *The Moneymakers International*. Cambridge, England: Black Bear Press, 1989.

Leavitt, Samuel. *Our Money Wars*. Boston, Massachusetts: Arena Publishing Company, 1894.

Littkefield, George Emery. *The Early Massachusetts Press, 1638–1711*. Boston, Massachusetts: The Club of Odd Volumes, 1907.

Logan, Herschel C. *The American Hand Press: Its Origin, Development and Use*. Whitier, California: The Curt Zoller Press, 1980.

Mather, Cotton. *The Life of Sir William Phips*. New York, New York: Covici-Friede, Inc., 1929.

Mather, Cotton. *Magnalia Christi Americana, or The Ecclesiastical History of New-England; From Its First Planning, in the Year 1620, Unto the Year of Our Lord 1698. (The Great Works of Christ in America)*. London, England: 1st edition. 1702. Hartford, Connecticut: Reprinted by Silas Andrus & Son, 1852.

McKay, George L. *Early American Currency: Some Notes on the Development of Paper Money in the New England Colonies, with 36 Reproductions of Engraved & Typographic Specimens*. New York, New York: Typophiles, 1944.

McShane, M. Patricia. *Wildcat Banking Practices and the Development of State Bank Supervision*. A thesis submitted to the Graduate School of Banking at Rutgers, The State University. June 1970.

MacKenzie, A.D. *The Bank of England Note: A History of its Printing*. Cambridge, England: Cambridge University Press, 1953.

Meier, Adolphus. *U.S. Treasury Notes to be the Circulation of the Country in Lieu of Bank Notes*. St. Louis, Missouri: Privately published by the author, 1861.

Melanson, Philip H. and Peter F. Stevens. *The Secret Service: The Hidden History of an Enigmatic Agency*. New York, New York: Carroll and Graf Publishers, 2002.

Melville, F.J. and John Easton. *Postage Stamps in the Making*. London, England: Faber and Faber, Ltd, 1949.

Mihm, Stephen. *Making Money, Creating Confidence: Counterfeiting and Capitalism in the United States, 1789–1877*. New York, New York: Doctoral Dissertation, New York University, 2003. UMI Dissertation No. 3089415. Ann Arbor, Michigan. 504 pages.

Mihm, Stephen. *A Nation of Counterfeiters: Capitalists, Con Men, and the Making of the United States*. Cambridge, Massachusetts: Harvard University Press, 2007.

Mitchell, Wesley Clair. *A History of the Greenbacks*. Chicago, Illinois: University of Chicago Press, 1903.

Mixer, Horace and John West. *The Age of Discovery: Or, An Infallible Guide to the Business Public; Compiled with Great Care under the Directions of a Bank Note Engraver; The Whole Forming An Infallible Theory, by which the Most Dangerous Counterfeit or Spurious Bank Notes can be Detected, No Matter How Well Executed They May Appear*. Chicago: Jameson & Moore, 1865.

Mogelever, Jacob. *Death to Traitors. The Story of General Lafayette C. Baker, Lincoln's Forgotten Secret Service Chief*. Garden City, New York: Doubleday & Company, 1960.

Monstier, Martin. *Art of Paper Currency*. London, England: Quarter Books, 1983.

Morris Jr., Thomas F. and Barbara R. Mueller. Editor. *The Life and Works of Thomas F. Morris, 1852–1898*. Privately published, 1968.

Neale, H.S. *The Art of Plate Printing*. Springfield, Massachusetts: Privately printed by the Linweave Association, 1927.

Newman, Eric P. *The Early Paper Money of America*. Racine, Wisconsin: The Western Publishing Company, 1976.

Newman, Eric P. (Editor) and Richard G. Doty. *Studies on Money in Early America*. New York, New York: American Numismatic Society, 1976.

Nolte, Vincent. *Memorial of Facts Connected with the History of Medallic Engraving and the Process of M. Collas*. London, England: Charles Tilt, 1838.

Ormont, Arthur. *Mr. Lincoln's Master Spy*. New York, New York: Julian Messner, 1966.

Ormsby, Waterman Lily. *A Description of the Present System of Bank Note Engraving, Showing Its Tendency to Facilitate Counterfeiting: To which is added a New Method of Constructing Bank Notes to Prevent Forgery*. New York, New York: Published by the author, 1852.

Ormsby, Waterman Lily. *Cycloidal Configurations or the Harvest of Counterfeiters. Containing Matter of the Highest Importance Concerning Paper Money. Also Explaining the Unit System of Bank Note Engraving*. New York, New York: W.L. Ormsby. (1862).

Partington, C.F. *The Engraver's Complete Guide: Comprising the Theory and Practice of Engraving, with Its Modern Improvements in Steel Plates, Lithography, &c., &c*. London, England: Sherwood, Gilbert and Piper. (1825).

Pellehn, Gustave. *Der Pantograph, 1603–1903. Von Urstorehsehnable zur modernen Zeichenmaschine*. Berlin, Germany: D. Reiner, 1903.

Peyton, George. *How to Detect Counterfeit Bank Notes: Or, An Illustrated Treatise on the Detection of Counterfeit, Altered, and Spurious Bank Notes with Original Bank Note Plates and Designs by Rawdon, Wright, Hatch & Edson,. . . .* New York, New York: Privately published by the author, 1856.

Phillips Jr., Henry. *Historical Sketches of the Paper Currency of the American Colonies, Prior to the Adoption of the Federal Constitution*. Roxbury, Massachusetts: Woodward's Historical Series, 1865. New York, New York: Reprinted by Burt Franklin, 1969.

Pierce, Wadsworth R. *The First 175 Years of Crane Papermaking*. Dalton, Massachusetts: Privately published for Crane & Company. (1977).

Portal, Sir Francis. *Portals. The Church, the State, and the People Leading to 250 Years of Papermaking*. London, England: Oxford University Press, 1962.

Preston, Robert E. *History of the Monetary Legislation and of the Currency System of the United States*. Philadelphia, Pennsylvania: John J. McKay, 1896.

Puglia, James Ph. *Forgery Defeated. Or a New Plan for Invalidating and detecting all Attempts of the Kind; for which a Patent has been obtained from the United States*. Philadelphia, Pennsylvania: Published by the author, 1822.

Pye, John. *Patronage of British Art, An Historical Sketch: Comprising an Account of the Rise and Progress of Art and Artist in London, from the Reign of George the Second . . . .* London, England: Longman, Brown, Green, and Longmans, 1845. London, England: Reprinted by Cornmaker Press, 1970.

Reed, Abner. *Diaries*. East Windsor, Connecticut: Connecticut Historical Society. Written by the author.

Rees, F.H. *The Art of Engraving*. Philadelphia, Pennsylvania: Keystone Publishing. 3rd Edition, 1909.

Renton, Edward. *Intaglio Engraving, Past and Present*. London, England: George Bell & Sons, 1896.

Rockoff, Hugh. *The Free Banking Era. A Re-Examination*. New York, New York: Arno Press, 1975. A revision of the author's doctoral dissertation at the University of Chicago, 1972.

Rogers, Daniel. Compiler. *The New-York City-Hall Recorder for the Year 1816, Containing Reports of the Most Interesting Trials and Decisions which have Arisen in the Various Courts of Judicature*. New York, New York: Charles N. Baldwin, 1817.

Rooks, Byron. *Our Paper Currency. The most Complete, Accurate and Reliable Instruction Extant in regard to All the Safeguards found on Genuine Paper Currency Which Furnish Infallible Information*. Portland, Oregon: Rutherford & Smith, 1891.

Rosencrantz, Herman. *The Life and Confession of Herman Rosencrantz; Executed in the City of Philadelphia on the 5th Day of May, 1770, for Counterfeiting and Uttering the Bills of Credit of the Province of Pennsylvania*. Philadelphia, Pennsylvania: Printed for James Chattin. 1770.

Savage, William. *A Dictionary of the Art of Printing*. London, England: Longman, Brown, Green, and Longman, 1841. New York, New York: Reprinted by Burt Franklin, 1965.

Savoy, H.S. *Geometric Turning: Comprising a Description of the New Geometric Chuck Constructed by Mr. Plant of Birmingham . . . .(etc)*. London, England: Longmans, Green & Co., 1873.

Scharf, J. Thomas and Thompson Westcott. *History of Philadelphia. 1609–1884*. Philadelphia, Pennsylvania: L.H. Everts & Co., 1884.

Schmeckebier, Laurence F. *The Bureau of Engraving and Printing. Its History, Activities and Organization*. Baltimore, Maryland: The Johns Hopkins Press, 1929.

Schraustadter Jr., Carl. *Photo-Engraving—A Practical Treatise on the Production of Printing Blocks by Modern Photographic Methods*. St. Louis, Missouri: Carl Schraustadter Jr., 1892.

Schriber Sr., Les. *Encyclopedia of Designs, Designers, Engravers, Artists of United States Postage Stamps, 1847–1900*. Published by the American Philatelic Society.

Schwan, Fred. *The Paper Money of the E.A. Wright Bank Note Company*. Port Clinton, Ohio: BNR Press, 1978.

Schweikart, Larry. *Banking in the American South from the Age of Jackson to Reconstruction*. Baton Rouge, Louisiana: Louisiana State University Press, 1987.

Scott, Kenneth. *Counterfeiting in Colonial America*. New York, New York: Oxford University Press, 1957.

Scott, Kenneth. *Counterfeiting in Colonial Connecticut*. New York, New York: The American Numismatic Society, 1957.

Scott, Kenneth. *Counterfeiting in Colonial New York*. New York, New York: The American Numismatic Society, 1953.

Scott, Kenneth. *Counterfeiting in Colonial Pennsylvania*. New York, New York: The American Numismatic Society, 1955.

Sewall, Samuel. *The Diary of Samuel Sewall, 1674–1729*. Edited from the manuscript at the Massachusetts Historical Society by M. Halsey Thomas. New York, New York: Farrar, Straus and Giroux, 1973.

Sharp, Granville. *The Gilbart Prize Essay. On the Adaptation of Recent Discoveries and Inventions in Science and Art to the Purpose of Practical Banking*. London, England: Groom bridge & Sons. 3rd edition, 1854.

Shepard, Elliott F. *Brief in Relation to the Bank Note Engraving and Printing Business*. Washington, D.C, 1877.

Siegel, Adrienne. *Philadelphia, Pennsylvania: A Chronological & Documentary History, 1615–1970*. Dobbs Ferry, New York: Oceana Publications, Inc., 1975.

Siegel, Alan A. *Out of Our Past. A History of Irvington, New Jersey*. Irvington, New York: The Irvington Centennial Committee, 1974.

Smee, Alfred. *Elements of Electro-metallurgy*. London, England: Longman, Brown, Green, and Longmans. 3rd Edition, 1851.

Smith, George W. *James Heath: Engraver to Kings and Tutor to Many*. Chelmsford, England: Published by the Author, 1989.

Smith, Lawrence Dwight. *Counterfeiting: Crime Against the People*. New York, New York: W.W. Norton Company, 1944.

Smithsonian Institution. *An Engraver's Potpourri: Life and Times of a 19th Century Bank Note Engraver*. Exhibition of the work of Stephen Alonzo Schoff, arranged by Elizabeth Harris, et. al., in the Hall of Printing and Graphic Arts. August 1979.

Smillie, James. *A Pilgrimage*. New York, New York: An unpublished autobiography, 1882.

Society for the Encouragement of Arts, Manufactures, and Commerce. *Report of the Committee of the Society of Arts, &c., Together with the Approved Communications and Evidence upon the Same, Relative to the Mode of Preventing the Forgery of Bank Notes*. London, England: Society of Arts, &c, 1819.

Standish, David. *The Art of Money: History and Design of Paper Currency*. San Francisco, California: Chronicle Books, 2000.

Song, Yingxing (alternate spelling is Sung, Ying-Hsing). *Chinese Technology in the Seventeenth Century*. University Park, Pennsylvania: Pennsylvania State University Press. Translated by É-tu Zen Sun and Shiou-Chuan Sun, 1966.

Stephens, Stephen DeWitt. *The Mavericks, American Engravers*. New Brunswick, New Jersey: Rutgers University Press, 1950.

Stimson, A.L. *A History of the Express Companies: and the Origin of American Railroads. Together with Some Reminiscences of the Latter Days of the Mail Coach and Baggage Wagon Business in the United States*. New York, New York: Privately printed and sold at Express Offices, 1858.

Stuart, William. *Sketches of the Life of William Stuart, the First and Most Celebrated Counterfeiter of Connecticut . . . .(etc.)*. Bridgeport, Connecticut: Privately published by the author, 1854.

Sumner, William Graham. *A History of American Currency*. New York, New York: Henry Holt and Co., 1874. New York, New York: Reprinted by Augustus M. Kelly, 1968.

Thomas, Isaiah. *The History of Printing in America with a Biography of Printers & an Account of Newspapers*. New York, New York: Weathervane Books, 1816. Reprint edition, 1970.

Todd, Richard Cecil. *Confederate Finance*. Athens, Georgia: University of Georgia Press, 1954.

Tomasko, Mark D. *The Feel of Steel. The Art and History of Bank Note Engraving in the United States*. Newton, Pennsylvania: Bird & Bull Press, 2009.

Tomasko, Mark D. *Two Hundred Years of American Bank Note Company: Security for the World*. New York, New York: Museum of American Financial History, 2006.

Tremmel, George B. *Counterfeit Currency of the Confederate States of America*. Jefferson, North Carolina: McFarland & Company, 2003. Atlanta, Georgia: Revised by Whitman Publishing, LLC, as *A Guide Book of Counterfeit Confederate Currency: History, Rarity and Values*, 2007.

Tucker, Stephen D. *History of R. Hoe & Company*. New York, New York: Privately printed by the author. (1887).

Underwood, Norman and Thomas V. Sullivan. *The Chemistry and Technology of Printing Inks*. New York, New York: D. Van Nostrand Company, 1915.

United States National Museum. *The Development of Electrical Technology in the 19th Century*. Washington, D.C.: Smithsonian Institution, 1962.

U.S. Treasury Department. *History of the Bureau of Engraving and Printing, 1862–1962*. Washington, D.C.: U.S. Treasury Department, 1962.

Victoria and Albert Museum. *Tools and Materials used in Etching and Engraving. A Descriptive Catalogue of a Collection Exhibited in the Museum*. London, England: His Majesty's Stationery Office, 1914.

Walling, George Washington. *Recollections of a New York Chief of Police*. New York, New York: Caxton Book Concern, Ltd, 1887.

Warner, Richard and Richard M. Adams. *Introduction to Security Printing*. Pittsburgh, Pennsylvania: PIA-GATF Press, 2005.

Weeks, Lyman Horrace. *A History of Paper Manufacturing in the United States, 1690–1916*. New York, New York: The Lockwood Trade Journal Company, 1916. New York, New York: Reprinted by Burt Franklin, 1969.

Whitley, Hiram C. *In It*. Cambridge: Riverside Press, 1894.

Whittemore, Hank. *Find the Magician! The Counterfeiting Crime of the Century*. New York, New York: Viking Press, 1980.

Wiborg, Frank B. *Printing Ink, A History. With a Treatise on Modern Methods of Manufacture and Use*. New York, New York, and London, England: Harper & Brothers, 1926.

Wilher, Edwin J. and Edward P. Eastman. *A Treatise on Counterfeit, Altered and Spurious Bank Notes . . . .* Poughkeepsie, New York: Privately printed by the authors, 1865.

Wilkie, Donald Ware. *American Secret Service Agent*. New York, New York: Frederick A. Stokes Company, 1934.

Wilkinson, W.T. *Photo-Engraving, Photo-Etching, and Photo-Lithography in Line and Half-Tone; and Collotype and Heliotype*. Revised and enlarged by Edward L. Wilson for the third (American) edition. New York, New York: Edward L. Wilson, 1888.

Willcox, Joseph. *Ivy Mills 1729–1866. Willcox and Allied Families*. Baltimore, Maryland: Lucas Brothers, Inc. Published for the author, 1911.

Williams, Charles Wye. *Considerations on the Alarming Increase of Forgery of the Bank of England, and the Neglect of Remedial Measures; with an Essay on the Remedy for the Detection of Forgeries and an Account of the Measures Adopted by the Bank of Ireland*. London, England: Longman, Hurst, Rees, Orme & Brown, 1818.

Williams, John Camp. *An Oneida County Printer: William Williams*. New York, New York: Charles Scribner's Sons, 1906.

Wroth, Lawrence. *Abel Buell of Connecticut. Silversmith, Type Founder, and Engraver*. New Haven, Connecticut: Yale University Press, 1926.

Wythes, M.D., William W. *A Description of the Cyclo-Ellipto-Pantograph*. Philadelphia, Pennsylvania: Henry Ashmead, 1858.

Public Documents

The publication of public documents began in 1845 when Congress contracted for that service with Little, Brown & Company of Boston, Massachusetts. The authority to publish was transferred by Congress in 1874 to the U.S. Government Printing Office. The laws and resolutions passed by Congress are known as the *United States Statutes at Large*. Representatives and Senate have been published since 1817 in the multi-volume *U.S. Congressional Serial Set*, commonly called the *Serial Set*. U.S. congressional documents are listed in this bibliography in chronological order.

British Government. The Currency Act of 1751. *United States Statutes at Large*. Volume 7. pp. 403 and 404. 24 George II, chapter 53.

British Government . The Currency Act of 1764. *United States Statutes at Large*. 4 George III, chapter 54.

The National Currency Act (later called the *National Bank Act*). *United States Statutes at Large*. 12 Stat., chapter 58, p.665. February 25, 1863.

U.S. Congress, House of Representatives Report No. 140. (38th Congress, 1st Session). *Report of the Select Committee to Investigate Charges Against the Treasury Department. United States Statutes at Large*. 12 Stat., Chapter 58, p.665, February 25, 1863. Washington, D.C.: The Treasury Department, 1864.

U.S. Congress, House of Representatives Executive Document No. 50. (38th Congress, 2nd Session). *Treasury Department Printing Bureau*. Washington, D.C.: The Treasury Department. February 4, 1865.

U.S. Congress, House of Representatives Executive Document No. 64. (38th Congress, 2nd Session). *Printing Bureau of the Treasury Department*. Washington, D.C.: Government Printing Office, 1865.

U.S. Congress, Senate Report No. 273. (40th Congress, 3rd Session). *Joint Select Committee on Retrenchment*. Washington, D.C.: No imprint. March 3, 1869.

U.S. Congress, House of Representatives Executive Document No. 45. (40th Congress, 3rd Session). *Engraving and Printing Bureau of the Treasury*. Washington, D.C.: Printed for the Committee.

U.S. Congress, House of Representatives Executive Document No., 188. (41st Congress, 2nd Session). *Money Paid to Bank-Note Companies, Etc*. Washington, D.C.: Printed by the Committee on Appropriations. March 14, 1870.

U.S. Congress, House of Representatives Report No. 150. (43rd Congress, 2nd Session). *Printing of United States Notes and Other Securities*. Washington, D.C.: Printed for the Committee. February 16, 1875.

U.S. Congress, House of Representatives Miscellaneous Document No. 43. (44th Congress, 2nd Session). *Bureau of Engraving and Printing. Testimony taken before the Committee on Expenditures in the Treasury Department, together with Reports and Correspondence*. Washington, D.C.: Government Printing Office, 1877.

U.S. Congress, House of Representatives Executive Document No. 224. (47th Congress, 1st Session). *Plate Printing by Steam-Power Presses*. Washington, D.C.: Government Printing Office, 1882.

U.S. Congress, Senate Miscellaneous Document No. 131. (50th Congress, 1st Session). *Printing of Government Securities*. Washington, D.C.: No imprint, 1888.

U.S. Congress, Senate Document No. 2604. (50th Congress, 2nd Session). *Report on Plate Printing by Committee on Finance, United States Senate*. February 15, 1889. This report was subsequently printed in book form as Treasury Department Document No. 1200, entitled *Plate Printing by Hand vs. Plate Printing by Steam*. Washington, D.C.: Government Printing Office, 1889.

U.S. Congress, Senate Document No. 109. (55th Congress, 3rd Session). *Report of the Committee to Investigate the Bureau of Engraving and Printing*. Washington, D.C.: Government Printing Office, 1899.

U.S. Congress, Senate Document No. 134. (55th Congress, 3rd Session). *Distinctive Paper for United States Bonds.* February 21, 1899.

U.S. Congress, House of Representatives. (60th Congress, 1st Session). *Transportation of Moneys by Express.* Washington, D.C.: Government Printing Office, 1908.

U.S. Congress, Senate Document No. 581. (61st Congress, 2nd Session). (1) *State Banking Before the Civil War,* by Davis R. Dewey, and (2) *The Safety Fund Banking System in New York, 1829–1866,* by Robert E. Chaddock. Washington, D.C.: Government Printing Office, 1910. New York, New York: Reprinted by Johnson Reprint Corporation, 1972.

U.S. Secret Service. *Counterfeiting and Other Crimes. A Digest for the information of Operatives of the Secret Service Division, Treasury Department.* Washington, D.C.: Government Printing Office, 1899.

U.S. Treasury Department. *Laws of the United States Relative to Counterfeiting Treasury Notes and other Securities and Coin of the United States and other Frauds Upon the Government.* Washington, D.C.: No agency or printer, but attributed to the U.S. Treasury Department.

U.S. Treasury Department. *Fines and Imprisonments in Counterfeiting Cases.* Washington, D.C.: Government Printing Office, 1935.

Journal Articles, Periodicals, and Lectures

Anonymous. "Cyrus Durand, the Machinist and Banknote Engraver." *The Illustrated Magazine of Art.* Volume III, 1854, pp. 267–270.

Anonymous. "Bank-Note Engraving in America." *The Illustrated Magazine of Art.* Volume III, 1854, pp. 308–312.

Anonymous. "Ninger ("im the Penman"), the Extraordinary Alleged Pen and Ink Counterfeiter." *Paper Money.* Whole Number 112, July/August 1984, pp. 178–180. A reprint of the story in the May 1896 edition of *Dickerman's United States Treasury Counterfeit Detector.*

Anonymous. "Miles Ogle and the $2 Counterfeits." *Paper Money.* Whole Number 115, January/February 1985, pp. 35 and 36. A reprint of the story in the November 1890 issue of *Dickerman's United States Treasury Counterfeit Detector.*

Anonymous. "Better Money from Improved Plates." *The Literary Digest.* December 18, 1926, p. 24.

Anonymous. "Currency of the Confederate States." *American Journal of Numismatics, and Bulletin of American Numismatic and Archeological Societies.* Boston, Massachusetts, volume XII, no. 1, July 1877, pp. 1–5.

Anonymous. "A Short History of the Modern Ink Mill." *The American Ink Maker.* September 1935, pp. 15–18.

Allan, Walter D. "The Young Angler. The Origins of Bank Note Vignettes #1." *Paper Money.* Whole Number 248, March/April 2007, pp. 155–157.

Allen, H.D. "The Paper Money of the Confederate States, with Historical Data" (series). *The Numismatist.* February 1919, pp. 50–56.

Anderson, William G. "U.S. National Debt (In the American Revolutionary Era)." *Paper Money.* Whole Number 105, May/June 1983, pp. 110–114. Dr. Anderson's article is an extract of his book, *The Price of Liberty: The Public Debt of the American Revolution,* published in 1983 by the University of Virginia Press.

Applegate, Howard B. Shelby. "A Visit to Security Columbian, United States Banknote, Inc." *Bank Note Reporter.* April 1982, pp. 16–19.

Applegate, Howard B. Shelby. "Men, Mythology and Symbolism on Stock Certificates." *Bank Note Reporter.* February 1982, pp. 30–32.

Appleton's Mechanics' Magazine and Engineer's Journal. New York, New York: D. Appleton & Company. A monthly periodical published 1852 through 1853.

Atwood, Dudley W. "An Episode in South Carolina Financing and Resulting Bank Note Designs." *Essay-Proof Journal.* Whole Number 120, Fall 1973, pp. 151–153.

Balazs, E. "The Birth of Capitalism in China." *Journal of the Economic and Social History of the Orient.* Volume III, Part 2, August 1960, pp. 196–216.

Ball, Douglas B. "Confederate Currency Derived from Banknote Plates." *The Numismatist.* Volume 85, no. 3, March 1972, pp. 339–352.

Bankers' Magazine. Title varies: (1) *Bankers' Weekly Circular and Statistical Record.* October 1845 to May 1846; (2) The *Bankers' Magazine and State Financial Register.* July 1846 to June 1849; (3) The *Bankers' Magazine and Statistical Register.* July 1849 to November 1894; (4) The *Bankers' Magazine.* December 1894 to June 1895; (5) *Rhodes' Journal of Banking* and the *Bankers' Magazine* consolidated. July to December 1895; (6) The *Bankers' Magazine.* January 1896 to June 1943.

Bankers' Magazine, The. "Toppan Carpenter and Company vs. The National Bank Note Company and Others, Infringement of Patent suite heard before the United States Circuit Court in Equity." *Bankers' Magazine.* Volume XII, New Series, July 1862, pp. 14–16.

Bankers' Magazine, The. "The Liabilities of Express Companies to Bankers." *Bankers' Magazine.* April 1864, pp. 806–808.

Bank Note Reporter. "British 'Adventure' World's Oldest Privately-held Stock." October 1988, front page.

Barth, B. and P. Grodzinski. "Micro-Writing, An Obsolete Art." *Industrial Diamond Review.* Volume 14, January 1954, pp. 12–17.

Berry, W.T. "Augustus Applegath. Some Notes and References." *Journal of the Printing Historical Society.* No. 2 1966, pp. 49–57.

Bettner, Karl H. "Inks for Printing Currency and Securities." *The American Ink Maker.* November 1935, pp. 14–17.

Bigsby, Captain V.L., USNR (Ret.). "Paper for Colonial Currency." *The Whitman Numismatic Journal*. June 1964, pp. 49–54 and August 1964, pp. 13–19

Blanchard, Julian. "A Specimen of Ormsby's Proposed Design for Bank Notes." *The Essay-Proof Journal*. Whole Number 60, pp. 169 and 170.

Blanchard, Julian. "Keatinge & Ball, Engravers." *The Essay-Proof Journal*. Whole Number 13, January 1947, pp. 7–9.

Blanchard, Julian. "National Bank Notes in the Early Years." *The Essay-Proof Journal*. Whole Number 22, April 1949, pp. 81–83.

Blanchard, Julian. "The Durand Engraving Companies." *The Essay-Proof Journal*. Whole Number 26, April 1950, pp. 81–89.

Blanchard, Julian. "The Durand Engraving Companies." *The Essay-Proof Journal*. Whole Number 27.

Blanchard, Julian. "The Durand Engraving Companies." *The Essay-Proof Journal*. Whole Number 29, January 1951, pp. 11–16.

Blanchard, Julian. "Waterman Lily Ormsby, 1809–1883, Bank Note Engraver." *The Essay-Proof Journal*. Whole Number 53, January 1957, pp. 10–30.

Blanchard, Julian. "End of the State Chartered Bank Notes." *The Essay-Proof Journal*. Whole Number 69, Winter 1961, p. 21.

Blanchard, Julian. "Government Portraits and Vignettes." *The Essay-Proof Journal*. Whole Number 77, 1963, p. 28.

Bloom, Murray Teigh. "Uncle Sam: Bashful Counterfeiter." *The International Journal of Intelligence and Counterintelligence*. Volume 2, no. 3, (Fall 1988), pp. 345–358.

Blum, William and Thomas F. Slattery. "The Electrolytic Reproduction of Engraved Printing Plates." *Chemical and Metallurgical Engineering*. Volume 25, no. 8, (August 24, 1921), pp. 320 and 321.

Bodenhorn, Howard. "Small-Denomination Banknotes in Antebellum America." *Journal of Money, Credit & Banking*. Volume 25, 1993.

Bolin, Benny. "Spencer M. Clark, Cornerstone of the Bureau of Engraving and Printing." *Paper Money*. Whole Number 135, May/June 1988, pp. 77 and 78, 80.

Bradbeer, William W. "New Jersey Paper Currency, 1709–1786." *Proceedings of the New Jersey Historical Society*, 1923. The New Jersey Frontier Guard.

Bradfield, Elston G. "Benjamin Franklin: A Numismatic Summary." *The Numismatist*. December 1956, pp. 1347–1353.

Brazer, Clarence W. "The Fine Art of Line Engraving." *The Essay-Proof Journal*. Whole Number 8, October 1945, pp. 195–202.

British American Bank Note Company. "The British American Bank Note Company's Ninety Years of Security Printing." Published by the company, reprinted in *The Essay-Proof Journal*, Whole Number 54, April 1957, pp. 67–88.

Buchner & Co., David. *Defenders and Offenders*. New York, New York: D. Buchner & Co., 1882. Originally published as "tobacco cards" which came in packages of chewing tobacco from the Gold Coin Tobacco Co. Each card, on its back, presented a police portrait of a criminal and a brief account of his crimes.

Carpenter, Frank G. "Making Our Paper Money 1893." *Paper Money*. Whole Number 110, March/April 1984, pp. 95 and 96. A reprint of an article syndicated in weekly newspapers concerning the Bureau of Engraving and Printing.

Chase, Philip H. "Confederate States of America Paper Money: Classification and Listing." *The Numismatist*. Part XVII, August,1946, pp. 912–915.

Chase, Philip H. "Confederate Treasury Notes: The Chemicograph Backs." *The Numismatist*. Volume 73, no. 4, April 1960, pp. 403–411.

Chase, Philip H. "The Mysterious Chemicograph Backs for Confederate Currency." *The Numismatist*. Volume 63, no. 3, March 1950, pp. 123–129.

Chorlton, Harry L. "Bank Note Etching on Steel." *The Essay-Proof Journal*. Whole Number 18, April1948, pp. 79–82.

Claudy, C. H. "Making and Destroying Paper Money: How the Bureau of Engraving and Printing and the Redemption Division Work." *Scientific American Supplement No. 2230*. September 28, 1918, pp. 200–202

Cochran, Robert E. "Genuine Counterfeits." *Paper Money*. Whole Number 132, November/December 1987, pp. 194–197.

Cochran, Robert E. "The Story of Cranky Tom Hale, and How He Was Captured by John Murray." *Paper Money*. Whole Number 165, May/June 1993, pp. 86–89.

Cowan, Arnold M. "More C.S.A. Engravers' Names Uncovered." *Bank Note Reporter*. September 1987, p.14.

Daniels, Forrest. "The New York State Free Banking Law." *Paper Money*. Whole Number 40, 4th Quarter, 1971, pp. 141–153.

Daniels, Forrest. "The New York State Free Banking Law." *Paper Money*. Whole Number 42, 2nd Quarter, 1972, pp. 74–79.

Daniels, Forrest. "The paper Money Laundry." *Paper Money*. Whole Number 165, May/June 1993, pp. 97–99.

Daniels, Forrest. "A Drawback Certificate." *Paper Money*. Whole Number 47, 3rd Quarter, 1973, pp. 135 and 136.

Davis, Andrew McFarland. "Certain Considerations Concerning the Coinage of the Colony and Public Bills of Credit of the Province of the Massachusetts Bay." *Proceedings of the American*

Academy of Arts and Sciences. Volume XXXIII, no. 12, (February 1898), pp. 190–211.

Davis, Andrew McFarland. "The Massachusetts Bay Currency, 1690–1750. The Plates." *Proceedings of the American Antiquarian Society*. New Series, volume XII, (October 1897–October 1898), pp. 410–425.

Davis, Andrew McFarland. "Occult Methods of Protecting the Currency. Sewall's Mnemonic Lines and their Interpretation." *Proceedings of the Massachusetts Historical Society*, December 1899, pp. 315–327.

Davis, Andrew McFarland. "Boston Banks, 1681–1740." *New England Historical and Genealogical Register*, July 1903.

Davis, Andrew McFarland. "Emergent Treasury-Supply in Massachusetts in Early Days." *Proceedings of the American Antiquarian Society*. April 26, 1905. Worcester, Massachusetts: Reprinted by the Hamilton Press, 1905.

Davis, Curtis Carroll. "The Craftiest of Men: William P. Wood and the Establishment of the United States Secret Service." *The Maryland Historical Magazine*. Volume 83, no. 2, Summer 1988, pp. 111–126.

Dickerman's United States Treasury Counterfeit Detector. New York, New York: John Holler Publisher.

Dickinson, Charles Wesley. "Copper, Steel, and Bank Note Engraving." *Popular Science Monthly*. Volume 46, March 1895, pp. 597–613.

Douglas, James. "Obituary Notice of Thomas Sterry Hunt." *Proceedings of the American Philosophical Society*. pp. 63–121. May 31, 1898.

Durand, Asher B. (?). "History and Progress of Bank Note Engraving." *The Crayon*. Volume 1, no. 8, February 21, 1855, pp. 116 and 117.

Durand, Roger H. "A Problem of Security." *Paper Money*. Whole Number 132, November/December 1987, pp. 187–190.

Dye, John S. *Dye's Government Counterfeit Bank Note Detector*. Philadelphia, Pennsylvania: S.E. Gumpert.

Eagan, Thomas F. "Pete McCartney, Counterfeiter." *Paper Money*. Whole Number 163, January/February 1993, pp. 22–28.

Eagan, Thomas F. "Pete McCartney, Counterfeiter, Part II." *Paper Money*. Whole Number 164, March/April 1993, pp. 43–48.

Eagan, Thomas F. "Counterfeiters in St. Louis." *Paper Money*. Whole Number 174, November/December 1994, pp. 203–205.

Elliott, Harrison. "The Portals: Paper-makers to the Bank of England." *The Paper-maker*. Volume 22, February 1953, pp. 38–42.

Essay-Proof Journal, The. Edited first by Clarence W. Brazer, 1944–1993.

Feller, R. L., et al. "The Kinetics of Cellulose Deterioration." *Historic Textile and Paper Materials*. Edited by H.L. Needles and S.H. Zeronian. American Chemical Society (Advances in Chemistry Series No. 212). Chapter 18, pp. 329–345, 1986.

Ferguson, John and Roger Davies. "A Survey of Tudor and Early Jacobean Rose Turning." The Society of Ornamental Turners, London, England. *Bulletin* No.83, pp. 133–144.

Ferreri, C. John. "America's First Historical Vignettes on Paper Money." *Paper Money*. Whole Number 157, January/February 1992, pp. 5–9.

Franklin, Benjamin. "A Modest Enquiry into the Nature and Necessity of a Paper-Currency." Andrew McFarland Davis's *Colonial Currency Reprints*, volume II, pp. 336–357.

Frazner, Arthur H. "Joseph Saxton and his Contributions to the Medal Ruling and Photographic Arts." *Smithsonian Studies in History and Technology*. No. 32. Washington, D.C.: U.S. Government Printing Office, 1975.

Gatlin, Dana. "The Monroe-Head Counterfeit." McClure's Magazine. Part of the series, "Great Cases of Detective Burns." Volume XXXVI, February 1911, pp. 542–556.

Gillingham, Harold E. "Old Business Cards of Philadelphia." *The Pennsylvania Magazine of History and Biography*. Volume 53, (1929), pp. 203–229.

Hammond, Bray. "The North's Empty Purse, 1861–1862." *American Historical Review*. Volume LXVII, no. 1, October 1961, pp. 1–18.

Hancock, Harold B. "The Gilpins and their Endless Papermaking Machine." *The Pennsylvania Magazine of History and Biography*. Volume 81, (October), pp. 391–405.

Harrison, William J. "Some Notes on The Harrison Family of Engravers." *The Essay-Proof Journal*. Whole Number 12, October 1946, pp. 195–203.

Hazen, William P. "Ninger, The King of Counterfeiters." *The Metropolitan Magazine*. Volume XXV, no. 1, (October 1906), pp. 82–84.

Heath Infallible Counterfeit Detector at Sight. By Authority from the United States Treasury Department. Boston, Massachusetts: Laban Heath. Several editions including the "Banking & Counting House Edition," and the "Pocket Edition." 1867.

Henry, Joseph. "Memoir of Joseph Saxton, 1799–1873." *Biographical Memoirs of the National Academy of Sciences*. Read before the National Academy, October 4, 1874. Volume 1, (1877), pp. 287–316.

Henshaw, D.M. "Donkin Pantagraph Engraving Machine with Rose Engine." *Transactions of the Newcomen Society*. Read at the Westminster Café, Holborn, London, January 23, 1935. Volume XV, 1934 and 1935, pp. 77–83.

Hessler, Gene. "Looking Closely at Portraits of Dom Pedro II." *Paper Money*. Whole Number 142, July/August 1989, pp. 116117, 126.

Hessler, Gene. "Spinner's Ladies." *Paper Money*. Whole Number 122, March/April 1986, p. 66.

Hessler, Gene. "Two Unique Interest-Bearing Treasury Notes from the Act of March 3, 1863." *Paper Money*. Whole Number 173, September/October 1994, pp. 174–176.

Hessler, Gene. "Working in Mirror Image." *The Numismatist*. December 1995, pp. 1529 and 1530.

Hill, Louis A. "Production of Steel Engraved Securities Which Defy Fraudulent Duplication." *The Essay-Proof Journal*. Whole Number 111, Summer 1971, pp. 101–103.

Hoober, Richard T. "Franklin's Influence on Colonial and Continental Paper Money." *The Numismatist*. December 1956, pp. 1357–1362.

Hood, James Franklin. "A Few Words on Wildcat Banking and Currency, Having Special Reference to the District of Columbia." Washington, D.C.: Privately printed by the author. An address to the Washington, D.C. Chapter of the American Institute of Banking on the Evening of December 9, 1915, 1916.

Horstman, Ronald L. "The First Greenbacks of the Civil War." *Paper Money*. Whole Number 135, May/June 1988, pp. 69–72, 76.

Horstman, Ronald L. "The Preparation of Demand Notes." *Paper Money*. Whole Number 148, July/August 1990, page 120.

Horstman, Ronald L. "National Customs Notes." *Paper Money*. Whole Number 150, November/December 1990, pp. 177–179.

Horstman, Ronald L. and Eric Newman. "Earliest Known Error on U.S. Paper Money." *Paper Money*. Whole Number 131, September/October 1987, pp. 156 and 157.

Hughes, Brent H. "Top Note Signers Served Confederacy Well." *Bank Note Reporter*. August 1993, pp. 22, 23, 26 and 27.

Hughes, Brent H. "Chemical Printing Saved the Confederacy." *Bank Note Reporter*. January 1998, pp. 46 and 47.

Huntoon, Peter. "The United States $500 & $1,000 National Bank Notes." *Paper Money*. Whole Number 136, July/August 1988, pp. 103–121.

Jeremy, David J. "Damming the Flood: British Government Efforts to Check the Outflow of Technicians and Machinery, 1780–1843." *Business History Review*. Volume LI, no. 1, (Spring 1977), pp. 1–34.

Kagin, Donald. "The First Attempts at Paper Currency in America." *The Numismatist*. Volume 86, no. 4, (April 1973), pp. 543–552.

Kagin, Donald. "Monetary Aspects of the Treasury Notes of the War of 1812." *The Journal of Economic History*. Volume XLIV, no. 1, (March 1984), pp. 69–88.

Kagin, Donald. "The Treasury Notes of the War of 1812." *Paper Money*. Whole Number 239, September/October 2005, pp. 323–334, 336, 338–340, 342–350.

Keatinge & Ball Bank Note Company. "Remarks on the Manufacture of Bank Notes and Other Promises to Pay." Published by the company. Reprinted by *The Essay-Proof Journal*. Whole Number 75, 1962, pp. 117–122.

Keatinge & Ball Bank Note Company. "Remarks on the Manufacture of Bank Notes and Other Promises to Pay." Published by the company, Reprinted by *The Essay-Proof Journal*. Whole Number 76, 1963, pp. 155–160.

Kelly, Jack. "Illegal Tender." *Invention & Technology Magazine*. Summer 2005, pp. 20–29.

Leonard, Eugenie Andruss. "Paper as a Critical Commodity during the American Revolution." *Pennsylvania Magazine of History and Biography*. Issue No. 4, (1950), pp. 488–499.

Marckhoff, Fred R. "Lith. By Ed. Mendel, Chicago." *Paper Money*. Whole No. 12, Fall 1964, pp. 79–83.

McCabe, Robert. "Waterman Lilly Ormsby and the Continental Bank Note Company." *Paper Money*. Whole No. 212, March/April 2001, pp. 163,165–170.

Meier, Henry. "The Origin of the Printing and Roller Press." *The Print Collector's Quarterly*. Volume 28, no. 1, (February 1941), pp. 8–55.

Morris II, Thomas F. "Our First National Bank Notes." *The Numismatist*. Volume LI, no. 7, July 1938, pp. 573–577.

Morris II, Thomas F. "The History of the Bureau of Engraving and Printing." *The Stamp Specialist*. Volume 11.

(Murray, John W.) "The Million Dollar Counterfeiting Ring." *Paper Money*. Adapted from *Memoirs of a Great Detective: Incidents in the Life of John Wilson Murray*. Whole No. 143, September/October 1989, pp. 141–146.

Nelson, Ronald L. "The Raid on Studivant's Fort." *Springhouse*. April 1998, volume 15, no. 2, pp. 25–32.

Newman, Eric P. "Counterfeit Continental Currency Goes to War." *The Numismatist*. January 1957, pp. 5–16. Continued in the February 1957 issue, pp. 137–147.

Newman, Eric P. "Earliest Known Error on U.S. Paper Money." *Paper Money*. Whole No. 131, September/October 1987, pp. 156 and 157.

Newman, Eric P. "Franklin and the Bank of North America." *The Numismatist*. December 1956, pp. 1368–1370.

Newman, Eric P. "Nature Printing on Colonial and Continental Currency." *The Numismatist*. Volume 77, February 1964, pp. 147–154, 299–305, 457–465, 613–623. Reprinted.

Newman, Eric P. "The Successful British Counterfeiting of American Paper Money During the American Revolution."

Patterson, Robert T. "Government Finance on the Eve of the Civil War." *The Journal of Economic History*. Volume 12, no. 1, (Winter 1952), pp. 35–44.

Peyton, George. "How to Detect Counterfeit Bank Notes." Reprinted in *The Essay-Proof Journal*. Whole No. 184, 4th Quarter, 1989, pp. 160–170. Originally printed by Rawdon, Wright, Hatch & Edson. Continued in *The Essay-Proof Journal*. Whole No. 185, 1st Quarter, 1990, pp. 17–22.

Pratt, Robert H. "The Birth of a Die." *The Essay-Proof Journal*. Whole No. 143, Summer 1979, pp. 103–115.

Raisig, L. Miles. "Memoirs of a C.S.A. Treasury Note Lithographer." *The Numismatist*. August 1951, pp. 838–842.

Raisig, L. Miles. "The Continental Currency Makers." *Numismatic Scrapbook Magazine*. Whole No. 296, October 1960, pp. 2825–2828.

Ralph, Joseph E. "The Production of Paper Money." *Paper Money*. Read before the New York Numismatic Club, February 10, 1911, by George Blake. Whole No. 104, March/April 1983, pp. 74–77.

Reed, III, Fred L. "Counterfeiting was Big Problem for C.S.A." *Bank Note Reporter*. Part II, October 2005, pp. 58, 60, 62, 64, 68.

Renker, Armin. "Moritz Friedrich Illig, 1777–1845, The Inventor of Rosin Sizing." *The Paper-maker*. Translated from the German. Volume 30, September 1961, pp. 37–43.

Rice, Foster Wild. "Antecedents of the American Bank Note Company of 1858." *The Essay-Proof Journal*. Whole No. 71, Summer 1961, pp. 91–103.

Rice, Foster Wild. "Antecedents of the American Bank Note Company of 1858." *Essay-Proof Journal*. Whole No. 72, pp. 139–152.

Rice, Foster Wild. "Corrections and Additions to *The Story of the American Bank Note Company*." *The Essay-Proof Journal*. Whole No. 121, Winter 1974, pp. 29–33.

Ringer, James. "Phips' Fleet." *National Geographic*. August 2000, pp. 72–81.

Rochette, Edward C. "A Darker Reason for Smaller Currency." *Paper Money*. Whole No. 199, January/February 1999, pp. 12 and 13.

Rolnick, Arthur J. and Warren E. Weber. "Explaining the Demand for Free Bank Notes." *Journal of Monetary Economics*. Volume 21, no. 1, 1988

Rolnick, Arthur J. and Warren E. Weber. "Free Banking, Wildcat Banking, and Shinplasters." *Federal Reserve Bank of Minneapolis Bulletin*.

Roth, Lillian. "Safety Papers." *Bibliographic Series*. No. 279, Institute of Paper Chemistry, 1978.

Scott, Kenneth. "A British Counterfeiting Press in New York Harbor, 1776." *The New York Historical Society Quarterly*. Volume 39, no. 273, April–July 1955, pp. 117–120.

Scott, Kenneth. "Counterfeiting in Colonial Virginia." *The Virginia Magazine of History and Biography*. Volume 61, no. 1, (January 1955), pp. 3–33.

Scott, Kenneth. "James Franklin on Counterfeiting." *Museum Notes*. New York, New York: The American Numismatic Society, 1958, VIII, pp. 217–220.

Scott, Kenneth. "New Hampshire Tory Counterfeiters Operating from New York City." *The New York Historical Society Quarterly*. Volume 34, 1950, pp. 31–57.

Scott, Kenneth. "Some Counterfeiters of Provincial Currency." *South Carolina Historical Magazine*. Volume 57, 1956, pp. 14–22.

Selgin, Geroge. "The Suppression of State Banknotes: A Reconsideration." *Economic Inquiry*. Volume 38, no. 4, October 2000, pp. 600–615.

Simons, Francis L. "Safety Papers—A Review of Theory and Practice." *TAPPI* (Technical Association of the Pulp and Paper Industry). Volume 34, no. 10, October 1951, pp. 113A–122A.

Smedley, Glen B. "The Story of the Western Bank Note & Engraving Co., Chicago." *The Essay-Proof Journal*. Whole No. 70, Spring 1961, pp. 55–59.

Smith, Arthur A. "Bank Note Detecting in the Era of State Banks." *Mississippi Valley Historical Review*. Volume XXIX, (December 1942), pp. 371–386.

Smith, David C. "The State of the Paper Industry in 1776." *TAPPI*. Volume 59, no. 7, (July 1976), pp. 56–59.

(Spaulding, Robert M.). "Edoardo Chiossone, Japanese Government Printing Bureau Engraver." *The Essay-Proof Journal*. Whole No. 177, 1st Quarter, 1988, pp. 16 and 17.

(Spaulding, Robert M.). "More on Edoardo Chiossone, Japanese Government Printing Bureau Engraver." *The Essay-Proof Journal*. Whole No. 181, 1st Quarter, 1989, pp. 36 and 37

Spencer, Asa. "Vindication of Claims to Certain Inventions and Improvements in the Graphic Arts." *American Journal of Science and Arts*. Volume XLIV, no. 1, April 1843.

Spinner, Francis E. "Abstraction of Twenty Thousand Dollars." *Paper Money*. Whole No. 51, May 1974, pp. 115, 119, 120. Extract from the 1870 *Annual Report* of U.S. Treasurer F.E. Spinner.

Stannard, William John. "Anaglyptography." Chapter taken from *Art Exemplar, A Guide to Distinguish One Species of Print from Another*. London, England: Privately printed by the author, 1859.

State of New Jersey vs. Joseph E. West 1847. Burlington County, New Jersey. 1785–1847.

State of New York. *Powers and Duties of the Agent of the Superintendent of the Banking Department, with Regulations in Relation to Engravers, Engraving and Printing Bank Notes*. Albany, New York: Wed, Parsons & Co., printers, 1855.

Stevens, Peter F. "King of the Coney Men: Master Counterfeiter Peter McCartney." *Traces of Indiana and Midwestern History.* Published by the Indiana State Historical Society. Volume 8, no. 2, Spring 1996, pp. 36–43.

Stock, Collard J. "Account of an 1881 Visit to Government Printing Works, Tokio." *The Essay-Proof Journal.* Whole No. 177, 1st Quarter, 1988, pp. 18–22.

Stoyle, F.W. "Printing Ink—Art, Craft, or Science." *Printing Technology.* Volume VIII, no. 2, December 1964, pp. 17–28.

Sullivan, Frank. "Paper, Papermaking, and the Patriots: Notes to Accompany the Papermakers' March to the Revolutionary War." *The Paper-maker.* Volume 20, September 1951, pp. 27–31.

Surasky, Charles. "The First and Last Postal Notes, 1883–1894." *Paper Money.* Whole No. 167, September/October 1993, pp. 154–157.

Sushka, Marie Elizabeth. "The Antebellum Money Market and the Economic Impact of the Bank War." *The Journal of Economic History.* Volume XXXVI, no. 4, (December 1976), pp. 809–835.

Sulla, Richard. "Forgotten Men of Money. Private Bankers in Early U.S. History." *The Journal of Economic History.* Volume XXXVI, no. 1, (March 1976), pp. 173–188.

Timberlake Jr., Richard H. "Denominational Factors in Nineteenth-Century Currency Experience." *The Journal of Economic History.* Volume XXXIV, no. 4, (December 1974), pp. 835–850.

Tomasko, Mark D. "The Republic Bank Note Company." *Paper Money.* Whole No. 145, January/February 1990, pp. 12–15.

Tomasko, Mark D. "ABNC Archive Sale Prompts Printing Metal Primer." *Bank Note Reporter.* February 2006, pp. 40, 42.

Tomasko, Mark D. "Central Banknote to Prominence with Estys." *Bank Note Reporter.* January 1998, pp. 14–16.

Tomasko, Mark D. "Notes on Bank Note Engravers and Artist Attribution." *Paper Money.* Whole No. 248, March/April 2007, pp. 144–154.

Tomasko, Mark D. "Identifying Bank Note Vignettes from A Family Firm, the American Bank Note Company." *Essay-Proof Journal.* Whole No. 199/200, 4th Quarter, 1993, pp. 86–92.

Toppan, Robert Noxon. "A Hundred Years of Bank Note Engraving in the United States." Read before the Trustees of the American Bank Note Company. New York, New York: American Bank Note Company, 1896.

Turner, Craig J. "Cyrus Durand: Inventive Genius." *Paper Money,* Whole No. 54, November 1974, pp. 243–251.

Tweedle, Norman. "The Rose Engine Lathe. Its History, Development and Modern Use." Issued in a series as a supplement to the *Bulletin* of the Society of Ornamental Turners (London). August 1, 1956.

Utley, H.M. "The Wild Cat Banking System of Michigan." *Report of the Pioneer Society of the State of Michigan.* Volume 5, 1864, pp. 209–227.

Voorn, Henk. "A Brief History of the Sizing of Paper." *The Paper-maker.* Volume 30, February 1961, pp. 47–53.

Voorn, Henk. "A Short History of the Glazing of Paper." *The Paper-maker.* Volume 27, no. 1, February 1958, pp. 3–10.

Wait, George W. "Banks That Changed Their Location Without Moving." *The Essay-Proof Journal.* Whole No. 74, Spring 1862, pp. 58 and 59.

Wakerman, Geoffrey. "Anastatic Printing for Sir Thomas Phillipps." *Journal of the Printing Historical Society.* No. 5, 1969, pp. 24–40.

Watson, Alan D, "Counterfeiting in Colonial North Carolina: A Reassessment." *North Carolina Historical Review.* Volume 79, no. 2, (2002), pp. 182–197.

Weaver, Ralph R. "Jacob Perkins, 1766–1849." *The Essay-Proof Journal.* Whole No. 74, Spring 1962, pp. 61–66, 93.

Weaver, Ralph R. "Jacob Perkins, 1766–1848." *The Essay-Proof Journal.* Whole No. 75, 1962, pp. 131–139.

Weaver, Ralph R. "Jacob Perkins, 1766–1848." *The Essay-Proof Journal.* Whole No. 76, 1963, pp. 169–175.

Weber, Warren E. "Early State Banks in the United States: How Many Were There and Where Did They Exist?" *Federal Reserve Bank of Minneapolis Quarterly Review.* Volume 30, no. 2, September 2006, pp. 28–40.

Weiss, Harry B. "The Number of Persons and Firms Connected with the Graphic Arts in New York City, 1633–1820." *Bulletin of the New York Public Library.* Volume 50, no. 10, (October 1946), pp. 775–786.

Weiss, Roger W. "The Issue of Paper Money in the American Colonies, 1720–1774." *The Journal of Economic History.* Volume XXX, no. 4, (December 1970), pp. 770–784.

Whitehand, W. A. "The Robbery of the Treasury of East Jersey in 1768 and Contemporaneous Events." *Proceedings of the New Jersey Historical Society.* Read before the New Jersey Historical Society on September 12, 1850. Volume V, pp. 49–65.

Whitfield, Steve and Ron Horstman. "Who Are These Guys?" *Paper Money.* Whole No. 235, January/February 2005, pp. 32–36,38–40, 42 and 43.

Wilkens, Ernest C. "F.E. Spinner and Fractional Currency." *The Essay-Proof Journal.* Whole No. 115, Summer 1972, pp. 103–111.

Williamson, Stephen D. "Private Money and Counterfeiting." Federal Reserve Bank of Richmond, Virginia's *Economic Quarterly.* Summer 2002, volume 88, Issue No. 3, pp. 37–57.

Winter, John. "Preliminary Investigations on Chines Ink in Far Eastern Paintings." *Advances in Chemistry.* Volume 138, no., 207, (1973), pp. 207–225.

Wolka, Wendell. "How They Did the Deal in 1861." *Paper Money*. Whole No. 210, November/December 2000, pp. 196, 198, 200, 202, 204, 206.

York, Norton D. "U.S. Unionism and the Power Four-Plate Printing Press." *Essay-Proof Journal*. Whole No. 91, Summer 1966, pp. 110–113.

Modern Topics

For readers interested in books and articles about new trends in the technology of bank notes, the following list may be of interest.

Bank Note Reporter. "BEP Ink Supplier Opens Fort Worth Plant." February 1992, p. 8.

Bank Note Reporter. "Press Stopped by Ink Problem." March 1992, p. 14.

Bank Note Reporter. "Search for missing $100 Plate." November 1991, p. 14.

Bank Note Reporter. "Inventor Ralph Wicker died Dec. 26." February 1998, p. 16.

Banks, W.H. "An Introduction to the Physics and Chemistry of Surfaces in Relation to Printing." *Printing Technology*. Volume VII, no. 1, July 1963, pp. 33–39.

Batelle Columbus Laboratories. *Evaluation of Visual Counterfeiting Deterrent Features (VCDFs)*. Final Report to the Board of Governors of the Federal Reserve System. Columbus, Ohio: Batelle Columbus Laboratories. May 1, 1985.

Cartwright, P.F.S. "Specifying the Rheological Properties of Lithographic Printing Inks." *Printing Technology*. Volume VIII, no. 2, December 1964, pp. 29–38.

Chambliss, Carlson R. "How Much U.S. Currency has Circulated?" *Bank Note Reporter*. May 1988, pp. 45–47, 73.

Coleman, Matt. "Portals Seeks Market Growth with New Security Papers Mill in U.S." *Pulp and Paper*. February 1984, pp. 110–113.

Currency News. "The Art and Science of Intaglio the Cornerstone of Security Printing." February 2005, volume 3, no. 2, pp. 8 and 9.

Currency News. "Optical Document Security." January 2003, volume 1, no. 1, p. 11.

Currency News. "Jura's Intaglio Developments." February 2005, volume 3, no. 2, p. 12.

Currency News. "Whatever Happened to . . . DuraNote?"

Currency News. "Document Security Hanging by a Thread." January 2003, volume 1, no. 1, p. 3.

Currency News. "Demetallization."

Currency News. "Quantum Dot Technology for Anti-Counterfeiting." March 2005, volume 3, no. 1, p. 9.

de Senarclens, Marina. "Security in Banknote Printing." *Towards New Dimensions: Guide to Swiss Economy and Business Opportunities*. Published by Swiss Quality Products. Third Issue (Autumn 1984), pp. 41–44.

Feller, R.I. et al. "The Kinetics of Cellulose Deterioration." *Historic Textile and Paper Materials*. Edited by Needles and Zeronian. American Chemical Society Advances in Chemistry Series, no. 212, Chapter 18, pp. 329–345.

Hall, Gene. "Mix it Up with Chemistry of Bank Note Inks." *Bank Note Reporter*. Volume 28, no. 4, April 2000, pp. 39, 40, 42.

Hanson, Victor F. "Determination of Trace Elements in Paper by Enery Dispersive X-ray Fluorescence." *Preservation of Paper and Textiles of Historic and Artistic Value II*. Washington, D.C.: American Chemical Society, 1981. pp. 143–168.

Haslop, John. "Mould-made Cotton Bank Note Paper and Plastic Substrate Alternatives." A paper given by Haslop, the Technical Manager of De La Rue's Security Paper and Print Division.

Healey, A.C. and J.S. Steggles. "Instrumental Studies of Copper Plate Inks." *Printing Technology*. Volume IV, no. 2, December 1960, pp. 5–22.

Hessler, Gene. "Comments on Current Czechoslovak Security Engraving. A Visit with Václav Fajt, Engraver of Czech Bank Notes and Postage Stamps." *The Essay-Proof Journal*. Whole No. 188, 4th Quarter, 1990, pp. 170–176.

Hively, Will. "Faking It." *Discover*. October 1998, pp. 87–96.

Huber, R.A. "The Latent Image and Its Role in Document Security." *Canadian Society of Forensic Science Journal*. Volume 10, no. 4, pp. 127–134.

Hughes, Brent H. "$160,000 Is Missing!" *Paper Money*. Whole No. 120, November/December 1985, pp. 263–265, 285.

Kawai, Junro. "Trends of Intaglio Printing and Security Printing." *Graphic Arts Japan* (?). Citation unknown (1979 or later), pp. 13–20.

Landress, M.M. and Bruce Dobler. *I Made it Myself*. New York, New York: Grosset & Dunlap, 1973. vii-x + 276 pp. One of the classic books by an actual counterfeiter.

National Research Council. *Counterfeit Deterrent Features for the Next Generation Currency Design*. Washington, D.C.: National Academy Press, Publication NMAB-472, 1993.

Oak Ridge National Laboratory. *Proceedings of the International Conference on Security Documents for the 21st Century*. Held at San Diego, California, April 1–3, 1987. Oak Ridge National Laboratories. CCNF-8704175, Contract.

Phillips, Roger W. "Optically Variable Films, Pigments, and Inks." *Optical Thin Films III: New Developments*. Proceedings of the Society for Photo-Optical Instrumentation Engineers, volume 1323, pp. 98–109. Bellingham, Washington: SPIE, the Society for Photo-Optical Instrumentation Engineers, 1990.

Purdy, Dan C. "The Xerox 6500 Colour Copier." *Canadian Society of Forensic Science Journal*. Volume 9, no. 3, September 1976, pp. 117–121.

Schafrik, Robert E. and Sara F. Church. "Protecting the Greenback." *Scientific American*. Volume 273, no. 1, July 1995, pp. 40–46.

Shaw, Merle B. and George W. Bicking. "Research on the Production of Currency Paper in the Bureau of Standards Experimental Paper Mill." *Technologic Papers of the Bureau of Standards*. Volume 21, 1926, pp. 89–108.

Shaw, Merle B. and George W. Bicking. "Further Experimental Production of Currency Paper in the Bureau of Standards Paper Mill." *Bureau of Standards Journal of Research*. Volume 3, December 1929, pp. 899–926. Reprinted by the U.S. Department of Commerce as Research Paper No. 121. Washington, D.C.: Superintendent of Documents.

Smith, Arthur A. "Bank Note Detecting in the Era of State Banks." *Mississippi Historical Review*. Volume 29, no. 3, December 1942, pp. 371–378.

Simmons, Francis L. "Safety Papers A Review of Theory and Practice." *TAPPI*. Volume 34, no. 10, October 1951, pp. 113A–122A.

Sugar, Steve. "Section 10, Bureau of Engraving and Printing. A Perfect 10." *Paper Money*. Whole No. 110, March/April 1984, pp. 82–86.

Thomas, C.T. and W. Blum. "The Production of Electrolytic Iron Printing Plates." Presented at the 57th General Meeting of the American Electrochemical Society. St. Louis, Missouri, May 29, 1930.

Ungerer, P.D. "The Ultimate Lathe." *Popular Science*. Volume 234, no. 4, April 1989, pp. 116–120.

Van Renesse, Rudolf I. Editors. *Optical Document Security*. Norwood, Massachusetts: Artech House, 1993. Ann Arbor, Michigan: Reprinted by UMI Books on Demand, 1997.

Weber, Charles G., Merle B. Shaw, and Martin J. O'Leary. "Suitability of Sweet Potato Starch for the Beater Sizing of Paper." *National Bureau of Standards Miscellaneous Publication M150*. Washington, D.C.: U.S. Government Printing Office. June 1935.

Wohlmannstetter, Elisabeth. "Manufacturing Banknotes: Paper beats Plastic." *Giesecke & Devrient Report 2/2001*.

U.S. Congress, House of Representative Serial No. 98-98. 98th Congress, 2nd Session. *The Currency Design Act*. Hearing

before Subcommittee on Consumer Affairs and Coinage of the Committee on Banking Finance and Urban Affairs, on H.R. 6005, "A Bill to Affirm the Authority of the Congress to Approve the Design of the Currency." Washington, D.C.: Printed by the Committee. July 1984.

U.S. Congress, House of Representatives Serial No. 99-27. 99th Congress, 1st Session. *The Currency Design Act*. Hearing before the Subcommittee on Consumer Affairs and Coinage of the Committee on Banking, Finance and Urban Affairs, on H.R. 48, "A Bill to Affirm the Authority of the Congress to Approve the Design of the Currency." Washington, D.C.: U.S. Government Printing Office, 1985.

U.S. Congress, House of Representatives Serial No. 103-154. 103rd Congress, 2nd Session. *Redesign of the Currency*. Hearing before the Committee on Banking, Finance, and Urban Affairs. Washington, D.C.: U.S. Government Printing Office, 1994.

U.S. Congress, House of Representatives Serial No. 105-22. 105th Congress, 1st Session. *Review of Department of the Treasury's Efforts to Combat Counterfeiting*. Hearing before the Subcommittee on General Oversight and Investigations of the Committee on Banking, and Financial Services. Washington, D.C.: U.S. Government Printing Office. July 10, 1997.

U.S. Congress, House of Representatives Serial No. 105-38. 105th Congress, 1st Session. *Printing Flaws on the Redesigned $50 Bill*. Hearing before the Subcommittee on Domestic and International Monetary Policy of the Committee on Banking and Financial Services. Washington, D.C.: U.S. Government Printing Office. October 1, 1997.

U.S. Congress, House of Representatives Serial No. 105-52. 105th Congress, 2nd Session. *Counterfeiting Using Personal Computers*. Hearing before the Subcommittee on Domestic and International Monetary Policy of the Committee on Banking and Financial Services. Washington, D.C.: U.S. Government Printing Office. March 31, 1998.

U.S. Congress, House of Representatives Serial No. 106-84. 106th Congress, 2nd Session. *Bureau of Engraving and Printing, Security Printing Amendments Act of 2000*. Washington, D.C. Government Printing Office. September, 14, 2000.

U.S. General Accounting Office. *Counterfeit U.S. Currency Abroad. Issues and U.S. Deterrence Efforts*. Report of the Honorable John M. Spratt Jr., House of Representatives. GAO / OGD-96-11. Washington, D.C. General Accounting Office, 1996.

About the Author

Bob McCabe is a retired chemist who grew up in southern Oklahoma during the 1940s. After graduating from the University of Oklahoma, his family moved to Florida. Bob's introduction to foreign bank notes began by chance during the late 1960s, when he was attracted to a number of very colorful French notes in an antiques and curios shop, and he decided to buy them. Bob soon began to buy notes from the few dealers around. His primary source was Jolie Coins in Roselyn Heights, New York, and Dwight Musser in Florida. In those days, most notes were less than $5 in uncirculated condition, and most of the Chinese notes were under $1 in uncirculated condition.

Bob's fascination with collecting notes evolved into an interest in how notes were made, especially the paper and ink chemistries, initially, followed by line and mechanical engraving, and eventually the entire subject of security printing. By taking working vacations at the Library of Congress (online at www.loc.gov), the New York Public Library, the Smithsonian Institution, the Philadelphia Historical Society of Pennsylvania, the Wintethur Museum, and many others, he was able to collect most of the literature written about these subjects in the last 300 years, which contributed to the research behind this book. He exchanged letters and phone calls with a number of experts in various fields, including author Murray T. Bloom. Bob and his children still live in Florida with three granddaughters and assorted dogs and cats.

Index

Index of British Patents

Index of German Patents

Index of U.S. Patents

Index of U.S. Statutes